Trust and Technology in a Ubiquitous Modern Environment:
Theoretical and Methodological Perspectives

Dominika Latusek
Kozminski University, Poland

Alexandra Gerbasi
California State University, Northridge, USA

INFORMATION SCIENCE REFERENCE

Hershey · New York

Director of Editorial Content:	Kristin Klinger
Director of Book Publications:	Julia Mosemann
Acquisitions Editor:	Lindsay Johnston
Development Editor:	Christine Bufton
Typesetter:	Gregory Snader
Production Editor:	Jamie Snavely
Cover Design:	Lisa Tosheff
Printed at:	Yurchak Printing Inc.

Published in the United States of America by
Information Science Reference (an imprint of IGI Global)
701 E. Chocolate Avenue
Hershey PA 17033
Tel: 717-533-8845
Fax: 717-533-8661
E-mail: cust@igi-global.com
Web site: http://www.igi-global.com/reference

Library of Congress Cataloging-in-Publication Data

Trust and technology in a ubiquitous modern environment : theoretical and methodological perspectives / Dominika Latusek and Alexandra Gerbasi, editors.   p. cm.
  Includes bibliographical references and index.
  Summary: "This book brings together scholars with significantly different backgrounds who share interests in the interplay between trust and technology, presenting novel theoretical perspectives on the topics of trust and technology, as well as some empirical investigations into the trust-building, trust-repairing, and trust-destroying practices in the context of technology"- -Provided by publisher.
  ISBN 978-1-61520-901-9 (hbk.) -- ISBN 978-1-61520-902-6 (ebook) 1. Technology--Psychological aspects. 2. Information technology--Psychological aspects. 3. Human-computer interaction--Psychological aspects. 4. Trust. I. Latusek, Dominika, 1981- II. Gerbasi, Alexandra, 1976- T49.5.T78 2010
  303.48'3--dc22
                    2009040710

British Cataloguing in Publication Data
A Cataloguing in Publication record for this book is available from the British Library.

All work contributed to this book is new, previously-unpublished material. The views expressed in this book are those of the authors, but not necessarily of the publisher.

List of Reviewers

Selcen Aykac, *Ozyegin University, Turkey*
David Boyns, *California State University, Northridge, USA*
Celeste Campos-Castillo, *The University of Iowa, USA*
Sylwia Ciuk, *Oxford Brookes University, UK*
Scott Erickson, *Ithaca College, USA*
Genoveffa Giambona, *University of Reading, UK*
Oren Golan, *New York University, UK*
Sonja Grabner-Kräuter, *Klagenfurt University, Austria*
Chanaka Jayawardhena, *Loughborough University, UK*
Dariusz Jemielniak, *Kozminski University, Poland*
Olga Morawczynski, *The University of Edinburgh, UK*
Lisa Slattery Rashotte, *University of North Carolina, USA*
Blaine G. Robbins, *University of Washington, USA*
Abigail Schoneboom, *City University of New York, USA*
Daniel B. Shank, *University of Georgia, USA*
Matthias Thiemann, *Columbia University, USA*
Monika Wańtuchowicz, *Warsaw University of Technology, Poland*
Andrew Wong, *Telenor Group Business Development and Research, Malaysia*

Table of Contents

Section 3
Applications of Technology: Impact on Trust

Section 4
Trust and Technology in Organizational Contexts

Detailed Table of Contents

Section 1
Trust and Technology: Theoretical Approaches

Chapter 1 presents an overview of basic principles of the Computer-Are-Social-Actors (CASA) paradigm, along with the review of landmark empirical works within this tradition. Based on the premise that people tend to treat computers socially, it further asks the question of how people assess trustworthiness of machines in human-computer interactions. The authors conclude that trust is an important category in human communication with computers and that computer users have a tendency to judge the trustworthiness of the equipment in the same way as they assess trustworthiness of other people.

This chapter discusses trust in the context of online communities and online marketplaces. The authors argue that the issue of trust in the virtual environment arises as a result of increasing interconnectedness which leads to vulnerability because computer users cannot control all "traces" they leave when surfing the internet. This study posits some fundamental questions about trust in the broad context of internet and provides sound theoretical framework for conceptual and empirical analysis of particular aspects of the use of internet.

Chapter 3

Daniel B. Shank, University of Georgia, USA

This chapter argues that structure and culture are among factors constituting antecedents of human trust toward technological actors. Using existing sociological theories the author develops his own propositions about individual's trust in technology as well as presents some initial empirical evidence of his model from existing literature.

Section 2
Trust and Technology in Interpersonal Contexts

Chapter 4

Andrew T. Fiore, University of California, USA
Coye Cheshire, University of California, USA

This chapter identifies major trust-related challenges associated with initiating romantic relationships through technology-mediated communication, for example trough online dating services or match-making services. In particular, the authors analyze the transformation of various types of trust through relationship's development. They also explore the theme of trustworthiness towards institutional actors (as websites) and individuals (website's users) in the context of online interactions.

Chapter 5

David Boyns, California State University, Northridge, USA

The growing popularity of participation in online communities brings about the issue of stability and order that keep groups together over time. This chapter presents an ethnographic study of one of virtual communities that grew around World of Warcraft, one of the "online worlds". It examines the process of constructing the normative order and social production of trust among players in a community which existence is limited exclusively to virtual space.

Chapter 6

Oren Golan, New York University, USA

This chapter presents the results of a qualitative study conducted among young internet users in Israel. It focuses on the exploration of factors that influence trust building during online socialization among youth. Particular emphasis is put on differentiating the virtual arena from other venues that have already been thoroughly studied, such as schools or clubs. As a result of this research three key features influencing (both as enablers and impediments) the formation of online trust are identified: lies and truths, anonymity and disclosure, and transparency and opacity.

This chapter describes an empirical study conducted among one of professional groups within a high-tech industry – independent web-designers in New York City area. It concentrates on the problem of trust building between the designers and their prospective client in the environment where face-to-face interaction (this, interpersonal trust-building) as well as institutional assurance structures are practically non-existent. This study finds that in such an uncertain environment trust building occurs through networks of referrals and informal recommendation systems.

Section 3
Applications of Technology: Impact on Trust

Chapter 8 presents results of a quantitative study aimed at testing two competing theories about the impact of technology on generalized trust – new institutional economics and overjustification and crowding theory. The findings confirm the presumptions of new institutional economics approach that technology, being mediated through formal institutions, fosters trust on a generalized level. The chapter concludes with outlining practical implications of the study for implementing technological innovations in organizations.

Chapter 9

This chapter draws upon two traditions in sociology: trust in technology and the sociology of technology, merging them into one perspective of looking at the question of how the social and cultural frameworks in which individuals are embedded can impact the process of technology adoption. The proposed model, built on existing theoretical and empirical literature, seeks to explain how the status of social actors can translate into trust towards technologies associated with them.

Kenya is a research site particularly well-suited for the study of social processes such as trust, as it lacks well-established institutions, norms, and overall stability. The study reported in chapter 10 is an ethnography of the process of implementing m-banking in this highly uncertain environment. Two types of trust – interpersonal and institutional trust – are found to play a key role in this process of technology adoption, with their relative importance varying over time.

Sonja Grabner-Kräuter, Klagenfurt University, Austria
Rita Faullant, Klagenfurt University, Austria

Chapter 11 investigates the types of online trust that play a role in the adoption of internet banking services. In particular, this study focuses on the distinction between trust towards particular online vendors and trust towards Internet as a general type of technology. It also tackles the important question about the influence of an individual's general propensity to trust others on their trust towards technologies. The conclusions are based on an empirical study conducted among bank customers in Austria.

Andrew Wong, Telenor Group Business Development and Research, Malaysia

In this chapter the author gives an account of a longitudinal qualitative research project conducted among actual and potential young mobile phone users from poor urban neighborhoods in Bangladesh. It investigates the practice of phone sharing, popular among those who otherwise cannot afford to have the device. Three processes are identified that play crucial role in domesticating new technology by youth: learning, sharing, and experimenting. A foundation for these processes is set by social trust which is cultivated at the level of interactions within groups.

Section 4
Trust and Technology in Organizational Contexts

Abigail Schoneboom, City University of New York, USA

Chapter 13 critically examines organizational responses towards the phenomenon of anonymous work-blogging. Actual strategies of addressing this problem seem to vary across a continuum characterized at one end by stringent control and surveillance, and, on the other end, by embrace and careful acceptance. The problem of work-blogging symbolizes that internet-related technologies have brought about additional ambiguity and tension in the workplace, for they further blurred the line between the public and the private spheres of employee's activities.

Genoveffa Giambona, University of Reading, UK
David W. Birchall, University of Reading, UK

Virtual teamwork has become increasingly popular as computer and communication technologies have advanced and became ubiquitous in contemporary organizations. The authors of this chapter analyze the impact of technology on teamwork and present a conceptual framework to assess trust requirements in virtual team-based organizations. They build their model on the premise that trust constitutes a vital precondition for effective work of virtual teams as it replaces more traditional ways of managerial control and coordination.

Anita L. Blanchard, University of North Carolina at Charlotte, USA
Lisa Slattery Rashotte, University of North Carolina at Charlotte, USA

Chapter 15 explores the question of how different features of certain technological applications affect trust development in online groups. The proposed model merges several traditions of academic investigation, especially research on group trust, social exchange, social identity, entitativity, and online groups. Special attention is also paid to the so-called identity technologies which are said to particularly support development of cohesion of online groups.

Denise Anthony, Dartmouth College, USA
James A. Kitts, Columbia University, USA
Christopher Masone, Google, USA
Sean W. Smith, Dartmouth College, USA

The experimental research project reported in this chapter was designed to investigate how different types and sources of information affect customers' trust towards online vendors as well as how they influence the decision to purchase goods from e-vendors. The authors distinguishing between two major sources of information (institutional third parties or recommendations from other customers) the experiments suggest that people are more willing to buy online when recommendation comes from institutional sources.

Kurt Komaromi, Ithaca College, USA
Fahri Unsal, Ithaca College, USA
G. Scott Erickson, Ithaca College, USA

The main goal of this chapter is to investigate the impact of social network websites on trust towards online vendors. It does it though a survey of three types of websites: two designed especially for e-commerce purposes and one functioning as a social networking site but with growing commercial component. The findings of this study indicate that, in general, individuals are more likely to purchase from websites based on institutional assurance rather than community-based assurance.

Sandro Castaldo, SDA Bocconi School of Management, Italy
Monica Grosso, SDA Bocconi School of Management, Italy
Charles Hofacker, Florida State University, USA
Katia Premazzi, SDA Bocconi School of Management, Italy

This chapter discusses the literature on interaction between online customers and e-vendors and presents results of a corresponding experimental research project. It seeks to explain e-shopping behavior in terms of trust individuals place in specific e-vendors, and, on the other hand, in terms of trustworthiness that various e-sellers generate. Trust in this context is claimed to be a key variable influencing the transformation from using the internet to just search for information to making actual purchases in virtual marketplaces.

Preface

The idea for this book originated from two observations. Firstly, ever since Fukuyama's (1995) and Putnam's (1993) influential books, trust has gained a prominent place at the center of academic scholarship in the social sciences. Scholars have claimed that trust serves many important roles in society, including a lubricant for social relations and economic exchange. Not only is trust key to satisfactory interpersonal relationships, but also for effective organizing, successful deal-making, as well as social and economic well-being (Barber, 1993; Fukuyama, 1995; Kozminski, 2009; Putnam, 1993; Sztompka, 1999). Scholarly interest in trust has intensified since the late 1990s as a result of the social, economic and political changes in the world. In the new, post cold war world order, trust has been seen as a primary component of social capital, and it has been viewed as a major key in creating stability in an increasingly global, democratized world.

Secondly, the omnipresence of technology in modern life makes it an important topic for academic exploration. As technology, in particular the Internet and associated tools became ubiquitous and gained millions of users, scholars quickly realized that we cannot discuss technology without bringing up the issue of trust. This became more apparent when problems such as privacy concerns, identity theft, hacking and cybercrime in general became a topic of heated discussions in the wider public, not merely among highly specialized groups of computer professionals.

On the other hand, users of the web know that the Internet, as an environment not limited by physical presence, may under some circumstances encourage opportunistic behavior and can be a fertile ground for dishonesty. Through sometimes painful experiences we have come to realize that our ability to control how technology is being used is limited. However, technology can create new opportunities to enrich human life and can increase social and economic well-being. In workplaces technology may encourage better communication and help build bridges between people that have never been able to contact each other before. But, it may also be used to put individuals' actions under surveillance, to track employees' movements and constantly record their activities. Oftentimes instead of building understanding and rapport between organizational members, the adoption of advanced technological solutions deepens the chasm between managers and their subordinates. Furthermore, trust issues arise not only in the areas of technology adoptions, but they concern technological devices themselves. For example, as personal computers, GPS transmitters and mobile phones become common and play a central role in our lives, we, its users, want to be sure that they are dependable and secure. Moreover, as we increasingly rely on the Internet, we also want to be certain that the interconnected environment that the web creates is safe and we are protected from fraud or abuse.

All these concerns, that we broadly term as trust issues are at the heart of academic interests of the individuals who contributed to this volume. The purpose of this collection is to present a variety of theoretical perspectives on the topics of trust and technology, as well as some empirical investigations into the trust-building, trust-maintenance, and trust-destroying practices in the context of technology.

It presents research positioned at the intersection of the issues of trust within and between individuals, and organizations, and technology under various guises, for example, high-tech work environments, computer-mediated communication, and the Internet as a business environment.

There are many publications about trust and technology as separate constructs, but there are no sources we know of which focus specifically on the interaction of both of the phenomena. Studies on trust abound, but only a small portion touch on issues of technology. Similarly, in the studies of technology, trust is present but usually it is treated as a supplementary or side issue. Trust and technology, as far as we know, have never simultaneously been treated as central themes of research.

Trust has been a topic of study of several disciplines, including management, economics, sociology and psychology. Technology, in turn, is becoming an important subject of academic inquiry as various technologies grow to be ubiquitous in our lives, both in professional and private contexts. On the one hand, trust has been praised as an indispensable lubricant of social life and social relations on multiple levels and in diverse contexts. On the other hand, the role of technology in both private and business reality is increasing. Therefore, at the intersection of both, important new questions arise: how does technology impact trust-building processes? Does technology support or inhibit trust-building? What are the possible applications of new technologies in trust-building projects? What happens to trust when the mode of communication becomes more "technologized"? Does technology breed distrust? What are the best strategies of applying technologies to support trust building in society (generalized trust), between or within organization (for instance, in virtual teams and in high-tech professions) or in our interpersonal dealings with others (for example, in romantic relationships)? In what ways does culture influence the process of technology adoption? Also, while there have been some discussions of interconnections and mutual influences between technology and trust, there have been few empirical studies that would clarify the relationship. These issues require sustained investigation in various contexts and they are precisely some of the questions that contributors to this volume chose to address.

In research on the relationship between trust and technology there are both theoretical and empirical gaps. The role of technology in building or destroying trust begs for more systematic and extensive investigation. Currently two major streams of research can be clearly discerned. They can be distinguished by their view on how technology affects trust. One tradition treats technology as a variable that positively influences trust through democratizing access to information and making it more accurate, thus improving the performance of organizations and generally making exchanges smoother. The second tradition is more critical of the effect of technology on trust, arguing that technology undermines trust between people as it increases monitoring and instead of empowering people it can be used to control them.

The chapters in this volume explore themes inspired by these two traditions and the previously mentioned questions. They examine trust and technology in a wide variety of settings and at different levels of analysis. This helps to deepen our understanding of the interaction between technology and trust. It also allows us to assess the current state of research centered on the issues of technology and trust. We hope that this collection will stimulate further studies and thus bring us to a clearer understanding of the relationship between technology and trust.

In the world of technology producers, the need for trust is explicitly recognized by leading figures in the industry. For example, in a keynote address at Davos, Bill Gates states: "Although complete trustworthiness has yet to be achieved by any technology -- power systems still fail, water and gas pipes rupture and telephone lines sometimes drop calls -- these systems are usually there when we need them and they do what we need them to do. For computers to play a truly central role in our lives, they must achieve this level of trust." From the academic point of view such claims, however, bring up an important question: can we actually "trust" the technology? Again, there seem to be two diverging perspectives. Sztompka (1999), for instance, maintains that people are the ultimate objects of trust. Therefore, if we say that we trust a certain application; we actually mean that we trust the people who created it. However, as Clifford Nass has consistently shown (Moon and Nass, 1996; Nass and Moon, 2000), people tend to treat technologies socially and sometimes ascribe to them human characteristics. If this is the case, then it would make sense to say that we trust a computer or a system. Nevertheless, we feel that trusting an individual and trusting a machine are qualitatively different. At the center of this debate lies the question of agency – while we can ascribe intentional actions (e.g. dimension of benevolence) to individuals, a machine acts according to some programmed protocols and it cannot choose whether to honor the trust placed in it.

We recognize that in a rather fragmented academic community there is a pressing need for more research that would bring together scholars from social sciences and technology-focused fields. One of our objectives when preparing this collection was to bring together scholars with significantly different backgrounds who share interests in the interplay between trust and technology. We are very happy to have gathered in this volume such a diverse group of experts – including business researchers, information system theorists, sociologists and communication scholars from both Europe and the United States. The interdisciplinary and international make-up of this group resulted in a set of highly diverse studies. They very across several dimensions: theoretical and empirical focus, conceptual underpinning, methodological approach (with quantitative, qualitative and experimental studies represented), specific subjects and objects of research, and the geographical areas and social groups where data were collected.

Organizing such a diverse set of chapters presented somewhat of a challenge. Eventually, we decided to open the collection with papers focused on theoretical considerations and then present works based on empirical studies clustered around three contexts: interpersonal relationships, adoption of technology, and interactions across organizational boundaries.

The chapters in Section 1 "Trust and Technology: Theoretical Approaches" set out a conceptual foundation for research presented in subsequent sections of the volume.

Clifford Nass and Jong-Eun Roselyn Lee give an extensive overview of Computers-Are-Social-Actors (CASA) research and explicate the basic principles of the CASA paradigm. Above all, they indicate that interaction with, or through, a technological device is a social experience full of emotions. In such situations, people tend to attribute an active role to the machine even if they "know" that they do not interact with real human being. The work reviewed in this chapter suggests that people do tend to treat computers as human beings and therefore assess their trustworthiness in similar ways. This claim offers one answer to the problem of the object of trust that we described above.

Then, Tina Gürthner and Guido Möllering turn our attention to the aspect of interconnectedness brought about by ubiquitously present technology. They argue that it is not the technology itself but the interconnection and interdependence it generates that creates an urgent need for trust in virtual environments. They call for a revision of much of what has been written on the topic of trust and technology and for a move towards a deeper analysis centered on the issues of interconnections, for this is precisely the source of our vulnerability in online activities. The authors review research that links trust and technology and conclude with an integrative framework for analyzing the phenomenon of online trust.

In Chapter 3 Daniel Shank takes us back to the social interaction issues posited by the CASA tradition. His approach to the problem of trusting technological actors utilizes sociological research on structure and cultural sentiments. He advocates a wider use of sociological theories in analyzing relations between humans and technologies. Two aspects of this novel work merit special attention. First, the strong claim that the study of trust towards technological actors cannot neglect the cultural attitudes towards technology. Second, he urges us to pay more attention to the influence of social structure on how trust towards technology develops in various groups in society.

Section 2 is organized around the theme of interpersonal interactions in numerous settings: among prospective romantic partners, gamers in an online world, in the subculture of young people, and high-tech professionals.

Andrew Fiore and Coye Cheshire present a theoretical perspective on online-initiated romantic relationships. The practice of online dating constitutes a unique setting offering insight into the evolution of trust as relationships develop. They describe the trajectory of the transformation of trust as the relationship changes qualitatively – goes from the "virtual" to the "real" world. They also discuss the evolution of different types of trust as the relationship progresses – from institutional trust being important when the relationship is initiated to interpersonal trust gaining importance as people meet face to face.

In matchmaking and dating services the ultimate goal is a face-to-face meeting and is the ultimate transformation of "virtual" trust into "interpersonal" trust. In contrast the interactions in the chapter by David Boyns take place entirely online. Boyns investigates the issues of trust creation and maintenance in the online gaming community of "World of Warcraft". Thanks to longitudinal ethnographic work Boyns is able to depict the intricate mechanisms that allow this exclusively virtual community to function smoothly.

Chapter 6 by Oren Golan is of a more general nature. Based on a qualitative study of Isreali youth Golan explores the process of trust creation in online interactions. He looks at the issue of trust building through the eyes of young people, and, following their lead, he identifies three components crucial for development of trust in virtual space (truth, disclosure, transparency).

Finally, Matthias Thiemann analyzes the work of freelance web designers in New York City. He points to the importance of personal experience in doing business online. Web designers, certainly representatives of one of the "high-tech" professions, face the challenge of building reputations in an exclusively virtual world. As it turns out, in the process of getting new orders, what matters for the web designers is either contact from the "offline" world or a network of references that, in the end, vouch for their trustworthiness.

The chapters in Section 3 touch on the broad theme of technology adoption. The studies in this section have particular relevance as their results can often be directly translated into advice for practitioners.

Blaine Robbins and Maria Grigoryeva examine the role that formal institutions play in the formation of generalized trust. Here, they argue technology has a mediating effect in the sense that – operating through institutional mechanisms - it encourages trust building. The results of the empirical study find strong support for the mediating role of institutions in the process of generating trust through technology. This has direct implications for various types of social transitions (both within organizations and in society) and suggests that more emphasis should be put on institution-building efforts if we seek to support generalized trust among individuals.

In Chapter 9 Celeste Campos-Castillo looks at trust in technology through a status value approach. The proposed model seeks to explain how the status of social actors can be grafted onto the technologies with which they are associated and can be used as a basis for trust. Linking together two traditions – research on trust in technology and the sociology of technology she attempts to address the question of how the social and cultural frameworks in which one is embedded can translate into trust and then influence technology adoption processes.

The interplay between institutional and interpersonal dimensions of trust is the main focus of Chapter 10 by Olga Morawczynski and Gianluca Miscione. They present an ethnographic study of the implementation of an m-banking (banking via mobile phone) application in Kenya, a rather unrepresented arena in social research. The observation of the process of trust building in an environment dominated by tribal affiliations and mistrust is particularly attractive for students of trust as we know that it is in unstable, changing environments lacking well-established institutional frameworks where social processes become particularly salient and observable.

The study by Sonja Grabner-Kräuter and Rita Faullant reported in Chapter 11 encompasses a similar industry – technology-mediated banking, but in the dramatically different setting of the Austrian banking sector. The authors find empirical confirmation for the notion of internet trust and thus support the position that technology, indeed, can itself be an object of trust. As this research shows, there is no uniform concept of "online trust".." Rather generalized trust towards certain technology (i.e., internet) should not be confounded with a more particular type of trust towards a certain agent (i.e., bank) using the Internet.

Finally, Andrew Wong (Chapter 12) presents an ethnographic study, conducted among poor young city dwellers in Bangladesh. It focuses on the prerequisites for sharing a mobile phone among a group of friends who otherwise cannot afford to use the device. Wong's answer emerges from the field data: he argues that it is social trust that enables key emerging processes that together allow for the successful adoption of new technology. Collective use of a mobile phone is an excellent example of how trust within groups develops and, moreover, actually is a prerequisite for the successful embracing of technological novelties. This work also forms a bridge to the final section of this collection. It shows how trust plays a crucial role in the process of group formation, as well as how it supports bonding and the transformation of individual thinking into a group-oriented mindset.

The chapters in Section 4 are centered on the question of how technology enables and constrains trust building within organizations as well as between an organization and its stakeholders.

Abigail Schonebom takes a critical stand towards the topic emphasizing the concept of "trust tension". Analyzing cases of workbloggers she presents how borders between work-related and private spheres may become blurred with the use of modern technologies. Technology, she argues, adds to ambiguity in the workplace and creates a challenge for established practices of organizing. There are two dominant patterns that companies adopt to deal with employees' blogging. Some organizations adopt an ideology of strict monitoring and surveillance. Other organizations, however, implement policies aimed at embracing workblogging and including it in organizational discourse. All these responses, eventually, have an impact on organizational performance, mainly through affecting group cohesiveness and employees' identification with organizations.

Genoveffa Giambona and David Birchall (Chapter 14) together with Anita Blanchard and Lisa Rashotte (Chapter 15) are interested in the impact of technology on new forms of group work enabled by the web. Virtual work is increasingly popular in organizations as information technology has become widespread and easily available. This creates additional challenges for teamwork. Not only can team members come from different backgrounds, cultures and with varying experience, but in a virtual environment they can be separated by distance and time zones.

Giambona and Birchall argue that trust is a key component for virtual team-based organizations. Trust is said to supplement and replace traditional management systems based on control. The authors maintain that new forms of organizing, such as web-based teams, require adequate governance styles - in particular, more reliance on trust. They offer a conceptual model that allows managers to analyze virtual teams and enables them to determine the minimum level of trust that needs to be established to assure the smooth functioning of a team.

In Chapter 15 Blanchard and Rashotte, in turn, focus on the internal cohesion of a virtual group. They distinguish key variables affecting group trust: sense of virtual community, entitativity, identity, and support. In their conceptual model technological features affect the commitment and attachment that lead to group trust. Therefore, of particular importance is the construct of identity technologies. They argue that solutions such as logs of members' activities and signature files allow for the construction of both personal identity and group identification in a virtual environment.

The three final chapters focus on the relationship between commercial organizations and their clients. Denise Anthony and her colleagues (Chapter 16) begin with the premise that the benefits of reputation systems for establishing trust online are limited; they usually only work well for closed networks. People who are outside of these networks can rely on two sources that "vouch" for the trustworthiness of online exchange partners: either interpersonal or institutional sources of information. They present experimental evidence that consumers tend to rely more on institutional sources of information, especially when they face great uncertainty about the vendor – as is the case with most first-time transactions. This has significant consequences for the organization of exchange online, as many existing marketplaces rely on peer recommendation systems.

In Chapter 17 Kurt Komaromi and his colleagues continue the investigation of the interaction between trust and technology in commercial settings. Specifically, they examine three types of websites (a retailer, an auction site, and a social networking site) from the perspective of trustworthiness these websites generate among the young generation and how this trustworthiness, then, translates into shopping behavior.

Sandro Castaldo and his colleagues ask a different question about customer behavior in online environments. They are concerned that although customers often rely on information from the web, they still are reluctant to actually make purchases online. The diagnosis by Castaldo and his colleagues is that people are still afraid of the uncertainties posited by virtual marketplaces, mainly privacy invasion, and that these concerns outweigh the actual possible gains from the transaction. Their study finds that trust appears to be the only variable influencing customers' willingness to disclose personal information to e-vendors, which suggests that, online vendors should put more effort into trust building initiatives with potential buyers.

Construed broadly, all of the chapters in this book examine problems and hopes for technology in the light of trust. They highlight some of the complexities and subtleties of phenomena related to trust and technology in a variety of contemporary contexts. Above all, they illustrate that the intersection of trust and technology still remains an underexplored area that can inspire further research.

As editors of this book we experienced the importance of both technology and trust in our collaboration throughout the process of putting this volume together. For the duration of this project we were separated by the Atlantic Ocean and we were avid users of modern technological devices. In the end, it seems important to realize that without trust in each other and without the support offered by modern technology we would not have been able to bring this project to a successful end.

REFERENCES

Barber, B. (1983). The logic and limits of trust. New Brunswick, NJ: Rutgers University Press: New Brunswick, NJ.

Fukuyama, F. (1995). Trust: the social virtues and the creation of prosperity. New York: Free Press.

Koźmiński, A., K. (2009). How it all happened? Warsaw, Poland: Difin.

Moon, Y., & Nass, C. (1996). How "real" are computer personalities?: Psychological responses to personality types in human-computer interaction. Communication Research, 23, 651-674.

Nass, C., & Moon, Y. (2000). Machines and mindlessness: Social responses to computers. Journal of Social Issues, 56(1), 81-103.

Putnam, R. D. (1993). Making democracy work: civic traditions in modern Italy. Princeton, NJ: Princeton University Press.

Sztompka, P. (1999). Trust: a sociological theory. Cambridge, UK: Cambridge University Press.

Section 1
Trust and Technology:
Theoretical Approaches

Chapter 1
Trust in Computers:
The Computers–Are–Social–Actors (CASA) Paradigm and Trustworthiness Perception in Human–Computer Communication

Jong-Eun Roselyn Lee
Hope College, USA

Clifford I. Nass
Stanford University, USA

ABSTRACT

Research based on the Computers-Are-Social-Actors (CASA) paradigm has documented that people's responses to computers are fundamentally "social"—that is, people apply social rules, norms, and expectations core to interpersonal relationships when they interact with computers. In light of the CASA paradigm, identifying the conditions that foster or undermine trust in the context of interpersonal communication and relationships may help us better understand the trust dynamics in human-computer communication. This chapter discusses experimental studies grounded in the CASA paradigm that demonstrate how (1) perceived people-computer similarity in personality, (2) manifestation of caring behaviors in computers, and (3) consistency in human/non-human representations of computers affect the extent to which people perceive computers as trustworthy.

INTRODUCTION

Although computers, when first invented, emerged in the image of a massive, beast-like machine (Laurel, 1993) or a "giant calculator" (Turkle, 1995), they have evolved to reside in almost every corner of our daily lives. We no longer use computers only as a computing tool, but use them for a variety of purposes including, but not limited to, learning, shopping, entertainment, and social interaction. In these various venues of computer use, people not just rely on computers for connecting and communicating with others (i.e., computer-mediated communication: CMC), but, in many cases, communicate *with* computers (human-computer communication: HCC).

Thanks to the advances in digital technologies and to the availability of higher bandwidths, the ways in which people communicate with computers and computer agents—pre-programmed digital

DOI: 10.4018/978-1-61520-901-9.ch001

representations that are controlled by computer algorithms (Bailenson & Blascovich, 2004; Isbister & Layton, 1995)—are becoming increasingly multimodal (Nass & Brave, 2005), enhancing the affordances for "richer" interaction. In addition, the roles played by computers in HCC are becoming remarkably diversified, ranging from trainers/tutors (W. L. Johnson, Rickel, & Lester, 2000) to personal assistants (Cassell & Bickmore, 2000; Maes, 1994) and social companions (Cassell, Sullivan, Prevost, & Churchill, 2000). As these changes take place in the landscape of HCC, with more and more computers and computer agents interacting and "working" with people, issues of people's trust in computers are particularly intriguing to study.

This chapter presents a number of research studies that investigated conditions under which computers and computer agents are perceived as trustworthy. This line of research is grounded in the assumption that computers and computer agents, which are lifeless digital artifacts, can and should be considered an object of trust. While it is true that people who use computers are well aware that a computer "does not warrant human treatment or attribution" (Nass & Moon, 2000, p. 82), our research program based on the Computers-Are-Social-Actors (CASA) paradigm has documented that people, despite their awareness that computers are not humans, do apply social rules, norms, and expectations to their interactions with computers, and treat computers as if they were "social actors" (Nass & Brave, 2005; Nass & Moon, 2000; Reeves & Nass, 1996).

In the context of interpersonal communication, trust is defined as "reliance upon," or confidence in, "the communication behavior of another person in order to achieve a desired but uncertain objective in a risky situation" (Giffin, 1967, p. 105). If we translate this definition of trust in interpersonal communication into HCC contexts, people's trust in computers may be understood as the extent to which people rely on or have confidence in a computer (computer agent),

particularly when they are seeking to achieve a goal (be it learning, receiving recommendations on commercial products, purchasing goods, or entertainment) in an uncertain or risky situation. The empirical evidence discussed in this chapter demonstrates that the conditions under which people perceive computers/computer agents as trustworthy closely reflect the conditions under which trust becomes fostered in the context of interpersonal communication. Before presenting these studies on trustworthiness perception of computers, we will first begin by discussing the CASA paradigm.

THE COMPUTERS-ARE-SOCIAL-ACTORS (CASA) PARADIGM

Research based on the CASA paradigm has demonstrated that people respond to computers in the same manner as they would toward other people, and such responses can be triggered once certain social cues are manifested by the computers (Nass & Brave, 2005; Nass & Moon, 2000; Reeves & Nass, 1996). That is, once a computer (or computer agent) looks, "talks" (via either text or speech), or behaves like a person —however minimal these cues might be—people would respond to it as if it were a real person (Nass, Takayama, & Brave, 2006). In this section, we describe some of the key CASA studies which have established the "social-ness" of people's responses to computers: studies on similarity attraction, reciprocity, and social stereotyping and categorization.

Similarity Attraction Operates in HCC

Can computers manifest personality characteristics? And when a computer exhibits personality-relevant cues, what responses would people show to the computer? And do social principles in human-human relationships such as similarity attraction (Byrne, Griffitt, & Stefanik, 1967) play out in human-computer relationships? These questions were addressed by some of the earliest CASA studies which focused on one of the key personality dimensions: dominance-submissiveness (Moon & Nass, 1996; Nass, Moon, Fogg, Reeves, & Dryer, 1995). Based on a standard dominance/submissiveness personality test, "dominant" and "submissive" respondents were categorized and were invited to participate in the experiment. These participants were paired with a computer that manifested either "dominant" or "submissive" personality via simple scripting of on-screen text. The findings showed that participants not only perceived the computer that exhibited dominant-personality cues through text as dominant and the computer exhibiting submissive-personality cues as submissive. Furthermore, consistent with the similarity-attraction principle of interpersonal relationships, participants showed greater attraction to the computer that exhibited characteristics matching their own personality than the one exhibited mismatching characteristics.

Follow-up studies demonstrated how far the effects of perceived similarity could get. For example, interesting effects were found for "personality changes" manifested by a computer over time (Moon & Nass, 1996). That is, when a computer's personality cues shifted from being dissimilar to being similar to the user' personality, the user exhibited greater attraction to the computer than when the computer's personality was either constantly similar, or constantly dissimilar, to the user's personality. Moreover, the power of cued similarity was so influential that it could even overcome self-serving bias (Moon & Nass, 1998). Namely, when a computer's "personality" matched the user's personality, the user was less likely to blame the computer for failure and more likely to give credit for success than when there was a computer-user personality mismatch (Moon & Nass, 1998).

These studies not only showed that computers—even with minimal cues—could manifest personality characteristics, but also documented that powerful social principles such as similarity

attraction play out in human-computer relationships as well.

People Reciprocate with Computers

Another interesting pattern uncovered by the CASA research is that people follow social rules and norms when they interact with computers. One such example is the rule of reciprocation, which is considered very powerful and pervasive in human culture (Cialdini, 1993). As Cialdini (1993) notes, "Each of us has been taught to live up to the rule, and each of us knows about the social sanctions and derision applied to anyone who violates it" (p. 19); reciprocation, in other words, is a type of over-learned, or "deeply ingrained," social behavior (Nass & Moon, 2000, p. 87). And although it is quite natural to presume that no one would ever feel obligated to follow the rule or would fear "social sanctions and derision" from violating the rule when interacting with a computer, the CASA studies have demonstrated that people nonetheless do "stick to" the rule, and do reciprocate to the computer.

In the first CASA experiment conducted on reciprocation (Fogg & Nass, 1997), participants performed two tasks. In Task 1, participants received "help" from a computer while doing web search; half of the participants worked with a computer that was helpful with the search, while the other half of the participants worked with a computer that was not helpful. Then in Task 2, participants were asked to create a color palette to best match human perception to "help" the computer. In one condition, participants performed the color palette task on the same computer they had used for the web search in Task 1; in the other condition, participants performed the task on a computer different from the one they used in Task 1. And the results showed that participants who interacted with a helpful computer for Task 1 and then worked on the same computer for Task 2 were willing to do a significantly greater amount of work for the computer than were those who used different computers for Task 1 and 2. When participants interacted with the not-so-helpful computer on Task 1, participants offered a significantly less amount of "help" when they used the same computer for Task 2 than did those who used different computers for Task 1 and 2, which suggested that participants even "retaliated" against the not-so-helpful computer when they were given a "chance" to do so (Nass & Moon, 2000).

Reciprocation in the context of HCC was also investigated with respect to self-disclosure (Moon, 2000).

In the context of interpersonal communication, intimate self-disclosure tends to be strongly governed by the rule of reciprocation; that is, people are willing to self-disclose to another person about themselves when the other party engages in self-disclosure first (Chaikin & Derlega, 1974). For testing whether reciprocal self-disclosure operates in HCC, Moon (2000) conducted an experiment which compared people's responses to a computer that "initiates" self-disclosure with people's responses to a computer that does not engage in such disclosive communication. In this study, participants were interviewed by a computer which asked some intimate questions (e.g., "What have you done in your life that you feel most guilty about?"). In the reciprocity condition, the computer first presented with some disclosive information about itself (e.g., "This computer has been configured to run at speeds up to 266MHZ. But 90% of computer users don't use applications that require these speeds. So this computer rarely gets used to its full potential"), and then asked the participant a related question ("What has been your biggest disappointment in life?"). By contrast, the control-condition computer did not present any "disclosive" information about itself; the computer, rather straightforwardly, solicited an answer to the interview question. The results showed that participants in the reciprocity condition were more likely to engage in intimate self-disclosure when compared with the participants in the control condition. The non-humanness of the computer was explicit; that is, the computer in the reciprocity condition never implied that it had "feelings," nor did it refer to itself as "I." Nonetheless, people reciprocated with the computer by engaging in intimate self-disclosure, which suggests that "over-learned" social norms such as the norms of reciprocity strongly govern HCC (Nass & Moon, 2000).

People Attribute Social Categories to Computers

Another avenue where the CASA paradigm established the social-ness of people's response to computers concerned social stereotyping and categorization of computers that exhibit category-associated cues. One line of research examined whether people would gender-stereotype computers when the voice output transmitted gender cues (Nass, Moon, & Green, 1997). In this study, participants interacted with a tutor computer, which had either female or male voice, and were presented with information on either a stereotypically masculine topic ("computers and technology") or a stereotypically feminine topic ("love and relationships"). The results were consistent with the way people attribute gender stereotypes to other people (Heilman, 1979): Whereas the male-voiced tutor computer was rated significantly more informative than the female-voiced computer for the "masculine" topic, the female-voiced computer received higher ratings than the male-voiced computer for the "feminine" topic.

People not only stereotyped computers, but also categorized and judged computers based on their expectations derived by category-relevant cues that were accessible. In an experiment which investigated the effects of ethnicity manifested by computer agents (Nass & Brave, Chapter 6), male participants, who were either Caucasian Americans or first-generation Koreans, were presented with an e-commerce website and then listened to product descriptions in English. Half of each ethnic group members were presented with product descriptions read by a Korean-accent voice agent, which was accompanied either by an image of a Korean male or by that of a Caucasian-Australian male; the other half heard the identical product descriptions read by an Australian-accent voice agent, which was accompanied either by an image of a Korean male or by that of a Caucasian-Australian male. And afterwards, participants were asked to rate the voice agents. The results showed that regardless of their' own ethnic identity, participants showed greater liking for the agents, and even for the products described by the agents, when the "ethnic" identity of the voice was consistent with the image featured by the agents than when there was inconsistency. These findings indicate that people, even when they interact with computers, would prefer not to have their "expectations" and "attributions" concerning social categories disrupted.

In sum, the CASA studies on manifestations of social categories in HCC suggest that although computers—as a lifeless digital artifact—do not "belong to" any social category groups based on gender or ethnicity, people still attribute social categories to computers when category-relevant cues are made available, and make judgments accordingly (Nass et al., 2006).

WHEN DO PEOPLE TRUST COMPUTERS? APPLICATION OF THE CASA PARADIGM

As reviewed in the previous section, research based on the CASA paradigm has documented that social rules, norms, and expectations that are core to interpersonal relationships do play out in the contexts of HCC. That said, in light of the CASA paradigm, understanding of the conditions that determine perceptions of trustworthiness in interpersonal situations may provide insights into the trust dynamics in HCC.

As Gambetta (1988) noted, "When we say we trust someone or that someone is trustworthy," we expect that the person "will perform an action that is beneficial or at least not detrimental to us" (p. 217); we then safely and willingly consider engaging in cooperation with that person (Gambetta, 1988). Then, when it comes to HCC, what are the conditions under which we perceive computers trustworthy, expecting that the computers would be "beneficial" or "at least not detrimental to us"? In this section, we present studies that have extended the previous CASA studies with an emphasis on perceptions of trustworthiness in computers. The key factors considered by these studies are: (1) perceived user-computer similarity in "personality"; (2) computers' manifestation of caring orientations toward the user; and (3) consistency in human/non-human representation of computers.

Perceived Similarity Breeds Trust in Computers

As discussed in the previous section, the CASA studies on the manifestation of dominance/submissiveness in computers documented that similarity attraction does govern people's perception of and attitudes toward computers. Then, just as people tend to trust those who have traits similar to their own (McAllister, 1995; Stiff, 1994; Zucker, 1986), would people find a computer more trustworthy when they find the computer "similar" to themselves (Fogg, 2003)?

The effects of perceived similarity on trustworthiness perception in HCC was investigated in a context where people interacted with a "talking computer," which communicated with users based on computer-synthesized speech (Nass & K. M. Lee, 2001). In this experiment, messages from the computer were presented via text-to-speech (TTS) systems, which could generate any speech-based content in real time (Olive, 1997). Use of computer-synthesized speech afforded a critical test of the CASA paradigm by providing people "consistent reminders that one is not interacting with a person," but with a lifeless digital artifact (Nass & K. M. Lee, 2001, p. 172). The personality dimension of interest was extroversion versus introversion (Digman, 1990; Winter, John, Stewart, Klohnen, & Duncan, 1998), particularly because the extroversion-introversion is clearly marked by vocal cues (e.g., intensity, frequency, frequency range, and speech rate) and can thereby be effectively manipulated via TTS systems.

In this study, participants interacted with a computer in the context of online shopping. On a website that looked similar to the interface used by *Amazon.com*, participants (who were selectively invited to participate in the study based on their extroversion/introversion personality scores) were presented with descriptions and reviews of five different books. These book descriptions/reviews were read either in an extrovert TTS voice or in an introvert TTS voice. Participants were then asked to rate the quality of the voice and that of the book reviews.

The results revealed interesting patterns with respect to people's perception of computer-synthesized, "machine-like" speech. First, people attributed extroversion and introversion to the synthesized voices: the "extrovert" computer voice was perceived as being significantly more extroverted, and the "introvert" computer voice as more "introverted." The data were also consistent with the similarity-attraction principle: the extrovert participants preferred the extroverted voice, while the introvert participants preferred the introverted voice. As for perceived trustworthiness, participants not only found the computer voice to be more trustworthy when it matched their own personality than when there was a personality mismatch. Interestingly, although the content of the book reviews were held constant, participants trusted the book reviewer more when the personality of the computer voice, through which the reviews were presented, matched participants' personality than when there was a mismatch. In

sum, these findings demonstrated how the power of similarity attraction could be extended into the realm of trustworthiness perception in HCC.

When Computers Care about Us: "Artificial" Caring that Fosters Trust

People, as social animals, appreciate being cared about by others (Aronson, 1972; Davis, 1996), and communication of caring is a key element of trust-building in interpersonal relationships (Burleson & Goldsmith, 1998). The positive effects of caring on trust have been documented in the context of intimate relationships. Specifically, caring is a key determinant of trust in romantic partners (Lock, Ferguson, & Wise, 1998), and violation of the expectation that one's partner would offer caring in times of distress tends to undermine trust (S. M. Johnson, Makinen, & Millikin, 2001). Clinical settings have also been extensively studied with respect to the trust-building effects of caring. Patients' trust in health practitioners tends to be positively affected by health practitioners' demonstration of caring through emotional commitment (Semmes, 1991); likewise, patients tend to show greater trust in health care providers who express caring orientations through compassionate gestures and empowering statements (Battaglia, Finley, & Liebschutz, 2003). Along similar lines, in teacher-student communication contexts, teachers' caring behaviors had positive effects on student perception of teachers' trustworthiness. (Teven & Hanson, 2004).

Caring orientations toward others may seem entirely irrelevant to computers (Brave, Nass, & Hutchinson, 2005), for a computer or computer-generated character is a "quintessential unfeeling artifact" (p. 162). Nonetheless, the CASA studies on the effects of "artificial" caring on people's trust in computers/computer agents have demonstrated that the positive effects of caring orientations on trust-building or trustworthiness perception do hold for HCC.

Computer Agents with "Empathy"

Empathy is a set of other-oriented emotional responses that reflects how one cares about another person's welfare (Batson, Polycarpou, Harmon-Jones, Imhoff, Mitchener, Bednar, & Klein, 1997). Viewing empathy as a core component of caring orientations, Brave et al. (2005) investigated how people respond to computer agents that express empathy toward them, using a competitive game-playing situation where the computer agent and the computer user did not have any shared goals or interest. In this experiment, participants played a Casino-style blackjack with a same gender computer agent, which had a human-like (i.e., non-humanoid) facial image. Participants were paired up with one of four versions of computer agents, which were created based on two factors: (1) expression of self-oriented emotion (absent vs. present) and (2) expression of empathic, other-oriented emotion (absent vs. present).

Specifically, this experiment manipulated the presence/absence of self-oriented emotion in the game-playing agent by varying the agent's reaction to its own performance on blackjack hands. The agent with self-oriented emotion displayed facial expressions that corresponded with the outcome of its own hand, while the agent without self-oriented emotion did not. And the presence/absence of empathic (other-oriented) emotion was manipulated by the agent's reaction to participants' performance on the game. That is, the empathy-present agent made a happy facial expression when the participant won a hand; when the participant lost a hand, the agent made a sad facial expression. The empathy-absent agent did not display any of these other-oriented emotional expressions.

The results showed that other-oriented (empathic), but not self-oriented, emotional expressions of the agent had a significant effect on perceived trustworthiness of the agent; that is, participants rated the agent to be more trustworthy when the agent displayed empathic emotion than when it did not. Although the agent was a computer-generated, lifeless artifact which lacked "genuine feelings," the computer user still found the agent more trustworthy when it manifested caring orientations toward the user than when it did not.

Colearner Agents Communicating Emotional Support

In another experiment, we examined the psychological mechanism behind the effects of "artificial" caring manifested by computer agents on perceived trustworthiness (J. R. Lee, Nass, Brave, Morishima, Nakajima, & Yamada, 2007). In this experiment, we used a computer interface designed for language learning, which featured a tutor agent and a colearner agent. Participants—Japanese college students who were all non-native speakers of English—took a lesson on English idioms led by the teacher agent.

The experiment session consisted of four parts: (a) instructions; (b) a brief video skit which presented a dialogue between two individuals; (c) an idiom lesson; and (d) a posttest questionnaire which included learning assessment. First, participants received instructions on how to use the interface. Upon finishing reading the instructions, participants were presented with a brief video skit on the computer screen. In the video, two individuals carried out a conversation in English using idioms that were to be explained in detail in the idiom lesson that followed. When participants finished watching the video skit, they were asked to click on the "Continue" button, which initiated the idiom lesson. First, the teacher agent asked a question on a given idiom (e.g., "What do you think the following statement means?") and offered a statement that included the idiom in question (e.g., "Lucy is a pain in the neck!"); three answer choices (e.g., "Lucy hurt her neck," "Lucy makes my neck hurt," and "Lucy is annoying") were provided and participants were asked to select one of the three answer choices. When an answer was submitted, the teacher agent provided a detailed explanation about the correct answer and about the specific usage of the given idiomatic expression.

While this general structure was shared by all three conditions of the experiment (i.e., the caring-colearner condition, the noncaring-colearner condition, and the control condition), the specific features of the idiom lesson differed across conditions. In the control condition which did not feature a colearner agent, the teacher agent called on the participant to select an answer choice for the given question. In the two experimental conditions (caring vs. noncaring colearner), the teacher agent asked either the participant or the colearner agent to give an answer to the question, alternating between the two.

The caring colearner and noncaring colearner conditions varied with respect to the colearner agent's behavior toward the participant. In the caring colearner condition, the agent showed empathic emotional expressions and made highly person-centered comforting remarks (Jones & Burleson, 1997)—"messages that acknowledge, elaborate, legitimize, and contextualize the feelings of the other" (p. 530)—to the participant. For example, when the participant gave a correct answer to the teacher agent, the caring colearner displayed positive emotional expressions and provided compliments such as: "Good job"; "That was hard, and you got it!"; "You're good at this"; "I'm impressed"; "I knew you'd get it right"; and "You are doing very well!" And when the participant provided an incorrect answer, the agent gave empathic and encouraging feedback such as: "That was a hard one"; "I didn't know that one, either"; "Don't worry – you are really good at these"; "I would have given the same answer; this is hard"; and "Good try." In the noncaring colearner condition, the colearner agent showed the same behavioral patterns as shown by the caring colearner agent except for the empathic, caring verbal feedback to participants.

Our results showed that participants in the caring-colearner condition (1) gave significantly higher ratings of the colearner agent in terms of trustworthiness and (2) performed better on the post-experiment learning assessment than did participants in the other two conditions. To better understand the process, we performed a mediation analysis in which the two experimental conditions were dummy-coded. The results of the mediation analysis revealed that the positive effects of "artificial caring" manifested by the caring colearner on the trustworthiness ratings and performance were mediated by participants' (self-reported) feelings of being supported. These findings demonstrated that communication of caring, which addresses the basic human need for affiliation and support, is important to fostering trust in the context of human–computer communication context. Namely, caring behaviors that are "artificial"—conveyed by a lifeless digital artifact that lacks genuine and natural feelings—still lead people to feel that they are supported in the given context, which in turn leads them to perceive the computer as trustworthy.

Should Computers Talk and Look like Human?: Consistency Matters

Advances in digital technologies allow interface designers and developers to incorporate various social cues into HCC. Text, although still widely used, is no longer the single dominant modality of HCC; rather, other types of modalities such as speech and graphics are increasingly being used for creating rich behavioral scripts for computers and computer agents (Gong & Nass, 2007). While such technological affordances offer ample opportunities for experimenting with various interface features, interface designers/developers, at the same time, are faced with challenges and choices that may be difficult to make. Particularly when the goal is to foster users' trust in computers, designers and developers should carefully decide what types of social cues they want to incorporate into the computer interface.

One interesting question is when computers/computer agents should (or should not) talk/

look like human and how human/non-human representations of computers would affect perceptions of trustworthiness. Although many different combinations could be derived when mixing and matching different types of representations and behaviors of computers/computer agents, the CASA paradigm illuminates one important rule that should be followed: consistency. In the person perception and interpersonal communication literature, inconsistency in communicative behaviors and traits (1) requires more cognitive processing effort (Schul, Burnstein, & Martinez, 1983); (2) elicits negative feelings (Hendrick, 1972); and (3) signals deception (Ekman & Friesen, 1969; Ekman & Friesen, 1974). And all of these undesirable consequences of social inconsistency may dismantle trust-building. Would these problems hold for HCC? Interestingly, studies based on the CASA paradigm have demonstrated that inconsistency in representations and behaviors of a computer/computer agent tends to have negative effects on perceived trustworthiness, which will be described below.

An "Attempt to Claim Humanness?": Computer Speech and Use of the First Person

Both the notion of self ("I") and the behavior of "speaking" are uniquely human, which lie at the core of our social expectations (Nass & Brave, 2005; Nass et al., 2006). Then, in what circumstances should speech-based computers/computer agents say or not say "I" when they interact with people? And under what conditions would synthetic voices be more appropriate than recorded (human) voices? These questions were addressed by an experiment which compared synthetic and recorded (i.e., human-like) speech interfaces with respect to use of the first person (Nass & Brave, 2005, Chapter 10).

In this experiment, participants were presented with an auction website. Half of the participants used an auction system based on a synthetic voice,

while the other half used a system based on a recorded voice. Then, for half of the participants who used the recorded-speech interface and for half of those who used the synthetic-speech interface, the system used the word "I" or "my"; here, the use of the first-person words represented only 5 percent of the entire words spoken by the system. By contrast, the other half of the participants of each group interacted with the "impersonal" system, which did not use the first-person words. For example, the system based on use of the first person remarked [italics added for emphasis]:

I will begin today's auction shortly. I have five items for auction today. I will read the descriptions for the items one by one. Please bid at the end of each item's description. My records indicate that you have $1,000 in your account. (...) The first item I have for you today is a cozy twin-size pine frame futon. The estimated retail price is around $180. It's a great piece of furniture for any room and very convenient when your friends come over. The cover is included. It is one of the top items I can offer to you today. (Nass & Brave, 2005, p. 118)

By contrast, the parallel message from the "impersonal" system was presented as follows:

Today's auction will begin shortly. There are five items for auction today. The descriptions for the items will be read one by one. Please bid at the end of each item's description. The records indicate that there is $1,000 in your account. (...) The first item today is a cozy twin-size pine frame futon. The estimated retail price is around $180. It's a great piece of furniture for any room and very convenient when your friends come over. The cover is included. It is one of the top items offered today. (Nass & Brave, 2005, p. 118)

The results presented solid evidence that consistency of humanness/non-humanness matters when it comes to users' trust in the system. That is, although the actual content displayed by the systems was basically the same, the recorded-voice system was perceived to be more trustworthy and useful when it used the first- person words than when it used impersonal expressions. And the synthetic-voice system was perceived to be less trustworthy when it used the first-person words than when it communicated in an impersonal way; there was no significant difference for the recorded-speech system. Furthermore, participants who interacted with the recorded-speech system actually bid significantly more when they heard the system say "I" and "my" than when they heard the impersonal system, whereas those who interacted with the synthetic-speech system bid more when the system communicated in an impersonal manner than when it used the first-person words. It is likely that the use of the first-person words shown by the synthetic-speech system—an "attempt to claim humanity"—was perceived as a "suspicious artifice" (Nass & Brave, 2005, p. 119) and hence had negative effects on the user's trust in the system. It is also possible that the inconsistency with respect to humanness/non-humanness representations of the system caused discomfort to the user, which might in turn have undermined trust in the system.

Human-Humanoid Inconsistency Hurts: The Case of Talking-Face Computer Agents

Regarding the consistency effects for humanness/ non-humanness representations, the aforementioned study investigated the effects of voice (recorded vs. synthetic) and speech style (self-referencing vs. impersonal) on trustworthiness perception, and demonstrated that consistency in terms of (1) what the computer sounds like and (2) what the computer says is key to fostering perceptions of trustworthiness.

As embodied computer agents (Cassell et al., 2000) are increasingly being used in computer applications, an important issue that should be examined is whether the consistency principle plays out with respect to computer agents' face-and voice-types (Nass et al., 2006). As faces and voices are two key biosocial attributes of humans, and as people have deeply ingrained social expectations about what constitutes humanness, any inconsistency between a face and a voice (e.g., a human face with a non-human voice or a non-human face with a human voice) manifested by a computer agent may undermine its perceived trustworthiness. This issue was investigated by an experiment that used talking-face agents (Gong & Nass, 2007) in an interviewing context which involved intimate self-disclosure.

In this experiment (Gong & Nass, 2007, Study 1), participants interacted with a computer agent playing the role of an "interviewer" that adopted one of four face-voice combinations: (1) human face and human voice; (2) human face and humanoid (synthetic) voice; (3) humanoid (computer-generated and computer-animated) face and human voice; and (4) humanoid face and humanoid voice. The human face was based on real people's photographic images, and the human voice, which was based on real people's recorded voice, sounded natural. The humanoid face, created based on a computer-generated facial animation model (Parke & Waters, 1996), looked computer-generated and synthetic; the humanoid voice was produced by a computer-speech engine and thus sounded synthetic (Massaro, 1998; Nass & Brave, 2005).

During the experiment session, the talking-face computer agents asked participants to respond to a series of self-disclosure questions (as used by Moon, 2000), which was employed as the main experiment task for assessing trust given that trust is a key factor that motivates intimate self-disclosure in interpersonal communication (Wheeless & Grotz, 1977). In this self-disclosure task, participants typed their answer to each question in a text box provided on the screen. After this task, participants responded to a post-experiment questionnaire that asked them to rate their experience with the computer agent.

The results provided support for the consistency effects, showing patterns similar to those of the study described earlier (Nass and Brave, 2005, Chapter 10). Participants, regardless of their gender, (1) engaged in significantly less intimate self-disclosure to the talking-face agent and (2) gave significantly lower ratings of trustworthiness when the agent's face and voice were inconsistent (i.e., a humanoid face paired with a human voice, or a human face coupled with a humanoid voice) than when they were consistent.

To sum up, in line with the CASA paradigm, the social rules and expectations regarding behavioral consistency in HCC do mirror the principle of "consistency attraction" (Nass & K. M. Lee, 2001). Just as inconsistency in communicative behaviors and traits shown by interactants hurts trust-building in the context of interpersonal communication, inconsistency in representations of computers/computer agents may undermine people's trust in computers in the HCC context.

FUTURE RESEARCH DIRECTIONS

One of the key take-home messages of the CASA research paradigm on trust in computers is that people tend to look for similar qualities of trustworthiness in computers as they do in other people (Takayama & Kandogan, 2006). In this light, the CASA paradigm opens up a host of avenues for identifying conditions under which people's trust in computers could be cultivated or dismantled, as we could leverage theories of trust in the context of interpersonal communication and test them in the context of HCC. That said, an intriguing question that has yet to be investigated is trust violation and repair in HCC. Although research based on the CASA paradigm has demonstrated what "social" attributes and qualities a computer should "possess" to be perceived as trustworthy, little research has been conducted on how trust could be repaired when a user's positive expectations about the technology are violated. Research

on trust violation in interpersonal settings has identified that trust repair can be done successfully when the mistrusted actor apologizes for violations concerning competence-related matters but denies responsibility for integrity-related matters (Kim, Ferrin, Cooper, & Dirks, 2004). It would be interesting to test whether similar dynamics play out in the context of HCC with respect to trust violation and repair.

Another critical issue that has yet to be tackled by the CASA paradigm is how the perceptions of trustworthiness would shape people's long-term "relationships" with computers. The CASA studies have contributed to identifying the factors that might determine trust in computers; however, all of these experiments have been based on one-time interactions. Future research should examine repeated or longer-term human-computer communication (Gong & Nass, 2007), which will provide helpful insights into how trusting long-term "relationships" could be developed and maintained between people and computers.

CONCLUSION

Research based on the CASA paradigm has demonstrated that interactions between people and computers are fundamentally "social," as people tend to apply social principles, rules, and expectations to the lifeless digital artifacts. The CASA paradigm has made important contributions to viewing communication between people and computers not just as a type of mediated communication but also as a type of interpersonal communication (Bracken & Lombard, 2004).

As demonstrated by the CASA studies described here, the social principles that govern us and the social expectations we hold with respect to trust-building in the interpersonal settings do translate into the context of human-computer communication. Just as we are more likely to trust those who are similar to us than those who are dissimilar to us, a computer that manifests "personality"-associated characteristics similar to one's own is more likely to be perceived to be trustworthy than a computer that does not manifest similarity. Just as we are more likely to trust people who make us feel cared about than those who do not, a computer that manifests caring behaviors toward its user is more likely to be perceived trustworthy than a computer that does not show caring orientations. Just as we are more likely to feel suspicious of deception and lose trust when we interact with people who lack consistency in their behaviors, inconsistency in representations and behaviors of a computer may negatively affect its perceived trustworthiness.

Trust is the basic building block of sound social relationships—"the loom on which we weave our social fabric" (Cassell & Bickmore, 2000, p. 50). As computer interfaces penetrate every corner of our social lives, many of important daily activities are performed through communication *with* computers. Computer users are constantly dealing with digital entities that offer opinions and recommendations; present products and services; deliver news and information; provide channels for social interaction with other individuals; and solicit and collect information from users (Gong & Nass, 2007). In all of our everyday activities performed *with* computers, trust serves as a critical factor. Beyond the theoretical frameworks and empirical evidence provided in this chapter, we hope that the CASA paradigm will continue to provide helpful insights into how trust could be promoted in human-computer relationships.

REFERENCES

Aronson, E. (1972). *The social animal*. New York: Viking.

Bailenson, J., & Blascovich, J. (2004). Avatars. In Bainbridge, W. S. (Ed.), *Encyclopedia of human-computer interaction* (pp. 64–68). Great Barrington, MA: Berkshire Publishing Group.

Batson, C. D., Polycarpou, M. P., Harmon-Jones, E., Imhoff, H. J., Mitchener, E. C., & Bednar, L. L. (1997). Empathy and attitudes: Can feeling for a member of a stigmatized group improve feelings toward the group. *Journal of Personality and Social Psychology, 72*, 105–118. doi:10.1037/0022-3514.72.1.105

Battaglia, T. A., Finley, E., & Liebschutz, J. M. (2003). Survivors of intimate partner violence speak out: Trust in the patient-provider relationship. *Journal of General Internal Medicine, 18*, 617–623. doi:10.1046/j.1525-1497.2003.21013.x

Bracken, C. C., & Lombard, M. (2004). Social presence and children: Praise, intrinsic motivation, and learning with computers. *The Journal of Communication, 54*, 22–37. doi:10.1111/j.1460-2466.2004.tb02611.x

Brave, S. B., Nass, C., & Hutchinson, K. (2005). Computers that care: Investigating the effects of orientation of emotion exhibited by an embodied computer agent. *International Journal of Human-Computer Studies, 62*, 161–178. doi:10.1016/j.ijhcs.2004.11.002

Burleson, B. R., & Goldsmith, D. J. (1998). How the comforting process works: Alleviating emotional distress through conversationally induced reappraisals. In Andersen, P. A., & Guerrero, L. K. (Eds.), *Handbook of communication and emotion: Research, theory, applications, and contexts* (pp. 245–279). San Diego, CA: Academic Press.

Byrne, D., Griffitt, W., & Stefanik, D. (1967). Attraction and similarity of personality characteristics. *Journal of Personality and Social Psychology, 5*, 82–90. doi:10.1037/h0021198

Cassell, J., & Bickmore, T. (2000). External manifestations of trustworthiness in the interface. *Communications of the ACM, 43*(12), 50–56. doi:10.1145/355112.355123

Cassell, J., Sullivan, J., Prevost, S., & Churchill, E. (2000). *Embodied conversational agents*. Cambridge, MA: MIT Press.

Chaikin, A. L., & Derlega, V. J. (1974). *Self-disclosure*. Morristown, NJ: General Learning Press.

Cialdini, R. B. (1993). *Influence: Science and practice*. New York: HarperCollins.

Davis, M. H. (1996). *Empathy: A social psychological approach*. Boulder, CO: Westview Press.

Digman, J. M. (1990). Personality structure: Emergence of the five-factor model. *Annual Review of Psychology, 41*, 417–440.

Ekman, P., & Friesen, W. V. (1969). Nonverbal leakage and clues to deception. *Psychiatry, 32*, 88–95.

Ekman, P., & Friesen, W. V. (1974). Detecting deception from the body or face. *Journal of Personality and Social Psychology, 29*, 288–298. doi:10.1037/h0036006

Fogg, B. J. (2003). *Persuasive technology: Using computers to change what we think and do*. San Francisco, CA: Morgan Kaufmann Publishers.

Fogg, B. J., & Nass, C. (1997). Do users reciprocate to computers? In *Proceedings of the CHI Conference '97* (pp. 331-332).

Gambetta, D. G. (1988). Can we trust trust? In Gambetta, D. G. (Ed.), *Trust* (pp. 213–237). New York: Basil Blackwell.

Giffin, K. (1967). The contribution of studies of source credibility to a theory of interpersonal trust in the communication process. *Psychological Bulletin, 68*(2), 104–120. doi:10.1037/h0024833

Gong, L., & Nass, C. (2007). When a talking-face computer agent is half-human and half-humanoid: Human identity and consistency preference. *Human Communication Research, 33*, 163–193. doi:10.1111/j.1468-2958.2007.00295.x

Heilman, M. E. (1979). High school students' occupational interest as a function of projected sex ratios in male-dominated occupations. *The Journal of Applied Psychology, 64*, 275–279. doi:10.1037/0021-9010.64.3.275

Hendrick, C. (1972). Effects of salience of stimulus inconsistency on impression formation. *Journal of Personality and Social Psychology, 22*, 219–222. doi:10.1037/h0032599

Isbister, K., & Layton, T. (1995). Agents: What (or who) are they? In Nielsen, J. (Ed.), *Advances in human-computer interaction* (*Vol. 5*). Norwood, NJ: Ablex Publishing Corporation.

Johnson, S. M., Makinen, J. A., & Millikin, J. W. (2001). Attachment injuries in couple relationships: A new perspective on impasses in couples therapy. *Journal of Marital and Family Therapy, 27*, 145–155. doi:10.1111/j.1752-0606.2001.tb01152.x

Johnson, W. L., Rickel, J. W., & Lester, J. C. (2000). Animated pedagogical agents: Face-to-face interaction in interactive learning environments. *International Journal of Artificial Intelligence in Education, 11*, 47–78.

Jones, S. M., & Burleson, B. R. (1997). The impact of situational variables on helpers' perception of comforting messages: An attributional analysis. *Communication Research, 24*, 530–555. doi:10.1177/009365097024005004

Kim, P. H., Ferrin, D. L., Cooper, C. D., & Dirks, K. T. (2004). Removing the shadow of suspicion: The effects of apology versus denial for repairing competence- versus integrity-based trust violations. *The Journal of Applied Psychology, 89*, 104–118. doi:10.1037/0021-9010.89.1.104

Laurel, B. (1993). *Computers as theater*. Reading, MA: Addison-Wesley Publishing Company.

Lee, J. R., Nass, C., Brave, S., Morishima, Y., Nakajima, H., & Yamada, R. (2007). The case for caring co-learners: The effects of a computer-mediated co-learner agent on trust and learning. *The Journal of Communication, 57,* 183–204. doi:10.1111/j.1460-2466.2007.00339.x

Lock, S. E., Ferguson, S. L., & Wise, C. (1998). Communication of sexual risk behavior among late adolescents. *Western Journal of Nursing Research, 20,* 273–294. doi:10.1177/019394599802000302

Maes, P. (1994). Agents that reduce work and information overload. *Communications of the ACM, 37*(7), 31–40. doi:10.1145/176789.176792

Massaro, D. M. (1998). *Perceiving talking faces: From speech perception to a behavioral principle.* Cambridge, MA: MIT Press.

McAllister, D. J. (1995). Affect- and cognition-based trust as foundations for interpersonal cooperation in organizations. *Academy of Management Journal, 38,* 24–59. doi:10.2307/256727

Moon, Y. (2000). Intimate exchanges: Using computers to elicit self-disclosure from consumers. *The Journal of Consumer Research, 26,* 323–339. doi:10.1086/209566

Moon, Y., & Nass, C. (1996). How "real" are computer personalities?: Psychological responses to personality types in human-computer interaction. *Communication Research, 23,* 651–674. doi:10.1177/009365096023006002

Moon, Y., & Nass, C. (1998). Are computers scapegoats?: Attributions of responsibility in human-computer interaction. *International Journal of Human-Computer Interaction, 49,* 79–94.

Nass, C., & Brave, S. B. (2005). *Wired for speech: How voice activates and advances the human-computer relationship.* Cambridge, MA: MIT Press.

Nass, C., & Lee, K. M. (2001). Does computer-synthesized speech manifest personality?: Experimental tests of recognition, similarity-attraction, and consistency-attraction. *Journal of Experimental Psychology. Applied, 7,* 171–181. doi:10.1037/1076-898X.7.3.171

Nass, C., & Moon, Y. (2000). Machines and mindlessness: Social responses to computers. *The Journal of Social Issues, 56,* 81–103. doi:10.1111/0022-4537.00153

Nass, C., Moon, Y., Fogg, B., Reeves, B., & Dryer, D. C. (1995). Can computer personalities be human personalities? *International Journal of Human-Computer Studies, 43,* 223–239. doi:10.1006/ijhc.1995.1042

Nass, C., Moon, Y., & Green, N. (1997). Are computers gender-neutral? Gender stereotypic responses to computers. *Journal of Applied Social Psychology, 27,* 864–876. doi:10.1111/j.1559-1816.1997.tb00275.x

Nass, C., Takayama, L., & Brave, S. B. (2006). Socializing consistency: From technical homogeneity to human epitome. In Zhang, P., & Galletta, D. (Eds.), *Human-computer interaction in management information systems: Foundations.* Armonk, NY: M. E. Sharpe.

Olive, J. P. (1997). The talking computer: Text to speech synthesis. In Stork, D. (Ed.), *Hal's legacy: 2001's computer as dream and reality* (pp. 101–130). Cambridge, MA: MIT Press.

Parke, F. I., & Waters, K. (1996). *Computer facial animation.* Wellesley, MA: A. K. Peters.

Reeves, B., & Nass, C. (1996). *The media equation: How people treat computers, television, and new media like real people and places.* New York: Cambridge University Press.

Schul, Y., Burnstein, E., & Martinez, J. (1983). The informational basis of social judgments: Under what conditions are inconsistent trait descriptions processed as easily as consistent ones? *European Journal of Social Psychology, 13*, 143–151. doi:10.1002/ejsp.2420130205

Semmes, C. E. (1991). Developing trust: Patient-practitioner encounters in natural health care. *Journal of Contemporary Ethnography, 19*, 450–470. doi:10.1177/089124191019004004

Stiff, J. B. (1994). *Persuasive Communication.* New York: Guilford Press.

Takayama, L., & Kandogan, E. (2006). *Trust as an underlying factor of system administrator interface choice.* Paper presented at the Conference on Human Factors in Computing Systems, Montréal, Canada.

Teven, J. J., & Hanson, T. L. (2004). The impact of teacher immediacy and perceived caring on teacher competence and trustworthiness. *Communication Quarterly, 52*, 39–53.

Turkle, S. (1995). *Life on the screen: identity in the age of the Internet.* New York: Simon & Schuster Paperbacks.

Wheeless, L. R., & Grotz, J. (1977). The measurement of trust and its relationship to self-disclosure. *Human Communication Research, 3*, 250–257. doi:10.1111/j.1468-2958.1977.tb00523.x

Winter, D. G., John, O. P., Stewart, A. J., Klohnen, E. C., & Duncan, L. E. (1998). Traits and motives: Toward an integration of two traditions in personality research. *Psychological Review, 105*, 230–250. doi:10.1037/0033-295X.105.2.230

Zucker, L. (1986). Similarity based trust. *Research in Organizational Behavior, 8*, 53–111.

Chapter 2
A Framework for Studying the Problem of Trust in Online Settings

Tina Guenther
Lecturer in Sociology, Founder and Author of Sozlog, Germany

Guido Möllering
Max Planck Institute for the Study of Societies, Germany

ABSTRACT

The chapter contributes to the conceptual foundations of research on trust in online settings by introducing a framework of the preconditions and constitutive elements of trust. Moving beyond simplistic, narrow, and vague applications of the notion of trust, researchers are enabled by this framework to recognize when trust is relevant and to address a broader range of elements and processes involved in the social constitution of trust. By way of illustration and differentiation, the authors discuss trust issues in online marketplaces and online communities in greater detail. An important message from the chapter is that the problem of trust does not only occur in specific activities on a particular website but, more importantly, through the interconnectedness of the websites used and the development of complex online biographies. Accordingly, the authors advocate research methods that are not only are well-grounded conceptually but also geared praxeologically toward the actual experience and enactment of trust.

INTRODUCTION

The possibilities for entering into social relationships via digital technologies such as the internet have undoubtedly multiplied since the beginning of the 21st century. If relationships established 'online' involve uncertainty and vulnerability just like 'offline' relationships, we need to take a close look at online trust. We conceptualize 'online trust' broadly as the social accomplishment of having positive mutual expectations in an online setting which may still be disappointed and abused. More importantly, we are concerned in this chapter with the fact that the 'online world' is, of course, not separate from offline reality, meaning in particular that any harm – as well as any good – done on the internet will mostly have offline consequences, too. This is the case, at least, in social relationships that are technologically mediated but ultimately connecting human actors.

DOI: 10.4018/978-1-61520-901-9.ch002

Our chapter contributes to a better understanding of online trust by outlining a framework that will enable researchers to assess and analyze more thoroughly, if and how trust is an issue in online settings. After giving some background considerations that motivate our chapter, we will discuss the preconditions for trust's relevance. This is followed by a description of the different elements involved in the constitution of trust and how they play out in online settings. We then discuss the implications of our framework, with particular emphasis on the methodological requirements and opportunities for empirical work in this area. In the conclusion, we highlight the value of a sound conceptual grounding of trust instead of invoking it too loosely in research on online relationships.

BACKGROUND

What is commonly called "Web 2.0" and also the "Social Web" – indicating already a new quality of online activities – comprises a wide spectrum of ideas, utopias, and business models. We can distinguish developments in technology, civil society, modes of production, and entrepreneurship that together and in interaction with each other make up the new possibilities of "Web 2.0".

First, in terms of technology, there are countless new applications such as weblogs, wiki webs, instant messaging, podcasts, RSS, social networking sites, and many more. The new technologies are designed to enable mass user participation and flexible reorganization of applications by users who create and recombine content, code, and metadata (Bruns, 2007; Guenther & Schmidt, 2008; Schmidt, 2006). Second, with this technological empowerment, "Web 2.0" can also denote an optimistic vision of a new civil society and the idea of a neo-Habermasian global public sphere of open discourse where critical discussions are possible, unconventional views can be expressed freely and the power of the state is counter-balanced (see Habermas, [1962]1989).

When the barriers to participation in new media are lowered, new arenas for exchanging information and opinions can emerge.

Third, the mode of production associated with "Web 2.0" is supposedly collaborative, heterarchical, and non-profit seeking. The content, code, and metadata going into such 'open source' products can challenge the proprietary solutions from the earlier days of the digital age (Benkler, 2006; Lessig, 2004). Fourth, it must be strongly emphasized, though, that the new opportunities are also part of a capitalist project that drives business and entrepreneurship ranging from e-commerce to a wealth of services and products offered by profit-seeking firms and individuals who use, maintain, or enhance the new technologies. It is by becoming more dynamic, integrative, interactive, and recombinant that the world of online media has entered into a new generation without a complete break from the internet of the 1990s.

The downside of increased connectedness is increased exposure. A highly dynamic world also carries higher uncertainty about the future. This makes trust a salient issue. The threats are well-documented by media reports, both online and offline, on crimes, privacy violations, and harassments made possible by the new digital media. Younger people are apparently less worried – though not less affected – by this, but middle-aged and older people are rather cautious, reluctant, and distrusting in their internet usage (Eimeren & Frees, 2008; PEW, 2005, 2008). It is important, though, to analyze clearly whether users merely see the possibility that nasty things can happen or whether they truly struggle to build and maintain trustful relationships with other users of online media. This is a complex matter because – as we will explore in this chapter – different realms of the online world as well as the online and offline worlds become increasingly interconnected, so that risks can spill over and grow to incalculable proportions. This brings trust into the picture even more.

Prior research has clearly recognized online trust as an issue, but tends to address it rather narrowly, focusing on security concerns to do with a particular kind of website, auctioning platform, e-commerce service, or social networking community (see Grabner-Kräuter & Kaluscha, 2003). We are missing a deeper analysis of the trust relationships involved, if any, and of the trust problems resulting from the use of multiple online services that may be rather harmless individually but can become dangerous when the various traces left by users are connected. Most studies on e-commerce in management, marketing, and organization capture only small parts of the overall problem (Belanger, Hiller & Smith 2002; McKnight & Chervany, 2002; McKnight et al., 2002; PEW, 2008; Shankar et al., 2002, 2003). Some work focuses just on the design of user interfaces (Brinkmann & Seifert, 2001; Gefen et al. 2003). Other authors broaden the picture by studying the effects of links between websites (Stewart, 2003) or the reputation systems that, ultimately, build on links between transactions and histories of user ratings (Bolton et al., 2004, 2008; Maztat, 2009). A different strand of research is concerned with privacy and surveillance issues, which comes closer to the broader picture that we look for, but usually portrays users in a rather passive role (Diaz, 2008; Hess, 2008; Zimmer, 2008).

Moreover, a fairly detailed study on trust in online communities by Thiedeke (2007) emphasizes the limitations of trust as a mechanism of complexity reduction and falls back on the maxim of "*Trust, but test!*" – i.e. the superiority of control over trust, which is a very common conclusion in research on online interaction. This view can be challenged, first, on the basis of research on the limited substitutability of trust and control, meaning that both are needed (Das & Teng, 1998; Long & Sitkin, 2006; Möllering, 2005) and, second, because it wrongly assumes that the online world can be clearly contained, e.g. by anonymity, so that none of the risks will spill over into the much less controllable offline world.

In working towards a deeper understanding of the problem of trust in online settings, we need to be clear under which conditions trust becomes relevant and we need to show how these preconditions apply in different online settings, for example internet-based markets and social networking sites. We address these points in the next section.

PRECONDITIONS OF THE RELEVANCE OF TRUST IN ONLINE SETTINGS

Defining and Delineating Trust

Mayer et al. (1995) propose that "trust is the willingness of a party to be vulnerable to the action of another party based on an expectation that the other party will perform a particular action important to the trustor, irrespective of the ability to monitor or control that other party" (p. 712). Rousseau et al. (1998) define trust as a "psychological state comprising the intention to accept vulnerability based upon positive expectations or behavior of another" (p. 395). These definitions complement each other. They identify positive expectations in spite of vulnerability and uncertainty as the essential characteristic of trust.

Trust requires that at least two actors are involved (Baier, 1986), a trustor and a trustee, but these actors do not have to be persons. We follow the literature in allowing for impersonal trust and trust in systems, as long as it is meaningful to attribute actions, intentions, and social relations to the entities involved (see McKnight & Chervany, 2002; Shapiro, 1987). Hence it makes sense to speak of trust in relation to a service provider, online community, or the general internet public under these conditions. Moreover, relationships may be structured in such a way that actors are trustors and trustees at the same time, either to each other in a dyad or to third parties in chains and networks of relationships. When trust is invoked, though, it is necessary to be as precise as possible about which actors are involved and in what kind of relationship they stand to each other. Actually, one of the practical issues of trust online is that the actors themselves often do not know who the others (really) are and what their networks of social relationships look like.

All the more, it is a precondition for trust's relevance that the actors we are interested in form more or less clear expectations about each other. Trust is a state of positive expectation, according to the definitions introduced above. If we cannot detect such expectations or if the actors we study are unable to form expectations, due to confusion or unfamiliarity, then trust is not applicable. More importantly, we should only speak of trusting expectations when they occur in the face of vulnerability and uncertainty (see Möllering, 2006). The social relationship between a trustor and a trustee is characterized by the fact that the trustor expects not to be harmed by the trustee, although the trustee is in a position to harm the trustor, and the trustor has neither perfect knowledge nor perfect control over the trustee's action. It is important to note that trust is the "willingness … to be vulnerable" (Mayer et al. 1995, p. 712) but not "willingness to be hurt." Online settings that involve little or no mutual expectations, vulnerability, and uncertainty are probably unsuitable for an analysis of trust as a relevant issue.

If trust presumes at least two actors in a social relationship, then it is imperative to explore the agency and the embeddedness of these actors further. Trust requires agency in the sense that the trustor and the trustee must have a choice to grant or withhold trust and to honor or exploit trust respectively. At the same time, the choices they make have to be meaningful and this requires a social context in which the actors are embedded and which structures any situational manifestations of trust or distrust. If these requirements are fulfilled, then it makes sense to analyze in detail how trust unfolds as a matter of embedded agency.

The effort of defining and delineating trust is much less important as a scholarly exercise in the interest of conceptual precision than as a practical task of establishing whether it makes sense to invoke trust as a relevant issue in a given online setting. We suggest actors, expectations, vulnerability, uncertainty, agency, and embeddedness as six preconditions that need to be considered. We contend that just being more explicit about these preconditions enhances our understanding of the role of trust in different settings already – including the likely insight that trust is less relevant in some settings than in others.

Relevance of Trust in Online Market Settings

In this subsection and the next we sketch the relevance of trust in two major settings, online marketplaces and social networking sites. We argue that the preconditions are generally fulfilled in both cases but in different ways. Looking at internet-based markets first, e-commerce takes place in the form of electronic markets, online shops, auction platforms, financial trading, private lending, and so on. There is broad agreement in the literature that online markets depend on trust to thrive (Belanger et al., 2002; Brinkmann & Seifert, 2001; Corritore et al., 2003; Gefen et al., 2003; Matzat, 2009; McKnight & Chervany, 2002; Bolton et al., 2004, 2008; Bolton & Ockenfels, 2006; Shankar et al., 2002, 2003; Wang & Emurian, 2005). Trust is required to enroll enough participants to a viable market and it is desired to reduce transaction costs caused by screening and other safeguarding mechanisms against opportunistic behavior by participants in the absence of trust and trustworthiness (e.g. Lorenz, 1988).

As a recent study shows for the United States (PEW, 2008), almost all internet users (93 percent) have engaged in economic activity online. On any day, more than a quarter of users engage in activities related to e-commerce such as searching for product information, making purchases or reservations, bidding in auctions, paying for downloads, or home banking including stock trading. This suggests that participation in online market places is a routine matter for most internet users. However, the same study also finds that users worry about security online. According to the PEW results, some 43 percent of online users have been frustrated by the absence or intractability of relevant information online; 32 percent are confused by information provided; and 58 percent have experienced at least one of these worries in connection with online shopping. Providers recognize the importance of trust and are willing to make efforts to increase the trustworthiness of their platforms. Research and practice are often short-sighted, though, in that they frame the trust problem in terms of technology, interface design, incentives, or regulation devices for a specific marketplace. While all of these factors may come into play, trust goes deeper.

Despite some variance at the individual level, internet users generally worry not only about the successful completion of online transactions as such (e.g. the delivery of a book ordered online and the correct billing to a credit card), but also about the traces they leave online, personal information in particular. They know that providers often use and sometimes abuse such digital footprints for purposes that go beyond individual sales transactions. Users, in return, can share information about the seller and tell other users about their good or bad experiences by using online media outside the provider's platform. In other words, apparently transient market transactions give rise to social relations between users and providers that may effectively become permanent. And these relationships extend into the offline world, because users and providers usually cannot remain completely anonymous but need to validate their identities, for example, for billing and delivery purposes.

A closer look at the six preconditions for trust's relevance outlined above draws our attention, first of all, to the various actors involved in online market places. Around the transaction between a buyer and a seller who, as users, perform a transaction using an online platform,

other actors come in as providers of the platform, as firms offering financial or logistics services, as data storage specialists, or as regulators and certification agencies. As the relevant actors are identified, different trust issues may emerge in the various dyads. From the point of view of the buyer, for example, the seller is responsible for product quality, the internet provider for data security, the financial intermediary for payment, the logistics partner for timely delivery, and so on. What makes trust more difficult, both analytically and practically, is that the identity of all the actors involved in a transaction may actually be unknown and hard to ascertain.

These examples already suggest that many things can go wrong when using online marketplaces. The actors do form positive expectations about each other's intentions and behaviors, at least in the moment when they make the deal, but these expectations can be disappointed. Beneath the overall expectation of truthful and cooperative interaction, there are many specifics about who should do what and who ought to abstain from abusing their position opportunistically in one way or another. This gives each trust relationship a slightly different quality according to the expectations it entails. While it is difficult to imagine that an online market transaction is entered into without positive expectations at all, it is quite possible that many expectations are implicit and hard to enforce. Borderline cases would be, for example, market gambling (a deal is made although it is unlikely to hold) or automated ordering and selling (a deal is made by software agents based on routine calculations).

Vulnerability is common in online market settings and we should distinguish at least two different qualities of vulnerability in this context. First, an online deal may fail when a party does not fulfill its contractual obligations and the others lose something as a result, i.e. a payment already made, a product or service already delivered, time wasted, or an alternative deal forgone. Second, parties are vulnerable to a possible abuse of information that was shared in order to perform the transaction, but can be used for other purposes, too. Fraud and libel denote the more dramatic forms of abuse, but spam and gossip can be harmful nuisances just the same. The first type of vulnerability (e.g. a failed deal) is far more calculable than the second type (e.g. abuse of credit card details), hence the former may be seen as a matter of risk, while the latter involves uncertainty in the Knightian sense where stakes and probabilities are unknown (see Knight, [1921]1971) and where trust goes beyond calculation. The precondition of uncertainty is also fulfilled in online marketplaces more generally, because the actors involved have imperfect knowledge and control. In particular, trust becomes relevant especially when unforeseen technical problems occur, which the actors handle responsibly or carelessly, proving or disproving their trustworthiness.

Finally, we can assume that the users and providers of online market places have a choice in whether they participate and that they exercise agency also in the way they treat their transaction partners and accept responsibility. Those who do not have positive expectations will most likely choose not to become active in online market settings, as long as there are still offline alternatives. At the same time, transactions in online marketplaces are embedded in larger institutional frameworks of both formal and informal rules ranging from specific rules for a given marketplace to more general rules of online trading to the national laws created offline but applicable to online activities, too, such as legal provisions on retail, banking, tax, anti-trust, consumer protection, and privacy. Given the internet's global reach and the sometimes vague identity of actors involved, it is often hard to assess which institutions are applicable and even harder to enforce rights and duties. This makes trust both more difficult and more important. Nevertheless, market activities on the internet are embedded in social structures that shape expectations and behaviors.

Relevance of Trust in Online Communities and Social Networking

While the e-commerce activities referred to above have existed for much longer and have evolved more gradually into more interactive formats, social networking sites are most typical for the new possibilities of "Web 2.0", because it is through MySpace, Facebook, LinkedIn, Friendfeed, Twitter, and the like that users shift and manage a significant part of their social lives onto the web where they upload, update, link up, and communicate personal information within more or less extensive networks. Social networking sites usually give their users various options, for example, in labeling information as private or public so that users have control, apparently, over what information can be accessed by whom (boyd/Ellison, 2007). This is where trust becomes relevant, though. First, the provider who stores the data knows everything and may alter or ignore the restrictions set by the user. Second, other users who are classified as friends and have access to more sensitive information may equally violate the restrictions and publish the information elsewhere. Third, relatively harmless public data stored on different sites may become quite powerful and potentially damaging when they are combined using search engines or applications such as Yasni. Hence, we observe how users struggle to manage their own online identities and reputations using technology such as OpenID or provider platforms such as ClaimID and myON-ID while other users and providers develop business models based on technologies that create links between traces and footprints that users leave online and exploit this information for dating, marketing, recruitment, or worse.

Considering the preconditions of trust's relevance more specifically, the main actors involved are the members of online communities (who use social networking sites), the providers (who run and maintain the sites), and third parties (who are interested in the data stored on the site). Social relationships in which trust plays a role are established between users who link up actively through the site but who may also gather information about each other without a confirmed bilateral link. Users also have a relationship with the site providers who may be connected to various third parties that are thus linked indirectly to the sites' users, too. Like in online marketplaces, different types of actors have different relationships and different trust issues. The overall trusting expectation, though, is that correct information is provided, for the sites would be useless without, and that the data must not be abused, or else users will withdraw them or no longer provide any. A social networking site without such positive expectations is bound to be a dysfunctional collection of errors and lies, but not a place for trust.

Vulnerability and uncertainty are still very salient in online community settings, though, because even a minority of actors can harm individual users and the whole community while there is no certainty that no such users will gain access to sensitive data. Even if many of the activities on social networking sites are rather playful and trivial, one must not forget that real actors with offline lives are behind the online users, providers, and onlookers. The damage can be emotional or material, light or severe. The common use of pseudonyms, usernames, avatars and other fictional identities does not solve trust issues. The harm mostly still gets through to the person behind the fake identity who may be unable, however, to establish the real identity of the perpetrator. Hence, we believe that this practice offers only limited protection but raises the perception of vulnerability and uncertainty – and thus the need for trust. This is exacerbated by the fact that the possibility of covering one's tracks and erasing one's footprints is very limited online.

Still, millions of people are very active in online communities. Social networking sites continue to be seen as an attractive business opportunity for providers, too. Nobody is forced to participate, but many choose to do so voluntarily and, more importantly, the main question is whether they do so responsibly. As long as there is also evidence of incompetent and malevolent agency, each user and provider faces a choice of being part of an online social network or not. Once again, this choice is not made in isolation but embedded in online and offline structures that influence the decision. For example, the choice may be limited to the range of existing sites, participation in one network may be more effective if one also uses other sites in parallel, and pre-existing offline communities may instigate their members to go online, too. Furthermore, online communities are governed by the same offline privacy regulations that apply to any association, organization, or individual, but that may be harder to control and enforce online.

Systemic Trust Problems Preventing Simplistic Solutions

In this section we support and extend the relevance of trust further by highlighting the systemic nature of trust issues in online settings. We have touched upon this point already, but it needs to be emphasized again, because much of the literature gives the impression that trust problems can be contained within particular applications, such as an online shop or social networking site, by implementing appropriate incentives and technologies to control access and information flows (Gefen et al., 2003; Wang & Emurian, 2005). In other words, the emphasis is on designing interfaces and applications in a 'trustworthy' fashion, but without paying much attention to the real actors and relationships that are (merely) mediated by technology and who have to accept any remaining vulnerability and uncertainty that cannot be eliminated by technology (nor, as Thiedeke [2007, p. 335 ff.] would argue, by distrust and power). Moreover, appealing and easy-to-use websites that elicit trust can be designed by honest and dishonest actors alike. This points to a signaling game that makes trust apparently impossible (Dasgupta, 1988) or a matter of faith (Möllering, 2009). According to Bacharach and Gambetta (2001, p. 159), only those signals of trustworthiness are reliable that would be too costly for an inherently untrustworthy trustee to fake. In contrast to Dasgupta (1988) who argues that an inherently untrustworthy trustee has an even bigger incentive to send (fake) signals of trustworthiness than the inherently trustworthy trustee – which means that the signals are actually useless per se – Bacharach and Gambetta (2001) point out that it may take substantially more effort to mimic a signal than to send it naturally. However, signaling theory only moves the trust problem to another level and, in practice, trust in an online website cannot be guaranteed by careful design but remains an individual accomplishment of the users (see Möllering, 2006, pp. 41 ff.) who suspend the possibility that a they may be deceived by a trustworthy-looking website or by the false and unverifiable claims of a platform provider (e.g. their policing of rogue users).

It should be noted again that, in times of "Web 2.0", it is simply too narrow to study whether users find the website of an online shop trustworthy or whether they are willing to risk buying something or entering their postal address at a particular site. The vulnerability and uncertainty that make trust relevant come increasingly from the dense interconnections between sites rather than from individual sites. Users cannot even draw on simple search engines or news pages anymore without entering a system that is designed to find out who they are and what they like, with the aim of tailoring advertising and content to their presumed interests and preferences (see various contributions in Zimmer & Spink [2008]).

The literature on reputation systems for online applications looks overly simplistic to us, too, because such systems, or rather provider platforms, give the impression that trustworthiness is calculable (e.g. 99 percent positive evaluations) and they mainly shift the problem to the reliability of the reputation system (e.g. that scores are not inflated or distorted in any way). At best, such systems are designed to increase control (see, for example the studies by Bolton et al., 2004, 2008; Bolton & Ockenfels, 2006), but they cannot eliminate vulnerability and uncertainty completely, which means that they leave the core of the trust problem unsolved. Furthermore, reputation systems also increase the interconnectedness of different online settings, especially when evaluations are invited, obtained, and posted by intermediaries such as price comparison services. The prospect that users will evaluate each other more and more on the internet, for everybody else to see, is not a very favorable one in our opinion, because these practices will create additional vulnerability and uncertainty for all involved, as past evaluations may forever haunt the poster just like the object.

Overall, we hope to have shown that trust is a general problem that is relevant in any online setting but that does not have a general solution to it, especially not one that addresses only the design of online media. We need to identify the actual social relationships that are (merely) technologically mediated, to establish the expectations, vulnerability, and uncertainty that they hold, and to take in both the agency of the individual actors as well as their embeddedness in social systems. The online world is a particular challenge for trust, because of the size and complexity of social networks that it enables and because of the broad but shallow embeddedness it draws on. In the next section, we address how trust can be socially constituted under these circumstances.

THE SOCIAL CONSTITUTION OF ONLINE TRUST

A General Framework for Explaining Trust

If trust is relevant in online settings, then we can draw on extensive literature aimed at explaining how trust comes about. In the following, we will use Möllering's (2006) integrative framework, which is derived from a critical review of existing trust theory. It distinguishes three perspectives on trust and highlights the leap of faith (*suspension*) as the key element required in all forms of trust.

In the first and most common perspective, trust is as matter of reason in the sense of a rational choice on the part of a trustor about his/her relationship with a given trustee. Accordingly, trust is based on a calculation of interest and utility, informed by the trustor's perception of the trustee's trustworthiness. There is much research on perceived trustworthiness and the types of criteria that trustors use, for example ability, benevolence, and integrity (Mayer et al., 1995). In the end, the trustor grants or withholds trust according to the expected value of the decision, like making a bet. This view suggests that trust can be increased through specific incentives, alignment of interests, and reliable signals of trustworthiness.

In the second perspective distinguished by Möllering (2006), trust is a matter of routine. In many social interactions in everyday life, it is taken for granted that people will give and honor trust – without calculating expected values every time. This trust is based on legitimate role expectations and appropriate role performances, and the recognition of what one should normally do. In other words, trust is not only protected by institutionalized rules, but institutionalized itself, that is, it is a usually unquestioned rule. Trust becomes stronger in this view, the less people think about it and the more they perform the trusting pattern automatically. Distrust, however, may equally become a hard-to-change routine.

In the third perspective that is very common in the literature, trust is a matter of reflexivity, meaning that it is based on experience and learning and has to be built more or less gradually. It is not a closed and static calculation, nor a mere repetition, but a combination of experimentation and reflection from one trust situation to the next. The trustor is able to engage with others even when calculations and routines are still impossible. Ac-

cordingly, trust is constituted when actors gain positive experiences in new situations.

We will discuss shortly how reason, routine, and reflexivity shape trust in online settings, but we need to emphasize that, in the framework we propose, trust is not to be confounded with its bases. In order to speak of trust as positive expectations in the face of vulnerability and uncertainty – beyond a rational choice, routine behavior, or past experience – there has to be a kind of leap of faith, i.e. the suspension of remaining doubt, uncertainty, and ignorance (Möllering, 2001). It is the special characteristic of trust that people interact *as if* things will go well, although they cannot be sure. This is a special emotional accomplishment and we will see what this means for users of online media.

In addition to the bases for trust and the leap of faith it involves, it is important to consider how the positive expectations of trust are experienced and enacted by the trustor. It is an empirical question, whether trust is experienced primarily as a positive emotion and intrinsic value, or whether trust is more of a burden and a source of anxiety even when positive expectations are in place. This is because in some settings actors would prefer to be able to interact without having to trust and in other settings it is the trust which makes the interaction particularly worthwhile. Similarly, when trust is present, it can be enacted in very different ways, even through inaction, or it may not be enacted at all.

The analysis of trust using the general framework outlined here needs to consider the part of the trustee, too. After all, the trustor responds to signals sent by the trustee regarding his/her interests and utility, trustworthiness, role acceptance, openness, and attitude towards vulnerability and uncertainty. Research and practice have an interest in understanding better the implications of the various, complex signaling games taking place online (see above; Bacharach & Gambetta, 2001). They give trustors and trustees many opportunities, and at least as many threats, to send

Figure 1. The trust wheel (Möllering 2006, p. 110)

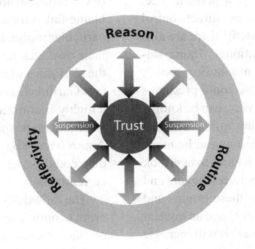

and receive trust-relevant signals responsibly, playfully, deceptively, and so on. While 'virtual' entities are accepted and welcome as part of the online world, fakes and liars are not. The question is how to facilitate leaps of faith – ultimately an 'illusion' of certainty – without misleading the trustor irresponsibly. Interestingly, deception may be both invited and avoided trough trust (see Möllering [2009] for a more extensive discussion).

We will demonstrate in the following sections that our framework is useful for gaining a better, more differentiated understanding of the constitution of trust in online marketplaces versus social networking media. The framework is based on the "Trust Wheel" (Figure 1, see Möllering 2006, p. 110) which shows that trust is based on reason, routine, and reflexivity, enabled by suspension. The positive expectation of trust is manifested in the experience and enactment on the part of the trustor.

Trust Constitution in Online Marketplaces

Online marketplaces would appear to be a paradigmatic setting for trust as a rational choice, based on calculating utility and assessing the trustworthiness of transaction partners. The calculative approach matches the relatively low complexity of the interactions, where vulnerability and uncertainty are supposedly limited to distinct transactions, i.e. relatively clear potential gains and losses, mostly standardized information requirements, short-term involvement with the exchange partner, and easy exit. Yet, all of these assumptions are problematic and the constitution of trust between strangers in markets is actually not as easily explained by reason as it seems.

To start with, as research on the moral hazard problem of online trading and auctioning platforms such as eBay demonstrates (e.g. Bolton et al., 2004, 2008; Bolton & Ockenfels, 2006), markets work better if the actors involved do not consider merely the immanent transaction but also their respective reputations which they gained in prior deals and which they need for future activities in the market. Hence the online market should become a market for reputation, as it were, in that a peer-to-peer control system is installed whereby transaction partners rate each other and prices are qualified by the perceived trustworthiness of the actors involved. Bolton, Ockenfels and their colleagues believe that trust problems in online markets can be solved rationally by setting the right incentives within the trading platform, especially the incentive to maintain a positive reputation based on past performance. Matzat (2009) shows that besides "direct control tools" such as these rating systems there are also the more contextual and relational "frame stabilizing tools" and "indirect monitoring tools". However, reliance on all these tools presumes that reputations and past behaviors can be known objectively, that the underlying online systems are safe, and that trading decisions can be made rationally. This kind of research tends to overlook that trust is not only an issue between buyers and sellers, but also between both these groups and the platform providers. The latter have an interest in inflated reputations, because this will increase trading activity. They also prefer not to incur high costs of monitoring and sanctioning the market participants. In sum, when designing markets with the aim of alleviating their inherent trust dilemmas, the rational trust problem is transferred partly to the market designers and providers.

If there are limits to explaining trust in online marketplaces as a matter of rational choice, then we need to look at routines, because online traders may be following certain scripts and play their prescribed roles without calculating utility and reputation in every transaction (Berger & Luckmann, 1966). Through isomorphism (DiMaggio & Powell, 1983), i.e. doing as everybody else does, it is likely that more and more actors become users of online marketplaces, because it is seen as 'normal' to buy certain things online on well-known websites, especially books, music, or holidays. From the perspective of trust research what is interesting in this regard is that trust is based on taken-for-grantedness and familiarity. Calculativeness re-enters only when things do not unfold as expected. The providers of online market places make use of this route to trust by designing interfaces in such a way that they look familiar to users (e.g. shopping carts and baskets) and by communicating impressive numbers of users, suggesting that 'everybody' is using this website and that it is completely normal to register and participate. Users themselves engage in a kind

of Garfinkelian normalization process when they blame failed transactions on the dishonesty of a particular transaction partner or perhaps even on their own incompetence rather than questioning the platform and its provider more fundamentally (see Garfinkel, 1967). This would be evidence of a highly routinized and institutionalized trust in an online marketplace, e.g. if everybody is using Amazon and eBay and nobody can imagine that they could be set up in any other way than they currently are.

The reflexivity perspective of trust is also relevant to online market places, besides reason and routine, because users may well find themselves in unfamiliar situations where they can neither calculate expected utility nor follow a routine script. Instead it is through learning by doing that they develop trust (or distrust) in other users and in a given platform and its provider. Thus, trading partners do not need to trust each other to the full extent at the outset of a trust relationship. They can engage in a form of as-if trust which can gradually produce genuine trust, or fail to develop further (Möllering, 2006, pp. 77-104; see also Beckert, 2005). For the trustful functioning of an online marketplace, it is important that trust is not only dyadic but develops throughout a network of users in their relationships with each other and with the platform provider. However, reflexivity-based trust takes time and effort – and it is not 'safe' either, because it may involve many disappointments and set-backs along the way. The leaps of faith required to get a positive spiral of trust started are particularly demanding, even when one follows what Luhmann (1979) called the principle of gradualness, i.e. starting with small steps into a new trust relationship. Engaging in online market places always requires the suspension of vulnerability and uncertainty (Möllering, 2006, pp. 105 ff.), because neither calculations, nor routines, nor experiential learning can be perfect. Users may always doubt what they see on the screen. If they choose to 'proceed to check-out' with positive expectations nevertheless, this is an enactment of their trust. In some instances, the behavior of online buyers and sellers may be better described as risk-taking, gambling, desperation, or foolishness. But we can speak of trust if an actor has positive expectations in spite of some remaining dangers.

As users of online platforms gain experience with this medium over time, their experiencing of trust in practice needs to be studied, too. It is telling in itself that some auction platforms advertise the excitement of participating in a bid, making even relatively trivial sales a matter of high emotional involvement. This extends to the question of whether the transaction partner will actually perform the deal after the auction is closed or the item has been ordered. At the same time, when users experience an auction positively or negatively in terms of trust, this always shapes their perception not only of their transaction partners but the platform providers, too. This is why it should be in the interest of platform providers to eliminate untrustworthy users, even if these users generate a lot of traffic, because their bad reputation may spill over to the whole platform. In order to enhance the users' positive experience, platform providers use techniques such a congratulating the transaction partners on their deal, thus making them feel good about their trust. Finally, to generate business, trust in online market places needs to translate into action. A platform cannot be sustained, if its users find each other trustworthy, but hardly anybody is really buying or selling anything. And the kind of trust that is involved in electronic markets is expressed most effectively by actual market activity. Leaps of faith are completed by mouse clicks, so to speak.

Trust Constitution in Online Communities and Social Networking

Reason, routine and reflexivity are categories that can be used to understand how trust is built in different settings. Comparing the online marketplaces considered above with online communities and social networking sites, the element of reason

and rational choice changes its meaning, because the utility of participating in online communities and social networks is often an end in itself. One participates not just to acquire items or pieces of information for offline use but in order to become part of a community. A good reputation and an extensive network of contacts here is not just a means to finding transaction partners but a measure of one's status and standing in the community. What this means is far less calculable in practice than the prices and percentage of satisfied customers in marketplaces. Online communities are designed to encourage their members to have as many contacts as possible, but beyond this maxim of "the more, the better", the exact motivations, payoffs and possible losses in online relationships are unclear. And it is a shallow basis for trust to believe that other users will not abuse their network contacts simply because they are afraid to lose some of these contacts as a result. As users join online communities and play with the different ways of managing their own identity and place in a network, the utility and trustworthiness of others are not calculated in advance but the product of participation. Nevertheless, social networking sites can be compared and distinguished meaningfully by the degree to which their members base their trust on estimated individual payoffs from participation (e.g. finding out about a job vacancy) versus taking participation to be the main payoff in itself (e.g. enjoying the chats with online friends). The utility for the provider of a networking platform might be just to enable a particular community of which the provider is a member, but it is often also a commercial interest of receiving participation fees, selling online advertising space, or collecting marketing profiles – which is much more interesting and problematic from a data protection and trust perspective. In order not to lose users, providers must signal the competent and benevolent treatment of personal information. In the end, though, users remain vulnerable to abuses by providers as well as other users.

Rational choice considerations are clearly relevant for trust in social networking, but also limited in explanatory power. Hence it should be fruitful to adopt the next perspective in our framework, i.e. trust as a matter of routines and taken-for-grantedness. To start with, while many older internet users may be reluctant to post their profiles on a website, younger users may already find this a completely normal thing to do in their daily lives. If, as far as they can see, everybody (in their offline world) is doing this and non-participation in Facebook, MySpace and so on is seen as the exception, then users will approach the online social media with relatively high trust in the websites and their users. It is important that this is not necessarily a naïve or even foolish type of trust, because the institutionalized rules and roles in established online communities and social networks may very well be highly reliable. Both the adherence to rituals such as a Twitter greeting in the morning or the inclusion of emoticons in text on the one hand and the reliable condemnation of unacceptable behavior among users on the other hand signal the normal working of an online community. What makes routine trust different from utility-based trust is that trustors do not have to calculate every time whether they should trust, but can adopt this as the default attitude and behavior – which is something that the providers of social media strongly promote, just like the providers of online marketplaces want users to think that it is completely normal to buy online. Even strongly institutionalized routines can still be broken, though, by untrustworthy users as well as providers. For example, when a provider changes the rules – as Facebook attempted in February 2009 – it may severely disrupt the routine expectations and undermine the trust in its services.

However, especially given the new formats for social networking and not to mention the new providers of such platforms that appear all the time, routines are not always in place yet and neither are reliable bases for rational decision making before entering a new community. This is where the re-flexivity perspective of trust applies. Users – and also providers as trustees – learn gradually about the trustworthiness of a website and the other users who seek to form a community over it or at least to find a forum for their own interests. Reflexivity as a basis for developing trust is also analytically important, as was already mentioned in relation to marketplaces, because users may be using multiple websites and their good or bad experiences with one online community will affect how they interact subsequently within other communities. According to the principle of gradualness (Luhmann 1979), people may leave only small and rather harmless pieces of information about themselves online, but then extend this and end up managing a complex personal identity online within their main communities. This is important when studying, for example, Facebook users. Among the hundreds of millions of users of this platform, many may be only experimenting a bit with a relatively low profile while others organize almost their entire social life around, within, and through this community. For providers, user recruitment may be facilitated if new users do not need to enter too much information initially when they first set up a profile. For users, the positive feedback from initial experiences with a community may lead them to enter ever more information about themselves and become somewhat imprudent, because the safety and trustworthiness of a community is overestimated based on extrapolations from the past that may not hold once really sensitive data are revealed. The reflexivity perspective makes us aware of the users' online and offline histories and reminds us that individual action is not just a matter of the general incentive structures and routines that can be drawn upon at a particular point in time in an online environment.

Participation in online communities always carries a degree of vulnerability and uncertainty that reason, routine and reflexivity cannot entirely eliminate. Even relatively innocent traces left online may be combined and abused by malevolent others, be it members of the same communities or outsiders who hack their way into the communities' databases. Against this background, users who participate with positive expectations have made a leap of faith. They act and interact as if the remaining dangers were unproblematic. It is hard to imagine that this is not what happens in most of the well-established online communities. The alternative would be that the majority of their members participate in a state of fear, coercion or desperation, not really expecting trustworthy behavior from the others but merely hoping that nothing bad will happen or even resigning to the fact that they will be taken advantage of. We cannot rule this scenario out completely, but when studying trust in online communities the more interesting question is how the other users and also the providers of the platforms promote the suspension of fear and doubt.

Enabling the leap of faith is closely related to the experiencing and enacting of trust in online communities. First, as in offline communities, the positive experience of feeling protected and respected within a trusted community is quite important. It needs to be maintained by the members of the community and in social networks this happens through the countless little messages that users send to support and comfort each other or to intervene when inacceptable behaviors occur. Trust is enacted not only by uploading personal information, but also by displaying one's responsibility, solidarity, and commitment to the other members. When trust is no longer enacted, an online community will become dysfunctional and probably dissolve before long, its members migrating to other platforms or withdrawing from online associations. In order to avoid this, online communities should be open for newcomers but display a virtual "Friends only!" sign above their virtual points of entry (see Möllering 2009, p. 146) as well as making sure that those who do not behave like friends are expelled. Friendship, here, is a matter of self-selection. By entering, the visitor commits himself to the rules of friendly behavior, irrespective of whether he or she is ac-

tually also an offline acquaintance of the owner of a weblog or profile.

The above reflections illustrate how our framework for studying trust in online settings can be applied to both online marketplaces and online communities. The main ideal-typical difference between the two forms of interaction on the internet remains that marketplaces are mostly used for short-term exchanges and brief encounters while communities are mostly used to manage longer-term identities and lasting relationships. Yet, the economic sphere of marketplaces and communal association in communities are densely interconnected. They have in common that the providers of the platforms want their users to "keep coming back" and that utility, routines, and learning processes are involved in the constitution of trust among users and between users and providers.

TOWARD A METHODOLOGY FOR THE EMPIRICAL STUDY OF ONLINE TRUST

Based on the analytical framework we have outlined and the specific issues around the complexity and interrelatedness between online settings as noted earlier on in the chapter, this section presents basic implications for the design of future empirical research in this field. The empirical study of trust online remains unsatisfactory, as long as trust online is conceptualized only as trust in a technology or incentive structure, because users do not only encounter specific websites but build their online biographies navigating across many parts of the internet. Their vulnerability lies much less in losing small things here and there than in losing control over their scattered online lives that are not disconnected from their offline realities. While online artifacts of all sorts represent important data, it is crucial to understand the various real and potential connections between all the traces, profiles, conditions of usage, and so on. To achieve this, we think that researchers need to meet with users in person to learn in depth about their intentions, decisions, and experiences related to the problem of trust. This is required to understand better the actual practices of using online marketplaces or social networks. We suggest a praxeological approach to trust, focusing on actors, their social relations, and their practices of integrating the internet into their daily lives. We think that trust in online settings is better explained on the basis of dense online biographies than on the basis of large datasets about isolated online interactions.

A variety of methods offer promising approaches for the empirical study of trust online. The methods that we advocate briefly below are all making use of online technology to a greater or lesser extent. This is an advantage when studying people who use such technologies already anyway. More conventional techniques are more appropriate perhaps for non-users or those who are have been upset by bad experiences on the internet. Each method can be used individually in smaller projects but a combination of these methods should be particularly fruitful in larger research projects on trust in online settings:

1. **Online surveys:** Respondents can be self-recruiting or be invited to the survey via email or regular mail. This method is problematic if it is not very open and interactive. Its potential can be increased if respondents are given the opportunity to offer detailed reflections and upload digital material that illustrates their online activities (Welker et al., 2005). It would also be desirable to create longitudinal panel data instead of just cross-sectional samples in order to get closer to the idea of analyzing online biographies. Qualitative interviews with at least a subsample of the survey respondents should also be considered.

2. **Laboratory experiments:** The main objective in using this method would be to observe users in real time as they are using online marketplaces and communities. Ideally, this should be with real websites that the users would go to outside of the lab situation, too, but more classical laboratory experiments with simulated websites and different treatments could be instructive, too, as long as the main interest is not in optimal web-design but in understanding how actors draw on their online histories when encountering a new site.

3. **Case studies:** This method aims for a dense description of an online marketplace or social networking platform and its offline context (see, for example, Geertz, 1977). Crucially, the research team needs to look behind the scenes. It is not enough to analyze the software and data involved in running the platform, i.e. the traces that are left naturally. Building on ethnographic techniques it is necessary to gain insights into the motivations and decisions of the platform providers and users, which will mostly not be documented already on the platform itself.

4. **Expert interviews:** This type of interviewing is not a data gathering exercise by an expert researcher but a conversation of the researcher with experts in the field who offer their insights and explanations on the phenomenon under study. For trust in online settings, the experts to be considered can be anyone with extensive experience, which includes users and providers as well as slightly more detached journalists, activists, IT specialists, or academics. The internet may be used to conduct the interviews (e.g. Skype). As an alternative to interviewing, the experts can also be asked to keep a diary on their online activities and reflections with regard to trust.

5. **Online forums:** Presuming that many trust issues in online settings are already discussed spontaneously by users in various chat rooms and blogs, it may be fruitful to create

a platform dedicated to this topic where all parties concerned can voice their concerns and report their experiences. Such an online forum (e.g. weblog) could be established as part of a website of a larger research project on online trust and be moderated by the researchers. The aim of this method would be to identify relevant issues and topical cases coming directly from the users' lives world, without claiming representativeness.

6. **Barcamps:** In the spirit of developing research methods that draw on new forms of interaction that have emerged form the online world, it would be particularly interesting to set up a self-organizing conference, known as a barcamp, on the topic of trust in online settings. The barcamp itself is an offline activity where anybody who is interested in the topic can meet with others face-to-face. The preparation of the barcamp is largely done online, though, and it is an important feature of this format that participants are posting their presentations, comments, twittering et cetera online, thereby creating qualitative data that can be used fruitfully in a trust research project.

These methodological suggestions build on conventional methods but encourage researchers, first, to make use of internet technology and online artifacts as well as, second, to try and get as close as possible to the practices and interpretations of users. In particular, the leap of faith that characterizes trust is an idiosyncratic, highly emotional accomplishment by trustors and this requires researchers to get close to the moment of experiencing and enacting trust (see also Barbarlet, 2009; Möllering, 2001)

CONCLUSION

In the offline world, trust is required in specific interactions and, more generally, as a basis for getting involved in the first place. Everybody using the internet is confronted with the choice to trust or to keep out, that is, limit the degree and scope of internet usage as long as they are distrusting. Everybody who chooses to participate, though, remains vulnerable, even if they have positive trusting expectations. The uncertainty about whether one will be harmed can only be suspended, not eliminated, because it is impossible to identify all sources of potential failure, transform them into risks, assign probabilities and mathematically manage risk in order to avoid failure (see Power, 2007, pp. 66-102). A wary, reluctant, and distrustful attitude paralyses users but contributes no additional security to the internet. Trust, in contrast, helps to overcome paralysis by combining good reasons with the benefit of the doubt and a cooperative, but not foolish, stance.

In our opinion, the sheer size, growth, and global interconnectivity of the internet rule out an effective centralized regulation of all online marketplaces, communities and the internet as a social sphere. Control or political governance as a more abstract form of control, if seen as an alternative to trust, is not a viable alternative in this field, contrary to the conclusions of, for example, Thiedeke (2007). Trust, in contrast, can be built up in decentralized processes and then lead to more generalized rules, roles, and routines that become institutionalized and taken for granted by all users across a range of online marketplaces and communities. In this chapter, we have proposed a broad framework that captures the elements involved in the constitution of trust. We underline that trust is not primarily an abstract property of a social system but a very personal and practical experience, stretching out in time and space, both online and offline. Hence it is not enough, in research or practice, to be concerned with the trust-effective design of individual websites or devices, as has been common to date. Trust is a social process spanning online biographies of users and the life course of provider platforms. Trusting actors are aware that trust concerns arise as a consequence of their participation, but they are prepared to make a leap of faith. Since users, providers, developers, and the general public alike are related to each other as trustors and trustees simultaneously, each party must offer a favorable self-definition and cooperate to produce a desirable internet of trust.

REFERENCES

Bacharach, M., & Gambetta, D. (2001). Trust in signs. In Cook, K. S. (Ed.), *Trust in Society* (pp. 148–184). New York: Russell Sage Foundation.

Baier, A. (1986). Trust and antitrust. *Ethics, 69*(2), 231–260. doi:10.1086/292745

Barbalet, J. (2009). A characterization of trust, and its consequences. *Theory and Society, 38*(4), 367–382. doi:10.1007/s11186-009-9087-3

Beckert, J. (2005). Trust and the Performative Construction of Markets. *MPIfG Discussion Paper 05/8.* Cologne, Germany: Max Planck Institute for the Study of Societies.

Belanger, F., Hiller, J. S., & Smith, W. J. (2002). Trustworthiness in electronic commerce: the role of privacy, security, and site attributes. *The Journal of Strategic Information Systems, 11*(3/4), 245–270. doi:10.1016/S0963-8687(02)00018-5

Benkler, Y. (2006). *The wealth of Networks. How Social Production transforms Markets and Freedom.* New Haven, CT: Yale University Press.

Berger, P. L., & Luckmann, T. (1966). *The Social Construction of Reality.* Garden City, NY: Doubleday.

Bolton, G., Loebecke, C., & Ockenfels, A. (2008). Does competition promote trust and trustworthiness in online trading? An experimental study. *Journal of Management Information Systems, 25*(2), 145–169. doi:10.2753/MIS0742-1222250207

Bolton, G. E., Katok, E., & Ockenfels, A. (2004). Trust among internet traders. A behavioral economics approach. *Analyse & Kritik, 26,* 185–202.

Bolton, G. E., & Ockenfels, A. (2006). *The Limits of Trust in Economic Transactions. Investigations of Perfect Reputation Systems.* Retrieved from http://ockenfels.uni-koeln.de/uploads/tx_ockmedia/Bolton_Ockenfels_Limits_of_Trust.pdf

Boyd, D. M., & Ellison, N. B. (2007). Social network sites: Definition, history, and scholarship. *Journal of Computer-Mediated Communication, 13*(1). Retrieved from http://jcmc.indiana.edu/vol13/issue1/boyd.ellison.html

Brinkmann, U., & Seifert, M. (2001). Face to Interface: Zum Problem der Vertrauenskonstitution im Internet am Beispiel von elektronischen Auktionen. *Zeitschrift für Soziologie, 30*(1), 23–47.

Corritore, C. L., Kracher, B., & Wiedenbeck, S. (2003). On-line trust: concepts, evolving themes, a model. *International Journal of Human-Computer Studies, 28*(6), 737–758. doi:10.1016/S1071-5819(03)00041-7

Das, T. K., & Teng, B.-S. (1998). Resource and Risk Management in the Strategic Alliance Making Process. *Journal of Management, 24*(1), 21–42. doi:10.1016/S0149-2063(99)80052-X

Dasgupta, P. (1988). Trust as a commodity. In Gambetta, D. (Ed.), *Trust: Making and Breaking Co-operative Relations* (pp. 49–72). Oxford, UK: Basil Blackwell.

Diaz, A. (2008). Through the Google Goggles: Sociopolitical bias in Search Engine Design. In Zimmer, M., & Spink, A. (Eds.), *Web Search. Multidisciplinary Perspectives* (pp. 11–34). Heidelberg, Germany: Springer.

DiMaggio, P. J., & Powell, W. W. (1983). The iron cage revisited: Institutional isomorphism and collective rationality in organizational fields. *American Sociological Review, 48*(2), 147–160. doi:10.2307/2095101

Eimeren, B., & Frees, B. (2008). *Internetzuwachs: Größter Zuwachs bei den Silversurfern. Ergebnisse der ARD/ZDF-Onlinerstudie 2008.* Retrieved from http://www.daserste.de/service/studie08_1.pdf

Garfinkel, H. (1967). *Studies in Ethnomethodology.* Englewood Cliffs, NJ: Prentice Hall.

Geertz, C. (1977). *The Interpretation of Cultures: Selected Essays.* New York: Basic Books.

Gefen, D., Karahanna, E., & Straub, D. W. (2003). Trust and TAM in online shopping: An integrated model. *Management Information Systems (MIS). Quarterly, 27*(1), 51–90.

Grabner-Kräuter, S., & Kaluscha, E. A. (2003). Empirical research in on-line trust: a review and critical assessment. *International Journal of Human-Computer Studies, 58*(6), 783–812. doi:10.1016/S1071-5819(03)00043-0

Guenther, T., & Schmidt, J. (2008). Wissenstypen im Web 2.0 – eine wissenssoziologische Deutung von Prodnutzung im Internet. In Willems (Ed.). Weltweite Welten. Figurationen aus wissenssoziologischer Perspektive (pp. 167-187). Wiesbaden, Germany: VS-Verlag.

Habermas, J. (1989). *The Structural Transformation of the Public Sphere: An Inquiry into a Category of Bourgeois Society.* Cambridge, MA: Polity Press. (Original work published 1962)

Hess, A. (2008). Reconsidering the Rhizome. A textual analysis of Web Search engines as Gatekeepers of the Internet. In Zimmer, M., & Spink, A. (Eds.), *Web Search. Multidisciplinary Perspectives* (pp. 35–50). Heidelberg, Germany: Springer.

Knight, F. H. (1971). *Risk, Uncertainty, and Profit.* Chicago: University of Chicago Press, Phoenix Books. (Original work published 1921)

Lessig, L. (2004). *Free Culture. The nature and future of creativity.* New York: Penguin.

Long, C. P., & Sitkin, S. B. (2006). Trust in balance: How managers integrate trust-building and task control. In Bachmann, R., & Zaheer, A. (Eds.), *Handbook of Trust Research* (pp. 87–106). Cheltenham, UK: Elgar.

Lorenz, E. H. (1988). Neither friends nor strangers: Informal networks of subcontracting in French industry. In Gambetta, D. (Ed.), *Trust: Making and Breaking Cooperative Relations* (pp. 194–210). New York: Blackwell.

Luhmann, N. (1979). *Trust and Power: Two Works by Niklas Luhmann.* Chichester, UK: Wiley.

Matzat, U. (2009). The Acceptance and Effectiveness of Social Control on the Internet: A Comparison between Online Auctions and Knowledge Sharing Groups. In Cook, K., Snijders, C., & Buskens, V. (Eds.), *Trust and Reputation.* New York: Russell Sage Foundation.

Mayer, R. C., Davis, J. H., & Schoorman, F. D. (1995). An integrative model of organizational trust. *Academy of Management Review, 20*(3), 709–734. doi:10.2307/258792

McKnight, D. H., & Chervany, N. L. (2002). What trust means in e-commerce customer relationships: An interdisciplinary conceptual typology. *International Journal of Electronic Commerce, 6*(2), 35–59.

McKnight, D. H., Choudhury, V., & Kacmar, C. (2002). The impact of initial consumer trust on intentions to transact with a web site: A trust building model. *The Journal of Strategic Information Systems, 11*(3/4), 297–323. doi:10.1016/S0963-8687(02)00020-3

Möllering, G. (2001). The nature of trust: From Georg Simmel to a theory of expectation, interpretation and suspension. *Sociology, 35*(2), 403–420.

Möllering, G. (2005). The trust/control duality: An integrative perspective on positive expectations of others. *International Sociology, 20*(3), 283–305. doi:10.1177/0268580905055478

Möllering, G. (2006). *Trust: Reason, Routine, Reflexivity*. Amsterdam: Elsevier.

Möllering, G. (2009). Leaps and lapses of faith: Exploring the relationship between trust and deception. In Harrington, B. (Ed.), *Deception: From Ancient Empires to Internet Dating* (pp. 137–153). Stanford, CA: Stanford University Press.

PEW Internet & American Life Project. (2007a). *Online identity management and search in the age of transparency*. Retrieved from http://www.pewinternet.org/pdfs/PIP_Digital_Footprints.pdf

PEW Internet & American Life Project. (2008a). *Online Shopping. Internet users like the convenience but worry about the security of their financial information*. Retrieved from http://www.pewinternet.org/pdfs/PIP_Online%20Shopping.pdf

Power, M. (2007). *Organized Uncertainty. Designing a World of Risk Management*. Oxford, UK: Oxford University Press.

Rousseau, D. M., Sitkin, S. B., Burt, R. S., & Camerer, C. (1998). Not so different after all: A cross-discipline view of trust. *Academy of Management Review, 23*(3), 393–404.

Shankar, V., Smith, A. K., & Rangaswamy, A. (2003). Customer satisfaction and loyalty in online and offline environments. *International Journal of Research in Marketing, 20*(2), 153–175.

Shankar, V., Urban, G. L., & Sultan, F. (2002). Online trust: A stakeholder perspective, concepts, implications, and future directions. *The Journal of Strategic Information Systems, 11*(3/4), 325–344. doi:10.1016/S0963-8687(02)00022-7

Shapiro, S. P. (1987). The social control of impersonal trust. *American Journal of Sociology, 93*(3), 623–658. doi:10.1086/228791

Stewart, K. J. (2003). Trust transfer on the World Wide Web. *Organization Science, 14*(1), 5–17. doi:10.1287/orsc.14.1.5.12810

Thiedecke, U. (2007). *Trust, but test! Das Vertrauen in virtuellen Gemeinschaften*. Konstanz, Germany: UVK.

Wang, Y. D., & Emurian, H. H. (2005). An overview of online trust: Concepts, elements, and implications. *Computers in Human Behavior, 21*(1), 105–125. doi:10.1016/j.chb.2003.11.008

Welker, M., Werner, A., & Scholz, J. (2005). Online-Research. Markt- und Sozialforschung mit dem Internet. Heidelberg, Germany: dpunkt.verlag.

Zimmer, M. (2008). The Gaze of the Perfect Search Engine: Google as an Infrastructure of Dataveillance. In Zimmer, M., & Spink, A. (Eds.), *Web Search. Multidisciplinary Perspectives* (pp. 77–99). Heidelberg: Springer.

Chapter 3
Trusting Technological Actors:
A Foundation in Structure and Cultural Sentiments

Daniel B. Shank
University of Georgia, USA

ABSTRACT

This chapter sets forth a theoretical foundation for studying trust toward technological actors as social actors using sociological research in structure and cultural sentiments. The introduction considers how modern intelligent technologies make human-technology trust a relevant and timely topic, while the background section reviews humans' social interaction with technology. Using social structure and cultural sentiments the author constructs four propositions about trusting technological actors. Two empirical research studies illustrate the cultural sentiment propositions showing trust in technological actors and violation of trust in computers. Throughout the chapter the author connects the sociological literature with everyday examples before providing grounded propositions that would be appropriate foundations for research in multiple disciplines.

INTRODUCTION

The source of any information affects people's trust in that information. We all have the experience of somebody believing something just because it came from a computer, sometimes according it higher trust for this reason, while others have the opposite response (Picard, 1997, p. 114)

It is not uncommon for people to trust global positioning systems to direct them to their destination, internet searches to bring up reliable information, stock prediction programs to make decent suggestions, and meteorology websites to predict upcoming weather. As developments are made in technology, there are several concurrent processes that are relevant to the importance of studying trust in technological actors. First, the capacity of technology allows it to be applied to new domains that previously were occupied only by humans. Domains where humans must trust in technologies to make

DOI: 10.4018/978-1-61520-901-9.ch003

decisions or predictions are vast including stock market and financial predictions, gaming, medical diagnostics, military and police intelligence, identity verification, online bidding systems, mobile network security systems, vehicle design configurations, vehicle stress simulations, and meteorology. Second, the complexity of the domains means that technologies are using stochastic and heuristic processes instead of deterministic processes. Artificial intelligence techniques used for designing systems in the aforementioned domains include pattern matching, simulated annealing, genetic and evolutionary algorithms, expert systems, rule-based learning with logic databases, distributed computing, simulations of environments and artificial neural networks. One domain and one technique I will use as an ongoing example is applying artificial neural networks to meteorological predictions. Artificial neural networks have been used in prediction of tornadoes, storms, solar radiation, carbon dioxide levels, pollutants, ozone concentration, sulfur dioxide concentration, and precipitation (Gardner & Dorling, 1998), tide charts (Steidley, Sadovski, Tissot, & Bachnak, 2005), ocean waves levels (Wedge, Ingram, McLean, Mingham, & Bandar, 2005), flash floods (Luk, Ball, & Sharma, 2000), fog (Nugroho, Kuroyanagi, & Iwata, 2002), air temperature (Jain, McClendon, Hoogenboom, & Ramyaa, 2003; Smith, McClendon, & Hoogenboom, 2006), and dew point temperature (Shank, Hoogenboom, & McClendon, 2008; Shank, McClendon, Paz, & Hoogenboom, 2008). Like artificial neural networks and weather prediction, a huge number of software applications, computational systems, and domains have important, nondeterministic technologies making trust in technological actors a timely topic.

In this chapter I begin by arguing that humans treat technologies socially, and therefore people's trust or distrust in them can be informed by sociological theory. Next, I review a limited sociological literature on trust, focusing on social structure and cultural sentiments as antecedents of

trust. As I review the literature, I apply theoretical principles from network theories and Affect Control Theory to technological actors in the form of propositions. Last, I conclude by reviewing two current Affect Control Theory research projects on cultural sentiments, trust, and technological actor interaction.

BACKGROUND

There are many different approaches to studying trust in technological actors. A number of studies investigate technologies' influence on organizations (DiMaggio, Hargittai, Neuman, & Robinson, 2001; Liker, Haddad, & Karlin, 1999; Podolny & Stuart, 1995; Shortliffe, 1993; Stuart & Podolny, 1996) and even how technological actors function as members of organizations (Carley, 2002). Actor-Network Theory (Callon & Latour, 1992; Latour, 2005) suggests that technology has been socially constructed to be a separate domain from the human-social realm, and to address this construction theorists analyze technology and humanity from the same standpoint. This moves technological actors, not humans, to the center of socio-cultural life and narratives (Latour, 1996). Likewise, science and technology studies look at science, technology, and knowledge as cultural products that are constructed (Bijker, 1995; Collins, 1995) and how they affect other systems such as culture, governments, communications (Jasanoff, Markle, Peterson, & Pinch, 1995), and privacy (Karat, Karat, & Brodie, 2008). All of these approaches contribute to the perspective adopted in this chapter, but are not fully reviewed within.

In Human-Computer Interaction (HCI) research one perspective called Computers Are Social Actors (CASA) is used as background for the propositions developed in this chapter. CASA is a research tradition based in psychological social-psychology and communications that proposes that people treat computers and other technologies socially. "Socially" means that the social-psychological processes that occur in human-human interaction are proposed to also be present in human-technology interaction. Scholars in the CASA tradition suggest that because humans are cognitive misers they will react automatically to social cues presented by technological actors (Nass & Moon, 2000). Further, this means that social cues from technology may be minimal, supported by much research that uses text manipulation as the only social cue (Ferdig & Mishra, 2004; Mishra, 2006; Moon & Nass, 1996; Nass, Fogg, & Moon, 1996; Nass, Moon, Fogg, Reeves, & Dryer, 1995; Nass & Reeves, 1996). Other cues that may contribute more to social presence have also been used in CASA research including voice (Nass & Steuer, 1993), onscreen characters (Isbister & Nass, 2000; Shinozawa, Reeves, Wise, Maldonado, & Naya, 2002), robots (Groom & Nass, 2007; Shinozawa, et al., 2002), and human-faces as agents (Brave, Nass, & Hutchinson, 2005).

Because the research suggests that even minimal cues can elicit social reactions in people, more complex technologies should as well. The research also indicates that filling a social position is enough to elicit social reactions (Nass & Steuer, 1993). For example, a website predicting air temperature is providing important information to people and thus occupying a social position of informer. Depending on how the information is presented (e.g., text-only, animated character, vocally, or through graphs) the type of social reaction may vary. The ability of a website to influence a person is related to not only the information presented at the website, but the perception of reliability of the website and the presentation and layout of the material (Fogg, 2003; Fogg, Cuellar, & Danielson, 2008; Karat, et al., 2008).

CASA researchers have broadly investigated a number of social processes. Many of the studies take known findings from psychology, findings that are generally based on human-human interaction, and replicate them for human-computer interaction. For example, people tend to perceive that human experts are more reliable and provide better information compared to human generalists regardless of the actual reliability or information quality. Nass and Reeves (1996) applied this to technology by labeling two televisions with "entertainment TV" and "news TV." They compared showing entertaining shows and news clips on the respectively labeled TVs (i.e., the expert) versus showing them on an unlabeled TV (i.e., the generalist). The same material was rated as more important, more informative, more disturbing, and more interesting on the expert news TV compared to the unlabeled TV, and funnier and more relaxing on the entertainment TV compared to the unlabeled TV. Other social-psychological processes replicated by CASA research include homophily, gender stereotyping, politeness, and attributions to computers (Ferdig & Mishra, 2004; Nass & Moon, 2000; Nass, et al., 1995; Nass, Steuer, & Tauber, 1994).

Trust has not been a particular focus of CASA research. Therefore, the theoretical foundation presented in this chapter is not based on empirical work from CASA, but instead rests on the general principles of human-computer interaction grounded in CASA research. Specifically, the following are background assumptions, derived from the CASA literature, for considering human trust in technology:

Assumption 1: A technological actor that exhibits at least minimal cues is a social actor and therefore can potentially be trusted by humans.

Assumption 2: A technological actor may have different characteristics (e.g., social cues and social position) that affect the way humans trust it.

These assumptions are about technology in human-technology trusting. In the next section I will use sociology and HCI literature on trust to make assumptions about the humans in human-technology trusting.

TRUSTING TECHNOLOGICAL SOCIAL ACTORS

Trust

A difficulty for theorizing about trust in technology derives from the many alternative definitions of trust from various academic traditions. Hardin has pointed out that trust has been confused with trustworthiness in many scholarly writings (2002). Specifically trustworthiness is a characteristic of an individual, whereas trust is the expectation in specific or general others to be trustworthy. Trust has been defined by some as having three distinct aspects: cognitive, affective, and behavioral (Lewis & Weigert, 1985) and considering them will be helpful in connecting to relevant literatures.

Consider visiting a website that predicted the next day's temperature. If you frequently visited that site and received predictions, you might have a specific cognitive trust toward the site, believing it will be correct in the future. Likewise you may depend on this site for accurate predictions, and if it crashed one day or gave extremely erroneous predictions, you may be angry or feel betrayed because you had an affective/emotional trust in it. Finally, these could alter your behavior, such as not putting on a jacket if the site predicted warm temperatures.

Cognition, affect, and behavior have been studied in regard to HCI and human-technology interaction. Emotions are vital in many types of human-technology interaction (Heise, 2004; Picard, 1997; Troyer, 2008), and the difference between emotion, mood, affect, and sentiment has been studied in relation to human-technology interactions (Brave & Nass, 2008). Byrne reviews historical cognitive approaches to HCI and three contemporary cognitive architectures approaches (2008). One of the most common behavioral connections of trusting technologies is willingness to take a risk as an indicator of trust. Furthermore, trust in computer software or websites is known to be influenced by many affective and cognitive fac-

tors including credibility, familiarity, predictability, quality of information, straightforwardness, degree of risk, information-control, transparency and external accreditation (Karat, et al., 2008).

CASA research suggests that social cues or occupying a social position would lead to social attributions and behavior toward technology. Thus,

Assumption 3: Humans can trust in technology cognitively, affectively, and behaviorally.

Aside from aspects of trust, there is variation in whether trust is conceptualized as a quality of an individual, thereby minimizing the importance of the trustee, or if trust is conceptualized relationally, taking into account the trustee. Studies in psychology have looked at generalized trust, which is also referred to as the personality trait or construct of trust. Studies from psychology include the Rotter Interpersonal Trust Scale (Rotter, 1967) and from sociology include a similar measurement of generalized trust (Yamagishi & Cook, 1993). These generalized trust studies have been criticized by some scholars for being so general that when applied to a situation, they do not take into account the difference in the cognitive, affective, and behavioral aspects of trust (Lewis & Weigert, 1985). The critics suggest that one may trust certain aspects of another and that these will vary by situation. I do not attempt to add to the debate here, but only to suggest those dimensions apply to trust in technological actors.

Reflecting again on the temperature prediction system, you might have more trust in it because you have a strong generalized trust. You tend to give every actor, human and technology, the benefit of the doubt. In contrast, it may be that this specific website has a particular reason to trust or distrust it. Perhaps the company that made it is not one you trust because of past encounters. The CASA research again would suggest the applicability of the specific versus generalized trust to technology. Because automaticity undergirds the social interaction with technology (Nass &

Moon, 2000), personality traits like generalized trust would play in to interactions with technology. Specifically,

Assumption 4: Humans' generalized trust will apply to trust in technology.

Social Structure and Trust

Recent sociological research by Lawler and colleagues highlights the process that connects cognitions and affect with behavior and is therefore applicable to theorizing about trust. Lawler and colleagues have developed two theories that apply: Relational Cohesion Theory (Lawler, Thye, & Yoon, 2000; Lawler & Yoon, 1993, 1996) and an Affect Theory of Social Exchange (Lawler, 2001; Lawler, Thye, & Yoon 2008). Both theories suggest that social structure enables and constrains interaction. Specifically, the Affect Theory of Social Exchange proposed that as individuals have positive interactions, these produce global emotions with a positive valence. These are then attributed differentially to other actors and groups based on the structure in which the individuals are embedded. The Relational Cohesion Theory shows how these positive emotions then produce relational cohesion and commitment. Lawler et al.'s model of relational cohesion measured concepts related to all three aspects of trust (2000). Related to the cognitive aspect of trust is the predictability of the exchange partner and related to the affective component is the positive emotions within an interaction. Both of these were theorized to lead to group cohesion, a cognitive-affective perception of the group's solidarity. This then led to behavioral outcomes such as gift giving and investment, indicating the behavioral outcomes of trust. All of these were resulting from a model that had an important antecedent structural condition. They found that greater total power increased agreement in interaction which, through several mediating variables, led to increased predictabil-

ity of exchange partners, positive emotion, and behavioral trust (Lawler, et al., 2000).

Structure as an antecedent to trust is a concept that can be applied to technological actors. Relational power in this tradition is the dependence on others for desired resources (Emerson, 1962). People are often dependent on technology for many types of resources, and therefore a technological actor holding those resources has some structural power over the dependent person. Examples of desired resources technological actors may possess includes information in an organizational setting (Carley, 2002; Liker, et al., 1999), ability for companionship (Sparrow, 2002), medical information (Shortliffe, 1993), housecleaning (iRobot Corporation, 2008), resources as a teammate (Groom & Nass, 2007), and airline reservations (Copeland & McKenney, 1988). The exact same resource might be differentially valuable to one person based on her dependence on it. If you are going to work in an office building all day, the predicted outside temperature might be slightly valuable, but if you are going to work outside all day it would be a much more valuable resource. Therefore, a website that predicted temperature would be powerful in some relations but not in others. This structural power of the website would be a separate factor affecting trust from the other factors that influence how much individuals trust websites (Fogg, 2003; Fogg, et al., 2008; Karat, et al., 2008). Based on the findings I propose the following:

Proposition 1: Holding constant the amount of positive interaction, the greater the dependence of a human on a technological actor for resources, the greater the trust.

A large body of research building on power-dependence suggests that the larger network of actors is important for considering how trust developed in dyadic relation (Burt, 2005; Cook, 2005; Cook & Emerson, 1978; Cook, Emerson, Gillmore, & Yamagishi, 1983; Lawler, 2001;

Lawler, et al., 2000; Molm, Takahashi, & Peterson, 2000). One condition that can increase trust is the embeddedness of actors in a dense or closed network. Drawing on Heider's Balance Theory, Burt argues that closed networks where actors' behavior does not go unnoticed decrease risks for individuals to trust each other (2005). This is due to both one's reputation as a type of information that is disseminated quickly through a dense network and to relationships which are highly likely between any actors in the dense network (Burt, 2005). This dovetails with all three aspects of trust with reputation, which is primarily cognitive, and relationships, which are more affective, producing trusting behavior. Burt further argues that the trust that develops takes time and that distrust may also develop similarly. Through the reputation and relationship present in long-standing closed networks, individuals have a clearly defined and greater level of trust or distrust for others in the network.

Based on CASA, I apply this network argument to technology where humans and technological actors are embedded in networks together. First, I consider a network of mainly human actors with one technological actor. In this case, reputation would function similarly to all human networks. You might ask a friend or coworker what website they use to get temperature predictions. If they vouch for the quality and accuracy of a particular website, then the reputation of this site will be cognitively validated. If everyone at your school or business gives reinforcing information about certain websites or other technologies, you will likely trust this technology over time. The affective dimension will also be present through relationships in this type of network. Even if you never receive information on the quality of a particular technology, the fact that your social network is utilizing and trusting in it may increase your ability to try it. A common example of this is when people have strong affective attachments to the PC or Macintosh brand of computers but are unable to articulate the actual benefits of their preferred

brand beyond hearsay. In fact, the reputation in that case is vague, but the relationship with the product is extremely clear.

A second type of network is that of technological actors with one human actor. Imagine you are considering trusting the forecast of a weather prediction website. Other technological actors may contribute to its reputation or relationship. The reputation might be enhanced by other websites that vouch for the quality of it (Karat, et al., 2008; Palmer, Bailey, & Faraj, 2000), such as your University's homepage recommending a particular weather prediction site. Also the University homepage may have a relationship by importing the temperature predictions onto its own site. Many technologies are produced and affiliated with companies and brand names for the purpose of reputation. If the websites you frequent use *Google* search and not *Yahoo!* search, then, using the social network logic of Burt (2005), I would suggest that you would be more likely to have increased trust in *Google* search compared to *Yahoo!* search. Additionally, the sponsored sites that appear when you do a search have a relational connection with your search engine: the sponsored site is vouched for by the search engine.

Technological actors have been researched as being a part of human social networks (Wellman, 2001) leading to organization networks that are hybrids between people and technologies (Carley, 2002). Actor-Network Theory makes a stronger claim that there is no fundamental distinction between human and non-human actors (Callon & Latour, 1992; Latour, 2005). This approach represents "a deep commitment to treating the humans and machines as members of a single community" (Collins, 1995, p295) and is compatible with the CASA literature and Assumptions 1 and 2. Any social actor can be a part of a network and principles of that network will apply, regardless of if the actor is human or technology. Furthermore, relationships between technologies in networks have been empirically studied as a "technological niche" where one innovation being adopted will become the foundation for newer technologies (Podolny & Stuart, 1995), compete with technologies in the same niche (Podolny, Toby, & Hannan, 1996), and make connections between companies affiliated with those technologies (Stuart & Podolny, 1996).

Reputation and relationship can contribute to trust in any combination of humans and technological actors in networks. Since the rise of the Internet, computers are in and part of networks, making these distinctions more theoretical than practical. Specifically, computer networks are facilitated by human social network connections, and human networks are facilitated by computer networks (Wellman, 2001). But these social networks are not just present for technological actors which exist on the Internet. Even machines, such as home appliances, are often thought of as connected through reputation and relationships. Brand names might contribute to the reputation of a technological actor, whereas compatibility between devices might contribute to the relationships between technologies. All these occur in the context of human actors making choices on what to buy, often with input from other people. In sum, the network positions of humans and technologies in relation to each other and other social actors are important as an antecedent of trust. This leads to the following proposition,

Proposition 2: A human and a technological actor embedded in the same dense network will have a greater magnitude of trust or distrust on average than if not embedded in the same dense network.

Cultural Sentiments and Trust

Cultural differences in the levels of generalized trust, in technology, and in the sentiments about those technologies will be important factors for trust in technological actors. Generalized trust affects the contributions of individuals in generalized social exchange (Yamagishi, 1988; Yamagishi & Cook, 1993), and these effects of generalized trust vary by the network structure (Yamagishi & Cook, 1993). I argued above that network structure is important for trust, but Yamagishi's research suggests that network structure may be differentially important in different cultures if generalized trust varied by culture. In a cross-cultural study of generalized trust, Yamagishi found that Americans had higher levels of generalized trust and cooperated more than Japanese when there was no sanctioning allowed (1988). Yet high levels of trust do not always lead to advantageous outcomes. Kiyonari et al. found that trust did not in fact lead to trustworthiness in one-shot interactions with anonymous partners (2006). Those that exhibited trust in their partners to divide up resources between them actually received *less* than those who divided up resources with no information or trust from their partners. For Americans this was statistically significant, suggesting there is a "reverse reciprocity" effect where trusting decreases reciprocity from those one trusted (Kiyonari, et al., 2006). These studies suggest that generalized trust may vary by culture, and that the level of generalized trust may affect the behavior, such as the behavioral trust of people in others. Therefore, and in congruence with Assumption 4, I suggest that cultural differences in generalized trust will be an important factor in trusting in technological actors.

Cultures may vary in their level of generalized trust; however, they also vary in their level of technology. Comparing cultures, noticeable differences could occur in the availability and sophistication of the technology and the views toward the purpose of technology. Although the internet has made access to some technologies nearly universal, access and language barriers still exist for many people. Mechanical technologies such as vehicles, mobile phones, and security systems are not as flatly available as web-based resources. Some cultures, countries, and populations within them have vastly different access to technology – a phenomenon commonly called the digital divide. Because familiarity is important for cognitive trust (Luhmann, 1979), it would not be farfetched to presume that cultural differences in trust would vary by accessibility and availability of the technology. The sophistication of the technology would also provide general cultural variation in levels of trust. A weather prediction website is a complex system that, if available in a culture, might necessitate a level of trust or distrust by its complexity. If the culture had many instances of artificial intelligence systems making important predictions, then there would be a high likelihood of a cultural perspective regarding such systems. Finally, the purpose of technology varies by culture. Backlashes to events such as eugenics in Europe or the atomic bomb in Japan may lead cultures to trust or distrust technology or specific types of technology in historically situated ways. Technological actors situated in a culture are simultaneously influenced by the evaluation of technology, the death or lifecycle of technology, the love of technology, and cultural narratives about the role and purpose of technology (see Latour, 1996).

Because of the potential for vast cultural variation between trusting humans and technologies and the variation between types of technologies, one approach to this cultural variation is to examine specific sentiments toward individuals concepts, actors, and objects that have been linguistically defined in that culture. This is the approach of Osgood and colleagues (Osgood, May, & Miron, 1975; Osgood, Suci, & Tannenbaum, 1957) who collected cross-cultural dictionaries of sentiments that varied on universal dimensions of meaning. They found a great deal of the variation on concepts in all cultures was due to three dimensions of meaning: Evaluation (also called valiance), Potency, and Activity (also called arousal). These respectively measure the meaning associated with the goodness, powerfulness, and liveliness of concepts in a particular culture. The sentiments toward a specific technology can then be determined on these dimensions and then, I suggest,

propositions involving those dimensions would be invariant to particularistic technological changes. Several data collections of the three dimensions of meaning have included technological actors such as *Automation, Automobile, Atomic Bomb, Airplane, Bus, Cinema, Electricity, Machine, Pocket Radios, Television, Telephone, Nuclear Submarine, Train* (Osgood, et al., 1975, Appendix F), *'Bot (King, 2001)*, and *Computer* (Troyer, 2004) and the first research example section of this chapter uses data from a recent technological actor collection project (Shank, 2010).

Based on this discussion of Osgood's universal sentiments, one way to study cultural differences in trusting technology would be to examine cultural sentiments of Evaluation, Potency, and Activity (EPA) of technological actors. But why would trust vary with the fundamental sentiments of technological actors? Affect Control Theory (ACT) suggests an answer. I will first introduce the main components of ACT, followed by details relating ACT to trust and then technology. This will culminate in propositions about the relations of cultural sentiments to trust in technological actors which I will illustrate with research examples.

Cultural Sentiments and Trust using Affect Control Theory

ACT (Heise, 1979, 2007; MacKinnon, 1994; Robinson & Smith-Lovin, 2006) proposes that people label actors, emotions, settings, and behaviors in interpersonal interaction and that these labels have an affective interpretation according to Osgood's three dimensions of meaning. These labels carry with them stable EPA (i.e., evaluation, potency, and activity) values known as fundamental sentiments. Because ACT's fundamental sentiments are based on the shared meanings by members of the culture, techniques have been developed for collecting new data on specific cultures or subcultures (Heise, 1970, 2010). Major collection projects, referred to as ACT Dictionaries have been collected for several cultures including Japan,

China, Germany, Northern Ireland, and multiple dictionaries in the United States and Canada (Heise, 2009). Additionally, supplemental dictionary entries have been collected, usually focusing on a subculture or on fundamental sentiments of a particular area of interest. Subcultural data has been collected for an internet subculture (King, 2001), a Jamband subculture (Hunt, 2008), and religious and homosexual subcultures (Smith-Lovin & Douglass, 1992).

Based on the fundamental sentiments of the elements of a situation, ACT can predict changes in the affect of the elements based on that interaction. The logic for this is contained in equations that were developed by Smith-Lovin (1987), and allow new affective sentiments, called transient impressions, to emerge in interaction. For example, if a *Teammate Trusts a Scoundrel*, the prediction using the fundamental sentiments of *Teammate, Trusts,* and *Scoundrel* for a male observer using the 1978 North Carolina ACT Dictionary and the equations suggest that after this interaction the *Teammate* would be seen as slightly less good, less powerful, and less active (lower EPA) and the *Scoundrel* would be seen as changing from quite bad to slightly bad (higher E), with the same amount of power and activity. Furthermore, that behavior of *Trusts* would be viewed as less good, less powerful, and more active than *Trusts* appears in general.

ACT is a negative feedback control theory (Robinson, 2007) and the situational meanings are being controlled by either a participant-observer or simply an observer. What is actually being controlled is a measure of the discrepancy in a situation referred to as deflection (D). Deflection is interpreted as the inverse of the likelihood that an event will occur – since most events are commonplace, discrepant events are rare compared to common ones. Deflection is operationalized as the squares of the difference between the fundamental sentiments and the transient impression of the EPA of all the elements in a situation. Deflection is signaled to participant actors through emotion and to observers through emotional expression (Robinson & Smith-Lovin, 1999; Robinson, Smith-Lovin, & Tsoudis, 1994).

When observers are controlling the meaning or definition of a situation, they are trying to reduce deflection. A participant in the situation would most likely reduce deflection through subsequent behavior (MacKinnon, 1994), but an observer or participant may reduce the deflection by cognitively reevaluating the situation by either relabeling elements of the situation, or adding emotion or trait modifiers to the actors in the situation (Heise & Thomas, 1989). In this way ACT makes theoretical predictions regarding behavior, cognition, and affect, meaning all three aspects of trust could be incorporated into ACT predictions. Currently, *Trust* is included as a behavior in the 1978 North Carolina ACT Dictionary and *Trusting* is included as a label for an actor in both the 1978 North Carolina and the Indiana 2003 dictionaries (Heise, 2009).

Not only is trust an appropriate concept to study with ACT, but technology is as well. Several technological actors have been rated in Osgood's EPA dimensions as previously listed; however, several Affect Control theorists have considered the potentials of interaction with technology as a social actor. King's study of Internet subculture found that technological actors, settings, and behaviors had cultural sentiments, but these varied based on how imbedded one was in the subculture (2001). Troyer collected pilot data on computers and interactions and showed how ACT could predict human-computer interactions similarly to human-human interactions (2004). ACT has been theorized to be a foundational component for incorporating emotional intelligence into simulated actors such as agents or bots in virtual environments (Troyer, 2008) or facial expressions on website's computerized agents (Heise, 2004).

To my knowledge this chapter's illustrative research is the first attempt to examine trust in technological actors from an Affect Control Theory perspective. As described above, the foundations of ACT predictions rest in the fundamental sentiments contained in the cultural dictionaries and the transient impressions built on those dictionaries combined with the transient impression equations. Therefore, I forward propositions related to each of those ACT cornerstones:

Proposition 3: Humans' trust in a technological actor will vary by the fundamental sentiments of that technological actor for a given culture.

Proposition 4: Humans' trust in a technological actor will vary by the transient impressions of that technological actor after social interaction.

Propositions 1 and 2 suggest ways in which network structure might influence trust in technological actors, while Propositions 3 and 4 suggest ways in which cultural sentiments might affect the same. I now zoom in from the broad propositional perspective and illustrate research under the umbrella of Propositions 3 and 4, including the development of related hypotheses.

Research on Fundamental Sentiments from Culture (Proposition 3)

The ACT dictionary I collected (Shank, 2010) consisted of 80 technology-related elements rated by approximately 30+ members of the United States culture on scales and methods developed by Osgood and colleagues (Osgood, et al., 1975; Osgood, et al., 1957) and revised by Heise (1970, 2010). The 80 items were selected to specifically capture a diversity of technologies that are well-known in United States culture but are not representative of all types of technology. Sixteen of the items were behaviors or human actors and the remaining 64 items were technological actors and are used for this exploratory analysis.

Although each technology has its own EPA rating, to look at broad categories of technological actors and to assess trust toward them I divided up the 64 technological actors into 27 categories. Following Robinson (1996), I divided up each of the three EPA dimensions, which ranged from -4 to +4, into Low (below -1.5), Medium (-1.5 to 1.5), and High (above 1.5) and classified all the technological actors into a category based on these (Table 1).

It is fascinating how specifically the technological actors divided up into the categories. Only 12 of the 27 potential categories (44.4%) had any actors classified in them. Notably, there were no technologies either high or low in Evaluation and low in Potency or Activity (HHL, HML, HLH, HLM, HLL, LHL, LML, LLH, LLM, LLL). Forty of the 64 items (62.5%) were in just four categories. I assigned category names to each group based on my perception of the characteristics of the technological actors that fell in that category. For example all the MHH are fast machines, all the MHM are large machines, and all the LHH are bombs. Although this analysis is more exploratory in nature, the labeling does lend support to the idea that technological actors are systematically distributed in EPA space in a culture.

What categories of technologies are most likely to be trusted based on cultural sentiments? The *D* column in Table 1 lists the deflections of the event *Human Trusts Technology*[1], where *Technology* was an EPA profile representing each technology category listed in Table 1 with High being set to 2.5, Medium to 0.0 and Low to -2.5. Lower deflections represent more likely events and higher deflections represent less likely event according to the theory. None of the deflections are extremely high (e.g., above 12). There is a difference between technologies medium and high in Evaluation with deflections ranging from 1.27 to 2.98 and those low in Evaluation ranging from 5.08 to 7.37. From this I draw an intuitive hypothesis that is now grounded in this exploratory analysis and ACT:

Table 1. Evaluation (E), potency (P), and activity (A) categorical divisions of technological actors and affect control theory simulation results: deflection (D) for human trusts technology. Data from Georgia 2008 ACT technology dictionary (Shank, 2010)

EPA*	Technological Actors	Category Name	N	D
MMM	*Minivan, Desktop Computer, Nonhybrid Vehicle, CD Player, Myspace, Fax Machine, Robot, Windows Computer, Android, Yahoo, Ebay*	*mixed middle category*	11	1.27
HMM	*Hybrid Vehicle, ATM, Antivirus Program, GPS, Bicycle, Car, FM Radio, Spyware Removal Program, Digital Camcorder, Artificial Limb, DVD Player, Internet Radio*	portable devices and small vehicles	12	1.39
HHM	*Biotechnology, Firewall*	intangible new technologies	2	1.92
MML	*VCR, Landline Phone*	older technologies	2	2.10
HMH	*PDA, TV Recording Device, Digital Audio Player, Cell Phone, Digital Camera, Macintosh, Laptop*	portable devices	7	2.26
MHM	*School Bus, Tank, SUV, Pickup Truck, Semi Truck*	large machines	5	2.36
MLL	*Cassette Player, AM Radio*	older technologies	2	2.36
HHH	*Ambulance, YouTube, Firetruck, Computer, HD TV, Wikipedia, Facebook, Google, Google Earth, Sports Car*	new technologies and popular websites	10	2.52
MHH	*Missile, Motorcycle, Police Car*	fast machines	3	2.98
LMM	*Web Error, Spam Email, Spyware*	web annoyances	3	5.08
LHM	*Computer Virus, Biological Weapon*	other harmful technology	2	6.73
LHH	*Weapons of Mass Destruction, Suicide Bomb, Nuclear Weapon, Car Bomb, Roadside Bomb*	bombs	5	7.37

*High = Above 1.5
Medium = -1.5 to 1.5
Low = Below -1.5

Hypothesis 1: People are less likely to trust technological actors with low Evaluation (bad) than technological actors with medium (neither good nor bad) or high Evaluation (good).

Research on Transient Impressions after Interaction (Proposition 4)

This example of transient impressions comes from an experiment I conducted comparing computers and humans in social exchange including affective sentiments (Shank, 2008) perceived justice, and behavioral reaction (Shank, 2009). This experiment did not measure trust *per se*, but it is appropriate because it instead dealt with a behavior that violates trust: coercion (see Molm, 1997). The experiment was a social exchange setting where ostensibly a subject interacts with several unseen actors arranged in a network that constrained the exchange of valued resources. It was modeled after theoretical work in the area of social exchange (Cook, Cheshire, & Gerbasi, 2006; Molm, 2003; Molm, et al., 2000) as well as being designed after a similar experimental paradigm (Molm, 1997; Molm, Quist, & Wiseley, 1993). This is related to Proposition 1 in that actors were in a power-dependent exchange relation to receive benefits from others but was not a test of Proposition 1. However, this experiment does set up a baseline for future testing of both Propositions 1 and 4 in conjunction: manipulating both the power-dependence of a structured interaction and the transient impression of that interaction.

In this experiment the strategy of one of the exchange partners was manipulated. In one condition the partner was cooperative, using a tit-for-tat reciprocal strategy, repaying valued resources with valued resources. The other condition was a coercive strategy, representing a blatant violation of generalized trust. The simulated partner using a coercive strategy would take away resources from the subject if the subject was not continuously giving positive resources back. The other manipulated condition was if the subject was told she was exchanging resources with computers or with other humans who were students. Dependent variable measurements included affective sentiments (i.e., EPA) toward the manipulated partner as well as the behavioral response (i.e., retaliation or resistance) of the subject via her exchanging.

An ACT simulation program (Heise, 2009) was used to simulate the interactions *Computer (or Student) Coerces (or Exchanges With) Student* and generate hypotheses about the differences in cooperative and coercive interaction with computers and humans (Shank, 2008). The EPA values for *Computer, Student, Coerce,* and *To Exchange With* come from the Georgia 2008 ACT Technology Dictionary (Shank, 2010). To generate hypotheses I simulated interactions for each of the factorial conditions in the experiment and then compared the transient impressions of the manipulated actor (i.e., the *Student* or *Computer*). The transient impression EPA averaged across gender of observer and behavior (i.e., *Coerces* or *Exchanges With*) for a *Student* was 1.18, 0.76, 1.80 and for a *Computer* was 1.64, 1.79, 1.56. The difference in Evaluation of 0.46 and Potency of 1.03 generated the following hypotheses[2]:

Hypothesis 2: After interaction, computers will be perceived as higher in Evaluation (more good) than students.

Hypothesis 3: After interaction, computers will be perceived as higher in Potency (more powerful) than students.

The results from this study indicated that overall computers were rated with higher Evaluation than students, supporting Hypothesis 2, and there was not a difference in Potency, not supporting Hypothesis 3. An interaction effect suggested that although computers and students did not differ in the potency, computers gained less potency than students did by engaging in coercive behavior compared to non-coercive behavior. A similar interaction effect in a different analysis shows the ratings of perceived justice of the behavior of one's partner were less just for students who coerced compared to computers who coerced leading to the subject increasing her resistance and retaliation (Shank, 2009).

Results only supported one of the two ACT hypotheses on transient impressions. One issue in research that combines a social exchange setting and ACT is that structural and cultural sentiments explanations have traditionally been in their own camps, ignoring the insight from each other. Yet there are a growing number of research traditions and theories that take the best elements from each (Clay-Warner & Robinson, 2008) including studying trust from a combined perspective (Gerbasi & Cook, 2008). Work on sentiments and interpersonal meaning is traditionally done by symbolic interactionists (McCall, 2006), but theories like Affect Control Theory, Identity Theory (Burke & Stets, 2009) and the Power-Status Theory of Emotion (Kemper, 1991) represent structural symbolic interactionism, which takes into account how structure shapes symbolic interaction. Research in network-based theories is now more likely to consider sentiments, affect, and emotions (Gerbasi & Cook, 2008; Molm, 2008) including the Affect Theory of Social Exchange and Relational Cohesion Theory. This chapter builds on the two camps to suggest the applicability of structure and cultural sentiments to trust in technological actors.

FUTURE RESEARCH DIRECTIONS

The assumptions and propositions set out in this chapter add sociological insights to the framing of a multidisciplinary study of trust toward technological actors. These insights themselves were often birthed in multidisciplinary traditions. The background work in CASA is grounded in a psychology, communications and HCI. The broad social exchange research paradigm (Proposition 1) is often studied in parallel by sociologists and economists. Social network research (Proposition 2) is popular in organizational science, business schools, and nonacademic institutions. The cultural research involving sentiments (Proposition 3 and 4) has drawn scholars and knowledge from anthropology, cultural studies, and engineering. The propositions in this chapter are already seated in disparate domain of multidisciplinary work including HCI and science and technology studies. And like the focus of this book, the study of trust and technology will continue to develop with ties to many parent disciplines.

The empirical research illustrates both a quantitative survey and a laboratory experiment. Future research should approach the study of trust in technological actors from many perspectives. Qualitative field work is necessary to identify specific factors in how actual daily interaction with technological actors creates, maintains, or inhibits trust. Additional survey research could illuminate views about technology in general and views about the aspects of specific technologies. In the study of organizations it would be important to study not only how technology might transform the ability of employees to conduct their jobs, but also how the interpersonal trust in technology may have implications beyond performance. In areas where computer systems are replacing workers, it is important to consider not only the situation of the displaced workers and the interaction of people with the new technology, but also how trust in the new technology might have secondary effects on trust in humans associated with that technology. Finally, the definition of a technological actor was purposely left ambiguous in this chapter because of the incredible need for development in the conceptualization of a technological actor (Collins, 1995). This is not a simple task as technologies come in many forms. They can be linked (e.g., websites), conceptual (e.g., biotechnology), embedded in each other (e.g., cartoon agent in a software program on a personal computer), scaled in magnitudes different than humans (e.g., nanotechnology, satellite system) and combined with humans (e.g., artificial heart, cyborgs). Conceptual and theoretical work in this area could provide a much needed focus to this emerging domain.

CONCLUSION

In this chapter I set forth several assumptions and propositions about trust in technological actors. First from Relational Cohesion and an Affect Theory of Social Exchange, I proposed that local structure would affect the power-dependence of technology and that people would trust technological actors they were dependent on for valued resources. Second from a social network perspective and drawing on Burt's concept of closure in dense networks, I proposed that larger social structure in terms of network embeddedness would increase the magnitude of trust or distrust in technologies that were embedded in that network. Third, I reviewed some empirical evidence of cross-cultural variation in trust then suggested Osgood's universal dimensions of meaning as relating to trust in technological actors across cultures and subcultures. ACT added to this cultural sentiments perspective by predicting changes due to interaction. I proposed those changes would be related to trust as well. Finally, I illustrated the final propositions with recent empirical data and specific hypotheses.

Studying human's trust in technological actors has grown in importance in recent years. Artificial intelligent systems, nanotechnology, autonomous vehicles, emotion-sensitive robots, human-machine mergers, and ubiquitous computing are some of the areas where technological sophistication is fundamentally changing the nature of human life. Futurists and transhumanists often warn us that these changes will happen quicker than we assume. Like the internet and mobile communications revolutions of the last two decades, technological changes will solve problems, create new ones, change fundamentals of social interaction, and generate important research questions for scientists. My hope is that through studying technologies as social actors, science will be better prepared to answer questions and rise to the challenge of understanding basic human life in the technology-saturated societies of the twenty-first century.

REFERENCES

Bijker, W. E. (1995). Sociohistorical Technology Studies. In Jasanoff, S., Markle, G. E., Peterson, J. C., & Pinch, T. (Eds.), *Handbook of Science and Technology Studies* (pp. 229–256). Thousand Oaks, CA: Sage.

Brave, S., & Nass, C. (2008). Emotion in Human-Computer Interaction. In Sears, A., & Jacko, J. A. (Eds.), *The Human-Computer Interaction Handbook: Fundamentals, Evolving Technology and Emerging Applications* (2nd ed., pp. 77–92). New York: Taylor & Francis.

Brave, S., Nass, C., & Hutchinson, K. (2005). Computers that Care: Investigating the Effects of Orientation of Emotion Exhibited by an Embodied Computer Agent. *International Journal of Human-Computer Studies*, *62*, 161–178. doi:10.1016/j.ijhcs.2004.11.002

Burke, P. J., & Stets, J. E. (2009). *Identity Theory*. Oxford, UK: Oxford University.

Burt, R. S. (2005). *Brokerage and Closure*. Oxford, UK: Oxford University.

Byrne, M. D. (2008). Cognitive Architecture. In Sears, A., & Jacko, J. A. (Eds.), *The Human-Computer Interaction Handbook: Fundamentals, Evolving Technology and Emerging Applications* (2nd ed., pp. 93–113). New York: Taylor & Francis.

Callon, M., & Latour, B. (1992). Don't Throw the Baby out with the Bath School! A Reply to Colins and Yearley. In Pickering, A. (Ed.), *Science as Practice and Culture* (pp. 343–368). Chicago, IL: University of Chicago.

Carley, K. M. (2002). Smart Agents and Organizations of the Future. In Lievrouw, L., & Livingstone, S. (Eds.), *The Handbook of New Media* (pp. 206–220). Thousand Oaks, CA: Sage.

Clay-Warner, J., & Robinson, D. T. (2008). *Social Structure and Emotion*. Amsterdam: Elsevier.

Collins, H. M. (1995). Science Studies and Machine Intelligence. In Jasanoff, S., Markle, G. E., Peterson, J. C., & Pinch, T. (Eds.), *Handbook of Science and Technology Studies*. Thousand Oaks, CA: Sage.

Cook, K. S. (2005). Networks, Norms, and Trust: The Social Psychology of Social Capital. *Social Psychology Quarterly*, *68*(1), 4–14. doi:10.1177/019027250506800102

Cook, K. S., Cheshire, C., & Gerbasi, A. (2006). Power, Dependence, and Social Exchange. In Burke, P. J. (Ed.), *Contemporary Social Psychological Theories*. Stanford, CA: Stanford University Press.

Cook, K. S., & Emerson, R. M. (1978). Power, Equity and Commitment in Exchange Networks. *American Sociological Review*, *43*, 721–731. doi:10.2307/2094546

Cook, K. S., Emerson, R. M., Gillmore, M. R., & Yamagishi, T. (1983). The Distribution of Power in Exchange Networks: Theory and Experimental Results. *American Journal of Sociology, 89*(2), 275–305. doi:10.1086/227866

Copeland, D. G., & McKenney, J. L. (1988). Airline Reservation Systems: Lessons from History. *Management Information Systems Quarterly, 12*(3), 353–370. doi:10.2307/249202

DiMaggio, P., Hargittai, E., Neuman, W. R., & Robinson, J. P. (2001). Social Implications of the Internet. *Annual Review of Sociology, 27,* 307–336. doi:10.1146/annurev.soc.27.1.307

Emerson, R. M. (1962). Power-Dependence Relations. *American Sociological Review, 27*(1), 31–41. doi:10.2307/2089716

Ferdig, R. E., & Mishra, P. (2004). Emotional Responses to Computers: Experiences in Unfairness, Anger, and Spite. *Journal of Educational Multimedia and Hypermedia, 13*(2), 143–161.

Fogg, B. J. (2003). *Persuasive Technology: Using Computers to Change What We Think and Do.* San Francisco: Morgan Kaufmann.

Fogg, B. J., Cuellar, G., & Danielson, D. (2008). Motivation, Influencing, and Persuading Users: An Introduction to Captology. In Sears, A., & Jacko, J. A. (Eds.), *The Human-Computer Interaction Handbook: Fundamentals, Evolving Technology and Emerging Applications* (2nd ed., pp. 133–146). New York: Taylor & Francis.

Gardner, M. W., & Dorling, S. R. (1998). Artificial neural networks (the multilayer perceptron) – A review of applications in the atmospheric sciences. *Atmospheric Environment, 32*(14-15), 2627–2636. doi:10.1016/S1352-2310(97)00447-0

Gerbasi, A., & Cook, K. S. (2008). The Effect of Perceived Trustworthiness on Affect in Negotiated and Reciprocal Exchange. In Clay-Warner, J., & Robinson, D. T. (Eds.), *Social Structure and Emotions* (pp. 142–166). Amsterdam: Elsevier. doi:10.1016/B978-0-12-374095-3.00009-4

Groom, V., & Nass, C. (2007). Can Robots be Teammates? *Interaction Studies: Social Behaviour and Communication in Biological and Artificial Systems, 8*(3), 483–500.

Hardin, R. (2002). *Trust and Trustworthiness.* New York: Russell Sage Foundation.

Heise, D. R. (1970). The Semantic Differential and Attitude Research. In Summers, G. F. (Ed.), *Attitude Measurement.* Chicago: Rand McNally.

Heise, D. R. (1979). *Understanding Events: Affect and the Construction of Social Action.* New York: Cambridge University Press.

Heise, D. R. (2004). Enculturating Agents with Expressive Role Behavior. In Payr, S., & Trappl, R. (Eds.), *Agent Culture: Human-Agent Interaction in a Multicultural World* (pp. 127–142). Mahwah, NJ: Lawrence Erlbaum Associates.

Heise, D. R. (2007). *Expressive Order: Confirming Sentiments in Social Actions.* New York: Springer.

Heise, D. R. (2009). *Interact.* Retrieved from http://www.indiana.edu/~socpsy/ACT/interact.htm

Heise, D. R. (2010). *Surveying Cultures: Discovering Shared Conceptions and Sentiments.* Hoboken, NJ: Wiley.

Heise, D. R., & Thomas, L. (1989). Predicting Impressions Created by Combinations of Emotion and Social Identity. *Social Psychology Quarterly, 52*(2), 141–148. doi:10.2307/2786913

Hunt, P. M. (2008). From Festies to Tourrats: Examining the Relationship between Jamband Subculture Involvement and Role Meanings. *Social Psychology Quarterly, 71*(4), 356–378. doi:10.1177/019027250807100405

iRobot Corporation. (2008). *About iRobot, 2008.* Retrieved from http://www.irobot.com/sp.cfm?pageid=74

Isbister, K., & Nass, C. (2000). Consistency of Personality in Interactive Characters: Verbal Cues, Non-Verbal Cues, and User Characteristics. *International Journal of Human-Computer Studies, 53*, 251–267. doi:10.1006/ijhc.2000.0368

Jain, A., McClendon, R. W., Hoogenboom, G., & Ramyaa, R. (2003). *Prediction of frost for fruit protection using artificial neural networks*. American Society of Agricultural Engineers.

Jasanoff, S., Markle, G. E., Peterson, J. C., & Pinch, T. (1995). *Handbook of Science and Technology Studies*. Thousand Oaks, CA: Sage.

Karat, J., Karat, C.-M., & Brodie, C. (2008). Human-Computer Interaction Viewed from the Intersection of Privacy, Security, and Trust. In Sears, A., & Jacko, J. A. (Eds.), *The Human-Computer Interaction Handbook: Fundamentals, Evolving Technology and Emerging Applications*. New York: Taylor & Francis.

Kemper, T. D. (1991). Predicting Emotions from Social Relations. *Social Psychology Quarterly, 54*, 330–342. doi:10.2307/2786845

King, A. B. (2001). Affective Dimensions of Internet Culture. *Social Science Computer Review, 19*(4), 414–430. doi:10.1177/089443930101900402

Kiyonari, T., Yamagishi, T., Cook, K. S., & Cheshire, C. (2006). Does Trust Beget Trustworthiness? Trust and Trustworthiness in Two Games and Two Cultures: A Research Note. *Social Psychology Quarterly, 69*(3), 270–283. doi:10.1177/019027250606900304

Latour, B. (1996). *Armis, or the Love of Technology* (Porter, C., Trans.). Cambridge, MA: Harvard University.

Latour, B. (2005). *Reassembling the Social: An Introduction to Actor-Network Theory*. Oxford, UK: Oxford University.

Lawler, E. J. (2001). An Affect Theory of Social Exchange. *American Journal of Sociology, 107*(2), 321–352. doi:10.1086/324071

Lawler, E. J., Thye, S. R., & Yoon, J. (2000). Emotion and Group Cohesion in Productive Exchange. *American Journal of Sociology, 106*, 616–657. doi:10.1086/318965

Lawler, E. J., Thye, S. R., & Yoon, J. (2008). Social Exchange and Micro Social Order. *American Sociological Review, 73*, 519–542. doi:10.1177/000312240807300401

Lawler, E. J., & Yoon, J. (1993). Power and the Emergence of Commitment Behavior in Negotiated Exchange. *American Sociological Review, 58*(4), 465–481. doi:10.2307/2096071

Lawler, E. J., & Yoon, J. (1996). Commitment in Exchange Relations. *American Sociological Review, 61*(1), 89–108. doi:10.2307/2096408

Lewis, J. D., & Weigert, A. (1985). Trust as Social Reality. *Social Forces, 63*(4), 967–985. doi:10.2307/2578601

Liker, J. K., Haddad, C. J., & Karlin, J. (1999). Perspectives on Technology and Work Organizations. *Annual Review of Sociology, 25*, 575–596. doi:10.1146/annurev.soc.25.1.575

Luhmann, N. (1979). *Trust and Power*. New York: Wiley.

Luk, K. C., Ball, J. E., & Sharma, A. (2000). A study of optimal model lag and spatial inputs for artificial neural network for rainfall forecasting. *Journal of Hydrology (Amsterdam), 227*, 56–65. doi:10.1016/S0022-1694(99)00165-1

MacKinnon, N. J. (1994). *Symbolic Interactionism as Affect Control*. New York: State University of New York.

McCall, G. J. (2006). Symbolic Interaction. In Burke, P. J. (Ed.), *Contemporary Social Psychological Theories*. Stanford, CA: Stanford University Press.

Mishra, P. (2006). Affective Feedback from Computers and its Effect on Perceived Ability and Affect: A Test of the Computers as Social Actors Hypothesis. *Journal of Educational Multimedia and Hypermedia, 15*(1), 107–131.

Molm, L. D. (1997). *Coercive Power in Social Exchange*. Cambridge, UK: Cambridge University.

Molm, L. D. (2003). Theoretical Comparison of Forms of Exchange. *Sociological Theory, 21*(1), 1–17. doi:10.1111/1467-9558.00171

Molm, L. D. (2008). The Structure of Reciprocity and Integrative Bonds: The Role of Emotions. In Clay-Warner, J., & Robinson, D. T. (Eds.), *Social Structure and Emotions*. Amsterdam: Elsevier. doi:10.1016/B978-0-12-374095-3.00010-0

Molm, L. D., Quist, T. M., & Wiseley, P. A. (1993). Reciprocal Justice and Strategies of Exchange. *Social Forces, 72*(1), 19–44. doi:10.2307/2580158

Molm, L. D., Takahashi, N., & Peterson, G. (2000). Risk and Trust in Social Exchange: An Experimental Test of a Classical Proposition. *American Journal of Sociology, 105*(5), 1396–1427. doi:10.1086/210434

Moon, Y., & Nass, C. (1996). How "Real" Are Computer Personalities? *Communication Research, 23*(6), 651–674. doi:10.1177/009365096023006002

Nass, C., Fogg, B. J., & Moon, Y. (1996). Can Computers be Teammates? *International Journal of Human-Computer Studies, 45*, 669–678. doi:10.1006/ijhc.1996.0073

Nass, C., & Moon, Y. (2000). Machines and Mindlessness: Social Responses to Computers. *The Journal of Social Issues, 56*(1), 81–103. doi:10.1111/0022-4537.00153

Nass, C., Moon, Y., Fogg, B. J., Reeves, B., & Dryer, D. C. (1995). Can Computer Personalities be Human Personalities? *International Journal of Human-Computer Studies, 43*, 223–239. doi:10.1006/ijhc.1995.1042

Nass, C., & Reeves, B. (1996). Technology and Roles: A Tale of Two TVs. *The Journal of Communication, 46*(2), 121–128. doi:10.1111/j.1460-2466.1996.tb01477.x

Nass, C., & Steuer, J. (1993). Voices, Boxes, and Sources of Message: Computers and Social Actors. *Human Communication Research, 19*(4), 504–527. doi:10.1111/j.1468-2958.1993.tb00311.x

Nass, C., Steuer, J., & Tauber, E. R. (1994). *Computers are Social Actors*. Paper presented at the SIGCHI Conference on Human Factors in Computing Systems: Celebrating Interdependence.

Nugroho, A. S., Kuroyanagi, S., & Iwata, A. (2002). A solution for imbalanced training sets problem by CombNET-II and its application on fog forecasting. *IEICE Transactions on Information and Systems. E (Norwalk, Conn.), 85-D*(7), 1165–1174.

Osgood, C. E., May, W. E., & Miron, M. S. (1975). *Cross-Cultural Universals of Affective Meaning*. Urbana: University of Illinois.

Osgood, C. E., Suci, G. J., & Tannenbaum, P. H. (1957). The Measurement of Meaning. [University of Illinois.]. *Urbana (Caracas, Venezuela)*, IL.

Palmer, J. W., Bailey, J. P., & Faraj, S. (2000). The Role of Intermediaries in the Development of Trust on the WWW: The Use and Prominence of Trusted Third Parties and Privacy Statements. *Journal of Computer-Mediated Communication, 5*(3).

Picard, R. W. (1997). *Affective Computing*. Cambridge, MA: MIT Press.

Podolny, J. M., & Stuart, T. E. (1995). A Role-Based Ecology of Technological Change. *American Journal of Sociology, 100*(5), 1224–1260. doi:10.1086/230637

Podolny, J. M., Toby, E. S., & Hannan, M. T. (1996). Networks, Knowledge, and Niches: Competition in the Worldwide Semiconductor Industry, 1984-1991. *American Journal of Sociology, 102*(3), 659–689. doi:10.1086/230994

Robinson, D. T. (1996). Identity and Friendship: Affective Dynamics and Network Formation. *Advances in Group Processes, 13,* 91–111.

Robinson, D. T. (2007). Control Theories in Sociology. *Annual Review of Sociology, 33,* 157–174. doi:10.1146/annurev.soc.32.061604.123110

Robinson, D. T., & Smith-Lovin, L. (1999). Emotion Display as a Strategy for Identity Negotiation. *Motivation and Emotion, 23*(2), 73–104. doi:10.1023/A:1021325011770

Robinson, D. T., & Smith-Lovin, L. (2006). Affect Control Theory. In Burke, P. J. (Ed.), *Social Psychology*. Stanford, CA: Stanford University Press.

Robinson, D. T., Smith-Lovin, L., & Tsoudis, O. (1994). Heinous Crime or Unfortunate Accident? The Effects of Remorse on Responses to Mock Criminal Confessions. *Social Forces, 73*(1), 175–190. doi:10.2307/2579922

Rotter, J. B. (1967). A New Scale for the Measurement of Interpersonal Trust. *Journal of Personality, 35,* 651–665. doi:10.1111/j.1467-6494.1967.tb01454.x

Shank, D. B. (2008). *Affect Toward Computers Who Coerce in Social Exchange*. Athens, GA: University of Georgia.

Shank, D. B. (2009). *Perceived Justice of Computers*. Paper presented at the Southern Sociological Society Annual Meeting, New Orleans, LA.

Shank, D. B. (2010). *Georgia 2008 Affect Control Theory Technology Dictionary*. Unpublished manuscript.

Shank, D. B., Hoogenboom, G., & McClendon, R. W. (2008). Dew Point Temperature Prediction Using Artificial Neural Networks. *Journal of Applied Meteorology and Climatology, 47*(6), 1757–1769. doi:10.1175/2007JAMC1693.1

Shank, D. B., McClendon, R. W., Paz, J., & Hoogenboom, G. (2008). Ensemble Artificial Neural Networks for Prediction of Dew Point Temperature. *Applied Artificial Intelligence, 22*(6), 523–542. doi:10.1080/08839510802226785

Shinozawa, K., Reeves, B., Wise, K., Maldonado, H., & Naya, F. (2002). Robots as New Media: A Cross-Cultural Examination of Social and Cognitive Responses to Robotic and On-Screen Agents. Submitted to the Information Systems Division of the International Communication Association.

Shortliffe, E. H. (1993). Doctors, Patients, and Computers: Will Information Technology Dehumanize Health-Care Delivery? *Proceedings of the American Philosophical Society, 137*(3), 390–398.

Smith, B. A., McClendon, R. W., & Hoogenboom, G. (2006). Improving air temperature prediction with artificial neural networks. *International Journal of Computational Intelligence, 3*(3), 179–186.

Smith-Lovin, L. (1987). Impression from Events. *The Journal of Mathematical Sociology, 13,* 35–70.

Smith-Lovin, L., & Douglass, W. (1992). An Affect-Control Analysis of Two Religious Groups. In Franks, D. D., & Gecas, V. (Eds.), *Social Perspectives on Emotion*. Greenwich, CT: Jai Press.

Sparrow, R. (2002). The March of the Robot Dogs. *Ethics and Information Technology, 4,* 305–318. doi:10.1023/A:1021386708994

Steidley, C., Sadovski, A., Tissot, P., & Bachnak, R. (2005). *Using an artificial neural network to improve predictions of water level where tide charts fail*. Paper presented at the Innovations in Applied Artificial Intelligence, Bari, Italy.

Stuart, T. E., & Podolny, J. M. (1996). Local Search and the Evolution of Technological Capabilities. *Strategic Management Journal, 17,* 21–38.

Troyer, L. (2004). *Affect Control Theory as a Foundation for the Design of Socially Intelligent Systems*. Paper presented at the American Association for Artificial Intelligence Symposium on Architectures for Modeling Emotion: Cross Disciplinary Foundations, Menlo Park, CA.

Troyer, L. (2008). A Strategy for Incorporating Social Intelligence in the Design of Virtual Environments. In Clay-Warner, J., & Robinson, D. T. (Eds.), *Social Structure and Emotion* (pp. 95–106). Amsterdam: Elsevier. doi:10.1016/B978-0-12-374095-3.00006-9

Wedge, D., Ingram, D., McLean, D., Mingham, C., & Bandar, Z. (2005). *A global-local artificial neural network with application to wave overtopping prediction*. Paper presented at the Artificial Neural Networks: Formal Models and Their Applications - ICANN 2005, Warsaw, Poland.

Wellman, B. (2001). Computer Networks as Social Network. *Science*, *293*, 2031–2034. doi:10.1126/science.1065547

Yamagishi, T. (1988). The Provision of a Sanctioning System in the United States and Japan. *Social Psychology Quarterly*, *51*(3), 265–271. doi:10.2307/2786924

Yamagishi, T., & Cook, K. S. (1993). Exchange and Social Dilemmas. *Social Psychology Quarterly*, *56*(4), 235–248. doi:10.2307/2786661

ENDNOTES

[1] *Human* was taken from the 2008 ACT Technology Dictionary and has an EPA profile for males of [1.23 1.16 0.84]; *Trusts* was taken from the North Carolina 1978 ACT Dictionary, because more resent ACT dictionaries did not have it. Its EPA profile is [2.11 0.99 -0.74].

[2] A criterion of at least 0.46 was calculated and used in Shank (2008) to determine the amount of difference between average transient impressions in order to reasonably generate a hypothesis based on ACT.

Section 2
Trust and Technology in Interpersonal Contexts

Chapter 4
The Role of Trust in Online Relationship Formation

Andrew T. Fiore
University of California, USA

Coye Cheshire
University of California, USA

ABSTRACT

Trust plays a key role in the formation of any romantic relationship, but it is particularly salient to the formation of relationships online. In this chapter, the authors examine how trustworthiness, relational trust, general trust, and confidence in systems shape the experience of online dating. The authors propose that each of these trust-related phenomena becomes salient at different points in the process of finding a potential date, contacting him or her, meeting face-to-face, and beginning an offline relationship. Moreover, the authors suggest that the constraints and affordances of online interaction have the potential both to help and to hinder the assessment of trustworthiness and the development of relational trust.

INTRODUCTION

"[Operation] Match feels that it has just scratched the surface in machine-age romance. Next step is a process called 'RealTime' that will allow a customer on any campus anywhere to fill in his questionnaire on a keyboard teletype (perhaps in the Student Union?) hooked up to a central computer. Within minutes, the keyboard will automatically type out the names and telephone numbers of five soul mates within driving range. Instant Eros, it seems, will be here long before 1984."

— *"My IBM Baby," Time Magazine, November 1965*

DOI: 10.4018/978-1-61520-901-9.ch004

In few areas of life do we entrust so much as with our romantic partners. To intertwine our emotional, financial, and familial future with another person requires a great deal of trust, given the high stakes of such a decision. Trust is a central component of many types of online relationships, but the development of intimate relationships through online dating and matchmaking services provides a unique window into the interplay of trust and related phenomena. Unlike many other types of online relationships, romantic relationships begun in computer-mediated environments are often expected to progress to face-to-face interaction. Researchers typically identify the point of the initial meeting as a clear risk, rife with various uncertainties (Green, 2007). However, we argue that there is much to gain from a wider view of the role of trust in activities that lead up to an in-person meeting and in subsequent interactions, as the relationship continues to develop.

In this chapter, we examine how four related phenomena — confidence in systems, trustworthiness, relational trust, and general trust — affect online relationship formation, in particular among people meeting through online dating systems. We begin by presenting a variety of theoretical perspectives on these phenomena, followed by an overview of interpersonal communication in computer-mediated communication environments in general and online dating systems in particular. Next, we consider the role of trust-related processes in online relationship formation: how computer-mediated self-presentation and interpersonal perception influence assessments of trustworthiness, how online communication affects the development of trust, and how people interacting through online dating systems seek to reduce uncertainty and build trust as they move toward meeting face-to-face. Finally, we suggest directions for future research that might deepen our understanding of trust in the context of computer-mediated relationship formation.

BACKGROUND

The Concept of Trust

Trust is an essential part of social interaction. As Trudy Govier (1997) argues, the benevolence and confidence that we associate with trust can act as a type of social glue, alleviating concerns of risk and uncertainty in interpersonal interaction. It is therefore unsurprising that trust is a central concept and the focus of research in diverse literatures such as psychology, sociology, social psychology, philosophy, computer science, communication, and economics. We begin by discussing four concepts that are essential for understanding trust and trust-like phenomena in online relationships: trustworthiness, relational trust, general trust, and confidence in systems. Since different literatures and research traditions speak more to some aspects of trust than to others, our goal is to highlight the key trust-related issues for online relationship formation from a range of theoretical and methodological approaches.

Uncertainty, Risk and Trustworthiness

When individuals initially interact with one another in the presence of risk and uncertainty, each party makes assessments, implicitly or explicitly, about the trustworthiness of the other. Risk is what is at stake in a given interaction (such as money or time), while uncertainty refers to the ambiguity of an outcome (Cook et al., 2005). Both risk and uncertainty influence one's assessment of another's trustworthiness in a given context. For example, assessments of trustworthiness might not be essential in situations with uncertain outcomes if the stakes are low. On the other hand, assessing the trustworthiness of others might be critical even in situations with relatively certain outcomes if the stakes are high.

Trust and trustworthiness are distinct concepts — the former results from a process of mutual risk-taking over time, while the latter is a *characteristic* of one who is trusted — yet the terms are frequently conflated in both academic literature and colloquial use. In particular, the use of "trust" when we mean "trustworthiness" is common, as is the misuse of "trust" in the context of one-time interactions between individuals. These non-repeated interactions are more accurately described as acts of risk-taking rather than examples of trust (Hardin, 1993; Hardin, 2002).

Key factors that affect our judgments of trustworthiness include the nature of the situation, including what is at stake and the mode of interaction, and perceptions about another's intentions and motivations (Cook et al., in press). An assessment of another person's trustworthiness helps us decide whether to take a risk with that person or not. People gauge the trustworthiness of those with whom they might interact based on various criteria, and they depend on these assessments in the presence of risk and uncertainty. However, when there are organizational or institutional mechanisms in place to shield individuals from betrayal, people tend to rely primarily on these third-party protections instead (see Cook, Hardin, and Levi, 2005).

When one person takes an initial risk, such as giving something of value to another, it acts as a signal of his or her intention to trust the other person. Some situations are more uncertain than others, but cooperative behavior over time consistently leads to high levels of trust in different kinds of social exchange interactions (Cheshire et al., 2009). Signaling one's intentions is especially important in online interactions, where limited information makes it difficult to assess the trustworthiness of others. The act of taking a risk in an online interaction is an important signal because the trustee knows that he or she has been entrusted with something of value, despite the uncertainties inherent in the interaction environment (Cheshire and Cook, 2004).

An act of risk-taking with another who is deemed trustworthy does not guarantee reciprocity or the development of trust. In fact, experimental research demonstrates that when individuals interact with complete anonymity in computer-mediated systems, acts of risk-taking are often not reciprocated at all (Cook et al., 2005; Yamagishi, in press). However, individuals tend to assess their partners as trustworthy and engage in increasingly risky exchanges if the system permits and the users maintain persistent identifiers over many interactions (Cheshire and Cook, 2004; Cook et al., 2005). In a cross-societal experimental study of trust and trustworthiness in the United States and Japan, Kiyonari and colleagues (2006) found that trust was not necessarily a simple reflection of trustworthiness. In particular, American participants reported high levels of trust yet perceived others as untrustworthy. However, at least some of this observed discrepancy between trust and trustworthiness was likely due to the structure of the interaction situations that were used in the study (Kiyonari et al., 2006).

Relational Trust

A track record of trustworthy behavior from others is extremely valuable in situations that include risk. When one's trust of another depends on an enduring relationship consisting of either direct or indirect interaction, then trust is considered relational (Hardin, 2002). The perpetual anticipation of trustworthy behavior from another person is a defining characteristic of a trust relation. A trust relation is stable because it "is too valuable to jeopardize by engaging in the kind of myopic opportunistic behavior that generates short-term gain but blocks the possibility of building a long-term relationship" (Cook et al., 2005, p. 122).

In a direct relationship between two individuals, trust occurs when "one party to the relation believes the other party has incentive to act in her interest or to take her interests to heart" (Cook, Hardin and Levi, 2005, p. 2). This view of pairwise, relational trust implies that each party encapsulates the other's interests (Hardin, 2002). For example, consider two long-time neighbors, Calvin and Veronica. Calvin *trusts* Veronica when he views Veronica to be trustworthy in a specific context, such as watching his cat while he is out of town. Using the encapsulated-interest view of trust, this means that Calvin views Veronica as trustworthy because Veronica's interests encapsulate his own: the cat is important and needs attention when Calvin is out of town. Calvin believes that Veronica is likely to act in a way that is consistent with these interests. Importantly, relational trust is context-specific (Hardin, 2002). The trust between Veronica and Calvin might or might not carry over to contexts beyond caring for a pet.

Relational trust can be cognitive, affective, or a combination of both types. Cognitive trust is based on our beliefs about another person's abilities, motivations, and intentions in a given situation (Hardin, 2002). Thus, cognitive trust is related to the amount of knowledge that we have — or *believe* we have — about someone else. In contrast, affective trust reflects the social and emotional connections between individuals. Affective trust does not depend on factual knowledge about another person, but it does require sufficient time to develop encapsulated interests and emotional bonds between individuals.

The cognitive and affective dimensions of trust relate to the duration of a given relationship. The initial act of risk-taking that can lead to a trusting relationship is distinct from the mature, emotional trust that develops over time (Hardin, 2002; Whitty, 2007). Thus, the earliest stages of a trust-building relationship are marked by gradually increasing risks (cf. Cook et al., 2005), an experience that can eventually lead to the encapsulated interests that underlie durable trust relations (Hardin, 2002). In the earlier example of Calvin and Veronica, the first time that Calvin left his cat with Veronica, it acted as a signal that Calvin viewed Veronica as trustworthy. As the two individuals continued to reciprocate over time by entrusting each other with objects of value, they were able to develop the stable, affective component of trust.

General Trust

Unlike relational trust, which constitutes a type of relationship with a specific individual, general trust comprises one's assumptions about the likely behavior of others in a given society or environment. Also known as social trust, it reflects an individual's basic attitudes about the trustworthiness of others. General trust varies across cultures and societies, with western societies consistently showing higher levels of general trust than eastern societies (Yamagishi et al., 2005).

High general trust corresponds to a belief in the benevolence of others' intentions, while low general trust corresponds to a guarded and skeptical view of others (Yamagishi, 1998). Thus, individuals with high general trust are more likely to accept risk and uncertainty in different social contexts than are those low in general trust. An important consequence of accepting uncertainty is that individuals with high general trust might also try new activities, despite their risks, more readily than those with low general trust (Yamagishi, 2001; Yamagishi et al., 1999). Individuals who are more trusting and less cautious interact with strangers more often, and they are more likely to confirm their expectations concerning the trustworthiness of others. More interactions might engender more mistakes, or situations where trustworthiness is misjudged and an act of risk-taking leads to loss. But despite these mistakes, increased interaction with others over time creates more opportunities for beneficial interactions (Hayashi, 1995). Those who are less trusting and more cautious end up with fewer beneficial interactions on average due to their lack of willingness to take risks (Orbell and Dawes, 1993).

Hardin (2002) argues that general trust is a purely dispositional construct, not tied to any specific context or association between individuals. In his view, general trust is neither cognitive nor relational. The idea that individuals carry around an overall disposition to trust might simply be considered optimism based on prior experience, not trust. This dispositional view of trust "is… merely an explanation of why some take risks more readily than others do or why some read the risks as less serious than others do" (Hardin, 2002, p. 198). Whether general trust constitutes trust *per se* or related but distinct concepts such as optimism and caution, it is useful to consider the role of default attitudes and beliefs — especially before engaging with others in risky or uncertain situations.

Confidence in the System

Scholars studying online trust have debated whether notions of trust that describe interpersonal relationships can be similarly applied to relationships with information systems, web sites, and computer programs. Trust in an information system primarily involves individuals' expectations about whether the technology will support the interactions expected by its users (Riegelsberger et al., 2007). In this view, trust is based on a holistic evaluation of a system, including issues such as integrity, survivability, and availability (cf. Schneider, 1999).

For some, the strict distinction between trust in person-to-person and person-to-system interactions is unnecessary (see Marsh and Dibben, 2003). However, Friedman and colleagues (2000) argue that this distinction is crucial because it makes little sense to say that individuals trust technology in the same way, with the same meaning and expectations, that they trust other people. One reason for this distinction is that the relational, interpersonal form of trust depends on the possibility of betrayal (Baier, 1986). Information systems and computer programs lack the agency and consciousness to *choose* to betray the trust placed in them. Whether a person is interacting with another human or a system, the truster must assess the likelihood that the trustee will respond in an expected manner. For human trustees, the response is a choice. For the information system, the response is pre-programmed or the result of

an algorithm. Therefore, the idiomatic use of the term "trust" to describe interaction with an information system is inaccurate.

This inapt but common use of "trust" might also stem from an incomplete view of the connection between humans and information systems, one that overlooks a key distinction. From the perspective of the human truster, there might be little difference in the evaluation of risk and uncertainty when interacting with a system or with another person. Indeed, on the surface, the process of evaluating a system seems very much like assessing the trustworthiness of a person. Yet any "trust" that develops in the context of an information system lacks the *relational* aspect that is the essence of the term — it is solely unidirectional.

On the other hand, there are good reasons to expect some similarities between the way that individuals behave toward information systems and the way they behave toward other people. When individuals interact with computers and information systems, there are many sources of uncertainty that might inhibit or engender trust-like behaviors. Online information systems can foster *system uncertainty*, or ambiguity about how interactions and contributions of information to a given system will be handled (Cheshire and Antin, in press). Individuals who face uncertainty and risk when interacting with a system use available information to assess the system's current behavior and anticipate its future actions, as they might in a risky situation with another human. In addition, experimental research indicates that humans generally treat computers and other information systems as social actors even when they know that the computers are not human (Nass et al., 1994).

As Nissenbaum (2004) suggests, the confusion between trust and trust-like concepts is likely due to common misunderstandings about the labels for these concepts. Conflating trust with terms such as confidence and surety "misses the point of why we care about [trust]" (Nissenbaum, 2004, p. 157). Trust-like behaviors towards computers and information systems are better described with concepts such as confidence, surety, reliability, credibility, and security (Cheshire and Cook, 2004), which allow for the possibility of disappointment or failure without attributing the agency necessary for betrayal. When we say that an individual "trusts" a system of social interaction or information exchange, it is more accurately a statement about one of these concepts. Thus, trust in a computer or information system is more appropriately described as *confidence in the system* (Nissenbaum, 2004).

Interpersonal Communication in Online Environments

Researchers in interpersonal communication have studied technologically mediated communication from a sociological and social psychological perspective for decades. Many of their theories seek to explain the differences between unmediated (i.e., face-to-face) and various kinds of mediated communication in terms of both psychological phenomena and information-theoretic concerns.

Studies of computer-mediated communication include such diverse topics as online collaboration (e.g., Grudin and Poltrock, 1997), collective action (e.g., Cheshire and Antin, 2008), and the production and interpretation of language (e.g., Herring, 2001). Wallace (1999) provides an overview of these issues and more. Here, though, we focus on those aspects of mediated communication that pertain most closely to the assessment of trustworthiness and the development of relational trust: how people present themselves and perceive others online, and how interaction changes given different mediating technologies with different constraints and affordances.

Self-Presentation and Interpersonal Perception

Goffman (1957) describes self-presentation as the performance of a "front," or a particular social identity, by means of signals or cues, such as manner of dress, use of words, and selection of facial expressions. He distinguishes between "giving" a signal on purpose as part of the performance and "giving off" a signal by accident, or as a side effect of an intended signal. In this view, self-presentation is a social process that includes not only the performance but also observers' interpretations — which don't always agree with the performer's intent (Goffman, 1957). In a face-to-face context, cues given off by accident, perhaps through body language, a fleeting expression, or an unbidden change in intonation, provide a great deal of information to observers and might affect their interpretations. Online, however, especially in media with few channels of communication to manage and plenty of time to manage them, people can control their self-presentation to a much greater degree. That is, they can choose to give off very little, though giving off nothing at all remains difficult.

Drawing on Goffman's framework and the related notion of signaling from biology, Donath portrays the online performance of self as a series of signals, classified as "conventional" or "assessment," that we attempt to give in order to convey a particular impression to others (Donath, 1999; Donath, in press). Assessment signals are unimpeachable indicators of a quality, typically requiring the quality in question and therefore difficult to fake. Lifting a heavy object is an assessment signal of strength. A conventional signal, on the other hand, does not require the quality it indicates; it can be faked. Donath gives the example of wearing a "Gold's Gym" t-shirt — it does not mean that the wearer is necessarily strong, even if he or she seeks to give that impression (Donath, 1999). Most signals in computer-mediated interaction are conventional signals, which makes the evaluation of trustworthiness perhaps more difficult online than face to face.

What photograph one displays, how one uses language, and which online pseudonym one selects are just a few of the vehicles for social signals in online environments. In an online dating profile, an individual might choose between a formal portrait and a flirtatious snapshot, write in organized paragraphs or casual stream of consciousness, and pick among nicknames that reflect a favorite hobby or suggest a professional affiliation. Readers of this profile might or might not interpret these choices as the author intends — the interpretation depends on each reader's particular knowledge, experience, and expectations, as suggested by Ellison and colleagues' interviews with online dating users (Ellison et al., 2006). Indeed, in online environments generally, the impressions that individuals form about one another are based not only on the cues provided, "but also on the conceptual categories and cognitive models people use in interpreting those cues" (Jacobson, 1999).

Interaction in Rich and Lean Media

Some theorists classify communication media as "rich" or "lean" depending on their multiplicity of cues, or how many types of information can be conveyed, and immediacy of feedback, or how quickly the conveyance and response occur (Daft and Lengel, 1986; Dennis and Kinney, 1998). Face-to-face interaction is a rich medium, whereas most computer-mediated communication systems are relatively lean, with mostly textual cues that might or might not be transmitted in real time.

Early theories of online interaction contended that communication in lean media was too impersonal for the formation of substantial relationships because of a dearth of social cues (Sproull and Kiesler, 1986) and the absence of a sense of "social presence" (Short et al., 1976). This would seem to preclude the development of relational trust. But subsequent researchers (Lea and Spears, 1995; Parks and Floyd, 1996) have suggested that a relative scarcity of social cues might not be as detrimental as the earlier work claimed and might in fact aid the formation of interpersonal connections in some circumstances.

In particular, Walther's (1992) theory of Social Information Processing asserts that individuals interacting online readily make inferences about others even from scant details gleaned from lean communication media. His notion of "hyperpersonal" interaction (Walther, 1996) goes a step farther — it suggests that people communicating in lean media, with limited cues and slow feedback, might form even higher levels of affinity for one another than they would face to face. This results from a tendency to fill in the blanks optimistically — that is, corresponding to what the perceiver wishes — when faced with limited information about a person. Laboratory and field studies have provided some empirical support for the theories of Social Information Processing and hyperpersonal interaction (Walther et al., 2001; McKenna et al., 2002; Ellison et al., 2006).

Online Dating Systems

Online dating systems constitute a genre of computer-mediated communication that has become a popular way to initiate contact with potential romantic partners. More than 7 million adults in the U.S. have gone on a date with someone they had met through an online dating site (Madden and Lenhart, 2006). Although they vary in the specifics, most online dating web sites include the following (Fiore and Donath, 2004):

- Personal profiles for each user, with demographic information, free-text and categorical self-descriptions, and often one or more photographs. Profiles on some sites also include audio or video clips and the results of personality tests.
- A mechanism to search the database of other users or to be matched automatically with potential dates.
- One or more means of private computer-mediated communication by which users can contact each other without disclosing an email address, phone number, or identifying information. Typically the communication mechanism is similar to email, but

some sites include audio or video chat as well.

Users of online dating systems typically seek to meet a potential partner face-to-face, though some users are content to keep their interactions solely online.

THE ROLE OF TRUST IN ONLINE RELATIONSHIP FORMATION

We now consider the four key trust-related concepts we have described—confidence in systems, trustworthiness, relational trust, and general trust — in the context of online dating. Each is more or less relevant to users at different times during the process of meeting someone through an online dating system. Initially, *confidence in the system* is essential for the user to believe that information about potential partners is reliable. Once the user identifies someone he or she would like to meet face-to-face, that person's perceived *trustworthiness* is the most important factor. The salience of trustworthiness peaks with the initial face-to-face meeting, a moment of great risk but also an opportunity for a great reduction in uncertainty. As the two people become better acquainted, *relational trust* can arise from their repeated interaction over time. Over time, the salience of relational trust — a product of mutual experience — surpasses that of trustworthiness, whose assessment relies on indicators rather than first-hand experiential knowledge of the other's behavior and interests. Thus, if relational trust develops, trustworthiness slowly becomes less relevant. Underlying this entire process is each person's *general trust*, or default tendency to be trusting or to show caution with others.

Figure 1 provides a schematic diagram of the hypothetical progression of the salience of these concepts in an online dating interaction that leads to a romantic relationship. In this diagram, we do not represent exact quantities on any particular scale but rather portray the trust-related concepts' *relative* importance to an online dater throughout the development of a relationship. We portray general trust as a diffuse shape rather than a sharp line, since it is an underlying characteristic that influences confidence in the system, assessments of trustworthiness, and the propensity to develop relational trust.

Confidence in Online Dating Systems

Confidence in the system is the first trust-related concept that becomes salient for people beginning the process of online dating. Will the system provide them with a suitable pool of potential partners? Will it safeguard their identities and allow them to interact effectively under a pseudonym? Do its searching and matching tools actually provide listings of the best matches for each user from among all the possibilities?

This type of confidence is intertwined with each online dating site's marketing and branding. Some sites promote themselves as matchmakers for marriage relationships; others focus on "casual encounters," or purely sexual interactions. Some present themselves as serious and rooted in relationship psychology — these often charge a higher membership fee — while others brand themselves as casual, playful, or irreverent. They market themselves according to these orientations. Adult Friend Finder advertises on its home page: "Meet real sex partners tonight!" On the other hand, eHarmony clearly focuses on matching people for successful marriages, touting "scientifically-based predictors of long-term relationship success." The brand becomes the reality to the degree that online dating users join sites whose goals align with their own. A user seeking a casual sexual encounter knows that he or she will likely not find it on a marriage-minded site and vice versa.

Figure 1. Schematic diagram of the salience of trust-related factors as a relationship formed through online dating progresses

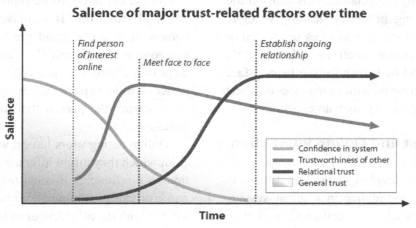

Confidence in a system primarily comprises users' assessments of reliability, security, and credibility. While branding clearly plays a large role in the perception of a system, users' control of and knowledge about how their own information will be managed and presented is equally important. Successful self-presentation is a key part of finding and attracting suitable partners in an online or offline environment, so it is crucial that users believe that their information will be displayed to others accurately and faithfully to their intent. In turn, users expect that the information that they find about others on a given site will be truthful. However, Carnegie Mellon University's *MySecureCyberspace* initiative bluntly describes a problem with these expectations: "Be warned that many of the profiles in an online dating web site are fake or have inaccurate information" (MySecureCyberspace, 2009).

This problem clearly affects assessments of the trustworthiness of the people portrayed in dating profiles, but the perception that content is inaccurate or intentionally deceptive can lead to an overall lack of confidence in the system as well. Perceived duplicity or carelessness on the part of the online dating service—whether real or merely suspected—can erode users' confidence in the reliability of information shared within the

system. For example, according to a 2009 *New York Post* article, a lawsuit was brought against a popular online dating web site for allegedly teasing paying subscribers with matches who were either canceled subscribers or people who had never subscribed at all (Golding, 2009). Whether or not this particular allegation is true, the existence of uncertainty and doubt can damage the credibility of the online dating site. Individuals cannot make reliable assessments about one another if they do not believe that the online system has restrictions or assurances in place to guard against fraudulent or fictitious profiles. To be clear, though, wholly fabricated or deceitful content of this sort is categorically distinct from lesser acts of exaggeration or omission in a real online dater's self-description. Self-enhancement and other minor misrepresentations are issues that we will explore more fully in the discussion of trustworthiness below.

Finally, confidence in matching technology plays a role even after two users have met through an online dating site. Users with a high level of confidence in the system, who thus believe that an online dating site has unique insight (scientific or otherwise) into the characteristics of their ideal partner, might begin a date or a relationship with their online match with higher expectations and a more positive attitude than those who do not believe the dating site's claims. This belief could be a self-fulfilling prophecy, leading to more pleasing interactions, if it induces pro-social or relationship-maintaining behavior (Karney et al., 2002), or it could be harmful if the face-to-face reality of interacting with the match does not meet the lofty standard set by such an expectation.

General Trust and Online Interaction

Each individual's level of general trust helps to determine their confidence in a given system, their evaluations of trustworthiness, and their readiness to develop relational trust with others. Since general trust is an underlying disposition to be more or less trusting of others, it is especially important in the formative periods of interpersonal relationships. General trust can serve as a threshold for a given individual, describing the likelihood that she will view others as trustworthy given the available information. In an online dating context, general trust is less relevant once two people begin to interact. At this point, the cognitive and affective aspects of trust become more relevant than general dispositions.

General trust can also influence the willingness of individuals to seek a partner through an online dating system at all. Those with high levels of general trust might place more faith in an online dating system to find an appropriate date or partner for them, or at least to provide the information necessary to make such a choice themselves, than would people with low levels of general trust. Similarly, those with high levels of general trust might more often judge other people on the site as trustworthy and thus suitable to risk contacting and perhaps meeting.

Assessing the Trustworthiness of Others

Once users have identified a potential date through an online dating system, they implicitly or explicitly evaluate the date's trustworthiness: Is this person likely to be representing himself or herself truthfully? If we make a date, will this person show up or stand me up? A sense that someone is "trustworthy" — that is, that it will be possible to form a trust relationship with him or her — follows from the perception of cues and signals from the person that indicate or imply fitness to trust.

Online dating users have a variety of signals from which they might infer trustworthiness, but none is infallible. Self-consistency in the profile and in private communications is one such indicator, but with the affordances of lean communication channels, a dedicated fabulist could construct a convincing false persona. Moreover, even if both participants are being truthful, each must evaluate the other's apparent interest in communicating, meeting, and perhaps beginning a relationship. Cues such as length, frequency, and timing of messages, as well as personalized content rather than generic come-ons, all serve as indicators (again imperfect) of genuine interest. Perceived trustworthiness is sometimes associated with attractiveness as well (Fiore et al., 2008).

Once two online dating users make plans to meet in person, trustworthiness becomes even more salient. The transition from online to face-to-face interaction is fraught with potential difficulties: First, will both parties show up for the date? Will they be on time? Will they be able to identify each other? Will they look like they do in their photos? In some ways the decision to show up for the date resembles a social dilemma — a situation in which the individual pursuit of self-interest leads to a situation in which everyone suffers (Yamagishi, 1995). Each party can choose to cooperate (keep the date) or defect (fail to keep the date). Both parties benefit by meeting even if they merely learn that they are not compatible, but each might be tempted to skip the date because of a lack of sufficient interest, nervousness, or competing demands on time, any of which might be more compelling than showing up. Of course, if the other party cooperates and waits for a date who never arrives, this is the worst individual result. Finally, if neither party keeps the date, the reward is minimal but so is the harm to either.

Deception and Self-Enhancement

In both research studies and popular-press interviews, some online daters claim that deception is rampant. In a medium dominated by Donath's (1999) conventional signals, it is easy to present oneself online very differently from how one appears face to face. However, an online dating user who misrepresents himself substantially will find his deception uncovered on the first date. Online dating users, then, walk a fine line between self-enhancement and honest self-presentation. Indeed, Gibbs and colleagues (2006) found in a survey of Match.com users that honesty was negatively associated with perceived success in self-presentation in online dating profiles. Even so, most respondents claimed they had not misrepresented themselves on purpose in their profiles, although at the same time they felt that others users' representations were not accurate (Gibbs et al., 2006). If users pursue a strategy of benign self-enhancement, these conditions are not necessarily contradictory.

Nonetheless, in a large enough pool of users, some number will likely misrepresent themselves intentionally. To investigate whether online dating users were lying about basic personal information, Hancock and colleagues (2007) measured and weighed online dating users, recorded their ages from their driver's licenses, and compared these quantities with those given in their online dating profiles. They found small but significant deviations from the truth about height and weight in directions that suggest intent — men slightly over-reported their height on average, and women slightly underreported their weight. However, most of these discrepancies were small enough that to call them "lies" would be an overstatement. Perhaps they constituted slight but deliberate self-enhancement, or perhaps these individuals were unconsciously presenting their ideal rather than their actual selves, a form of wishful thinking that Ellison and colleagues (2006) documented in their interviews with online dating users.

Finally, the perception that deception is commonplace in online dating might also stem from the effects of mediation. Walther's (1992) theory of Social Information Processing holds that individuals interacting online readily make substantial inferences about others even from scant details gleaned from lean communication media. If these inferences lead to incorrect impressions, the people behind the profiles might appear to have lied when their true characteristics are found to contradict the impressions formed online — but as a result of misperception, not deception.

Laying the Groundwork for Relational Trust

When two online daters begin communicating, each seeks to evaluate the other as a potential date and, perhaps, romantic partner. Questions of trust and trustworthiness are implicit in this exchange: Is this person who she says she is? Is he truly interested in me, or is he being disingenuous? Although an assessment of trustworthiness provides a starting point for the development of trust, relational trust as we define it can result only when individuals consistently engage in reciprocal acts of entrusting with the same person over time. Trustworthiness inferred from cues or indicators can remain useful over the course of a relationship, but we argue that the deeper, encapsulated-interest form of relational trust becomes more salient as a committed romantic relationship develops.

Individuals who use online dating services always begin with some form of computer-mediated communication before meeting in person. Can the online interaction promote or even accelerate the development of relational trust? Henderson and Gilding (2004) suggest that the heightened sense of affinity that people feel for each other when interacting through lean communication media encourages reciprocal self-disclosure. Similarly, Joinson (2001) found that individuals spontaneously told their partners more about themselves in text-based discussion than in face-to-face conversation and in visually anonymous versus visually identifiable contexts. Since self-disclosure is important for the development of intimacy and trust, we might expect to find higher levels of trust in computer-mediated communication than in face-to-face interactions. However, in a laboratory study of cooperation and defection in a social dilemma context, Rockmann and Northcraft (2008) found lower levels of both cognitive trust and affective trust as well as higher levels of deception when participants interacted via a lean computer-mediated channel than when they interacted face to face.

Building Trust, Reducing Uncertainty

If Walther's hyperpersonal effect operates in the online dating context, it could be risky for users to interact too much online before meeting face-to-face, because they might develop an artificially inflated sense of affinity for each other, leading to disappointment in person. Yet at the same time, the promise of online dating lies in the ability to evaluate many potential partners quickly. How might online dating systems facilitate relationship formation, including the initial development of relational trust?

Frost (2005) proposes "virtual dates," online activities that provide a venue for shared experiences prior to meeting in person. In contrast to profiles and private messages, in which users *describe* their personal characteristics — a notoriously difficult thing to do accurately (cf. Ellison et al., 2006) — virtual dates allow users to *demonstrate* their personality, sense of humor, and other characteristics. The experience of virtual dates could help to "[bring] expectations for [offline] dates more in line with reality" (Frost, 2005).

We propose that there is a "sweet spot" in

the amount of interaction two users undertake online — and thus how much information they gain or uncertainty they eliminate about each other — before they meet in person. Certainly, users need to gain a modicum of information simply to evaluate one another's attractiveness and suitability as a partner. (In one study, more information provided in an online dating profile led to lower levels of liking on average [Norton et al., 2007], perhaps due to the ability of users to better *discern* whom they like when they have more complete information.) To evaluate many potential dates quickly, to establish that a potential date is trustworthy enough to meet, and to begin building relational trust, users needs to engage in some online communication. But to avoid the pitfalls of hyperpersonal interaction and artificially high expectations in the transition from online to offline, users must also avoid too much online involvement before meeting face-to-face.

FUTURE RESEARCH DIRECTIONS

Our present understanding of how trust and related factors like trustworthiness operate in the context of online relationship formation derives from theoretical and empirical findings about trust, computer-mediated communication, and their intersection. However, little research has focused on assessments of trustworthiness or the development of relational trust specifically in the context of online dating.

Since the development of relational trust is a process that occurs over time, future work in this area should adopt a longitudinal approach in order to gain a better understanding of how trust-related phenomena develop and change in relative importance over the early course of a relationship. Following a cohort of online dating users as they find, evaluate, meet, and date potential partners will improve our understanding of how trustworthiness assessments change and relational trust develops during the establishment of a new relationship. Moreover, in such a study, comparing objective behavioral metrics and subjective experiences between online dating users with low levels of general trust and those with high levels of general trust should provide us with a clearer picture of exactly how this dispositional factor affects the progression of relationships begun online.

CONCLUSION

The assessment of trustworthiness and the development of relational trust are just as important online as offline, but they are considerably more fraught with ambiguity and uncertainty in computer-mediated interactions. In this chapter, we argued that confidence in online dating systems, trustworthiness, relational trust, and general trust are related to different aspects of online relationship formation over time. In the context of online dating, general trust and confidence in the system are especially salient when individuals first begin to use an online dating service. As individuals gain information about others through the system, they form perceptions and beliefs about the trustworthiness of potential partners. Individuals have control over their own self-presentation in most online dating systems, but this freedom also creates uncertainty about the truthfulness and reliability of others' profile information.

Relationships initiated through online dating face distinctive challenges compared to those begun face-to-face. Computer-mediated interactions are associated with higher amounts of spontaneous self-disclosure, but individuals also appear prone to develop unrealistically favorable impressions of those whom they meet online. Thus, the development of relational trust in couples who meet through online dating requires that they reconcile potentially exaggerated expectations conceived online with face-to-face reality.

The earliest attempts at computer matchmaking services go as far back as the 1960s, but the appropriation of communication technology for romantic purposes began much earlier, with the telegraph and postal mail (cf. Whitty, 2007). The benefits of using today's technologies to meet romantic partners are clear — they limit risks by enabling communication before a meeting, allow individuals to search for an ideal mate using a variety of criteria, and give individuals a great deal of control over their own self-presentation. Yet the research reviewed in this chapter suggests that although it is easier in some ways to assess trustworthiness and build trust in an online context than it is face-to-face, in other respects it can be more difficult. Online and offline environments provide distinct contexts for social interaction that influence the development of trust in different ways. Continued study of these important differences in the context of online dating will deepen our understanding not only of trust but also of relationship formation both online and face-to-face.

REFERENCES

Baier, A. (1986). Trust and Antitrust. *Ethics, 96,* 231–260. doi:10.1086/292745

Cheshire, C., & Antin, J. (2008). The Social Psychological Effects of Feedback on the Production of Internet Information Pools. *Journal of Computer-Mediated Communication, 13*(3). doi:10.1111/j.1083-6101.2008.00416.x

Cheshire, C., & Antin, J. (in press). Order, Coordination and Uncertainty. In Cook, K. S., Snijders, C., Buskins, V., & Cheshire, C. (Eds.), *eTrust and Reputation*. New York: Russell Sage Foundation.

Cheshire, C., & Cook, K. S. (2004). The Emergence of Trust Networks: Implications for Online Interaction. *Analyse & Kritik, 28*.

Cheshire, C., Gerbasi, A., Cook, K. S., & Harkness, S. (2009, August). *Trust and Structural Shifts in Modes of Exchange*. Paper presented at the meeting of the American Sociological Association, San Francisco, CA.

Cook, K. S., Cheshire, C., Gerbasi, A., & Aven, B. (in press). Assessing Trustworthiness in Online Goods and Services. In Cook, K. S., Snijders, C., Buskins, V., & Cheshire, C. (Eds.), *eTrust and Reputation*. New York: Russell Sage Foundation.

Cook, K. S., Hardin, R., & Levi, M. (2005). *Cooperation Without Trust?* New York: Russell Sage.

Cook, K. S., Yamagishi, T., Cheshire, C., Cooper, R., Matsuda, M., & Mashima, R. (2005). Trust Building via Risk Taking: A Cross-Societal Experiment. *Social Psychology Quarterly, 68*(2). doi:10.1177/019027250506800202

Daft, R. L., & Lengel, R. H. (1986). Organizational Information Requirements, Media Richness and Structural Design. *Management Science, 32*(5), 554–571. doi:10.1287/mnsc.32.5.554

Dennis, A. R., & Kinney, S. T. (1998). Testing media richness theory in the new media: The effects of cues, feedback, and task equivocality. *Information Systems Research, 9*(3). doi:10.1287/isre.9.3.256

Donath, J. (1998). Identity and Deception in the Virtual Community. In Smith, M., & Kollock, P. (Eds.), *Communities in Cyberspace*. London: Routledge.

Donath, J. (in press). *Signals, Truth and Design*. Cambridge, MA: MIT Press.

Ellison, N., Heino, R., & Gibbs, J. (2006). Managing Impressions Online: Self-Presentation Processes in the Online Dating Environment. *Journal of Computer-Mediated Communication, 11*(2). doi:10.1111/j.1083-6101.2006.00020.x

Fiore, A. T., & Donath, J. S. (2004). Online Personals: An Overview. *Extended abstracts of ACM Computer-Human Interaction 2004.*

Fiore, A. T., Shaw Taylor, L., Mendelsohn, G. A., & Hearst, M. (2008). Assessing Attractiveness in Online Dating Profiles. In *Proceedings of ACM Computer-Human Interaction 2008*, Florence, Italy.

Friedman, B., Kahn, P., & Howe, D. (2000). Trust Online. *Communications of the ACM, 43*(12). doi:10.1145/355112.355120

Gibbs, J. L., Ellison, N. B., & Heino, R. D. (2006). Self-presentation in online personals: The role of anticipated future interaction, self-disclosure, and perceived success in Internet dating. *Communication Research, 33*(2), 1–26. doi:10.1177/0093650205285368

Goffman, E. (1956). *The Presentation of Self in Everyday Life*. New York: Doubleday.

Golding, B. (2009, June 10). Dot-com has 'Date' in Court. *New York Post*. Retrieved August 26, 2009, from http://www.nypost.com/seven/06102009/news/regionalnews/dot_com_has_date_in_court_173449.htm

Govier, T. (1997). *Social Trust and Human Communities*. Montreal, Canada: McGill-Queen's Press.

Green, M. C. (2007). Trust and social interaction on the Internet. In Joinson, A., McKenna, K., Postmes, T., & Reips, U.-D. (Eds.), *The Oxford Handbook of Internet Psychology*. Oxford, UK: Oxford University Press.

Grudin, J., & Poltrock, S. E. (1997). Computer-Supported Cooperative Work and Groupware. In M. Zelkowitz (Ed.), Advances in Computers, 45, 269–320.

Hancock, J. T., Toma, C., & Ellison, N. (2007). The truth about lying in online dating profiles. *Extended abstracts of ACM Computer-Human Interaction 2007.*

Hardin, R. (1993). The Street-Level Epistemology of Trust. *Politics & Society, 21*, 505–529. doi:10.1177/0032329293021004006

Hardin, R. (2002). *Trust and Trustworthiness*. New York: Russell Sage Foundation.

Hayashi, N. (1995). Emergence of Cooperation in One-shot Prisoner's Dilemmas and the Role of Trust. *Japanese Journal of Phycology, 66*(3), 184–190.

Henderson, S., & Gilding, M. (2004). 'I've Never Clicked this Much with Anyone in My Life': Trust and Hyperpersonal Communication in Online Friendships. *New Media & Society, 6*, 487–506. doi:10.1177/146144804044331

Herring, S. C. (2001). Computer-mediated discourse. In Schiffrin, D., Tannen, D., & Hamilton, H. (Eds.), *The Handbook of Discourse Analysis* (pp. 612–634). Oxford, UK: Blackwell.

Jacobson, D. (1999). Impression Formation in Cyberspace: Online Expectations and Offline Experiences in Text-based Virtual Communities. *Journal of Computer-Mediated Communication, 5*(1).

Joinson, A. N. (2001). Self-disclosure in computer-mediated communication: The role of self-awareness and visual anonymity. *European Journal of Social Psychology, 31*, 177–192. doi:10.1002/ejsp.36

Karney, B. R., McNulty, J. K., & Bradbury, T. N. (2002). Cognition and the Development of Close Relationships. In *The Blackwell Handbook of Social Psychology: Interpersonal Processes*. Hoboken, NJ: Wiley-Blackwell.

Kiyonari, T., Yamagishi, T., Cook, K. S., & Cheshire, C. (2006). Trust and Trustworthiness in Two Games and Two Cultures. *Social Psychology Quarterly, 69*(3). doi:10.1177/019027250606900304

Madden, M., & Lenhart, A. (2006). Online Dating. *Pew Internet and American Life Project*. Retrieved August 26, 2009, from http://www.pewinternet.org/~/media/Files/Reports/2006/PIP_Online_Dating.pdf.pdf

Marsh, S., & Dibben, M. R. (2003). The Role of Trust in Information Science and Technology. *Annual Review of Information Science & Technology, 37*, 465–498. doi:10.1002/aris.1440370111

McKenna, K. Y. A., Green, A. S., & Gleason, M. E. J. (2002). Relationship Formation on the Internet: What's the Big Attraction? *The Journal of Social Issues, 58*(1), 9–31. doi:10.1111/1540-4560.00246

My, I. B. M. *Baby*. (1965, November 19). Time Magazine. Retrieved August 26, 2009, from http://www.time.com/time/magazine/article/0,9171,834652,00.html

MySecureCyberspace. (n.d.). *Online Dating*. Carnegie Mellon University. Retrieved August 26, 2009, from http://www.mysecurecyberspace.com/encyclopedia/index/online-dating.html

Nass, C. I., Steuer, J., & Tauber, E. R. (1994). Computers are social actors. In *Proceedings of ACM Computer-Human Interaction 1994*, Boston, MA.

Nissenbaum, H. (2004). Will Security Enhance Trust Online, or Supplant It? In Kramer, R., & Cook, K. (Eds.), *Trust and Distrust Within Organizations: Emerging Perspectives, Enduring Questions* (pp. 155–188). New York: Russell Sage Publications.

Norton, M., Frost, J., & Ariely, D. (2007). Less is more: The lure of ambiguity, or why familiarity breeds contempt. *Journal of Personality and Social Psychology, 92*(1), 97–105. doi:10.1037/0022-3514.92.1.97

Orbell, J. M., & Dawes, R. M. (1993). Social Welfare, Cooperators' Advantage and the Option of Not Playing the Game. *American Sociological Review, 58*, 787–800. doi:10.2307/2095951

Riegelsberger, M., Sasse, A., & McCarthy, J. D. (2007). Trust in mediated interactions. In Joinson, A., McKenna, K., Postmes, T., & Reips, U.-D. (Eds.), *The Oxford Handbook of Internet Psychology*. Oxford, UK: Oxford University Press.

Rockmann, K. W., & Northcraft, G. B. (2008). To be or not to be trusted: The influence of media richness on defection and deception. *Organizational Behavior and Human Decision Processes*, *107*(2), 106–122. doi:10.1016/j.obhdp.2008.02.002

Schneider, F. B. (Ed.). (1999). *Trust in Cyberspace. Commission on Information Systems' Trustworthiness*. Washington, DC: National Research Council.

Wallace, P. (1999). *The Psychology of the Internet*. Cambridge, UK: Cambridge University Press.

Walther, J. B. (1992). Interpersonal effects in computer-mediated interaction: A relational perspective. *Communication Research*, *19*(1), 52–91. doi:10.1177/009365092019001003

Walther, J. B. (1996). Computer-mediated communication: Impersonal, interpersonal, and hyperpersonal interaction. *Communication Research*, *23*(1), 3–44. doi:10.1177/009365096023001001

Walther, J. B., Slovacek, C., & Tidwell, L. C. (2001). Is a picture worth a thousand words? Photographic images in long term and short term virtual teams. *Communication Research*, *28*(1), 105–134. doi:10.1177/009365001028001004

Whitty, M. (2007). Love letters: The development of romantic relationships throughout the ages. In Joinson, A., McKenna, K., Postmes, T., & Reips, U.-D. (Eds.), *The Oxford Handbook of Internet Psychology*. Oxford, UK: Oxford University Press.

Yamagishi, T. (1995). Social Dilemmas. In Cook, K., Fine, G. A., & House, J. S. (Eds.), *Sociological Perspectives on Social Psychology* (pp. 311–334). Boston, MA: Allyn and Bacon.

Yamagishi, T. (1998). *The Structure of Trust*. Tokyo, Japan: University of Tokyo Press.

Yamagishi, T. (2001). Trust as a form of social intelligence. In Cook, K. S. (Ed.), *Trust in Society* (pp. 121–147). New York: Russell Sage Foundation.

Yamagishi, T., Foddy, M., Makimura, Y., Matsuda, M., Kiyonari, T., & Platow, M. (2005). Comparisons of Australians and Japanese on group-based cooperation. *Asian Journal of Social Psychology*, *8*(2), 173–190. doi:10.1111/j.1467-839x.2005.00165.x

Yamagishi, T., Kikuchi, M., & Kosugi, M. (1999). Trust, gullibility and social intelligence. *Asian Journal of Social Psychology*, *2*(1), 145–161. doi:10.1111/1467-839X.00030

Yamagishi, T., Matsuda, M., Yoshikai, N., Takahashi, H., & Usui, Y. (in press). Trust and Reputation. In Cook, K. S., Snijders, C., Buskins, V., & Cheshire, C. (Eds.), *eTrust and Reputation*. New York: Russell Sage Foundation.

Chapter 5
The Savory Deviant Delight:
A Study of Trust & Normative Order in an Online World

David Boyns
California State University, Northridge, USA

ABSTRACT

Massively Multiplayer Online worlds (MMOs), like World of Warcraft (WoW) have been established as increasingly prominent, technologically-based communities. Because MMOs require high-levels of cooperative activity, and are organized in an anonymous, virtual space, the establishment of a normative order among participants is essential. Trust is a key component of that normative order. This study examines trust and normative order among WoW game-players, and is based upon an ethnographic analysis of the gaming community. The results identify four primary techniques of normative order maintenance that are both formally institutionalized in the game, and informally organized within the player community itself. Trust is identified as a key resource through which players manage the uncertainties of their technologically-based community, and maintain the integrity of WoW's normative order. The study concludes that the construction of a normative order within online worlds is crucial and that trust plays an important role in their stability.

INTRODUCTION

The title of this study is a spoof on the name of a cooking recipe found in the Massively Multi-Player Online Role-Playing Game (MMORPG or MMO) *World of Warcraft* (WoW*)*. When cooked, this recipe, "the savory *deviate* delight," transforms the countenance of a player's in-game avatar and

alters its true identity. The recipe is quite popular among players in the game as the "deviate" disguise provides a character with a "deviant" appearance, and although the transformation is singly cosmetic, it introduces an element of surprise, entertainment and humor into the game.

The effects of eating the "savory deviate delight" provide an analyst of WoW with a metaphor of the game itself and the relationship that many players have toward their game-play. In the same way that

DOI: 10.4018/978-1-61520-901-9.ch005

the "savory deviate delight" allows characters to transform their in-game appearance, WoW allows players to become quite extraordinary compared to their real-life selves. Much like the "delights" of this deviate recipe, WoW permits players the opportunity not only to become something unexpected compared with their real-life identities but, also, to take on mischievous and frequently deviant roles in a technologically-mediated environment already permeated with illusion and fantasy.

WoW is the most prominent of a genre of MMOs that have become increasingly popular over the past three decades. MMOs are the contemporary synthesis of role-playing games (like *Dungeons and Dragons*) and online virtual communities (like Multi-User Dungeons). Released in November of 2004, WoW boasts nearly 12 million subscribers, and heralds players from every continent worldwide. Because of its mass appeal and the complexity of its design, WoW provides an interesting sociological environment for the study of community organization, social identity construction and technologically-mediated communication. Given that players in the game are largely anonymous by real-life standards, and that no player could possibly be in real-life the character they portray, WoW creates an intriguing sociological context for the study of normative order, the emergence of trust in social relationships, the techniques that engender its maintenance, and the consequences of its transgression.

This study is based upon an ethnographic analysis of one WoW community, and investigates the techniques of normative order construction that are both institutionalized within the game's design, and are created more informally among players themselves. Of specific interest is the degree to which trust is cultivated among players, and the tacit role that trust plays in managing the uncertainties of social interaction in a virtual environment largely circumscribed by anonymity and pretense. The study begins with a synopsis of WoW game-play as a sociological environment. It then moves to a review of the relevant litera-

tures on normative order and trust with specific implications for online social environments. The results of the analysis outline and describe four techniques of normative order maintenance that emerge among players who work to construct a basis for trust within the WoW community. The cultivation of trust within WoW is explored with respect to both the formal structure of the game and the informal culture that is created among the players themselves.

BACKGROUND

A Synopsis of World of Warcraft

WoW is the largest and most well-known of a series of MMOs that are on the cutting edge of online social worlds. Thematically, WoW is based upon a fantasy world that is imbued with magic and sword-play, fantastic treasures, powerful monsters and puzzle-solving adventure. As a character-driven game, one of the fundamental objectives in WoW is for players to create and advance their avatars by enhancing their skills and abilities through the completion of ever-increasing complex tasks. To begin their game-play, players select a server on which they will play. There are unique server types, and each server can contain tens-of-thousands of characters. Next, players, choose to participate in one of two competing factions (Alliance or Horde). These factions are opponents in the game and players are not able to directly interact across factions except through non-verbal "emotes." Within each faction, players choose among a set of races for their character[1], select a gender (female or male), and ornament their character with a variety of physical attributes (hair styles, facial features, skin pigmentation, etc.). After the selection of a character's race, players choose among a set of racial-specific classes[2] each of which has specified abilities and are designed to bring specific attributes to group game-play.

Once a character has been created, the initial objective of WoW is for a player to "level up" their character. This is accomplished through the acquisition of "experience points" by defeating monsters and completing complex "quests." Much of the leveling of characters is designed for solo play, though players frequently form small "parties" in order finish more difficult tasks. When players complete their leveling they advance to WoW's "end game," where the most sophisticated and multifaceted aspect of game-play resides. Here, players must form large "raid" groups varying in size from ten to forty players in order to master labyrinthine dungeons and defeat their most powerful inhabitants. Raids require sophisticated coordination, a balance of players and classes, and a significant amount of social interaction. The completion of end-game raid objectives are important for WoW game-play as is it here that the rarest and most desirable "loot" is to be discovered through which characters can gain increased attributes and can become powerful. Raid events typically involve several hours of consecutive play and may require several days of periodic game-play to complete. Some dungeons may require months of intermittent play to master, and raid groups may practice on and off for weeks before they are able to defeat individual foes. While some raid groups are created "on the fly" as "pick up groups," the majority are established as extensions of in-game guilds.

Guilds are the most permanent and complex social group in the WoW community. While guilds can vary in size and composition, those pursuing end-game objectives can house hundreds of players and their characters. For many end-game guilds, their *raison d'etre* is to develop an experienced membership, matched with a set of raiding strategies, for the primary purpose of completing high-end, raid dungeons. Guild membership is the most direct means by which players can advance their characters and increase their power and skill. But, guilds do not merely serve the instrumental purpose of end-game character progression; they also are important communities for coordinating the game's social life. Many players form and join guilds primarily as an outlet for socializing in the game, and while players can leave a guild at any time, many remain in the same guild, immersed in a common social community, for months or even years.

For game designers, guilds represent the social aspect of the MMO that is perhaps its most unique feature (Bartle, 2003). MMOs are not simply video game environments; they are also complex sociological environments that allow players to develop sophisticated forms of social interaction and create their own culture (Boyns, Forghani and Sosnovskaya, 2009; Duchenaut and Moore, 2004; Duchenaut, Moore and Nickell, 2004; Duchenaut, Yee, Nickell, Moore, 2006, 2007). In WoW, players are able to cultivate significant social relationships, build lists of characters they identify as "friends," and communicate in-game through a variety of Instant Message (IM) chat channels. Players are also encouraged to interact economically through the trade of goods and services, some exchanged formally through the game's "auction house" system, and others through informal bartering and negotiation.

For the purposes of this paper, perhaps the most salient aspect of WoW is that it is explicitly designed to facilitate the development of a sociological reality among its players. Within the confines of WoW's graphics, and the formal "physics" outlined by the game's computer algorithms, players are able to create a normative culture that is both an ongoing accomplishment and structured around stable conventions. WoW players generate their own normative world complete with cultural practices, in-game etiquette, normative expectations for behavior, deviant roles, and systems of sanctioning. The cultural life of WoW is multifaceted, extending beyond the confines of the game's computer code, and often beyond the computer screen itself (Boyns, Forghani and Sosnovskaya, 2009; Taylor, 2006). It is the development of this normative order within the sociological life of WoW that is the focus of this study.

Normative Order, Trust and the Societal Community

Normative order has been an enduring concern of sociologists at least since the work of Durkheim (1984[1893]). Following this tradition of thought, sociologists like Parsons (1951, 1971), Goffman (1967) and Luhmann (1995) have explored the means through which frameworks of cultural norms, values and beliefs are institutionalized within a societal community and impose systems of social order and their concomitant means of social control. While these normative systems are frequently formalized, expressed in codified laws and organized mechanisms of punishment and adjudication, they are also organized informally through social interaction, collective decision-making and face-to-face sanctioning (Blau, 1973). In fact, through this informal dimension, normative order can be subject to a significant process of negotiation. This "negotiated order" has been the object of a impressive tradition of theorizing in symbolic interactionist analysis, which argues that while normative conventions can be externally and coercively imposed as Durkheimian (1982[1895]) "social facts," they are always subject to the deliberation and interpretation of participants in face-to-face situations (Blumer, 1969; Fine, 1984; Strauss, 1978).

Trust has been theorized as an essential component of normative order (Durkheim, 1984[1893]; Luhmann, 1979; Misztal, 1996; Simmel, (1978[1900]); Sztompka, 1999). While it is common for societal communities to establish formal means of social control, compliance and conformity are, on some level, typically problematic for the members of such communities as actors are always presented with the option to challenge normative, group expectations, or to "free ride" on the collective efforts of the group (G. Hardin, 1968; Olson, 1965). In the face of normative order, uncertainty and risk are commonly identified as endemic problems for community organization, social control, exchange relationships, and group

continuity (Cook, 2005; Kollock, 1994; Molm, Takahasi and Petersen, 2000). In fact, both risk and uncertainty have been identified as among the preeminent problems of the contemporary social world, particularly in conditions infused with cultural ambiguity, an absence of tradition, rapid technological innovation, and flexible identity construction (Bauman, 1997; Beck, 1992; Giddens, 1990, 1991).

Of general concern in the literature on trust, and of specific relevance for the present study, is how individuals seek to maintain trust both in specific, interpersonal relationships (often called "relational trust") (Jones, et al, 1997) and how a broader context of trust can be created in largely anonymous social environments (frequently referred to as "generalized trust") (Rotter, 1971, 1980). While a clearly delineated normative order can be understood as a general precondition for the emergence of both relational and generalized trust, this normative order never produces complete security in trust relationships. Both interpersonal relationships and the social communities they compose are always circumscribed by concerns related to trust (relational and generalized) and its fallacies.

The primary factors that serve to undermine trust have been very usefully theorized as *risk* and *uncertainty*, both of which are produced by different sociological dynamics. Following the model proposed by Guseva and Rona-Tas (2001), trust is understood as a means of managing the uncertainties that stem from ambiguities in social relationships. Here, trust is seen as specifically embedded in interpersonal relationships and is a product of, and is organized around, the ties within social networks. Whereas the uncertainties of personal relationships are mitigated by trust, risks produced within societal communities are mediated by the rational calculations of probable outcomes. In order to circumvent risks, norms for behavior and exchange are established through the formal institutionalization of risk-reducing social structures that facilitate the estimation of successes (or failures) resulting from social relationships. Such formalized norms are frequently inflexible and constitute a normative order that is disembedded from the negotiations of interpersonal relationships.

Using this model, normative order can be seen as an outcome of mechanisms that mitigate both risk and uncertainty. Because normative order can be fragile, and approached with trepidation by members of a common community, both the risks and uncertainties of engaging in, and relying upon, social relationships pose salient, sociological problems for members of social groups. Risks are managed through the formal institutionalization of generalized norms circumscribing relationships and exchanges (oftentimes codified in institutional practices) and allow for individuals to predict the probable likelihood of specific outcomes. Uncertainties, however, are wrought with much more ambiguity and are mediated through trust that is cultivated and negotiated informally through specific social relationships.

Virtual communities pose interesting problems for the analysis of normative order and the management of both risk and uncertainty. While the evolution of normative order within online worlds provides important parallels with that created in real-life communities, the technological environment of the Internet creates new problems for societal organization. In virtual environments, trust takes on new and more particularized relevance in the constitution of normative order. Because online worlds are shrouded in interpersonal anonymity, and frequently in normative ambiguity, the establishment and maintenance of trust can take significant effort and informal negotiation.

Trust and the Virtual Normative Order

It has been commonly recognized that trust is an important concern associated with virtual worlds (Bierhoff and Vornefeld, 2004; Dutton and Shepard, 2006; Henderson and Gilding, 2004;

Kollock, 1999; LaFrance, 1996; Lunn and Suman, 2002; Vishwanath, 2004; Zimmer and Hunter, 2003). Not only do virtual worlds provide new forms of, and contexts for, social interaction and interpersonal relationships, but they also create new problems associated with the establishment of normative conventions and social control. As they have been explored in social science research, the ambiguities surrounding trust in the Internet typically deal specifically with the risks and uncertainties of economic exchange (Dutton and Shepard, 2006; Kollock, 1999; LaFrance, 1996; Vishwanath, 2004; Zimmer and Hunter, 2003). The prevalence of such concerns have led social Internet scholars to describe the economic environment of virtual worlds as a "culture of risk" (Castells, 2001:112) where issues of "cybertrust" in exchange transactions (Dutton and Shepard, 2006) are central. Because e-commerce occurs in an environment of effective anonymity, with real money often exchanged for unseen, or even virtual, goods, and because trade partners are not in close proximity, the concerns of trust management are very high. However, e-commerce is generally mediated by risk-mitigating techniques that serve to set ground-rules for transactions, technologically structure bartering relationships, and formally institutionalize a normative system for exchange. Studies of e-commerce have suggested that because the Internet is an "experience technology" (Dutton and Shepard, 2006; Lunn and Suman, 2002), the more that individuals engage in successful, virtual transactions, the more likely formal, normative systems of Internet exchange are to be experienced as reducing risk.[3]

While studies of trust with respect to e-commerce have generated significant interest by social science investigations, it is the research into the socio-emotional nature of online social worlds that has received the most attention. Several studies stand out as harbingers in the exploration of the violation of trust within Internet communities" like Dibbell's (1998) now classic study of a sexual assault in cyberspace, and Rheingold's

(1995) account of the virtual suicide that shook the early Internet community the WELL. These studies, and others like them, reveal that online communities can be permeated with significant levels of trust, the violation of which can cause striking antipathy among individuals who have considerable emotional investment in, and personal identification with, their online relationships.

When more abstract, negotiated and socio-emotional goods are at stake (i.e. social identities and interpersonal relationships), the dynamics of virtual exchange take on a different complexion. Here, virtually constructed identities and relationships, as well as environments of general sociability, are important resources at play (Ben-Ze'ev, 2004; Henderson and Gilding, 2004; Mandelli, 2002; Rheingold, 1995; Turkle, 1995; Wallace, 2001). The research into the construction of virtual identities and relationships has suggested that, unlike e-commerce exchanges, socio-emotional goods are much more saturated with uncertainty and are often solely negotiated through normative conventions established and maintained "on the fly" by users themselves. Such relationships can be wrought with deception, or at least the fear of deception (Ben-Ze'ev, 2004; Green, 2007; Rheingold, 1995; Riegelsberger, et al, 2007), and generally require a "leap of faith" in order to establish enduring and trusting relationships (Henderson and Gilding, 2004).

Research Questions

The present study builds upon this literature and explores the intersection of research on online worlds and the social constitution of normative order. It follows prior studies of the social life of MMOs (Boyns, Forghani and Sosnovskaya, 2009; Duchenaut and Moore, 2004; Duchenaut, Moore and Nickell, 2004; Duchenaut, Yee, Nickell, Moore, 2006, 2007; Taylor, 2006) and approaches WoW as a sociological space in which both normative order and trust are issues of considerable significance. This investigation is guided by two primary research questions: (1) How is normative order established, violated and maintained in technologically-mediated virtual environments? (2) What are the primary techniques that allow for the construction of WoW's normative culture by which trust is created and preserved?

METHODOLOGY

This study is the result of an ethnographic investigation of WoW game-play conducted from November 2005 to April 2009. The methodological orientation of this study is largely inductive and descriptive, and is indebted to the "grounded theory" approach (Charmaz, 2006; Glaser and Strauss, 1967; Strauss, 1987) commonly used in ethnographic analysis. This research is also based upon the emerging tradition of Internet or "virtual" ethnography[4] (Baym, 2000; Hine, 2001; Kendall, 2002; Kozinets, 2006; Markham, 2004, 2005; Miller and Slater, 2000) which emphasizes the "thick description" (Geertz, 1973) of online communities and their inhabitants. Such research relies upon a researchers' immersion in online environments to explore community organization, identity negotiation and the indigenous production of meaning.

Hundreds of hours of ethnographic observations of game-play were logged during the course of this study, some focusing on the analysis of in-game interaction in common "chat" channels, and others emphasizing active participation in the community life of WoW. The observations stem from the analysis of one specific gaming environment, the Impala realm, a Player-versus-Environment (PvE) server.[5] Ethnographic analysis required the creation and development of WoW characters on this realm, and the "leveling" of specific characters for game-play at the "end game" level. Membership in a high ranking guild and active participation in the guild community were an intrinsic aspect of the ethnographic field research.[6] Direct interaction with players was conducted textually through in-game IM chat channels, as well as by voice via proprietary Voice over Internet Protocol systems. Participation in guild discussions (both in-game and via external sources like guild webpages) and in multi-player, guild activities were fundamental to the study's ethnographic field work.

In addition to direct involvement in WoW game-play, significant observations were made of Impala's in-game IM chat channels. Observations of these interactions yielded considerable information about the community life and social organization created by players on Impala. Because discussions in IM chat channels are conducted textually, serial screen-shots of chat windows were taken so that the contents of interaction could be transcribed for future content analysis.

Finally, an examination of forums on WoW related websites was undertaken to complement the analysis. It is in these forums that many of the "rules" of WoW game-play are debated among players, as are strategies for the most effective game performance. On realm-specific forums, particular issues related to activities on individual game servers are highlighted, including conversations about problematic players and their actions, guild misconduct, and efforts to coordinate in-game activities among players who normally do not meet in the flow of their game-play.

RESULTS

The results of this study suggest that WoWs' normative order is established and maintained through a definable set of techniques that are both formally instituted within the game environment and informally organized among players themselves. Within this normative order, inter-player trust is established as an indispensable aspect of the games' community life. Both game designers and players rely upon the continuity of this normative order to create a sense of trust through which the integrity of game experience is preserved. The results of this study articulate a specific set of techniques through which a sense of normative order is created and preserved. Because WoW is played within a technologically-mediated, virtual space that facilitates high levels of anonymity and many ephemeral social relationships, both risk and uncertainty pose significant concerns for players. Trust emerges as an important resource for players in maintaining the continuity and integrity of their game experience.

Paralleling the theories of normative order in real world communities (Durkheim, 1984[1893]; Luhmann, 1979; Misztal, 1996; Simmel, (1978[1900]); Sztompka, 1999), a sense of trust in both the game environment and its players is facilitated by the normative order ensconced in the WoW's virtual world. When this normative order is challenged by players, a sense of distrust is created which generates both conflict among players and also between game designers and the players they serve. At times, this distrust creates inertia toward the use of social control mechanisms that reinforce WoW's normative order; at other times, distrust is sustained as an integral aspect of the sociology of WoW game-play itself. As presented in these results, the outcomes of this study document the role that trust plays in constructing the techniques of normative order within WoW.

Techniques of Normative Order Maintenance

The game environment of WoW is monitored and controlled through both formal and informal sanctions. On the one hand, formal sanctions are organized around direct mediation by Game Masters (GMs), the prescribed monitoring of characters, the suspension of players, and the banning of player accounts. On the other hand, informal sanctions are facilitated through conversations in global game chat, the establishment and enforcement of guild ethos, appeals to guild leaders, selective grouping decisions, and the stigmatization of specific characters.

At its broadest level, the normative order of WoW is formally organized around the game's End User License Agreement (EULA) and the Terms of Use Agreement (ToU), which outline the basic proscriptive and contractual expectations that circumscribe game-play. Before they can play, all players must agree to the game's EULA and ToU, both of which delineate the baseline expectations for game-play, a matrix of punishable offenses, and the conditions of sanctions for violations. These formal norms create the basic, structural expectations around which the normative order of WoW is established and constitute a framework in which the social participation in WoW emerges. It is through this formal dimension of WoW's normative order that primary issues of risk are managed for players. However, WoW's game environment is sufficiently interactive to allow for cultural conventions to emerge beyond the basic design of the game and allow for the development of an environment of trust-based sociability that is an emergent property of the players in the game (Duchenaut and Moore, 2004; Ducheneaut, Moore, and Nickell, 2004; Ducheneaut, Yee, Nickell, and Moore, 2006). What evolves within the formal organization of the game can be described as a "participatory culture" (Raessens, 2005) that is informally generated and maintained by the players themselves, and is distinct from the normative conventions that are outlined by the structure of the game design. It is within the participatory culture that considerable uncertainties emerge, and implicit trust is enacted that becomes central not only to the social world of WoW but also to the fundamental aspects of its game-play.

The results of this study indicate four primary techniques through which the normative order of WoW is established both formally by the game's design and informally within the participatory culture created by players. These results also document the means through which trust contributes to the continuity and integrity of these techniques of normative order. These techniques are:

1. Institutionalized Risk Mitigation
2. Formal Petitions to Higher Authority
3. Appeals to the Community
4. Expulsion, Ignoring and Stigmatization

In the following sections, each of these techniques are taken up in turn and discussed with respect to the means by which they create expectations for trust.

Institutionalized Risk Mitigation

Like all computer games, the logic of MMO design provides an overarching "physics" and social structure for game-play (Bartle, 2003). In many ways, WoW's design intentionally serves to establish a common space in which players can experience and enjoy the game without much interference from other players, and thus limit the potential risks that they might encounter. WoW's game designers have embedded some important elements into the game for the purposes of allowing players to estimate the probable outcomes of specific social interactions. WoW's rules of game-play provide a formalized, and somewhat inflexible, social structure through which cultural expectations are coordinated for players, trust among players is cultivated, and consequently risk is mitigated. These rules begin with the graphical contours of the game's landscape, but extend through the formal systems within which players are compelled to act, and which at times sharply limit the scope of their social interaction.

One of the basic risk-mitigation techniques is the designation of specific server types for game-play, each of which has specific norms for social interaction. Most important here is the distinction made between Player-versus-Player (PvP) and Player-versus-Environment (PvE) servers. On PvP servers, players from opposing world factions (Alliance and Horde) can be attacked and killed at will when they are not in territories designated as "neutral." While this PvP dimension to the game is commonly identified by players as exciting and challenging, at times, it can become extremely disruptive for game-play. It is not unusual for players to report being killed by opposing players and then "camped" and killed over and over each time they resurrect; sometimes players on both sides of the combat will recruit their allies to support them and join in the melee. Such "camping" of players is not technically in violation of the game's rules, and although it provides an added sport to game-play, it also can be a source of endless frustration for players who are trying to accomplish some of the game's other goals. PvE servers provide players with the option of engaging in PvP combat where players can only attack one another when they are "flagged" to do so. Often labeled "care bear" servers, PvE environments attract players who prefer to focus on the "questing" aspect of the game and who do not want to be worried about being "ganked" by opposing players. As an element of game design, the distinction between PvP and PvE environments permits players a choice in the kind of gaming experience they would like to have and, in essence, produces a sense of what is commonly called "generalized trust" (Rotter, 1971, 1980), and allows them some certainty regarding the potential risks they might encounter while they play.

Other risk-mitigation techniques create for participants increased confidence regarding their interaction both with players and with objects in the game. Central here are the "tagging" and "looting" systems of game design. The tagging system allows players to engage in combat with one of the game's monsters, earn credit for the monster's death, and be assured of winning the creature's "loot" when it is killed. Without the ability to "tag" a monster, players would have considerable uncertainty regarding the distribution of loot as anyone could appropriate the rewards of the kill irrespective of whether or not they participated in the fight. Risks associated with the distribution of rewards are further mediated with the use of a looting system based upon random probability

rolls of the dice. When players formally group together in accomplishing specific tasks, the design of the game allows them to select specific looting rules for reward allocation. Because the acquisition of loot is one of the primary objectives of WoW, and is a fundamental basis for character development, it is vital to have a system in which ambiguity regarding the allocation of rewards is sharply minimized. Although players can sometimes "ninja" the loot (as discussed below), the mitigation of risk regarding rewards is fundamental to WoW's social environment and the trust that players cultivate both toward the game and toward one another.

The existence of formal frameworks for social interaction (e.g. PvP and PvE environments), as well as tools like the tagging and looting systems, help to minimize the risks that players might encounter during their game-play. These techniques allow players to reasonably estimate the probable outcomes of their gaming experience, take the "leap of faith" required for the generation of trust in anonymous online environments (Green, 2007; Henderson and Gilding, 2004; Riegelsberger, et al, 2007), and serve to establish the foundation for the normative order within which game-play occurs.

Formal Petitions to Higher Authority

Within this formally institutionalized, normative order, players have very little elasticity except as enforcers of cultural norms through "petitions" to Game Masters (GMs). Dibbell's (1998) work documents the central role that GMs play not only in mediating conflict in online worlds but, also, in reaffirming a climate of trust once the normative order to the world has been violated. In WoW, as in many other MMOs, Game Masters are put in place as the environment's "higher authority" to address concerns of players that emerge in the course of their game experience (Bartle, 2003). These matters can involve structural issues related to the game, like bugs encountered during game-play, or technical issues related to sound or graphical display. More importantly for the purposes of this study, GMs also are called upon to address players more sociological concerns. Typical examples of such issues requiring GM intervention are harassment and the use of offensive language. Such sociological matters are usually addressed by players who "report" offenders to GMs. GM issued sanctions can involve "account penalties" that range from warnings, to 3-hour suspensions, to "bans" of a day or more, to permanent account closures. The following excerpt[7] taken from a forum on a popular WoW related website provides a telling instance of WoW's system of formal sanctioning:

Topic: Temp ban for "sexual harassment"

From: The Lurker[8]

So i recently got banned for "sexually harassing" another player I think i remember the episode that led to the ban. Some guy was being a total douche in AB [Arathi Basin, a PvP Battleground] yelling and screaming for people to DEFEND FFS[9] etc. You know the type. Eventually i told him to go smoke a co*k. With the asterix included. He was apparently shocked and said he was going to report me to GM. And he did…with gold sellers, scammers, hackers and bugs running rampant i dont think chasing swearwords whould be a priority for the GMs.

PS. Dont forget to go to church on Sunday.

From: Riotgrrl

Personally I agree with your ban. I have nothing against you but heres why. I am a 25 year old woman. I play WoW for fun and for socialising with friends. I also hate the "defend ffs" and "omg[10] disc priest is dpsing more than healing wtf[11]?" comments in battlegrounds but thats what the ignore feature is there for. I log on to chat, have fun, play the game and level my character. I wouldn't use language like that and I don't appreciate others using it to me. While I would just ignore you and not report it, it is against the ToS and if it is your first offense its just a 3 hour ban or whatever to get you to cool down … Swearing in your guild with people who accept it and use the same language doesn't hurt anyone. But on a public channel that is classed as offensive and the ToS tell you not to do it. You broke the rules, you got banned. Sorry but thats what happens. Thats not sexual harrassment though, you should be banned for language/offensive behaviour.

What is important about this account is that it illustrates the overlapping dimensions of normative order enforcement that can exist simultaneously during WoW game-play. At its base level, there is an assumption made by both game designers and players that participants in the WoW community will adhere to the basic policies of WoW sociability. However, within this framework of risk reduction resides a great deal of uncertainty regarding players' actual adherence to this formal, normative order. It is in this sociological space of normative uncertainty that trust becomes most salient.

Both game designers and players trust that participants in the game will adhere to the conventions prescribed by the game and report violators. In the excerpt above, comments like "I agree with your ban … You broke the rules, you got banned. Sorry but thats what happens" illustrate the importance that players hold toward adherence to WoW's formal, normative conventions. As these formal norms constitute the game's fundamental trust inducing mechanisms, these players' reinforcement of these norms also exemplify the degree to which they entrust one another to abide by the rules of the game and minimize the risks for all players. At the same time, as this excerpt also demonstrates, players also place a significant trust in the WoW community that they will not be reported for momentary or inconsequential violations of WoW's formal norms. In the same way that normative order in real life communities has important formal dimensions (Luhmann, 1979; Misztal, 1996; Sztompka, 1999), WoW's normative order also is significantly, and even technologically, formalized. However, WoW's normative structures are also subject to significant, interpersonal negotiation; and it is these interpersonal negotiations that shape the dynamics of trust within WoW game-play. It is within the formalized normative order that the "negotiated order" (Blumer, 1969; Fine, 1984; Strauss, 1978) of WoW emerges and provides the basis for the generation of a more informally produced, "relational trust" within the game.

Appeals to the Community

While players depend upon GMs to support and enforce the formally institutionalized norms of WoW game-play, outside of these structural "rules" players are confronted with a high degree of uncertainty. Although they are bound by the policies of the game, within the confines of WoW's "physics" players can do and say virtually anything they choose. It is in this realm of "participatory culture" (Raessens, 2005) that players must make important decisions regarding WoW's normative world, and establish cultural "ground rules" for interaction, etiquette, game-play, and ultimately for the trust that they will rely upon for the integrity of their gaming experience. Decisions involving

"relational trust" typically concern issues regarding who to group with, how to distribute loot, membership in guilds, or whether or not a person deserves to be reported to a GM. Players have discovered that some of the uncertainty regarding their gaming experience can be managed though appeals made within the WoW community. It is here that the sociological basis of the normative order of WoW's social world is constructed, and players must rely upon their own ingenuity in negotiating an informal, cultural world in which their game-play occurs. It is in these community relations that trust, and its violation, emerges as an indispensable component of WoW game-play.

At its broadest level, WoW's informal culture is established within discussions among the general community. On the Impala server, players frequently use the in-game IM system to post questions about game activities, request information, share strategies, discuss problematic players, and negotiate sanctions for violators of game norms.[12] Because much of the group life of WoW is ephemeral and can be composed of players who have little prior experience with one another, social interactions can be imbued with considerable uncertainty. When a player's trust is violated, as frequently occurs in online worlds (Dibbell, 1998; Henderson and Gilding, 2004; Rheingold, 1995), appeals are commonly made to the entire server community to help resolve the issue.

Frequently, however, WoW players take their appeals to more local levels where troublesome characters who commit egregious violations of trust can be reported to guild leaders. Because players are normally dependent upon their guilds for game-play at advanced levels, guild leaders can carry considerable influence over the behavior of their guild members. Players who harass or use abusive language toward another player can be called upon to justify their actions in the face of their guild community. In instances of serious transgression, characters can be kicked out their guild and then their actions publicly rebuked in the broader server community. Because of the pressure that many guilds can exert upon their members, guilds are typically responsible for negotiating much of the uncertainty inherent in WoW's social life and provide an important source of stability to WoW's normative order.[13]

One of the most common violations of collective trust that is typically met with appeals to the broader community occurs when players "spam" common chat channels. "Spamming" in WoW is identified as repetitive posting of text by players to common chat channels or to individual characters. Spam occurs most frequently in global game chat and is considered annoying because it fills chat windows with irrelevant text, preventing individuals from following and engaging in more meaningful discussions. In essence, spammers violate the generalized trust of members of the WoW community, and distort not only the integrity of game-play but, also, the sense of trust that players have among the anonymous denizens that inhabit their technological world.

It must be emphasized that WoW game-play relies upon IM chat in a number of different channels (e.g. channels for "General," "Trade," "Guild," "Raid," "Party," or personal chat). Although players may attend only to messages in specific channels, the conversations in all channels are broadcast in the same chat window simultaneously, with messages in each channel distinguished by their display in a unique color. Because many, distinct conversations among disparate groups all occur simultaneously in the same interaction window, any attempt to clutter that chat "space" with senseless spam in common chat channels can significantly interrupt game-play and become instantly frustrating to players.

Once it is initiated in common chat channels, spam sequences can, persist for nearly an hour with dozens of players facilitating, and exacerbating the spam. Interestingly enough, the public outrage directed at the spam, when posted in the same channels, can have the same effect as the spam itself, cluttering the chat windows with needless

text and making individual conversations difficult to follow. The following account documents one such instance of spam observed within the realm's "Trade" channel, which could be seen by all players with Alliance characters situated in one of the realm's major cities. In this instance, players are illustrating a common practice of spamming the name of a game item (the "Giant Stalker's Belt") embedded in the title of a film.[14] The spam begins with an innocent, initiatory post by Dogeatdog, is followed by a series of imitative posts by other players (Cheshire, Cruzier, Pallypolice, etc.), all of which are contested by annoyed players (Furrious, Decimus, Surferrosa, Equality, etc.) expressing their frustration:

[2. Trade] [Dogeatdog]: knock knock, who's there? [Giant Stalker's Belt]

[2. Trade] [Cheshire]: [Giant Stalker's Belt] on a plane

[2. Trade] [Dogeatdog]: [Giant Stalker's Belt] and his cultural learnings of American to make benefit glorious nation of khazakstan

[2. Trade] [Cruzier]: Once upon on a [Giant Stalker's Belt]

[2. Trade] [Furrious]: [Giant Stalker's Belt] can suck my balls part 3 all you noobs better stop spamming

[2. Trade] [Decimus]: This is not funny at all

[2. Trade] [Crusier]: Dude, Where's my [Giant Stalker's Belt]

[2. Trade] [Equality]: dude just stop

[2. Trade] [Surferrosa]: shutup

[2. Trade] [Pallypolice]: how I met you [Giant Stalker's Belt]

[2. Trade] [Decimus]: shut up guys, seriously

[2. Trade] [Equality]: omfg[15] shut up

[2. Trade] [Nighthyme]: be mature

While this account only documents segments of the first few minutes of a session of spam that persisted for nearly 30 minutes before dissipating, it reveals several characteristics that are indicative of most instances of spam: they frequently emerge as a parody of game play, are engaged in by a number of different characters, oftentimes providing an entertaining distraction for game-play, consume large amounts of the space of the IM chat window, and evoke outrage from members of the general community.

The presence of spam, matched with the outrage it provokes, helps to illustrate the importance of WoW's common space for players of the game, and highlights the trust that players have about its responsible use. Spammers violate the normative order of the WoW community by attempting to monopolize the game's public IM chat. The fact that instances of spam, even if they manifest only through a few lines of repetitive text, are almost always met with some public resistance and sanctioning, is illustrative of the existence of a sense of trust that is informally negotiated among WoW players, and marks the degree to which inter-player trust is fundamental for the integrity of the game's community.

Even with the outrage that spam evokes, it is important to note that spam can also make positive contributions to the in-game culture that emerges among players. Spammers generate a sense of outrage against a violation of the use of common, public space and produce an attempt to "normalize" that violation through community sanctioning. The outrage spam incites illustrates the presence of informal trust between players and the efforts that will be taken toward its maintenance. The combined effect of spam, the trust it violates, the outrage it induces, the sanctioning mechanisms it generates, and the entertainment it provides, illustrate important expression of WoW's normative order which is rich in its dynamism and complexity.

Expulsion, Ignoring and Stigmatization

At its most informal level, WoW's normative order is negotiated among the players themselves in the flow of their game-play. Because much of

WoW's group life is transitory and occurs between characters who are relatively unknown to one another, players frequently have to use improvised means in making decisions about whom to trust and how to manage the uncertainties of the game. Here, players are frequently compelled to make grouping decisions with the expectation that the group may not work out, or that things could go disastrously wrong.[16] Players also make choices about whom to interact with and about the topics of conversation. Characters that are found to be unreliable, unskilled or generally untrustworthy, can be expelled from groups (and even from more stable guild communities), or formally silenced through the game's "ignore" system which prevents players from receiving IM messages from those characters added a player's "ignore" list. At extreme levels, a series of expulsions and ignores can result in the stigmatization of specific characters both in local communities and in the broader WoW community. Such degraded characters frequently become floaters within the server, unattached to specific guilds or social groups; they may also become "guild hoppers," serially leaving (or being "kicked" from) guilds.[17]

On Impala, several characters were observed who seemed to delight in their stigmatization. One such character, Drtrust, earned a notable reputation as a "ninja" and became the server's most infamous and stigmatized player. The label of "ninja" is frequently given to WoW's most untrustworthy players and is commonly used to describe someone who has engaged in-game thievery and deception, where items won in group play are appropriated for individual use, or when individuals abscond with traded goods without reciprocal compensation. Ninjas are likely the most bemoaned of WoW's deviant "identities," as they free-ride on the trust of other players, and illustrate perhaps the most egregious transgression of the generalized trust embedded in the game's normative order.

Because ninja looting is not technically against the formal rules of game-play, players must negotiate looting rules upfront and come to a consensus about how loot is to be distributed. Many guilds whose members raid together on a permanent basis, establish formal strategies for loot distribution. Among more ephemeral groups, a tacit, generalized trust forms the basis of loot distribution, and its violation becomes a frequent subject of discussion in WoW's public forums. While ninja-ing loot is technically not in direct violation of WoW's formal rules of game-play, it is certainly a violation of the informal trust created and maintained by players themselves. Prior research has highlighted the importance of maintaining the reliability of this trust, particularly in virtual environments where deception is a significant concern and players must frequently make a "leap of faith" in establishing trusting relationships (Ben-Ze'ev, 2004; Dibbell, 1998; Green, 2007; Henderson and Gilding, 2004; Rheingold, 1995). Ninja looting highlights the importance of trust in maintaining WoW's social life as it exposes a vulnerability in the game experience that cannot be avoided except through inter-player cooperation. Ninjas transgress the foundation of the tacit, generalized trust cultivated within the game and pose a direct challenge to the integrity of the game's community life by elevating the uncertainties of teaming up with other players in game activities.

The presence of stigmatized players like Drtrust highlight not only the normative dimensions of WoW game-play but, also, the degree to which the game's societal community will go in enforcing its culture and protecting the interpersonal trust it works to construct. The presence of Drtrust also illustrates the salience of individuals in the WoW community who adopt "violator roles" that intentionally elevate the degree of risk and uncertainty experienced by players. These kinds of characters are common in WoW's game environment and pose interesting problems for the maintenance of WoW's normative order and the sense of trust it embraces.

FUTURE RESEARCH DIRECTIONS

This study has outlined techniques through which WoW's normative order is created by the cultivation of trust among its players. While it relies upon ethnographic observations made about the game environment, it does so from a relative distance. Because interviews are not used as a methodological technique in this research, the means through which normative order, the maintenance of trust, and the effects of its violation are not investigated as they might be indigenously experienced by players themselves. It is likely that interview data might yield additional dimensions of normative order construction, other more covert violator roles, and a richer account of the importance of trust in the experience of WoW's sociological world.

Future research should also explore additional techniques of trust-based, normative order constitution that are only hinted at by the present study. For example, the anonymity inherent in online worlds like WoW not only produces ambiguity about the identities of players in real life contexts but, also, generates uncertainty about the capabilities and experience of the characters they play. A skilled player may be called upon to operate a character that does not have the requisite capabilities to complete a given task. In this way, players may place a high degree of trust in one another, but they may distrust the competence of one another's characters.

Related topics for investigation also involve a character's presentation of their identity within the public community as trustworthy, or untrustworthy. Players do significantly engage in what Goffman (1959) would describe as "identity work" for their characters. Some players intentionally seek to disguise their identities though character transformation tools (like the "savory deviate delight") or by donning low-level or "vanity" gear. Other players, who have acquired extremely rare items will seek to attract attention by displaying their characters within the game in high traffic areas so their unique accomplishments can be publicly recognized by passersby. Still other players who violate the tacit trust of other players are forced to negotiate the "repair" their stigmatized identities, a process which can take considerable effort in the anonymous space of WoW's sociological world. Such topics related to the trust and distrust of specific character identities would provide important, additional dimensions of the study of online social worlds.

CONCLUSION

The focus of this study has been to investigate the interrelationship of normative order and the social production of trust within the online community of World of Warcraft. Because WoW is a technological environment in which advanced game-play is dependent upon a rich community life, and where the interaction of most players is sustained through virtually anonymous relationships, the issues of both normative order and trust pose compelling sociological problems. In many ways, the emergence cultural norms within WoW resonate with systems of normative order that develop in real life communities. In both online and real life worlds, formally institutionalized and informally negotiated dimensions of cultural order evolve in order to shape social interaction, codes of behavior, etiquette, and establish a sense of trust among community members. However, in online worlds, because of the highly salient and recognized anonymity of social relationships, trust is a broader, more disconcerting, and more complex issue (Bierhoff and Vornefeld, 2004; Dutton and Shepard, 2006).

The results of the present study support prior research which contends that trust is a central problem for inhabitants of virtual worlds like WoW (Bierhoff and Vornefeld, 2004; Dutton and Shepard, 2006; Green, 2007; Henderson and Gilding, 2004; Kollock, 1999; Riegelsberger et al, 2007; Zimmer and Hunter, 2003). Here, the concerns of "cybertrst" (Dutton and Shepard,

2006) extend beyond the boundaries of economic exchange and into the socio-cultural arena of WoW's sociological organization. Not only are mechanisms for the management of trust structurally built into WoW's game design, but the game is also organized around a community life in which trust must be negotiated and established among players themselves. Parallel to the literature on trust in real life communities (Luhmann, 1979; Misztal, 1996; Sztompka, 1999), trust is an essential part of WoW's normative order and is monitored by systems of sanctioning that are embedded within game-play. In some ways, these sanctioning mechanisms are formalized and institutionalized within the rules of the game as a form of "generalized trust" (Rotter, 1971, 1980); in other ways, sanctions are organized informally as a form of "relational trust" (Jones, et al, 1997) and imposed by the members of the WoW community. It is the combination of the formal and informal dimensions of WoW's normative order that serve to create a foundation for trust that is the cornerstone of its rich sociological world.

Following the model of risk and uncertainty proposed by Guseva and Rona-Tas (2001), the construction of WoW's normative order can be outlined with respect to central theoretical issues related to the social production of trust. It is clear that WoW's game environment poses specific issues associated with risk and uncertainty, both of which evolve as salient challenges to the constitution of WoW's normative order. On the one hand, players can experience threats to WoW's normative order that can be specifically managed through the formal, institutionalization of techniques of risk mitigation with the game's design. Such threats are overcome by embedding within the game structural "rules" for maintaining and monitoring the integrity of the implicit trust that guides game-play, and are organized around systems that allow players to sustain that trust though the submission of formal petitions to the game's higher authorities. Some players do transgress these institutionalized norms, and such violations of "generalized trust" are met with formal sanctioning and punishment. On the other hand, and notwithstanding the formal rules of the game, the threats to WoW's normative order are permeated with high degrees uncertainty that can only be negotiated informally by sustaining a "relational trust" among the members of the WoW community, a claim that is commonly made about online worlds in general (Henderson and Gilding, 2004). Such a result supports the broader claims that trust plays a basic role in group continuity, organization and integrity (Cook, 2005; Kollock, 1994; Molm, Takahasi and Petersen, 2000). It is in the sociological space of WoW that "relational trust" plays a central role in coordinating the game's community life and inter-player activities. Here, a sense of trust is maintained through discussions held with in the broader game community, appeals to local guild leaders, and by the stigmatization of specific players. Because players must put their trust in one another, the game's sociological world is rather fragile; but it is this same fragility that provides some of the more creative and compelling dimensions of the game.

While this investigation's results point to some of the community dynamics that emerge in online worlds, some may question the relevance of such a study to the non-virtual world. Some may contend that a study of virtual gaming worlds and their normative organization is of little consequence of the understanding the dynamics of trust and community life among real people in real social spaces. However, as the use of the Internet expands world-wide, and more dimensions of everyday social life are conducted online, it is likely that gaming environments with their rich, sociological complexity will serve as models for other forms or online community organization (Castronova, 2005, 2007). In particular, because the social life of WoW is permeated with salient issues related to the social, cultural, political and economic orders, it provides a compelling simulation of the social organization of trust that could be directed toward real world concerns. The investigation of the massive virtual spaces devoted to gaming can help to identify and clarify the more pragmatic concerns related to trust in the constitution of virtual communities, particularly those directly ensconced in real world activities. It is hoped that this study is contribution toward that goal.

REFERENCES

Bartle, R. (2003). *Designing virtual worlds*. Indianapolis, IN: New Riders Publishing.

Bauman, Z. (1997). *Postmodernity and its discontents*. Cambridge, MA: Polity Press.

Baym, N. (2000). *Tune in, log on*. Thousand Oaks, CA: Sage.

Beck, U. (1992). *Risk society: Towards a new modernity*. Newbury Park, CA: SAGE Publications.

Ben-Ze'ev, A. (2004). *Love online: Emotions on the Internet*. Cambridge, UK: Cambridge University Press. doi:10.1017/CBO9780511489785

Bierhoff, H.-W., & Vornefeld, B. (2004). The social psychology of trust with applications in the Internet. *Analyse & Kritik, 26*, 48–62.

Blau, P. (1973). *The Dynamics of Bureaucracy*. Chicago: University of Chicago Press.

Blumer, H. (1969). *Symbolic interaction: Perspective and method*. Englewood Cliffs, NJ: Prentice Hall.

Boyns, D., Forghani, S., & Sosnovskaya, E. (2009). MMORPG worlds: On the construction of social reality in World of Warcraft. In Heider, D. (Ed.), *Living virtually: Researching new worlds* (pp. 67–92). New York: Peter Lang.

Castells, M. (2001). *The Internet galaxy: Reflections on the Internet, business and society*. Oxford, UK: Oxford University Press.

Castronova, E. (2005). *Synthetic worlds: The business and culture of online games*. Chicago: University of Chicago Press.

Castronova, E. (2007). *Exodus to the virtual world: How online fun is changing reality*. New York: Palgrave Macmillian.

Charmaz, K. (2006). *Constructing grounded theory: A practical guide through qualitative analysis*. Thousand Oaks, CA: Sage Publications.

Cook, K. (2005). Networks, norms, and trust: The Social psychology of social capital. *Social Psychology Quarterly, 68*(1), 4–14. doi:10.1177/019027250506800102

Dibbell, J. (1998). *My tiny life: Crime and passion in a virtual world*. New York: Holt.

Ducheneaut, N., & Moore, R. J. (2004). The social side of gaming: A study of interaction patterns in a massively multiplayer online game. In *Proceedings of the ACM conference on computer-supported cooperative work*, Chicago, IL (pp. 360-369).

Ducheneaut, N., Moore, R. J., & Nickell, E. (2004). Designing for sociability in massively multiplayer games: an examination of the third places of SWG. In J. H. Smith & M. Sicart (Eds.), *Proceedings of the other players conference*. Copenhagen, Denmark: IT University of Copenhagen.

Ducheneaut, N., Yee, N., Nickell, E., & Moore, R. J. (2006). Alone together? Exploring the social dynamics of massively multiplayer games. *Conference proceedings on human factors in computing systems CHI2006* (pp. 407-416). Montreal, PQ, Canada.

Ducheneaut, N., Yee, N., Nickell, E., & Moore, R. J. (2007). The life and death of online gaming communities: A look at guilds in World of Warcraft. In *Proceedings of CHI 2007* (pp. 839-848). New York: ACM.

Durkheim, E. (1982). *The rules of sociological method*. New York: The Free Press. (Original work published 1895)

Durkheim, E. (1984). *Division of labor in society*. New York: The Free Press. (Original work published 1893)

Dutton, W. H., & Shepard, A. (2006). Trust in the Internet as an experience technology. *Information Communication and Society, 9*(4), 433–451. doi:10.1080/13691180600858606

Fine, G. A. (1984). Negotiated orders and organizational cultures. *Annual Review of Sociology, 10*, 239–262. doi:10.1146/annurev.so.10.080184.001323

Geertz, C. (1973). *The interpretation of cultures*. New York: Basic Books.

Giddens, A. (1990). *The consequences of modernity*. Stanford, CA: Stanford University Press.

Giddens, A. (1991). *Modernity and self-identity: Self and society in the late modern age*. Stanford, CA: Stanford University Press.

Glaser, B. G., & Strauss, A. L. (1967). *The discovery of grounded theory. Strategies for qualitative research*. Chicago: Aldine Publishing Company.

Goffman, E. (1959). *The presentation of self in everyday life*. Garden City, NY: Basic Books.

Goffman, E. (1967). *Interaction ritual: Essays on face-to-face behavior*. New York: Anchor Books.

Green, M. (2007). Trust and social interaction on the Internet. In Joinson, A., McKenna, K., Postmes, T., & Reips, U.-D. (Eds.), *The Oxford Handbook of internet psychology* (pp. 43–52). New York: Oxford University Press.

Guseva, A., & Rona-Tas, A. (2001, October). Uncertainty, risk and trust: Russian and American credit card markets compared. *American Sociological Review, 66*, 623–646. doi:10.2307/3088951

Hardin, G. (1968). Tragedy of the commons. *Science, 162*, 1243–1248. doi:10.1126/science.162.3859.1243

Henderson, S., & Gilding, M. (2004). 'I've never clicked this much with anyone in my life': Trust and hyperpersonal communication in online friendships. *New Media & Society, 8*(4), 487–506. doi:10.1177/1461444804044331

Hine, C. (2001). *Virtual ethnography*. London: Sage.

Jones, W. H., Couch, L., & Scott, S. (1997). Trust and betrayal: The psychology of getting along and getting ahead. In Hogan, R., Johnson, J., & Briggs, S. (Eds.), *Handbook of Personality Psychology* (pp. 465–483). San Diego: Academic Press. doi:10.1016/B978-012134645-4/50020-2

Kendall, L. (2002). *Hanging out in the virtual pub: Masculinities and relationships online*. Berkeley, CA: University of California Press.

Kollock, P. (1994). The emergence of exchange relationships: An experimental study of uncertainty, commitment, and trust. *American Journal of Sociology, 100*, 313–345. doi:10.1086/230539

Kollock, P. (1999). The economies of online cooperation. In Smith, M. A., & Kollock, P. (Eds.), *Communities in Cyberspace* (pp. 220–239). New York: Routledge.

Kozinets, R. V. (2006). Netnography 2.0. In R. W. Belk (Ed.), Handbook of qualitative research methods in marketing (129-142). Northampton, MA: Edward Elgar Publishing.

LaFrance, M. (1996). Why we trust computers too much. *Technology Studies, 3*(1), 163–178.

Luhmann, N. (1979). *Trust and power*. New York: Wiley.

Luhmann, N. (1995). *Social Systems*. Stanford, CA: Stanford University Press.

Lunn, R. J., & Suman, M. W. (2002). Experience and trust in online shopping. In B. Wellman & C. Haythornthwaite (Eds.), The Internet in everyday life (549-577). Malden, MA: Blackwell Publishing.

Maines, D. R., & Charlton, J. (1985). Negotiated order approach to the analysis of social organization. *Studies in Social Interaction*, (Supplement 1), 271–308.

Mandelli, A. (2002). Bounded sociability: Relationship costs and intangible resources in complex digital networks. *IT & Society, 1*(1), 251–274.

Markham, A. (1998). *Life online: Researching real experience in virtual space*. Lanham, MD: AltaMira Press.

Markham, A. (2004). Internet communication as a tool for qualitative research. In Silverman, D. (Ed.), *Qualitative research: Theory, method, and research* (pp. 95–124). Thousand Oaks, CA: Sage.

Markham, A. (2004). The methods, politics, and ethics of representation in online ethnography. In Denzin, N. K., & Lincoln, Y. S. (Eds.), *Handbook of qualitative research* (3rd ed., pp. 793–820). Thousand Oaks, CA: Sage.

Miller, D., & Slater, D. (2000). *The Internet: An ethnographic approach*. Oxford, UK: Berg.

Misztal, B. (1996). *Trust in Modern Societies*. Cambridge, UK: Polity Press.

Molm, L., Takahasi, N., & Peterson, G. (2000). Risk and trust in social exchange: An experimental test of a classical proposition. *American Journal of Sociology, 105*(5), 1396–1427. doi:10.1086/210434

Olson, M. Jr. (1965). *The logic of collective action*. Cambridge, MA: Harvard University Press.

Parsons, T. (1951). *The social system*. New York: The Free Press.

Parsons, T. (1971). *The system of modern societies*. New York: Prentice Hall.

Raessens, J. (2005). Computer games as participatory media culture. In Raessens, J., & Goldstein, J. (Eds.), *Handbook of compute game studies* (pp. 373–388). Cambridge, MA: MIT Press.

Rheingold, H. (1995). *The virtual community: Homesteading on the electronic frontier*. Reading, MA: Addison-Wesley.

Riegelsberger, J., Sasse, M., & McCarthy, J. (2007). Trust in mediated interactions. In Joinson, A., McKenna, K., Postmes, T., & Reips, U.-D. (Eds.), *The Oxford Handbook of internet psychology* (pp. 53–70). New York: Oxford University Press.

Rotter, J. B. (1971). Generalized expectancies for interpersonal trust. *The American Psychologist, 26*, 443–452. doi:10.1037/h0031464

Rotter, J. B. (1980). Interpersonal trust, trustworthiness, and gullibility. *The American Psychologist, 35*, 1–7. doi:10.1037/0003-066X.35.1.1

Simmel, G. (1978). *The Philosophy of Money*. London: Routledge. (Original work published 1900)

Strauss, A. (1978). *Negotiations: Varieties, processes, contexts, and social order*. San Francisco: Jossey-Bass.

Strauss, A. (1987). *Qualitative analysis for social scientists*. Cambridge, UK: Cambridge University Press. doi:10.1017/CBO9780511557842

Sztompka, P. (1999). *Trust: A sociological theory*. Cambridge, UK: Cambridge University Press.

Taylor, T. L. (2006). *Play between worlds: Exploring online game culture*. Cambridge, MA: MIT Press.

Turkle, S. (1995). *Life on the screen: Identity in the age of the Internet*. New York: Simon and Schuster.

Vishwanath, A. (2004). Manifestations of interpersonal trust in online interaction: A cross-cultural study comparing the differential utilization of seller ratings by eBay participants in Canada, France, and Germany. *New Media & Society, 6*(2), 219–234. doi:10.1177/1461444804041441

Wallace, P. (2001). *The psychology of the Internet*. Cambridge, UK: Cambridge University Press.

Zimmer, E. A., & Hunter, C. D. (2003). The Internet and risk: Perception and reality. In Strate, L., Jacobson, R., & Gibson, S. B. (Eds.), *Communication and Cyberspace: Social Interaction in an Electronic Environment* (pp. 183–202). Cresskill, NY: Hampton Press.

ENDNOTES

[1] Alliance races are: Human, Night Elf, Dwarf, Gnome and Draenei; Horde races are: Orc, Troll, Undead, Tauren and Blood Elf.

[2] Players may select from the following classes: warriors, mages, druids, priests, paladins, warlocks, shaman, rogues, hunters and death knights.

[3] Other studies have revealed that successful use of computer technologies and their applications creates new forms of trust, not in relationships between individuals but, in the technological systems themselves (Bierhoff and Vornefeld, 2004; LaFrance, 1996).

[4] Kozinets (2006) describes a specific set of techniques for virtual ethnographic analysis as "Netnography."

[5] In the interest of confidentiality, Impala is used here a pseudonym and is not the actual name of the server examined in the study. There are over 240 distinct *WoW* realms, each of which facilitates the game-play of thousands (or even tens-of-thousands) unique characters. While Impala is a PvE realm – some realms emphasize Player-

versus-Player (PvP) combat, and others involve a more direct Role-Playing (RP) of characters – it assumed that many of the dynamics outlined in this study are present across unique server types.

6   Characters were only developed and leveled within the Alliance faction on the Impala realm. Because direct interactions across factions are not made possible within the game design, interaction and community organization among the players of the other faction (the Horde) are not included in this study. However, there is sufficient, though largely anecdotal, evidence to suggest that the dynamics of game-play and social interaction are consistent across factions – particularly because many players play characters on both the Alliance and Horde factions.

7   This series of posts has been slightly edited for the sake of brevity to remove redundant or irrelevant discussion regarding the topic.

8   This is not the character's true name. For the purposes of confidentiality, all player names reported in this study have been replaced with pseudonyms.

9   Internet slang for "for f*ck's sake."

10   Internt slang for "oh my god."

11   Internet slang for "what the f*ck."

12   On Impala, a broad range of non-game topics are frequently included in these forums, like debates about political issues, current events or sports teams, as well as nonsense issues related to player's "mothers" or their sexual activities.

13   Guilds also are known to generate their own policies for interaction and comportment (Duchenaut, Yee, Nickells and Moore, 2007). During the course of this study, it was frequently noted that those characters that were identified as serious violators of interpersonal trust did not belong to a guild, or were known to move frequently between guilds. These observations suggest that not only are guilds successful in the mitigation of the uncertainties inherent in WoW's social life, but also that players find more freedom to be untrustworthy if they are not tied to a guild community.

14   Only the text from the 'Trade' channel is displayed in the excerpt below, though interactions in other channels were embedded in the space of the chat window.

15   Internet slang for "oh my f*cking god."

16   After all, a player joining a group in order to complete a game objective could potentially be partied with an unskilled six-year old, a person playing on-the-side while they are at work, or a parent whose primary attention is devoted to the care of their small child … or all of the above.

17   At the most acute levels, characters may even transfer servers and change their character's name in order reconstruct both their game identity and their community relations anew among an entirely different group of players.

Chapter 6
Impediments to and Affordances of Creating Trust over the Internet:
The Case of Israeli Youth*

Oren Golan
New York University, USA

ABSTRACT

In spite of obstacles to trust-building over the Internet, as well as continuous warnings on the part of educators, parents and social movements about the dangers of unsupervised web surfing by children and adolescents, an avid culture of youth has emerged over the Internet and created spaces for trust-building. This paper aims to display the key impediments encountered in the formation of trust relations over the Internet among youth, and the ways that these obstacles are engaged. Observations and conversations with Israeli adolescents yielded three intertwined impediments to online trust: (1) Lies and truths. (2) Anonymity/Disclosure (3) Transparency/Opacity. Uncovering the ways that youth create and maintain trust may illuminate our understanding of how youth communicate and fraternize in today's Information and Communication Technology society. Basing itself on these findings, this study contributes to the understanding of challenges and bridges for instilling social integration through computer-mediated-communication (CMC).

INTRODUCTION

The Internet has been lauded for its ability to foster interaction among innumerable individuals. However, this interaction among strangers has been accompanied by apprehension and uneasiness. This concern has been magnified in the case of children and youth, who are often considered susceptible to

DOI: 10.4018/978-1-61520-901-9.ch006

adult harassment and are viewed as requiring adult and state protection.

In spite of continuous warnings on the part of educators, parents and social movements about the dangers of unsupervised web surfing by children and adolescents, an avid culture of youth has emerged over the Internet, whose tracts have created spaces for trust-building.

In sociological literature, trust[1] has been perceived as a major building block of social solidarity and society's various productions. Furthermore, trust has been seen as a precondition for securing economic relations and for coping with conflict (Durkheim, 1949; Barber, 1983; Gambetta, 1988; Sztompka, 1999). Trust may be defined as "confidence in the reliability of a person or system" (Giddens, 1990). Among scholars, social trust has been linked to a number of positive outcomes. For example, trust has been linked to social solidarity and cohesion, to strong economic performance (Yamagishi and Yamagishi, 1994; Fukuyama, 1995) and is viewed as a source of support for democratic ideals (Muller and Seligson, 1994; Cleary and Stokes, 2006). In theories of social capital, social trust is both an outcome and a cause of high levels of civic involvement (Putnam, 2000; Kelly, 2008) and also curbs non-normative behavior.

Early studies of the Internet expressed disbelief in the possibility of creating and maintaining interpersonal and collective trust due to the inhuman lack of face to face interaction (Kiesler, Siegel and McGuire, 1984; Beninger, 1987; Heim, 1992; Stoll, 1995). Later on, with the rise of the Internet and the intense activity it engendered, social scientists and intellectuals noted the rise of online trust, occasionally as a surprising finding, and measured the outcomes of these ties in the exchange of individual goods, production of public goods, the existence of stable social networks, online community building, and the formation of social norms over the net (see Silverstone, 1999; Parks and Floyd, 1996; Kollock and Smith, 1999; Baym, 2000; Raymond, 2001; Dutton and Shepherd, 2006). Researchers also delineated the paradoxical emergence of trust within online cultures that foster deviant behavior (e.g. mass infringements on copyrights, plagiarism), and is best illustrated in the case of Hackers (Taylor, 1999). These studies contributed to an understanding of the new forms and dynamics of trust over the Internet, but were less concerned with the ways trust is created among specific social sub-groups, cultures and social categories. In this study, I aim to focus on the generation of trust among youth.

BACKGROUND

Youth serve as an important case study for observing online trust for the use of new technologies is prevalent among adolescents. Surveys and social indicators point not only to the extensive involvement of youth in Internet and technological activities, but also to a high degree of expertise manifested in the use of these technologies. Rather than limit them to specific areas, schools or community centers for example, youth integrate these activities into the overall matrix of their daily lives (Rideout et.al., 2005; Thurlow and McKay, 2003; Livingstone, 2002; Johnsson-Smargdi, 2001; Holloway and Valentine, 2003; Hecht, 2001). Furthermore, the question of trust formation is viewed as particularly important for young people's integration into society and their outreach beyond the confines of the family (Jarrett, Sullivan and Watkins, 2005; Eisenstadt, 1974).

As the Internet has rapidly become an integral part of youth's everyday lives and is an important venue for adolescents to socialize with their peers, this paper aims to examine the formation of trust in a social arena that is very different than more documented venues of socialization and fraternization among youth (e.g. schools, youth movements, dance clubs). Among more traditional settings, trust relations are based on a direct, face-to-face interaction, as well as being embedded in communal social networks (in the neighborhood, school etc). These features are absent in computer-mediated-relations and raise questions regarding the ability and ways for creating trust over the Internet given the Internet's own social and technological affordances and challenges (on this comparison in a controlled environment see Wilson, Straus and McEvily, 2006). More specifically, I ask what are the impediments identified by youth for online trust and how do they confront these obstructions?

Methodology

In carrying out the research, I wished to utilize the advantages of the traditional methods of the social sciences (i.e. interviews, participant observation) together with research tools developed within the new forms of cybernetic ethnography (also referred to as "inter-view analysis" - see Wilhelm, 2000:26), multimedia and mediation of instruments (Markham, 1998; Danet, 2001; Kendall, 2002)

Information was obtained, mainly, by two methods: in-depth interviews and observational and ethnographic analyses.

(a) **In-depth interviews** were conducted with 38 youngsters between the ages of 12-21, between 2000 and 2004. Most of the interviews were conducted face-to-face in the private environment of the adolescents' homes[2], while the interviewer sat together with the youngsters at the teenagers' personal computers. These interviews enabled the interviewer to investigate their activities and uncover their preferred chat rooms, newsgroups, game activities, and more. Interviews were further used as an aid for interpreting observations by use of key informants – the benefits, procedure and reasoning for this research strategy will be discussed further on.

(b) The other research method employed was **observation and analysis** of chat rooms, four Israeli youth-dominated newsgroups (Walla 16 plus minus; Fresh software, Tzahevet and Diablo), personal homepages, and blogs. Online sites were then chosen to correspond to the interviewees' accounts of their net activity. This method is grounded in the natural setting of youth's digital activities and facilitates an in-depth insight into the signs and metaphors of the rich multi-media world of Internet culture (including sounds, colors, verbal style and other features). Furthermore, it involves minimal researcher intervention in the investigated activities. As Internet culture, by nature, is textual and open, this avenue of research is appropriate and serves as an unobtrusive means of investigation (see, for example, on net analysis, Markham, 1998; Baym, 2000; Wilhelm, 2000; Danet, 2001).

Data Analysis

The data were analyzed using categorization techniques (Strauss & Corbin, 1990). The purpose of this analysis is to identify central themes in the data, to find recurrent experiences, and to link different categories to form central themes. The coding process was guided by principles set forth by Glaser and Strauss (1967) for comparative analyses. To ensure reliability, two independent researchers analyzed the entire data set (Strauss & Corbin, 1998). The two sets of categories obtained from the separate analyses were compared and discussed (Marshall & Rossman, 1995). This procedure led to the identification of patterns of youth engagement with trust impediments over the Internet. To further increase reliability, the analysis was reviewed by two independent readers (Marshall & Rossman, 1995). Finally, comparisons were made with the literature on trust building so as to increase validity (Bogdan & Biklen, 1982; Strauss & Corbin, 1998)

Challenges for Research

Two challenges that this design for studying online trust yielded stem from the study of online youth's social and symbolic worlds, as well as from the difficulties of studying the Internet. First, the study of children and youth present an array of dilemmas that invoke classical ethnographic challenges such as the outsider/insider issues and the relationship between researcher and researched (Best, 2006; Lewis, 2004). Accordingly, the present study raised a possible conceptual rift between myself, as an adult researcher, and the worldviews and cultural knowledge of my adolescent subjects. In particular, this gap challenged my ability to interpret the online conceptions and productions (e.g. posted texts, online dialogue, pictures) of youth online. To mitigate this gap the study utilized the aid of interviews and key informants that interpreted the online happenings. This was done face to face with interviewees, or occasionally using an Instant Messenger to continuously communicate with informants and ask them about online happenings (in forums, blogs etc.) I encountered. The second challenge involves the study of the social worlds of the Internet. The study of online trust may present a dilemma for researchers as the ephemeral nature of the Internet, combined with the impediments mentioned in this study may limit researchers' ability to validate their data. This is not to say that traditional interaction may not yield trust-related shortcomings of research. Margaret Mead, for example, may have been fooled by her informants in her face to face engagement (Freeman, 1999). However, the limitations of cyberspace compound the shortcomings familiar to social scientists. In this study an attempt to confront this potential obstacle was provided by triangulating information obtained by face to face interviews, interpretations of key informants together with observations of online activity. This mitigated the problems of reduced presence and the ability to misrepresent and disclose information online, with a wealth of information derived from direct conversations with adolescents. Furthermore, as exploring the activities and symbolic worlds of surfers are expressed visually; the analysis draws upon a semiotic analysis of interface culture and visual representation (see also Johnson, 1997). Danet's pioneering studies on IRC folk art (2001) demonstrates a clear case of ethnographic interpretive observations on virtual groups that based their activities on the exchange of virtual art. In this study, I draw upon Danet's work, but aim to enrich the observational perspective by interviews with informants on their own activities as well as their interpretations of the groups' behavior.

FINDINGS

Observations and conversations with adolescents yielded three intertwined categories of impediments to online trust as well as their enabling aspects:

1. **Lies and Truths** – Dispensing sincere, fabricated and/or false information online.
2. **Anonymity/Disclosure** – Masking and divulging limited information of the surfers' self over the net.
3. **Transparency/Opacity** - Willingness to impart otherwise concealed information about the surfers' virtual assets (e.g. music files, pictures, videos).

1. Lies and Truths over the Internet

A key issue in the study of trust is the question of reliability in relationships. This reliability is in contradistinction to the possibility of lying and dispensing misinformation over the net. Over the Internet, it is difficult, and often impossible, to monitor surfers who post information. For example, cross-dressing is relatively scarce offline, is obviously quite overt in face-to-face interaction, and is prevalent over the web (Danet, 1996). This is compounded by other personal and primordial factors that are blurred, concealed or misrepresented with regard to the surfers' identity (e.g. ethnicity, age, religion). Under these circumstances, suspicion is aroused and the chances for creating trust decrease.

Online observations revealed the ways adolescents view and respond to the prevalence of online lies. For example, on December 15, 2007 a surfer known as "the best D" complained that he had been cheated by a member of the forum known as "Dustin". According to "the best D", "Dustin" offered to upgrade his game avatar on the "Club Penguin" MMORPG and after disclosing his details, "Dustin" appropriated his virtual assets. Following "the best D"'s complaint several members responded and offered their help to restore "the best D" to his former status in the game. Furthermore, they posted several angry messages addressed to "Dustin". For example, this is what "Yoni3000" wrote (15.10.2007):

I would call you a 'f*** up', but I won't descend to your level, and besides I do this [help kids like "the best D"] because of liars like yourself. Stop lying, believe me – I caught bigger liars than you including kids that cannot be persuaded to tell the truth. This is not a problem for me… if you send lots of messages from different [user] names and won't help you so just stop trying to dupe everyone.

"Yoni 3000"'s post formed a well known public response to social deviance by attempting to expose "Dustin"'s transgression and put him, and more importantly, his deceit, to shame. "Yoni 3000" and other surfers tried to compensate his victim ("the best D") ostracize the offender and restore trust to the group. This awareness of lies and deceit continuously recurred among interviewees.

For example in the words of 15-year-old Dan from Tel Aviv:

Q - Do you lie over the Internet?

Dan - I'm one of those people that tell the truth, and I can tell you from experience, that there are lots of liars.

Dan expresses a point of view common to most of my interviewees in that he views other surfers' conduct over the net as untrustworthy.

According to the Pew reports (Lenhart, Rainie & Lewis 2001) about a third of adolescents claimed that they were lied to in Emails or Instant Messengers. This raises the question of how communication can exist in conditions of high suspicion and distortions of reality. This dilemma was presented to me by Tamir, a 14-year-old adolescent from Jerusalem:

Q - How would you describe the trust with your peers online?

Tamir- Not too high; lots of people do not believe [what others are saying]. You say things, and they don't believe you. Sometimes I don't believe them either. This is because you do not activate all your senses; you cannot see them and cannot hear them. The fact that you cannot see them and do not know them makes you not believe them.

Tamir emphasizes that the conditions of cyberspace constitute a space for anonymous interaction with limited sensual exposure. His further comments display his distrust of online relationships:

Tamir - …This is an important point: there is no trust among people who meet over the Internet. There really isn't - even though you can be a real good friend of his. For example, this kid called Liron, all through the summer vacation, everyone was good friends with him; lots of people spoke to him. However, there was a lot of distrust. We spoke to him every day, but still there was distrust. Lots of people used to say to him online - [disparagingly] yeah yeah, sure, sure. There was something that happened to Liron, who is a friend of mine. You see the more you win [online multiplayer] games, the better your score. So this boy had an amazing score, and Liron saw him, and didn't believe it. He kept telling me that somehow he cheated.

Q- Is this guy someone you and Liron consider a friend?

Tamir – Yes, he is.

Q – He is a friend and yet you haven't ever met him?

Tamir - No, everything is online.

Q- Do you know if he is older than you?

Tamir – Yes, he is much older.

Q- Did you ever speak to him over the phone?

Tamir – Sure, there are phone calls back and forth.

Tamir depicts a deviant situation where someone who has little credibility is communicating with a group of computer gamers. Further conversations I held with Tamir and with other gamers made me aware that the question of lies is of particular importance in this field. I learned that by hacking game programs, players can lie to the community, represent themselves as high scorers and thus reinforce their informal status in the community (On the social meanings of cheating in gaming culture and strategies for power leveling see Consalvo, 2007). Furthermore, they can manipulate multiplayer games and corrupt the rules of the game which is premised upon the assumption that all players are on an equal footing. In doing so, these deviant players promote an atmosphere of wrongdoing, particularly among veteran players who place particular value on player abilities and fair competition.

Tamir's account is one that demonstrates the ways suspicion regarding the manipulation of a game threatened the trust relations. Even frequent phone conversations did not rectify this impression and yet the connection was not brought to a close, in spite of the group's unease and disbelief.

Interviewees discussing online lies pointed to strategies used by adolescents to confront the dishonesty over the Internet. A common strategy mentioned was a continuous effort for evaluating the truth. I discussed the question of online lies with Nir, a 14-year-old youth from Haifa:

Q- Do you believe people you meet online?

Nir – Yes, often I believe them. You can tell if a man is telling the truth or not.

Nir feels that he can distinguish between lies and truth-telling over the web. This sense of control and understanding provides him with a sense of security and enables him to develop trust with other web surfers.

In contrast to Nir's intuitive self-reliance, other surfers use online, or offline, friends to help them evaluate the trustworthiness of their interlocutors.

Maya, a 16-year-old girl from Jerusalem told me that she would often spend time in chat rooms with a girl friend.

Q- How do you represent yourselves online?

Maya – Not as ourselves. It depends on how he [the interlocutor] represents himself. If he says he is 18, then we are 17, if he is 25 – we run off.

Maya and her friend relied on each other's discernment to evaluate the information they received from their counterparts and net-suitors.

Interviewees discussed other ways of learning about their fellow surfers. This included verifying the information provided by other surfers and comparing them to the adolescents' established knowledge, holding extended conversations and utilizing other forms of media (e.g. phones, SMS texting). These ways of learning about the trustworthiness of interlocutors were demonstrated in the following cases:

For example verification of the interlocutor's information by cross-checking it with existent, personal knowledge can be found in the words of 15-year-old Zachi from Herzliya:

Q- In what way do people lie?

Zachi – Let me give you an example – my cousin Ben loved to say [online] that he is a girl and ask people all kinds of questions. He would say that he is a girl from New York and ask people how they feel about living in Israel. All kinds of questions like that.

In this case, Zachi describes someone masquerading to experience a different role in life – that of a stranger living in the US. He describes these actions as a prank, or a humorous activity, rather than a destructive act against other surfers or an online community. He does mock the interlocutors that responded to the lie or prank in a naïve manner, and views his cousin's act as skillful and amusing. However, beyond the expressive aspects of Ben's endeavor, we can see how his impersonation enables him to verify the reliability of other surfers. He asks them questions about things he is already knowledgeable about. This enables him to detect discrepancies and determine the others' honesty.

Another way to verify the integrity of surfers is by prolonging the interaction and expanding it to additional channels of communication. This is what Noy, a 16-year-old girl from Tel Aviv said:

I should say that sometimes when you chat with someone, you might want to meet, or date him. A good friend of mine wanted to meet this boy. She really wanted to. Spoke to him for a long time online.

The account by Noy of her friend's phone calls with a virtual suitor enabled her to validate information already obtained online (e.g. gender, age) as well as receive overt and covert information that is not available through text-based interaction (e.g. ethnic accent, voice demeanor).

Subsequent to expanding the means of communication, adolescents provide additional means

of interaction. Yael a 16-year-old girl from Jerusalem said:

Q- Would you provide people with additional means for communicating with you? The people whom you've spoken to on the phone, would you provide them with an email address, your home address or any other means to contact you?

A- If I saw that he was just a j*** I wouldn't give it to him.

The questionable existence of reliability in online relations arises from an inability to enforce any physical or monetary sanctions on the other. This creates a symmetry or situation of equivalence among youth that challenges them to improvise and develop skills for detecting lies, and forging relationships with trustworthy partners over the net. Adolescents described their use of various means for truth detection and verification of information received as well as of assessing the integrity of the interlocutors. These tests enabled them to evaluate the risks involved in interacting with anonymous strangers and to manage their relations.

2. Anonymity/Disclosure

The Internet can be characterized as an innate tension between anonymity and disclosure. On the one hand, the availability of information over the Internet has long been seen as its basic property; on the other hand, the quest for privacy and the ability to have a limited or even masked representation is also seen as a normative option over the net. Critical information that might reveal the surfers' full identity is concealed through use of pseudonyms and avatars while detailed information about the self and the issue at hand is mostly imparted in other ways.

According to Luhmann (1988), familiarity is a key feature for creating trust. This familiarity is threatened in modern society. As trust is nourished by a reciprocal encounter, anonymity can be seen as a characteristic that constitutes a buffer obstructing this engagement. This tension between engagement and disengagement is accentuated online. Over the Internet, anonymity enables sheltering of the self and lying to others, particularly because of the lack of visual traits present in face-to-face relations (e.g. race, gender, age) facial cues, body demeanor and symbolic representation (e.g. clothes, makeup) that communicate much of each party's intentions and social status. This can elevate suspicions among participants in the online surroundings. This would lead to the conclusion that under online conditions the possibilities for creating meaningful and trusting relations would be low.

Among youth, this study revealed the ways an interplay of anonymity and disclosure of personal characteristics served to enhance trust. This disclosure is affected by the sharing of personal information and creating a process of mutual knowledge and understanding. Paradoxically, the impediment of minimized disclosure may be transformed into a trust-building feature as youth find creative ways to impart personal information and foster group discussion and support, while at the same time shelter themselves from criticism and ridicule by not disclosing their full identities.—This can be viewed as the creation of a state of moratorium by youth, as developed by Erikson (1968) and further by Kahane (1997) where a selective permissiveness to divulge limited information, on the part of the virtual peer group, and playful or even occasionally provocative playfulness, on the part of youthful surfers, may lead to deep, if often transitory, commitment on the part of youth (see Erikson, 1968:157; Kahane, 1997:28).

The interplay of anonymity and disclosure can be demonstrated in several illustrative cases. For example, forum websites often enable, and even require registered members to display a picture and provide some basic information (e.g. age, place of residence etc). This information is posted alongside the text of the speaker, and implies a stable persona that represents the surfer. Figure 1 demonstrates a typical way of public disclosure on a youth-dominated gamer forum (posted March 3, 2009) that involves a pseudonym ('R4ZoR'), a monster avatar-figure and the number of posts (9520) submitted by 'R4ZoR' on this forum. 'R4ZoR' further states that he is from: Max Payne 3, referring to a computer game, rather than a place.

In this case, 'R4ZoR'' demonstrates a feature commonly used by surfers in general, and adolescent Internet users in particular, by selecting an avatar that is representative of themselves and shows them as having a stable and unchanging persona within the specific website. Here 'R4ZoR' uses humor to complement his persona, thereby creating a friendly and lighthearted representation of himself and inviting future interaction (Golan, 2009).

'R4ZoR''s case is one that I have often encountered online and that complements other studies (Danet, 2001; Blais, 2001) where the self is represented by a stable set of signs (e.g. avatars, pseudonyms) that combine with the persona's demeanor and behavior (e.g. humorous, aggressive, considerate). In spite of the surfer's anonymity, his/her nature is revealed to the peer group and a sense of familiarity is fostered. It is this familiarity that establishes a sense of trust (Luhmann, 1988).

In addition to the issue of familiarity, youth addressed the anonymity/disclosure impediment by sharing personal information and in turn generating intimacy. An example of the sharing of sentiments may be seen in requests for advice in romance and exposing personal concerns as demonstrated by "Yuval the lover" posted on a young people's Israeli newsgroup (Walla 16 plus/minus 5/3/2002):

I am a student in the 11th grade in [the town of] Beer Sheva and I am looking for a serious [meaningful] relationship. I worked at the "Burger Ranch" for a while until I left (I quit). While I worked I gained a lot of weight and am very fat now. Another thing that makes things tough for me is that I became

Figure 1. Personal information posted on Israeli gamer forum

more religious and I now keep kosher and observe the Sabbath. Up till now I could not find anyone who would be right for me. Can girls be flexible and accept a boyfriend that doesn't look so hot and observes the Sabbath and can't go out on Friday nights? With regard to character, I think I am a mature person. I am pretty sensitive; however I have a lot to give. Thanks in advance to whomever will assist me.

Yuval

PS the issue is very serious!!! Please address appropriately.

"Yuval the lover" describes a personal issue, which vexes him as an adolescent. Rather than addressing specific dating newsgroups, Yuval chooses to address a newsgroup centered on his peer age-group, with the intention of obtaining advice and emotional support. Shortly after his posting, a girl named Amalia replied (8/3/02):

For every pot there is a cover [colloquial Israeli idiom]

You'll find someone like yourself, who is traditional and doesn't go out on Friday nights. In addition, I am sure that aside from all your shortcomings I am sure there are some advantageous points. With regard to your weight – there are plenty of girls that prefer guys who are a bit "heavy". It may be that for the time being you may have difficulties finding such a girl, a kind that understands that a connection isn't based on external appearances and going out on Friday nights but reaching out for a deep connection.

Amalia's response, as are other responses to Yuval, is empathic to his situation. She does not offer him a specific plan or avenue of conduct (i.e. addressing a therapist or dating network) but offers her emotional support.

Yuval's emotional exposure is directed at creating a sympathetic response. The exposure of a weakness is a sensitive and familiar issue for adolescents, and the response of other surfers, headed by Amalia, establishes a sense of obligation and trust towards the intimate account exposed. The climate of acceptance of weaknesses and supporting the other parallels the dynamics created in support groups and generates trust among surfers of this specific forum.

The case of Yuval represents other cases of self-disclosure that once again seem familiar, yet do so by focusing on sensitive and intimate information that strengthens online bonds.

To sum up, youth have countered the impediment of anonymity and disclosure with forms of enhancing familiarity, either by creating stable relationships, albeit semi-camouflaged ones and by forming intimacy. Paradoxically, anonymity over the Internet facilitates greater self-disclosure and familiarity, all of which generate virtual intimacy and trust among youth.

This is achieved by concealing critical information that might reveal the surfers' full identity, while imparting detailed information about the self and the issue at hand. This partial anonymity stimulates a meaningful interaction as the adolescent feels that she/he is not fully exposed to mockery and personal contempt, while at the same time the young person has access to meaningful dialogue and support.

3. Transparency/Opacity

In organized social institutions, transparency is considered a key form of creating trust (Jahansoozi, 2006). The issue of transparency has been studied in various contexts and disciplines. Scholars focusing on organizational studies frequently use this term to emphasize aspects of transparency in regard to decision making and sharing information within the organization and beyond its perimeters. Hence, transparency is referred to as an effort to publicly reveal internal information of the organization (especially monetary issues).

Concurrently with the aspects emphasized by organization researchers, the psychological legacy of the term emphasizes transparency as a constructed bias or "illusion" – a tendency for people to overestimate the extent to which others can discern their internal states (Gilovich, Medvec and Savitsky, 1998).

Among CMC researchers the emphasis on transparency has been on the ability of the interface to enable its users to maximize their understanding of the applications' capabilities and the affordances of available information (in terms of the programs interface and code, for example) (Begole et al., 1997)

In spite of their different disciplinary origins, these definitions are all means of constructing alliances and fostering trust. In this paper I wish to draw on the psychological and organizational studies and add an interpersonal dimension to the original CMC definitions. Here I refer to it as the deliberate attempt to move from a secretive or opaque relationship to one that encourages open access to information, which ultimately creates a higher level of trust among stakeholders. However, over the Internet, transparency can be viewed as a key impediment to creating trust as the surfer does not know what his online peer's assets are. This is to say that there is little way of knowing if other surfers have different abilities (e.g. bandwidth, computer virtuosity), knowledge and digital goods (e.g. music, movies, pictures), which they are concealing and refrain from sharing. Under these circumstances, surfers find it difficult to assess the outcome of their interaction, and may be hesitant to engage in a meaningful exchange and form a trustworthy relationship.

One way of achieving transparency is through peer-to-peer file-sharing programs. This refers to the distribution of electronically stored information such as games, movie files, computer programs and hacking devices. Adolescents informed me that they use popular programs for this file-sharing (e.g. emule, Kazaa) and other means (such as the mIRC dcc options, or exchange of files using public storage domains such as Rapidshare or Megaupload while posting materials on Blogs and other electronic message boards).

Yossi, a 17-year-old teenager from Jerusalem discussed his frequent use of these file-sharing programs:

Today it [acquiring songs and computer files] is my most prevalent use of the Internet. I download songs, software, games...

On these file-sharing programs surfers enable other users to browse through their virtual collections (of music, movies, etc.) and to download items of their choice. This form of transparency is limited by the scope of assets, as the user may limit sharing to a specific niche (library or sub-library on her/his personal computer), as well as defining the rate of exchange (upload speed).

In addition to transparency that is obtained by using software that encourages sharing, among youth, a starting point for achieving a more personal or community-oriented transparency over the Internet can be found when approaching a specific community (such as the fans' or gamers' websites observed in this study). First, these sites are youthful in the sense that the surfers know from previous experience, from friends' recommendations as well as the discourse relayed in these public spaces, that they limit themselves to a large number of surfers of a similar age group. This ensures, to some extent, a similar social background and set of interests (e.g. connection to the family, army service, school, attitudes towards the opposite sex). Second, the Israeli online setting, bounded by the Hebrew language, ensures a similar background in terms of nationality and cultural acquaintance. In this sense, participation in a public space ensures a sense of belonging to an 'imagined community' to use Anderson's term (1991).

However, taking part in an "imagined community" of one's peers is not enough to dissipate the transparency impediment. The symbolic space promotes further trust towards each other by instigating acts of generosity and altruism. For example, the dissemination of information about multiplayer games being started up, the launch of a new and improved version of current software, hacking tips, and so on can all be considered actions that foster transparency and therefore generate trust.

To demonstrate, on the 'Tzahevet' forum that focuses on fans of a popular Israeli basketball team, Maccabi Tel Aviv, two participants who call themselves 'Nir' and 'Alona H'maximona'

posted some virtual wallpapers[3] for members of the group that were in fact modified pictures of their venerated players (figure 2).

After displaying these wallpapers, a significant number of respondents wrote comments like:

- 'OFIR@' Wrote: "wowwwwww, what great wallpapers, thanks Alona and Nir" (August 9, 2004).
- 'Galequiem' wrote: "wowwwwww, they are all beautiful (August 5, 2004).
- Avner wrote: "Good for you! Two Pistols!" [idiom meaning "you are extremely talented"] (July 26,2004).
- Noam wrote: "Wow Wow Wowwww! It came out great Nir and Alona. It's so great to see these things and be proud that I know you. (June 15, 2004)
- Avi wrote: "Good for you! Straight to my computer. You really did well ☺ (June15, 2004)

These short comments of support from the community accentuate and promote not only the created object, but point out the talent of its creators, and express gratitude for their act of revealing their virtual assets and sharing them. 'Alona H'maximona' and 'Nir' strengthened their personal position in the community, and in their act of giving, fostered a reciprocal system that is non-personal per se, but nevertheless generated a 'community spirit', that inclined towards a generally positive disposition of giving. By the act of giving not only have 'Alona H'maximona' and 'Nir' participated in an act of gifting (on gift giving over the net see Kollock, 1999) but have conveyed a sense of transparency towards the group, revealing the virtual artifact they created, and implying the nature of online possessions that they are producing and are willing to share with the group.

The challenge of transparency continues to persist among online surfers. In face-to-face interaction, symbols communicate social status and imply aspects of transparency. However, symbols

Figure 2. Wallpaper posted on a fan forum ('Tsahevet')

that represent a person's assets are lacking online. Surfers do not know the body of 'virtual wealth' that their interlocutors have and are willing to share. Adolescents demonstrated how they are avid collectors and contributors to this shared wealth, expose their knowledge, share their virtual creations and either directly or covertly disclose the virtual assets and display positive intentions of giving and committing towards the virtual group. In an environment that does not require transparency, and may facilitate opacity, youth-controlled sharing of information and virtual assets accentuate the meaning of this endeavor and foster a sense of trust among their peers.

CONCLUSION

The sociological legacy of trust largely focuses on the social conditions that enable relations. It demonstrates the process of institutionalizing trust by exploring the transformation from interpersonal to generalized trust in social arrangements that facilitate its emergence (e.g. in a system of laws, moral precepts, and cultured based norms) (Sztomka, 2008). As an environment that is ubiquitous and ever changing, the Internet poses a threat to surfers as it facilitates the encounter between strangers whose interests, intentions

and capabilities are unknown. The emergence of trust in such an environment seems unlikely, and is infrequent among many (such as the elderly), thus creating what can be seen as a digital trust gap. In this sense, much of the digital gap that is widely explored by researchers and policymakers can be seen as stemming from a trust impediment, rather than an economic or educational variance. The present study uncovered three intertwined impediments to online trust, and the ways that youth approached these challenges. (1) Lies and truths. (2) Anonymity/Disclosure (3) Transparency/Opacity. All three describe the disclosure and concealment of different aspects of the surfers' digital worlds. The first two can be viewed as an active effort of the surfer to unveil information that has been partially concealed by others. It can be seen as stemming from youth's view of cybersociety as a sphere of danger and distrust. In this perilous space, adolescents improvise strategies to mitigate these threats. In contrast, the third impediment of transparency/opacity may be viewed as a proactive effort of trust building. In a voluntary act of disclosure youth perpetuate a generalized sense of trust, cultivate the common good and advance community solidarity.

Adolescents accept the impediments of the Internet and use them to forge a playful and expressive sphere where they use lies, masks, partial disclosure of personal representation, virtual goods and ultimately generate trust. In this sense the Internet can be seen as a space of moratorium where youth can experiment in trust building with other surfers, and engage in trial and error with tempered and calculated risk taking. Hence, experimenting with trust building over the Internet can be seen as a form of self-socialization for social skills, where the adolescent may perpetuate or disengage her/his relationship at any time. This moratorium is constantly threatened by various agents aimed at regulating the conduct of surfers in general, and that of youth in particular.

Occasionally state initiatives are publicly discussed regarding the question of "securing the web". Policymakers express their concern for the misgivings that occur online and propose ways of expanding or coercing disclosure and transparency of net participants thus enabling a more monitored and secure surfing experience. These ideas may contribute to facilitate aspects of the Internet (e.g. e-commerce) yet may infringe not only on democratic ideals such as privacy and free speech, but bears significance to the very charismatic allure of the Internet, particularly among youth. In his study, Kahane points to an inherent conflict between youth and adults with regard to control/autonomy in socializing organizations (Kahane, 1975). Whereas an increase in youth autonomy may lead to delinquent and anti-social behavior, its existence can be seen as a fundamental condition for the formation of meaningful relations. The ways youth autonomously explore the Internet and actively negotiate their relations with other surfers lend to the strength of their new found connections, adds to their skills for mobilizing social capital and fostering trust with others. Adult supported monitoring, as well as perceptions of the Internet as an untrustworthy space can lead to a safer environment, yet may impede on the benefits of the Internet for youngsters, as well as its charismatic appeal.

Exploring the impediments and dilemmas faced by youth while approaching this new medium, unveiled the ways that youngsters, as digital natives navigate within the social worlds of cyberspace and find new sources of social (friendships, communities), cybernetic (e.g. files, games) and cultural capital (online habitus, in Bourdieu's terms) through confronting challenges and improvising ways the formation of online trust relations. As they grow into society, perhaps these digital natives may instill their social sensibilities and further advance a cybernetic culture that will approximate some of the goals predicted by the utopic visionaries of the Internet.

In this study an exploration of online youth has fostered the convergence between theories of trust building, Internet interaction and youth activity. The sociological legacy of trust emphasized the social conditions that fostered the emergence of trust. These studies discussed the significance of social institutions, norms and the law to foster and maintain trust building. This tradition has been revisited by Jarvenpaa, Tractinsky & Vitale (2000) that have studied online trust in e-commerce and shown how equivalent mechanisms of trust building have been established, and further reified by Silverstone (1999). In the present study, rather then viewing trust as a product of establishing order, this study points to the ways that the Internet facilitates the formation of trust through playful, and improvisational behavior. In youth's online experience, the formation of trust can be seen as stemming from moratorium and autonomy, rather then regulation, institutionalization and control. In this sense, the current study may enable us to re-examine the social circumstances that foster trust, and invite further research in additional social and cultural settings.

REFERENCES

Anderson, B. (1991). *Imagined communities: Reflections on the origin and spread of nationalism*. London: Verso.

Barber, B. (1983). *The Logic and Limits of Trust*. Piscataway, NJ: Rutgers University Press.

Baym, N. K. (2000). *Tune in log on: soaps, fandom and online community*. Thousand Oaks, CA: Sage.

Begole, J., Struble, C. A., Shaffer, C. A., & Smith, R. B. (1997). Transparent Sharing of Java Applets: A Replicated Approach. In G. Robinson, & C. Schmandt (Ed.), *Proceedings of the 10th annual ACM symposium on User interface software and technology*, Banff, Alberta, Canada, October 14 - 17, 1997 (pp. 55-64). New York: ACM Press

Beninger, J. R. (1987). Personalization of mass media and the growth of pseudo-community. *Communication Research*, *14*, 352–371. doi:10.1177/009365087014003005

Best, A. L. (2006). Introduction. In Best, A. L. (Ed.), *Representing Youth: Methodological Issues in Critical Youth Studies* (pp. 1–38). New York: NYU Press.

Blais, D. (2001). 'Walla chat': An Ethnographic View of an Israeli Internet Chat Site [in Hebrew]. *Kesher*, *30*, 77–92.

Bogdan, R. C., & Biklen, S. K. (1982). *Qualitative Research for Education: An Introduction to Theory and Methods* (2nd ed.). Boston: Allyn and Bacon.

Cleary, M., & Stokes, S. C. (2006). *Democracy and the culture of skepticism: Political trust in Argentina and Mexico*. New York: Russell Sage Foundation.

Consalvo, M. (2007). *Cheating: Gaining Advantage in Videogames*. Cambridge, MA: MIT Press.

Danet, B. (1996). Text as mask: Gender, play and performance on the Internet. In Jones, S. G. (Ed.), *Cybersociety 2.0: Revisiting computer-mediated communication and community* (pp. 122–138). Thousand Oaks, CA: Sage.

Danet, B. (2001). *Cyberpl@y*. London: Berg.

Durkheim, E. (1949). *The Division of Labor in Society*. Glencoe, IL: Free Press.

Dutton, W. H., & Shepherd, A. (2006). Trust in the Internet as an experience technology. *Information Communication and Society*, *9*, 433–451. doi:10.1080/13691180600858606

Eisenstadt, S. N. (1974). Friendship and the structure of trust and solidarity in society. In Leyton, E. (Ed.), *The compact: Selected dimensions of friendship* (pp. 138–145). Toronto, Canada: University of Toronto Press.

Erikson, E. H. (1968). *Identity: Youth and Crisis*. New York: Norton.

Freeman, D. (1999). *The Fateful Hoaxing of Margaret Mead: A Historical Analysis of Her Samoan Research*. Boulder, CO: Westview Press.

Fukuyama, F. (1995). *Trust: The social virtues and the creation of prosperity*. New York: The Free Press.

Gambetta, D. (1988). Mafia: the Price of Distrust. In Gambetta, D. (Ed.), *Trust: Making and breaking cooperative relations* (pp. 158–175). New York: Basil Blackwell.

Giddens, A. (1990). *The Consequences of Modernity*. Stanford, CA: Stanford University Press.

Gilovich, T., Savitsky, K., & Medvec, V. H. (1998). The Illusion of Transparency: Biased Assessments of Others' Ability to Read One's Emotional States. *Journal of Personality and Social Psychology*, *75*(2), 332–346. doi:10.1037/0022-3514.75.2.332

Glaser, B. G., & Strauss, A. (1967). *The Discovery of Grounded Theory: Strategic for Qualitative Research*. Chicago: Aldine.

Golan, O. (2010). Symbols and Language of Youth on the Internet: Rhetoric, idioms and icons [in Hebrew]. *Israeli Sociology*, *11*(2), 389–416.

Hecht, J. (2001). Digital Youth. *Mashabei Enosh*, *167*, 38–50.

Heim, M. (1992). The Erotic Ontology of Cyberspace. In Benedikt, M. (Ed.), *Cyberspace: First steps* (pp. 59–80). Cambridge, MA: MIT Press.

Holloway, S. L., & Valentine, G. (2003). *Cyberkids: Children in the Information Age*. London: Routledge.

Jahansoozi, J. (2006). Organization-stakeholder relationships: exploring trust and transparency. *Journal of Management Development*, *25*(10), 942–955. doi:10.1108/02621710610708577

Jarrett, R. L., Sullivan, P. J., & Watkins, N. D. (2005). Developing social capital through participation in organized youth programs: Qualitative insights from three programs. *Journal of Community Psychology*, *33*, 41–55. doi:10.1002/jcop.20038

Jarvenpaa, S. L., Tractinsky, N., & Vitale, M. (2000). Consumer Trust in an Internet store. *Information Technology and Management*, *1*, 45–71. doi:10.1023/A:1019104520776

Johnson, S. (1997). *Interface Culture: How New Technology Transforms the Way we Create and Communicate*. New York: Basic Books.

Johnsson-Smaragdi, U. (2001). Media use styles among the young. In Livingston, S., & Bovill, M. (Eds.), *Children and their changing media environment: A European comparative study* (pp. 113–140). London: Lawrence Erlbaum Associates Publishers.

Kahane, R. (1975). Informal Youth Organizations: A General Model. *Sociological Inquiry*, *45*(4), 17–28. doi:10.1111/j.1475-682X.1975.tb00345.x

Kahane, R. (1997). *The Origins of Postmodern Youth*. Berlin: De Gruyter.

Kendall, L. (2002). *Hanging out in the virtual pub: Masculinities and relationships online*. Berkeley, CA: University of California Press.

Kiesler, S., Siegel, J., & McGuire, T. W. (1984). Social Psychological aspects of computer-mediated communication. *The American Psychologist*, *39*(10), 1123–1134. doi:10.1037/0003-066X.39.10.1123

Kollock, P., & Smith, M. A. (1999). Communities in Cyberspace. In Smith, M. A., & Kollock, P. (Eds.), *Communities in Cyberspace* (pp. 3–28). London: Routledge.

Lenhart, A., Rainie, L., & Lewis, O. (2001). Teenage Life Online. *Pew Internet & American Life Project Reports*. Retrieved April 11, 2009, from http://www.pewinternet.org/pdfs/PIP_Teens_Report.pdf

Lewis, V. (2004). Doing Research with Children and Young People: An Introduction. In Fraser, S., Lewis, V., Ding, S., Kellett, M., & Robinson, C. (Eds.), *Doing Research with Children and Young People* (pp. 1–11). London: Sage.

Livingstone, S. (2002). *Young people and new media: Childhood and the changing media environment*. London: Sage.

Luhmann, N. (1988). Familiarity, confidence, trust: Problems and alternatives. In Gambetta, D. (Ed.), *Trust: Making and breaking cooperative relations* (pp. 94–107). New York: Basil Blackwell.

Markham, A. (1998). *Life online: Researching real experience in virtual space*. London: Sage.

Marshall, C., & Rossman, G. (1995). *Designing Qualitative Research*. Thousand Oaks, CA: Sage Publications.

Muller, E. N., & Seligson, M. A. (1994). Civic culture and democracy: The question of causal relations. *The American Political Science Review*, *88*, 635–652. doi:10.2307/2944800

Neyland, D. (2007). Achieving Transparency: The Visible, Invisible and Divisible in Academic Accountability Networks. *Organization*, *14*(4), 499–516. doi:10.1177/1350508407078050

Parks, M. R., & Floyd, K. (1996). Making Friends in Cyberspace. *The Journal of Communication*, *46*(1). doi:10.1111/j.1460-2466.1996.tb01462.x

Raymond, E. S. (2001). *The cathedral and the bazaar: Musings on Linux and Open Source by an accidental revolutionary*. Cambridge, MA: O'Reilly.

Rideout, V., Roberts, D. F., & Foehr, U. G. (2005). Generation M: Media in the lives of 8-18 Year-Olds. *Kaiser Family Foundation*. Retrieved April 11, 2009, from http://www.kff.org/entmedia/upload/Generation-M-Media-in-the-Lives-of-8-18-Year-olds.pdf

Silverstone, R. (1999). *Why Study the Media?* London: Sage.

Stoll, C. (1995). *Silicon Snake Oil*. New York: Doubleday.

Strauss, A., & Corbin, J. (1990). *Basics of qualitative research: Grounded theory procedures and techniques*. London: Sage Publications.

Strauss, A. L., & Corbin, J. (1998). *Basics of qualitative research: Techniques and procedures for developing grounded theory* (2nd ed.). Thousand Oaks, CA: Sage.

Sztompka, P. (1999). *Trust: A sociological theory*. Cambridge, UK: Cambridge University Press.

Sztompka, P. (2008). Trust Review of Democracy and the Culture of Skepticism: Political Trust in Argentina and Mexico by M. Cleary & S. C. Stokes. *International Sociology, 23*(2), 215–234. doi:10.1177/0268580907086377

Taylor, P. A. (1999). *Hackers: Crime in the Digital Sublime*. London: Routledge. doi:10.4324/9780203201503

Thurlow, C., & McKay, S. (2003). Communication Technologies in Adolescence. *Journal of Language and Social Psychology, 22*(1), 94–103. doi:10.1177/0261927X02250060

Wilhelm, A. G. (2000). *Democracy in the digital age: Challenges to political life in cyberspace*. New York: Routledge.

Wilson, J. M., Straus, S. G., & McEvily, B. (2006). All in Due Time: The Development of Trust in Computer Mediated and Face-to-Face Teams. *Organizational Behavior and Human Decision Processes, 99*, 16–33. doi:10.1016/j.obhdp.2005.08.001

Yamagishi, T., & Yamagishi, M. (1994). Trust and Commitment in the United States and Japan. *Motivation and Emotion, 18*, 129–166. doi:10.1007/BF02249397

ENDNOTES

[*] I wish to thank the Israeli Internet Association (ISOC-IL) as well as the Israel Foundation Trustees for financial assistance towards the completion of this article and the Levi Eshkol Institute for Social, Economic and Political Research in Israel. I also wish to thank Ori Eyal and Batia Siebzehner for their many helpful comments, as well as Sandra Fine for her editing assistance and important remarks.

[1] The term itself has engendered much debate among scholars who discuss its fundamental nature and relationship with society at large. For a good example of conceptual discussions of the term see Luhmann, 1988.

[2] A few (5) were conducted in other venues including "public zones" (e.g. coffee shop, burger bar).

[3] Wallpaper refers to a graphics file that can be displayed in computer applications behind or around the main dialogue boxes, working display areas, etc. for decoration. It should be noted that wallpaper choice and collection is a common activity among net surfers in general, and youth in particular, who swap and often change their choices for display. This is a feature that has been insufficiently studied as a personalized object of self expression.

Chapter 7
The Role of Trust in Interactive High Tech Work:
The Case of Freelance Web–Designers in NYC

Matthias Thiemann
Columbia University, USA

ABSTRACT

With regard to the spread of self-presentations of individuals and small firms on the internet, this chapter inquires into the role of trust and trust-building techniques of freelance web-designers in spreading the application of high-technology to end-consumers. Engendering relationships of trust is a predominant necessity for the freelancers in a market lacking structural assurances, making that group an ideal object of study for trust-enhancing strategies in client interaction. Methodologically, it proposes a way to study the adaptation of entrepreneurs to the requirements of trust, enlarging the focus on dramaturgic action of the trust-taker in exchange situation to markets for cooperation, in which cooperative experiences are a major trust-building factor. The analysis suggests that in those markets dramaturgical action is not only directed at clients but also at the referral networks in which they are embedded in, having important repercussions for the negotiating power of freelancers.

INTRODUCTION

In the 1990s, in theoretical and empirical work on developments of modernity, the topic of trust occupied center stage. During that period, several authors detected a decline in trust and claimed a potential malfunctioning of government (Putnam, 1995) or a threat to beneficial cooperation that needs trust (Misztal, 1996; Sztompka, 1999). As Cook, Hardin

and Levi (2005, pp.190-196) show, much of this debate has overstated the importance of trust in and for modern societies, given the increase of complexity that necessitates the substitution of trust with other measures less dependent on interpersonal relations (Luhmann 1967,1979). The legal and governmental institutions as well as professional codes and self-binding documents free us from much personal scrutiny by those with whom we are cooperating. However, in this enlarging modernity of abstracted relationships with the other based on standardized

DOI: 10.4018/978-1-61520-901-9.ch007

procedures and institutions that lessen the danger inherent in interaction, we can discern new countervailing trends. One of those is the emergence of an increasingly unregulated sector of service-workers, who as independent contractors offer their services and make their livings on their own. Here, the necessity for the monitoring of quality is transferred from the organization that offers its services to the customer who needs to assess the qualities of the independent contractor. This now poses at least as much a problem to these independent contractors as to their customers. In order to maintain a steady stream of work and income, contractors do need to bridge the gap of a lack of institutionalized trust (Zucker, 1986) as regards their qualifications, quality of work and price that come with a largely unregulated market for their services. Cooperation and exchange in these markets both entail risk and necessitate trust on the part of the principal (client) regarding the agent (freelancer). Principals are uncertain about the capabilities and the intentions of the freelancer as well as vulnerable, because money and time are at stake. These markets for interactive service work therefore seem quite appropriate as a means of studying the way the necessities of trust and trustworthiness structure the behavior and interaction of economic agents that are directly dependent on succeeding in generating trust.

Trust is a reflexive process in which trust needs to be actively built up. With that in mind, the questions pursued in this chapter are: how do freelancers overcome the gap of trust that resides in an unregulated exchange structure in which institutionalized signs of trustworthiness as well as commonly established price markers are missing? How do they reduce the perception of vulnerability of the trust-giver while, at the same time, decreasing the uncertainty regarding their ability for successful cooperation and their benevolence regarding their clients? The problematic circularity of this particular market makes entry into new information circuits an important concern for the freelancers. The importance of trust in this market

is heightened when one takes into account that freelancers, as well, face the risk of being taken advantage of by their clients through theft of ideas (Fenwick, 2006) and refusal to pay. Not only do clients need to assess trustworthiness, also freelancers do in order to avoid unpleasant surprises.

When we frame the problem of trust in terms of principal agent theory (see Dasgupta, 1988), we see the importance of reputation to overcome a lack of trust, the importance of signals to separate trustworthy from untrustworthy agents (Spencer, 1974) and the power of the shadow of the future in transforming non-cooperative equilibria into cooperative ones as concepts at hand for the researcher. In the research on trust in the game theoretical literature, however, one finds relatively little on the role of networks and information flow or on the role of cooperation. This chapter focuses on the constraints and adaptations of rational actors to the conditions of freelance work that are given by huge information asymmetries and risks on both sides. In the theory of repeated games and reputation, a certain degree of continuous interaction of different actors or their observability by an exterior third is assumed, guiding the rational decision-making of actors (e.g. Gibbons, 2001). Rather than taking these constellations as a given, the actors under observation struggle in order to perpetuate relationships and to turn at least some of their relationships into reoccurring ones and to embed themselves in a stable network of information flow, in which their respective reputations become valuable assets.[1]

THE RESEARCH ON TRUST-SHIFTING FROM THE TRUST-GIVER TO THE TRUST-TAKER

Trust is an "elusive concept" (Gambetta, 1988, p. ix), which stems from its manifold usage in common language. In Luhmann's fundamental essay (1967, 1979) on trust he grounds trust in the necessity to cope with the freedom of will of the other, making trust an indispensable element of human life. Trust is understood as a functional answer to the fact that a person can neither entirely control an other's action nor does he or she even have a base for such control based on a common understanding of the situation, as the other's wishes and attitudes remain opaque. It is in the social interaction that actors develop a shared understanding of the social situation and the other's values. As these starting assumptions clarify, an approach of "calculative trust" (Williamson, 1993, p. 453) cannot fully capture the problems inherent in the moment of trusting. Rather, trust should be understood as a "tranquilizer in social relations enabling the trust-giver to remain calm despite the uncontrollable freedom of action of the trust-taker" (Beckert, 2005, p.18).

To act on trust exposes one to the potentially harmful action of others that cannot be controlled and therefore requires the suspension of distrust. It is useful to see trust as a continuous variable, where initial trust can rather be described as "conditional trust" (Jones and George, 1998, pp. 535-536) depending on continued signs of shared interpretive schemes of the situation and mutual role taking, which can then either evolve into unconditional trust or devolve into distrust. Factors that constrain the occurrence of conditional trust for newly forming business relationships regard the size of the stake in an interaction (vulnerability), the uncertainty regarding the benevolence, ability and integrity of the other (Heimer, 2001; Mayer et al, 1995; Cook et al., 2005, p.6) as well as the structural assurances (e.g. regulations, guarantees, legal recourse) that the context provides in which the interaction takes place (McKnight et al., 1998, pp. 479-480). These factors interact with the disposition to trust, which depends on individual and on situational characteristics. Regarding the latter, certain situations such as door-to door sales marketing are entered into with distrust, whereas a social gathering of friends and acquaintances is more prone to initial trust even in newly forming relationships.

The research on the trust-giver's decision making process and the factors in her/his decision to trust clarify the obstacles for entering into a business relationship which freelancers need to overcome. One branch of the research on trust has focused on the systemic antecedents for trust to happen. Every time interactions are socially fixed by programs or rules and accompanied by taken-for-granted accounts (thus institutionalized), trust is almost automatic since "it may be literally unthinkable to act otherwise" (Zucker, 1986, p. 58). Structural assurances beliefs (McKnight et al., 1998, p. 479) are almost entirely missing for web-design freelancers in New York City, as there are no professional codes or regulations as to what web-design is or who is allowed to call himself a web-designer. This lack of institutionalization of roles comes with a lack of scripts of interaction that can guide interaction, such as those for guiding doctor-patient encounters.

As Heimer (2001) has pointed out, vulnerability and uncertainty are the two core conditions of the trust giver in the moment of trust giving. Any process that invokes trust needs to reduce uncertainty and to decrease vulnerability in order to increase the chances for entrusted action to occur. One way of reducing uncertainty, while only slowly increasing the vulnerability of trust givers lies in gradually increasing the stakes (Luhmann, 1979, p. 41), thus allowing the trust-giver to get to know the characteristics of the trust-taker before having too high stakes. However, for many of the freelancers interviewed, many customers were not returning and/or came with "major" requests right from the beginning. This peculiarity stems from the specifics of their work: when building web-sites mostly for individuals and small businesses the first job often already involves the building of a site. Due to this fact, the principle of gradualness does not play out on the individual level, but as this chapter tries to show on the level of the networks of acquaintances, within which the reputation of a freelancer "travels."

Given the distrust freelancers need to overcome in initiating collaboration, the question emerges whether or not freelancers actively attempt to overcome the structural distrust inherent in their position in an unstructured market. In this context, one can ask with Moellering (2006, p.74) if one can conceive of a "kind of trust entrepreneur who actively shapes context in a trust-enhancing manner?" Recent work on signaling in trust games, which naturally pays more attention to the trust-taker, should allow us to appreciate better the specific conditions for generating trust which these actors are facing and how they creatively adapt to them. In an innovative article, Bacharach and Gambetta (2001) propose to analyze the trust game in terms of signaling theory, treating "trust as the product of underlying trust-worthy making character features" (p. 150). They postulate a potential difference of raw pay-offs (the pay-offs of short-term rational actors) and all-in pay offs, which transform pay-offs through specific qualities of the trust-taker, as for example moral guilt when defrauding other people, honesty or a long-term perspective.

These features of the trust-taker are conceptualized as *krypta* (the desired qualities of a trust-taker, which are unfortunately indiscernible to the trust-giver) and *manifesta*, signals that indicate that the signal-emitter has such *krypta*, which are the only observables in the game. The problem thus is shifted to a "secondary problem of trust" in which trust-givers must judge if signals of the trust-taker actually can be trusted. Actors of a malignant nature who intend not to cooperate will have every incentive to emit *manifesta* that signal trustworthiness, even though they do not possess the respective *krypta* if the production of *manifesta* is cheaper than the expected pay-off from the defected cooperation. Trust-givers are confronted with a "mimic-beset trust game." The important practical question is if a trust-giver can trust this sign of a *krypton*, and only once this question is resolved, the primary trust game can

be decided. *Manifesta* on which to build one's positive decision rationally are then those that cost little to the honest agent and much to the dishonest trust-taker.

The great breakthrough of these two authors lies in focusing the attention on the assessment of "signaling management strategies" (ibid) of the potential trust-takers by the trust-givers. Their allusion to "semiotic warfare regarding the values of signs" (p. 167) already brings into the picture the action of the signalers; however, their focus still mostly lies with the decision of the trust-giver. Jens Beckert (2005) shifts this focus and proclaims that the "functioning of trust in markets has not been properly understood" (p. 5) due to a lack of attention to the actions of the potential trust-taker:

Yet that is precisely what represents an essential element for overcoming possible exchange barriers in markets. The operational principles of trust are only revealed through the study of the performative acts of the trust-taker, with which he tries to produce the impression of trust-worthiness. (ibid)

The shift of attention for Beckert can be grounded in the insight that "the trust taker always has an interest in entering the trust game, independent of the intention of defection or cooperation" (p. 9), which leads him to state that "assuming that the trust-taker is aware of this centrality in the game, one can hypothesize that such games are primarily initiated by the trust taker" (ibid). His approach focuses on the production of the willingness to trust by the trust-taker and therefore his investment into signaling strategies that make him appear trustworthy. Dramaturgical means of self-presentation are used to convey authenticity, the identity of manifesta and krypta, in order to generate the advance concession of the trust-giver. The characteristics of markets he enumerates that are boosting the importance of such dramaturgical action are remarkably fitting for web-design in New York City. When asymmetric information between principal and agent (trust-taker) regarding the quality and value of goods is given, coupled with the capacity of the trust giver to choose between different offers, the importance of trust-management increases (ibid, p.22). Beckert's argument for the increased role of trust in exchange relationships is their rising complexity and flexibility. Interactive service work's complexity however derives from the fact that the exchange relation is at the same time a relation of cooperation in which the product to be exchanged does not yet exist at the moment of initial interaction.

To grasp the problems of trust inherent in such a relationship analytically, one needs a more nuanced picture of problems of trust in cooperation than the one provided by Beckert and most economic theorists. The simple dichotomy of cooperative and non-cooperative behavior used to classify the risks for potential exchange needs to be deepened for actual cooperation. Rather than separating the problem of pricing from the problem of opportunistic behavior (ibid, p.21), one needs to consider moments in which both fall together. The risk of overcharging that only emerges in the cooperation due to hourly billing can hardly be grouped into the category of non-cooperative behavior. Trust and its build-up are not only threatened by non-cooperative, defecting behavior, but also by the danger of overcharging and misrecognition of desires of the client in the process of production. The significance of reputation and relationships of trust characteristic for such an embedded market (see Granovetter 1985, p. 490) is intensified through the aspect of creative cooperation in interactive service work which gives special importance to the modality of producer-client interaction. "As the client sees in interactive service work not only the product, but also the production, he also sees the producer. Production and producer therefore become in tendency an aspect of the product itself" (Voswinkel, 2000, p.179, translated by author).

One specific problem of project-work with respect to trust is that once a project is started,

it is hardly possible for the client not to pay at least a partial amount for something has been produced and efforts have been expanded. In an initial encounter, the client must, thus, make a commitment to a production process, only within which he will find out the actual cooperative behavioral characteristics of the freelancer. In this respect, Nooteboom's remark that trust "is as much the result of cooperation as a condition for it" (Nooteboom, 1996, p. 989) proves to be true, however it is often prior cooperation with acquaintances of the client that are the condition for cooperation with him.

FREELANCE WEB-DESIGNERS AS THE MOST DISADVANTAGED SEGMENT OF THE WEB-MARKET

Freelance web-designers in New York are engaged in the production of web-sites mostly for individuals and small businesses, ranging from design of the user interface and video-animation to programming the code and connecting it to other sites and databases (database development). The eleven freelance web-designers I interviewed are part of a growing stratum in knowledge and cultural services, one-person enterprises selling services via service contracts (see Ertel and Pröll 2004, p. 3). In contrast to traditional self-employed people, they don't possess fixed capital like offices (if one thinks, for instance, of other professional categories such as doctors or lawyers); rather, they are engaged in changing projects in a non-space-bound environment. As part of the independent contractors in the US, the freelancers of my sample are excluded from unemployment insurance, health care or work accident insurance, which increases the importance of assuring a steady flow of work on their own. The most important difference between these workers and traditional self-employed is the lack of professional regulation, of clear boundaries of occupational images, and of necessary professional qualification or self-regulation via professional bodies (see Christopherson, 2004, p. 552). There are no minimum-prices, certificates of quality or other regulations that usually protect professionals from unqualified competition and exploitation. This lack of clear signals leads to an increased importance of interpersonal networks of clients to overcome principal-agent problems which generate regionally-specific labor markets (see Batt et al, 2001; Gottschall and Henninger, 2005). In their study of freelance web-designers in Germany, Gottschall and Henninger (2005) accordingly call the initial client contact the central "needle eye" (ibid, p.162) for freelancers, with both recommendations and past experiences cooperation playing large roles. Active client acquisition is rather rare due to high uncertainty of clients regarding the ability of the freelancers, which as they state promotes an *informal governance* based on communication, trust and reputation (ibid; see also Batt et al., 2001, p.18).

A prior, rather extensive study on the web-design industry in New York City (Damarin, 2004; 2006) documented that freelancers are the most disadvantaged segment of the web-design market. Besides having to keep up with accelerating technology, they also have to overcome the uncertainty of their work orders and volatility of income. Given the lack of contacts into the corporate world which would help them to acquire new orders, the low income and high volatility of work might actually prove to be self-sustaining problems. Their clients, which are often non-web businesses, usually have only a few jobs to be done so that there is the danger of a sudden drying up of information regarding new jobs. The challenges that freelance web-designers thus face to generate a steady demand for their work are the need to create awareness of their capabilities among potential clients, to overcome the distrust that is connected to an unregulated relationship of exchange and cooperation and the information asymmetry that is embedded in the expert-layman relationship regarding web-technology.

METHODOLOGY

The original research question of the empirical study was "How do people in unstructured labor markets create both a steady demand for their work and stable income flows, thereby overcoming the uncertainty inherent in freelance work?" I investigated this question through in-depth interviews with two experts and semi-structured interviews with eleven freelance web-designers aged 25 to 49 (six male, five female). The participants were reached through internet contact, personal contact and at an event of the freelancers union. Requirement for participation was that those interviewed were working for at least 6 months working as freelance web-designers and that they earned more than 50% of their total income through this activity. They were earning between $10,000 and $80,000 dollars a year with an average work experience as a freelancer of about three years in New York City. Six of the interviewed were below 30 years of age; four were between 30 and 40; and one was above 40. The interviews lasted an average of 75 minutes. The semi-structured format allowed me to encourage the interviewees to focus on their experiences of client acquisition, client interaction and the potential problems of volatile work load and income while allowing them to insert relevant topics that were not foreseen by the interviewer. While allowing me to capture the subjective ways of coping with market-mediated employment, the consistent guideline makes comparison possible.

For purposes of analysis, the interviews were transcribed and then coded, using the method of "Grounded Theory" (see Glaser and Strauss, 1967) in order to generate context-specific hypotheses about market behavior from recurring topics in these semi-structured interviews.[2] While in the field, the analysis of the first interviews revealed the importance of client relationships for work acquisition as well as highly different "average prices" for an hour of work in different circles of clients which led to a sharper focus on these aspects. After a phase of open coding in which I established comparable categories under which certain behavior could be subsumed, I analyzed the different categories in relation to each other to grasp what dynamics I could observe. Particularly helpful was the suggestion of Granovetter (1985) to analyze the action of market actors in embedded markets under the assumption of rationality while looking for environmental factors that make seemingly irrational action rational (Granovetter, 1985, p. 504).

The comparison of the experiences of freelancers, the success of their different strategies and their market position combined with their common description of conditions in the market place allowed me to gain a better grasp of the market in which they are embedded. Looking for the factors they ascribed their success to and the factors that stand out from a comparative analysis between different freelancers, trust as social capital as well as its management rapidly emerged as a dominant topic.

MAKING A LIVING IN A FRAGMENTED MARKET: A FREELANCER'S WORKING SITUATION

Analyzing the sample for common factors influencing the precariousness of their working situation, the length of being a freelancer and the contact networks established in that time, establishing oneself in a specific niche and the specific way of entertaining client relationships emerge as the most important factors. The dominant mechanism by the help of which work is found in the sample is the *referral*. Other mechanisms (in the decreasing order of importance) are the return of old clients or respectively the updating of old jobs, online postings (5 out of 11), outsourcing of specific jobs from/to other freelancers (seven interviewees) and the use of recruiting agencies (three respondents). Freelancers themselves are well aware of the importance of referrals.

"I think everything is about networking and putting your name out and having other people say 'oh, I know this designer'" (Maria, line 35).[3]

Referrals themselves are seen as generating a feeling of familiarity:

"Just because…word of mouth really helps, just because people feel a little bit more comfortable when they know that oh, my friend so-and-so-worked with you" (Tom, line 117f).

To reduce the fear of being taken advantage of, freelancers do not charge for the first meeting in which they encounter the client to understand the project, thus reducing the costs of first contact. In this moment, the freelancer not only needs to capture what the clients want, but also to consult with as well as to bond with them. Asked what accounts for the jobs they obtained, some of the interviewees mentioned the ability of understanding what the client needs:

"That was more of if I managed to establish the connection with the client, if I got what they want" (Giovanni, line 220f).

"One of my skills I am good at seeing what you want on your site, I am good at giving you descriptions back that make you go, 'Yes, that is what I am talking about'" (Tom, line 526f).

The sign of competence in the first encounter is evidently important, also for taking the fear of the client faced with an unknown situation of building an internet representation (an e-commerce site for example). Specializing in a specific niche is here of advantage, as freelancers can provide clients with consultancy as to what they might need.

I think like the thing that are my strongest skills is being able to sort of analyze your business, to tell you what you need, because like as

I said, a lot of people never thought about a lot of those issues that I thought about, because I had multiple clients, you know, and so in that sense I am kind of reassuring, because if they are clueless and scared, I can inform them about some things. (Helena, line 292ff)

The different elements involved in that moment (presentation of capability, consultancy as well as bonding) can be well seen from the following account of the first phone interview:

So it is like creating an instant relationship and a connection to them, that to me is pitching, sort of like being a consultant and teaching them that you have a lot of expertise but also at the same time learning about them so that you create a bond that goes past a phone call. (John, line 59ff)

The peculiar nature of interactive service work gives specific importance to a management of client cooperation that proves satisfying for the clients. Web design is strongly dialogical work, and due to the potential of follow-up orders and recommendations this interaction becomes very important to the freelancer with a potential for an amplifying positive feedback loop from client satisfaction to client acquisition. Proactively addressing fears of clients, some freelancers can convert the structural constraints of the market into strengths of their respective business models. Much of the uncertainty of clients resides in the expert-layperson relationship that is intertwined with a real fear of interacting with technology itself that becomes necessary for a successful interaction between the designer and the client. The designer has to convey the range of the possible as well as to encourage the input from the client to generate a satisfactory final product that often becomes a very personal representation on the internet.

One freelancer explains:

There is a lot of fear about technology and you know it can be really overwhelming, and I am really nice with people and I take a lot of time, like whatever time they need, I take, and I mean they are paying for it, so why should I be in a hurry. (Alina, line 336ff)

She and Helena actively engage their clients to become co-producers who have a strong say in the design of the site. This has at least two beneficial outcomes. The first is that once the fear of technology is overcome and clients are involved, they will be willing to exceed their budget-limits to reach their optimal result. The second is that clients are usually very satisfied with the results and the process (in which they feel themselves heard) which will increase the number of referrals one gets. This intense cooperation corresponds with a way of budgeting that already includes time for contingencies and change requests, increasing the flexibility of the freelancers and, if not fully used, allowing for refunds to the client. Rather than demarcating their own skills from the client, they invite him or her to participate which reduces his or her fears. The success of this strategy contrasts with freelancers who see clients as a barrier to good design and, thus, are not able to bind clients and to establish themselves in social circles.

The second biggest challenge I think is that everybody thinks they are a designer, so even though they want me to design it for them, they are telling me how to design. So sometimes it gets a little crazy... because they want to design too, but you hired me to do it. (Maria, line 52ff)

It is this self-assertion that hinders mutual role taking and the integration of the client in the process of web-site design, which reduces the satisfaction process with the production process.

One widespread pattern in the career of the freelancers is the gradual shift from a competitive online-postings and bidding market in the beginning to a less competitive one mediated by recommendations, for which the following quote is paradigmatic:

In the beginning, I would have to source clients, I didn't have like sort of a name or people for whom

I was doing it, so I would have to source clients naturally, but after like most people became aware or even my clients liked the level of my work or they would refer me to other people, so it is, then it was snowball, after a year of me going alone by myself, trying to source clients (Ariane, line 245ff).

Given that it also implies a structural shift in the environment from one lacking trust to one embedded in mechanisms depending on and creating trust, this shift has a positive connotation. At online postings not only are web-designers competing with low quality competitors who impact the prices clients are willing to pay, but also it is very difficult to establish trust.

"You can send them all the information you want and like this and that and they will still think that you are trying to rip 'em off" (Maria, line 515f).

At the same time, online postings also have the disadvantage that the persons one is cooperating with are strangers who have not even an indirect connection to the freelancers, the spotty character of the exchange therefore increasing the risk of ending up unpaid. As Peter in the following quote reflects, business relationships in a legally unregulated space require building personal relationships.

Well, there are, in a sense, as a freelancer it is more of a personal relationship at least to me...It is not just clear-cut business or you do stand the chance of just getting screwed over by a client, so in terms of coverage, that especially legally, it is very loose, you don't have any coverage (Peter, line 159ff).

Building personal relationships over time can also help one to establish oneself in a certain circle of acquaintances. Asked what she meant by personal relationships to her clients, Helena answered,

Just that it is not, I guess they can call me and ask me questions and I am not going to charge them for answering the question. You know it is like, or they don't remember how to do something that I have already taught them how to do, and so, you know and so I will explain it to them and so it is not like that is not in the contract, so I feel like I kind of have an ongoing relationship with their business...So I have some ongoing relationships and so I think, that helps that then if somebody says, oh, I need a web developer, they think oh, this person keeps helping me out, and they, you know, so they tend to refer me, because they have sort of a personal relationship." (Helena, line 145ff, emphasis mine)

Teaching clients technology, thereby reducing their dependence on the freelancer, as well as not charging for the occasional help binds clients and freelancers together in a mutually beneficial process. In this sense, I detected gradualness of trust in the exchange relationships of freelance designers with clients, but mostly not in specific client relationships but with a network of acquaintances where experiences that are communicated in referrals build the trust. Asked why people – who have never even met her, trust her, Helena replies,

I have no idea. There is no reason. I don't know if people are just naïve or – I mean I obviously I think I have a good reputation from the referrals – and I think that is essential. I think that is the biggest thing (Helena, line 354ff)

The shift from a competitive segment into social circles in which one is the address for web-design work is also connected with a possible ascendance of prices which are set by custom rather than by competition. An entry into a market segment that is mediated by referrals and thus trust-relationships can mean an important improvement for freelancers in terms of stabilization of income, which, however strictly, depends on the number of orders and the resources of clients in the specific niche. On at her rather steady orders, Helena reflects,

I don't know, I mean partially it is just people who are gonna spend more money talk to other people who have done other big projects, so I think you know if you have a more sophisticated business, you will gonna talk to someone who has had that experience, so the more of those I do, the more people will mention my name when it comes to it. (Helena, line 555ff)

E-businesses with rather bigger budgets or NGOs with a constant fluctuation of personnel that independently of the freelancer transfers the freelancer's reputation to new customers are beneficial niches, while other potential niches have too few resources to prove sufficient.

So, by that time, I actually realized that there was actually a niche in the market, because students, fresh especially when graduating, they needed to have a web presence to show your website to prospective employers, so I started I had to do at least two people where I had to do their portfolio of work, ... so it could have been a market just with the students, but then your rates would have to be lower, because they could not really pay that high rates (Ariane, line 529ff)

As one can see from the above quotes, niches of clients who have the same needs and who know each other can be very beneficial to freelancers, so that placing oneself into these information circuits and gaining a good reputation in them become part of the reflections and action of freelancers. The most extreme example of deliberate action is Tom, who seeks out musicians in New York City:

I am actually building on a niche right now because I am so involved with music communities, so I do work a lot with musicians on their sites and growing them out.... But I am sort of trying to track down mostly musicians and artists, and it is kind of interesting niche to grow, especially in an area like New York, there are so many musicians, it is almost like an infinite resource to work with. (Tom, line 191ff)

Niche building strategies are connected to conscious attempts of trying to enter into social circles where their skills are in high demand. Freelancers here take the route of social acquaintances who introduce them into social situations, rather than approaching the group directly or entering into a conversation that eventually will lead to a discussion of each other's occupations. Instead of bringing up their services themselves, they are waiting for the topic of profession to occur such that their services are offered incidentally.[4]

Somebody asked me like a networking question, and I say, "Just sort of find one thing. Just find one thing that they are interested in and then you can roll on it to whatever you need to talk about." ...So I just stand around and somebody will say something and then start talking, I am like, "Oh, I have this, like I have something on my computer," and "Oh, I have something like on my computer," and "I just had something doing this," and I am like, "No," and that will roll into like "And, what do you do?" "Oh, I am a web designer." And, that is how that rolls. (Tom, line 937ff)

This category of jobs, the "Oh, you happen to be there jobs" (A.B.), forms for two of the freelancers in the sample a considerable amount of jobs received, but is pursued by at least four. The idea is not one of consciously setting people up to meet, but rather, to avoid the situation of offering one's services directly to people, as the role of solicitant induces doubts about the quality of the freelancers and also gives substantial negotiating power to the solicited. Instead, when asked if one could do something for somebody, the freelancer starts with trust conferred upon him by the mutual acquaintance or at least a lack of distrust in an incidental situation and has much more leeway to accommodate the other, while finding ways that are advantageous to him- or herself.

A good example is on Saturday I went to- I actually missed my friends show, because I was at another show that was before that, but he was hanging out, so I came around and said hi, and his guitarist has his own company, that are off selling guitars, trying to get that off base, and he goes and says, "Well we really don't have a website." So, it is like, "Wow, Tom here is a Web- Designer," and it then just rolls from there, and so we are in talks right now. (Tom, line 211ff)

This trust management that puts the freelancer into the position of being asked, rather than the one that is asking translates into a broader feature of exchange relationships that freelancers prefer. The position of being sought after, as for example when being referred to by a former client, allows them to be more "in the driver's seats" and to grant favors to clients rather than to ask for favors from them. This has important repercussions for the efforts expanded for a specific price, as can be seen in the following quote:

With an estimate or a quote it is more like they come to you because they are looking for something and they heard that maybe you are a good person for it and so they are really sort of courting you in a way…And, then, they go, "Oh, well, you know, I don't have that amount of money." And, you go, "Well I could- I could do it in this way. I could scale back and then I could afford to do it at that premium." So it is more like, it is more like you are in more you know the driver's seat, with the project (Alina, line 473ff).

In contrast to bidding processes of several freelancers for the same project, processes that are characterized by lowering the price for the same work, here the freelancer can lower the work load for the same price.

Given the importance of reputation in these circuits of information for the freelancer to find work, some behavior that seems irrational in the short-term becomes rational, for example sending clients to cheaper, better-suited competitors or building small devices free of charge if the client does not have the sufficient budget to

make it worthwhile. In such a way, freelancers establish a reputation of putting the clients' welfare first, generating trust in their networks and for the person. Such acts of gift-giving generate referral networks for the freelancer and bind the gift-recipients for the long term.

And I would always go and tell a client, if I can't do it or if I consider it could be done better in some other way, because ultimately, I want the client more than I would want the project, I would much rather have them saying: "This guy is straight with us. I am going to use him again," than try to do something just to get the money and then not do a good job.' (Giovanni, line 196ff)

Giovanni's goal is thus to bind or to bond with the client rather than having the short-term gain. This behaviour, however, competes with the tendency of freelancers to "oversell" themselves and to learn the skills on the job, where a delicate balance needs to be found. The more clients one has, the easier it is to let an ill-fitting client go, a fact that has further beneficial implications, as the following quote shows:

It is always in the interest of the person, you know, that I am turning them down, so it is not like I am turning them down because I am a jerk, but it is because you know, it is not a good match …It is weird, because it is usually the opposite, we get more work out of a situation like that because the client really understands that we are looking out for them and care about them and to care about their project, so they then tend to send more people to us and to come back to us with other projects….They like knowing this is a person that not only is she not trying to screw me over, she is turning down the job you know because she thinks it would be better if it would be done by somebody else. So people really like that. (Alina, line 573ff)

As we can see, the asset of a reputation of personal disinterest in dealing with clients has the effect of returning clients and an increased number of referrals; thus, the short-term loss becomes a long-term gain. Such effects can be explained by the integrity and benevolence as well as filled order books that are communicated by these signals, which points to competence. While such signs alleviate the difficulties of finding work for some, it is also an effect that further stratifies the market. Those who have a filled order book can afford to send people away, emitting signals of trustworthiness that might increase their orders. Tom summarizes the image that he is trying to convey by actions like offering free scaffolds for web-sites rather than charging clients with small budgets as "being a friendly guy that helps you out, …and I will try to work in your budget if I can. If I can't, I will help you find somebody or something that will" (Tom, line 493ff). As he says, helping others if they cannot afford your services also protects one's price levels, while generating referrals.

CONCLUSION

In this chapter, several viable strategies to make a living as a freelancer are identified; however, all of them include attempts to create a personal relationship with clients, overcoming the gap of trust that is inherent in interpersonal cooperation and exchange relationships which are not highly legally structured. To integrate the client in interactive service work into the process of production such that he can identify with the final product and potentially even enjoy the process itself is a precondition for client satisfaction. Indeed, the data seems to suggest that this is a predominant uncertainty for clients in website production. One of the ways to achieve this is to overcome the distance of users of technology to the technology itself and to increase their confidence in their capacities as designers, which allows for a stronger engagement of clients in the process of designing a site, directly leading to more work hours. This leads to more satisfaction, further referrals and longer-lasting relationships between client and designer.

Binding a network of clients is crucial for a steady flow of requests, income and work. The importance of the cooperative process in creating a web-site and of trustworthiness as a condition for contracting cause the segmentation of the market for web-design into several social circles within which the reputation of a freelancer circulates on the one hand, and an anonymous bidding market occurs on the other hand. The market for web-design work thus needs to be conceptualized as an imperfectly connected information space, clamped by different networks. The entrance into communication channels and the building up of a good reputation in them is crucial for a freelancer's working situation. For that reason, freelancers try to embed themselves into certain niches. They do so by generating "personal relationships" with their clients that go beyond the market exchange or by seeking out social networking situations, thereby decreasing the uncertainty of clients and generating a suspension of the feeling of vulnerability. These strategies, however, do not always generate sufficient orders. [5] Such social capital cannot provide full employment security to freelancer, but what it implies is that as entrepreneurs of their own labor power, they also become entrepreneurs of trust. Freelancers engage in image and reputation management built through signs of integrity and benevolence. These advance investments then have their impact as much on the clients themselves as on the referral networks they are embedded in.

The empirical evidence points to an understanding of markets of interactive service work as essentially an ecology of spaces of information flow that are differentiated by the ways in which the problems of uncertainty and vulnerability of the different actors are solved. On the one hand, there is the anonymous market in which sellers are bidding for work and overcoming the gap of trust is complicated by anonymous means of communication (e-mail). On the other hand, there are different information networks (niches), in which specialized freelancers have established their reputations and find work through recommendations. Their specialized statuses allow them to decrease the feeling of uncertainty of clients by consulting the client in the process of production helped by their past experiences. In this way, the fear of technology is overcome, while their reputation as capable agents who look after the interests of their clients decreases the fear of being taken advantage of. The freelancers react to these different specific market-constraints by engaging in the production of signs of trustworthiness and trust-breeding practices that prove beneficial when embedding in certain resourceful niches is achieved. Given that many of these strategies were emerging from work-experience rather than through intentional design, an analogy to evolutionary game theory seems appropriate. "The units that are subject to selection pressure in evolutionary biology are 'strategies'…, which are conditional strategies from available menus so as to further their projects and purposes" (Dasgupta, in press). As an analogy, we can say that the freelancers who successfully manage trust-relationships establish themselves in niches and have a higher chance of persisting in that position. Besides the factor of chance, we can also observe self-reinforcing effects of positive feedback loops: the better one is embedded (e.g. in terms of number of job offers), the better one can follow trust-enhancing strategies.

Overall, this chapter shows that Beckert's suggestion to focus on the trust-taker's initiating behavior opens up a fruitful avenue of research. However, such dramaturgic action not only relates to clients directly but also to acquaintances of clients who can be reached via referral. This insight and the specific focus on trust-enhancing strategies in cooperation are the specific lessons for trust research this chapter proposes.

REFERENCES

Bacharach, M., & Gambetta, D. (2001). Trust in signs. In Cook, K. S. (Ed.), *Trust in Society* (pp. 148–184). New York: Russell Sage Foundation.

Batt, R., Christopherson, S., Rightor, N., & van Jaarsveld, D. (2001). *Net working: Labor market challenges for the new media workforce*. Washington, DC: Economic Policy Institute.

Beckert, J. (2005). Trust and the performative construction of markets. *MPIfG Discussion Paper* 05/8. Koeln, Germany: Max Planck Institut fuer Gesellschaftsforschung. Retrieved May 1, 2009, from http://www.mpifg.de/pu/mpifg_dp/dp05-8.pdf

Christopherson, S. (2004). The divergent worlds of new media: How policy shapes work in the creative economy. *Review of Policy Research, 21*(4), 543–558. doi:10.1111/j.1541-1338.2004.00093.x

Cook, K. S., Hardin, R., & Levi, M. (2005). *Cooperation without trust?* New York: Russell Sage Foundation.

Damarin, A. K. (2004). *Fit, flexibility, and connection: Organizing employment in emerging web labor markets. New York City 1993-2003*. Unpublished doctoral dissertation, Columbia University, New York.

Damarin, A. K. (2006). Rethinking occupational structure - The case of web site production work. *Work and Occupations, 33*(4), 429–463. doi:10.1177/0730888406293917

Dasgupta, P. (1988). Trust as a commodity. In Gambetta, D. (Ed.), *Trust: Making and Breaking Co-operative Relations* (pp. 49–72). Oxford, UK: Basil Blackwell.

Dasgupta, P. (in press). Trust and Cooperation among Economic Agents. In Philosophical Transactions of the Royal Society B

Ertel, M., & Pröll, U. (2004). Arbeitssituation und Gesundheit von „neuen Selbständigen im Dienstleistungssektor. [Working situation and health of new self-employed in the service sector]. *Arbeit, 1*, 1–12.

Fenwick, T. (2006). Contradictions in portfolio careers: Work design and client relations. *Career Development International, 11*(1), 65–79. doi:10.1108/13620430610642381

Gambetta, D. (1988). Introduction. In Gambetta, D. (Ed.), *Trust: Making and breaking co-operative relations*. Oxford, UK: Basil Blackwell.

Gibbons, R. (2001). Trust in social structures: Hobbes and Coase meet repeated games. In Cook, K. S. (Ed.), *Trust in Society* (pp. 332–353). New York: Russell Sage Foundation.

Glaser, B., & Strauss, A. L. (1967). *The discovery of grounded theory-Strategies for qualitative research*. New York: Aldine.

Gottschall, K., & Henninger, A. (2005). Freelancer in den Kultur- und Medienberufen: Freiberuflich, aber nicht frei schwebend. [Freelancer in the culture and media professions: freelance but not free pending] In Mayer-Ahuja, N., & Wolf, H. (Eds.), *Entfesselte Arbeit- Neue Bindungen* (pp. 156–184). Berlin, Germany: Ed. Sigma.

Granovetter, M. (1985). Economic action and social structure: A theory of embeddedness. *American Journal of Sociology, 91*(3), 481–510. doi:10.1086/228311

Gross, P. (1983). *Die Verheißungen der Dienstleistungsgesellschaft* [The promises of the service society]. Opladen, Germany: Westdeutscher Verlag.

Heimer, C. A. (2001). Solving the problem of trust. In Cook, K. S. (Ed.), *Trust in Society* (pp. 40–88). New York: Russell Sage Foundation.

Jones, G. R., & George, J. M. (1998). The Experience and Evolution of Trust: Implications for Cooperation and Teamwork. *Academy of Management Review, 23*(3), 473–490. doi:10.2307/259293

Luhmann, N. (1979). *Trust and power: Two works by Niklas Luhmann*. Chichester, UK: Wiley. (Original work published 1967)

Mayer, R. C., Davis, J. H., & Schoorman, F. D. (1995). An integrative model of organizational trust. *Academy of Management Review, 20*(3), 709–734. doi:10.2307/258792

Mcknight, D. H., Cummings, L. L., & Chervany, N. L. (1998). Initial trust formation in new organizational relationships. *Academy of Management Review, 23*(3), 473–490. doi:10.2307/259290

Misztal, B. A. (1996). *Trust in modern societies*. Cambridge, UK: Polity Press.

Moellering, G. (2006). *Trust: reason, routine and reflexivity*. Oxford, UK: Elsevier.

Nooteboom, B. (1996). Trust, opportunism and governance: A process and control model. *Organization Studies, 17*(6), 985–1010. doi:10.1177/017084069601700605

Putnam, R. D. (1995). Bowling alone: America's declining social capital. *Journal of Democracy, 6*(1), 65–78. doi:10.1353/jod.1995.0002

Spence, M. A. (1974). *Market signaling: Informational transfer in hiring and related screening processes*. Cambridge, MA: Harvard University Press.

Sztompka, P. (1999). *Trust: A Sociological Theory*. Cambridge, UK: Cambridge University Press.

Voswinkel, S. (2000), Das mcdonaldistische Produktionsmodell - Schnittstellenmanagement interaktiver Dienstleistungsarbeit. [The mcdonald production modell- Interface management in interactive service work] In H. Minssen (Ed.), Begrenzte Entgrenzungen. Wandlungen von Organisation und Arbeit (pp. 177-203). Berlin, Germany: Ed. sigma.

Williamson, O. E. (1993). Calculativeness, trust, and economic organization. *The Journal of Law & Economics, 36*(2), 453–486. doi:10.1086/467284

Zucker, L. G. (1986). Production of trust: Institutional sources of economic structure, 1840–1920. In Staw, B. M., & Cummings, L. L. (Eds.), *Research in Organizational Behavior* (*Vol. 8*, pp. 53–111). Greenwich, CT: JAI Press.

ENDNOTES

[1] A comment made by a freelance video-cutter whom I interviewed at an event of the Freelancer's Union revealed to me the value of a mass of returning clients: he said that, although he has a job offer, he is not returning to the corporate world, as he would lose all his clients. This further justifies seeing clients as entrepreneurial capital with a relationship of trust that is hard to achieve.

[2] To code the material, I used the qualitative analysis software "Nvivo 8," which facilitates storing and ordering the codes.

[3] For reasons of confidentiality I have changed the names of the interviewees.

[4] Prior research (Damarin 2004) mentions the occurrence of such jobs, actually in substantial numbers, but does not offer any further analysis of it.

[5] Indeed, 8 of 11 freelancers have experienced serious droughts of work and shortages of income. A special danger of a stock of clients that generates referrals is a general market downturn which could wipe out the close clients one has.

Section 3
Applications of Technology:
Impact on Trust

Chapter 8
Technology:
A Bane or Boon for Cross–National Levels of Generalized Trust?

Blaine G. Robbins
University of Washington, USA

Maria S. Grigoryeva
University of Washington, USA

ABSTRACT

The country-level determinants of generalized trust that usually command the most research are ethnic homogeneity, institutional performance, civic culture, and economic development. Despite the popularity and insight of this research, there is little quantitative empirical evidence that explores the impact of technology—a necessary and exogenous condition for many of these determinants—on generalized trust. In this chapter, technology measures from the World Bank are combined with a generalized trust measure from the World Values Survey and other country-level predictors from various data sources to test two competing theories of generalized trust across 57 countries. One theory, new institutional economics, argues that technology will yield formal institutions, which structure incentives and reduce uncertainty, that, in turn, increase generalized trust. The other perspective, overjustification and crowding theory, argues that actors constrained by extrinsic motivators, such as technology and institutional incentives, will attribute trust to the incentive rather than to the individual, and generalized trust, as a result, will decrease. Structural equation model results confirm the new institutional economics claim that the positive effects of technology on generalized trust are positively mediated by formal institutions. The authors conclude by outlining various managerial implications and directions for future research.

DOI: 10.4018/978-1-61520-901-9.ch008

INTRODUCTION

In his foundational text *The Division of Labor in Society*, Emile Durkheim ([1893] 1984) famously argued that the evolution from a traditional and personal community to a modern and impersonal society would not necessarily lead to the eventual demise of social solidarity, as Tönnies ([1887] 1963) and other communitarians forebode. Instead, this evolution would lead to a new social solidarity founded not on likeness and similarity, but on interdependence and trust. This is because a complex division of labor activates social processes, such as trust, that emerge to resolve problems of solidarity brought about by individualistic social relationships. Durkheim rendered a radical and counterintuitive conclusion: as individuals ostensibly become more autonomous and liberated from their community bonds, they become ever more dependent on society. The key to this dependence is trust.

Since *The Division of Labor in Society*, research within sociology (e.g., Blau, 1964; Coleman, 1990; Yamagishi & Yamagishi, 1994), psychology (see Kurzban, 2003; Tyler & Kramer, 1996), economics (see Arrow, 1974; North, 1990; Williamson, 1985), and political science (e.g., Hardin, 2006; Levi, 1998; Putnam, 1993) reveals that a number of general determinants and consequences of trust exist beyond those outlined by Durkheim (see Nannestad, 2008; Welch, Rivera, Conway, Yonkoski, Lupton, & Giancola, 2005 for a review). Institutions (Delhey & Newton, 2005; Knack & Keefer, 1997), social relationships (Putnam, 2000), homophily (Brewer, 1981; Putnam, 2007), and cultural values (Uslaner, 2000) are often cited as determinants of trust, while lower rates of corruption (Uslaner, 2002), economic performance (Zak & Knack, 2001), "good government" (Knack, 2002; Putnam, 1993), and life satisfaction (Bjørnskov, 2003) are recognized as its consequences.

Although the role of technology in generating or undermining trust remains empirically underexplored, existing theoretical literature provides two competing models of technology and trust that can be tested to fill this empirical void. In the first model, new institutional economics, technology is often treated as an exogenous variable–a dimension or concept lacking explanation–that is used as the catalyst for larger, more complex models. For instance, in Douglas North's (1990) model, technologies provide effective standardized measurements that better assess the price and quality of goods, and increase monitoring capacity of institutions and organizations, which results in swifter enforcement and greater constraint on individual action. This reduces uncertainty and increases information that results in greater trust. Technology, then, has a theoretically indirect and historically distant, although necessary, positive effect on trust.

In the second theoretical perspective, the overjustification and crowding model, the motivation to trust is derived from intrinsic and extrinsic sources. According to the theory, extrinsic motivators, such as technologies and institutions, undermine and *crowd out* intrinsic reasons to trust (Bohnet, Frey, & Huck 2001; Enzle & Anderson, 1993; Fehr & Falk, 2002; Malhotra & Murnighan, 2002; Mulder, van Dijk, De Cremer, & Wilke, 2006). This occurs because individuals attribute trust to the external motivation rather than to the internal disposition of the trustee (Deci, Koestner, & Ryan, 1999). Recent investigations in administrative science support this notion. Economic organizations often adopt information technologies, such as surveillance devices, to increase employee trustworthiness and enhance productivity. Ironically, the increased monitoring and sanctioning capacity brought about by these technologies undermines the intrinsic motivation to trust (Cialdini, 1996). Resulting in distrust of the organization and fellow coworkers as well as heightened employee malfeasance.

As of yet, very few research efforts have attempted to resolve the debate over trust and technology. A primary goal of the current volume is to rectify this issue. The present study, therefore, addresses the role that technology has on cross-national rates of trust. As such, we test a new institutional model of trust (Greif, 2006; North, 1981, 1990), while contrasting this approach with divergent predictions from an overjustification and crowding perspective (Bohnet, Frey, & Huck, 2001; Cialdini, 1996; Deci, Koestner, & Ryan, 1999; Enzle & Anderson, 1993). We demonstrate with structural equation models (SEM) that formal institutions foster generalized trust. To the extent that technology encourages generalized trust, it does so indirectly, operating through these institutional mechanisms. Such mediating effects of formal institutions are observed because technology alters relative prices and/or strengthens monitoring and sanctioning capacity. These factors promote the emergence and expansion of formal institutions that then reduce perceived uncertainty and cultivate trust.

BACKGROUND

In this section we begin with a definition of what we mean by trust: the unconditional belief of actor *i* that stranger *j* or anonymous other *k* takes their interests into account. This is also referred to as generalized trust. We then provide an overview of the two competing perspectives that attribute either trust or distrust to technology. In the first perspective, new institutional economics, trust is seen as a consequence of formal institutions. Since institutions provide secure exchange and reduce uncertainty, they afford opportunity for the belief that others can be trusted. To show how this process occurs, we highlight what institutions do, what conditions lead to institutional emergence, and what exogenous factors—with an emphasis on technology—spark the evolution from informal to formal institutional structures. We contrast this first perspective with overjustification and crowding theory, which suggests that trust is a product of perceived internal dispositions and moral motivations to sustain an agreement. According to this view, external motivators, such as institutional

incentives, *crowd out* the perception that others are internally motivated to cooperate. As a result, technologies that bolster formal institutions and their accompanying enforcement mechanisms will foster distrust. To stress the differences between these two standpoints, we summarize the basic theoretical model and key empirical insights from the overjustification and crowding perspective.

Generalized Trust

Trust is usually classified along two dimensions: rational choice or norm-based, and particularized or generalized. According to the rational choice camp, trust is both cognitive and relational, where *i* trusts *j* under condition *y* (Cook, Hardin, and Levi, 2005). For one to trust, the truster must believe that the trustee takes their interests into account. This trust is also situational; for instance, a client may trust a lawyer for legal advice but they will rarely trust them to perform surgery. Norm-based versions of trust, on the other hand, conceptualize trust as a moral or personal attribute of individuals, where trust is a product of the value-system and cultural milieu in which individuals are embedded (Durkheim, [1893] 1984; Mansbridge, 1999; Uslaner, 2002). Under such stipulation, trust is non-strategic and often unconditional. People simply internalize values that teach them how to trust others—it becomes "…a general outlook on human nature… (Uslaner, 2002, p. 17)."

Along with the second dimension, trust varies as either particularized or generalized. The former, which is synonymous with "thick, personal trust", suggests that people are only capable of trusting identifiable and known others situated within a specific context. Frequent face-to-face interactions characteristic of tightly knit social networks such as small town associations, sports teams, and religious communes foster this type of trust. In contrast, generalized trust, or "thin, impersonal trust", claims that trust can extend to strangers and anonymous others of which the truster knows very little, and under conditions that are not well specified. This type of trust occurs when people do not expect their valuables to be stolen if they enter a crowded bus, or have their children kidnapped if they leave them unattended in a department store.

The poles along these two dimensions tend to complement each other. It is difficult for a goal-oriented purposive actor to perform cost-benefit calculations under the "generalized" extreme, because information concerning the trustee and the situation is poor; that is, actor i does not know actor j with respect to unfamiliar situation w. The norm-based approach to trust formation, on the other hand, lends itself to the "generalized" pole. Individuals who internalize optimistic and egalitarian world-views are more likely to trust regardless of the situation or paucity of information (Uslaner, 2002); if actor i believes all people are good and moral, actor i will trust actors j, k, or l regardless of condition x, y, or z. However, while these two dimensions have their affinities (i.e., particularized rational trust and generalized norm-based trust), the rational choice dimension can be general and the norm-based dimension can be particular. With the rational choice approach, just because a truster has little information on either the trustee or the context does not mean that the truster will not calculate, or attempt to calculate, possible misconduct (see Herreros & Criado, 2008). With the norm-based approach, individuals will trust others regardless of if the trustee is a close friend or a stranger

Presently available data do not allow us to ascertain whether the choice to trust is rational or normative. The measure of trust we employ is used by virtually all cross-national survey studies of trust and asks, "In general, do you think that most people can be trusted, or you can't be too careful in dealing with people." It is difficult to determine from this question if the choice to trust is due to cost-benefit calculations or internalized codes of action. To adjudicate this issue with survey methods is problematic, if not impossible. Therefore, we remain neutral with respect to this

dimension. We can, however, assess whether trust is generalized or particularized. The survey item asks about "most people" (not a specific person) and does not identify conditions in which trust holds; these are two necessary factors for generalized trust. For the same reasons, this survey question is an invalid measure of particularized trust: specific types of actors are not identified and situations are unknown.

In summary, a lack of valid measurement for rational, norm-based, and particularized trust constrains the present analysis. Because of this, our results should be restricted to discussions of generalized trust. While this ostensibly limits the generalizability of the conclusions, there is a large literature on generalized trust that engages in similar theoretical and empirical debates in which we can situate our findings (see Nannestad, 2008; Welsh et al., 2005). In the next section, we outline the theoretical role of technology in producing generalized trust by reviewing competing theories that specify *how* technology impacts generalized trust and *whether* technology creates or destroys generalized trust.

New Institutional Economics

According to new institutional economics (NIE), technology can indirectly affect trust in four ways, all of which operate through formal institutions: (1) it can improve the precision of measurement, (2) it can increase the transportation of commodities, (3) it can confer military advantages to countries, and (4) it can facilitate communication and strengthen the enforcement capacity of institutions. The first three factors motivate actors to change their institutional environments so as to abstract greater gains from exchange. This often results in the emergence of formal institutions, such as states, that internally control and externally protect trade. The fourth factor buttresses and expands the reach of pre-existing institutional enforcement. Ultimately, these four processes spark the assemblage of formal institutions and augment the effectiveness and efficiency of their control, which then aid in the development of trust. Thus, to fully comprehend how technology produces trust we will theoretically outline the causes and consequences of institutions. To accomplish this task, we first outline the historical roots of NIE, offer a definition of institutions, and point to the core issue of the paradigm—transaction costs. We then sketch the relationship between transaction costs and trust, and trace the conditions under which institutions will arise and the key factors leading to their emergence. Finally, we illustrate how technology fits in with this perspective and then provide a falsifiable theoretical model.

Neoclassical economics models assume that actors have perfect information, stable preferences, and the ability to perform complex calculations. Under such conditions, institutions play a minor role in the economy (i.e., the resolution of entitlements and rights should take place through the market) because transactions with perfect information are expected to be fairly costless and efficient. According to this framework, the impact of institutions varies by levels of market competitiveness. If markets are not competitive, institutions and firms have a large, albeit negative, influence on the economy by setting prices and stunting economic growth. Conversely, institutions and organizations are much less influential within fully competitive markets. They are subject to the price mechanism and are merely passive reflections of market forces. In short, the neoclassical framework relegates institutions and social organizations to entities that either follow the ebb and flow of the market or push economies towards economic stagnation.

Knowing that no market, sector, or economy exists as neoclassical economists assume, Ronald Coase challenged the model in two seminal papers entitled "The Nature of the Firm" (1937) and "The Problem of Social Cost" (1960). In these papers, Coase forcefully argued against the assumption of perfect information, noting that principles in the market often do not know the quality of the good being exchanged or if agents will credibly commit to agreements. This lack of knowledge and information produces economic friction, or what Coase calls transaction costs: costs above and beyond the costs of the good being exchanged, which include search costs, bargaining costs, and monitoring and sanctioning costs. Mechanisms that reduce these costs solidify commitment and decrease uncertainty. Institutions and organizations, according to Coase, do not play a tertiary role as specified in the neoclassical model. Instead, formal rules and firms suppress certain types of market exchange as a means to economize on transaction costs. By doing so, they render impossible types of exchange possible.

The Coasian framework set the foundation for a branch of research on institutions and economic action, what we now call new institutional economics (e.g., Alchion & Demsetz, 1973; Brinton, 1992; Brinton & Nee, 1998; Cheung, 1974; Cook & Levi, 1990; Demsetz, 1967; Eggertsson, 1990; Ellickson, 1991; Grief, 2006; Hechter & Opp, 2000; Hodgson, 1988; Hopcroft, 1994; Knight, 1992; North, 1981, 1990; Williamson, 1975, 1985). Although not a cohesive group, the writers in this area generally see institutions as (a) formal or informal rules of the game that limit or enable the choice set of individuals through proscriptive or prescriptive enforcement mechanisms, and (b) as key to economic development and social order in general. It is not supply and demand that dictates prices as the neoclassical model suggests, but the power and authority found in institutions, which both directs prices and economizes on transaction costs. Here the core issue related to transactions costs is the problem of trust. When transaction costs are high, information is incomplete or asymmetric. The result is that credible commitments are difficult to secure and actors are unsure of who will take their interests into account during an exchange. For these reasons, individuals are unlikely to trust others. The primary function of an institution, then, is to reduce these transaction costs, so actors have clear expectations of possible malfeasance and can direct their trust towards credible exchange partners.

Suppose, for instance, that actor i is need of commodity z, but it is difficult for actor i to assess the quality of z or determine who can provide z at the least expense. As a result of this uncertainty, actor i must expend resources to find a reputable exchange partner j or invest resources in devices that effectively appraise z. The expenditure of resources in either case constitutes *search costs* that institutions and technology can help reduce.[1] In rotating credit associations and micro-lending banks, for example, the structure of these institutions allows group members to open and close membership as they see fit, massively reducing search costs (see Cook, Hardin, & Levi, 2005). Moreover, if these organizations are accepting new members, telephones and computer-mediated communication can amplify the speed at which possible recruits of good repute are found (Ciborra 1993).

Now, presume that actor i found an actor j who can supply commodity z. More than likely, actor j will not supply z for free, so both actors must specify terms of exchange, which creates *bargaining costs*. Often this will result in either an informal or formal contract that details who gets what, when, where, and why, and punishes misconduct according to particular agreed upon sanctions. The cost of contract preparation is dependent on the ease of communication and convention, which are conditional on transportation and information technologies. For example, the number of airports or the density of communication systems in a country, such as phone and internet lines, can heighten the efficiency of contract preparation among distant trading partners; thus, reducing bargaining costs.

Once actors i and j have outlined terms of exchange and prepared a contract, agreements must be enforced to ensure that both parties maintain their end of the bargain; otherwise, the contract is a hallow promise where neither actor has an incentive to comply. Institutional enforcement,

such as monetary sanctions or status rewards, guarantees that actors will oblige contract for reasons that it is in the interests of both actors to avoid or receive incentives. The problem is that doing so creates *monitoring and sanctioning costs*. Military and communication technology can reduce these costs by bolstering the monitoring capacity of institutions—through satellites and video surveillance, for instance—so sanctioning mechanisms are swiftly applied. Note that institutions and technology in all phases of the exchange process alter transaction costs, reduce uncertainty, foster credible commitments, and, as a result, encourage trust.

Since, as illustrated, institutions are critical for the solidification of trust, it is necessary to describe when they come about. First, and most importantly, institutions are emergent social processes that develop from repeated social exchange among actors (Nee & Ingram, 1998). Without social interaction, institutions would cease to exist, let alone emerge. Second, inherent within every social interaction are one of three distinct strategic problems that institutions attempt to resolve. These situations include problems of coordination (Schelling, 1960; Ullmann-Margalit, 1978), externalities and competition (Coleman, 1990; Eggertsson, 1990; Hechter, 1987), and the allocation of resources (Knight 1992). When faced with one of these issues, actors will jointly produce and uphold norms to create common benefits if and only if the benefits for each actor are greater than the costs (Nee & Ingram, 1998). In sum, institutions emerge to encourage various types of behavior under one of these three abstract conditions.

Yet institutions vary widely in their form and structure. Some institutions are hierarchical and cover an entire territory, while others are horizontally organized and limited to a single community. To be more specific, institutions are either enforced by group members (i.e., decentralized) or a third-party (i.e., centralized), and are either applicable to everyone (i.e., public) or to a particular group (i.e., private) (Ingram & Clay,

2000). It is impossible to predict the constellation of organizational structures and institutional forms by only considering the three strategic problems outlined above. This is because none of the situations identify exogenous parameter shifts that would lead to public-centralized institutions versus private-decentralized institutions.

One of the first NIE scholars to theoretically specify when and how informal norms become formal institutions is Douglas North (1981, 1990). Drawing on Demsetz (1967), North's central claim is to theoretically illustrate how state institutions (i.e., property rights) determine the structure of incentives and thereby the trajectory of an economy. North argues that property rights are important for the economy because they reduce uncertainty and foster exchange. Without such a system of rights and control, complex exchanges within markets through time and space are difficult to create and sustain.

For North, all societies rely on personalized exchange, informal norms, and subjective mental models to secure credible commitments. Given that modern economies depend on impersonal exchange to promote growth and prosperity, the only way to sustain such exchanges without becoming mired in high transaction costs is with formal institutions and third-party enforcement. To explain how and when these institutions come about, Avner Greif (2006) and Douglas North (1990) identify three critical necessary conditions: population density, impersonal or individualist social relations, and technological advances (see also Levi 1988).

Following Durkheim ([1893] 1984) and Weber (1979), both North and Greif argue that increases in population density decrease information and increase uncertainty during economic exchange. This occurs because individual action under such conditions is difficult to control. Within large populations, anonymity and personal obscurity becomes commonplace and creates incomplete and asymmetric information. To resolve these information problems, individuals and organizations are likely to develop formal institutions capable of managing and controlling large numbers of individuals.

Furthermore, both North and Greif argue that prior ideologies, cultural beliefs, and social organization can either inhibit or facilitate the development of formal institutions and trust, much like Durkheim suggested in *The Division of Labor in Society*. Greif categorizes social organization in terms of collectivist and individualist (i.e., mechanical and organic), while North refers to this type of social organization as personal and impersonal, respectively. Collectivism is marked by high levels of information, thick communication and gossip networks, and segregated social relations in which each individual interacts with members of a specific religious, ethnic, and/or familial group. Actors embedded within collectivist societies are highly dependent on the group, and group-specific collective punishments, such as social and moral sanctions, are effective at controlling group members.

Low levels of communication and high levels of integration among diverse individuals within a society, on the other hand, characterize individualism. With individualism, the dependence of any one individual on the group is weak because exit options are available for those actors. This limits the control capacity of private-order enforcement since individuals can simply leave and avoid collective sanctions such as exclusion. An essential solution to the problem of individualist social order, then, is the implementation of a formal third-party sanctioning system (Greif, 1993, 1994).

Finally, besides population density and individualist social relations, Greif and North argue, along with many others (see Demsetz 1967; Foreman-Peck, 1995; Obstfeld & Taylor, 2003; Weber, 1979), that technological advance is a critical force in motivating the emergence and change of formal institutions. It does so through four key processes. First, technologies alter the precision of measurement of goods and commodities. This generates recurrent exchange among a variety of actors, which, in turn, produces more complex and frequent contract disputes. As a result, formal institutions emerge to control, and resolve, the increased volume and variety of economic conflict. Second, technologies increase the speed at which commodities are exchanged. To illustrate, advances in transportation, such as the wagon and galley, increased the rate of exchange among anonymous parties, and required formal institutions to reduce the returns to malfeasance that followed these types of exchange. Both of these technological developments—measurement and transportation technology—cause changes in relative prices. According to North (1990), this motivates organizations to create, or implement incremental changes in, formal institutions so as to abstract greater benefits from the institutional environment. Third, technologies, specifically military technologies, increase geopolitical military pressure and the threat of land warfare. This promotes the development of formal state structures and revenue seeking elites (Hintz, 1913; Levi, 1988; Tilly, 1975). Fourth, and finally, technologies augment the enforcement capabilities of institutions. Observation technologies, such as video cameras, and transportation technologies greatly boost the monitoring capacity of institutions and widen their range of control. Moreover, these technologies increase communication to facilitate swift and immediate punishment. In sum, technologies promote the development of formal institutions and increase their effectiveness and efficiency.

Invoking Greif and North, the NIE model of generalized trust we test is as follows: population density, impersonal and individualist social relations, and technology are the key exogenous parameters that lead to the creation of formal institutions. Legal property rights, the rule of law, and third-party enforcement—all characteristics of formal institutions—increase information and reduce transaction costs, which leads to less uncertainty and greater generalized trust. Additionally, to adequately test this model, we need to embed it within a predictive model of generalized trust that

takes into account other known determinants. To do so, we borrow a model outlined by Delhey & Newton (2005) in which ethnic homogeneity and religious traditions (i.e., Protestantism) produce formal institutions, income inequality, and national wealth that then impact generalized trust. We also connect technological advances to national wealth, suspecting that technology increases economic efficiency and growth (North, 1990). See Figure 1 for the causal model.

Overjustification and Crowding Theory

While new institutional economics suggests that informal and formal institutions generate trust, the overjustification and crowding perspective emerging out of political science, administrative science, and social psychology argues that formal institutions can lead to trust's demise (Berhnheim & Whinston, 1998; Fox, 1985; Ghoshal & Moran, 1996; Sitkin & Roth, 1993; Taylor, 1987; Ullmann-Margalit, 2004). The underlying cause of trust for these scholars is not necessarily certainty provided by institutional incentives, but rather the truster's perceptions of intrinsic benevolence and integrity. In other words, for trust to develop, commitment to cooperate must be a reflection of the trustee's internal disposition or motives, not the assurance provided by monitoring and sanctioning mechanisms (Gambetta, 1988). The emergence of trust, then, can only happen when the motivation to cooperate is not driven by an external incentive (Mayer, Davis, & Shoorman, 1995).

Within this perspective, there are two primary explanations for why institutions reduce trust. The first has to do with institutional dependence (Taylor, 1987). When third-party enforcers such as managers, police officers, and judges are present to secure contracts, individuals depend on those institutions, rather than each other, to resolve conflict (Horne, 2000). Actors become unwilling to expend personal costs on enforcing informal norms if the state is available to do so, and coop-

Figure 1. Theoretical model of generalized trust

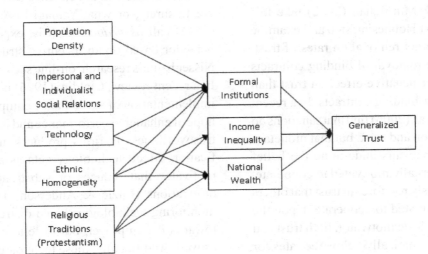

eration becomes less a result of interdependence among actors and more a result of institutional incentives (Erikson & Parent, 2007). The result is a breakdown in community, fewer acts of altruism, and a self-reinforcing dependence on state institutions to foster social order. If one believes that spontaneous cooperation is impossible without state intervention, trust will fail to manifest (see also Ullmann-Margalit, 2004).

The second explanation is rooted in social psychology, specifically attributional and overjustification research, and places individual cognition and extrinsic motivators at the center of its analysis (Deci, 1971; Deci, Koestner, & Ryan, 1999; Fehr & Falk, 2002; Green, Sternberg, & Lepper, 1976). The argument put forth by the scholars in this area is that when an actor is intrinsically motivated to perform a given act, and is subject to a reward or punishment, the actor will attribute their personal motivation, and eventual action, to the extrinsic device rather than their intrinsic desires. In effect, external motivational forces replace, or *crowd out*, internal ones, and, as a result, the actor's intrinsic motivation to perform the act decreases (Deci at al., 1999). Yet the scope of the overjustification

effect is not limited to just the self, and is frequently attributed to others as well. For instance, if two actors enter an exchange and negotiate a binding contract, both interacting parties will attribute their cooperation to the contract and not to each other's moral or ethical motives. This very example shows how and why institutional mechanisms can reduce trust: in the presence of high monitoring and sanctioning capacity or third-party enforcement, individuals will attribute cooperation to those situational controls instead of any dispositional or intrinsic motivation of the actor to trust. The implication is that trust will flourish only under conditions of weak external control, and that trust will wane, although not disappear, under conditions of strong external control.

Recent experimental work reveals support for these types of trust-control dynamics. Bohnet et al. (2001), for instance, show that levels of interpersonal trust are conditional on (a) a prior history of a contractual agreement, and (b) the type of contract. They find that present levels of trust depend on previous levels of contract enforceability, such that higher levels of trust are the result of weak contract enforcement and lower levels of trust are the result of average contract enforcement. Malhotra & Murnighan (2002) take this research to the next Hobbesian step and examine the effects of contract removal on rates of trust. They find that the removal of binding contracts has a much greater negative effect on trust than the removal of non-binding contracts. In a recent analysis, Mulder et al. (2006) find that sanctions do increase cooperation and trust, but that monetary enforcement mechanisms undermine the belief that others are internally motivated to cooperate, while simultaneously reinforcing trust that others are externally motivated to cooperate. Upon the removal of the extrinsic motivator, both trust and cooperation fell dramatically below the rates for those who had no prior exposure to the external sanctioning system. This is what the authors call *the paradox of sanctioning systems*. Although our focus in this section has exclusively centered on the dynamics between trust and control, the association between technology and trust is very similar. Technologies spur the creation of formal institutions and augment their effectiveness and efficiency. The usage of a contract by two or more actors becomes much less costly—communication technologies facilitate bargaining and surveillance, and ensure that contracts are carried out according to the pre-specified agreements. As noted earlier, the prevalence of contracts reduces the prevalence of trust. Thus, technologies directly and indirectly undermine trust: individuals attribute cooperation not to the individual, but to the technology and institution that is motivating them to act pro-socially.

The negative effects of technology on trust have been documented (see Cialdini, 1996; Nissenbaum, 2004). Nissenbaum (2004), for instance, cites how the popular solution to social order in on-line interactions is a set of technical security mechanisms aimed at creating interpersonal trust among internet users; what Nissenbaum calls *trust through security* (author's own emphasis). Nissenbaum writes from a similar standpoint as other overjustification scholars, suggesting that

these securities will not enhance trust but instead create surety, or what Yamagishi & Yamagishi (1994) call *assurance*. That is, expectations of behavior based on an incentive structure, or, in Nissenbaum's research, on-line security systems. In a recent review, Cialdini (1996) notes that the implementation of surveillance equipment in the hope of enhancing performance and interpersonal trustworthiness in firms produces an overjustification effect: technology acts as an extrinsic motivator that reduces or substitutes intrinsic motivations (Enzle & Anderson, 1993). Such monitoring technologies breed distrust not only towards the employer, but to fellow employees as well. Additionally, these technologies can exacerbate malfeasance. The actor subject to such monitoring devices attempts to find imperfections with the monitoring system. If incomplete monitoring is discovered, even those employees who are intrinsically honest and moral will try to cheat the monitoring system.

Below we begin to empirically explore these two competing theories, the new institutional economics and the overjustification and crowding perspective. We use structural equation modeling (SEM) to determine *how* technological advances connect to generalized trust, as specified by Avner Grief and Douglas North. We then explore *whether* technological advances lead to the growth or demise of generalized trust.

DATA AND METHODS

The data for this study are derived from numerous country-level sources that match on the year in which a country conducted their fourth wave (roughly the year 2000) of the World Values Survey (WVS). These sources of data include Polity IV (Marshall, Jaggers, & Gurr, 2005), the Economic Freedom of the World project (Gwartney, Lawson, & Samida, 2000), the World Bank and Governance Matters, the CIA World Fact book and the book of world rankings (Kurian, 2001), and Freedom

House. Missing data in the WVS and country-level data sets narrow the sample to 57 countries. See Table 1 for a list of the countries and Table 2 for sources of data.[2]

Variables

As noted earlier, to measure our dependent variable, trust, we use the common question of trust found in the WVS that is phrased as follows: "In general, do you think that most people can be trusted, or you can't be too careful in dealing with people?" We then take the natural log of the proportion of individuals in each country who answer 'yes' to this question. While this question is used extensively in research on generalized trust (e.g., Bjørnskov, 2007; Newton & Delhey, 2005; Herreros, 2004; Paxton, 2002, 2007), it suffers from validity and reliability problems (Ahn, Ostrom, Schmidt, & Walker, 2002; Glaeser, Laibson, Scheinkman, & Soutter, 2000;

Table 1. List of countries

Albania	Malta
Argentina	Mexico
Austria	Morocco
Bangladesh	Netherlands
Belarus	Peru
Belgium	Philippines
Bosnia and Herzegovina	Poland
Bulgaria	Portugal
Canada	Republic of Moldova
Chile	Republic of Korea
China	Republic of Macedonia
Czech Republic	Romania
Denmark	Russian Federation
Estonia	Serbia and Montenegro
Finland	Singapore
France	Slovakia
Germany	Slovenia
Great Britain	South Africa
Greece	Spain
Hungary	Sweden
Iceland	Tanzania
India	Turkey
Ireland	Uganda
Italy	Ukraine
Japan	United States
Kyrgyzstan	Venezuela
Latvia	Vietnam
Lithuania	Zimbabwe
Luxembourg	

Miller & Mitamura, 2003). Yet we feel justified in using this question because (a) the literature is extensive, and (b) the invalidity or unreliability of the question remains open to debate (see Holm & Danielson, 2005; Nannestad, 2008).

In our study we have five exogenous dimensions: population density, impersonal and individualist social relations, technology, ethnic homogeneity, and religious traditions. To measure population density, we use one indicator from the World Bank that measures the logged number of people per square kilometer. This is a common valid measure that has been used in other research on generalized trust (Delhey & Newton, 2005). We use two variables from the fourth wave of the WVS to measure the dimension of impersonal and individualist social relations. First, to capture impersonal social exchange we aggregate a series of questions from the WVS that asks whether the respondent belongs to a particular organization. The question is as follows: "Please look carefully at the following list of voluntary organizations and activities and say…which, if any, do you belong to?" Aggregating the responses produces a single ordinal variable ranging from 0 (does not belong to any group) to 11 (belongs to every group). We sum this aggregate variable, divide by the country sample size to generate a country mean-level, and then natural log the values to alleviate skew. Note we assume that individuals who belong to few organizations will have personal ties, while those who belong to many organizations will have impersonal ties. Second, to capture the psychological foundations of individualism (see Oyserman, Coon, & Kemmelmeier 2002) we include a measure from the WVS asking a respondent if "Independence is an important child quality." Like the previous WVS questions, we sum and divide the question by the country sample to generate a country mean level of "independence."

With regards to technology, we use three information technology variables from the World Bank to measure this latent dimension. First, the telephone mainlines per 1,000 people in a coun-

try divided by 100. Second, the log international internet bandwidth bits per person in a country. And, third, the natural log internet users per 100 people in a country. From the CIA World Fact book and the book of world rankings (Kurian, 2001), we use the percent largest ethnic group within a nation to measure ethnic homogeneity (see Paxton, 2007). Following Delhey & Newton (2005), we include the percent of a country's population that is protestant to measure religious traditions. The data is from the CIA World Fact book and the book of world rankings.

And, finally, there are three endogenous independent dimensions that predict generalized trust: formal institutions, income inequality, and national wealth. We measure formal institutions with five country-level variables from various sources. First, we use the measure of legal property rights found in the Economic Freedom of the World data set. We also include two measures from Freedom House measuring freedom of the press and political rights. Additionally, we include a rule of law measure from the World Bank Governance Matters data set. And, finally, we use the Polity IV measure of democracy and autocracy. These specific indicators measure (a) the effectiveness and efficiency of state incentives, (b) the constraints on political leaders to act in the interests of the citizenry, and (c) the common knowledge and universal applicability of laws. All of these have been extensively used in prior research on generalized trust (e.g., Berggren & Jordahl, 2006; Bjørnskov, 2007; Delhey & Newton, 2005; Herreros, 2004; Paxton, 2002, 2007), and are key causal indicators for both the new institutional economics (i.e., incentives) and overjustification and crowding (i.e., extrinsic motivators) perspective. To measure income inequality we log the gini coefficient for each respective country. Data for this measure comes from the World Bank, and is a common measure found in other studies of generalized trust (e.g., Bjørnskov, 2007; Herreros & Criado, 2008; Hooghe, Reeskens, Stolle, & Trappers, 2009). Finally, we use the log gross domestic product in constant year 2000 US dollars to measure national wealth. This indicator is from the World Bank and, like the gini coefficient, is also commonly used in research on generalized trust (see Berggren & Jordahl, 2006; Delhey & Newton, 2005).

All descriptive statistics and data sources can be found in Table 2.

Results

To test the validity of our dimensions, we first run an initial confirmatory factor analysis (CFA) where we set one lambda path for each latent variable equal to 1.0. We assume that each of the indicators for generalized trust, population density, ethnic homogeneity, religious traditions, income inequality, and national wealth are perfectly measured,

Table 2. Descriptive statistics and data sources

Variables	Mean	SD	Min	Max	Source
Generalized Trust					
Ln trust	-1.45	0.52	-2.55	-0.41	WVS
Population Density					
Ln population density	4.45	1.33	1.02	8.73	WB
Impersonal and Individualist Social Relations					
Social relations	-0.45	0.75	-2.74	0.89	WVS
Independence	0.48	0.18	0.18	0.84	WVS
Technology					
Telephone/100	3.12	2.20	0.02	7.36	WB
Ln bandwidth	2.81	2.52	-2.14	9.19	WB
Ln internet	1.73	1.49	-1.96	3.94	WB
Ethnic Homogeneity					
Percent largest ethnic group	0.82	0.17	0.4	0.99	WF
Religious Traditions					
Percent protestant	0.18	0.26	0	0.91	WF
Formal Institutions					
Legal property rights	6.47	1.94	2.6	9.6	EFW
Democracy	8.4	2.78	0	10	PIV
Free press	1.44	0.71	0	2	FH
Rule of law	0.43	1.03	-1.25	1.89	GM
Political rights	2.35	1.84	1	7	FH
Income Inequality					
Ln gini	3.54	0.22	3.18	4.06	WB
National Wealth					
Ln gdp	8.37	1.53	5.51	10.66	WB

Note. EFW = Economic Freedom of the World; PIV = Polity IV; GM = Governance Matters; FH = Freedom House; WB = World Bank; WF = CIA World Fact book (Kurian, 2001); WVS = World Values Survey.

and, as a result, we set their measurement errors equal to 0. To assess fit, we use the chi-square (χ^2), comparative fit index (CFI), incremental fit index (IFI), and the root-mean-square error of approximation (RMSEA). A model that perfectly captures the observed data should produce CFI and IFI values equal to 1.0, and RMSEA values equal to 0.0; CFI and IFI values greater than 0.9 and RMSEA values smaller than 0.08 suggest adequate fit (Hu & Bentler, 1999). Based on these criteria, and after correlating a number of substantively relevant error structures, the results of our CFA reveal that the measurement model produces a good fit (χ^2 = 71.27, CFI = 0.992, IFI = 0.992, RMSEA = 0.042).[3] Moreover, each one of our indicators significantly relates ($p < 0.05$) to the respective latent dimension. This suggests convergent validity of our model (Hair, Anderson, Tatham, & Black, 1998).

We then test the causal model specified in Figure 1 using structural equation models. Note that Figure 1 is a simplified model: it does not show measures, error terms, correlated errors, or covariances among the exogenous dimensions. All five exogenous dimensions are set to covary.[4] To begin, the SEM fit statistics in Table 3 closely resemble the CFA fit statistics (χ^2 = 97.7, CFI = 0.974, IFI = 0.976, RMSEA = 0.067). This suggests that the structural equation model specified in Figure 1 conforms well to the observed data.[5]

The overall results reveal mediocre support for the NIE model of institutions but strong support for the NIE model of generalized trust. Technology significantly, and positively, relates to formal institutions.[6] The other theoretical NIE predictors do not fare as well. Both population density and individualist social relations are statistically insignificant, while one of the exogenous parameters specified by Delhey & Newton (2005), ethnic homogeneity, appears to positively increase formal institutions. These five variables account for a large percentage of the variation in formal institutions, as indicated by the R^2 of 0.90. As for the other endogenous dimensions, nothing in the model relates to income inequality while all of the specified exogenous dimensions significantly produce national wealth. The R^2 reveals that the model explains only 4 percent of the variation for income inequality but 93 percent of the variation for national wealth. Finally, the model shows that formal institutions increase generalized trust and that this relationship is statistically significant, with 28 percent of the variation explained. The other specified causal factors, income inequality and national wealth, are statistically insignificant and appear not to produce generalized trust.[7]

FUTURE RESEARCH DIRECTIONS

While the present findings are particularly enlightening, our research suffers from obvious limitations, and future investigations that resolve these issues would greatly contribute to our understanding of the relationship between technology and trust. First, our measure of technology—information technologies—does not fully capture the technological spectrum. We have argued that these technologies increase the communication capacity of formal institutions that then increase generalized trust, but what are the effects of other technological advances? For instance, advents in military technology that allow for swifter control within countries could facilitate the state's infringement on citizen rights and foster conditions under which individuals distrust the government and others (Erikson & Parent, 2007; Rothstein, 2000; Rothstein & Stolle, 2008). As such, future cross-national studies should take different measures of technology into account, and pay special attention to their possible differential effects on generalized trust.

Second, the technology dimension we use does not adequately measure surveillance technologies, which is a primary factor that reduces generalized trust according to the overjustification and crowding perspective (see Cialdini, 1996). In essence, our measures of technology may only be capturing

Table 3. Latent dimension structural equation model predicting generalized trust[a]

	Outcome Dimensions							
	Formal Institutions		Income Inequality		National Wealth		Generalized Trust	
	b	SE	b	SE	b	SE	b	SE
Population Density	0.05	0.05						
Impersonal Social Relations	0.21	0.17						
Technology	0.67*	0.07			1.12*	0.10		
Ethnic Homogeneity	0.84*	0.35	-0.20	0.13	0.97*	0.47		
Religious Traditions	-0.16	0.33	-0.10	0.11	-0.63*	0.27		
Formal Institutions							0.23*	0.14
Income Inequality							-0.10	0.23
National Wealth							0.03	0.10
R^2	0.90		0.04		0.93		0.28	
Goodness-of-Fit								
χ^2	97.7							
CFI	0.974							
IFI	0.976							
RMSEA	0.067							
N	57							
[a] Robust standard errors (one-tailed)								
* $p < 0.05$								

the possible positive effects of technology while ignoring the negative effects. Including a measure of surveillance technologies per capita in our model would resolve this issue. As of yet, however, such cross-national data is unavailable. The next step would be to employ case study methods that examine the effects of surveillance technologies among multiple organizations and between different economic sectors. Doing so would greatly contribute to the debate and shed light on if and how information and surveillance technologies differ with respect to generalized trust.

Third, and finally, while our study ostensibly provides strong support for the new institutional economics model, our results may actually favor overjustification and crowding theory. Recall that in a recent investigation by Mulder at al. (2006), the researchers find that extrinsic motivators simultaneously undermine intrinsic trust and bolster extrinsic trust. This is a dynamic labeled the paradox, or double-edged sword, of sanctioning systems. The observed trust enhancing effects of technology and formal institutions may, in fact, be capturing only one side of this sword, the belief that others are extrinsically motivated to trust, while the other side of the sword, albeit unmeasured and unobserved, tacitly lowers levels of intrinsic generalized trust within the population. In other words, it is possible that what we and other scholars of generalized trust are observing is not the *crowding out* effect of intrinsic generalized trust, but the *crowding in* effect of extrinsic generalized trust.

The implication is that current methods may be inappropriate to adequately test overjustification and crowding theories. The reason has to do with the fundamental problem of causal inference coupled with the difficulty, and unavailability, of using survey research to differentiate between extrinsic and intrinsic sources and forms of trust. Thus, it is our firm belief that the greatest understanding of the relationship between technology and trust will not come from cross-national surveys, ethnographies, or even comparative organizational studies, but from experiments. Our hope is that the present research will provide the necessary insight to inform such future research.

Managerial Implications

In spite of the limitations and necessity for future investigations, the present research has compelling managerial implications. The authors find that formal institutions are critical for generating trust and that the effect of technology on trust is fully mediated by these institutions. This mechanism indicates that firm executives who adopt technological innovations from other organizations without the accompanying institutional frameworks will likely fail to reap the benefits of this new technology. As Cordella (2006) makes explicitly clear, technology without institutions creates massive complexities that can actually amplify transaction costs and possibly diminish trust. The increased information provided by technology only reduces transaction costs if the flow of information "...is equally balanced by an improvement in the ability to manage it (Cordella, 2006, p. 199)." For instance, although electronic marketplaces may provide an abundance of consumption options, such a profusion of information can confuse and stifle the consumer, increasing the need for institutional brokers to help match consumers and producers (Bailey & Bakos, 1997). Here, technology increases information and reduces uncertainty, but

also increases search costs. To reduce these search costs, firms that adopt internet-based technologies in order to enter the electronic marketplace need to provide institutional mechanisms that cull and review necessary facts from the impeding flood of information for the consumer. Thus, those that espouse technology should be aware of its impact not only on information, but also on complexity, as well as the role of institutions in managing this complexity.

CONCLUSION

In this chapter, we tested two competing theories of how technology may impact generalized trust. The first theory, new institutional economics, argues that technology will indirectly, and positively, produce generalized trust. It does so through the mechanism of formal institutions. As states become more technologically advanced they develop formal rules and centralized organizations to accommodate these changes. The more effective and efficient a state's institutions, the more generalized trust its citizens will display. The second perspective, overjustification and crowding theory, presents a competing hypothesis for trust production. Technologies and institutions act as extrinsic motivators that crowd out intrinsic reasons to trust others. Two parties subject to an incentive will attribute the cooperation of the other to the enforcement mechanism and not to personal moral convictions. As a result, these technical and social controls will diminish trust. We tested these theories using structural equation models, a wide range of data sources, and a sample of 57 countries. The results lend support to the new institutional economics model of generalized trust.

Although the present research exhibits some limitations that warrant future investigations, it appears that technology is a great, albeit indirect, boon for trust. Trust continually ebbs and flows with uncertainty. To the extent that technology provides certainty, it has the power to generate trust.

REFERENCES

Ahn, T.-K., Ostrom, E., Schmidt, E., & Walker, J. (2003). Trust in two-person games: Game structures and linkages. In Ostrom, E., & Walker, J. (Eds.), *Trust and reciprocity*. New York: Russell Sage Foundation.

Alchian, A., & Demsetz, H. (1973). The property rights paradigm. *The Journal of Economic History*, *33*, 16–27.

Arrow, K. (1974). *The limits of organization*. New York: Norton.

Bailey, J., & Bakos, J. Y. (1997). An exploratory study of the emerging role of electronic intermediaries. *International Journal of Electronic Commerce*, *1*, 7–20.

Berggren, N., & Jordahl, H. (2006). Free to trust: Economic freedom and social capital. *Kyklos*, *59*, 141–169. doi:10.1111/j.1467-6435.2006.00324.x

Berhnheim, B. D., & Whinston, M. D. (1998). Incomplete contracts and strategic ambiguity. *The American Economic Review*, *88*, 902–932.

Bjørnskov, C. (2003). The happy few. Cross-country evidence on social capital and life satisfaction. *Kyklos*, *56*, 3–16. doi:10.1111/1467-6435.00207

Bjørnskov, C. (2007). Determinants of generalized trust: A cross-country comparison. *Public Choice*, *130*, 1–21. doi:10.1007/s11127-006-9069-1

Blau, P. (1964). *Exchange and power in social life*. New York: Wiley.

Bohnet, I., Frey, B. S., & Huck, S. (2001). More order with less law: On contract enforcement, trust, and crowding. *The American Political Science Review*, *95*, 131–144. doi:10.1017/S0003055401000211

Brewer, M. B. (1981). Ethnocentrism and its role in interpersonal trust. In Brewer, M. B., & Collins, B. E. (Eds.), *Scientific inquiry and the social sciences* (pp. 345–359). New York: Jossey-Bass.

Brinton, M. (1992). *Women and the economic miracle: Gender and work in postwar Japan*. Berkeley, CA: University of California Press.

Brinton, M., & Nee, V. (Eds.). (1998). *The new institutionalism in sociology*. Stanford, CA: Stanford University Press.

Cheung, S. (1974). A theory of price control. *The Journal of Law & Economics*, *12*, 53–71. doi:10.1086/466784

Cialdini, R. (1996). The Triple tumor structure of organizational behavior. In Messick, D. M., & Tenbrunsel, A. E. (Eds.), *Codes of conduct* (pp. 44–58). New York: Russell Sage Foundation.

Ciborra, C. U. (1993). *Teams, markets and systems*. Cambridge, UK: Cambridge University Press.

Coase, R. (1937). The nature of the firm. *Economica*, *4*, 386–405. doi:10.1111/j.1468-0335.1937.tb00002.x

Coase, R. (1960). The problem of social cost. *The Journal of Law & Economics*, *3*, 1–44. doi:10.1086/466560

Coleman, J. (1990). *Foundations of social theory*. Cambridge, MA: Harvard University Press.

Cook, K. S., Hardin, R., & Levi, M. (2005). *Cooperation without trust?* New York: Russell Sage Foundation.

Cook, K. S., & Levi, M. (1990). *The limits of rationality*. Chicago: University of Chicago Press.

Cordella, A. (2006). Transaction costs and information systems: Does IT add up? *Journal of Information Technology*, *21*, 195–202. doi:10.1057/palgrave.jit.2000066

Deci, E. L. (1971). Effects of externally mediated rewards on intrinsic motivation. *Journal of Personality and Social Psychology*, *18*, 105–115. doi:10.1037/h0030644

Deci, E. L., Koestner, R., & Ryan, R. M. (1999). A meta-analytic review of experiments examining the effects of extrinsic rewards on intrinsic motivation. *Psychological Bulletin, 125,* 627–668. doi:10.1037/0033-2909.125.6.627

Delhey, J., & Newton, K. (2005). Predicting cross-national levels of social trust: Global pattern or Nordic exceptionalism? *European Sociological Review, 21,* 311–327. doi:10.1093/esr/jci022

Demsetz, H. (1967). Towards a theory of property rights. *The American Economic Review, 57,* 347–359.

Durkheim, E. (1893). *The division of labor in society.* London: MacMillan. (Original work published 1984)

Eggertsson, T. (1990). *Economic behavior and institutions.* Cambridge, UK: Cambridge University Press. doi:10.1017/CBO9780511609404

Ellickson, R. (1991). *Order without law.* Cambridge, MA: Harvard University Press.

Enzle, M. E., & Anderson, S. C. (1993). Surveillant intentions and intrinsic motivations. *Journal of Personality and Social Psychology, 64,* 265–279. doi:10.1037/0022-3514.64.2.257

Erikson, E., & Parent, J. M. (2007). Central authority and order. *Sociological Theory, 25,* 245–267. doi:10.1111/j.1467-9558.2007.00307.x

Fehr, E., & Falk, A. (2002). Psychological foundations of incentives. *European Economic Review, 46,* 687–724. doi:10.1016/S0014-2921(01)00208-2

Foreman-Peck, J. (1995). *A history of the world economy.* Hempstead, UK: Harvester Wheatsheaf.

Fox, D. R. (1985). Psychology, ideology, utopia, and the commons. *The American Psychologist, 40,* 48–58. doi:10.1037/0003-066X.40.1.48

Gambetta, D. (1988). Can we trust trust? In Gambetta, D. (Ed.), *Trust: Making and breaking cooperative relationships* (pp. 213–237). Cambridge, MA: Blackwell.

Ghoshal, S., & Moran, P. (1996). Bad for practice: A critique of the transaction costs theory. *Academy of Management Review, 21,* 13–47. doi:10.2307/258627

Glaeser, E. L., Laibson, D. L., Scheinkman, J. A., & Soutter, C. L. (2000, August). Measuring Trust. *The Quarterly Journal of Economics,* 811–847. doi:10.1162/003355300554926

Green, D., Sternberg, B., & Lepper, M. R. (1976). Overjustification in a token economy. *Journal of Personality and Social Psychology, 34,* 1219–1234. doi:10.1037/0022-3514.34.6.1219

Greif, A. (1993). Contract enforceability and economic institutions in early trade: The maghribi traders' coalition. *The American Economic Review, 83,* 525–548.

Greif, A. (1994). Cultural beliefs and the organization of society: Historical and theoretical reflection on collectivist and individualist societies. *The Journal of Political Economy, 102,* 912–950. doi:10.1086/261959

Greif, A. (2006). *Institutions and the path to the modern economy: Lesson from medieval trade.* Cambridge, UK: Cambridge University Press.

Gwartney, J., Lawson, R., & Samida, D. (2000). *Economic freedom of the world 2000: Annual report.* Retrieved from http://www.freetheworld.com.

Hair, J. F., Anderson, R. E., Tatham, R. L., & Black, W. (1998). *Multivariate data analysis.* Upper Saddle River, NJ: Prentice-Hall.

Hardin, R. (2006). *Trust.* Cambridge, UK: Polity.

Hechter, M. (1987). *Principles of group solidarity.* Berkeley, CA: California University Press.

Hechter, M., & Opp, K.-D. (Eds.). (2001). *Social norms*. New York: Russell Sage Foundation.

Herreros, F. (2004). *The problems of forming social capital. Why trust?* London: Palgrave. doi:10.1057/9781403978806

Herreros, F., & Criado, H. (2008). The state and the development of social trust. *International Political Science Review, 29*, 53–71. doi:10.1177/0192512107083447

Hodgson, G. M. (1988). *Economics and institutions: A manifesto for a modern institutional economics*. Cambridge, UK: Polity Press.

Holm, H. J., & Danielson, A. (2005). Tropic trust versus Nordic trust: Experimental evidence from Tanzania and Sweden. *The Economic Journal, 115*, 505–532. doi:10.1111/j.1468-0297.2005.00998.x

Hooghe, M., Reeskens, T., Stolle, D., & Trappers, A. (2009). Ethnic diversity and generalized trust in Europe. A cross-national multilevel study. *Comparative Political Studies, 42*, 198–223. doi:10.1177/0010414008325286

Hopcroft, R. (1994). The social origins of agrarian change in late medieval England. *American Journal of Sociology, 99*, 1559–1595. doi:10.1086/230454

Horne, C. (2000). Community and the state: The relationship between normative and legal controls. *European Sociological Review, 16*, 225–243. doi:10.1093/esr/16.3.225

Hu, L., & Bentler, P. M. (1999). Cutoff criteria for fit indexes in covariance structure analysis: Conventional criteria versus new alternatives. *Structural Equation Modeling, 6*, 1–55. doi:10.1080/10705519909540118

Ingram, P., & Clay, K. (2000). The choice-within-constraints new institutionalism and implications for sociology. *Annual Review of Sociology, 26*, 525–546. doi:10.1146/annurev.soc.26.1.525

Knack, S. (2002). Social capital and the quality of government: Evidence from the state. *American Journal of Political Science, 46*, 772–785. doi:10.2307/3088433

Knack, S., & Keefer, P. (1997). Does social capital have an economic payoff? A cross-country investigation. *The Quarterly Journal of Economics, 112*, 1251–1288. doi:10.1162/003355300555475

Knight, J. (1992). *Institutions and social conflict*. Cambridge, UK: Cambridge University Press. doi:10.1017/CBO9780511528170

Kurian, G. T. (2001). *The book of world rankings*. New York: Facts on File.

Kurzban, R. (2003). Biological foundations of reciprocity. In E. Ostrom & J. Walker, Trust and reciprocity (pp. 105-127). New York: Russell Sage Foundation.

Levi, M. (1988). *Of rule and revenue*. Berkeley, CA: California University Press.

Levi, M. (1998). A state of trust. In Braithwaite, V., & Levi, M. (Eds.), *Trust and governance* (pp. 77–101). New York: Russell Sage Foundation.

Levi, M., & Stoker, L. (2000). Political trust and trustworthiness. *Annual Review of Political Science, 3*, 475–507. doi:10.1146/annurev.polisci.3.1.475

Malhotra, D., & Murnighan, J. K. (2002). The effects of contracts on interpersonal trust. *Administrative Science Quarterly, 47*, 534–559. doi:10.2307/3094850

Malone, T. W., Yates, J., & Benjamin, R. I. (1987). Electronic markets and electronic hierarchies: Effects of information technology on market structure and corporate strategies. *Communications of the ACM, 30*, 484–497. doi:10.1145/214762.214766

Mansbridge, J. (1999). Altruistic trust. In Warren, M. E. (Ed.), *Democracy and trust* (pp. 290–309). Cambridge, UK: Cambridge University Press. doi:10.1017/CBO9780511659959.010

Marshall, M., Jaggers, K., & Gurr, T. R. (2005). Polity IV dataset. Computer file version p4v2004. College Part, MD: Center for International Development and Conflict.

Mayer, R. C., Davis, J. H., & Shoorman, F. D. (1995). An integrative model of organizational trust. *Academy of Management Review, 20,* 709–734. doi:10.2307/258792

Miller, A. S., & Mitamura, T. (2003). Are surveys on trust trustworthy? *Social Psychology Quarterly, 66,* 62–70. doi:10.2307/3090141

Mulder, L. B., Dijk, E. V., De Cremer, D., & Wilke, H. A. M. (2006). Undermining trust and cooperation: The paradox of sanctioning systems in social dilemmas. *Journal of Experimental Social Psychology, 42,* 147–162. doi:10.1016/j.jesp.2005.03.002

Nannestad, P. (2008). What have we learned about generalized trust, if anything? *Annual Review of Political Science, 11,* 413–436. doi:10.1146/annurev.polisci.11.060606.135412

Nee, V. (2005). The new institutionalism in economics and sociology. In Smelser, N. J., & Swedberg, R. (Eds.), *The handbook of economic sociology* (pp. 49–74). Princeton, NJ: Princeton University Press.

Nee, V., & Ingram, P. (1998). Embeddedness and beyond: Institutions, exchange, and social structure. In Nee, V., & Brinton, M. (Eds.), *New institutionalism in sociology* (pp. 19–45). Stanford, CA: Stanford University Press.

Nissenbaum, H. (2004). Will security enhance trust online, or supplant it? In Kramer, R. M., & Cook, K. S. (Eds.), *Trust and distrust in organizations.* New York: Russell Sage Foundation.

North, D. (1981). *Structure and change in economic history.* New York: Norton.

North, D. (1990). *Institutions, institutional change, and economic performance.* New York: Cambridge University Press.

Obstfeld, M., & Taylor, A. M. (2003). *Global capital markets: Growth and integration.* Cambridge, UK: Cambridge University Press.

Oyserman, D., Croon, H. M., & Kemmelmeier, M. (2002). Rethinking individualism and collectivism: Evaluation of theoretical assumptions and meta-analyses. *Psychological Bulletin, 128,* 3–72. doi:10.1037/0033-2909.128.1.3

Paxton, P. (2002). Social capital and democracy: An interdependent relationship. *American Journal of Sociology, 67,* 254–277. doi:10.2307/3088895

Paxton, P. (2007). Association memberships and generalized trust: A multilevel model across 31 countries. *Social Forces, 86,* 47–76. doi:10.1353/sof.2007.0107

Putnam, R. (1993). *Making democracy work: Civic traditions in modern Italy.* Princeton, NJ: Princeton University Press.

Putnam, R. (2000). *Bowling alone: The collapse and revival of American community.* New York: Simon and Schuster.

Putnam, R. (2007). E pluribus unum: Diversity and community in the twenty-first century. The 2006 Johan Skytte Prize Lecture. *Scandinavian Political Studies, 30,* 137–174. doi:10.1111/j.1467-9477.2007.00176.x

Rothstein, B. (2000). Trust, social dilemmas and collective memories. *Journal of Theoretical Politics, 12,* 477–501. doi:10.1177/0951692800012004007

Rothstein, B., & Stolle, D. (2008). How political institutions create and destroy social capital: An institutional theory of generalized trust. *Comparative Politics, 40.*

Schelling, T. C. (1960). *The strategy of conflict.* Cambridge, MA: Cambridge University Press.

Sitkin, S. B., & Roth, N. L. (1993). Explaining the limited effectiveness of legalistic 'remedies' for trust/distrust. *Organization Science, 4*, 367–392. doi:10.1287/orsc.4.3.367

Taylor, M. (1987). *The possibility of cooperation.* Cambridge, UK: Cambridge University Press.

Tönnies, F. (1963). *Gemeinschaft und gesellshaft.* Darmstadt, Germany: Wissenschaftliche Buchgessellschaft. (Original work published 1887)

Tyler, T. R., & Kramer, R. M. (1996). Whither trust? In Kramer, R. M., & Tyler, T. R. (Eds.), *Trust in Organizations* (pp. 1–15). Thousand Oaks, CA: Sage.

Ullmann-Margalit, E. (1978). *The emergence of norms.* Oxford, UK: Oxford University Press.

Ullmann-Margalit, E. (2004). Trust, distrust, and in between. In Hardin, R. (Ed.), *Distrust* (pp. 60–82). New York: Russell Sage Foundation.

Uslaner, E. M. (2000). Producing and consuming trust. *Political Science Quarterly, 115*, 569–590. doi:10.2307/2657610

Uslaner, E. M. (2002). *The moral foundations of trust.* Cambridge, UK: Cambridge University Press. doi:10.1017/CBO9780511614934

Weber, M. (1979). *Economy and society.* Berkeley, CA: University of California Press.

Welch, M. R., Rivera, R. E. N., Conway, B. P., Yonkoski, J., Lupton, P. M., & Giancola, R. (2005). Determinants and consequences of social trust. *Sociological Inquiry, 75*, 453–473. doi:10.1111/j.1475-682X.2005.00132.x

Williamson, O. E. (1975). *Markets and hierarchies: Analysis and antitrust implications.* New York, NY: Free Press.

Williamson, O. E. (1985). *The economic institutions of capitalism.* New York: The Free Press.

Yamagishi, T., & Yamagishi, M. (1994). Trust and commitment in the United States and Japan. *Motivation and Emotion, 18*, 129–166. doi:10.1007/BF02249397

Zak, P., & Knack, S. (2001). Trust and growth. *The Economic Journal, 111*, 207–243. doi:10.1111/1468-0297.00609

ENDNOTES

[1] Cordella (2006) argues that technology can reduce search, bargaining, and enforcement costs only if institutions and organizations have the ability to efficiently process that new information (see also Malone, Yates, & Benjamin, 1997). Otherwise, information will become asymmetric, and although uncertainty will decrease it comes at the price of increased complexity and greater opportunism (Williamson, 1975, 1985).

[2] I use multiple imputation techniques found in STATA 10 to maintain statistical power and a sizable country level sample. Note that none of the imputed variables have greater than 10 percent missing cases. I imputed legal property rights values for Belarus and democracy values for Luxemburg and Malta.

[3] We correlate the following exogenous indicator error structures as indicated by an LM test: (1) democracy and political rights; (2) political rights and free press; (3) ln internet and ln bandwidth; (4) democracy and free press; (5) democracy and legal property rights; (6) telephone/100 and inequality; (7) democracy and ethnic homogeneity; (8) telephone/100 and ln bandwidth; and (9) telephone/100 and ln internet.

[4] A correlation or covariance matrix of indicators is available upon request.

[5] Diagnostics reveal that outliers and multicollinearity do not bias the results. Outliers do exist when predicting formal institutions and

income inequality but their exclusion does not alter the results beyond those presented here. Results available upon request.

[6] We use robust standard errors to remedy the presence of skewness and kurtosis

[7] We finished with a post hoc analysis to determine if any direct effects from the exogenous variables to generalized trust would improve model fit. In other words, we are determining if the specified endogenous independent variables truly mediate the exogenous dimensions; the results from a LaGrange multiplier test suggest that this is the case. Including a direct effect from any of the five exogenous variables does not statistically significantly improve model fit.

Chapter 9
Trust in Technology:
A Status Value Approach to Understanding Technology Adoption

Celeste Campos-Castillo
The University of Iowa, USA

ABSTRACT

The notion of trust in technology has recently flourished through translating what researchers know about interpersonal trust into the realm of technology. What has been missing from this movement is a sociological perspective on trust in technology, an understanding of how the social and cultural framework in which one is embedded can shape outcomes like trust. To fill this void, the author develops a framework for understanding how these macrostructures can become imported into the local context (e.g., the workplace) to influence trust in technology. Specifically, this framework takes a status value approach (Berger & Fisek, 2006) to explain how the status of social actors (e.g., people, organizations) can transfer to the technologies to which they are associated and be used as a basis for trust. The author focuses the discussion of this theory around implications for technology adoption and offers suggestions for future applications of the theory in other domains.

INTRODUCTION

A recent observation about two popular social networking sites – MySpace and Facebook – is that their customers are divided along social class lines, with the working class individuals concentrated in MySpace and the middle class individuals gathering on Facebook (boyd, 2007). What might account

for this differential adoption of technologies that mediate social networking?

In a world increasingly reliant on technologies to mediate tasks like social networking, there has been a growing interest regarding trust in technology (Lee & See, 2004), which I am defining here as the belief that the technology will perform a set of delegated tasks with minimal risk. Essentially, the probability that a person will adopt a technology depends on the person's trust in that technology (Lee & Moray,

DOI: 10.4018/978-1-61520-901-9.ch009

1992, 1994; Lewandowsky, Mundy, & Tan, 2000; Muir, 1987; Parasuraman & Riley, 1997). Weber (1947) saw technology as a means to move beyond finite human capacity and rationalize a process; if a human controller does not trust technology, then how can technology increase productivity? Can you trust that the directions from your car's GPS unit will lead you to the correct destination and not a dead end road? How do you determine if you will spend your money, for instance, on the books that Amazon.com recommends while you peruse around their website? Or how about trusting websites like eHarmony.com to match you and the person with whom you will be presumably spending the rest of your life?

A number of explanations for the extent to which technologies are trusted exist in the literature. Some have focused on how stable individual differences in the propensity to trust (Rotter 1971) influence trust in technology (e.g., Parasuraman, Singh, Molloy, & Parasuraman, 1992). Others have looked at how the design of the technology might alter trust (e.g., Lee & Moray, 1994). While much has been written on the role of trust in technology, there is a missing piece to the picture – a sociological perspective. I build on Lee and See's (2004) suggestion that macrostructures shape the evolution of trust in technology by providing a theory of *how* larger macrostructures can become imported into the local context (e.g., workplace) and have influence over trust in technology. A primary emphasis in sociology is that the local context is influenced by the larger social and cultural framework in which it is embedded. The social structure and personality perspective within sociology (McLeod & Lively, 2003), for instance, focuses on the multiple, interconnected layers of social milieu that shape individual outcomes such as which social networking site to use. Of course, a sociological understanding of technology is not new. For example, sociology has provided explanations for the digital divide, which is a term used to describe differential access to and ownership of technology. A variable often used in sociological

models – socioeconomic status – has been shown to be a primary correlate of access to computer technology (Bimber, 2000; Calvert et al., 2005; Wilson, Wallin, & Reister, 2003).

These two literatures – trust in technology and the sociology of technology – have for the most part evolved separately from one another. I merge together these two literatures to initiate a sociological perspective on trust in technology. I use status value theory (Berger & Fisek, 2006) from the expectation states program (Berger & Webster, 2006), a family of theories that explains how inequalities in the larger social structure get imported into the local context. Several of these theories (including status value theory) revolve around status, which is the prestige, honor, and esteem conferred to a social actor by a particular culture. As an example, many cultures tend to confer more status to men than women, all else being equal (Pugh & Wahrman, 1983).

Status has been recently discussed as a signal for trustworthiness (Cook, 2005; Cook, Hardin, & Levi 2005). A working paper (Campos & Schultz, 2009) suggests that a model of trust by Mayer and his colleagues (Mayer, Davis, & Schoorman, 1995) can be used to understand how status influences trust, shaping mobility in the workplace. I suggest that we can use a similar logic when discussing trust in a technology. Technologies that have higher status value than others will be trusted more and have a higher rate of adoption. At the same time, the designation of status value in technology is a social construction. Status value theory (Berger & Fisek, 2006) posits that initially unvalued objects, like new technologies, can become imbued with status value when they are associated with elements that hold status value (e.g., individuals or organizations); the status value of these elements spreads to the unvalued objects.

I suggest how this status value approach to understanding trust in technology can be used to predict technology adoption. Explanations from classic economic theories highlight the rational decision-making of autonomous agents in adoption. However, these agents are almost always embedded in a social and cultural framework that colors decision-making. Because trust in technology influences adoption of the technology, as in selecting online shopping services (Kollock, 1999), we can use this status value approach to understand the adoption process. The theory can be extended to inform other concerns surrounding trust in technology, such as reliance in automation within the field of human factors engineering.

I begin with the theoretical background for the theory on trust in technology. I review the literature on technology adoption to set the stage for the current application of the theory. I then make links to trust and status value theory. Afterwards, I formally present the propositions in the theory. I end the chapter with ideas on future directions with the current theory and avenues for theoretical extensions.

BACKGROUND

Technology Adoption

The diffusion of a new technological innovation is generally slower than many other contagion processes (Geroski, 2000; Rogers, 1995). Adopting new technologies involves acquiring new skills, abilities, and knowledge, causing the process to be sluggish among individuals and organizations. Markets tend to exhibit inertia and are biased toward existing products (Katz & Shapiro, 1992), causing proponents of new technologies to face the daunting task of convincing consumers to switch from their current preferences. Consequently, there is a slow incremental trend in technological innovation and the emergence of new dominant designs occurs mostly through technological discontinuities, which are innovations that dramatically affect the ratio of price to performance and create stochastic shocks to the system (Anderson & Tushman, 1990; see also Loch & Huberman, 1999). Yet, it is precisely these

large deviations from the slow trend that produce the most uncertainty when deciding whether to adopt (Rogers 1995), begging the question: What causes the initial adoption of a new technology? Early explanations of adoption have focused on mechanisms that are drawn from classical economic notions of reasoning. More recently, there has been a movement toward explanations that focus on the social context of rational thought.

Classic Approach to Adoption

Classic sociological explanations of rational thought are often rooted in Weber's (1947) anthology of observations, some of which revolved around the bureaucratic form of economic organization. For Weber (1947), bureaucracies were a form of achieving ends through rational means, particularly because they concentrate the means of economic production. Technologies rationalize production through mechanization – a reduction of uncertainty in economic exchange through standardization. The technical core of an organization – the segments where inputs are transformed into outputs – was seen as such an important element in the rationalization of production that managers were advised to seal off the core from environmental disturbances (Thompson, 1967).

Which technologies afforded the best means to achieve ends? The classical view of rational thought generally conceives of a top-down approach in decision-making, where higher-ranking offices stated goals beforehand and actions in the lower-ranking offices were the result of pursuing those goals. In regards to deciding whether to adopt a technology, goals would be used to weigh the costs and benefits of technology adoption (Reinganum, 1981). Adoption occurs when expected returns exceed a threshold, which depends solely on idiosyncratic goals (e.g., Davies, 1979).

Dissents from the classic approach contend that actors can make decisions based on "gut reactions" and rationalize them after the fact (Feldman & March, 1981; Weick, 1995). Rational thought was once envisioned as a process removed from emotions, but now a more common view filtering into the literature is that decisions need an emotional substrate (Damasio 1999). It is not that reasoning is no longer seen as rational, but rather that it is perceived as rational given social exigencies.

Social Approach to Adoption

Research examining technology adoption has relied on the perceived characteristics of the technology and social processes underlying the adoption. The two are not necessarily independent of one another. The perception of a technology's utility and ease of use is directly related to the acceptance of a new technology (Igbaria, Guimaraes, & Davis, 1995), yet these perceptions can be subject to the social context. The classic study of the diffusion of a medical innovation (Coleman, Katz, & Menzel, 1957) highlights the role of peers. Burt (1987) revisited the data and proposed that competitive forces can increase the propensity for structurally equivalent doctors to adopt new innovations. In another related line of research, the attractiveness of a consumer good, such as technologies, is largely based on its sales history (Katz & Shapiro, 1986). This is referred to as demand-side economies of scale, whereby the durability of a good largely depends on the number of consumers who buy compatible products. For example, during the videotape format war in the 1970s and 1980s, both VHS and Betamax (and a few other formats) competed for a share of the market. The durability of a Betamax videotape was largely based on how many consumers bought Betamax video systems. If others were buying VHS players, consumers would be better off following these others to ensure durability of their purchase.

We can connect our discussion of social processes to our previous discussion of uncertainty. Weber's (1947) rationalization is but one solution to uncertainty. A social approach to the problem comes from neoinstitutionalism (e.g., DiMaggio & Powell, 1983; Meyer & Rowan 1977), which suggests that the social and cultural framework in which an organization is embedded, or the institutional environment (DiMaggio & Powell, 1983; Meyer & Rowan 1977), can provide guidance under uncertainty. The institutional environment informs us of what is considered legitimate, creating a homogenization of preferences and behavior because organizations overwhelmingly adopt these legitimate practices to increase their viability in the field.

With respect to technology adoption, we would expect that technologies that were perceived as legitimate would be more likely to be adopted (DiMaggio & Powell, 1983). An organization, for instance, would mimic other organizations and adopt their technologies. As a result, technical requirements would be decoupled from actual practice because of the emphasis on seeking legitimacy over technical function. Technological innovations that would greatly increase efficiency might be neglected and those that are in actuality inefficient could be revered (Abrahamson, 1991).

Also found within a cultural framework is status information, which are consensual beliefs about actor traits in regards to their relative prestige, honor, and esteem (Berger et al., 1977). Status can be used as a cue to infer quality under uncertainty (Podolny, 1994; Podolny et al,. 1996), such as hiring and promotion decisions (Foschi 2000; Ridgeway & Correll 2004) and the pricing of consumer products (Benjamin & Podolny, 1999). Status has also been linked to technological innovations, with many current innovations building from the prior ones of high status organizations (Podolny & Stuart, 1995; Podolny, Stuart, & Hannan, 1996). While much research has been conducted linking status to inferences of quality in decision-making, little work has been developed to understand how trust mediates the relationship. Trust has been cast as the definitive solution to the problem of uncertainty because it minimizes transaction costs (Williamson, 1981).

Trust

The majority of the research on trust revolves around trust between a person and another person (i.e., interpersonal trust) or a person and a "generalized other" (see Mayer, Davis, & Schoorman, 1995; Rousseau, Sitkin, Burt, & Camerer, 1998 for reviews). The literature on interpersonal trust has been the primary basis for understanding human-technology trust (Lee & See 2004). Because evidence suggests that humans treat computers as social actors (Reeves & Nass, 1996), a motivation existed among researchers (e.g., Lee & Moray, 1992, 1994; Muir 1987) to translate what is known about interpersonal trust to human-technology trust.

Adopting a new technology involves considerable risk and uncertainty, potential breeding conditions for trust (Cheshire & Cook, 2004; Kollock, 1994; Molm, Takahasi, & Peterson, 2000). Anonymity in computer-mediated interaction creates uncertainty and risk, particularly in situations like internet markets where there is asymmetry in information between buyers and sellers (Yamagishi & Matsuda, 2003). For an organization, changes to its technical core can lead to an increase in susceptibility to mortality (Hannan & Freeman, 1984). Increasingly, the technical core of organizations is becoming computerized (Malone, Laubacher, & Morton, 2003), escalating the need for a full understanding – one that includes sociological explanations in addition to traditional ones – of how trust in technology operates.

Reputation systems, like those used on eBay, are often used to infer trustworthiness (Kollock, 1999). Reputation is a characteristic assigned to an actor by other actors, based on past behavior. Actors refrain from opportunism or malfeasance because their reputation can quickly spread in an embedded network (Granovetter, 1985). Firms want to not only continue to conduct business with the same partners, but also be able to conduct business with other partners in the future (Macaulay,

1963). Among diamond merchants, for example, defecting from normatively prescribed business behaviors would result in a loss of family, religious, and community ties (Coleman, 1988).

Reputation is considered an intangible asset, with a firm's name conveying its reputation developed from prior performance (Kreps, 1990; Tadelis, 1999). A firm with a bad reputation may attempt to shed its name to disassociate itself from previous bad choices, like the troubled insurer American International Group (AIG) changing signs outside its Manhattan office to read, "American International Underwriters" (AIU) (Goldsmith & Siemaszko, 2009). Buyers are even willing to pay 8.1% more for the same items from an established eBay seller than from a new seller with little sales history (Resnick et al., 2006). With respect to technologies, reputation can be seen driving trust decisions as implied by eHarmony commercials that highlight their (purported) reputation for matching couples who eventually marry one another. Another example is when a prospective user might seek reputation information by asking his or her network alters for their past experiences with the technology (DiMaggio & Louch, 1998).

In the absence of reputation information – as in the case of new technologies – buyers tend to rely on status information (Benjamin & Podolny, 1999). In a review of interpersonal trust, Mayer et al. (1995) contend that the three person traits that lead to trust in the individual are competence, benevolence, and integrity. I propose that trust in a technology is a socially constructed process driven by status information that shapes the perception of these three traits. In other words, larger macrostructures with status value information can be imported into the local context and influence trust decisions.

Status Value

Berger and Fisek's (2006) status value theory is a refinement of Ridgeway's (1991) status construction theory in that it extends its scope and provides alternative mechanisms for the construction of status value. Both suggest ways in which nominal characteristics of actors come to be imbued with status value. Status construction theory focuses on the role of unequal resources in the formation of status value, while status value theory suggests that the differential distribution of status elements can influence the spread of status value. Both theories comprise a branch of the expectation states research program (Berger & Webster, 2006), where many theories within the program focus on how larger macrostructures influence the local context.

Expectations States Program

The expectation states theories seek to explain how performance expectations for oneself and another are formed and maintained (Berger & Webster, 2006). The research program is a family of interrelated theories – such as status characteristics theory (e.g., Berger et al. 1977), reward expectations theory (e.g., Berger et al., 1985), second-order expectations theory (e.g., Troyer & Younts, 1997), and status construction theory (e.g., Ridgeway 1991) – that use the basic notion of an expectation state in different domains. The scope of these theories is defined as situations in which actors are task-oriented and must work together to achieve a valued outcome. I review three theories that will be the focus of our discussion: status characteristics theory, status construction theory, and status value theory.

Status Characteristics Theory

Initial work in the expectations states program revolved around status characteristics, which is essentially any person characteristic with at least two states that can be ordered according to amount of prestige (i.e., status value) conferred by a given culture (e.g., gender, with the male state receiv-

ing higher status than the female state). Research in status characteristics theory was primarily centered on the differential attributions of task competence that resulted from statuses of task group members. Later research would study other inferences that resulted from status differences. Of particular importance to our current discussion is the belief that high status group members are more group-oriented (Ridgeway 1982) and are more likely to be given the "benefit of the doubt" (Foschi 2000) than low status members. These two attributions, along with the attribution of competence, correspond to the three traits in an individual Mayer et al. (1995) discuss as prerequisites to trusting the individual.

Status Construction Theory

Over the past few decades, we have seen a progressive growth in theory and research to explicate the dynamics of status relations (see Berger & Webster, 2006). These works begin with the assumption that there already exists a consensus on which characteristics of the population receive which differential value in esteem and competence (i.e., status characteristics.) Ridgeway (1991) developed status construction theory to unfold how any nominal characteristic (N) in a given population with two initially unvalued states comes to be imbued with social value. Essentially, Ridgeway (1991) posits that a correlation between the two states of the nominal characteristic (N_a and N_b) and level of resources (high vs. low) that systematically favors one state (say, N_a) over the other (N_b) can cause consensus among members of the population that the favored state has more status value than the unfavored state.

There have been several refinements of Ridgeway's (1991) original formulations (e.g., Webster & Hysom 1998; Ridgeway et al., 1998; Ridgeway & Correll, 2006; Ridgeway & Erickson, 2000). Of relevance to the current discussion is Berger and Fisek's (2006) status value theory.

Status Value Theory

While the original formulation of status construction theory (Ridgeway, 1991) focused solely on the role of unequal resources in creating status value, Berger and Fisek's (2006) status value theory broadens the possible mechanisms that can create status value. When objects become associated with status characteristics or other status elements, they come to be imbued with the concomitant status value. An example of this is found in Thye's (2000) lab experiment, where different colored poker chips were ascribed different value, based on the relative status of the individuals with whom they were associated. A green poker chip associated with a high status member was valued more than a purple poker chip associated with a low status member.

Berger and Fisek (2006) propose that the chips in Thye's (2000) experiment can be used as status cues (i.e., become status elements), spreading their value to others. Their theory captures Veblen's (1953[1899]) contention that the conspicuous consumption of objects like fashion and silver eating utensils are used to signal one's quality of life. Status is a resource that many seek to achieve (Huberman, Loch, & Önçüler, 2004; Willer 2009), motivating the acquisition of status elements. Very little work has been conducted to test or extend their theory. One exception is a recent experiment that tested Berger and Fisek's (2006) theory, Hysom (2009) showed that the differential assignment of both a fictitious title and a special certificate was enough to create status differences among interactional partners. We can use the theory to understand how the status of social actors transfers to the technologies with which they are associated.

THEORY

A status value approach can inform us under what conditions a focal actor (P) would adopt a technology. It is important to note that status value theory, as with all theories in the expectation states program, is a relational theory. That is, status value is not necessarily a static trait of a person, organization, or object but rather an attribute of a relationship between them. A person may be high on status value in one context, but low in another. The theory therefore applies to settings where the social units are differentiated on status to make value comparisons. The boundaries of a theory are referred to the scope conditions of the theory (Cohen 1989).

Scope Condition 1: Social units (e.g., individuals, organizations) are differentiated on status value.

An additional scope condition is necessary, because status value information is not always relevant to the situation. Status characteristics theory (and many other theories in the expectations states program) states that status is used as a marker for task performance expectations when groups are both task and collectively-oriented (Berger et al. 1977). Groups that fall outside of this scope condition would not exhibit the proposed behavioral inequalities outlined in the theory. I translate this scope condition into the realm of choosing a technology to adopt. Task-orientation in a group refers to P's motivation to complete the task and achieve a desired outcome. When P is choosing which technology to adopt, P must be motivated to complete the task, which entails selecting a "proper" technology (where P – or others - specifies what qualifies as "proper," e.g., efficient, effective, decorative). Collective-orientation in a group refers to P's belief that it is legitimate to take into consideration the input of others. With respect to technology adoption, this would refer to P believing that it is legitimate to consider others' previous decisions when deciding which technology to adopt.

Scope Condition 2: P is task and collectively-oriented.

The theory also necessitates that P already be aware of the new technology. This is more of a simplifying assumption, as the literature on how P might become aware of the technology (sometimes referred to as the rate of awareness-knowledge) deserves its own separate discussion (see Rogers, 1995 for one).

Assumption: P is aware of the focal new technology.

I will now take the different ideas I have presented to formally construct a theory of how status value can influence trust in technology. We can organize social units, such as individuals and organizations, based on status to form a status hierarchy (Berger et al., 1977; Podolny 1993; Stinchcombe, 1965). The status value of these units is the result of a social construction process. For example, the law school rankings of *U.S. News World and Report* can create a status hierarchy among law schools (Sauder & Lancaster 2006). Similarly, status construction theory (Ridgeway 1991) explains how an initially unvalued nominal trait becomes imbued with status value. Berger and Fisek (2006) posit that the status of social units can spread to nonvalued objects (see also Thye, 2000). Within organizational theory, we see a similar process with the status of organizations being spread to their affiliations (Stuart, 2000; Stuart, Hoang, & Hybels 1999). I apply these insights to technological innovations.

Proposition 1: Unvalued technologies that are associated with valued social units (e.g., individuals, organizations) that are higher (lower) status than P are more likely to be perceived with the concomitant status value of the social units.

Status characteristics theory (Berger et al., 1977) explains how task competency expectations are formed and used to organize interaction in a collectively oriented task group. Other inferences that result from status include perceptions of being benevolent toward the group (Ridgeway, 1982) and integrity in actions, resulting in giving the "benefit of the doubt" (Foschi, 2000). Along parallel lines, we can posit how technologies imbued with status lead to similar inferences about them.

We can extract from interpersonal, human-to-human processes and apply them to human-technology processes. Oftentimes people will treat technologies as social actors (Reeves & Nass, 1996). When researchers give a human voice to media, such as a computer, humans begin to apply social rules and expectations to these media (Reeves & Nass, 1996).

To understand how status influences perception of technology, we will need to translate the prior-mentioned inferences (see also Lee & Moray, 1992) into the language of technology. With respect to a technology, task competency would be akin to effectiveness in its scope of application. Viewing people as benevolent, or group-motivated, is similar to viewing a technology as helpful in achieving group aims. Integrity in individuals is seen as consistency in actions and values. In technology, this is referred to as reliability.

Proposition 2: The more status value a technology has relative to P, then the more likely P will perceive the technology to be effective (competent), helpful (benevolent), and reliable (integrity).

Mayer and his colleagues (2005) contend that people who appear to possess these three traits are more likely to be trusted. In other words, these three traits (competency, benevolence, and integrity) that are inferred from status can be used as a basis for trust in people (Campos & Schultz, 2009). Similarly, we can posit that these three traits can influence trust in technology (see also Lee & Moray, 1992).

Proposition 3: The more P perceives a technology to be effective (competent), helpful (benevolent), and reliable (integrity), the more P trusts it.

The adoption of a technology, as I described earlier in this paper, can involve risk and uncertainty. Trust manages risk and uncertainty (Williamson, 1981). Trust in technology is the belief that it will execute a set of tasks with minimal risk. The perception that the technology is effective (competent), helpful (benevolence), and reliable (integrity) increases the trust in technology, thus increasing the likelihood of its adoption (e.g., Lee & Moray, 1992, 1994).

Proposition 4: The more P trusts a technology, the more likely P will adopt it.

FUTURE DIRECTIONS

There are a number of directions we can take with the theory. It suggests ways in which organizations can increase the adoption of a high risk technology they are marketing, such as the new nanotechnologies (Petersen et al., 2007), by associating the technology with high status actors. We would hypothesize that if a set of technology choices were equally risky, the one associated with the high status actor would be the most likely to be trusted and adopted. The story behind the class divisions between MySpace and Facebook (boyd, 2007) that opened this chapter falls in line with this prediction.

Another extension might be to expand the scope of *Proposition 4*. As I mentioned before, I was merely discussing technology adoption for demonstration purposes. Technologies that are trusted more may lead to other outcomes, such as greater financial investments in the technology. In other words, the theory would advise managers of technological innovations to attach their new technologies to high status actors to increase investments. Here, we would predict that when a set of technology choices are equally risky, the one associated with a high status actor would bring in the greatest financial investment.

There is such a thing as too much trust in a technology, leading to its misuse. Misusing technology refers to the overreliance on it (Parasuraman & Riley, 1997). Relying too much on the cruiser control system on your car, for example, is an instance where too much trust could be an issue. The recent Continental Connection airplane crash near the Buffalo Niagara International Airport in February 2009, are vivid reminders of potential risks of relying on such automation systems. The theory I presented suggests that trust varies directly with the status of actors associated with it. Misusing technology could be caused by too much trust being conferred to it, because of the large status differences between P and the social unit associated with the technology.

Because status value theory suggests that the technologies would be imbued with status value, they would now become status elements. Much like an organization's alliances can signal its quality (Stuart 2000; Stuart, Hoang, & Hybels, 1999), the technologies it adopts would also signal its quality. The theory explains the phenomenon surrounding a surge in adoption of "cool" technologies like the iPod, which has its very own culture (Levy, 2006). Adopting a trusted technology would increase the likelihood that others will decide to exchange with us using the technology. eBay has increasingly become the preferred format for online auctioning; new platforms would have to compete with eBay and establish their status as a trustworthy technology. A seller interested in finding exchange partners would be better off using eBay than a newer platform. One possible line of research would compare the effects of adopting trusted technologies on exchange partner selection.

Lastly, although the theory currently focuses on the social construction of trust in technologies, it can certainly be broadened to explain trust in other entities like other objects or even people. Essentially, any object or person that can be imbued with status value as a result of being associated with status valued elements (Berger &

Fisek, 2006) can receive trust concomitant to the status value being spread. We would only need to replace the word "technology" with the entity of interest in the above propositions. For example, to explain how the spread of status value influences trust in a person, we would develop the following propositions:

Proposition 5: A person who is associated with valued social units (e.g., individuals, organizations) that are higher (lower) status than P are more likely to be perceived with the concomitant status value of the social units.

Proposition 6: The more status value a person has relative to P, then the more likely P will perceive the person to be competent, benevolent, and possess integrity.

Proposition 7: The more a person is perceived to be competent, benevolent, and full of integrity, the more the person is trusted.

The last proposition would depend on the area of interest. For example, the prestige of one's undergraduate, graduate, or professional school is often associated with job outcomes (e.g., Sauder & Lancaster, 2006). In this case, we would theorize that the prestige of these schools transfer to a job applicant, whose trustworthiness is determined by the level of prestige.

CONCLUSION

Two literatures – trust in technology and the sociology of technology – have largely been developed independently from one another. My goal in this paper was to connect the two and show how a sociological understanding of how the social and cultural framework in which one is embedded can influence trust in technology. In my explication,

I linked ideas from status value theory (Berger & Fisek 2006) and trust (Mayer et al., 1995) to understand technology adoption. Previously, researchers have suggested that status could be used as a signal for trust (Cook 2005; Cook et al., 2005). There is some research that is beginning to directly look at this link (e.g., Campos & Schultz, 2009). The theory I developed adds to this blossoming body of knowledge on status-based trust.

I took much of what we know from interpersonal trust and translated it into the realm of trust in technology. There are some who suggest that trust is fundamentally interpersonal (Friedman, Kahn, & Howe, 2000; Olson & Olson, 2000). Because there has been research that suggests that people can treat technologies like other people (Reeves & Nass, 1996), I proceeded with my intentions. There are certainly some challenges with extrapolating from the research on interpersonal trust to understand trust in technology (Lee & See, 2004). Underlying interpersonal trust is faith in the intentionality of the trustee, because transferring control to the trustee is thought to minimize risk. How can we infer intentionality of technology? A user might consider the intentionality of the technology's designers (Rasmussen, Pejterson, & Goodstein, 1994), thus switching from person-to-technology trust to person-to-person trust. Downloading software off of the internet, for example, might be a case where we consider if the designers are attempting to transfer computer viruses (e.g., Trojans) onto our computer for malicious intent. Another possibility is that a user might attribute intentionality based on the social aspects (e.g., speech) of the computer, as seen in research suggesting that computers can be treated as social actors (Nass & Lee, 2001). Because high status actors are trusted more than low status actors (Campos & Schultz, 2009), we would expect that people would trust personal computers with the voices of men (high status) more (on average) than personal computers with the voices of women (low status). There may be other issues, but future research will need to be conducted to tease out to what extent the concept of trust from interpersonal relationships can proliferate in human-computer interaction.

I focused my theoretical discussion on the domain of technology adoption. There are certainly other realms to which we can extend the theory, like financial investments. Adopting a new technology involves risk and uncertainty as we can never be completely certain that the technology will be competent, reliable, or helpful. We often look to our social and cultural environment for signals regarding which technologies to choose from. One source of those signals is the association of technologies with status valued actors, such as individuals or organizations. I have suggested that the status value from these actors gets spread to the technologies with which they are associated. The status information of a technology can supply cues of its trustworthiness and can affect adoption rates and perhaps other arenas of interest regarding technology.

REFERENCES

Abrahamson, E. (1991). Managerial fads and fashions: The diffusion and rejection of innovations. *Academy of Management Review, 16*, 586–612. doi:10.2307/258919

Anderson, P., & Tushman, M. L. (1990). Technological discontinuities and dominant designs: A cyclical model of technological change. *Administrative Science Quarterly, 35*, 604–633. doi:10.2307/2393511

Berger, J., & Fişek, M. H. (2006). Diffuse status characteristics and the spread of status value: A formal theory. *American Journal of Sociology, 111*, 1038–1079. doi:10.1086/498633

Berger, J., Fisek, M. H., Norman, R. Z., & Wagner, D. G. (1985). The formation of reward expectations in status situations. In Berger, J., & Zelditch, M. Jr., (Eds.), *Status, reward, and influence: How expectations organize behavior* (pp. 215–261). San Francisco: Jossey-Bass.

Berger, J., Fisek, M. H., Norman, R. Z., & Zelditch, M. Jr. (1977). *Status characteristics and social interaction*. New York: Elsevier.

Berger, J., & Webster, M. (2006). Expectations, status, and behavior. In Burke, P. (Ed.), *Contemporary social psychological theories* (pp. 268–300). Stanford, CA: Stanford University Press.

Bimber, B. (2000). Measuring the gender gap on the internet. *Social Science Quarterly, 81*, 868–876.

Boyd, D. (2007, June 24). Viewing American class divisions through Facebook and MySpace. *Apophenia Blog Essay*. Retrieved June 20, 2009, from http://www.danah.org/papers/essays/ClassDivisions.html

Burt, R. (1987). Social contagion and innovation: Cohesion versus structural equivalence. *American Journal of Sociology, 92*, 1287–1335. doi:10.1086/228667

Calvert, S. L., Rideout, V. J., Woolard, J. L., Barr, R. F., & Strouse, G. A. (2005). Age, ethnicity, and socioeconomic patterns in early computer use: A national survey. *The American Behavioral Scientist, 48*, 590–607. doi:10.1177/0002764204271508

Campos, C., & Schultz, M. (2009). *Status-based trust and its effects on workplace mobility*. Presented at the annual meeting of the American Sociological Association, San Francisco, CA.

Cheshire, C., & Cook, K. S. (2004). Uncertainty and the emergence of trust networks: Implications for research on the internet. *Analyse & Kritik, 28*, 220–240.

Coleman, J. S. (1988). Social capital in the creation of human capital. *American Journal of Sociology, 94*, S95–S120. doi:10.1086/228943

Coleman, J. S., Katz, E., & Menzel, H. (1957). The diffusion of an innovation among physicians. *Sociometry, 20*, 253–270. doi:10.2307/2785979

Cook, K. S. (2005). Networks, norms, and trust: The social psychology of social capital. *Social Psychology Quarterly, 68*, 4–14. doi:10.1177/019027250506800102

Cook, K. S., Hardin, R., & Levi, M. (2005). *Cooperation without trust?* New York: Russell Sage.

Davies, S. (1979). *The diffusion of process innovations*. New York: Cambridge University Press.

DiMaggio, P., & Louch, H. (1998). Socially embedded consumer transactions: For what kinds of purchases do people most often use networks? *American Sociological Review, 48*, 619–637. doi:10.2307/2657331

DiMaggio, P., & Powell, W. W. (1983). The iron cage revisited: Institutional isomorphism and collective rationality in organizational fields. *American Sociological Review, 63*, 147–160. doi:10.2307/2095101

Feldman, M. S., & March, J. G. (1981). Information in organization as signal and symbol. *Administrative Science Quarterly, 26*, 171–186. doi:10.2307/2392467

Foschi, M. (2000). Double standards for competence: Theory and research. *Annual Review of Sociology, 26*, 21–42. doi:10.1146/annurev.soc.26.1.21

Friedman, B., Kahn, P., & Howe, D. (2000). Trust online. *Communications of the ACM, 43*, 34–40. doi:10.1145/355112.355120

Geroski, P. (2000). Models of technology diffusion. *Research Policy, 29*, 603–625. doi:10.1016/S0048-7333(99)00092-X

Goldsmith, S., & Siemasko, C. (2009, March 23). This isn't AIG…it's AIU! Insurance giant takes down sign on Water St. offices. *New York Daily News*. Retrieved on May 28, 2009, from http://www.nydailynews.com/money/2009/03/23/2009-03-23_this_isnt_aig__its_aiu_insurance_giant_t.html

Granovetter, M. (1985). Economic action and social structure: The problem of embeddedness. *American Journal of Sociology, 91*, 481–510. doi:10.1086/228311

Hannan, M. T., & Freeman, J. H. (1984). Structural inertia and organizational change. *American Sociological Review, 49*, 149–164. doi:10.2307/2095567

Huberman, B. A., Loch, C. H., & Önçüler, A. (1994). Status as a valued resource. *Social Psychology Quarterly, 67*, 103–114. doi:10.1177/019027250406700109

Igbaria, M., Guimaraes, T., & Davis, G. B. (1995). Testing the determinants of microcomputer usage via a structural equation model. *Journal of Management Information Systems, 11*, 87–114.

Katz, M. L., & Shapiro, C. (1986). Technology adoption in the presence of network externalities. *The Journal of Political Economy, 94*, 822–841. doi:10.1086/261409

Katz, M. L., & Shapiro, C. (1992). Product introduction with network externalities. *The Journal of Industrial Economics, 40*, 55–83. doi:10.2307/2950627

Kollock, P. (1994). The emergence of exchange structures: An experimental study of uncertainty, Commitment, and Trust. *American Journal of Sociology, 100*, 313–345. doi:10.1086/230539

Kollock, P. (1999). The production of trust in online markets. *Advances in Group Processes, 16*, 99–123.

Kreps, D. M. (1990). Corporate Culture and Economic Theory. In Alt, J. E., & Shepsle, K. A. (Eds.), *Perspectives on Positive Political Economy* (pp. 90–143). New York: Cambridge University Press.

Lee, J. D., & See, K. A. (2004). Trust in automation: Designing for appropriate reliance. *Human Factors, 46*, 50–80.

Levy, S. (2006). *The perfect thing: How the iPod shuffles commerce, culture, and coolness*. New York: Simon & Schuster.

Lewandowsky, S., Mundy, M., & Tan, G. P. A. (2000). The dynamics of trust: Comparing humans to automation. *Journal of Experimental Psychology. Applied, 6*, 104–123. doi:10.1037/1076-898X.6.2.104

Loch, C. H., & Huberman, B. A. (1999). A punctuated-equilibrium model of technology diffusion. *Management Science, 45*, 160–177. doi:10.1287/mnsc.45.2.160

Macaulay, S. (1963). Non-contractual relations in business: A preliminary study. *American Sociological Review, 28*, 55–67. doi:10.2307/2090458

Malone, T. W., Laubacher, R., & Scott Morton, M. S. (2003). *Inventing the organizations of the 21st Century*. Cambridge, MA: MIT Press.

Mayer, R. C., Davis, J. H., & Schoorman, F. D. (1995). An integrative model of organizational trust. *Academy of Management Review, 20*, 709–734. doi:10.2307/258792

Meyer, J. W., & Rowan, B. (1977). Institutionalized organizations: Formal structure as myth and ceremony. *American Journal of Sociology, 83*, 340–363. doi:10.1086/226550

Molm, L. D., Takahashi, N., & Peterson, G. (2000). Risk and trust in social exchange: An experimental test of a classical proposition. *American Journal of Sociology, 105*, 1396–1427. doi:10.1086/210434

Muir, B. M. (1987). Trust between humans and machines, and the design of decision aids. *International Journal of Man-Machine Studies, 27*, 527–539. doi:10.1016/S0020-7373(87)80013-5

Nass, C., & Lee, K. M. (2001). Does computer-synthesized speech manifest personality? Experimental tests of recognition, similarity-attraction, and consistency-attraction. *Journal of Experimental Psychology, 7*, 171–181.

Olson, J. S., & Olson, G. M. (2000). i2i trust in e-commerce. *Communications of the ACM, 43*, 41–44. doi:10.1145/355112.355121

Parasuraman, R., & Riley, V. (1997). Humans and automation: Use, misuse, disuse, abuse. *Human Factors, 39*, 230–253. doi:10.1518/001872097778543886

Parasuraman, S., Singh, I. L., Molloy, R., & Parasuraman, R. (1992). Automation-related complacency: A source of vulnerability in contemporary organizations. *IFIP Transactions A – Computer Science and Technology, 13*, 426–432.

Petersen, A., Anderson, A., Wilkinson, C., & Allan, S. (2007). Nanotechnologies, risk and society. *Health Risk & Society, 9*, 117–124. doi:10.1080/13698570701306765

Podolny, J. M. (1993). A status-based model of market competition. *American Journal of Sociology, 98*, 829–872. doi:10.1086/230091

Podolny, J. M., & Stuart, T. E. (1995). A role-based ecology of technological change. *American Journal of Sociology, 100*, 1224–1260. doi:10.1086/230637

Podolny, J. M., Stuart, T. E., & Hannan, M. T. (1996). Networks, knowledge, and niches: Competition in the worldwide semiconductor industry, 1984-1991. *American Journal of Sociology, 102*, 659–689. doi:10.1086/230994

Pugh, M. D., & Wahrman, R. (1983). Neutralizing sexism in mixed-sex groups: Do women have to be better than men? *American Journal of Sociology, 88*, 746–762. doi:10.1086/227731

Reeves, B., & Nass, C. (1996). *The media equation: How people treat computers, television, and new media like real people and places*. New York: Cambridge University Press.

Reinganum, J. F. (1981). On the diffusion of new technology: A game theoretic approach. *The Review of Economic Studies*, *48*, 395–405. doi:10.2307/2297153

Resnick, P., Zeckhauser, R., Swanson, J., & Lockwood, K. (2006). The value of a reputation on eBay: A controlled experiment. *Experimental Economics*, *9*, 79–101. doi:10.1007/s10683-006-4309-2

Ridgeway, C. L. (1982). Status in groups: The importance of motivation. *American Sociological Review*, *47*, 76–88. doi:10.2307/2095043

Ridgeway, C. L. (1991). The social construction of status value: Gender and other nominal characteristics. *Social Forces*, *70*, 367–386. doi:10.2307/2580244

Ridgeway, C. L., Boyle, E. H., Kuipers, K. J., & Robinson, D. T. (1998). How do status beliefs develop? The role of resources and interactional experience. *American Sociological Review*, *63*, 331–378. doi:10.2307/2657553

Ridgeway, C. L., & Correll, S. J. (2004). Motherhood as a status characteristic. *The Journal of Social Issues*, *60*, 683–700. doi:10.1111/j.0022-4537.2004.00380.x

Ridgeway, C. L., & Correll, S. J. (2006). Consensus and the creation of status beliefs. *Social Forces*, *85*, 431–453. doi:10.1353/sof.2006.0139

Ridgeway, C. L., & Erickson, K. G. (2000). Creating and spreading status beliefs. *American Journal of Sociology*, *106*, 579–615. doi:10.1086/318966

Rogers, E. M. (1995). *Diffusion of Innovations*. New York: Simon & Schuster.

Rotter, J. B. (1971). Generalized expectancies for interpersonal trust. *The American Psychologist*, *26*, 443–452. doi:10.1037/h0031464

Rousseau, D. M., Sitkin, S. B., Burt, R. S., & Camerer, C. (1998). Not so different after all: A Cross-discipline view of trust. *Academy of Management Review*, *23*, 393–404.

Sauder, M., & Lancaster, R. (2006). Do rankings matter? The effects of *U.S. News and World Report* rankings on the admissions process of law schools. *Law & Society Review*, *40*, 105–134. doi:10.1111/j.1540-5893.2006.00261.x

Stinchcombe, A. L. (1965). Social structure and organizations. In March, J. G. (Ed.), *Handbook of Organizations* (pp. 219–223). Chicago: Rand-McNally.

Stuart, T. E. (2000). Interoganizational alliances and the performance of firms: A study of growth and innovation rates in a high-technology industry. *Strategic Management Journal*, *21*, 791–811. doi:10.1002/1097-0266(200008)21:8<791::AID-SMJ121>3.0.CO;2-K

Stuart, T. E., Hoang, H., & Hybels, R. C. (1999). Interorganizational endorsements and the performance of entrepreneurial ventures. *Administrative Science Quarterly*, *44*, 315–349. doi:10.2307/2666998

Tadelis, S. (1999). What's in a name? Reputation as a tradable asset. *The American Economic Review*, *89*, 548–563.

Thompson, J. D. (1967). *Organizations in action: Social science bases of administrative theory*. New York: McGraw Hill.

Thye, S. R. (2000). A status value theory of power in exchange relations. *American Sociological Review*, *65*, 407–432. doi:10.2307/2657464

Troyer, L., & Younts, C. W. (1997). Whose expectations matter? The relative power of first- and second-order expectations in determining social influence. *American Journal of Sociology*, *103*, 692–732. doi:10.1086/231253

Weber, M. (1947). *The theory of economic and social organization*. New York: Oxford Press.

Webster, M., & Hysom, S. J. (1998). Creating status characteristics. *American Sociological Review, 63*, 351–379. doi:10.2307/2657554

Weick, K. E. (1995). *Sensemaking in organization*. Thousand Oaks, CA: Sage.

Willer, R. (2009). Groups reward individual sacrifice: The status solution to the collective action problem. *American Sociological Review, 74*, 23–43. doi:10.1177/000312240907400102

Williamson, O. E. (1981). The economics of organization: The transaction cost approach. *American Journal of Sociology, 87*, 548–577. doi:10.1086/227496

Wilson, K. R., Wallin, J. S., & Reiser, C. (2003). Social stratification and the digital divide. *Social Science Computer Review, 21*, 133–143. doi:10.1177/0894439303021002001

Chapter 10
Trustworthy Mobile Transactions:
A Longitudinal Study of M–PESA in Kenya

Olga Morawczynski
The University of Edinburgh, UK

Gianluca Miscione
International Institute for Geo-Information Science and Earth Observation, The Netherlands

ABSTRACT

This chapter will focus on one vital determinant of m-banking adoption and use—trust relations. It presents the case of M-PESA, an m-banking application that quickly achieved a remarkable local embeddedness in large segments of Kenyan society. Data for this case was gathered during a fourteen month ethnographic study that took place in two locations—one urban and one rural. The chapter identifies four categories of trust (interpersonal, extended, presumptive, institutional) that were a prerequisite for mobile banking, and a lubricant for its sustainability and growth. It shows that institutional trust relations were strong during the early stages of adoption whilst the interpersonal ones were weak. This means that customers trusted Safaricom, the mobile service provider offering M-PESA. They did not, however, trust the agents that facilitated cash in and cash out. The chapter also gives attention to the changing nature of these relations through time. For example, it shows that interpersonal trust relations between customers and agents strengthened with increased interaction. The chapter concludes by identifying areas for future research and delineating recommendations for managers.

INTRODUCTION

The pervasiveness of the mobile phone in developing countries has recently instigated the development of applications designed to alleviate poverty. One of the most recent is m-banking—a platform for the delivery of financial services via the mobile phone. Studies discussing these technologies tend to focus on their accessibility and adoption, addressing whether these applications have the potential to

DOI: 10.4018/978-1-61520-901-9.ch010

be "transformational", or appropriated by a large segment of the unbanked population (Ivatury & Pickens, 2006; Porteous, 2006; 2007). To date, there is very little empirical work examining the adoption of m-banking applications and discussing the numerous barriers to this process. The relevance of such barriers to understanding ICT adaptation in the context of emerging economies has also been given little attention. We will suggest that the lessons learned from the case presented here are relevant beyond the context of the "developing world" or "the South". This is because processes of social change are not solely localized in a place, but are the unfolding product of the encounter between quite different social worlds in "the South" and in "the North". The ethnographic methodology helps in unpacking such constructions. We also highlight how concepts like "institution" can be powerful in explaining this and similar cases, as far as they include local social models (tribes, as an example from this case).

This chapter will focus on one vital determinant of m-banking adoption and use—trust relations. As several authors have observed, economic transactions are contingent upon trust (Luhmann, 1979; Mayer, Davis & Schoorman, 1995; Putnam, 1993). This study presents the case of M-PESA, an m-banking application that quickly achieved a remarkable local embeddedness in large segments of Kenyan society. Data will be used from an ethnographic study that was conducted in two locations: Kibera, and informal settlement outside Nairobi; and Bukura, a village in Western Kenya. This study took place over a period of fourteen months and tracked the adoption, usage and impact of M-PESA. Using data from these two sites, the chapter identifies three classes of actors that were vital to the establishment and maintenance of trust—users, agents and Safaricom (mobile operator). It further illustrates how trust relations between these actors changed through time. The findings presented here contribute to the aforementioned m-banking literature by highlighting

the numerous trust relations that must be in place before an m-banking application becomes "transformational" (Porteous, 2006, 2007).

TRUST AS THEORETICAL LENS

There exists a wide body of literature on the topic of trust. However, a concise definition of the term remains elusive as it holds a variety of meanings across disciplines. Because we are examining trust in the context of m-banking exchange, we will appropriate a definition that is inherently relational (Kramer, 1999; Mayer et al., 1995; McAlister, 1995; Mishler & Rose, 2001). The starting point to our definition of trust is that it emerges as a property of relations between two or more social actors. These actors can be individuals, or organizations such as corporations and political parties (Smith, 2007). They are interacting in some way and have expectations regarding each other's future behaviour (Barber, 1983; Dasgupta, 1988). For example, they expect that the other actor will fulfil their obligations, behave in a predictable manner, and will act fairly in situations of opportunism. In this regard, trust is the expectation that actors have of each other, and of the organizations with which they deal.

Several categories of trust relations exist within the literature. Some scholars pay attention to the trust relations that emerge between individuals. This is known as *interpersonal trust* (Boon & Holmes, 1991; Bran & Foddy, 1988; McAlister, 1995). This type of trust is established between two or more individuals whose interaction over a given period of time allows them to learn about one another, increasing the ability of each party to make judgements regarding the other's disposition, intentions and motives. The discussion below will make clear that such trust relations were weak during the early stages of M-PESA. Several authors have also pointed to something called *extended trust* to explain trust relations that extend beyond those that we know personally (Raiser, Haerpfer, Nowotny, & Wallace, 2001). They have argued that such trust is essential for an efficient market economy because it fosters co-operation between individuals who may not have prior information about each other. Several explanations have been given as to why individuals choose to rely on each other, and co-operate, even without direct knowledge about the other actor. Some argue that an individual's role in society can form a basis of *presumptive trust*. It is not the actual person that is trusted but the system of expertise that produces and sustains role-appropriate behaviour (Kramer, 1999). For example, Dawes (1994) asserts that "we trust engineers because we trust engineering and believe that engineers are trained to apply valid principles of engineering, moreover, we have evidence everyday that these principles are valid when we observe planes flying". As will be discussed below such extended trust relations between users and agents, and beyond, were vital at later stages of adoption.

Whilst some pay attention to relations that emerge between individuals, others examine those that exist between individuals and organizations such as corporations or political parties, commonly referred to as *institutional trust* (Mishler & Rose, 2001; Williamson, 1985).[1] This differs from interpersonal trust in so far as the relationship is based on trust in institutional arrangements rather than in between people. Institutional trust, however, also includes an element of interpersonal trust, since beliefs held about a particular institution can be contingent upon the personnel whom they staff (Smith, 2007). For example, Zimmer (1972) argued that institutional leaders can greatly affect the way in which the entire institution is perceived. To make this point, Zimmer examined the impacts of the Watergate scandal on perceptions of trust by the public of the government. He concluded that the violated trust of Nixon led to a generalized distrust for the American government. Our findings concur with that of Zimmer. As we will describe, organizational leaders affect institutional trust relations.

These four types of trust relations—interpersonal, institutional, extended and presumptive—will be used to frame the discussion. Data from various stages of the adoption process will be incorporated into the analysis. We will make clear the trust relations that were vital during the early phases of adoption and explain how these relations emerged, and were sustained, in the two research sites. This will facilitate an understanding of how trust evolved, and was sustained, between the aforementioned actors.

RESEARCH QUESTIONS AND APPROACH

In this paper, we aim at answering the following theory-driven research questions:

1. How do the four types of trust relations (interpersonal, extended, presumptive, institutional) help our understanding the nature of mobile transactions in Kenya?
2. How do these trust relations change over time?

The following trust relations will be examined as focal points to answer the previous questions:

a. Inter-personal
    ○   among customers, and
    ○   between the customers and agents,
b. Institutional
    ○   between the customer and Safaricom—the mobile service provider offering the M-PESA service
c. Extended and presumptive
    ○   between customers and agents

METHODOLOGY

This study draws data from an ethnographic study, which extended over fourteen months (September 2007-December 2008). A variety of methods were used to collect data during this period. Over 350 semi-structured, and twenty one group, interviews were conducted. Three classes of informants were chosen: users, non-users, and agents. The majority of these took place in the homes of the informants. Public locations such as the agent shops, churches and marketplaces were also used for the interviews. The duration of the interviews varied. The group interviews usually lasted over one hour. The individual interviews tended to be shorter, spanning anywhere from fifteen minutes to one hour. Many of the informants were interviewed more than once. This facilitated an understanding of changing trust relations over time. Participant observation was also used, especially in the shops offering M-PESA. Such observations made were vital for understanding trust relations between customers and agents.

The first few months were spent in Kibera. The money trail was thereafter followed to Bukura. It must be noted that the research strategy changed over time and was led by the findings in the field. For example, the decision was made to conduct a multi-sited ethnography because of the strong urban-rural relations in Kenya. At the early stages of the research one shop offering M-PESA was chosen in each location. However, as the research progressed, other shops were visited. This was especially the case in Kibera, where there was a high penetration of agents. Because there was only one agent in Bukura, neighboring village shops offering M-PESA were visited. The incorporation of other agent shops allowed for additional insights into the nature of trust relations. A research assistant was hired to facilitate the data collection. This assistant had strong connections in each of the two sites. Although he lived in Kibera, his rural home was in Bukura. He thus acted as a vital support for data collection throughout the research. He also acted as a translator. This was especially the case in Bukura, where many of the informants only spoke the local language (Kiluhya).

BACKGROUND: INTRODUCING M-PESA

M-PESA is an m-banking application that facilitates various financial services via the mobile phone. Users can check their account balance, make deposits and withdrawals, pay bills, purchase mobile phone credit, and transfer such credit to other users. It targets the unbanked, prepaid segment of the population and was officially introduced onto the Kenyan market in March of 2007 by Safaricom, the Kenyan mobile service provider (Vaughan, 2007). It was funded by Department for International Development (DFID), a department of the UK government that provides aid to developing countries in conjunction with Vodafone, a UK telecommunications company (Hughes & Lonie, 2007). Since its introduction, M-PESA has grown rapidly. In December of 2008, less than two years after the launch of the application, the user base had grown over 5 million.[2] The gross M-PESA transaction rates are also impressive. The cumulative value of money transfers at May of 2009 was over £994 million (120 billion Kenyan Shillings [KSh]).

To access M-PESA services, individuals must register at one of the retail agent outlets, and deposit cash. This cash is thereafter reflected as e-money in a virtual account that is managed by Safaricom. This is called the non-bank led model of m-banking because the customer has no direct relationship with a bank. After this account is created, and an e-money balance established, all of the aforementioned transactions can be conducted. To access e-money transferred via M-PESA, the recipient must also visit a retail agent. They provide the agent with identification, verify the transaction number, and convert the e-money balance on their phone into cash. The M-PESA agents are vitally important to the functioning of the entire system. Not only do they transact cash withdrawals and deposits, but they facilitate the smooth operation of the system by providing customer support services. The majority of these agents are located in shops offering M-PESA services. Usually, there are one or two agents working in each shop. Most of these shops offer products and services aside from M-PESA. They sell airtime, mobile phones and associated accessories. Many also sell other goods, including food and other items for domestic consumption.

EMPIRICAL SETTING

To answer these questions the study will draw on data from an ethnographic study, which extended over a fourteen month period (September 2007 - December 2008). The research began in Kibera, an informal settlement outside Nairobi. Kibera is situated close to the city centre and covers about 2.5 km² of land. Over 1 million people reside in Kibera, typically living in mud walled houses with iron sheet roofs. Although the informal settlement is ethnically diverse, the majority of the residents belong to the Luo or Luhya ethnic group. Most migrate from villages in Western Kenya where it is difficult to find work. Whilst residing in Kibera, they usually find employment as casual laborers or in the informal sector. Only 10% are reported to be formally employed (Ilako & Kimura, 2004). These informal, or casual jobs, provide migrants with little job security. As such, it is common for them to move between Kibera and their rural home—returning when they can no longer afford to live in the city (Ishihara, 2003).

There are no formal financial institutions within Kibera. The residents must travel into town, or outside Kibera, to access the banks and money transfer services. The under-representation of these organizations could be explained by the lack of security. There is very little police presence within the informal settlement. There are, however, over forty M-PESA agents scattered around Kibera. According to Safaricom, this number is expected to increase in the coming months.

Many of the urban migrants interviewed confirmed that they came to Kibera from Western Kenya. A segment of these interviewees noted that their rural home was in, or around, Butere-Mumias district. They also noted that several agents were offering M-PESA services in the area. After a visit to this area, a village called Bukura was chosen as the second site. The M-PESA agent at Bukura was one of the busiest in Butere-Mumias. Frequent queues were observed outside of the shop. The urban migrants also provided contacts to their rural relatives, who were the recipients of money, in the district. The majority of the study was thus focused in these two areas.

Bukura has a population of just over 20,000 residents and covers 30 km². Kakamega, the nearest town, is situated over 20 km away from Bukura. The majority of the residents are subsistence farmers holding one to five acres of land. On this land they usually grow food crops for domestic consumption. There are very few opportunities for employment within and around Bukura. To make extra money, some of the residents sell their crops in the local market. Many of the households depend on remittances sent by friends and family in urban areas such as Kibera. According to many of the interviewees, these remittances make up a substantial part of the household income. Some even asserted that 50-100% of such income was derived from remittances. There are no formal financial organizations within Bukura. As such, many of the villagers do not have a bank account. Money transfer services, however, are available within the village centre. There is a PostaPay, the money transfer service offered by the Post Office. Some of the residents travelled to Kakamega to retrieve their money from one of the bus or Matatu companies. There is also one M-PESA agent in the village centre. This agent would service not only Bukura, but also the surrounding villages.

A variety of qualitative methods were used to collect data within these two sites. This includes participant observation, semi-structured and group interviews. In the earlier stages of the research, such observation and interviews were conducted in retail shops offering M-PESA. The goal at this stage was to identify the user base and to monitor interaction between users and agents. At latter stages, time was also spent in the households of the informants and other public spaces. This facilitated understanding of how interpersonal trust relations between customers affected adoption.

FINDINGS FROM THE FIELD

Usage

Before the aforementioned research questions are addressed, we will provide an analysis of the usage patterns. There are two ways in which we monitored usage. Firstly, we counted the number of transactions that were recorded in the agent's logbook, and noted the transaction type. We also discussed usage patterns with customers in the shop. In regards to transaction patterns, they differed in the two sites. The shop in Bukura was the busiest of those studied, with 150-200 transactions conducted per day. The majority of these transactions were withdrawals. Most customers were retrieving money that was sent by their relatives from the urban areas. In Kibera, there were 70-185 transactions per day in the shops visited. The majority of these transactions were deposits. Such deposits were made by the urban migrants, who were sending money back to their rural homes. It must be noted that these differing transaction rates were not related to the demand of the service but to the representation of agents. As mentioned above, there was only one M-PESA shop in Bukura. There were over thirty in Kibera.

As time went on, we noted a change in the nature of these transactions. In Bukura, there was a slight increase in the number of deposits. In Kibera, there was a substantial increase in the number of withdrawals. According to the agents,

this was occurring because customers were using M-PESA as a savings mechanism. Customers confirmed this finding. Many asserted that they used the application to store money because it was accessible (as mentioned above, there were no banks in Kibera or Bukura). Most residents thus had to travel to access financial services. Informants further claimed that it was "cheaper to save with M-PESA". Most banks in Kenya charged a monthly maintenance, as well as per transaction fee. Such fees were not conducive to frequent transactions or the storage of small amounts of money. Informants asserted that they did not store money in the bank because their "small savings" would quickly be "wiped out". With M-PESA, customers only paid to make withdrawals. Deposits were free, and there was no maintenance fee for the storage of money. This is because the pricing structure was designed for money transfers, and not for savings.

Many of the female informants in Kibera further asserted that M-PESA provided them with a safe place to keep their money. The women explained that before M-PESA they stored their money at home. However, this method was "risky" because the money could be found, and stolen, by their husbands. They preferred to store this money outside of the house to decrease this risk. It must be noted that M-PESA was used more frequently for savings in Kibera than Bukura, investment being preferred to the depositing of savings in the latter district. Many of the women would purchase, and re-sell, items such as maize and sugar cane. This allowed them to make "something small" from their money. The rural residents explained that such profits would not be made if the money was sitting idle in a savings mechanism. M-PESA was also increasingly used for top-ups, especially in Kibera and especially at night. As mentioned above, security was an issue in the informal settlement. Many informants explained that they preferred M-PESA to scratch cards because they did not need to leave their homes to top-up their phones.

Interpersonal Trust

We found that interpersonal trust relations were most important during the early stages of adoption. In particular, the relationship between customers and agents was a vital determinant of usage. In Kibera, such interpersonal relations were initially weak. Customers did not trust agents with their money, yet they continued to use M-PESA because they trusted Safaricom, the mobile operator offering the service. This will be discussed in more detail below.

The agents often complained that they would receive the blame for all the problems with the M-PESA system. Because M-PESA utilizes the same data channel as text messages, it often becomes congested at 'peak texting times'. The result is that many M-PESA transactions fail. They are either not processed in the system, or are processed but the SMS that confirms the M-PESA transaction to the agent and customer is not sent. The agents asserted that in both of these cases, they were accused of stealing the customer's money after a deposit was made and no confirmation SMS received. A conversation with an M-PESA agent in Kibera revealed the following:

I asked the agent whether she, or her customers, had lost money when the system became congested. She said no. She then added that on several occasions her customers 'thought that they had lost their money'. Last week, she explained, she had a customer come in to make a deposit. He wanted to send the money to his relatives. This customer gave her the money and he was told to wait for the confirmation SMS. However, after waiting for nearly an hour, he told the agent that he had to leave for work and would be back if he did not receive the confirmation. He came back the next day to 'hassle' her, she explained. She tried to make it clear to him that the money was 'in the system', but the customer demanded his 'stolen' money back. He then became 'angry' and began to 'quarrel'. She had to call the Safaricom people

to reverse the transaction so that she could give the man his deposit.

Most of the Kibera agents interviewed had similar stories. They explained that they were also accused of stealing money from the customers. Such accusations were not as frequent in Bukura. Bernard, the owner of the Bukura shop, was a local farmer and business man. He knew, and was even related to, many of the customers who came in to transact. He had established interpersonal trust relations with his customers before the application was introduced.

Our data further revealed that some customers in Kibera did not expect others to trust the agents. In fact, the agents told us that some customers would come into the shop with their debtors and attempt to withdraw money. This was even when the customers did not have enough money in their accounts to make the requested withdrawal. We saw one incidence of this with a man who had a debt with a peanut seller:

We heard some yelling outside of the shop before we saw a man stumble in with a cigarette in one hand and a pack of peanuts in the other. He smelled of alcohol and his white shirt had large brown stains, and what appeared to be cigarette burns. He was followed by another man who was holding a large basket of peanuts...The man in the white shirt entered the shop and yelled "get the money from the agent". He then pointed at Cheryl [the agent]. Before the peanut seller could make his way into the shop, the man in the white shirt pushed passed him and they ran out into the street. They continued to yell at each other, and a crowd was beginning to gather.

Once they left, we all started to laugh. My research assistant turned to me and explained that the man told the peanut seller to collect the "5 bob"[3] for peanuts from Cheryl. The peanut seller demanded his money in cash, and refused to believe that the man in the white shirt had "5 bob" in an M-PESA account. Cheryl explained that this sort of thing happens very often. Customers who are in debt will come in with their debtors and try to withdraw money from their M-PESA account. The agent will check the account and realize that the customer does not have enough money for the requested withdrawal and inform the customer. The customer will then become angry and inform the debtor that the agent is lying and that the agent does not want to give the customer their money. Cheryl emphasized that 'it is always our fault'.

Our interviews with the customers in Kibera confirmed that many did not trust the M-PESA agents. On one occasion, an angry customer complained to us that the agent in Kibera had stolen money from him. He asserted that he had made a deposit of "400 bob" the week before and when he checked his balance that morning he only had "399 bob". He demanded that the agent return the "1 bob" that was stolen. The M-PESA agent had to spend several minutes explaining that there was "1 bob" deducted from his account every time that he checked his balance. The man was not convinced and asked for some evidence. The agent showed him a leaflet with the different transaction costs. The customer then stamped out the door with the leaflet in hand.

The trust relations between customers and agents changed over time. At the later stages of the fieldwork, many of the agents asserted that conflict with the customers had significantly decreased. They were no longer constantly questioned about transaction fees. Some further noted that the regular customers did not wait for the SMS confirming the transaction before leaving the shop. "These guys have finally learned that we are not corrupt", explained one of the Kibera agents.

Interpersonal trust relations amongst customers also instigated M-PESA adoption rates. Many of the rural informants asserted that they initially did not want to adopt M-PESA. Some asserted that they were "confused by technology" and did

not know how the application functioned. Others claimed that they were "unsure" about the agents. These informants continued that they only adopted the application because they were "convinced" to do so by their urban relations. One elderly woman, who sold clothing in Bukura market, explained:

I had no idea how this thing [M-PESA] worked… I was confused. My son sends me money from Nairobi. He convinced me to register. At first I said no. I wanted him to use Posta [post office]. At least I understood this thing. But he convinced me finally. He said M-PESA was fast and safe. So I started using it.

Many of the urban migrants confirmed that they influenced their rural relatives to sign up with M-PESA. They explained that M-PESA was faster and more accessible than the other services. They did not need to travel outside Kibera to send money. The pricing structure was also designed so that money transfers were significantly cheaper if both the sender and the recipient were registered. For example, it would cost the urban migrant 30 KES to send 6000 KES if the recipient was registered. That same transaction would cost 175 KES if the recipient was not registered. Such transaction costs incentivized many urban migrants to convince their rural relatives to register. So, the rate scheme leveraged the existing trustworthy relations to increase the number of registered users.

Finally, distrust relations between husband and wife also increased adoption. As was mentioned above, many of the unbanked urban women asserted that they adopted M-PESA for their "secret savings". Several of the women explained that their husbands would regularly search their homes for hidden money. One woman added that, "I eventually ran out of places to hide the cash". The wives continued that the money was usually taken by their husbands after it was found. To avoid this risk, many of the women opened an M-PESA account to keep their savings. The women explained that this reduced the risk of the money being stolen. The husbands were not aware that this account existed, and thus could not steal the savings.

Institutional Trust

Institutional trust relations were also vital at an early stage. We noted above that many of the informants did not trust the agents. Our findings further show that informants continued to use M-PESA because they trusted Safaricom. Most informants claimed that it was safe to store money in M-PESA because it would be protected by the mobile operator (MO). How did Safaricom build such good trust relations with customers? The MO has a history in Kenya. It has provided mobile services since 1997, began targeting the low income-segment in early 2000, and had a 70% of the Kenyan market by 2008. Many of the M-PESA customers have been using Safaricom as their mobile service provider before M-PESA was introduced. They have had time to assess the quality of the institutional arrangements and make judgments about the company. The establishment of institutional trust relations before the launch of M-PESA was vitally important to its success. Users were making deposits into an account managed by Safaricom. Such an action indicated that they had faith that the MO would protect their cash, and make it accessible when needed. It must be noted that the nature of institutional trust relations also changed during the fieldwork. One event instigating this change was the Safaricom initial public offering (IPO), which was announced in mid-March of 2008. After hearing the announcement many of the informants questioned whether the company was "in trouble". Such questions continued to be asked after share prices fell dramatically. To protect their money, many of the informants withdrew some, or all, of their savings from M-PESA. They thereafter kept that cash somewhere else. There was another reason why institutional trust relations between the customer and Safaricom were strong. An interview with an M-PESA customer revealed the following:

Andrew made clear that there were several problems with Equity [name of his bank]. I leaned forward and asked him what they were. "I don't mean to be tribal" he replied, "but the president of Equity is too close to Kibaki [the President of Kenya]". I asked him to explain and he told me that the president of Equity Bank, who was Kikuyu like Kibaki, was giving "too much" of the "common man's" money to support Kibaki's electoral campaign. If this went on, he emphasized, the bank would crash and the money of the "common man" would be lost. He then said that this is why spreading out your money in several accounts was a "good idea"...I asked him whether he was afraid that Safaricom would crash and that he would lose the money in his M-PESA account. He shook his head. He said that everyone knew that Safaricom would not involve themselves in "tribal politics" because Micheal Joseph (the president of Safaricom) did not belong to any of Kenya's tribes...He was just a mzungu [white person].

This shows how ethnic tensions are also part of institutional trust relations. Like Andrew, many trusted Joseph because he did not have tribal affiliations. He was exempt from accusations of tribal favoritism because of his South African background. Many also attributed the success of Safaricom to Joseph. They claimed that Joseph "made talking cheap" and provided "phone services for the common man". Such a finding confirms Zimmer's (1972) argument that institutional leaders can affect the way that the entire organization is assessed, and whether it is trusted. Ethnicity was a crucial determinant also during the post-election violence[4] in Kibera. One of the agents, who belonged to the Luo ethnic group, explained:

Guys were difficult before and after the violence, but the Kikuyu [different ethnic community] were the worst. They kept on questioning everything... even guys who were regular customers. They refused to leave without the confirmation SMS...One of the regulars even lost it when the confirmation did not come through. He tried to get behind the bars and attack me!

Many of the agents confirmed that customers of different ethnic communities became especially "difficult" during this period. In Kibera, the majority of the M-PESA agents closed their shops during the post-election to avoid violence. Such ethnic tensions between customer and agents were not as prominent in Bukura. This is because the majority of the residents belonged to one ethnic community—the Luhya. However, several neighboring villages had Kikuyu agents. These agents closed the shop and fled during the violence. Many did not return, even after a peace agreement was signed.

Extended and Presumptive Trust

Extended and presumptive trust relations were also important, but at a later stage of adoption. Many of the customers in Kibera asserted that they visited the same agent after signing up with M-PESA. They noted that they wanted to "test out" the system and decrease the chances of money being stolen by the agent. As they became more familiar with the application they began to "branch out" and visit some of the other agents. One farmer in Bukura, who had recently signed up with M-PESA, explained:

You have to be careful with agents in these parts... Some are good and others are thieves. They will take your cash and disappear... You should always wait for the confirmation (SMS). I visit the guys in Bukura because I know them well. Bernard lives by my place... I know where to find him if cash gets lost.

The farmer was interviewed again after a few months. At that point, he noted that he had visited other agents in Kakamega, the neighboring town, when Bernard ran out of cash float.[5] When asked

if he had any difficulty with the other agents he shook his head. He explained that most of the agents were "honest" and would not steal his cash. He further noted that he would wait for the confirmation SMS before leaving the shop to ensure that the transaction had been processed through the Safaricom system. From this finding we can argue that interpersonal trust relations are important for the development of extended trust. Many customers preferred to establish trust relations with one agent when "testing out" the system. Once they gained trust in the agent and system, they began to branch out and visit unknown agents.

Another interesting finding, in regards to presumptive trust, emerged in Bukura. As mentioned above, the agent at Bukura was from the area. He had interacted with the residents and established interpersonal trust relations before the application was introduced. He explained that such relations sometimes brought problems. Many of his relatives refused to take him "seriously" as an agent. They would not bring their IDs when transacting, and would tell Bernard that there was no need for such documentation. Others would come into the shop and demand to be served first because they were his relatives. Bernard explained that they would become angry and "bring issues" to his wife if he did not meet their demands. We can use these findings to argue that strong interpersonal relations affect the establishment of presumptive trust. Those who knew Bernard before the application was introduced did not take him "seriously" as an agent, but continued to treat him as a relative, or friend, negatively impacting on his operations. Agents in Kibera did not face this problem. As mentioned above, many had not established interpersonal trust relations with residents before M-PESA was introduced. Some noted, however, that they avoided "getting close" to customers. One agent in Kibera explained:

I try to keep some distance with the customers. If not then these guys ask for too many favors. They want to be served first... They don't want to wait like the others. This gets the other customers mad. You can't serve well when you favor customers…

These agents in Kibera did not want to face the problems experienced by Bernard. They thus maintained their professionalism by keeping their distance from customers.

CONCLUSION

This chapter used four categories of trust relations to explain the growth of M-PESA—interpersonal, institutional, presumptive, and extended. It showed how all four of these categories shaped adoption and usage patterns, albeit at different stages. For example, institutional trust relations were vitally important during the early stages of adoption. In fact, they acted as a conduit for the development of interpersonal trust. This was especially the case in Kibera. Many of the informants did not initially trust the agents in the informal settlement. They did, however, trust Safaricom. Most owned a mobile phone and had exposure to the company before the application was introduced. Michael Joseph, the CEO of Safaricom, was one reason for the establishment of such trust. Joseph's political neutrality, and lack of affiliation with any of Kenya's tribes, was especially important during the post-election period. Because he was a *mzungu* [white person], he was spared from accusations of tribal favoritism. This decreased the fear of Safaricom crashing, and money of the "common man" disappearing. Interpersonal trust relations between customers and agents were stronger in the smaller town of Bukura. The shop owner was a local farmer and businessman. He had established trust relations before becoming an M-PESA agent. Many of the customers were his neighbors, relatives, and friends. He noted, however, that such relations had unintended consequences. Some of his customers did not take him "seriously" as an agent. They would demand favors, which made it more difficult for him to operate. The empiri-

cal evidence also showed that interpersonal trust relations changed over time. In both sites they were strengthened by increased interaction. The agents noted that accusations of theft and corruption decreased as customers became accustomed to M-PESA.

Presumptive and extended trust was also important, albeit at later stages of adoption. In this case, the establishment of interpersonal trust relations between customers and agents was often a precondition for presumptive and extended trust. Many customers asserted that they interacted with one agent when first adopting the application. With increased usage they extended their network and began to choose agents on the basis of proximity or convenience, rather than histories of interaction. Institutional trust was also important for the formation of these extended relations. Many of the customers noted that they would look for the M-PESA brand before transacting with unknown agents. They further relied on the confirmation SMS, which was sent by Safaricom, to validate the transaction. The empirical evidence also showed that local institutions such as tribes shaped the trajectory of growth. In particular, they strengthened trust relations between the customers and Safaricom during the post-election violence whilst weakening those between customers and agents. Numerous agents noted that some members of different tribes became especially "difficult" during the violence. Some agents closed their shops to avoid attacks. This finding is interesting as tribal affiliations have not been given attention within the trust literature.

FURTHER RESEARCH

The existing literature needs to pay more attention to the various processes of trust negotiation that must occur before, and during, widespread adoption and usage. The role of these processes in shaping the trajectory and nature of transformational m-banking applications should also be made clear. Such findings can provide an important basis for the development of future research about transformational dimension of ICTs, mostly – though not exclusively – in 'developing contexts'. Here, we have presented just one case of trust establishment and evolution. It is likely that the four types of trust relations would develop differently in other contexts. It is further likely that a different set of actors would be involved. Such research would complement the findings presented in this chapter, and allow for generalizations regarding the establishment and maintenance of trust in m-banking transactions as well as ICT development and usage.

RECOMMENDATIONS

Public and private organizations, system designers, and decision-makers, who are thinking of introducing an m-banking service, can draw several lessons from this analysis. The first is related to institutional trust. The service providers must realize that their brand name is vitally important to the establishment and maintenance of trust relations. It provides a basis for the development of interpersonal and extended trust relations, both of which are important for widespread deployment. Secondly, the factors shaping the evolution of trust relations are different in Kenya than other "Western" settings. For example, trust associated to an organization depends on aspects like tribal belonging of its key members. This introduces new dimensions to institutional analysis. Such dimensions must be given careful attention by stakeholders, as they help to explain local adaptation and evolution of m-banking systems. They can further help designers and implementers to understand users' behavior, especially the rejection of a technology, and its unexpected uses. Finally, rapid adoption, and frequent usage, is more likely if features that reinforce institutional trust relations are built into the application. These features are

especially important when intermediaries, in this case the agents, are used for the extension of financial services.

REFERENCES

Barber, B. (1983). *The logic and limits of trust.* New Brunswick, NJ: Rutgers University Press.

Boon, S., & Holmes, J. (1991). The dynamics of interpersonal trust: Resolving uncertainty in the face of risk. In Hinde, R. A. (Ed.), *Cooperation and prosocial behavior* (pp. 167–182). New York: Cambridge University Press.

Brann, P., & Foddy, M. (1988). Trust and the consumption of a deteriorating resource. *The Journal of Conflict Resolution, 31*(4), 615–630. doi:10.1177/0022002787031004004

Dasgupta, P. (1988). Trust as a commodity. In Gambetta, D. (Ed.), *Trust: Making and breaking cooperative relations* (pp. 49–72). New York: Basil Blackwell.

Dawes, R. M. (1994). *House of cards: Psychology and psychotherapy built on myth.* New York: Free Press.

Hughes, N., & Lonie, S. (2007). M-PESA: Mobile Money for the "unbanked": Turning cellphones into 24-hour tellers in Kenya. *Innovations,* Winter and Spring.

Ilako, F., & Kimura, M. (2004). *Provision of ARVs in a resource-poor setting: Kibera slum.* Paper presented at the International Conference on AIDS, Nairobi.

Ishihara, S. (2003). *The informal economy of Kibera slums.* Unpublished doctoral dissertation, SOAS, London.

Ivatury, G., & Pickens, M. (2006). *Mobile phone banking and low-income customers: Evidence from South Africa.* Consultative Group to Assist the Poor/The World Bank.

Klopp, J., & Kamungi, P. (2008). Violence and elections: Will Kenya collapse? *World Policy Journal, 24*(4), 11–18. doi:10.1162/wopj.2008.24.4.11

Kramer, R. (1999). Trust and distrust in organizations: Emerging perspectives, enduring questions. *Annual Review of Psychology, 50*, 569–598. doi:10.1146/annurev.psych.50.1.569

Luhmann, N. (1979). *Trust and power.* New York: Wiley.

Lynch, G. (2008). Courting the Kalenjin: The failure of dynasticism and the strength of the ODM wave in Kenya's Rift Valley province. *African Affairs, 107*(429), 541–568. doi:10.1093/afraf/adn060

Mayer, R., Davis, J., & Schoorman, F. D. (1995). An integrative model of organizational trust. *Academy of Management Review, 20*, 709–734. doi:10.2307/258792

McAlister, D. J. (1995). Affect- and cognition based trust as foundations for interpersonal cooperation in organizations. *Academy of Management Review, 38*(1), 24–59. doi:10.2307/256727

Mishler, W., & Rose, R. (2001). What are the origins of political trust? Testing institutional and cultural theories in post-communist societies. *Comparative Political Studies, 34*(1), 30–62. doi:10.1177/0010414001034001002

Porteous, D. (2006). *The enabling environment for mobile banking in Africa.* Boston: DFID.

Porteous, D. (2007). *Just how transformational is m-banking?* Finmark Trust.

Powell, W., & DiMaggio, P. J. (Eds.). (1991). *The new institutionalism in organizational analysis.* Chicago: The University of Chicago Press.

Raiser, M., Haerpfer, C., Nowotny, T., & Wallace, C. (2001). *Social capital in transition: a first look at the evidence.* Working Paper No. 61, European Bank.

Smith, M. (2007). *Confianza a la Chilena: A comparative study of how e-services influence public sector institutional trustworthiness and trust.* Unpublished doctoral dissertation, London School of Economics, London.

Vaughan, P. (2007). Early lessons from the deployment of M-Pesa. In *The transformational potential of m-transactions* (pp. 6–10). Newbury, UK: Vodafone Group PLC.

Williamson, O. E. (1985). *The economic institutions of capitalism.* New York: Free Press.

Zimmer, T. (1972). The impact of Watergate on the public's trust in people and confidence in the mass media. *Social Science Quarterly, 59*, 743–751.

ENDNOTES

[1]   We distinguish organizations from institutions by defining the latter as the accepted social models which the former embody. For example, the financial system is a socially accepted model of handling money (an institution which a remarkable number of people recognize and accept), the banks are actual organizations conducting such activities. Adhering to new institutionalism (Powell and DiMaggio, 1991), we use this distinction to note how organizations and institutions affect each other, as discussed later.

[2]   This is in a country of 38 million. It is estimated that Safaricom has over 80% of the market share.

[3]   'Bob' is the slang name used for Kenyan shilling.

[4]   The disputed presidential elections of December 2007 eventually erupted into wide-scale violence. As a result of this violence 1500 people lost their lives. Another 600,000 were displaced from their homes. For more

information about the violence consult Lynch (2008) or Klop & Kamungi (2008).

5 The M-PESA agents had to maintain a cash float to operate. Such maintenance was espe-

cially important in the rural area, where the majority of transactions were withdrawals. Most agents made frequent trips to the bank to withdraw cash, and top-up their float.

Chapter 11

Internet Trust as a Specific Form of Technology Trust and its Influence on Online Banking Adoption

Sonja Grabner-Kräuter
Klagenfurt University, Austria

Rita Faullant
Klagenfurt University, Austria

ABSTRACT

The construct of trust is important for online banking, because it underlines what is conducive to an enabling online banking environment. This chapter reports on an empirical study of 381 bank customers in Austria that investigates the role of Internet trust as a specific form of technology trust in the context of Internet banking. Furthermore the impact of propensity to trust as a facet of personality on Internet trust is investigated. The findings stress the importance of Internet trust as a determinant of consumer attitudes toward Internet banking and its adoption. In addition, the results show that propensity to trust is a determinant not only for trust in interpersonal relationships but also for trust in technological systems.

INTRODUCTION

Trust in general, is an important factor in many social interactions, involving uncertainty and dependency. Trust is central to any economic transaction, whether conducted in a retail outlet in the real offline world or over the Internet, by means of a website. However, trust is even more important in an online situation (Riegelsberger, Sasse, & McCarthy, 2005; Walczuch & Lundgren, 2004). One reason for the importance of trust in e-commerce is the fact that in a virtual environment the degree of uncertainty of economic transactions is higher than in traditional settings. Internet-based commercial transactions are accompanied by several risks that either are caused by the implicit uncertainty of using open technological infrastructures for the exchange of information (system-dependent uncertainty) or can be explained by the conduct of actors who are involved in the online transaction (transaction-specific uncertainty) (Grabner-Kräuter, 2002).

DOI: 10.4018/978-1-61520-901-9.ch011

Internet banking can be regarded as an especially suitable research context for examining questions related to risk and trust, as particular features of Internet banking render a unique environment, in which trust is of crucial importance. Compared to face-to-face transactions, Internet banking transactions have some unique characteristics, such as the extensive use of technologies, the distant and impersonal nature of the online environment, and the implicit uncertainty of using an open technological infrastructure for financial transactions (Gan, Clemes, Limsombunchai, & Weng, 2006; Yousafzai, Pallister, & Foxall, 2003). Indeed, recent literature on online banking shows that the lack of trust has to be considered to be one of the main reasons why consumers are still reluctant to conduct their financial transactions online (Flavian, Guinalıu, & Torres, 2006; Luarn & Lin, 2005; Mukherjee & Nath, 2003; Rotchanakitumnuai & Speece, 2003). In Austria (and in many other countries) potential users object to conducting their financial transactions online, despite the huge amount of money banks have spent on building user-friendly Internet banking systems. This points out the need to further investigate the factors that hinder consumers' acceptance of Internet banking.

Using numerous different theoretical approaches and models several researchers have investigated the factors that impact the decisions of customers to adopt Internet banking (for recent reviews see e.g. (Hernandez & Mazzon, 2007; Sayar & Wolfe, 2007)). Concerning different types of barriers to Internet-based financial transactions, trust-related issues are of critical importance (Rotchanakitumnuai & Speece, 2003). Most empirical studies on consumer online trust focus on interpersonal trust, where the object of trust is the Internet vendor (e.g. Gefen, 2000; Gefen, Karahanna, & Straub, 2003; Koufaris & Hampton-Sosa, 2004; Pavlou, 2003; Suh & Han, 2003), whereas the influence of technology or system trust on online consumer behavior is largely neglected (Grabner-Kräuter & Kaluscha, 2003).

This paper adds both to technology adoption research and to trust research in marketing by examining the role that different types of online trust play in the adoption of Internet banking. The focus is on the concept of Internet trust, analyzing if it is a distinct type of trust that influences the consumer's perceived risk of Internet banking and the consumer's attitude toward Internet banking. To form a more complete picture of factors influencing consumer decisions to use the Internet as a medium for conducting financial transactions we encompass selected psychological antecedents of Internet trust in our study. In several studies the consumer's general disposition to trust was found to have an impact on the consumer's initial trust in an online vendor (Gefen, 2000; McKnight, Choudhury, & Kacmar, 2002; Teo & Liu, 2007). However, little research has addressed the question whether an individual's propensity to trust other people also has a major influence on his/her trust in technical systems (Grabner-Kräuter & Faullant, 2008; Kaluscha, 2004; McKnight, et al., 2002; McKnight & Chervany, 2002). Hence, another aim of our study is to shed light on the potential influence of dispositional trust on trust and risk perception in the context of Internet banking. Furthermore, we include self-efficacy as a dimension of perceived behavioral control that might influence Internet trust and online banking adoption in our research model.

The paper continues as follows: Below, in the first section, we give an approximate and brief overview of several theoretical frameworks that have been used to investigate the adoption of online banking. The subsequent discussion focuses on the central construct Internet trust, followed by the development of hypotheses regarding antecedents and consequences of Internet trust in the context of online banking. Then, methodology, results, and hypotheses testing are presented. The final section discusses the study's findings, contribution, and theoretical and managerial implications.

BACKGROUND

The adoption of Internet banking is an instance of information technology acceptance and use within a setting that combines technology adoption with bank marketing elements, and it thus requires distinct theorization within the information systems and the consumer behavior literature (Pavlou & Fygenson, 2006). The analysis of factors that impact the decisions of customers to adopt innovative retail services such as Internet banking has extensively focused on the issue of user technology acceptance (Hernandez & Mazzon, 2007; Lai & Li, 2005; Ravi, Carr, & Sagar, 2006; Wang, Wang, Lin, & Tang, 2003). Several theoretical approaches have been used and many competing models have been developed to investigate the determinants of acceptance and adoption of new information technology. These theoretical approaches have been discussed extensively in the literature (for comprehensive reviews see e.g. (Hernandez & Mazzon, 2007; Venkatesh, Morris, Davis, & Davis, 2003), thus we only briefly sketch out the relevant theoretical frameworks.

Especially in the information systems literature questions related to user technology acceptance have received wide and intense interest. For years researchers have focused on a relatively mutual subset of factors for predicting technology adoption and use: individual attitudes (for example, attitude toward using computers), behavioral intention to use the technology, and personal perceptions (most frequently perceived ease of use and perceived usefulness) (McElroy, Hendrickson, Townsend, & DeMarie, 2007). The technology acceptance model (TAM) first proposed by Davis (1989) incorporates these variables. TAM has been widely applied in technology acceptance research and is an adaptation of the Theory of Reasoned Action (TRA) (Ajzen & Fishbein, 1980). TRA posits that overt behavior of a person is predicted by the person's intentions toward this behavior, while the behavioral intention is a function of both the attitude toward the behavior and subjective norms

regarding the behavior (Ajzen & Fishbein, 1980). The Theory of Planned Behavior (TPB) (Ajzen, 1991) is an(other) expansion of TRA, for situations where people do not have complete control over their behavior. TPB additionally includes the exogenous variable of perceived behavioral control, a construct that reflects how people perceive the internal and external restrictions to their behavior (Eriksson, Kerem, & Nilsson, 2008).

Unlike TRA and TPB, general models that are applicable to all kinds of human behavior, TAM was especially designed for the case of users' acceptance or adoption of new information systems. TAM does not include the construct of subjective norms, because technology adoption is typically assumed to be voluntary, and because the influence of subjective norms is difficult to unravel from the effects of attitude on behavioral intention (Davis, 1989). It has been criticized that TAM with its focus on perceived usefulness and perceived ease of use as determinants of the attitude toward using the technology might not adequately consider the potential influence of other psychological and situational factors (Dabholkar & Bagozzi, 2002). Therefore, extensions and modifications of TAM have been suggested by several researchers (for an overview see Chau & Lai (2003)). For example, (Gefen, et al., 2003) have integrated antecedents of online trust and trust in the online vendor and the technological attribute-based antecedents of intended use found in TAM into an extended theoretical model to explain intended use of a business-to-consumer website. In a similar way, Pavlou (2003) integrated trust toward the web retailer and consumer perceived risk with TAM.

A second line of research has investigated acceptance and use of new information technologies from the perspective of the Innovation Diffusion Theory (IDT) (Rogers, 1995). This stream of research also focuses on individual acceptance of technology by using behavioral intention or adoption as dependent variables, but the determinants are usually established according to the characteristics of the new technology

(Hernandez & Mazzon, 2007; Venkatesh, et al., 2003). Analyzing past research on the diffusion of innovation Rogers found that the most important factors influencing technology adoption are user's perceptions regarding relative advantage, compatibility, complexity, trialability, and observability of the innovation (Rogers, 1995).

Most research on the adoption of Internet banking either builds on TAM models (e.g. Chau & Lai, 2003; Lassar, Manolis, & Lassar, 2005; Pikkarainen, Pikkarainen, Karjaluoto, & Pahnila, 2004; Sukkar & Hasan, 2005; Wang, et al., 2003) or on IDT frameworks (Eriksson, et al., 2008; Gerrard & Cunningham, 2003; Ndubisi & Sinti, 2006; Polatoglu & Ekin, 2001). Lassar et al. (2005) integrate TAM and the adoption of an innovation framework to predict online banking acceptance. Gounaris & Koritos (2008) investigated the underutilized Perceived Characteristics of the Innovation framework (an extension of the IDT framework) vis-à-vis the TAM and IDT frameworks and found a significantly improved explanatory power of the former. In this study, we focus on Internet trust as a determinant of online banking acceptance. As both Internet banking adopters and non-adopters were examined, we did not integrate the technological attribute-based antecedents of intended use found in TAM or the IDT based characteristics of Internet banking as a new technology in our research model. Rather the proposed hypotheses are formulated in accordance with a reduced theory of reasoned action framework. To be placed in a TRA or TPB framework, trust must be defined with respect to a behavior through a well-specified target, action, and context (Pavlou & Fygenson, 2006).

THE CONCEPT OF INTERNET TRUST

The importance of initiating, building, and maintaining trust between buyers and sellers as key facilitators of successful e-commerce is increasingly being recognized in academic as well as in practitioner communities. Meanwhile a number of studies have investigated the role of trust in the specific context of business-to-consumer electronic commerce, having their roots in different scholarly disciplines and focusing on different aspects of this multi-dimensional construct [see the overview in Chang, Cheung & Lai, 2005; Grabner-Kräuter & Kaluscha, 2003]. The concept of trust has been defined by researchers in many different ways, which often reflect the paradigms of the particular academic discipline of the researcher. Some definitions overlap, but more often each definition offers an explanation of a different aspect of trust. Thus there are literally dozens of definitions of trust, which many researchers find contradictory and confusing (Gulati & Sytch, 2008). These problems apply particularly to e-commerce domain research (McKnight & Chervany, 2002).

In the organizational trust literature trust is mostly defined as a belief or expectation about the other (trusted) party, or as a behavioral intention or willingness to depend or rely on another party, coupled with a sense of vulnerability or risk if the trust is violated [e.g. Mayer, Davis, & Schoorman, 1995; Rousseau, Sitkin, Butt, & Camerer, 1998]. Accordingly, online trust is most often defined as a belief or expectation about the website, the web vendor and/or (less frequently) the Internet as the trusted party or object of trust or as a behavioral intention or willingness to depend or rely on the trusted party (McKnight & Chervany, 1996; McKnight, et al., 2002; McKnight & Chervany, 2002). In the context of Internet banking, the trustor is typically a consumer who has to decide whether to adopt Internet banking or stay with more traditional ways of undertaking her/his financial transactions.

Especially within the research disciplines of relationship marketing and organizational theory several scholars have offered trust definitions that highlight trust related attributes of the trusted party. Researchers have defined trust as a multi-dimensional construct and included specific characteristics of the trusted party in their trust definitions such as ability, integrity, benevolence, predictability, credibility or dependability [e.g. Mayer, et al., 1995; Palmer & Bejou, 1994; Selnes, 1998]. These characteristics or attributes of the trusted party are often referred to interchangeably as elements, antecedents, underlying dimensions or determinants of online trust (Wang and Emurian 2005). Fundamentally, these attributes of the trustee reflect different components of trustworthiness, a concept that again is defined differently by a number of researchers (e.g. Riegelsberger et al. 2005). In line with a multi-dimensional idea of trust more commonly found in the marketing and organization theory literature (e.g. Morgan & Hunt 1994) we propose to include specific characteristics of the trusted party in the definition of online trust. Basically, two broad dimensions of online trust can be distinguished. The 'hard dimension' of online trust has a functionality-based nature, involving the ability, competence, and predictability of the trusted object. The trustor's judgement of the hard dimension is based primarily on cognition. This dimension is relevant for all objects of trust in the context of e-commerce: the e-commerce website, the merchant that the website represents, and the underlying technology. The 'soft dimension' of trust comprises characteristics or attributes such as honesty, integrity, benevolence and credibility that refer to the intrinsic, value-based motivation of the trustee to act in the interest of the trustor. The trustor's perception of the soft dimension is mainly affect-based. The operationalization of this trust dimension respectively of its sub-dimensions makes sense only in interpersonal trust relationships, or more specifically, when the trusted party is another individual person.

The analysis of online trust in the context of Internet banking should not focus exclusively on interpersonal relationships but has to consider impersonal forms of trust as well. The technology itself – serving as a transmission medium for conducting financial transactions and including security services and technical solutions embedded in e-commerce technologies – has to be considered as an object of trust (Corritore, Kracher, & Wiedenbeck, 2003; Pennington, Wilcox, & Grover, 2003/2004; Ratnasingam, 2005; Rotchanakitumnuai & Speece, 2003; Shankar, Urban, & Sultan, 2002). Ratnasingham (1999) proposes the term technology trust and suggests that dimensions of security services such as confidentiality mechanisms, authentication mechanisms, and access control mechanisms contribute to the enhancement of technology trust from a capability process that serves to support the privacy, accuracy, authenticity of authorized parties, and accountability of e-commerce transactions. Mukherjee & Nath (2003) view the customers' orientation towards e-commerce technology and the extent to which they trust the electronic system as a proxy for their trust in Internet banking.

When investigating the influence of technology trust on online consumer behavior it makes sense to define this construct as a belief, for example about the reliability and security of the e-commerce infrastructure, combined with a willingness to rely on the Internet as a medium for economic transactions. Trust in technical systems is mainly based on the perceived functionality (e.g. reliability, capability, correctness and availability) of a system (Lee & Turban, 2001; Thatcher, Loughry, Lim, & McKnight, 2007). Therefore, we argue that only the 'hard dimension' of trust is relevant for the conceptualization and operationalization of Internet trust. We conceptualize Internet trust as trusting beliefs in the reliability and predictability of the Internet and the willingness of the consumer to depend on the Internet with regard to economic transactions.

ADOPTION OF INTERNET BANKING: HYPOTHESES' DEVELOPMENT

The proposed hypotheses are formulated in accordance with an adapted theory of planned behavior framework.

Attitude and actual behavior. The concept of attitude can be considered a key factor in most consumer behavior models. Attitude has long been shown to influence behavioral intentions and actual behavior (Ajzen, 1991). Most studies on the acceptance of Internet banking focus on attitudes and/or behavioral intentions and not on actual behavior (Grabner-Kräuter & Faullant, 2008). In our research model the dependent variable is the frequency of Internet banking adoption for private purposes. For reasons of parsimony we do not include intention in our research model. We expect a positive direct relationship between the attitude toward Internet banking and its adoption. Based on Venkatesh's definition of attitude toward using technology (Venkatesh, et al., 2003), attitude toward Internet banking is defined as an individual's overall affective reaction to using the Internet for his/her banking activities. We propose that

H1: Favourable attitude toward Internet banking positively influences its adoption.

Internet trust. *The prevailing view of consumer trust in the e-commerce literature contends that trust has a direct positive effect on attitudes and behavior (Jarvenpaa, Shaw, & Staples, 2004; Kim & Prabhakar, 2000; Pavlou, 2002; Suh & Han, 2003; Teo & Liu, 2007). The consumers' trusting beliefs about the trusted party or trusted object affect their attitude toward the trusting behavior. The relationship between trust and attitude draws on the notion of perceived consequences (Pavlou & Fygenson, 2006). Internet trust enables favourable expectations that the Internet is reliable and predictable and that no harmful consequences will occur if the online consumer uses the Internet as a transaction medium for his/her financial transactions. Therefore, we propose that*

H2: Internet trust positively influences the consumer's attitude toward Internet banking.

Perceived risk of Internet banking. *The concept of consumer-perceived risk has been widely dealt with in the marketing literature and has been shown to influence consumer behavior to varying degrees and in varying contexts (Cunningham, Gerlach, & Harper, 2005; Mitchell, 1998). Consumer behavior researchers most often define perceived risk in terms of the consumer's perceptions of the uncertainty and potential adverse consequences of buying a product or service (Littler and Melanthiou 2006). Many studies have shown that consumers perceive different facets or components of risk and that their predictive value for total risk and risk-reducing behavior depends very much on the product class (Gemünden, 1985). Distinct facets of risk (e.g. social, financial, security, and performance risk) may be perceived independently of one another as they can arise from different kinds of sources. The influence of risk perception on consumer attitudes and behavior may be different in situations that are dominated by different types of risks, e.g. either by high social risk or high financial risk (Mandrik & Bao, 2005). Conducting economic transactions on the Internet presents numerous risks for consumers, over and above the transaction process itself being perceived as risky (Einwiller & Will, 2001). In the online environment criminal acts can be performed at extremely high speed, and without any physical contact (Cheung & Lee, 2006). If an unauthorized individual is able to gain access to the online banking portfolio of a user, a considerable amount of financial information may be jeopardised and there might be significant financial losses. Hence, the most important categories of perceived risk associated with Internet banking are likely to be financial risk and security risk related to the potential loss because of deficiencies in the operating system or misappropriation of funds through illegal external access (Awamleh & Fernandes, 2006; Littler & Melanthiou, 2006; Rotchanakitumnuai & Speece, 2003; Sarel & Marmorstein, 2003).*

Drawing on the work of Luhmann (1989) trust can be seen as a mechanism to reduce the complexity of human conduct in situations where people have to cope with uncertainty. In this functional perspective Internet trust can be seen as a mechanism that reduces the uncertainty of using open technological infrastructures for the exchange of information, i.e. system-dependent uncertainty. With regard to Internet banking or online shopping system-dependent or exogenous uncertainty primarily relates to potential technological sources of errors and security gaps or, to put it economically, to technology-dependent risks that can not be avoided by an agreement or a contract with another actor who is involved in the transaction (Grabner-Kräuter 2002). In the context of online shopping, several studies have confirmed the expected risk-reducing impact of trust (Chang, et al., 2005; Gefen, et al., 2003; Jarvenpaa, Tractinsky, & Vitale, 2000; Pavlou, 2003). Hence, we conclude that Internet trust is a mechanism that reduces the perceived system-dependent risks of economic transactions on the Internet. We propose that

H3: Internet trust is negatively related to perceived risk of Internet banking.

Similar to trust, perceived risk can also be regarded as a situational belief about the likelihood of gains and losses (Mayer, et al., 1995; Teo & Liu, 2007). In several studies a significant negative impact of risk perception on the attitude towards online shopping or likelihood to purchase online was found (Jarvenpaa, et al., 2000; Kuhlmeier & Gary, 2005; Laforet & Li, 2005; Teo & Liu, 2007). Drawing on these findings we posit that

H4: Perceived risk of Internet banking is negatively related to the consumer's attitude toward Internet banking.

Propensity to trust. Propensity to trust or dispositional trust is the extent to which a per-

son displays a tendency to be willing to depend on others across a broad spectrum of situations and persons (McKnight, et al., 2002). This type of trust has its roots in personality psychology (e.g. (Rotter, 1967)) and can be seen as a stable intra-individual characteristic which influences interpersonal interaction with others. Despite its wide use in literature and also in empirical studies the concept of dispositional trust has mostly been conceptualized as a stand-alone trait without relation to the theoretical understanding of the personality structure which has emerged in recent years in psychology. Mooradian, Renzl, & Matzler (2006) were among the first to empirically relate propensity to trust to the hierarchical structure of the Five Factor Model, and investigate the relationship between trait and state trust in the context of knowledge sharing. We also argue that the concept of dispositional trust needs to be related to recent findings in personality research. By splitting the Big Five into 30 narrower facets, additional information is thought to be gathered about individuals over and above what could be obtained from the five common factors (McCrae & Costa, 1992). The lower-level facets might therefore be more closely related to overt and observable behaviors (Paunonen, Haddock, Forsterling, & Keinonen, 2003). We propose the trust facet of the Five Factor Model to adequately reflect the stand-alone perceptions of the propensity to trust concept. Furthermore, we propose that the concept of propensity to trust is not exclusively applicable to interpersonal situations but is extendable towards technical systems (see also Grabner-Kräuter & Faullant, 2008). First evidence in this regard can be found in Siegrist, Gutscher, & Earle (2005) who found that general trust (as disposition) might influence perceptions of new technologies. We posit that propensity to trust influences both Internet trust and the perceived risk of Internet banking.

H5a: People with high/low scores on the trust-scale display higher/lower levels of internet trust.

H5b: People with high/low scores on the trust-scale display lower/higher levels of perceived internet banking risk.

Self-efficacy. Self efficacy is a dimension of perceived control and can be defined as individual judgements of a person's capabilities to perform a behavior (Pavlou & Fygenson, 2006). Self-efficacy is associated with beliefs and behavior and has been shown to have a critical influence on decisions involving computer usage and adoption (Igbaria & Iivari, 1995). Management information systems research suggests that individuals who have high computer self-efficacy are more likely to use information technology (Igbaria & Iivari, 1995; Thatcher, et al., 2007). Applied to Internet banking, self-efficacy reflects the belief that consumers have about their ability to use the computer and the Internet effectively to conduct their banking activities (Torkzadeh, Chang, & Demirhan, 2006). We propose that

H6a: Self-efficacy is positively related with Internet trust.

H6b: Self-efficacy is positively related with Internet banking adoption.

STUDY

Sample. To test the proposed relationships, data from customers from different Austrian banks who are also Internet users (both adopters and non-adopters of Internet banking) were collected. Subjects for the study were randomly selected people that have been approached at different locations (airport, park, shopping precincts) in bigger and smaller cities more or less all over Austria. Data collection took place in August 2007. The interviewers randomly selected airport passengers and passers-by, asked them to participate in the study (if they used the Internet and had a

bank account) and to complete the standardized, self-administered questionnaire. In most cases respondents did not need any help with answering the questions. As an incentive, interviewees received a soft drink. 381 usable questionnaires were collected. Table 1 displays the characteristics of the sample.

Measures. A standardized questionnaire with closed-response questions using 5-point (self-efficacy and frequency of Internet banking adoption) and 7-point (all other constructs) rating scales was developed (see appendix). All measurement items were drawn from the literature, and they were adapted using standard psychometric scale development procedures. Internet trust was measured with 4 items, 2 items measuring the perceived reliability and predictability of the Internet (e.g. "When performing a transaction on the Internet I know exactly what will happen", and 2 items measuring the willingness to depend on the Internet (e.g. "I trust the Internet"). The items were adapted from McKnight et al. (2002) and McKnight & Chervany (2002) and the brand trust scale developed by Chaudhuri & Holbrook (2001). Perceived risk of Internet banking (5 items; e.g. "I am afraid that other people might get access to information about my Internet banking transactions") was adapted from Awamleh & Fernandes (2006) and Meuter, Bitner, Ostrom & Brown (2005), self-efficacy (2 items; e.g. "How comfortable do you feel using the Internet?" from Lassar et al. (2005). Attitude toward online banking (3 items; e.g. "I think it is good for me to use Internet banking") was based on scales developed by Lai & Li (2005), Wu & Chen (2005) and Chau & Lai (2003). The measure for propensity to trust was taken from Costa and McCrae's (1992) NEO-Personality-Inventory-Revised (NEO-PI-R).

Reliability and validity. Structural equation modeling was used to analyze the data (AMOS 7.0). Confirmatory factor analysis (CFA) was conducted to test the measurement model and establish the convergent and discriminant validity of the constructs. As a result of the refinements

Table 1. Characteristics of the sample

Characteristic		%
Gender	Male	48.6
	Female	51.4
Age	Less than 20 years	10.5
	20-29 years	23.1
	30-39 years	20.5
	40-49 years	23.4
	50-59 years	13.6
	60-69 years	5.5
	More than 70 years	3.4
Education	Primary	4.7
	High school	36.7
	Vocational school or apprenticeship	29.7
	University	26.5
	Other	2.4
Internet Banking	Adopters	59.1
	Non-Adopters	40.9

and purification, the initial measurement instrument of 22 items was reduced down to 17 items for the final, refined measurement model. The final measurement model reached or succeeded all recommended thresholds for global fit indices, with a goodness-of-fit index (GFI) of .953, an adjusted goodness-of-fit index (AGFI) of .932; the root mean square error of approximation (RMSEA) is .036, the Tucker-Lewis index (TLI) is .986 and the comparative fit index (CFI) is .989. Thus, it can be concluded that the model fits the data reasonably well. In order to evaluate the local fit of the structural components, reliability and validity of the measures were tested calculating the composite reliability (CR) of the constructs, the average variance extracted (AVE) and the Fornell-Larcker-Ratio (FLR) (Fornell & Larcker, 1981) to test discriminant validity. The results are reported in Table 2, showing good psychometric properties of the measures. For the endogenous constructs Internet trust, perceived risk of Internet banking and attitude toward Internet banking, and the exogenous construct self-efficacy all indices clearly

exceed their respective common acceptance levels recommended by previous researchers (indicator loading > .4, t-value significant, composite reliability > .6, average variance extracted > .5, Fornell-Larcker-Ratio <1). One indicator loading of the exogenous construct propensity to trust is lower than the recommended threshold.

Hypothesis testing results. Figure 1 displays the results of the basic model with the main effects, the explained variance of endogenous latent constructs and the strength of structural relationships.

R^2 values of the endogenous constructs are .39 (Internet trust), .37 (perceived risk of Internet banking), .57 (attitude toward Internet banking), and .55 (adoption Internet banking). Hence, the personality facet propensity to trust and self-efficacy influence Internet trust, explaining 39% of its variance. Both propensity to trust and Internet trust influence perceived risk of Internet banking, explaining 37% of its variance. Internet trust has a strong positive effect and perceived risk of Internet banking has a medium negative effect on the attitude toward Internet banking, and together

Table 2. Psychometric properties of the scales in the basic model

	Item	Indicator loading	t-Value factor loading	Composite reliability	Average variance extracted	Fornell-Larcker-Ratio
Internet Trust	ITRUST2	.694	16.691***	0.88	0.65	0.87
	ITRUST3	.636	15.905***			
	ITRUST4	.680	16.497***			
	ITRUST5	.578	--			
Perceived Risk Internet Banking	RISK_IB3	.654	20.384***	0.92	0.74	0.49
	RISK_IB4	.681	19.827***			
	RISK_IB5	.851	24.668***			
	RISK_IB6	.784	--			
Attitude toward Internet Banking	ATT1	.836	--	0.95	0.87	0.65
	ATT2	.893	32.988***			
	ATT3	.878	32.169***			
Self-efficacy	SE_Comp	.745	--	0.93	0.87	0.41
	SE_Inter	.974	19.027***			
Trust propensity	Agree1_6	.600	9.916***	0.80	0.59	0.07
	Agree1_7	.881	9.167***			
	Agree1_8	<u>.267</u>	--			
Frequency adoption Internet banking	FREQ_IB	<u>1.00</u>				0.53

Figure 1. Relationships in the basic model

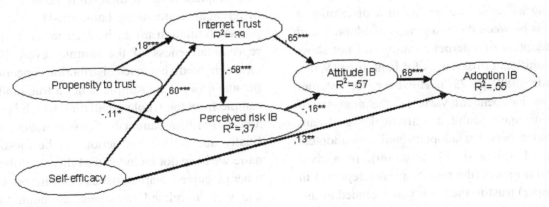

*** p = ,000; ** p< ,01; *p< ,05;
Notes: CMIN/DF 1,450; p=,001; GFI=,952; AGFI=,934; TLI=,987; CFI=,990; RMSEA=,034

these variables explain 57% of the variance of attitude. 55% of the variance of Internet banking adoption is explained by attitude toward Internet banking, which has a strong positive impact on adoption of Internet banking (ß=.68; p=.000), and self-efficacy, which has a direct positive impact on adoption of Internet banking (ß=.13; p=.001) and, additionally, an indirect impact on Internet trust and attitude. The results of the main effect model provided support for hypotheses 1 to 6b. Self-efficacy has a strong positive effect impact on Internet trust (ß=.60; p=.000). Internet trust has a strong and positive impact on attitude toward Internet banking (ß=.65, p=.000) and a strong and negative impact on perceived risk of Internet banking (ß=-.58, p=.004). Perceived risk of Internet banking has a negative impact on attitude toward Internet banking (ß=-.16, p=.002). In support of H5a and H5b, propensity to trust has a significant positive impact on Internet trust (ß=.18, p=.000) and a significant negative impact on perceived risk, (ß=-.11, p=.027). 3

Discussion. The results of this study provide strong support for the proposed influence of Internet trust on risk perception and consumer attitudes toward Internet banking. In the original survey, the variable bank trust was also included, as we expected it to influence the adoption of Internet banking as well. The results of a discriminant analysis between the two groups of adopters and non-adopters of Internet banking did not show any significant differences for bank trust (Wilks Lambda=.988, p=.731). However, for Internet trust as independent variable, the analysis of discriminance found a statistical significant difference between adopters and non-adopters (Wilks' Lambda=0.673; p=0.000). In a rival structural model (the results are not reported in this paper) trust in the bank was included as another antecedent of the attitude toward Internet banking. Bank trust did not show any impact on the attitude toward Internet banking and there was only a small intercorrelation between bank trust and Internet trust. Thus it can be concluded that

trust toward the bank or the Internet vendor in a broader sense and trust toward the Internet must not be confounded or treated as different dimensions of the same construct "online trust", but have to be regarded as two distinct constructs that influence online consumer behavior in different ways. Another contribution of this study to the trust literature is the confirmation of the hypothesized impact of propensity to trust on Internet trust as a specific form of technology trust. The question whether the psychological concept of dispositional trust or propensity to trust is extendable towards technical systems is controversially discussed in the literature (Kaluscha, 2004; McKnight, et al., 2002; McKnight & Chervany, 2002). Our findings assert that not only people may be the object of dispositional trust, but trust propensity might be a generalized tendency both across different situations and different objects of trust (Grabner-Kräuter & Faullant, 2008).

FUTURE RESEARCH DIRECTIONS

In the previous sections we have already mentioned some of the limitations of our study, amongst others the combined analysis of adopters and non-adopters (even if there were no significant differences concerning bank trust). One important limitation might be seen in the lacking representativeness of the sample, even if we have achieved a balanced distribution concerning the age groups, the sample is not a true random sample from the whole population which is why a selection bias cannot be fully excluded. And finally, due to space restrictions on the questionnaire we have not included usability, usefulness, other perceived characteristics of online banking and website-related questions, although there might be interaction effects with the psychological constructs investigated in the present study. This could be a valuable research goal for future studies, as the relative importance of Internet trust in the adoption process of Internet banking might be related to external stimuli provided by the website interface.

Research focusing on the investigation of the dimensionality of online trust poses another fruitful avenue for trust researchers. Scholars either view trust as being one-dimensional or multi-dimensional, but clear empirical evidence is lacking that would help to favour one of these views. In line with the theoretical reasoning of (Gefen & Straub, 2004) and the findings of their empirical study we believe that the dimensions that constitute trust are context-specific and that the meaning and consequences of trust can be better analyzed and understood when different trust dimensions are viewed separately. Thus the relevant trusting beliefs or expectations that determine trust-related behavior depend on the circumstances of the interaction. In the case of Internet trust, the relevant trusting beliefs dimensions are predictability and reliability, whereas benevolence and integrity are dimensions of trustworthiness that are relevant only for interpersonal or interorganizational trust concepts.

The findings of our study showed that Austrian consumers tend to have low trust in the Internet as a medium to conduct their personal banking activities. Across Europe, Internet banking adoption rates are markedly different (Meyer, 2006). For example, in Norway and Finland 70-80% of Internet users adopt online banking, in Austria and Germany about 40%, whereas in Greece and Romania less than 10% of the Internet users make use of online banking or brokerage (Meyer, 2006). On the other hand, in Brazil the Internet banking growth rate over the past years has exceeded that of the Internet itself (Hernandez & Mazzon, 2007). Factors influencing the adoption of Internet banking have been investigated in numerous different countries (e.g. (Akinci, Aksoy, & Atilgan, 2004; Eriksson, et al., 2008; Karjaluoto, Mattila, & Pento, 2002; Kuisma, Laukkanen, & Hiltunen, 2007; Laforet & Li, 2005; Mukherjee & Nath, 2003; Rotchanakitumnuai & Speece, 2003; Sukkar & Hasan, 2005; Wan, Luk, & Chow, 2005)).

Consequently, cross-cultural effects on consumers' online trust may prove to be another fruitful topic for future research. One of the ways in which culture affects trust is through dispositional trust. But culture can also affect the perception of different trust dimensions and the importance given to each of these dimensions (Schoorman, Mayer, & Davis, 2007). In any case, we conclude in line with several other researchers that the relationship between (online) trust and culture needs to be further investigated (Gefen, 2000; Lee & Turban, 2001; Schoorman, et al., 2007; Shankar, et al., 2002; Teo & Liu, 2007).

CONCLUSION

As yet, most studies on consumer online trust have focused on trust-related characteristics of the Internet firm or the website interface. In order to derive effective implications for enhancing consumer trust in e-commerce a number of empirical studies have attempted to identify the elements that are pertinent to the formation of online trust. Because the willingness to buy online or adopt Internet banking depend both on the consumer's trust in a specific party (website or online merchant) and in the Internet as underlying transaction medium, not only characteristics of the merchant but also characteristics of the website and the underlying technology infrastructure are factors that affect online trust. We conceptualized Internet trust as trusting beliefs in the reliability and predictability of the Internet and the willingness of the consumer to depend on the Internet with regard to economic transactions and thus we did not include any characteristics of the bank or the bank's website in our definition. The results of this study confirm the expected influence of Internet trust on risk perception (strongly negative) and on consumer attitudes toward Internet banking (strongly positive).

Researchers propose a number of different instruments and measures Internet retailers can use to influence the trusting beliefs, intentions and behaviors of online consumers (see the overview in Grabner-Kräuter & Kaluscha (2003)). Basically, these instruments and measures can be seen as potential signals of trustworthiness as they aim at increasing the perceived trustworthiness of the website and the online vendor (Bart, Shankar, Sultan, & Urban, 2005). Implications for the design of trust-inducing websites are mainly presented in the growing body of literature in the field of human computer interaction that focuses on how to implement graphical e-commerce interfaces that are perceived as trustworthy by online consumers (Wang & Emurian, 2005). However, these recommendations might not be sufficient to overcome consumers' reluctance to conduct their financial and other economic transactions on the Internet, as consumers might refrain from visiting websites designed for e-commerce or Internet banking because they do not consider the Internet infrastructure to be reliable and secure. Fuelled by media reports, there is a growing perception that the Internet is insecure and unsafe (Gorman, 2007). To attract more Internet banking customers and increase the acceptance of online banking services in Austria, it is definitely not enough to make the Internet banking system convenient and easy to interact with. Rather it is of paramount importance, to address the issue of security in order to improve the rate of Internet banking adoption [see also Laforet & Li, 2005; Mukherjee & Nath, 2003]. To ensure the security of their online banking systems banks use security features such as firewalls, filtering routers, callback modems, encryption biometrics, smart cards, and digital certification and authentication (Mukherjee & Nath, 2003). However, for the majority of consumers it is beyond the scope of their technological understanding to fully comprehend the meaning and functionality of these security features. Therefore the attention of bank managers might be fruitfully focused on training and promotion approaches with the aim to influence their customers' perception of online security and

to improve their customers' knowledge about privacy and security mechanisms and concepts such as encryption methods.

REFERENCES

Ajzen, I. (1991). The theory of planned behavior. *Organizational Behavior and Human Decision Processes*, *50*(2), 179–211. doi:10.1016/0749-5978(91)90020-T

Ajzen, I., & Fishbein, M. (1980). *Understanding attitudes and predicting social behavior*. Englewood Cliffs, NJ: Prentice-Hall.

Akinci, S., Aksoy, S., & Atilgan, E. (2004). Adoption of Internet banking among sophisticated consumer segments in an advanced developing country. *International Journal of Bank Marketing*, *22*(3), 212–232. doi:10.1108/02652320410530322

Awamleh, R., & Fernandes, C. (2006). Diffusion of Internet Banking amongst educated consumers in a high income non-OECD country. *Journal of Internet Banking and Commerce*, *11*(3).

Bart, I. Y., Shankar, V., Sultan, F., & Urban, G. L. (2005). Are the Drivers and Role of Online Trust the Same for all Web Sites and Consumers? A Large Scale Exploratory Empirical Study. *Journal of Marketing*, *69*, 133–152. doi:10.1509/jmkg.2005.69.4.133

Chang, M. K., Cheung, W., & Lai, V. S. (2005). Literature derived reference models for the adoption of online shopping. *Information & Management*, *42*, 543–559. doi:10.1016/S0378-7206(04)00051-5

Chau, P. Y. K., & Lai, V. S. K. (2003). An Empirical Investigation of the Determinants of User Acceptance of Internet Banking. *Journal of Organizational Computing and Electronic Commerce*, *13*(2), 123–145. doi:10.1207/S15327744JOCE1302_3

Chaudhuri, A., & Holbrook, M. B. (2001). The chain of effects from brand trust and brand affect to brand performance: The role of brand loyalty. *Journal of Marketing, 65*, 81–93. doi:10.1509/jmkg.65.2.81.18255

Cheung, C. M. K., & Lee, M. K. O. (2006). Understanding consumer trust in internet-shopping: a multidisciplinary approach. *Journal of the American Society for Information Science and Technology, 57*(4), 479–492. doi:10.1002/asi.20312

Corritore, C. L., Kracher, B., & Wiedenbeck, S. (2003). On-line trust: concepts, evolving themes, a model. *International Journal of Human-Computer Studies, 58*, 737–758. doi:10.1016/S1071-5819(03)00041-7

Cunningham, L. F., Gerlach, J., & Harper, M. D. (2005). Perceived risk and e-banking services: An analysis from the perspective of the consumer. *Journal of Financial Services Marketing, 10*(2), 165–178. doi:10.1057/palgrave.fsm.4770183

Dabholkar, P. A., & Bagozzi, R. (2002). An attitudinal model of technology-based-self-service: Moderating effects of consumer traits and situational factors. *Journal of the Academy of Marketing Science, 30*(3), 184–201.

Davis, F. D. (1989). Perceived usefulness, perceived ease of use, and user acceptance of information technology. *Management Information Systems Quarterly, 13*(3), 318–340. doi:10.2307/249008

Einwiller, S., & Will, M. (2001). *The Role of Reputation to Engender Trust in Electronic Markets.* Paper presented at the Proceedings of the 5th International Conference on Corporate Reputation, Identity, and Competitiveness, Paris.

Eriksson, K., Kerem, K., & Nilsson, D. (2008). The adoption of commercial innovations in the former Central and Eastern European markets. The case of internet banking in Estonia. *International Journal of Bank Marketing, 26*(3), 154–169. doi:10.1108/02652320810864634

Flavian, C., Guinalıu, M., & Torres, E. (2006). How bricks-and-mortar attributes affect online banking adoption. *International Journal of Bank Marketing, 24*(6), 406–423. doi:10.1108/02652320610701735

Fornell, C., & Larcker, D. F. (1981). Evaluating structural equation models with unobservable variables and measurement error. *JMR, Journal of Marketing Research, 18*, 39–50. doi:10.2307/3151312

Gan, C., Clemes, M., Limsombunchai, V., & Weng, A. (2006). A logit analysis of electronic banking in New Zealand. *International Journal of Bank Marketing, 24*(6), 360–383. doi:10.1108/02652320610701717

Gefen, D. (2000). E-commerce: the role of familiarity and trust. *Omega-The International Journal of Management Science, 28*, 725–737. doi:10.1016/S0305-0483(00)00021-9

Gefen, D., Karahanna, E., & Straub, D. W. (2003). Trust and Tam in Online Shopping: an integrated model. *Management Information Systems Quarterly, 27*(1), 51–90.

Gefen, D., & Straub, D. W. (2004). Consumer trust in B2C e-commerce and the importance of social presence: experiments in e-products and e-services. *Omega-The International Journal of Management Science, 32*, 407–424. doi:10.1016/j.omega.2004.01.006

Gemünden, H. G. (1985). Perceived risk and information search. A systematic meta-analysis of the empirical evidence. *International Journal of Research in Marketing, 2*, 79–100. doi:10.1016/0167-8116(85)90026-6

Gerrard, P., & Cunningham, B. J. (2003). The diffusion of Internet banking among Singapore consumers. *International Journal of Bank Marketing, 21*(1), 16–28. doi:10.1108/02652320310457776

Gorman, G. E. (2007). Who am I, and where's my money? Issues in online security. *Online Information Review, 31*(5), 561–565. doi:10.1108/14684520710832298

Gounaris, S., & Koritos, C. (2008). Investigating the Drivers of Internet Banking Adoption Decision: A Comparison of Three Alternative Frameworks. *International Journal of Bank Marketing, 26*(5), 282–304. doi:10.1108/02652320810894370

Grabner-Kräuter, S. (2002). The Role of Consumers Trust in Online Shopping. *Journal of Business Ethics, 39*, 43–50. doi:10.1023/A:1016323815802

Grabner-Kräuter, S., & Faullant, R. (2008). Consumer Acceptance of Internet Banking: the Influence of Internet Trust. *International Journal of Bank Marketing, 26*(7), 483–504. doi:10.1108/02652320810913855

Grabner-Kräuter, S., & Kaluscha, E. A. (2003). Empirical research in on-line trust: a review and critical assessment. *International Journal of Human-Computer Studies, 58*, 783–812. doi:10.1016/S1071-5819(03)00043-0

Gulati, R., & Sytch, M. (2008). The dynamics of trust. [Book review]. *Academy of Management Review, 33*(1), 276–278.

Hernandez, J. M. C., & Mazzon, J. A. (2007). Adoption of internet banking: proposition and implementation of an integrated methodology approach. *International Journal of Bank Marketing, 25*(2), 72–88. doi:10.1108/02652320710728410

Igbaria, M., & Iivari, J. (1995). The effects of self-efficacy on computer usage. *Omega, 23*(6), 587–605. doi:10.1016/0305-0483(95)00035-6

Jarvenpaa, S. L., Shaw, T. R., & Staples, S. (2004). Toward Contextualized Theories of Trust: The Role of Trust in Global Virtual Teams. *Information Systems Research, 15*(3), 250–267. doi:10.1287/isre.1040.0028

Jarvenpaa, S. L., Tractinsky, N., & Vitale, M. (2000). Consumer trust in an Internet store. *Information Technology and Management, 1*, 45–71. doi:10.1023/A:1019104520776

Kaluscha, E. A. (2004). *The importance of Initial Consumer Trust in B2C Electronic Commerce*. University of Klagenfurt, Klagenfurt.

Karjaluoto, H., Mattila, M., & Pento, T. (2002). Factors underlying attitude formation towards online banking in Finland. *International Journal of Bank Marketing, 20*(6). doi:10.1108/02652320210446724

Kim, K., & Prabhakar, B. (2000). *Initial trust, perceived risk and the adoption of internet banking*.

Koufaris, M., & Hampton-Sosa, W. (2004). The development of initial trust in an online company by new customers. *Information & Management, 41*, 377–397. doi:10.1016/j.im.2003.08.004

Kuhlmeier, D., & Gary, K. (2005). Antecedents to internet-based purchasing: a multinational study. *International Marketing Review, 22*(4), 460–473. doi:10.1108/02651330510608460

Kuisma, T., Laukkanen, T., & Hiltunen, M. (2007). Mapping the reasons for resistance to Internet banking: A means-end approach. *International Journal of Information Management, 27*, 75–85. doi:10.1016/j.ijinfomgt.2006.08.006

Laforet, S., & Li, X. (2005). Consumers' attitudes towards online and mobile banking in China. *International Journal of Bank Marketing, 23*(5), 362–380. doi:10.1108/02652320510629250

Lai, V. S., & Li, H. (2005). Technology acceptance model for Internet banking: an invariance analysis. *Information & Management, 42*, 373–386. doi:10.1016/j.im.2004.01.007

Lassar, W. M., Manolis, C., & Lassar, S. S. (2005). The relationship between consumer innovativeness, personal characteristics, and online banking adoption. *International Journal of Bank Marketing, 23*(2), 176–199. doi:10.1108/02652320510584403

Lee, M. K. O., & Turban, E. (2001). A Trust Model for Consumer Internet Shopping. *International Journal of Electronic Commerce, 6*(1), 75–91.

Littler, D., & Melanthiou, D. (2006). Consumer perceptions of risk and uncertainty and the implications for behaviour towards innovative retail services: The case of Internet Banking. *Journal of Retailing and Consumer Services, 13*, 431–443. doi:10.1016/j.jretconser.2006.02.006

Luarn, P., & Lin, H.-H. (2005). Toward an understanding of the behavioral intention to use mobile banking. *Computers in Human Behavior, 21*, 873–891. doi:10.1016/j.chb.2004.03.003

Luhmann, N. (1989). Vertrauen. Ein Mechanismus der Reduktion sozialer Komplexität (3rd ed.). Stuttgart.

Mandrik, C. A., & Bao, Y. (2005). Exploring the Concept and Measurement of General Risk Aversion. *Advances in Consumer Research. Association for Consumer Research (U. S.), 32*, 531–539.

Mayer, R. C., Davis, J. H., & Schoorman, D. F. (1995). An integrative Model of organizational trust. *Academy of Management Review, 20*(3), 709–734. doi:10.2307/258792

McCrae, R. R., & Costa, P. T. (1992). Discriminant validity of NEO-PIR facet scales. *Educational and Psychological Measurement, 52*, 229–237. doi:10.1177/001316449205200128

McElroy, J. C., Hendrickson, A. R., Townsend, A. M., & DeMarie, S. M. (2007). Dispositional Factors in internet use: Personality versus cognitive style. *Management Information Systems Quarterly, 31*(4), 809–820.

McKnight, D. H., & Chervany, N. L. (1996). The Meanings of trust. *MISRC Working Paper.* Retrieved October 2002, from http://www.misrc.umc.edu/wpaper/WorkingPapers/9604.pdf

McKnight, D. H., Choudhury, V., & Kacmar, C. (2002). Developing and Validating Trust Measures for e-Commerce: An Integrative Typology. *Information Systems Research, 13*(3), 334–359. doi:10.1287/isre.13.3.334.81

McKnight, H. D., & Chervany, N. L. (2002). What trust means in e-commerce customer relationships: An interdisciplinary conceptual typology. *International Journal of Electronic Commerce, 6*(2), 35–59.

Meuter, M. L., Bitner, M. J., Ostrom, A. L., & Brown, S. W. (2005). Choosing Among Alternative Service Delivery Modes: An Investigation of Customer Trial of Self-Service Technologies. *Journal of Marketing, 69*, 61–83. doi:10.1509/jmkg.69.2.61.60759

Meyer, T. (2006). *Online banking. What we learn from differences in Europe.* Frankfurt am Main: Deutsche Bank Research.

Mitchell, V.-W. (1998). Consumer perceived risk: conceptualisations and models. *European Journal of Marketing, 33*(1/2), 163–195. doi:10.1108/03090569910249229

Mooradian, T., Renzl, B., & Matzler, K. (2006). Who Trusts? Personality, Trust and Knowledge Sharing. *Management Learning, 37*(4), 523–540. doi:10.1177/1350507606073424

Mukherjee, A., & Nath, P. (2003). A model of trust in online relationship banking. *International Journal of Bank Marketing, 21*(1), 5–15. doi:10.1108/02652320310457767

Ndubisi, N. O., & Sinti, Q. (2006). Consumer attitudes, system's characteristics and internet banking adoption in Malaysia. *Management Research News, 29*(1/2), 16–27. doi:10.1108/01409170610645411

Palmer, A., & Bejou, D. (1994). Buyer-Seller Relationships: A Conceptual Model and Empirical Investigation. *Journal of Markeliiig Management, 10*, 495–512.

Paunonen, S., Haddock, G., Forsterling, F., & Keinonen, M. (2003). Broad versus Narrow Personality Measures and the Prediction of Behaviour Across Cultures. *European Journal of Personality, 17*, 413–433. doi:10.1002/per.496

Pavlou, P. A. (2002). *What drives electronic commerce? A theory of planned behavior perspective.* Academy of Management Proceedings.

Pavlou, P. A. (2003). Consumer Acceptance of Electronic Commerce: Integrating Trust and Risk with the Technology Acceptance Model. *International Journal of Electronic Commerce, 7*(3), 101–134.

Pavlou, P. A., & Fygenson, M. (2006). Understanding and predicting electronic commerce adoption: an extension of the theory pf planned behavior. *Management Information Systems Quarterly, 30*(1), 115–143.

Pennington, R., Wilcox, D. H., & Grover, V. (2003/2004). The Role of System Trust in Business-to-Consumer Transactions. *Journal of Management Information Systems, 20*(3), 197–226.

Pikkarainen, T., Pikkarainen, K., Karjaluoto, H., & Pahnila, S. (2004). Consumer acceptance of online banking: an extension of the technology acceptance model. *Internet Research, 14*(3), 224–235. doi:10.1108/10662240410542652

Polatoglu, V. N., & Ekin, S. (2001). An empirical investigation of the Turkish consumers' acceptance of Internet banking services. *International Journal of Bank Marketing, 19*(4), 156–165. doi:10.1108/02652320110392527

Ratnasingam, P. (2005). E-Commerce relationships: The impact of trust on relationship continuity. *International Journal of Commerce & Management, 15*(1), 1–16.

Ratnasingham, P. (1999). Risks in low trust among trading partners in eletronic commerce. *Computers & Security, 18*, 587–592. doi:10.1016/S0167-4048(99)82005-7

Ravi, V., Carr, M., & Sagar, N. V. (2006). Profiling Of Internet Banking Users In India Using Intelligent Tequniques. *Journal of Service Research, 6*(2), 61–73.

Riegelsberger, J., Sasse, A. M., & McCarthy, J. D. (2005). The mechanics of trust: a framework for research and design. *International Journal of Human-Computer Studies, 62*, 381–422. doi:10.1016/j.ijhcs.2005.01.001

Rogers, E. (1995). *Diffusion of Innovations.* New York: Free Press.

Rotchanakitumnuai, S., & Speece, M. (2003). Barriers To Internet Banking Adoption: a qualitative study among corporate customers in Thailand. *International Journal of Bank Marketing, 21*(6), 312–323. doi:10.1108/02652320310498465

Rotter, J. B. (1967). A new scale for the measurement of interpersonal trust. *Journal of Personality, 35*, 651–665. doi:10.1111/j.1467-6494.1967.tb01454.x

Rousseau, D. M., Sitkin, S. B., Butt, R. S., & Camerer, C. (1998). Not so different after all: A cross-discipline view of trust. *Academy of Management Review, 23*(3), 393–404.

Sarel, D., & Marmorstein, H. (2003). Marketing online banking services: The voice of the customer. *Journal of Financial Services Marketing, 8*(2), 106–118. doi:10.1057/palgrave.fsm.4770111

Sayar, C., & Wolfe, S. (2007). Internet banking market performance: Turkey versus the UK. *International Journal of Bank Marketing, 25*(3), 122–141. doi:10.1108/02652320710739841

Schoorman, F. D., Mayer, R. C., & Davis, J. H. (2007). Editor's Forum: An Integrative model of organizational trust: Past, Present, and Future. *Academy of Management Review, 32*(2), 344–354.

Selnes, F. (1998). Antecedents and consequences of trust and satisfaction in buyer-seller relationships. *European Journal of Marketing, 32*(3), 305–322. doi:10.1108/03090569810204580

Shankar, V., Urban, G. L., & Sultan, F. (2002). Online trust: a stakeholder perspective, concepts, implications, and future directions. *The Journal of Strategic Information Systems, 11*, 325–344. doi:10.1016/S0963-8687(02)00022-7

Siegrist, M., Gutscher, H., & Earle, T. C. (2005). Perception of risk: the influence of general trust, and general confidence. *Journal of Risk Research, 8*(2), 145–156. doi:10.1080/1366987032000105315

Suh, B., & Han, I. (2003). The Impact of Customer Trust and Perception of Security Control on the Acceptance of Electronic Commerce. *International Journal of Electronic Commerce, 7*(3), 135–161.

Sukkar, A. A., & Hasan, H. (2005). Toward a Model for the Acceptance of Internet Banking in Developing Countries. *Information Technology for Development, 11*(4), 381–398. doi:10.1002/itdj.20026

Teo, T. S. H., & Liu, J. (2007). Consumer trust in e-commerce in the United States, Singapore and China. *Omega-The International Journal of Management Science, 35*, 22–38. doi:10.1016/j.omega.2005.02.001

Thatcher, J. B., Loughry, M. L., Lim, J., & McKnight, D. H. (2007). Internet anxiety: An empirical study of the effects of personality, beliefs, and social support. *Information & Management, 44*, 353–363. doi:10.1016/j.im.2006.11.007

Torkzadeh, G., Chang, J. C.-J., & Demirhan, D. (2006). A contingency model of computer and Internet self-efficacy. *Information & Management, 43*, 541–550. doi:10.1016/j.im.2006.02.001

Venkatesh, V., Morris, M. G., Davis, G. B., & Davis, F. D. (2003). User Acceptance of Information Technology: Toward a Unified View. *Management Information Systems Quarterly, 27*(3), 425–478.

Walczuch, R., & Lundgren, H. (2004). Psychological antecedents of institution-based consumer trust in e-retailing. *Information & Management, 42*, 159–177.

Wan, W. W. N., Luk, C.-L., & Chow, C. W. C. (2005). Customers' adoption of banking channels in Hong Kong. *International Journal of Bank Marketing, 23*(3), 255–272. doi:10.1108/02652320510591711

Wang, Y. D., & Emurian, H. H. (2005). An overview of online trust: concepts, elements, and implications. *Computers in Human Behavior, 21*, 105–125. doi:10.1016/j.chb.2003.11.008

Wang, Y.-S., Wang, Y.-M., Lin, H.-H., & Tang, T.-I. (2003). Determinants of user acceptance of Internet banking: an empirical study. *International Journal of Service Industry Management, 14*(5), 501–519. doi:10.1108/09564230310500192

Wu, I.-L., & Chen, J.-L. (2005). An extension of trust and TAM model with TPB in the initial adoption of on-line tax: an empirical study. *International Journal of Human-Computer Studies, 62*, 784–808. doi:10.1016/j.ijhcs.2005.03.003

Yousafzai, S. Y., Pallister, J. G., & Foxall, G. R. (2003). A proposed model of e-trust for electronic banking. *Technovation, 23*, 847–860. doi:10.1016/S0166-4972(03)00130-5

APPENDIX

Items Questionnaire

Internet Trust (adapted from Chaudhuri and Holbrook, 2001; McKnight et al., 2002; McKnight and Chervany, 2002)

1. With adequate safety measures on a website I don't hesitate to enter my credit card information. (willingness to depend on the Internet)
2. I trust the Internet. (willingness to depend on the Internet)
3. When performing a transaction on the Internet I know exactly what will happen. (trusting beliefs - predictability)
4. Internet transactions (e.g. online shopping or online hotel reservations) always function as expected. (trusting beliefs - reliability)

Perceived Risk of Internet Banking (adapted from Awamleh and Fernandes, 2006 and Meuter et al., 2005)

5. I am afraid that other people might get access to information about my Internet banking transactions.
6. I believe it can rather easily happen that money is stolen if using Internet banking.
7. I am afraid that the confidentiality of my financial transactions might get lost when using Internet banking.
8. I think that privacy is not guaranteed when using Internet banking.

Attitude Toward Internet Banking (adapted from Lai & Li, 2005; Wu & Chen, 2005; Chau & Lai, 2003)

9. In my opinion it is desirable to use Internet banking.
10. I think it is good for me to use Internet banking.
11. Overall, my attitude toward Internet banking is favourable.

Self-Efficacy (adapted from Lassar et al., 2005)

12. How comfortable do you feel using the Computer?
13. How comfortable do you feel using the Internet?

(Propensity to) Trust (Costa & McCrae, 1992)

14. My first reaction is to trust people.
15. I tend to assume the best about people.
16. I have a good deal of faith in human nature.

Adoption Internet Banking

17. How frequently do you use Internet banking for private reasons?

Chapter 12
Social Trust as Seed:
Cases of Early Mobile Phone Domestication Among Poor Urban Youth in Bangladesh

Andrew Wong
Telenor Group Business Development and Research, Malaysia

ABSTRACT

This chapter examines the role the mobile phone plays in the poor urban youth's social life. This chapter argues that one can better grasp their social life by looking through the new technology lens. It seeks to examine the collective-mediated learning, sharing, and experimenting with the emergent patterns of trust in the social context. The emergence of three types of social trust genres that correspond respectively to the stage of domestication by the poor urban youth are described: social trust as a seed for peer-to-peer learning, social trust as a seed for group underground sharing, and social trust as a seed for fueling the experimental spirit. It concludes that social trust functions as a seed for increasing positive interdependent towards others play an important role in nurturing trust among the poor urban youth as they domesticate new media technology, such as the mobile phone, into their everyday lives.

INTRODUCTION

A group of youth forms a circle, focusing intently on a small device that excites them. It acts as a small radio station, blaring out catchy tunes. A gang of three youths keeps snapping pictures from a portable device as they take turns posing with different backgrounds and animated faces. What kind of object are they all examining? That central object is the omnipresent mobile phone. What the youth are doing have almost identical patterns in other parts of Bangladesh; they form a group and then use the mobile phone as one of their everyday central life focus points. The mobile phone is quickly becoming a fixture in everyday life in Bangladesh, and there is a growing sense of it as a familiar presence.

For the past two years, reflecting on several trips for fieldwork taken to Bangladesh, this author's questions about the mobile phone simply as a communication and coordination tool had changed to: How is mobile communication integrated into youth life as part of their emancipation towards adult-

DOI: 10.4018/978-1-61520-901-9.ch012

hood? Can society learn something about why the youth are more willing to share a mobile phone collectively, and how this collective behavior influences the group dynamics and trust among them? For the past two years, while studying the poor urban youth and mobile communication, this author has learned to direct attention at such moments. The stories told usually revolved around the mobile phone and its influences on their collective-mediated learning, sharing, and experimenting.

"When we group together, we are like a family, although we are not. That I think is something special about us" Dhaka Youth, Female, around 18 years old.

"We learn together and sometimes fall out together. Never mind the fall out between us. That's ok. It is part of the learning." Chittagong Youth, Male, 21 years old.

"We learn, share and learn, and grow together by using different ways to learn." Sylhet Youth, Male, 25 years old.

These three voices, all from the fieldwork, have much in common. They refer to the process of exploring the use and the domestication of mobile phones into everyday life. The process that braids all these together is a path of collective-mediated learning, then the sharing of collective practices, and finally, having the courage to experiment imaginatively. As a consequence, this path sparks a new way of domesticating the mobile phone. To further explore these ideas, these chapters seek to answer several key questions: How and what are the mobile use particularities of the poor urban youth? How does social trust play a role in mobile use and domestication? What are the different genres of social trust that emerge from their interaction with the mobile phone?

This chapter starts with a literature review about the domestication of new media, and describes the constructionism perspective in a domestication context. It also connects the characterization of social trust in the new media context. Then, a general logic of social trust based on the economic and sociology perspective is outlined. Next, this chapter describes the ethnography work of the mobile phone domestication, and its related subjects. In the findings and discussion section, this chapter discusses collective-mediated learning, sharing, and experimenting through the social trust lens. Then this chapter focuses on three case studies of social trust as the most promising – social trust as seed – explanations relevant to collective-mediated learning, sharing, and experimenting: peer-to-peer learning, underground sharing practices, and experimenting to connect. Finally, it concludes by showing that the existing evidence points toward the fact that groups who succeed in cultivating social trust are most likely to domesticate new media technology with sustained confidence.

BACKGROUND: CHARACTERIZATION OF SOCIAL TRUST IN THE NEW MEDIA DOMESTICATION AND EMERGING COUNTRY CONTEXT

In order to grasp the mobile use domestication, a theoretical framework is needed to capture the complexity of the matter at hand. The first two subsections postulate that new media domestication, such as the mobile phone, can be studied based on consumption-, sociology- and anthropology-wide perspectives. By delving deeper to examine the inner workings of mobile use and domestication, it is important to understand not only the system (way of workings), but also the structure (the frame that a process follows). This will allow a grasp of the phenomenon in an orderly manner. Based on the empirical findings from different cases, the mobile use and domestication falls distinctively under a developmental framework; there is a process a person will go through, and this process runs from knowing the basic steps to advancing towards greater complexity of use. Henceforth, a constructionist perspective of the domestication context allows progress in thinking about a person's mobile use, which follows certain patterns. Linking closely with domestication is the notion of trust, which is an important element that amplifies the domestication process. The last subsection studies the collective manner in which trust is formed; therefore, the term social trust is adopted in this chapter to exemplify the importance of how social trust is important in a collective society like Bangladesh.

New Media Domestication

Domestication as a concept comes to mind in large part from consumption of sociology and anthropology studies. Recently, it has moved towards studies of new media, such as the mobile phone and Internet, as part of the information and communication technologies (ICTs) tools (Pantzar, 1996; Haddon, 2006). The domestication framework looks beyond the use and adoption of technology; it also covers behavioral sequences, such as gratification, benefits, and expectations (Silverstone & Haddon, 1996). In the new media context, several studies have been conducted on the personal computer (Lally, 2002), the Internet (Haddon, 1999; Ward, 2005), and the mobile phone (Haddon, 2003). Domestication of new media takes time. This is especially true for the poor youth who have little prior knowledge about new technology. According to Silverstone (1995), and Lie and Sørensen (1996), domestication is evolutionary, rather than revolutionary, because experience needs to commingled over a long period of time. Thus, in the context of this chapter, domestication is defined beyond usage, as it also involves the cultural and socio-techno influence that creates a unique way in which technology or

new media are introduced and embedded as part of everyday life.

A special interest of this chapter is the role that communication tools play in the lives of the poor urban youth, especially in Bangladesh, which ranks among the least-developed countries. Relative to other ICT tools, the mobile phone holds the edge in both the volume of ownership and degree of closeness to the owner's everyday lives. In the International Telecom Union (ITU, 2008) publication of the Global Information Society, the mobile phone subscribers' statistics show its significance: 92 per 100 habitants (developed countries), 33 per 100 habitants (developing countries), and 10 per 100 habitants (least-developed countries). As compared with Internet subscribers' statistics, the mobile phone differentiates itself as the leading ICT tool for communication and interaction purposes: 24 per 100 habitants (developed countries), 4 per 100 habitants (developing countries), and 0.2 per 100 habitants (least-developed countries). There is growing evidence that new media technology, more commonly known as ICT, plays a role in poverty relief and as an asset for better livelihood (Narayan et al, 2000; Marker et al., 2002; Slater & Kwami, 2005; Souter et al., 2005; CIDA, 2002). There are already plenty of anecdotes and real data indicating that the impact of mobile use in developing countries is wide and reaches even the poorest population, and is deep enough to touch people's lives in every imaginable way from poverty alleviation to entertainment during social hours (Kenny, 2002; Bell, 2005; Kamssu, 2005; Rao & Mendoza, 2005; Anderson, 2006; Hudson, 2006; Castells, Qiu, Fernandez-Ardevol & Sey, 2007; Garbacz & Thompson, 2007). Abraham (2006) details economic gain through mobile use for the fishing industry in India, and Aminuzzaman (2002) studies the village pay phone impact on society, and its consequences on rural and urban communication in Bangladesh.

Hynes and Rommes (2005) rightly argue that the importance of experience or a matter of good experience will have an influence on whether people find a place for technology in their lives or reject it. Aside from the experience standpoint, there are other factors in non-adoption, and poverty is one of the main reasons (Silverstone & Haddon, 1996). Evidence from the ITU report (ITU, 2008) shows new media technology, such as the mobile phone, is influential as it permeates everyday lives, especially in the poorer countries such as Bangladesh. However, there is little research to understand the domestication process, or how the poor find alternative ways to domesticate new media technology as a result of their social and economic constraints.

Constructionism Perspective in the Domestication Context

Constructionism theories suggest that learning is an active process, whereby learners actively construct and discover mental models and ideas of the world around them. Constructionism stresses the importance of learning by actively making meaning in the real world. In the early 1980s, Seymour Papert, a mathematician and computer scientist, wrote about how a childhood toy car had brought him into science through his experience toying around with the wheels and its parts. In the view of Papert (1980), voicing our inner feelings and ideas is the key to learning. In other words, expressing ideas make them real and shareable, which in turn shapes and sharpens these ideas and enables us to communicate better. Like learning to use a mobile phone, it is a cycle of self-directed learning, as well as an iterative process by which learners invent for themselves different ways of communicating through the device that will give them meaningful communication. Papert further argues that learning is grounded in contexts and shaped by constant uses, and use of external mediation is essential to create a good learning environment. Vygotsky (1978) expands the effective learning boundary by arguing that social facilitation is an important element in the learning process, in addition to individual learning.

Constructionists see themselves as constructivists, as they view children as builders of their own cognitive tools and real world realities, as well as having a view themselves of being developmentalists, where knowledge and skill are formed incrementally. In Papert's words, becoming one with the phenomenon under study is a key to learning. In addition, "diving" into unknown situations is also an important part of learning (Papert, 1980). In many ways, the domestication process holds the developmentalist stand. Silverstone, Hirsch, and Morley (1992) hold almost similar viewpoints that human-machine encounters are a dialectic process. They further distinguish four phases of domestication: appropriation, which relates to practices of ownership and possession; objectification, which focuses on the object and its display in a geography context; incorporation, which details uses and functions of an object in and over time; and lastly, conversion, which refers to the ways in which the object is employed as a currency for indicating membership in relations with the outside. The research perspective of this chapter marks two departures from the four domestication phases as suggested by Silverstone et al. First, the ownership of an object is rare for poor youth; rather, the shared object is more prevalent. Therefore, a different mindset is needed to examine the domestication process. Second, Silverstone et al. focus on human-machine encounters, mainly from the individual ownership perspective. The poor youth in the developing countries are more collective in nature, because of their need to share resources out of social and economic necessity. Therefore, this study will characterize domestication of new media technology from a collective domestication perspective.

Sociological and Economic Perspectives of Social Trust

Much of the public debate and research on new media have focused on how they go beyond the limit of space and time, thereby opening up multifariousness of communication and engagement possibilities. An example of this is the debate on social trust. Boslego (2005) argues that a precise definition of social trust is difficult to pin down. An often-cited definition of trust is one by Gambetta (1998), "Trust (or, symmetrically, distrust) is a particular level of the subjective probability with which an agent will perform a particular action, both before [we] can monitor each action (or independently of his capacity of ever being able to monitor it) and in a context in which it affects [our] own action." According to Boslego (2005), social trust is the motivation or impetus for social relations that form a basis for interaction and foster relationships. Trust or social trust is often considered as a valuable commodity, and is therefore a creator of wealth and prosperity (Dasgupta, 1998; Fukuyama, 1995). In a broader perspective, social trust is part of social capital created by strong ties within a social network of a group or in a society (Fukuyama, 1995; Hearn, 1997). According to Field (2003), the central thesis of social capital theory is that relationships matter and those social networks are a valuable asset. Putnam (1995 & 2000) regards social capital as social networks, and their associated reciprocity as the byproducts of the network. One of the byproducts is social trust.

Trust between individuals thus becomes trust between strangers and trust of a broad fabric of social institutions; ultimately, it becomes a shared set of values, virtues, and expectations within society as a whole. Without this interaction, on the other hand, trust decays; at a certain point, this decay begins to manifest itself in serious social problems... The concept of social capital contends that building or rebuilding community and trust requires face-to-face encounters. (Beem 1999, p. 20)

Whether it is viewed from the economic or the sociological perspective, social trust constitutes the core of social life. The sociological perspective of trust focuses on developing and maintaining those social ties. According to Misztal (1996), the definition of trust states that trust is believing from our own standpoint that the consequences of someone's intended action will be appropriate. Hearn writes an elaborate explanation of trust and its elements:

Trust and trustworthiness, and the moral individuals, who embody them, arise in communitarian interdependencies and social institutions that instill in people the habits of reciprocity and responsibility and the sense of moral obligation whose presence affords the strongest grounds people have for trusting one another. (Hearn, 1997, p. 97)

There are a few reasons for how trust is developed and cultivated that are relevant to the study of the domestication of new media technology, especially within the group level. Brickham, Becker, and Castle (1979) argue that a collective knowledge of motivation within a group will develop and enhance trust in each member. Sorrentino, Hanna, Holmes, and Sharp (1995) examine the process of doing things in a repetitive mode, which in turn increases the chances of interaction within a group. In the case of the mobile phone, as a group interacts more, they are likely to form greater bonds with each other. Time embeds trust deeper within a group.

Similarly, Macy and Skvoretz (1998) elaborate that as time passes, individuals in a group grow to learn with each other, and are therefore familiar and comfortable with each other. The familiarity with each other is usually not one dimensional. It involves the characteristics of the individuals, and their values, interests, and motivation, among others. Nee and Sanders (2001) find that a similarity of attributes, such as interests and values will enhance the trust with each other. Molm, Takahashi, and Peterson (2000) found an interesting phenomenon, in that if individuals believe that they benefit equally from a group through the exchange of information and knowledge, then the trust in each member becomes stronger.

The economic perspective of social trust is considers as part of a valuable resource. In an economic sense, it is a way to balance information asymmetry between buyers and sellers involved in an economic transaction (Akerlof, 1970; Resnick et al, 2000). It is a valuable resource in itself, as it decreases the transaction costs associated with doing business with an unknown person (Wolfe, 1989; Fukuyama, 1995). Arrow (2000) furthers the argument for the importance of social trust as a promoter of economic progress by leveraging the collective cooperation that in turn fosters trust. Trust enhances economic exchange, as over time people tend to become familiar with each other through interaction, thereby enhancing the level of cooperation (Krishna, 2000).

In conclusion, the differences between the social and economic perspectives of social trust are between treating social trust as a resource to enhance social interaction and exchange, and treating social trust as an interaction process to build up cooperation and reciprocity in the social relation context.

BACKGROUND ON BANGLADESH AND THE ETHNOGRAPHY ON THE POOR YOUTH

As a country, Bangladesh can be seen as a collective effort of people living in a small country with high population density. The collective sentiment of having their language – the Bengali – triggered the cry for independence from Pakistan, and to date this sentiment is still very much alive. It is both social and economic. For example, take the case of groups sharing and pooling their money to share Internet surfing time. Financial constraint is not the only reason, as this is also done to share the experience of chatting and discussing what they discover on the Internet. Traditions in Bangladeshi families run deep. Attitudes and mindsets of parental authority on restricting or allowing Internet and mobile phone use among family members affect the extent of ICT access, use, and adoption among family members. There is a strong need for families to connect with other members, even with distant relatives with extended ties in Bangladesh. This suits their practical as well as emotional needs. In a practical sense, communicating to coordinate daily activities and ensuring the safety of family members is essential. In an emotional sense, communicating to bond and nurture relationships through social activities is considered important.

The study reported here is a synthesis of several ethnographic studies on the poor households and individuals. Fetterman (1998) defines "…ethnography is the art and science of describing a group or culture" (p. 1). This ethnography research is to document and describe the lives of the young urban poor, and their use of the mobile phone in different contexts. In the context of this work, the young urban poor are defined with several characteristics: A dependent, typically living in an urban household with less than 7000 Takas per month, aged between 12 and 25 years, and mostly still in school and college or working at odd jobs. The research design, according to Pelto (1970), "…involves combining the essential elements of investigation into an effective problem-solving sequence" (p. 331). In drawing up a robust research design, this article relied on interviews with individuals, family interviews, observations, and interpretative analysis, in an effort to synthesize and appreciate the idea that the socio-cultural and economic situation of the poor youth can be understood better from the point of view of the youth themselves, rather than our own hypotheses. This is in line with Geertz's argument for writing in depth through "thick description" (Geertz, 1976 and 20002000). The analysis of this research draws upon work across mobile information and communication that were framed by three key genres of using the mobile phone: solely for entertainment purposes, as a means to create a greater network, and being creative to maximize per minute airtime usage by means of SIM-switching and coded missed calls. These three genres of using mobile phones are a way of describing different degrees of usage sophistication and socialization intent in mobile communication engagement, with reference to socialization context, rather than producing "hard data" on the percentage of calls per day or average number of calls.

To understand their engagement with the mobile phone, this article draws from Seymour Papert's constructionism perspective. In the adaptation of Papert's constructionism, this study seeks to examine collective-mediated learning, sharing, and experimenting as agents of change, and the mobile phone as a mechanism of change, in everyday interaction. Based on this model, this paper argues that social trust acts as a seed to enhance collective-mediated learning, sharing, and experimenting with the mobile phone. The collective-mediated process itself cultivates social trust.

All of these research scopes were extensions of this author's existing research into mobile communications and poor households and individuals. This research seeks to understand how mobile information and communication are integrated and negotiated into ongoing, everyday social and economic interactions, and as a result, how it transforms them in different ways and contexts.

A youth sample of 32 individuals was drawn from the three ethnographic studies mentioned earlier. The breakdowns of participants by cities are 14 in Dhaka, 7 in Sylhet, and 11 in Chittagong. These sites were selected as major cities in Bangladesh with differing cultural, socio-economic, and outside influences, such as returning family members from overseas. The difference in the number of participants in each city was due to availability and suitability issues, and the time that the researchers had at each location to conduct the fieldwork. In order to create anonymity for the participants, each youth's quote was named based on their geographical location. For example, if the quote came from a participant residing in Dhaka, then this person was named "Dhaka Youth".

DISCUSSION AND CASE STUDY

Emergence of Three Social Trust Genres

Based on the interviews and observations on the ground, trust in a group or in a social context plays a crucial role in the early use of a mobile phone by poor youth. Among poor urban youth, it is a known fact that social trust is important. In the context of this chapter, the definition of social trust is this: It is the collective manner in which trust is formed that brings forth social bonding, solidifying group identity, and enabling trustworthy communication and interaction among a group at large. In one sense, social trust nurtures greater levels of group bonding, knowledge sharing, and reciprocity. Also, the existence of social trust solidifies group identity, rules, and boundary. Hence, social trust is a liberator of social gathering, as it enables trustworthy and open communication in the key social genres among youth, such as: friendship seeking, friendship bonding, group identity search, and social reciprocity.

Similarly, the participants conceive an interesting and homogenous worldview about the importance of trust in a social context, and how it is interwoven with how they learn, share, and experiment with the mobile phone. The crux of the matter is that social trust does amplify collective-mediated learning, sharing, and experimenting with the mobile phone. The participants draw on social trust when contemplating issues that could significantly influence the way their group endures in social relationships. Social trust for them is the seed of the three different stages of their mobile phone adoption and domestication: social trust as a seed for mustering confidence in learning; social trust as a seed in the reinforcing agent in sharing; and social trust as a seed for risk-taking in experimenting. A few quotes below are illustrative of:

Social trust as a seed for mustering confidence in learning:

When I started out to use mobile phone, actually at that time, I don't have a mobile phone, I just borrowed it once in a while from my elder brother. I don't have money to buy one. I don't see the need to get one. However, I have a different opinion, when my friends decided to get one, you know, just to try it out. It just gives us some confidence to buy a phone, to just try out anything, since this is our phone. Sylhet Youth, Male, 18 years old, exerts the need for a spirited group workout so that the group members can learn from each other.

Social trust as a seed in the reinforcing agent in sharing:

I don't have much money to spend on luxury items such as a mobile phone, however, when I share the cost of owning a mobile phone with another two of my best friends, owning a phone is no longer a luxury. Not only have we shared the cost of owning a phone. I think more importantly we shared our fun moments together to learn about calling and SMSing. We laughed. We enjoyed. I think that's give us time to learn to be comfortable with each other. Dhaka Youth, Male, 17 years old, elaboration about importance of social trust as a reinforcing agent is testified by his accounts of previously sharing a mobile phone.

Social trust as a seed for risk-taking in experimenting:

There are a lot of risk, especially for us young people, not knowing how to operate a phone and therefore, not able to fully use it to our advantage. I think when we operate as a group we are becoming more adventurous, trying way of using the mobile phone, like we come out with a way to

do missed call to each other, especially at night, when we have nothing much to do. Dhaka Youth, Female, 18 years old, believes that as a group they are stronger in spirit and more adventurous.

As discussed in the introduction, it is advantageous to develop a context of what was discussed earlier as grist for new ways of thinking about how social trust influences collective-mediated learning, sharing, and experimenting. The narrative of case studies exemplifies three different states of engagement with the mobile phone. The goal is to provide descriptions that present the native point of view and phenomenology of mobile use domestication in everyday life in Dhaka, Sylhet, and Chittagong. In Case 1, the examples of social trust functioning as a seed for peer-to-peer learning are recounted. Common to the examples in Case 1 is the co-presence of others as an important factor in building social trust, and in turn, how co-presence drives peer-to-peer learning. In Case 2, the examples of how social trust plays a role as a seed for group underground sharing practices are examined. The examples shown in Case 2 uncover the practices that are difficult to recognize without first understanding the real motive behind it. In Case 3, the importance of social trust in fuelling the experimenting spirit among the poor urban youth is emphasized. Several examples related to risk-taking play a major role in fuelling an experimenting spirit, and social trust plays a role in sustaining it.

Case 1

Co-Presence: A Case of Social Trust Seeding Peer-To-Peer Learning

When people are about to learn something new, they move from knowing nothing to knowing something. This process could be in the form of: learning through the instruction manual, asking a friend who has had the problem before, learn from a web forum or watching YouTube, and just self-learning, since we have (at some point) learned to use other similar devices. Particularly when learning about new media technology, such as the Internet and mobile phone, for the youth who live in a more developed society and are better off economically, consuming a new gadget or subscribing to a new service appears to be a non-event.

This behavior is fuelled by our reservoir of past knowledge that 1) enables us to see the whole picture, therefore knowing the form of a new gadget or a new service, 2) enables us to dissect the whole into parts, therefore knowing the functionality of a new gadget or a new service, 3) enables us to synthesize the whole and parts, therefore building self-confidence to learn through toying around, and 4) enables us to appreciate and enact more nuanced sensitivity towards the domestication of the newfound knowledge into everyday life.

In contrast, the poor youth have a reversal in circumstances. This is an uncharted territory for them. In the interviews and observations, the more common practice of learning to use new media such as the Internet and mobile phone is somewhat more complex, due to their need to search for a diversity of information. For example, in an uncomplicated situation, such as learning to make a call to another person, this author observed that poor youth have several decisions to make. The decisions do not mainly concern knowing the whole and parts, per se. Despite the fact that this act seems trivial to most, poor youth need to make at least three decisions, 1) In the first place, do I really need to make a call? 2) Is there an alternative way of doing so? 3) What are the benefits of my doing so (with emphasis on benefits, instead of just a benefit)? These questions, to them, supersede questions that most people commonly ask themselves when toying with a new gadget or a new service. It could be an indication of not having a well-developed mindset to accept and adopt new media technology, it could be an indication of a lack of a crystallizing mindset to synthesize with previous experience, or it could be an indication of the hesitation to unlearn due to lack of willingness and fear.

Quotes from *Dhaka Youth* and *Sylhet Youth* are illustrative in this regard:

I always wonder how it feels like to own a mobile phone. I have this feeling it is kind of cool and I will feel special. At that point, I use to go to the PCO (Public Calling Office) to make my call; however, I feel I wish to do more than just calling. How about receiving calls? That will be nice. Somehow, I don't know whether this additional advantage will benefit me. Dhaka Youth, Female, 25 years old, recounts her experience when trying to resolve her dilemma about what to do.

I talked to a lot of people. They told me about their experiences using a mobile phone. I think I get some form of idea of what it means to use and own a mobile phone. At that point, I feel the urge to buy one. You know because of seeing my friends having one. I don't want to be left out. Sylhet Youth, Male, 18 years old, explains further on his dilemma about whether there is really a need and what it means for him to be connected.

A case in point is how social trust is part of the seed to encourage peer-to-peer learning. Several interesting interviews confirmed this article's belief that social trust acts as the prerequisite seed to foster peer-to-peer learning. This author noted different dimensions of learning difficulty for the poor urban young that turns learning into a problematic effort. The learning process is steep, and an emotionally fearful process. The learning process is a harder alternative than depending on another person to do the task. The learning process is not sequential; rather it is a perplexing web of confusion and anxiety. The learning process is largely individualistic in nature.

In essence, the co-presence of familiar faces makes learning a less daunting effort. To them, familiar faces extend the notion that: I trust you that we can learn together; I trust you that we can rely on each other; and I trust that the sum of us learning together is greater than an individualistic effort. This need for co-presence as a result of sharing one particular mobile phone breeds several behavioral sequences: co-presence builds familiarity, familiarity over time builds up group norm, group norm over time strengthens group cohesion, group cohesion over time builds trust among members, and trust over time fosters social trust that allows tolerance with each other and democratization of decision-making (i.e. we are all equal) within the group.

Case 2

SIM-Switching and Missed Calls: A Case of Social Trust Seeding Group Underground Sharing Practices

Once a group learns the form and functionality of a mobile phone, and are able to use the mobile phone as a tool for socializing, they are now ready and able to go beyond the basics. The ability to practice together for a long duration of time is vital for knowledge to be coalesced and yoked. The limits on individual learning are becoming clear. In dealing with the mobile phone in the context of the poor youth, a variety of information pieces need to be blended together. It is hard for the first timer to do so individually. There are concerns about where to search for information, what the information means, how can a person use the information to advance his knowledge, whom can he use as source for advice in case he gets stuck, and so on. The formation from learning as a group, to solidifying the group learning into group sharing practices was observed. As the shared learning occurred over time, the amount of accumulated knowledge could double or triple as a result, as illustrated by the quotes:

I enjoy learning much more now. I feel I learned more as a group. We add on to each other knowledge. Dhaka Youth, Male, 18 years old, indicates that he is learning at a greater speed due to the advantages of collective memory.

Learning as a group is something that all of us as a group enjoy. We are like this big head, instead of just many small heads. We think faster as we enjoy ourselves. Sylhet Youth, Female, 22 years old, shares similar experience with Dhaka, with greater enthusiasm.

In the interviews about their sharing experiences, the poor youth in Dhaka, Sylhet, and Chittagong described how they learn about new things and how they intend to capture knowledge and synthesize the knowledge. This synthesis of knowledge, in turn, creates a space for the group to mingle, explore, and form a new basis for sharing even more. This paper's take on this issue involves a sharing continuum. At one end of the continuum, socializing is a part of enjoyment. It concerns interaction with others; the co-presence of others meliorates sharing culture with the group. At the other end of the continuum are the issues concerning everyday survival, or whether sharing creates value for the group as a whole. From these sharing dimensions, a formulation of a shared, unique culture emerges as a result. As the shared culture matures over time, the youth become capable of envisioning other possibilities that are quite different from what they think as individuals; therefore, deepening the social contract among them.

We feel we are as one. All is equal. Equal in opinion and in our favorite.

Sylhet Youth, Female, 21 years old, describes what she perceives as shared culture.

We need to be with each other. Otherwise there is no point to be a part of the group. I think just being with each other is as important as respecting each other. Dhaka Youth, Male, 23 years old, talks about the simpler concept of just being with each other as part of the buildup towards shared culture.

Accordingly, a generic formula can be put forth for the fostering of sharing culture among the poor urban youth. Following a period of open adjustment and readjustment, untrammeled exploration of each other's motives, expectations, and preferences, they come to trust each other. The interactions in the following period expose even more of the contours of their lives. This social playground of interaction is the foundation of social trust.

Sylhet Youth and Chittagong Youth explain that being in-sync with their share practice is important:

We swapped our SIM card frequently. It is fun. It is part of cost saving for us. Of course, we are doing missed calls as well. We bond as a result. I think of we know each other well and comfortable with each other, to know each other well. Chittagong Youth, Male, 24 years old, justifies his group underground practices as part of the embedded trust within the group.

We believe in each other. And, I think that's an important source for us to share our mobile phone together. No trust, no sharing, as simple as that. Sylhet Youth, Female, 22 years old, shares her experiences on the importance of trust, as trust conduces sharing.

Reflecting at greater length on the poor urban youth, for them sharing is a form of earning social capital. Among the poor youth, the motivation to earn social capital currency provides the proximal context in which possible modes of social capital are made available. Here, it was observed that several different modes of social capital exist and are valued to them by: friendship currency (to have more friends or relationships), trust currency (to be trusted and gain good reputation), knowledge currency (to be seen as knowledgeable and dependable), influence currency (someone who attains influencing power within and outside of the group), and interaction currency (someone who can interact with others effortlessly). Such a variety of social capital currency and its impact also establish a practically grasped, shared sense of reality for the youth – a social field. This social field provides the basis for the recognition of stronger group dynamics and bonding, two important elements for greater expressiveness and social activity when using the mobile phone. As an actor in the social field, they will offer or exchange their social capital currency. For instance, if a person has a lot of knowledge currency, he will offer his knowledge, or exchange with another person who has a higher trust currency.

Case 3

Experiment to Connect: A Case of Social Trust Seeding Experimenting Spirit

In the mobile phone use context, many forms and contexts in which the poor youth do experiment were observed. The definition of experiment to them implied a different meaning. To them, experiment is not only about learning to be creative, but also a need. The importance of "doing an experiment" was noted in several instances, one of which was maneuvering small steps to accomplishing a larger task. Although it seems like a simple task, for a person or a group who has only a faint idea of the bigger picture, it is hard to imagine. The mind and hand have to work together to make sense and absorb the new experience.

In the group behavior context, they experimented with new ways of negotiating among them for resources, such as additional time to use the mobile phone, the good manners of using a mobile phone, and understanding each other's expectations, among others. In the economic context, they experimented with new ways of reducing the cost of using and owning a mobile phone. As mentioned earlier, a group may have a particular underground share practice, such as SIM-switching, based on their interactions with other groups. However, as the group matures, they tend to formulate their own underground practices. This formulation process comes through many trials and errors. In the social context, they experiment new ways of bonding with the outside party through the mobile phone. As a group, they can easily communicate with others, as they are comfortable and know each other's expectations. With an outsider, they need to be conscientious, as to not step beyond the boundary, so to speak.

These experimental cases exemplify a crucial point. It describes the "constant perplexing state" of the poor youth. Because there is always something that they do not know, they constantly search for new information and constantly face the risk of not knowing. They need many different ways of searching for opinions and inspiration. Gardner (2006) explains this through the concept of multiperspectivalism, an approach that distinguishes different analytic perspectives that can contribute to the elucidation of an issue or problem.

One example that illustrated why the urban poor youth take the risks to be connected to the rest of the world, and how they do so, inspired this author to look at them differently. Observation at the street level revealed something unusual. Whenever a few groups were asked about what excites them right now about mobile use, they all mentioned getting connected to the world through mobile instant messaging. Most of the groups that this author spoke with have been together for more than a year, and they were all excited about a messaging service called *MiG33*. All of the groups that were spoken to mentioned that they heard about it from others; however, it is really up to them to try it out. The experiment has many failures, but the reward of having the opportunity to talk to someone far away is irresistible. Also, knowing someone far away is something to be proud of; a highly-regarded type of social capital in one sense.

At first it is all trial and trial. No success. No fun. Then, after a few days we feel we are getting

there. Then, boom and it happened. We know how to do so. Chittagong Youth, Male, 21 years old, expresses his joy of finding Eureka!

Knowing something is about practice and being analytical. Be optimistic and we will get there. We know it because we have done it. Dhaka Youth, 23 years old, rationalizes why there is a need for trial in multiple series in order to get it.

In summary, the emergence of three types of social trust genres that correspond respectively to the stages of domestication experience by the poor urban youth were described: social trust as a seed for peer-to-peer learning, social trust as a seed for group underground sharing, and social trust as a seed in fueling the experimenting spirit. The practices described earlier as collective-mediated learning, sharing, and experimenting, are inseparable from group dynamics and context, and they grow out of the patterns of mobile phone domestication that have been established through different types of mobile exchanges.

CONCLUSION

This chapter has described how social trust plays an important role in collective-mediated learning, sharing, and experimenting as part of the domestication of the mobile phone in the everyday lives of poor urban youth. Although there is much variability in the specifics of social and economic backgrounds of the poor youth in Dhaka, Sylhet, and Chittagong that were studied, there is an apparent uniform view on social trust as a seed to amplify collective-mediated learning, sharing, and experimenting that may proffer a deeper meaning. It suggests that the grooming of social acceptance and the process of collective learning requires an element of trust in order to interweave all the information and knowledge. It also suggests that the process of collective sharing requires an element of trust to interweave the reason to share and the reason to believe in sharing, and that the process of collective experimenting requires an element of trust to believe in each other to take risks for the group betterment. Arguably, the poor urban youth realize that for them to domesticate the mobile phone, it is a long process of adjustment to accommodate one another. It is an assiduous process of examining what is expected and the reaction of others, motivated by social and economic elements.

Significantly, the cultivation of social trust is a key factor that promotes greater chances of success in domesticating mobile phone in their everyday lives. In particular, social trust plays an important role in nurturing the collective behavior and dynamics of a group. Moreover, social trust provides the foundation on which a group can grow collectively, and transcend individual thinking into group thinking. And at least in this analysis, one point stands out. Those groups who succeed in cultivating social trust are most likely to domesticate new media technology with sustained confidence. Therefore, social trust functions as a seed for increasing positive interdependent towards others and plays an important role in nurturing trust among poor urban youth as they domesticate new media technology, such as the mobile phone, into their everyday lives.

This study has limitations, due to the small convenience sample of 32 individuals from low-income backgrounds in three different cities in Bangladesh. However, the richness of the findings gives several options for the design of insightful future research. Already in this study, ethnographic data opens for reflection on the cultural contexts that can explain the differences in attitudes and behavior of mobile use among the youth. A next step would be to explore the national culture more deeply. Based on such an inquiry, cases from other cultural contexts and sub-cultures within these contexts (e.g., social class, geographical location, different age cohort) could be strategically added. Since this study has achieved some

fundamental understanding of the mobile use of poor youth, an obvious future project would be to explore how these mobile uses will change over time, and how they vary in different income and education backgrounds. In order to explore these important issues, this paper proposes that the current study comprises an important first step in a longitudinal ethnographic study of social trust, and the positive interdependent processes in poor youth mobile use. A further implication of this study is the development of new technologies. It will be beneficial for the mobile industries' developers to have an in-depth understanding of the importance of social trust on the mobile use domestication process, and thereafter create services, applications, and incentives that can build on social trust within a group. The obvious benefit will be the increasing attractiveness of mobile use, as the group has more trusting relationships with each member.

REFERENCES

Abraham, R. (2006). *Mobile phones and economic development: Evidence from the fishing industry in India.* In The international conference on information and communications technologies and development, (ICTD 2006) conference proceedings. Berkeley, CA: IEEE.

Akerlof, G. A. (1970). The market for Lemons: Quality uncertainty and the market mechanism. *The Quarterly Journal of Economics*, *84*(3), 488–500. doi:10.2307/1879431

Aminuzzaman, S. (2002). Cellular phones in rural Bangladesh: A study of the village pay phone of Grameen bank. In Goldstein, A., & O'Connor, D. (Eds.), *Electronic commerce for development.* Paris: OECD Development Centre Studies.

Anderson, J. L. (2006). A structured approach for bringing mobile telecommunications to the world's poor. *Electronic Journal of Information Systems in Developing Countries*, *27*(2), 1–9.

Arrow, K. J. (2000). Observations on social capital. In Dasgupta, P., & Serageldin, I. (Eds.), *Social capital: A multifaceted perspective* (pp. 3–5). Washington, D.C.: The World Bank.

Beem, C. (1999). *The necessity of politics. Reclaiming American public life*. Chicago: University of Chicago Press.

Bell, G. (2005). The age of the thumb: A cultural reading of mobile technologies from Asia. In Thumb culture: The meaning of mobile phones for society, eds. P. Glotz, S. Bertschi and C. Locke, Boslego, J. (2005). Engineering social trust what can communities and institutions do? International Health, 27 (1) – Spring.

Brickham, P., Becker, L. J., & Castle, S. (1979). Making trust easier and harder. *Journal of Personality and Social Psychology, 62*(6), 989–1002.

Castells, M., Qiu, J. l., Fern'andez-Ard`evol, M., & Sey, A. (2007). *Mobile communication and society: A global perspective (information revolution and global politics)*. Cambridge, MA: MIT Press.

CIDA. (2002). CIDA's strategy on knowledge for development through information and communications technologies, available at: www.acdi-cida.gc.ca/ict, (accessed 5 January 2009).

Dasgupta, P. (1988). Trust as a commodity. In Gambetta, D. (Ed.), *Trust: Making and breaking cooperative relations* (pp. 49–72). New York: Basil Blackwell.

Fetterman, D. M. (1998). *Ethnography: Step by Step*. London: Sage Publication.

Field, J. (2003). *Social Capital*. London: Routledge.

Fukuyama, F. (1995). *Trust: The social virtues and the creation of prosperity*. New York: The Free Press.

Gambetta, D. (1998). *Can We Trust Trust?* Oxford, UK: University of Oxford.

Garbacz, C., & Thompson, H. G. (2007). Demand for telecommunication services in developing countries. *Telecommunications Policy, 31*(5), 276–289. doi:10.1016/j.telpol.2007.03.007

Gardner, H. (2006). *Five minds for the future*. Boston, MA: Harvard Business School Press.

Geertz, C. (1973). *The interpretation of culture*. New York: Basic Books.

Geertz, C. (2000). *Local knowledge: Further essays in interpretive anthropology*. New York: Basic Books.

Haddon, L. (1999, June). *European perceptions and use of the Internet*. Paper presented at the conference Usages and Services in Telecommunications, Arcachon.

Haddon, L. (2003). Domestication and mobile telephony. In Katz, J. (Ed.), *Machines that become us: The social context of personal communication technology* (pp. 43–56). New Brunswick, NJ: Transaction.

Haddon, L. (2006). The contribution of domestication research to in-home computing and media consumption. *The Information Society, 22*(4), 195–203. doi:10.1080/01972240600791325

Hearn, F. (1997). *Moral order and social disorder: The American search for civil society*. New York: Aldine de Gruyter.

Hudson, H. E. (2006). From rural village to global village: Telecommunications for development. In *The information age*. Mahwah, NJ: Lawrence Erlbaum Associates.

International Telecom Union. (2008). *The global information society: A statistical view*. New York: United Nations Publication.

Kamssu, A. J. (2005). Global connectivity through wireless network technology: A possible solution for poor countries. *International Journal of Mobile Communications, 3*(3), 249–262. doi:10.1504/IJMC.2005.006583

Kenny, C. (2002). Information and communication technologies for direct poverty alleviation: Costs and benefits. *Development Policy Review, 20*, 141–157. doi:10.1111/1467-7679.00162

Krishna, A. (2000). Creating and harnessing social capital. In Dasgupta, P., & Serageldin, I. (Eds.), *Social capital: A multifaceted perspective* (pp. 71–93). Washington, DC: The World Bank.

Lally, E. (2002). *At home with computers.* Oxford, UK: Berg.

Lie, M., & Sørensen, K. (1996). Making technologies our own? Domesticating technology into everyday life. In Lie, M., & Sørensen, K. (Eds.), *Making technologies our own? Domesticating technology into everyday life* (pp. 1–30). Oslo: Scandinavian University.

Macy, M. W., & Skvoretz, J. (1998). The evolution of trust and cooperation between strangers: A computational model. *American Sociological Review, 63*(5), 638–660. doi:10.2307/2657332

Marker, P., McNamara, K., & Wallace, L. (2002). *The significance of information and communication technologies for reducing poverty.* London: DFID.

Misztal, B. (1996). *Trust in modern societies.* Cambridge, UK: Polity.

Molm, L., Takahashi, N., & Peterson, G. (2000). Risk and trust in social exchange: An experimental test of a classical proposition. *American Journal of Sociology, 105*(5), 1396–1427. doi:10.1086/210434

Narayan, D., Chambers, R., Shah, M. K., & Petesch, P. (2000). *Voices of the Poor: Crying out for Change.* New York: Oxford University Press. doi:10.1596/0-1952-1602-4

Nee, V., & Sanders, J. (2001). Trust in ethnic ties: Social capital and immigrants. In K. S. Cook (Ed.), Trust in society: Vol. 2. The Russell Sage Foundation Series on Trust (1st ed., pp. 374–392). New York: Russell Sage Foundation.

Pantzar, M. (1997). Domestication of everyday life technology: Dynamic views on the social histories of artifacts. *Design Issues, 13*(3), 52–65. doi:10.2307/1511941

Papert, S. (1980). *Mindstorms: Children, computers and powerful ideas.* New York: Basic books.

Pelto, P. J. (1970). *Anthropological research: The structure of inquiry.* Cambridge, UK: Cambridge University Press.

Putnam, R. D. (1995). Bowling Alone: America's Declining Social Capital. *Journal of Democracy, 6*(1), 65–78. doi:10.1353/jod.1995.0002

Putnam, R. D. (2000). *Bowling along: The collapse and revival of American community.* New York: Simon & Schuster.

Rao, M., & Mendoza, L. (Eds.). (2005). *Asia unplugged: The wireless and mobile media boom in the Asia-Pacific.* Thousand Oaks, CA: Sage.

Resnick, P., Kuwabara, K., Zeckhauser, R., & Friedman, E. (2000). Reputation systems. *Communications of the ACM, 43*(12), 45–48. doi:10.1145/355112.355122

Silverstone, R. (1995). *Television and everyday life.* London: Routledge.

Silverstone, R., & Haddon, L. (1996). Design and the domestication of information and communication technologies: Technical change and everyday life. In Silverstone, R., & Mansell, R. (Eds.), *Communication by design: The politics of information and communication technologies* (pp. 44–74). Oxford, UK: Oxford University Press.

Silverstone, R., Hirsch, E., & Morley, D. (1992). Information and communication technologies and the moral economy of the household. In Silverstone, R., & Hirsch, E. (Eds.), *Consuming technologies: Media and information in domestic spaces* (pp. 15–31). London: Routledge. doi:10.4324/9780203401491_chapter_1

Slater, D., & Kwani, J. (2005). *Embeddedness and escape: Internet and mobile use as poverty reduction strategies in Ghana.* Report No. 4, Information Society Research Group, London.

Sorrentino, R. M., Hanna, S. E., Holmes, J. G., & Sharp, A. (1995). Uncertainty orientation and trust in close relationships: individual differences in cognitive styles. *Journal of Personality and Social Psychology, 68*(2), 314–327. doi:10.1037/0022-3514.68.2.314

Souter, D., Scott, N., Garforth, C., Jain, R., Mascarenhas, O., & McKemey, K. (2005). *The economic impact of telecommunications on rural livelihoods and poverty reduction: A study of rural communities in India (Gujarat).* Mozambique and Tanzania: Report, Commonwealth Telecommunications Organisation Report for U.K. Department for International Development.

Vygotsky, L. (1978). *Mind in society: The development of higher psychological processes.* Cambridge, MA: Harvard University Press.

Ward, K. (2005). Internet consumption in Ireland—Towards a connected life. In Silverstone, R. (Ed.), *Media, technology and everyday life in Europe* (pp. 107–123). Aldershot, UK: Ashgate.

Wolfe, A. (1989). *Whose keeper? Social science and moral obligation.* Berkeley, CA: University of California Press.

Section 4
Trust and Technology in Organizational Contexts

Chapter 13
Anonymous Workblogging and Organizational Coping Strategies

Abigail Schoneboom
City University of New York, USA

ABSTRACT

In recent years, the rise of blogging has led to debate about whether employees should be free to talk about their employers on the Internet, and whether they should be able to blog on company time. Several high-profile cases of fired bloggers between 2002 and 2006, drew attention to important labor and civil rights issues that led to debate among human resources and employment law experts in the mainstream media. The negative publicity surrounding the cases of fired bloggers has given rise to an alternative management strategy – a cautious embrace of blogging by employers, who saw the practice as a potential opportunity for marketing and professional development. However, efforts by bloggers to retain their right to blog anonymously signify continuing tensions, revealing the contradictions between workplace surveillance and an "enlightened" management doctrine based on openness and trust, indicating a refusal by some employees to align their blogging endeavors with the interests of their employer. This chapter examines the workblogging phenomenon as an intersection of organizations, technology, and trust, and makes some tentative connections between Guerra et al.'s (2003) concept of "trust-tension" and the critical management literature.

INTRODUCTION

Ever since workblogs – online diaries about work entered the mainstream in 2002, bloggers' rights have been controversial, and the fight for blogger freedoms has raised labor and civil rights is-

sues that go far beyond the act of blogging itself. High-profile cases of fired bloggers have helped to shape the debate and led to discussion about free speech in the workplace, the right of workers to organize, employees' freedom to do what they like when off-duty, and the encroachment of work into personal space.

DOI: 10.4018/978-1-61520-901-9.ch013

This debate has placed management in an uncomfortable position: employers who have disciplined or fired bloggers in order to remove what they perceive as a potential threat to their company have been subjected to hydra-like retaliation from the blogging community. For business as a whole, the media focus on fired workbloggers has created bad publicity, drawing attention to the economic vulnerability of workers and revealing cracks in a corporate ideology that is ostensibly founded on openness and mutual trust.

The goal of this chapter is to question whether employers have contained the blogging phenomenon, surveying media coverage and blog content, and looking in particular at the limitations of both surveillance and more "trust-based" management strategies that have been used to deter or co-opt bloggers. The study, which is strictly exploratory and not aimed at offering practical advice, situates the practice of employee blogging (or "workblogging") in relation to the sociological literature on workplace resistance, trust, and blogging. Arguing that the content of these blogs mirrors the criticisms of modern work culture that have been raised by writers such as Hochschild and Ross, the literature review contextualizes workblogging in terms of recent studies of worker recalcitrance. This chapter makes an exploratory connection between this critical management literature, which highlights ongoing employee discontent in today's "enlightened" workplaces, and Guerra et al.'s (2003) concept of "trust-tension."

Exploring how organizations have coped with the workblogging phenomenon, the chapter analyzes two key cases: Dooce (a.k.a. Heather Hamilton), a Los Angeles-based web designer who lost her job in 2002 after her supervisor found irreverent comments about the company on her blog; and Petite Anglaise (a.k.a. Catherine Sanderson) whose dismissal in 2006 led to a successful labor tribunal and a lucrative book deal. These cases are set against a backdrop of emerging management responses to employee blogging, which range from draconian surveillance measures to a cau-

tious embrace of the practice by companies such as Yahoo and Sun Microsystems. Looking at these developments, this chapter illustrates how some employees have publicly refused to align themselves with management policies that attempt to co-opt and contain blogging, and traces organized efforts to protect bloggers' rights to anonymous and non-corporate sponsored self-expression.

BACKGROUND

Knowledge organizations demand free-flowing information, employee autonomy, and flexibility. However, this can create anxiety for the organization in terms of minimizing worker behaviors that might threaten the organization. This chapter examines the workblogging phenomenon as an intersection of organizations, technology, and trust, and draws some tentative connections between the trust literature and the critical management sphere.

The wide-ranging debate about trust and technology examines the relationship between proximity or familiarity with technology and one's willingness to engage in online social or economic transactions (Dutton & Shepherd, 2006); the impact of the loss of physical cues (Wallace, 2001), and the possibility for alternative trust-generating mechanisms such as the availability of high-quality online information in computer-mediated interactions (Ben-Ner & Putterman, 2002; Riegelsberger, Sasse, & McCarthy, 2003). Of particular interest to this study, however, is Guerra et al.'s (2003) notion of trust-tension.

In their discussion of e-commerce transactions, Guerra et al. emphasize the transfer of data that must take place in order to establish accountability, but point out how this flow of personal information creates anxiety over the potential misuse of the information: "In this way, there is a 'trust-tension' between privacy and identity: absence of data impedes trust as accountability is limited, but data gathering creates trust problems regarding the use of the data in question and intrusions on privacy"

(2003, p.5). Guerra et al., draw on Bacharach and Gambetta's (2001) three-component definition of trust: uncertainty, exposure on the part of the trustor, and temptation on the part of the trustee. This chapter posits that the concept of trust-tension might also apply to internet use in the workplace, where knowledge organizations demand free-flowing information for their smooth functioning, yet this creates anxiety among managers because this information might be used or represented by employees in ways that are damaging to the firm, especially in the presence of the Internet's rapid dissemination infrastructure.

As we have transitioned from the rule-bound certainty of Taylorized workplaces to "looser" management cultures based on normative control, the interplay of organizational exposure and worker temptation has become a central component of the workplace. By granting autonomy, management exposes the organization to disruption. On the one hand, knowledge work has been facilitated by corporate cultures that promise self-actualization through non-hierarchical teams, flexible schedules, and strong social ties, which produce loyalty and hard work in the absence of command and control structures (Deal & Kennedy, 1982; Drucker, 1973, 1994; Peters & Waterman, 1982). However, this openness also creates vulnerability, as organizational exposure to the outside world is increased and workers are tempted to indulge in behaviors that are not sanctioned by the employer. These concerns are amplified by Internet connectivity, which transcends organizational boundaries, and potentially connects recalcitrant workers to mainstream media.

As illustrated by the testimony later in this chapter, the practice of anonymous workblogging has been perceived by some legal and business interests as a breach of the trust that has been placed in today's knowledge workers by employers. However, efforts to restrict anonymous workblogging have resulted in negative publicity since punitive measures clash with organizational philosophies that are ostensibly based on autonomy. Aware of the ideological disconnect presented by anonymous workbloggers, savvy corporations have, instead of banning the practice, begun to accept blogging, by promoting employer-sanctioned blogs and open discourse between workers and their supervisors. However, the energetic pursuit of anonymizing strategies and legal protections on the part of the blogging community indicates that bloggers continue to see a conflict between company interests and their creative freedom.

Building on Guerra et al.'s concept of trust-tension, it appears that the contemporary knowledge organization is in a quandary. From a critical management perspective, it might be argued that, despite the promises of management gurus, underlying conflict between workers and management precludes complete openness between organizations and employees. On the part of employers this has resulted in a complex interplay of blogging deterrents, moral injunctions, and pro-blogging maneuvers. Meanwhile, anonymous workblogging persists, albeit in a significantly suppressed form.

The persistence of workblogging is consistent with Thompson and Ackroyd's (1995) claim that even today's relatively comfortable workplaces cannot eliminate worker misbehavior. In their study, *All Quiet on the Workplace Front*, Thompson and Ackroyd call for renewed study of worker resistance in environments where workers are not necessarily physically oppressed – the well-lit, Internet-enabled offices that nourish today's bloggers are a far cry from the grueling labor process endured by yesterday's factory workers, yet there still seems to be a need to resist or push back. Anonymous workbloggers are often productive employees but they make fun of management buzzwords, celebrate time-wasting on the job, and express a lack of motivation and an underlying conviction that their labor is meaningless (Schoneboom, 2007).

Their writings mirror the claims of a critical sociological literature that includes the work of Hochschild (1997) and Ross (2002), which exposes the insidious consequences of corporate culture in terms of time-scarcity and self-exploitation. As an act of ironic distancing from one's job, anonymous workblogging is reminiscent of the complex navigation of organizational self outlined by Kunda (1992), where workers use dramatization and irony to resist the colonization of their private thoughts and emotions by the company. However, I argue that the highly networked, Internet-based nature of the blogosphere[1] affords employees the opportunity to transcend organizational boundaries, form alliances, and connect with traditional media in ways that go beyond the individualized and easily contained resistance demonstrated by Kunda.

Recent studies have revealed that workbloggers generally do not see themselves as engaged in a labor struggle, and tend to characterize their blogging activity as a form of creative self-expression rather than an act of resistance or defiance (Lenhart & Fox, 2006; Richards, 2007). The blog cases featured in this chapter fit this description. Dooce's blog, at the time of her firing, was a well-written narrative about her daily life, which happened to include details about her job; Petite Anglaise's blog touched on work very rarely before her firing, and focused on Paris, her love life, and childrearing, not on a systematic critique of the labor process. However, I argue that when bloggers have been fired, their blogs become sites of resistance, loosely organizing diffuse employees and other interested parties around common concerns. Where cases of fired bloggers have become *causes célèbres*, the debate has focused on labor issues, especially knowledge workers' sense of vulnerability and their rejection of job-centered fulfillment. While these efforts are relatively diffuse and ephemeral, I argue that they are useful to the labor movement, and that they signal future organizing possibilities for labor, in spite of management's ongoing effort to contain and co-opt the blogging phenomenon.

This study was originally part of my PhD dissertation, which examines the practice of workblogging as a creative act of resistance. The research for this section consisted of an informal exploration of the phenomenon, followed by three case studies (two of which are included in this chapter). In order to familiarize myself with the phenomenon, I downloaded and read several hundred postings and comments from 25 bloggers who had been fired between January 2002 and December 2006, which had been identified through the *Morpheme Tales* blog (Hopkins, 2009), reading postings dates three months before and after each firing and following all links from these postings to news and blog coverage of firings. I narrowed this sample to three blogs (*Dooce*, *Petite Anglaise* and *The Woolamaloo Gazette*), reading all postings submitted 12 months before and after the firing. I also performed Google searches for journalism and policy articles related to these three bloggers. Two of the case studies (*Dooce* and *Petite Anglaise*) are detailed in this chapter, while the third is being developed as a longer journal article. I analyzed the blog postings, comment streams, and news articles using techniques drawn from grounded theory (Glaser & Straus, 1968). This entailed coding content related to specific issues and aligning common material with particular concepts that emerge from the blog. For the 2004-2006 period, I adopted a virtual ethnographic stance as a blog reader, regularly reading workblogs as part of my dissertation research. I followed firing events as they unfolded on blogs, and analyzed the impact of the mainstream media coverage as it echoed through the blogs and new sources that I was monitoring. One obvious shortcoming of this method is that no direct participation and observation of fired bloggers was built into the study. However, I am concerned less with measuring blog realities against "real life" events than with evaluating the media effect and social interaction to which these events led. I have therefore focused on the blogosphere as the "field" of study, exploring it as a loosely cohesive and unfolding social network that is open to virtual ethnographic analysis (Beaulieu, 2004; Hakken, 1999).

FIRED WORKBLOGGERS AND ORGANIZATIONAL POLICY

Being Dooced: The Fired Blogger Phenomenon

In February 2002, Los Angeles-based web designer Heather B. Hamilton was fired from her job because of comments posted on her blog, *Dooce* (http://www.dooce.com). She had not mentioned the company by name and had concealed her identity, using only the pseudonym "Dooce," but someone emailed top executives at the company, informing them that she was writing about the company on her blog and she was fired shortly thereafter. The firing of Dooce immediately became a hot topic in the blogging community and she was flooded with emails from her readers. The press picked up on the issue and before long the term "dooced," to be fired from one's job because of one's blog, had become part of the blogging lexicon.

Dooce's blog was notable because it was extremely well written, irreverent, and funny. Her postings in 2002 were varied but many described her experiences in the workplace, offering vivid and scathing caricatures of her colleagues. In "The Proper Way to Hate a Job" (Hamilton, 2002b), she counseled readers on "successfully avoiding any work related to your actual job," suggesting that readers spend the afternoon conducting, "seemingly academic experiments with bandwidth by seeing how many simultaneous downloads of 'Get Ur Freak On' your CPU can handle." At other times her portraits of colleagues were cleverly evocative, as in this description of her boss, entitled "Intimidation": "When she talks with her hands she looks like she's molesting the air around her, sticking her fingers in holes and around forbidden curves. Often the air around her is the air around me, and my air doesn't appreciate it" (Hamilton, 2002a). Dooce's posts were littered with cynical references to team meetings and PowerPoint presentations, making fun of corporate buzzwords like "consumerizing," "creative shaping," and "expandable flow linkage," and demonstrating contempt for the company's cultural norms and its butchery of the English language.

As a well-paid employee of a high-tech company that had embraced contemporary management thinking, Dooce's comments emerged from a workplace that afforded workers a significant degree of freedom to manage their time and set their own schedules, and her writing pointed to the exploitative and frustrating aspects of a boundaryless labor process. Yet prior to her firing, Dooce was in good standing at the company and was far from being perceived as a disgruntled worker in the eyes of her supervisor. In addition to providing a place to vent about interpersonal conflicts, Dooce's blog gave her a way of distancing herself from those aspects of her job that she could not reconcile with her own value system, helping her to maintain an organizational self that could perform well on the job without having to submit entirely to the company's culture.

As Kunda (1992) has shown, workers respond to the new emphasis on employee participation in a strong corporate culture in diverse ways, using irony, humor, and dramatic metaphors to negotiate an "organizational self" that meets the demands of the job while maintaining some distance from the company's claims on their private resources and emotional lives. In this sense, "The organizational self becomes an active and artful construction, a performance, a tightrope walk, a balancing act of organizational reality claims, fluctuating between contradictory modes of relating to the organization and always threatened with the threat of burnout, or the exposure of its own illusions" (p. 216).

Dooce's blog is an example of individualized role-distancing (Kunda, 1992), or innocuous blowing off of steam about minor workplace frustrations (Barsoux, 1993). However, the tone of her writings, the public nature of her blog and the media attention that her firing generated, suggests an altogether more explosive ideological disconnect, and represents a more threatening situation

Figure 1. Curt Hopkins' blog posting "Statistics on Fired Bloggers." (© 2009, Curt Hopkins. Used with permission.)

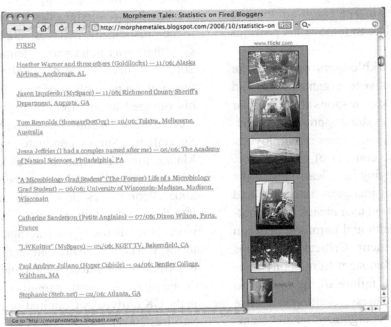

that goes beyond the type of self-contained and largely apolitical employee behavior analyzed by Kunda or Barsoux. Dooce's commitment to free self-expression, regardless of the consequences, persists as an inspiration to the community of bloggers who continue to risk being "dooced" by writing about their job or blogging on company time: "I made a conscious decision when I conceived dooce.com that I would never bow to the intimidation of others, including employers or pussy-ass cocksmacks who think I should just stop complaining and be a good worker bee already" (Hamilton, 2002).

Dooce's firing was the first of many highly publicized blogging cases between 2002 and 2006 that caught the attention of the mainstream media, drawing attention to labor issues and demonstrating the reach that could be commanded by individual employees. These included Delta employee Ellen Simonetti, who was fired in 2004 for posting photos of herself in uniform on her blog, and the UK's first fired blogger, Joe Gordon,

a Waterstone's bookstore employee who lost his job because of irreverent comments he had made about his boss on his blog, *The Woolamaloo Gazette*. In 2004, San Francisco-based writer Curt Hopkins began to keep track of fired bloggers via his posting, "Statistics on Fired Bloggers." This posting has been updated many times, based on information provided by readers, and has become an authoritative source of information on people around the world who have lost their jobs because of blogging (Hopkins, 2009). Between 2002 and 2006, Hopkins lists 42 fired bloggers from organizations as diverse as Richmond County Sheriff's Department and the *Ladies' Home Journal*. Most of these firings appear to have occurred without being generating a media furor, but a small percentage garnered international media attention.

During this period, some popular workplace blogs disappeared without warning, raising suspicions that authors had been discovered by their employees and forced to take down their blogs. For example, Dr. Dre's blog, *Doing Less Harm*, based on the perspective of a National Health Service employee, was removed suddenly in January 2004, leading to suggestions in *The Guardian* that the NHS had forced Dr. Dre to remove his postings (Butler, 2005).

The firing of workbloggers points to an interesting tension between organizational and private selves and raises questions about how far organizational mandates about appropriate behavior extend into the personal lives of employees. Again drawing on the concept of trust-tension, anonymous workblogging has clearly tested the limits of a system that increases autonomy and free-flowing information as a means of promoting organizational health and harmony between workers and management. Critical revelations about the workplace that stem from anonymous workblogs represent a failure of the system to maintain complete openness, resulting in a sense of over-exposure for the organization and signifying that, with the Internet at their fingertips, temptation on the part of recalcitrant workers is too difficult to resist.

The following sections explore the ways in which organizations have responded to the workblogging phenomenon, tracing a growing awareness among employers that summarily firing employees could lead to damaging publicity. I show that employers who wished to promote workplace cultures based on trust and openness were moved to accept and co-opt blogging rather than prohibit it. However, organized efforts to protect anonymous workblogging indicate that many employees do not wish to align their identities with corporate interests. Irreverent workplace blogs may, I contend, reflect fundamental criticisms of contemporary work culture, which may ultimately be of use to the labor movement.

Technology Policies with Teeth: Employers Respond to Bloggers

Organizational reactions to the blogging phenomenon range from disciplinary action to the development of "enlightened" strategies that cautiously encourage employees to blog about work, while reminding them of the firm's trust in their responsible behavior. On the disciplinary side, there was an increased demand in 2004 and 2005 for surveillance of employees' computer use, and the promotion of blogging policies that discouraged anonymous blogging about work. According to the 2005 Electronic Monitoring and Surveillance Survey conducted by the American Management Association (AMA) and the ePolicy Institute (American Management Association, 2005), "companies increasingly are putting teeth into their technology policies," with 26% firing workers for misusing the Internet and 76% monitoring workers' website connections. According to guidelines on Internet and email policies, produced by ACAS, similar trends were identifiable in the UK (Advisory Conciliation and Arbitration Service, 2004).

According to AMA data, firms were intensifying their monitoring of Internet use and adopting technological surveillance tools to "battle people problems" (American Management Association, 2005). The AMA survey reports that 89% of firms inform employees that their Web usage is being tracked but that only 20% had policies on operating personal blogs on company time. Firms were encouraged by the ePolicy Institute to institute specific blogging policies that would supplement existing policies on Internet and email use. Law experts argued that such a policy could protect an employer from appearing heavy-handed when it came to disciplinary action. For example, in February 2005, the UK employment law firm Cobbetts (2005) advised employers, "failure to have such a policy in place may result in claims that sanctions imposed are too draconian and may lay an employer open to claims in the employment tribunal."

During 2004 and 2005 an alternate corporate strategy emerged that is in some ways a tacit acknowledgement of the ideological limitation of punitive workplace policies that result in bloggers being fired. This new strategy has been promoted by David Sifry, founder and CEO of Technorati, which monitors trends in the blogosphere and advises businesspeople about commercial opportunities. In October 2004, Sifry announced in his blog, "there is still a tremendous opportunity for forward-thinking companies and management to have a significant positive impact on their public perception by encouraging an enlightened blogging policy, encouraging openness both within and outside of the organization" (Sifry, 2004). Sifry announced that forward-thinking companies such as Sun Microsystems were encouraging their workers to have personal blogs, while other firms, including Boeing and General Motors, were setting up corporate blogs where they invited employees to post authoritatively on new developments and products. This news marked a new corporate embrace of blogging, with firms competing to adopt these "enlightened" strategies that reflected the latest management thinking.

In this spirit of open embrace of employee blogging, several companies, including IBM and Yahoo, officially encouraged public posting and discussion of their blogging policies. Writing in May 2005, IBM employee and blogger James Snell praised IBM's policy as a triumph over anonymous blogging, noting the company's endorsement of IBM bloggers and its enlistment of employees in devising and formalizing the policy:

IBM today is publishing an announcement on its Intranet site encouraging all 320,000+ employees worldwide to consider engaging actively in the practice of "blogging" [...] The core principles – written by IBM bloggers over a period of ten days using an internal wiki – are designed to guide IBMers as they figure out what they're going to blog about so they don't end up like certain notable ex-employees of certain notable other companies. (Snell, 2005)

Snell dismisses as "crap," a CNN article offering advice on anonymous workblogging, and

reminds IBMers, "this isn't a policy that IBM is imposing upon us – it is a commitment that we all have entered into together." The guidelines emphasize IBM's corporate values of "open exchange and learning" and "trust and personal responsibility in all relationships," and encourage IBM bloggers to identify themselves and their role in the company. Company-hosted blogs are to be written in a way that "adds value" to the company, and, while the guidelines indicate that what employees do outside of work is their own business, they are cautioned that, "activities in or outside of work that affect your IBM job performance, the performance of others, or IBM's business interests are a proper focus for company policy" (Snell, 2005).

The development of corporate blogging as a strategic response to anonymous workblogging signifies the ability of organizations to respond quickly to perceived threats and minimize potential damage by devaluing acts of resistance. Corporate blogging policies such as those launched by IBM, cleverly restore to employees the idea of self-management and self-determination, while subtly impugning the moral value to workers who blog under a pseudonym. However, such openness creates uncertainty over how information might be shared or misused, leading to some organizational anxiety over how to control or limit the potential for such behavior without leading to negative publicity.

Anonymous Blogging Continues

In 2004 and 2005 period, corporate blogging strategies aimed at co-opting or condemning anonymous workblogging were received skeptically by many in the blogging community, and the mainstream media continued to express concerns that an employer-sanctioned blog would be no substitute for one written in complete freedom. In the *Daily Telegraph*, James Hall (2005) captured this reaction, commenting that, "The very point of blogs is that they are open and honest. But how can blogs that have been sanctioned by a company be objective, wary bloggers ask." Amid proposals that employees should obtain permission from their employer before starting their blog, *The Guardian*'s Patrick Butler (2005) argued that employer-sanctioned workblogs by definition lacked the satirical edge that made them capable of revealing truths and perspectives that could be gained elsewhere. In some cases, bloggers themselves were given a mouthpiece by mainstream media sources. In an August 2005 *New York Times* Op-Ed column, Jeremy Blachman, who had been "outed" in December 2004 as the author of the very popular blog *Anonymous Lawyer* argued for the continuation of anonymous blogging about work:

Now that everyone can publish online, we can get these incredible glimpses into worlds we might otherwise never get to see. People across the world can share stories, commiserate and connect with each other. Potential employees can see beyond the marketing pitches. (Blachman, 2005)

The promotion of corporate blogging by David Sifry, James Snell, and other supporters was met by a vigorous rebuttal from non-profit organizations and individual bloggers devoted to anonymous blogging. Most prominently, in April 2005, The Electronic Frontier Foundation (EFF, http://www. eff.org), a US-based nonprofit organization dedicated to protecting Internet freedoms, published its guide, "How to Blog Safely about Work or Anything Else" (2005a) which clearly stated the EFF's support for anonymous blogging and provided concrete advice on how workers could blog without revealing their identity.

The EFF guide describes blogs as "personal telephone calls crossed with newspapers," and counsels bloggers not to give away telling details about their workplace, as well as strongly advising against blogging while at work due to the high probability of detection. It outlines anonymizing technologies and services, such as Tor, Invisiblog, and Anonymous Surfing software, which conceal

the IP address of a computer, potentially helping bloggers to elude surveillance efforts. The EFF issued popular FAQs that explain bloggers' legal rights, reminding non-unionized US employees that in most states they are hired "at will," a status that affords workers very few protections from being arbitrarily fired. The Labor Law FAQ (2005b) informs US-based bloggers that, under the First Amendment, they cannot be fired for talking about unionizing or (so long as they notify the appropriate regulatory body first) for whistle blowing, and it explains the protected category of "concerted speech," where two or more people may legally blog about their working conditions, such as the pay scale or vacation policy, without fear of retaliation.

By reminding employees of their at-will status and their right to organize, EFF reaffirmed the role of unions in protecting workers' rights and reinvigorating labor questions that may previously have seemed irrelevant or anachronistic. Although EFF's guides focus on US employment law, the organization's efforts toward protecting the right to anonymous and free speech on the Internet generated considerable interest and support in the UK, revealing the need for a similar organization specializing in UK issues and triggering an Internet campaign that led to the formation of the UK-based Open Rights Group (http://www.openrightsgroup. org) in November 2005 (Doctorow, 2005).

For members of the blogging community who write irreverently or critically about their work, it has been difficult to avoid the cautionary tales about fired bloggers, and some have responded to the warnings by reevaluating their practice. Many of the anonymous workblogs that flourished in 2004 and 2005 were discontinued by 2006. These included fairly widely read blogs such as *Doing Less Harm*, and the supermarket blog *Life of a Morrison's Employee*, which was suddenly taken down and replaced by a link to an employee forum. Some bloggers removed only their work-related postings, leaving those that could not get them in trouble, while others took down their entire blogs. Google's addition of blog searchability in

Figure 2. Graphic promoting the Electronic Frontier Foundation's resources protecting bloggers' rights. (Courtesy Electronic Frontier Foundation. Used with permission.)

2005 (Sifry, 2005) made it hard for bloggers to hide in obscurity, creating an additional deterrent for those who wished to blog even occasionally about work. As "Dan," a blogger in the north of England, comments:

One thing I don't write about now, although I used to, is my work. I had written a series of posts, starting out quite harmless, but ending up a lot more risky- there was one all about racist remarks made by a colleague, one comparing a visiting VIP visitor from company HQ to a particularly self-important Roman Emperor, and another about

my unwillingness to take on a move to another team because, among other things, it sounded a bit too much like hard work and I would have less time to devote to the blog. I started to worry about being found out (it would at that time have only taken a Google search for my name) so one day took them all down. But those stories are all just in hibernation really and the day will come when they reappear in some untraceable online place – I even have the title of my new blog all worked out. (Dan, personal communication, November 11, 2005)

Dan has been alarmed at the prospect that blogging might threaten his livelihood but he hasn't given up hope of continuing once he has covered his tracks better. However, the concerted effort to protect bloggers' rights indicates a more sustained threat, made possible by Internet-enabled, loosely networked bloggers who, like Dan, have been temporarily cowed but remain committed to the ideal of non-corporate self-expression.

The Case of Petite Anglaise

Exemplifying this commitment, the 2006 firing of the Paris-based blogger Petite Anglaise, confirms the persistence of recalcitrant blogging despite corporate attempts to control it. Petite, whose real name (as revealed by the press) is Catherine Sanderson, was terminated from the accounting firm of Dixon Wilson in April 2006 after her employer found out about her blog, accused her of blogging on company time, and of potentially bringing the firm into disrepute through her writings. Sanderson, who worked as a bilingual secretary, had never identified the firm or referred to the accounting industry in her blog, and wrote only rarely about incidents at work.

The sacking of Petite was in some ways anachronistic – her firm was notably conservative and clearly oblivious to the learning curve that many organizations have followed with regard to the negative publicity that could result from firing an employee for blogging. However, the case also represented a maturing of the blogging community and confirmed the persistence of anonymous workblogging in spite of corporate attempts limit or prohibit it. Petite's case highlights widespread attachment in the blogging community to principles of free speech and the right to maintain a detached and even critical orientation to the labor process. Her firing, and the explosive media and Internet coverage that it generated, awakened a "sleeping giant": the possibility that any employee could be connected to a powerful and vocal network. The case also highlighted knowledge workers' dedication to making use of workplace resources and networks for their own creative projects, pursuing self-fulfillment through avenues other than their formal work duties. Further, Petite Anglaise illustrated the power of creative writing itself in cultivating a following, creating a sense of intimacy among a diffuse group of readers, and nurturing countercultural values that clash, albeit subtly, with the idea of job commitment.

Catherine Sanderson started writing *Petite Anglaise* in July 2004 after reading about blogging on *The Guardian*'s website and following links to blogs such as Belle de Jour, the now discontinued blog of a London call girl (Anglaise, 2007a). Writing pseudonymously as "Petite," Sanderson's blog chronicles her personal struggles in raising a child, coping with the ends and beginnings of relationships, and trying to survive financially in the French capital. It was already a relatively popular blog before her firing, commanding a readership of about 3000 visitors per day (Randall, 2006), but this number swelled ten-fold to 30,000 a day immediately afterwards (Frost, 2006).

In Sanderson's entire blog, only a handful of anecdotes pertain to workplace events and characters – Petite gives the number as 12 out of 384 posts (Anglaise, 2006a). In one, "titillation," she describes the accidental baring of her cleavage during a videoconference hookup, making reference to the conservatism and sexism that prevails at the firm. In a passage that was repeatedly cited in the press, she writes of one of the firm's partners: "This other boss is very old school. He wears braces and sock suspenders (although I don't have any firsthand experience of those), stays in gentlemen's clubs when in London, and calls secretaries 'typists'" (Anglaise, 2005b). Petite also intimated in her blog that she had taken time off from work on a false excuse in order to spend time in a hotel room with her new lover (Anglaise, 2005a). And, as became important in the later legal tribunal, it was evident from the timestamps on her blog entries that she had blogged during work hours.

Figure 3. One of Petite's postings from July 2006, telling the story of her firing and its aftermath. (© 2006, Catherine Sanderson. Used with permission.)

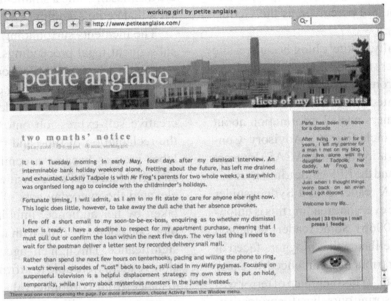

Petite wrote about her firing in July 2006 and was immediately bombarded with comments from readers, provoking interest from a Paris-based *Daily Telegraph* reporter who broke the story in the mainstream press, quoting Sanderson as taking a moral stand, "defining the boundaries between personal and professional activities, where the line should be drawn for bloggers who touch on the events of their working life in their writing" (Randall, 2006). Multiple press and radio interviews followed and the story was picked up by Associated Press and syndicated worldwide. In *The Guardian*, Petite described herself as a "competent and dependable worker" (Sanderson, 2007), commenting in *The Times* that she objected to otherwise good workers being sanctioned for their blogging activity (Bremner, 2007). In the following months, she was given opportunities to write opinion pieces for *The Guardian* (Sanderson, 2007) and *New Statesman,* and secured a book deal worth close to a million dollars with Penguin (Rickett, 2006). A memoir based on her blog was released in 2008. In March 2007, Petite

won a legal victory against her employer, when a French labor tribunal granted an unfair dismissal verdict and ordered her firm to pay 44,000 Euros in damages. She told *The Guardian* that she hoped her case would, "send out reassuring signals to the millions of people blogging in France" (Johnson, 2007).

In the aftermath of Petite's firing, regular followers of the blog were joined by new readers who had heard of Petite's plight, and the slew of comments immediately following the media publicity overloaded the server that hosted Sanderson's blog (Anglaise, 2006a). The comment box at *Petite Anglaise* became a gathering place for people who wanted to offer their sympathies, express their support for free speech, and report on how the story had been covered in their local media. Readers from places as far afield as Estonia and China posted comments about how the story had reached their local and national newspapers. While not all comments were supportive, the vast majority were, leading a reader called O. to comment, "there are literally thousands of readers supporting you," while a visitor called Monty chimed in with, "You represent the people and to all our eyes you are perceived as the victim" (Anglaise, 2006b).

More specifically, Petite's blog became a site where other workers talked about their own fears about blogging from work. Several "Dooced" bloggers commented about having themselves been fired, and others posted information about employee rights, including the Advisory Conciliation and Arbitration Service (ACAS) Internet guidelines (2006) and the EFF guide to anonymous blogging (2005). A reader called Sydneysnider commented, "hope everyone reading this is unionized" (Anglaise, 2006b). Some readers lamented the increased surveillance that bloggers faced at work – as the labor tribunal commenced, a reader called Morgan wrote, "This e-climate of terror will have most of us censoring ourselves for protection, even though we write because we believe in free speech and rights to personal, non-corporate opinion" (Anglaise, 2007b). Among the comments, were several demonstrations of solidarity with Petite in asserting the right to blog from work, with visitors commenting that they were reading through the comments and posting from work on company computers in their own workplaces. According to one commenter, Petite's fans temporarily detonated a Google bomb (influencing the ranking of a given page in results returned by the Google search engine), associating the search term "Dixon Wilson" with the Wikipedia definition of stupidity (Anglaise, 2006a).

Although most of the comments were one-off remarks, at times, readers responded to each other, building on previous comments and bringing forth diverse viewpoints amidst the largely supportive tone of the discussion. In response to the tribunal result, a reader called Paul Reichel interrupted the generally supportive vein of opinion by posting an opposing view: "You used their time and their facilties [sic] - both of which they and not you had paid for." A debate ensued, with some readers defending Petite's right to blog on company time

or to be given fair warning rather than an immediate dismissal, while a smaller number upheld the view that Petite's employer was partly in the right.

The incidents surrounding Petite's firing and subsequent legal proceedings, gave her readers – many of whom were bloggers themselves – an opportunity to reflect on their orientation to their organizational role and to elevate their acts of creative self-expression onto a plane in which the reclamation of time and resources from the labor process became a communal rather than an individual act. Petite's widely publicized case elevated the everyday acts of resistance undertaken by her audience, imbuing the reading of blogs on company time with moral and political significance. Through engagement in the discussion, readers were able to affirm their ideological distance from corporate values, renewing their commitment to writing anonymously on their own blogs. Regular readers who had been attracted to the blog by the quality of Petite's writing, became united around shared values – such as a lack of job commitment – that were subtly present in the blog before the incident but became overt after the firing. By demonstrating their intellectual sophistication – expressing contempt for tabloid newspapers, for example – Petite's readers attempted to distinguish themselves as educated, critical thinkers, ready to contribute their ideas and analysis to the case.

While Petite's readers made no move toward any kind of long-term political organization, their willingness to engage in discussion about the labor process demonstrated a creative need for unfettered self-expression and a commitment to borrowing time from the work day for dialogue and artistic endeavors. Research on workblogs has indicated that bloggers do not identify their activity as resistance (Richards, 2007), and has highlighted the personal nature of the phenomenon (Lenhart et al., 2006), emphasizing that most anonymous workbloggers blog as an act of creative self-expression rather than an act of defiance. Amidst the media furor over her firing, Sanderson referred to her blog as a personal endeavor, yet acknowledged its inherently public nature: "I've often thought it's a little like being an actor on the stage and not being able to see the audience because of the lights. You can kind of forget that they're there and just write for yourself" (Frost, 2006). Her blog underscores the connection between creative writing and resistance, reconciling the seeming contradiction between writing that is intimate and personal yet able, albeit ephemerally, to precipitate large-scale political mobilization in support of worker's rights. In the long-term, Petite's blog, and others like it, helps members of the blogging community to strengthen their adherence to iconoclastic values, making subtle connections between their writing and a literary culture that rejects traditional career values and fuels its members' individual efforts to limit their participation in a labor process that they find somewhat alienating.

FUTURE RESEARCH DIRECTIONS

Assessing the potential impact of anonymous workblogging is difficult, since the practice is a moving target that shifts continually in response to workplace computing policies and rapidly evolving Internet technology. The case studies presented here are very specific to the technological and social moment in which they emerged and, as such, they are not presented as generalizable phenomena, but rather as unique manifestations of technologically enabled employee recalcitrance that, it is suggested, is likely to continue in as yet undetermined forms.

Blogging technology is constantly morphing, and blogs themselves will inevitably be replaced by other social technologies. As Internet-enabled cell phones become the norm, reliance on workplace networks in order to blog from work is no longer a necessity, and new developments such as "microblogging" (see Twitter, http://www.twitter.com/) may take advantage of SMS text capabilities,

being driven by postings from handheld devices rather than desktop computers.

Some commentators have observed that amateur blogging is already very much on the decline (Boutin, 2008), and that there has been a mass migration to Facebook as an alternative communication medium. Future research might explore whether these developments represent new avenues for dissent, permitting workers to circumvent company network surveillance and use their own wireless technologies for workplace-based resistance. Another relevant task for researchers is to assess the degree to which the human need to elude surveillance drives the development of new Internet technologies, rather than merely responds and adapts to technological developments.

Recent discussion in the media has pointed to concern among neuroscientists that newer tools such as Facebook lack any sustained narrative and lead to atomized and self-absorbed communication. As blogs give way to Twitter and Facebook, it may be interesting to explore the presence (or absence) of narrative in these newer tools, which may have implications in terms of organizing power or media impact.

Workplace policies and management ideology must be a central focus of future research and must be regarded as in dialogue with emerging technologies and behaviors. An intriguing issue, as blogging morphs into newer forms of social technology, is whether workers will be able to stay one step ahead of workplace policies, creating new opportunities for disruption of the labor process. Today's anonymous workbloggers could be tracked longitudinally to see how they take advantage of emerging tools, while also scanning emerging Internet-based social realms for new voices of resistance. In broadening the analysis, it may be interesting to move beyond the study of workblogging and related practices in purely Western contexts, and incorporating a more international perspective on what is essentially a global phenomenon.

CONCLUSION

From the employer's perspective, blogging has presented a form of trust-tension (Guerra et al., 2003), where free-flowing information is necessary to organizational health, yet lack of control over how this information is used creates a sense of over-exposure and vulnerability. Drawing on critical management literature, this chapter has shown how organizations have coped with the anonymous workblogging phenomenon, revealing limitations of punitive anti-blogging policies and questioning blogging strategies that promote transparency between workers and employers.

Critics of corporate culture such as Hochschild (1997), Ross (2002) and, in the UK, Bunting (2004), have argued that the colonization of workers' emotions and creative impulses in the service of salaried time has led to overwork, time-scarcity, and neglected families and communities. Looking at workers in a high-tech environment who are simultaneously seduced by the company culture yet wary of its encroachment into their private space, Kunda (1992) adds an important and subtle dimension to this analysis, focusing on how white-collar workers engage in minor acts of resistance yet, in the absence of a compelling alternative, return to the organization as their principal source of affirmation. Thompson and Ackroyd (1995) have criticized Kunda for promoting a "Foucauldian turn" in organizational sociology that forecloses the possibility of resistance in the knowledge workplace. They advocate a revival of academic research into informal and subtle forms of resistance.

The mainstream media, in covering the high profile cases of fired bloggers, has often treated anonymous workblogging as a political phenomenon, characterizing bloggers as recalcitrant employees engaged in conscious acts of rebellion. However, recent studies of blogging have cautioned against regarding the workblogging phenomenon as a conscious act of defiance and have downplayed the idea of blogs as public forums for rhetoric and debate (Lenhart et al., 2006; Richards, 2007). Yet, analysis of the relationship between personal creative writing and political mobilization in the blogosphere reveals a subtle yet concrete process of ideological convergence around anti-corporate, anti-work, and generally iconoclastic values that represent a firm and sustained detachment by some bloggers and their readers from the labor process in which they are engaged.

The containment of blogging through periodic tightening of Internet surveillance and institution of blogging guidelines has stifled workplace and work-themed blogging. Furthermore, corporate blogging policies that cautiously welcome employee bloggers under a banner of mutual trust and openness, have promoted the idea that anonymous bloggers are morally questionable. However, as recent high-profile workblogging controversies have illustrated, anonymous blogging is a potentially disruptive, highly networked phenomenon that makes use of rapidly evolving Internet technologies to create new opportunities for dialogue and action.

Anonymous workblogging highlights a kind of trust-tension in organizations that require free-flowing information for their health, yet might be threatened by over-exposure in the blogosphere or the media. Efforts to suppress anonymous blogging by increasing surveillance and discouraging the practice through written policies have encountered ideological limitations, since they clash with corporate culture based on employee freedom and self-management. Some of these limitations have been surmounted by the powerful new corporate strategy of permitting blogging as an integral aspect of the corporate culture and encouraging employees to blog openly and candidly about their work. Yet, although this "corporate blogging" strategy has garnered vocal support from prominent employees of influential organizations and has been hailed as a moral victory over anonymous blogging, employer-sanctioned blogs fail to accommodate the continued need for unfettered critical distancing from the labor process. As newer technologies are ushered in, the viability of management philosophies that are based on openness and trust remains an intriguing question.

REFERENCES

Advisory Conciliation and Arbitration Service. A. (2004). *Internet and e-mail policies.* Retrieved November 30, 2006, from http://www.acas.org.uk/index.aspx?articleid=808

Advisory Conciliation and Arbitration Service (ACAS). (2006, September). *Internet and e-mail policies.* Retrieved June 22, 2007, from http://www.acas.org.uk/index.aspx?articleid=808

American Management Association. A. (2005). *2005 Electronic Monitoring and Surveillance Survey--Many companies monitoring, recording, videotaping and firing employees.* Retrieved November 30, 2006, from http://www.amanet.org/press/amanews/ems05.htm

Anglaise, P. (2005a, September 21). Hotel. *Petite Anglaise.* Retrieved June 19, 2007, from http://www.petiteanglaise.com/archives/2005/09/

Anglaise, P. (2005b, May 13). Titillation. *Petite Anglaise.* Retrieved June 18, 2007, from http://www.petiteanglaise.com/archives/2005/05/

Anglaise, P. (2006a, July 20). Suspendered. *Petite Anglaise.* Retrieved June 18, 2007, from http://www.petiteanglaise.com/archives/2006/07/20/suspendered/#comments

Anglaise, P. (2006b, July 18). Things fall apart. *Petite Anglaise.* Retrieved June 18, 2007, from http://www.petiteanglaise.com/archives/2006/07/

Anglaise, P. (2007a). *About Petite Anglaise.* Retrieved June 18, 2007, from http://www.petiteanglaise.com/about-this-site/

Anglaise, P. (2007b, March 22). Twist. *Petite Anglaise.* Retrieved June 20, 2007, from http://www.petiteanglaise.com/archives/2007/03

Bacharach, M. O. L., & Gambetta, D. (2001). Trust in signs. In Cook, K. (Ed.), *Trust and social structure* (pp. 148–184). New York: Russell Sage Foundation.

Barsoux, J.-L. (1993). *Funny business: Humour, management and business culture.* London: Cassell.

Beaulieu, A. (2004). Mediating ethnography: Objectivity and the making of ethnographies of the Internet. *Social Epistemology, 18*(2-3), 139–163. doi:10.1080/0269172042000249264

Ben-Ner, A., & Putterman, L. (2002). *Trust in the new economy.* Minneapolis, MN: University of Minnesota, Industrial Relations Centre.

Blachman, J. (2005, August 31). Job posting. *New York Times,* p. 19.

Boutin, P. (2008, October 20). Twitter, Flickr, Facebook make blogs look so 2004. *Wired Magazine,* 16.

Bremner, C. (2007, March 30). Secretary sacked for blog on office life wins £30,000. *The Times.*

Bunting, M. (2004). *Willing slaves: How the overwork culture is ruling our lives.* London: HarperCollins.

Butler, P. (2005, February 4). Reality bytes: What's up, Doc? NHS blogger in mystery moonlight flit. *The Guardian.*

Cobbetts. (2005, February). Danger! Bloggers at work. *Employment Matters.*

Deal, T. E., & Kennedy, A. A. (1982). *Corporate cultures: The rites and rituals of corporate life.* Reading, MA: Addison-Wesley.

Doctorow, C. (2005, July 24). Would you give a fiver a month for a UK tech/civil liberties org? *BoingBoing*. Retrieved 30 November 2006, from http://boingboing.net/2005_07_01_archive.html.

Drucker, P. (1973). *Management*. New York: Harper & Row.

Drucker, P. (1994). *Knowledge work and knowledge society: The social transformations of this century*. Paper presented at the 1994 Edwin L. Godkin Lecture. Retrieved 1 August 2006, from http://www.ksg.harvard.edu/ifactory/ksgpress/www/ksg_news/transcripts/drucklec.htm

Dutton, W. H., & Shepherd, A. (2006). Trust in the Internet as an experience technology. *Information Communication and Society*, *9*(4), 433–451. doi:10.1080/13691180600858606

Electronic Frontier Foundation. (2005a, May 31). *How to blog safely (about work or anything else)*. Retrieved January 5, 2006, from http://www.eff.org

Electronic Frontier Foundation. E. (2005b). *Bloggers' FAQ: Labor Law*. Retrieved November 30, 2006, from http://www.eff.org/bloggers/lg/faq-labor.php

Frost, V. (2006, July 24). Virtually famous. *The Guardian*.

Glaser, B. G., & Straus, A. L. (1968). *The discovery of grounded theory: Strategies for qualitative research*. London: Weidenfeld and Nicholson.

Guerra, G. A., Zizzo, D. J., Dutton, W. H., & Peltu, M. (2003). *Economics of trust in the information economy: Issues of identity, privacy and security*. OII Research Report No. 1.

Hakken, D. (1999). *Cyborgs@Cyberspace? An ethnographer looks to the future*. New York: Routledge.

Hall, J. (2005, April 9). Big Business battles to keep up with the bloggers. *Daily Telegraph*.

Hamilton, H. (2002, February 27). Tell it to their face for Christ's sake. *Dooce*. Retrieved June 14, 2007, from http://www.dooce.com/archives/daily/02_27_2002.html

Hamilton, H. (2002a, February 6). Intimidation. *Dooce*. Retrieved November 30, 2006, from http://www.dooce.com/archives/daily/02_06_2002.html

Hamilton, H. (2002b, February 17). The proper way to hate a job. *Dooce*. Retrieved November 30, 2006, from http://www.dooce.com/archives/daily/01_17_2002.html

Hochschild, A. R. (1997). *The Time bind: When work becomes home and home becomes work*. New York: Metropolitan Books.

Hopkins, C. (2009, January 29). Statistics on fired bloggers. *Morpheme Tales*. Retrieved March 18, 2008, from http://morphemetales.wordpress.com/2009/01/29/statistics-on-fired-bloggers/

Johnson, B. (2007, March 30). Briton sacked for writing Paris blog wins tribunal case. *The Guardian*.

Kunda, G. (1992). *Engineering culture: Control and commitment in a high-tech corporation*. Philadelphia: Temple University Press.

Lenhart, A., & Fox, S. (2006). *Bloggers: A portrait of the internet's new storytellers*. Pew Internet and American Life Project.

Peters, T., & Waterman, R. H. (1982). *In search of excellence*. New York: Harper and Row.

Randall, C. (2006, July 17). Wrote blog and got the sack. V bad. Will sue. *Colin Randall's Paris Blog*. Retrieved June 18, 2007, from http://www.telegraph.co.uk/news/main.jhtml?xml=/news/2006/07/18/wblog18.xml

Richards, J. (2007). *Unmediated workplace images from the Internet: An investigation of workblogging*. Paper presented at the 25th International Labour Process Conference.

Rickett, J. (2006, September 30). Joel Rickett on the latest news from the publishing industry. *The Guardian*.

Riegelsberger, J., Sasse, M. A., & McCarthy, J. D. (2003). The researcher's dilemma: Evaluating trust in computer-mediated communication. *International Journal of Human-Computer Studies, 58*, 759–781. doi:10.1016/S1071-5819(03)00042-9

Ross, A. (2002). *No collar: The humane workplace and its hidden costs*. New York: Basic Books.

Sanderson, C. (2007, April 2). Blogger beware! *Comment is Free*. Retrieved June 18, 2007, from http://commentisfree.guardian.co.uk/catherine_sanderson/2007/04/blogger_beware.html

Schoneboom, A. (2007). Diary of a working boy: Creative resistance among anonymous workbloggers. *Ethnography, 8*(4), 403–423. doi:10.1177/1466138107083559

Sifry, D. (2004, October 17). Oct 2004 State of the Blogosphere: Corporate bloggers. *Sifry's Alerts*. Retrieved November 30, 2006, from http://www.sifry.com/alerts/archives/000390.html

Sifry, D. (2005, September 14). Welcome to the Blogosphere, Google! *Sifry's Alerts*. Retrieved November 30, 2006, from http://www.sifry.com/alerts/archives/000340.html

Snell, J. (2005, May 16). Blogging@IBM. *Chmod 777 Web*. Retrieved November 30, 2006, from http://www-128.ibm.com/developerworks/blogs/dw_blog_comments.jspa?blog=351&entry=81328

Thompson, P., & Ackroyd, S. (1995). All quiet on the workplace front? A critique of recent trends in British industrial sociology. *Sociology, 29*(4), 615–633. doi:10.1177/0038038595029004004

Wallace, P. (2001). *The psychology of the Internet*. Cambridge, UK: Cambridge University Press.

ENDNOTE

[1] A collective noun commonly used to describe all the blogs in existence.

Chapter 14
Building and Maintaining Business Relationships in a Virtual Environment:
The Role of Trust in New Forms of Organisation Based on Virtual Teaming

Genoveffa Giambona
University of Reading, UK

David W. Birchall
University of Reading, UK

ABSTRACT

In this chapter the authors propose a framework based on team characteristics to assess the trust requirements in virtual team-based organisations. They start off by looking at what is meant by new forms of organisation and the drivers for new forms by reviewing relevant literature. They proceed to an examination of factors impacting on the effective working of the virtual organisation emphasising the role of virtual teams in such organisations. This leads to a discussion of the reliance on trust rather than on management through control systems and processes. It is then recognised that there is considerable diversity in the form and purpose of virtual teams. This leads to the development of a conceptual framework for assessing the need for trust for a team to be effective rather than managerial processes and control mechanisms. Finally, areas for further research and exploration are put forward.

INTRODUCTION

The many changes that are taking place in the business environment are forcing companies to look closely at the way they operate (Kalakota and Robinson, 1999; Harigopal, 2006). The complexities of business have grown over the last few decades to the point where it is not possible to directly employ people with all the specialist skills and knowledge needed to tackle complex decisions and their implementation across ever-globalising businesses (Smallbone and Rogut, 2005). Moreover, as they face up to global competition, businesses are getting increasingly focused on 'lean' working as they

DOI: 10.4018/978-1-61520-901-9.ch014

attempt to reduce their fixed cost base in order to increase their competitiveness (Cruet et al., 2008).

It is widely accepted that several new organisational forms emerged simultaneously during the 1980s: globalisation, reduced technology cycles, shifting demographics, changing expectations among workers and customers, the restructuring of capital markets, the exponential expansion of information technology and computer networks, the rapid advances of information science, as well as the dismantling of hierarchy, are all examples of trends acting as drivers for changes in organisations (D'Aveni, 1994; Beatty and Ulrich 1993).

As identified early by Stewart (1993), one of the consequences of these trends is the frantic pace of change in technology, geopolitics and markets, which has left many organizations vulnerable. Computerised information systems have led to lower unit costs and higher productivity: sheer size is no longer sufficient for large companies to dominate in a world of fast-moving, flexible, smaller organizations; moreover, rapidly changing technology has made the concept of the experience curve obsolete as a strategic competitive tool, and the customer and consumer are both smarter and more demanding. In addition, emerging around the trends identified above is the whole new information economy in which the fundamental sources of wealth are knowledge and communication, rather than natural resources and labour (Robertson and Hammersley, 2000).

Developments in information technology have freed up much work from a physical location so that virtual working is increasingly commonplace for the individual (Birchall et al., 2008). Virtual team working with team members distributed across nations and cultures is also, increasingly, the norm for staff in global organisations. More and more, the old models of control within organisations are being eroded and, increasingly, work is being performed across time and space without necessarily strong contractual ties between parties, with an open-source model, whether in software, R&D or the innovation process (Castells, 2004;

Harigopal, 2006). However, in order for these virtual teams to work effectively, a certain degree of trust is required (Birchall et al., 2008; Birchall and Giambona, 2007). Trust allows teams to organise their work more quickly, manage themselves better and work more creatively (Lipnack and Stamps, 2000; Handy, 1995).

In this chapter the authors propose a framework, based on team characteristics, to assess trust requirements in virtual team-based organisations. They start off by looking at what is meant by new forms of organisation and the drivers for new forms by reviewing relevant literature. They proceed to an examination of factors impacting on the effective working of the virtual organisation emphasising the role of virtual teams in such organisations. This leads onto a discussion of the reliance on trust rather than management through control systems and processes. It is recognised that there is considerable diversity in the form and purpose of virtual teams. This leads to the development of a conceptual framework for assessing the need for trust for a team to be effective rather than managerial processes and control mechanisms. Finally areas for further research and exploration are put forward.

THE VIRTUAL ENTERPRISE: ITS ORIGINS AND FORM

Alternative forms of organisation have been of interest to thinkers, researchers, and organisational leaders for not just decades but probably the whole of the last century: the advent of the Internet in the 1990s has given a fresh stimulus to the debate as increasing connectivity was seen as offering possibilities to bring changes in work organisation not seen in earlier periods other than in exceptions (Harigopal, 2006). Not only did the development of the Internet, accompanied by the emergence and rollout of 3G, play a part in this, but also societal changes were having an impact on business effectiveness (Birchall and Lyons, 1996).

Still, after all these years, the notion of new organisational forms is not very well defined. Early on, this idea was associated with the adoption of organisational practices such as the Quality of Working Life, Total Quality Management, Business Process Reengineering and outsourcing (Bowman and Singh, 1993). Moreover, new organisational forms were seen as typical ways of organising in the knowledge age (Miles et al., 1997). As a consequence, management scholars and practitioners all over the world began to promote concepts such as 'knowledge economy' and 'new information economy' (Halal, 1998). Nowadays it is accepted that there are several names for these new organisational forms, among them: 'flexible firms' (Kalleberg, 2003); 'shamrock organisations' (Handy, 1995; Harris, 2001; Bridge et al., 2003); 'network firms' (Chetty and Blankenburg, 2000; Dyer and Nobeoka, 2000); 'boundaryless organisations' (Ashkenas et al., 1995; Baruch, 2004).

In these organisational forms, temporary workers, contractors and inter-organisational alliances provide an effective extension of the 'core' staff and functions. In particular, the notion of 'boundaryless organisation' underpins much of the current research on new organisational forms (Robertson and Hammersley, 2000). Thanks to boundary-spanning activities people can acquire knowlegde and information which are vital to acquiring market value (Swan et al., 1999). Moreover, the boundaryless organisation can take forms such as network-based design (Osterloh and Frey, 2000) and self-organising clusters (Lei et al., 1999; Defilippi, 2002).

The concept of 'shamrock organisation' was first discussed by Charles Handy (1995) to give an example of how he perceived organisations were changing. Handy uses the symbol of the shamrock to describe the three bases on which people are often employed and organisations linked. According to this author, people who are linked to an organisation often fall into three categories which have different expectations and are managed and/or rewarded differently. The first category is a core of qualified technicians and managers; they are essential to the continuity of the organisation and have deep and detailed knowledge of it. They are highly paid and committed, this commitment being demonstrated by the fact that they work long hours; they are mobile and operate within a task culture. The second category is made up of contracted specialists who are often used for functions such as R&D, advertising and computing. They operate in an existential culture and their contribution to the organisation is measured in outputs and results rather than in hours and time devoted to the firm. The third category consists of a flexible labour force, called in on an ad hoc basis, depending on the task at hand. These people operate within a role culture. According to Handy, although these staff operate on a casual basis, it is important that they are managed not casually but in a way that recognises the worth of their knowledge to the organisation. Many of the processes and procedures applied to the management of the performance of permanent staff do not fit well with temporary engagements. Whilst contracted to achieve certain outputs, success is often not based on time contribtions but rather on individuals fulfilling epectations. Those responsible for managing contract staff often have to put trust in these indiciduals relying on their professionalism.

According to Robbins (1998: 565), the boundaryless organization 'seeks to eliminate the chain of command, have limitless spans of control, and replace departments with empowered teams'. In such an organizational structure, vertical boundaries are removed to flatten the hierarchy, and horizontal boundaries are removed in order to replace functional departments with cross-functional teams and to organize activities around processes. When fully operational, boundaryless organizations remove the barrier of geographic distance from external constituencies. Such organizations are thus characterized by a decreased dependence on a command-and-control style of leadership; a breakdown of hierarchies: an increasing commitment to virtual technologies; reliance on teamwork: greater flexibility; and knowledge centres that interact largely through mutual interest and electronic systems, rather than authority.

However, despite extensive interest in the literature, Kasper-Fuehrer and Ashkanasy (2001: 238) recognise that 'there is still little common understanding of the concept as evidenced by the multitude of labels applied to virtual organisations (VOs)'. Kasper-Fuehrer and Ashkanasy (2001) also looked at control vs. trust and reported that with a lack of a legal framework for the formation, operation or dissolution of a VO, the VO members have to develop their own formal or informal guidelines for the operation of the enterprise. Such agreements were found to include clarification of the members' tasks and responsibilities, contracts, the allocation of funds, potential liability, how members will contribute their expertise and how they will seek to reach agreement on shared organizational objectives. Importantly, the authors see trust between the parties as a substitute for the traditional control mechanisms available in hierarchical organisations and formal guidelines set out in the early stages of the partnership serve to reduce misperceptions and facilitate the establishment of trust. A high level of trust, then, is seen as having the potential to reduce the need for specific contractual specifications of future transactions and to reduce transaction costs. However, Kasper-Fuehrer and Ashkanasy add that, if the relationship goes sour, the costs of conflict resolution may well be high. Hence, in order to establish trust, the VO needs to go through the usual contractual negotiations as well as trust building processes but also needs to have processes in place to deal with the issues arising in maintaining the trust levels needed.

Gallivan (2001) makes a useful distinction which adds to the definition of the VO from Kasper-Fuehrer and Ashkanasy (2001). He distinguishes between the virtual organisation and more narrowly defined terms such as: *virtual corporations* which are profit-making forms of the virtual organisation; a *virtual team* which is a group of individuals collaborating with a specific objective and usually with finite duration; and *virtual work or virtual workplaces* which are the practice of using ICT to perform one's job duties. But, for much of their work, virtual organisations depend on virtual teams. To be seen as 'virtual', a team should meet three basic attributes (Gibson and Manuel, 2003):

1. It must be a functioning team, i.e. members must be interdependent in task management and must have shared responsibility with regard to outcomes;
2. Team members must be geographically dispersed;
3. Team members must rely on technology-mediated communication to carry out their tasks.

However, the mere use of technology to communicate does not make a team 'virtual' as even co-located teams rely on technology to work together. Hence, we agree with Zakaria et al. (2004: 16) when they say that 'what is paramount is the degree of reliance on electronic communication… as virtual teams have no option as to whether or not to use it, since they depend on virtuality': more often than not, virtual team members never meet face-to-face.

RESEARCH INTO THE SUCCESS OF THE VIRTUAL ENTERPRISE

One application of the VO of particular interest because of the nature and complexity of the knowledge work involved has been studied by Finholt in the form of the 'collaboratory' (2003). Finholt describes the 'collaboratory' as a laboratory without walls where the Internet creates possibilities for the organisation of joint scientific work amongst geographically dispersed collaborators. Their collaboration is based on accessing information in digital libraries, data sharing and data exploration, as well as the remote use of instruments and facilities. Even the equipment might be distributed – a 'cyber-infrastructure'. Therefore, the possibility also exists for the design of experiments to be undertaken within dispersed groups as well as the sharing of activities comprising less integrated research experiments carried out by independent groups. Because of the nature of the tasks, this clearly is going to be dependent on advanced IT systems which are not generally required to support virtual teaming. Finholt suggests to include tools to support both frequent interaction amongst virtual collaborators and data viewers that display the current modes and status of remote equipment and services that provide scientifically critical data. In contrast to co-location, he sees this as moving the development of scientific discoveries away from a situation of relative isolation within small tight-knit and exclusive teams where competitive rivalries can lead to collaboration being undermined, to one of mega-collaborations. He sees this development as suited to tackling critical problems such as those facing nation states which have the potential for global impact unless concerted action is taken internationally. He sees this as being achieved by combining the skills and insights of all key scientists in the field wherever based. Whilst one might see this as 'distributed intelligence' embracing those who otherwise were marginalised, he does recognise the possibility that those who are on the margin may well fail to get into the inner and somewhat elitist group - the 'balkanisation effect'. He concludes that whilst the development of the collaboratory probably exceeds the early projections of Wulf (1993), actual developments are rather modest. His overall conclusion is that this results from a huge difficulty in supporting complex group working in a virtual setting. The sharing of expensive equipment seems to have been achieved to some degree. But Finholt sees less evidence that collaboratories have qualitatively

changed scientific work. So the provision of a shared platform in itself does not overcome all the issues in managing groups across language and cultural barriers even though there is a common professional language. This may well in part be due to the lack of relationship building between the scientists involved: the result is a lack of trust between members who suspect others will not fulfil obligations and act in ways which are not serving the common good. Finholt concludes that scientific collaborations appear to require face-to-face contact at least initially: collaboratories may well augment rather than replace proximity; for elite scientists collaboratories may be more of an imposition than a benefit. Many of his proposed solutions relate in part to the creation of conditions where participants are more likely to trust each other. Finholt's findings are worthy of consideration in relation to trust development in any virtual teaming.

This view is reinforced by Olson and Olson (2001) who state that for some tasks co-location is still essential, e.g. where tasks are closely coupled and dependent on frequent interaction and feedback amongst collaborators. Olson et al. (2000) also refer to collaboration readiness (the psychological preparedness of participants) and collaboration technology readiness (the sufficiency of the technology infrastructure and the availability of local technology expertise, both implicit and explicit).

Thomas and Bostrom (2008) investigated trust building and cooperation in virtual teams involved in information systems development (ISD) work. In their view, ISD work necessitates continual co-operation across internal barriers and resolution of ongoing conflicts. Failure to resolve task conflict between groups that are themselves prone to raise social defences that disable cooperation will result in negative reactions. In turn, this will lead to failed cooperation which interrupts the normal flow of communications necessary for cooperative work. This results in trust and relationship breakdown. The researchers build on Jarvenpaa et al.'s (2004) suggestion that perceptions of ability, benevolence (a feeling that the other parties feel inter-personal care and concern and a willingness to go beyond that which is purely personal gain), integrity in others (adherence to a set of principles thought to result in dependability and reliability) are the antecedents of interpersonal trust and predict the existence of trust. Their findings also build on Wastrel's (1999) suggestion that social defences can be heightened or minimised by the ICT in use and that conflict resolution may be enabled by successful technology adaptation. Specifically, Thomas and Bostrom's interest is in the design of workflow or other systems to allow greater transparency for all to see the weight of each other's contribution. This, in turn, is assumed to reduce the level of misunderstanding. They found that workflow systems can be used to enable progress to be viewed thus enhancing the perception of integrity. Moreover, modelling technology can give the non-trustors a comfortable model for understanding the quality of work so as to improve their perception of other members' ability (Thomas and Bostrom, 2008). They concluded that those in a virtual team comprising members from different organisations may well not have compatible IT systems and hence even basic data such as calendars and email systems may not be capable of being shared. They also report that relational trust breakdowns between team members were critical and generally debilitating and needed to be dealt with by leaders. Virtual team leaders did not always recognise how they might bring about technology adaptation to achieve commonality in systems used although they did recognise the trade-off between personal use of a more forceful vs. a more facilitative style. Thomas and Bostrom also reported experiencing difficulty in getting developers to use the systems provided particularly project management reporting. In conclusion they suggest that ICT usage failures can have a domino effect that erodes team productivity. Trust and cooperation are seen a central reason for technology adaptation. This piece of research stresses the impact of the technology platform as an enabler of relationship building and trust development. Not only is a common platform seen as important but also by design of processes to make the transparency of individual contributions explicit thus enabling all to assess the degree to which team members are meeting commitments as a factor in trust development. They also emphasise the role of the leader in resolving conflicts without expanding on means by which this might be achieved in a virtual environment.

Given the diversity in the nature of virtual organisations, it is not surprising that clear conclusions about factors leading to success have not been established. However, relationships seem to be a prerequisite for effective virtual teaming which, in turn, is the basic unit of many virtual organisations. Trust between stakeholders is essential and for this to be present there are a number of recognised enablers. The leader clearly has a role in developing team member trust through creating a supportive culture and patterns of communication, but enabling technologies and processes are also impactful.

TRUST VS. ORGANISATIONAL CONTROL SYSTEMS AND PROCESSES

As trust seems to be an important theme in studies on the effectiveness of VO functioning, a number of key elements recognised as standing at its basis must be borne in mind. Specifically:

1. *Risk*: Trust always involves an element of risk and doubt (Lewis and Weigert, 1985);
2. *Expectation*: Trust implies that one party expects another one to be honest, reliable, competent and, based on such expectations, is willing to become 'vulnerable' (Ishaya and Macaulay, 1999; Mishra, 1996).
3. *Inability to monitor another party and need to act despite uncertainties*: If trust exists,

Table 1. Main types of trust emerging from the literature

Categories of trust	Based on	Main researchers
Deterrence-, knowledge-, identification-based trust	Fear of punishment Knowledge of the other party Common values	Shapiro et al., 1992 Lewicki and Bunker, 1996 Jarvenpaa and Leidner, 1999
System trust	Formal structures	Creed and Miles, 1996 Luhmann, 1979
Swift trust	Category-driven Actors deal with each other more as roles than as individuals	Meyerson et al., 1996 Jarvenpaa and Shaw, 1998

the lack of constant monitoring must be accepted, even when the other party's actions have a bearing on one own's choices (McEvily et al., 2003).

The main categories of trust are referred to in the literature as shown in Table 1 below.

Lewicki and Bunker (1996) affirm that these three categories of trust are interdependent, while Jarvenpaa and Leidner (1999) maintain that Deterrence- and Knowledge-based trust are difficult in virtual environments due to the lack of social interaction. Many researchers also suggest that an embedded predisposition to trust or propensity to trust amongst team members will contribute to the process of trust production (see for example Jarvenpaa et al., 1998; Mayer and Davis, 1999; Becerra and Gupta, 2003).

Lewis and Weigert (1985) list four rules which govern trust development:

1. The greater the homogeneity of the group, the higher the level of trust.
2. The greater the connectedness of a social network, the greater the level of trust.
3. The greater the size and complexity of a community, the lower the level of trust.
4. The greater the social change, the lower the level of trust.

These rules seem to suggest that teams within one organisation are likely to develop trust in a different way and in different forms to teams

made up of members from different organisations. Moreover, many virtual teams are likely to experience rapid change as well as feeling 'separated' from the main organisation, so for them the route to trust development will be different from that of teams more firmly based within the organisation.

As already mentioned, effective leadership/facilitation is linked to trust development. The research of Kayworth and Leidner (2000) suggests that the leader has a crucial role in providing a setting for group socialisation and cohesiveness building as a means to developing trust. The building of relationships between team members should be a fundamental concern of leaders/facilitators (Pauleen and Yoong, 2001). Pauleen and Yoong also see effective communication as key in building relationships which, in turn, influence team effectiveness.

However, Ariss et al. (2002) focus attention on the means by which one can side-step the need for high levels of trust by introducing control mechanisms, thereby avoiding what appear to be areas of potential challenge for the leader of the virtual team. They point out that traditional organisations, in order not to be reliant on trust, have checkpoints and control systems. The researchers observe that many managers persist with old ways of thinking about trust by installing software to monitor employee computer activities when they are working virtually. But close monitoring of staff can have negative effects on motivation where it results in a pacing of work, lack of involvement, reduced social support from peers and supervisors and fear of job loss. Some studies have even linked anxiety, depression and nervous disorders to the pressures induced by workplace monitoring (see for example Fairweather, 1999). The resulting feeling for team members is a denial of self-respect which instead comes from being trusted to do the job correctly. Rather than dependence on a formal organisational code of ethics, a strong deterrent to deviant behavior is the employees' personal code of ethics, although the impact of this may be negated by strong attempts at managerial control. Moreover, research by Piccoli and Ives (2003) suggests that the leader's exercise of behavioral control mechanisms has unexpected and unintended negative consequences on team trust in virtual settings: some of the behavioral control mechanisms needed in a virtual setting may be different from those needed in non-virtual settings. Possibly, however, of long-term significance is the influence of tight control systems on innovation behavior and as a result a shortfall in achieving goals. This seems to reinforce Henttonen and Blomqvist's (2005) view that virtual teams are focal and flexible units in the networked economy which can be used to collect and combine diverse information and knowledge from different locations and thus enhance the organizational ability to learn and innovate.

The issue of the impact of the organisation's control system on the individual's sense of trust is the theme of the research undertaken by Gallivan (2001). This research is of particular interest here since, as an example of virtual organisations, it examines open source software (OSS) development by groups of unpaid contributors. These groups are self-forming, they cross national and cultural divides and successfully achieve complex product development in a virtual environment. He suggests that this is one of the clearest and most successful examples of VOs and that the OSS movement is a prototypical virtual organization in part because it relies not on trust *per se* but rather on an overarching set of control mechanisms that ensure performance. Through an analysis of

cases and written documents, he explores how mechanisms of social control and self-control serve to ensure effective performance. He builds on Husted's (1998) categorisation of trust as:

- Knowledge-based underpinned by prior history of transactions;
- Characteristic-based where the attributes of the other party lead to trusting behavior;
- Institutional-based trust where a trusting environment ensured by guarantor agencies exists;
- Justice-based trust where procedural justice leads to effective procedures being in place;
- Swift trust where a limited trust exists in quickly constituted teams.

His main thesis is that, by controlling the conditions for collaboration and the norms of behavior, any member can have confidence in other members of the virtual organisation thus obviating the need for trust. OSS development is seen as taking place in an 'e-lance' economy where e-lancers join together into fluid and temporary networks. Gallivan concludes that trust is either relatively unimportant in OSS projects or its existence remains unacknowledged and taken for granted. Where he found evidence of references to trust, it appeared that trust existed amongst software developers willing to share and that the developers had trust in the 'wisdom and fairness' of project leaders who have control over the given project. The quality of leadership was acknowledged as a factor - the promise of open-source software is not just access to the source code but trust in human leadership (Aoki et al., 2001). Trusting the judgement of others is the basis of the peer review process. Thus, despite emphasising control systems as a mechanism for ensuring effective team working, Gallivan acknowledges that they do not obviate the need for trust in providing the basis for team work. Markus et al. (2000) suggest that, despite the potential for chaos, these projects are surprisingly disciplined through the action of multiple interacting governance The consequence of rule violation is reduced likelihood that the violator's contribution will be taken seriously or even noticed (Lee and Cole, 2000). Members can be voted out, privileges can be reduced and people can be excluded in the first place. This seems to tie in with O'Leary et al.'s research (2001) which concluded that trust and control rather than being opposites or substitutes are closely intertwined and often mutually reinforcing approaches to managing distributed work: three practices – socialisation, communication and participation – are especially important sources of trust and control. One might conclude that, in these teams, trust is a multi-faceted concept. Where control mechanisms seen as legitimate exist within the team, it appears that trusting relationships are likely to prosper and flourish whereas without some control, unless the members are highly motivated to work together and develop their own code, there is unlikely to be a sufficiency of trust to enable the members to operate together. However trust is built up through communication between members, and transpires from a process of participation and socialisation.

Dani et al. (2006) were also interested in the issue of control systems and examined the impact of organisational culture on trust in the working of virtual teams. They see low trust regimes as being characterised by management's general mistrust and suspicion of employees, with a perceived need for continuous surveillance over many aspects of behavior. They categorise companies on the basis of level of trust and level of regulation. They see high trust and high regulation as being present in companies where there is the need for high levels of measurement for product or service traceability reasons such as in lean manufacture. They see this as leading to a confrontation mode of behavior between management and labour. In global teams involved in knowledge work, made up of diverse skills, with a limited history of working together and only limited prospects of working together again, interpersonal relations are likely to be built

on similar personal relationships and professional characteristics and swift trust is the order of the day. Where there is cultural diversity trust relationship building will take longer. Members' initial actions, as well as their responses, are critical to trust development. Swift trust is observed where the situation is weak and where ambiguity and uncertainty are high. Cultural differences are seen as leading to coordination problems and creating barriers to effective communication. Less obvious and more subtle differences among team members may also impact on performance. They see the possibility that people work where there are standard operating procedures that prescribe their work pattern and limit the scope for autonomy but the overall company environment is trusting. Whilst swift trust was evident in teams, they report the need for face-to-face meetings to get through the early phase in team development and achieve rapport. Those working in virtual teams were found to prefer a high trusting organisation.

However, although trust and control are both seen as means for reducing uncertainty (Das and Teng, 1998), Crisp and Jarvenpaa (2000) rightly point out that most of the literature on virtual organisational forms concludes that high levels of uncertainty limit the use of control mechanisms, requiring instead the presence of trust. Finally, according to Godar and Ferris (2004) the most effective virtual teams are found to be those that can regulate and manage themselves and where independent members function autonomously and self reliant. But this undoubtedly is very much dependent upon the development of a high level of member trust.

We support the view that in virtual interactions collaboration can be effective only if the parties enter into it with the willingness to open up to one another and cooperate to achieve a goal, carry out a task and solve problems. Trust is the factor which binds collaborators by fostering faith that both parties will do their bit without acting opportunistically. It is with this in mind that we adopt Mayer and Davis's (1999: 712) definition of trust which they see as 'the willingness of a party to be vulnerable to the actions of another party based on the expectation that the other party will perform a particular action important to the trustee, irrespective of the ability to monitor or control that other party.'

A FRAMEWORK TO ASSESS TRUST REQUIREMENTS IN VIRTUAL TEAMS

The main factors which, according to Birchall et al. (2008), have a deep impact on trust development are presented in Figure 1. In summary, the significant dimensions can be categorised as: the personal qualities of the virtual team members, characteristics of the team and its purpose, the parent organisation and the client organisation, all within the context of a dynamic business environment.

According to Giambona et al. (2009), particularly important factors impacting on the levels of trust in virtual teams are:

1. Virtual team member characteristics including dimensions of personality relating to disposition to trust, personal motivation, competence levels and their fit to the needs of the team, and prior experiences of virtual team working.

2. The anticipated lifespan for the virtual team is an important influencing factor on the need for trust development. Short-term teams appear to operate on swift trust and the team members act as if trust is present from the outset. Emphasis is placed on completing the task rather than spending time on the soft side of team working such as the handling of emotions and relationships. In contrast, longer-term teams have more likelihood of having to face up to issues in developing and maintaining deeper trust as well as finding ways of introducing new members as and when needed. This is likely to include tackling the soft issues in working together by devoting energy to establishing personal relations with other team members.

3. Task complexity and the potential for process codification are important influences over the extent to which the team needs to focus on behavioral aspects of the tasks such as cognitive activities, collaboration and conflict resolution. These will influence the degree of interdependency which in turn influences the extent to which the team behavior needs to be either based on trust or on alternative means of regulation. The degree of autonomy, the means assumed for establishing control over team activity and the processes through which the team is established are important determinants of trust development.

4. The management style is likely to have an impact on the degree of autonomy afforded the team in practice. An inappropriate management style for the particular team may be reinforced by the culture within the employing organisation which may counter the degree of autonomy of virtual teams. Systems for monitoring team performance are dysfunctional where differences in team member contributions are highlighted in the process. Reward systems based on team performance strengthen team working but can also lead to friction where disparities in performance are felt to exist. The rate of change within the parent organisation will impact on the functioning of the team particularly where the main points of contact, or processes and systems, are being changed, as this impacts on the working methods of the team. The communications infrastructure may inhibit the team's ability to undertake all the functions needed to solve complex problems, particularly those which involve negotiation where team members are in disagreement about working methods.

Figure 1. The factors impacting on trust development in virtual teams

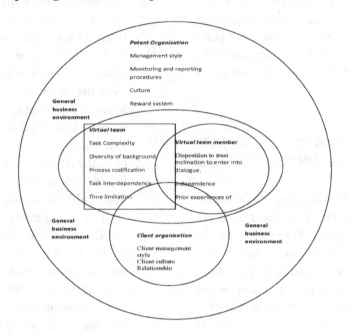

We have used the typology of virtual teams introduced by Duarte and Tennant-Snyder (1999) as the basis of a framework to review the characteristics of the virtual teaming impacting on trust development. The researchers define teams as follows:

1. **Networked teams:** team membership is fluid and members can be either internal or external to the organisation;
2. **Parallel teams:** usually these teams have a short lifespan and they are distinct from the rest of the organisation; they often undertake special assignments and tasks;
3. **Project or product development teams:** they are usually formed to manage projects specifically aimed at customers; their tasks are non-routine ones and the outcomes are measurable;
4. **Work or production teams:** they deal with ongoing work and have a clearly defined membership;

5. **Service teams:** teams which offer, for example, network support on a 24/7 basis;
6. **Management teams:** members of this type of team are rarely cross-organisational or geographically dispersed;
7. **Action teams:** these are teams that need to act quickly to respond to specific situations; membership is often cross-organisational, e.g. crisis management.

This approach enables a review of both the degree to which trust is essential and the nature of the trust which will enable effective team working. It is suggested that the following characteristics demand higher levels of team member trust:

1. High task complexity with associated higher risk of task failure;
2. High team member interdependence resulting from the need to combine member capabilities in order to achieve task completion;
3. Lack of codification of processes along with high process uncertainty requiring joint

efforts to find/create solutions and resolve differences of opinion;

4. Long term working is likely to lead to issues becoming important which for their resolution depends upon high levels of trust;

5. Complex boundary spanning relationships where the team includes those employed by different organisations adds complexity and will lead to greater challenges if trust is not present;

6. High degree of team autonomy from parent organisation leading to self-management with the team establishing their won norms of behavior and self control requires high level of trust to be created to sustain this and work effectively.

On the other hand, the following characteristics of teamwork require swift trust:

1. Short time period to achieve required outcomes making relationship trust infeasible;

2. Fluidity in team membership with constant changes in membership with the frequent need to integrate new capabilities into team working;

3. High client-demands with limited time to build relationships;

4. Limited contact with parent organisation through the project phases.

In Table 2, based on a review of the literature (see Birchall et al, 2008) we present the framework designed to suggest the degree of trust needed for different forms of virtual team working to be successful. The framework can be used as an assessment tool to gauge the potential effectiveness of virtual teams:

Table 2 shows that Action Teams normally require both a high level of overall trust (high task complexity, team interdependency, low process codification, high boundary spanning and high autonomy) and swift-trust (short time period, unstable membership). In contrast, work or production teams appear to require much less trust in order to perform, although high trust levels may well improve overall performance. By firstly categorising the type of team being examined into the framework shown and then following this by weighting the characteristics of the team it is then possible to form a view of the level of trust ideally present to ensure effective working.

We have shown what we see to be the presence of each characteristic in each form of team working, showing in some cases that there is a range from low to high requirement for trust, depending on the specifics of the situation. Each case of team working has to be assessed in turn, although it is expected that the presence of the characteristics will fall within the range indicated. The weightings are presented as illustrative of how the table might be used, either as a framework to guide future research or as a guide to management practice.

The framework is useful to management in order to assess what form of trust is a prerequisite of effective team working for different types of activity in different contexts; what type of supervision is potentially needed in different teams and, where trust is identified as below the acceptable threshold, what tactics virtual team members and supervisors need to adopt in order to take corrective action and make sure that the right level of trust is in place. The framework can thus help assess whether the teams can have a fluid membership and can develop effective working relationship.

CONCLUSION AND AREAS FOR FURTHER EXPLORATION AND RESEARCH

There is little doubt that new forms of organisation are emerging as the competitive landscape grows both more global and uncertain. Whether firms seek to introduce more networked organisational forms or not, they are gradually being forced to adopt these new ways of working if they wish to remain in business. We have proposed here

Table 2. Assessing different types of virtual teams and the degree to which teamwork characteristics are present

Type of virtual team	Complexity of task/ Codification of knowledge	Team inter-dependence	Codification of Processes	Temporary/ fixed and short time period (swift trust)	Crossing organisation boundaries	Stability of membership	Team independence of management structures.
Networked teams	H-L	M-H	L	L-M	H	L	L-M
Parallel Teams	H-L	M	H-L	L	H-L	M	L
Project or Product Development Teams	H	H	L-M	M-H	H-L	H-L	H-L
Work or Produc-tion Teams	H-L	L-M	H	L	L	H	L
Service Teams	H-L	L-M	H	L	L	H	L
Management Teams	H	M-H	L	L	L	H	L
Action Teams	H-M	H	L	H	H	L-M	H

Key: H – high presence; H-M – high to medium presence; M - Moderate presence: M-L – medium to low presence: L – low presence

that these new forms of organisation are based largely around virtual team-working. However, prior research has shown that these new forms of organisation and virtual teaming can take on various forms. We have also highlighted that these new forms of organisation cannot rely on traditional ways of managing the workforce by constantly observing what staff are doing and managing working methods. Neither can they rely on processes and procedures, rules and regulations to control the behavior of members of virtual teams and their results. It has been recognised that such mechanisms in themselves are inadequate even for the management of traditionally structured enterprises and success is only achieved where the informal organisation supports performance. In order to be successful, these new organisational forms depend upon relationships between stakeholders. In turn, for these relationships to be effective, they should undoubtedly be based upon the establishment of a working level of trust between members and groups.

In this chapter we have presented a conceptual framework for assessing the nature of a variety of forms of virtual teaming so as to establish the minimum levels of trust needed for effective working. This framework can lead on to the development of a series of hypotheses for subsequent research. However, in developing research in this area, for it to be of practical benefit, it is important to introduce outcome variables in the form of appropriate measures of team effectiveness. At the end of the day managers are interested in what practices with lead to effective virtual teaming and high performance outcomes. Trust is an enabler of performance and in any model will be an intervening variable.

One of the key issues for research in relation to the practice of virtual teaming is to establish means by which managers and those being consulted for advice can assess the effectiveness of the working of any team and identify appropriate interventions to turn around non-performing teams. However this is an age-old issue confronting managers of teams whether collocated or virtual and despite the wish for a scientific approach leading to clear prescriptions for action, this will not be achieved given the complexity and dynamics of the relationships between people.

REFERENCES

Aoki, A. Hayashi, K., Kishida, K., Nakakoji, K., Mishawaka, Y., Reeves, B., Tkashima, A., & Yamamoto, Y. (2001). A case study of the evolution of Jun. An object oriented open source 3D multimedia library. In *Proceedings of the 23rd International Conference on Software Engineering*, Toronto, Ontario, Canada (pp. 524 - 533).

Ariss S., Nykodym, N., & Cole-Laramore, A. A. (2002). Trust and Technology in the Virtual Organization. *SAM Advanced Management Journal*, 22-25.

Baruch, Y. (2004). Transforming careers: from linear to multidirectional career paths: Organizational and individual perspectives. *Career Development International*, 9(1), 58–73. doi:10.1108/13620430410518147

Beatty, R. W., & Ulrich, D. O. (1993). *Re-energising the Mature Organisation. Managing Change: Cases and Concepts*. New York: McGraw-Hill.

Becerra, M., & Gupta, A. (2003). Perceived trustworthiness within the organization: The moderating impact of communication frequency on trustor and trustee effects. *Organization Science*, 14(1), 32–45. doi:10.1287/orsc.14.1.32.12815

Birchall, D., & Lyons, L. (1995). *Creating Tomorrow's Organisation*. London: Pitman.

Birchall, D. W., & Giambona, G. (2007). SME manager development in virtual learning communities and the role of trust: A conceptual study. *Human Resource Development International*, 10(2), 187–202. doi:10.1080/13678860701347164

Birchall, D. W., Giambona, G., & Gill, J. (2008). Who is on the other side of the screen? Learning in a virtual environment. In Kautonen, T., & Karjaluoto, H. (Eds.), *Trust and New Technologies*. Cheltenham, UK: Edward Elgar Publishing.

Birchall, D. W., & Tovstiga, G. (2005). *Capabilities for Strategic Advantage – Leading through Technological Innovation*. London: Palgrave.

Bowman, E. H., & Singh, H. (1993). Corporate restructuring: Reconfiguring the firm. *Strategic Management Journal*, 14(2), 5–14. doi:10.1002/smj.4250140903

Castells, M. (2004). *Informationalism, Networks and the Network Society: A Theoretical Blueprint*. Retrieved March 27, 2009, from http://ascweb.usc.edu/pubs/faculty/Informationalism.pdf

Chetty, S., & Blankenburg, H. D. (2000). Internationalisation of small to medium-sized manufacturing firms: a network approach. *International Business Review*, 9(1), 77–93. doi:10.1016/S0969-5931(99)00030-X

Crisp, C. B., & Jarvenpaa, S. L. (2000). *Trust over Time in Global Virtual Teams*. Austin, TX: University of Texas Publishing.

D'Aveni, R. A. (1994). *Hypercompetition: Managing the Dynamics of Strategic Manoeuvring*. New York: The Free Press.

Dani, S. S., Burns, N. D., Backhouse, C. J., & Kochhar, A. K. (2006). The implications of organizational culture and trust in the working of virtual teams. *Journal of Engineering Manufacture, 220*(B), 951-960.

Das, T. K., & Teng, B. (1998, July). Between trust and control: developing confidence in partner cooperation in alliances. *Academy of Management Review, 23*, 491–512. doi:10.2307/259291

Defilippi, R. J. (2002). Organizational models for collaboration in the new economy. *Human Resource Planning, 25*(2), 24–35.

Duarte, D., & Tennant-Snyder, N. (1999). *Mastering Virtual Teams: Strategies, Tools and Techniques that Succeed*. San Francisco: Jossey-Bass Publishers.

Dyer, J. H., & Nobeoka, K. (2000). Creating and managing a high-performance knowledge-sharing network: The Toyota case. *Strategic Management Journal, 21*(3), 345–367. doi:10.1002/(SICI)1097-0266(200003)21:3<345::AID-SMJ96>3.0.CO;2-N

Fairweather, N. B. (1999). Surveillance in employment: The case of teleworking. *Journal of Business Ethics, 22*(1), 39–49. doi:10.1023/A:1006104017646

Finholt, T. A. (2003). Collaboratories as a new form of scientific organization. *Economics of Innovation and New Technology, 12*(1), 5–25. doi:10.1080/10438590303119

Gallivan, M. J. (2001). Striking a balance between trust and control in a virtual organization: a content analysis of open source software case studies. *Information Systems Journal, 11*(4), 277–304. doi:10.1046/j.1365-2575.2001.00108.x

Giambona, G., Silburn, N. J. L., & Birchall, D. W. (2009). Trust, virtual teams and grid technology. In Bessis, N. (Ed.), *Grid Technology for Maximising Collaborative Decision Management and Support: Advancing Effective Virtual Organisations.* Hershey, PA: IGI Publishing.

Gibson, C. B., & Manuel, J. A. (2003). Building Trust: Effective Multicultural Communication Processes in Virtual Teams. In Cohen, S. G., & Gibson, C. B. (Eds.), *Virtual Teams That Work Creating Conditions for Virtual Team Effectiveness.* San Francisco: Jossey-Bass.

Godar, S. H., & Ferris, S. P. (2004). *Virtual and Collaborative Teams: Process, Technologies And Practice.* Hershey, PA: IGI Publishing.

Halal, W. E. (1998). *The New Management: Bringing Democracy and Markets Inside Organisations.* San Francisco: Berrett-Koehler Publishers.

Handy, C. (1995). *The Age of Unreason.* New York: Arrow Business Books.

Harigopal, K. (2006). *Management of Organizational Change: Leveraging Transformation.* Thousand Oaks, CA: Sage.

Henttonen, K., & Blomqvist, K. (2005). Managing distance in a global virtual team: the evolution of trust through technology-mediated relational communication. *Strategic Change, 14,* 107–119. doi:10.1002/jsc.714

Husted, B. W. (1998). the ethical limits of trust in business relations. *Business Ethics Quarterly, 8,* 233–248. doi:10.2307/3857327

Ishaya, T., & Macaulay, L. (1999). The role of trust in virtual teams. In P. Sieber, & J. Griese (Eds.), *Organizational Virtualness & Electronic Commerce, Proceedings of the 2nd International VoNet - Workshop,* September 23-24, Bern (pp. 135-152).

Jarvenpaa, S. L., & Leidner, D. E. (1999). Communications and trust in global virtual teams. *Organization Science, 10*(6), 791–815. doi:10.1287/orsc.10.6.791

Jarvenpaa, S. L., & Shaw, T. R. (1998). Global virtual teams: Integrating models of trust. In P. Sieber & J. Griese (Eds.), *Organizational Virtualness Proceedings of the 1st Vo Net - Workshop,* April, Bern, (pp. 35-51).

Jarvenpaa, S. L., Shaw, T. R., & Staples, D. S. (2004). The role of trust in global virtual teams. *Information Systems Research, 15*(3), 250–267. doi:10.1287/isre.1040.0028

Kalakota, R., & Robinson, M. (1999). e-Business: Roadmap for success. Reading, MA: Addison Wesley.

Kalleberg, A. L. (2003). Flexible firms and labour market segmentation. *Work and Occupations, 30*(2), 154–175. doi:10.1177/0730888403251683

Kasper-Fuehrer, E. C., & Ashkanasy, N. M. (2001). Communicating trustworthiness and building trust in virtual organizations. *Journal of Management, 27,* 235–254. doi:10.1016/S0149-2063(01)00090-3

Kayworth, T. R., & Leidner, D. (2000). The global virtual manager: A prescription for success. *European Management Journal, 18*(2), 183–194. doi:10.1016/S0263-2373(99)00090-0

Lee, G. K., & Cole, R. E. (2000). *The Linux Kernel Development as a Model of Open Source Knowledge Creation. Unpublished working paper*. Berkeley, CA: Haas School of Business, University of California.

Lei, D., Slocum, J. W., & Pitts, R. A. (1999). Designing organizations for competitive advantage: the power of unlearning and learning. *Organizational Dynamics*, (Winter): 24–38. doi:10.1016/S0090-2616(99)90019-0

Lewicki, R., & Bunker, B. B. (1996). Developing and maintaining trust in work relationships. In Kramer, R., & Tyler, T. (Eds.), *Trust in Organizations: Frontiers of Theory and Research*. Thousand Oaks, CA: Sage.

Lewis, D., & Weigert, A. (1985). Trust as a Social Reality. *Social Forces, 63*(4), 967–976. doi:10.2307/2578601

Lipnack, J., & Stamps, J. (2000). *Virtual Teams*. New York: John Wiley.

Luhmann, N. (1979). *Trust and Power*. New York: John Wiley.

Markus, M. L., Manville, B., & Agres, C. E. (2000). What makes a virtual organization work? *Sloan Management Review, 42*, 26.

Mayer, R. C., & Davis, J. H. (1999). The effect of the performance appraisal system on trust for management: A field quasi-experiement. *The Journal of Applied Psychology, 84*(1), 123–136. doi:10.1037/0021-9010.84.1.123

McEvily, B., Perrone, V., & Zaheer, A. (2003). Trust as an organising principle. *Organization Science, 14*(1), 91–103. doi:10.1287/orsc.14.1.91.12814

Meyerson, D., Weick, K., & Kramer, R. (1996). Swift trust and temporary group. In Kramer, R., & Tyler, T. (Eds.), *Trust in Organizations: Frontiers of Theory and Research*. Thousand Oaks, CA: Sage.

Miles, R. E., Snow, C. C., Mathews, J. A., Miles, G., & Coleman, H. J. (1997). Organizing in the knowledge age: Anticipating the cellular form. *The Academy of Management Executive, 11*(1), 7–20.

Mishra, A. (1996). The Centrality of Trust. In Kramer, R., & Tyler, T. (Eds.), *Trust in Organizations: Frontiers of Theory and Research*. Thousand Oaks, CA: Sage.

O'Leary, M., Orlikowski, W., & Yates, J. (2001). Distributed work over the centuries: trust and control in the Hudson's Bay Company (1670-1826). In Hinds, P., & Kiesler, S. (Eds.), *Distributed Work*. Cambridge, MA: MIT Press.

Olson, G. M., Finholt, T. A., & Teasley, S. D. (2000). Behavioral aspects of collaboratories. In Koslow, S. H., & Huerta, M. F. (Eds.), *Electronic Collaboration in Science*. Mahwah, NJ: Lawrence Erlbaum Associates.

Olson, G. M., & Olson, J. S. (2001). Distance Matters. *Human-Computer Interaction, 15*(2), 139–178. doi:10.1207/S15327051HCI1523_4

Osterloh, M., & Frey, B. S. (2000). Motivation, knowledge transfer and organisational forms. *Organization Science, 11*(5), 538–550. doi:10.1287/orsc.11.5.538.15204

Pauleen, D. J., & Yoong, P. (2001). Relationship building and the use of ICT in boundary-crossing virtual teams: A facilitator's perspective. *Journal of Information Technology, 6*(4), 205–221. doi:10.1080/02683960110100391

Piccoli, G., & Ives, B. (2003). Trust and the unintended effects of behavior control in virtual team. *Management Information Systems Quarterly, 27*(3), 365–395.

Robbins, S. P. (1998). *Organizational Behavior: Concepts, Controversies, Applications*. Upper Saddle River, NJ: Prentice Hall.

Robertson, M., & Hammersley, G. (2000). Knowledge management practices within a knowledge-intensive firm: the significance of the people management dimension. *Journal of European Industrial Training, 24*(2), 241–253. doi:10.1108/03090590010321205

Shapiro, D. L., Sheppard, B. H., & Cheraskin, L. (1992). Business on a handshake. *Negotiation Journal, 8*(4), 365–377. doi:10.1111/j.1571-9979.1992.tb00679.x

Smallbone, D., & Rogut, A. (2005). The challenge facing SMEs in the EU's new member states. *The International Entrepreneurship and Management Journal, 1*(2), 219–240. doi:10.1007/s11365-005-1130-x

Stewart, T. A. (1993). Welcome to the Revolution. *Fortune, 128*(15), 66–80.

Thomas, D., & Bostrom, R. (2008). Building trust and cooperation through technology adaptation in virual teams: Empirical field evidence. *Information Systems Management, 25*(1), 45–56. doi:10.1080/10580530701777149

Zakaria, N., Amelinckx, A., & Wilemon, D. (2004). Working together apart? Building a knowledge-sharing culture for global virtual teams. *Creativity and Innovation Management, 13*(1), 15–29. doi:10.1111/j.1467-8691.2004.00290.x

Chapter 15
The Role of Technology in the Development of Group Trust

Anita L. Blanchard
University of North Carolina at Charlotte, USA

Lisa Slattery Rashotte
University of North Carolina at Charlotte, USA

ABSTRACT

In this chapter, the authors will elaborate a theoretical model for the development of group trust and the role that technology plays in that process. They first will articulate the particular nature of group trust, as opposed to individual trust or generalized trust. The authors then discuss the variables which affect group trust, such as sense of virtual community, entitativity, identity, and support. The authors will present a model that posits that technological features affect the commitment and attachment that lead to group trust. Technological features include group and personal identification cues (e.g., signature files, member activity). Future research directions utilizing this model are discussed.

INTRODUCTION

Trust is an important component of online groups. Trust develops in these groups when the members feel as though they can rely on the information provided and believe in the other members. In this chapter, we are interested in examining how group trust develops in online groups that are supported by varying technologies in the forms of bulletin/discussion boards or newsgroups. We focus on these groups because they are a relatively common internet application and have a substantial history

DOI: 10.4018/978-1-61520-901-9.ch015

of use dating back to the first online communities (Finholt & Sproull, 1988; Rheingold, 1993; Sproull & Keisler, 1991). This provides us with a substantial body of knowledge within which to develop our conceptual model of trust and technology.

This chapter addresses the conceptual characteristics of the technologies and not the specific applications of the technologies. For example, in our model development, we will focus on the construct of identity technologies - of which signature files and group-specific emoticons are but two concrete examples. Our goal is to develop a theoretical model that will be applicable to bulletin boards and newsgroups but may also be applied to other online groups which are either in existence or may emerge in the future (e.g., the groups forming on social networking sites like Facebook).

Overall, our model posits that technological features are one mechanism affecting how identity, structure, and interaction create the commitment and attachment that lead to group trust. Technological features can include identification cues (e.g., signature files, member activity), message organization structure, and moderation.

BACKGROUND

Trust and Online Research

In this chapter, we focus on group or social trust, as opposed to individual trust. Group trust is the belief that each member of a group "(a) makes good-faith efforts to behave in accordance with any commitments, (b) is honest in whatever negotiations preceded such commitments, and (c) does not take excessive advantage of another even when the opportunity is available" (Cummings & Bromiley, 1996, p. 303). Although trust can be examined between individuals, we feel that trust between members of a group, i.e., social trust (cf., Welch, et al., 2005), is of primary importance in understanding online *group* interactions. Social trust, as opposed to individual/interpersonal trust, is directed toward the group rather than specific individuals.

Trust requires risk (Gambetta, 1988; Luhmann, 1979; Sztompka, 1999). If members of a group do not perceive some risk in participating, there is no need for them to develop trust in the other group members. Risks in online groups include deception, embarrassment, and having someone take advantage of the member. Deception is an issue when a member is not participating truthfully about his or her identity. Deception in online groups is very upsetting to group members (Birchmeier, Joinson, & Dietz Uhler, 2005; Joinson & Dietz-Uhler, 2002; Utz, 2005). The popular media

has also spent a great deal of time warning the public about the risks interacting with people on line who are deceiving them, some of whom are potentially malevolent (e.g., Schwartz, 2008).

Embarrassment occurs when members participate and then are either ignored or mocked by the rest of the group. One participant in a previous study described posting messages as broadcasting one's opinions to the group with a loudspeaker (Blanchard & Markus, 2004). If a member unintentionally violates the group's norms of conduct or expresses an unpopular opinion, he or she could be singled out by the group for unwanted negative attention.

Finally, members risk being taken advantage of if they continually give information and support, but never receive any in return. This violation of the near-universal norm of reciprocity (Goulder, 1960) could cause members to lose trust as they feel the group is taking advantage of them. This risk may also explain why some researchers and activists have such negative views about lurkers, members who read messages but who do not participate in group discussions.

We recognize that these risks are also possible in face-to-face (FtF) groups. However, all of these risks are at least as strong if not stronger online. The first risk, deception, is much more likely to be an issue online and represents the primary risk of online groups because of the limited amount of information interactants have about one another (other that what each chooses to provide to the group). In FtF groups, only those in the same physical proximity have the potential to cause another member embarrassment (Wellman & Guilia, 1999). Online, everyone has the potential to see someone called out for their behavior, even considerably after the fact, and thus cause the target to be embarrassed.

Now that we have established that trust is important in online groups, we can turn our attention to the antecedents of trust. We will discuss the variables which affect group trust, such as identity, structure, and interaction. Of course, we

Figure 1. Model of the role of technology in the development of group trust.

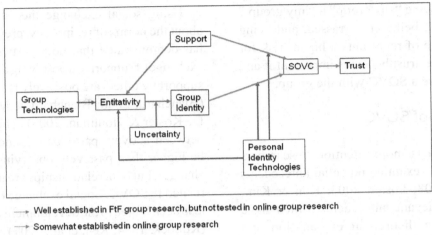

cannot include all antecedents of group trust in a single model. Here, we leave out those which are not connected to the technologies we consider relevant. Thus, we do not include leadership, organizational context, individual characteristics, and motivations, among other concepts. Some elements of our model have been established for online communication, some for face-to-face groups, and some – those related to the characteristics of the technology – are new. Our model is presented in Figure 1. We will examine the various relationships depicted in the model in turn, beginning with the established ones.

Sense of Virtual Community

Sense of Virtual Community and Trust

We propose that sense of virtual community is important in understanding group level trust. Sense of virtual community (SOVC) is defined as members' feelings of identity, belonging and attachment to an online group. SOVC derives from the concept of FtF sense of community (SOC), which has been a longstanding and important component of FtF community psychology research (Chipuer & Pretty, 1999; Fisher, Sonn, & Bishop,

2002; McMillan & Chavis, 1986; Obst & White, 2004). Virtual community researchers have begun to pay attention to these feelings in online groups as well (Blanchard & Markus, 2004; Koh & Kim, 2003; Obst, Zinkiewicz, & Smith, 2002; Rheingold, 1993; Roberts, Smith, & Pollock, 2002).

The relationship between SOVC and trust may actually be more important in online groups than in FtF communities. The reason is that member entry and departure has higher costs in FtF communities (and other FtF groups) than in online ones. At the most extreme end, one has to physically move one's residence to enter or leave a FtF community. At a less extreme end, one has to at least decide to show up and physically attend a FtF group meeting. This is not true online, where attending a meeting can be accomplished by a few clicks of a mouse and perhaps filling out an application to become a member. While this denotes some effort, it is not the same as physical movement and dedication of time to attend a meeting.

In addition, online there may be hundreds or even thousands of options for groups related to a particular topic (Ren, Kraut, & Kiesler, 2007). With entry costs so low and so many options for different groups, when does participation become risky and therefore require trust? We propose that when members develop a strong attachment to a group, a sense of virtual community, the group changes from being "any group" to "my group." Being deceived, being embarrassed, and being taken advantage of represents a higher risk for them. Therefore, trust becomes important if and only if they have a SOVC with the group.

Antecedents of SOVC

As SOVC attracts more attention, researchers are beginning to examine potential antecedents (Blanchard, 2008; Foster, 2004; Koh & Kim, 2003). Two relevant antecedents which have developed both theoretical explanation and empirical support are exchanges of support and the development of a group identity. Increased levels of both lead to higher levels of SOVC. In addition, these antecedents of SOVC are also antecedents of trust.

Support

Exchanging informational and socio-emotional support is an important - if not essential - characteristic in online groups (Baym, 1997; Rothaermel & Sugiyama, 2001; Wellman & Guilia, 1999). Exchange of support is also important in FtF SOC (McMillan & Chavis, 1986). Members exchange support in a variety of ways in online groups. Support may be actively exchanged publicly in posts for the entire group to read or may occur privately through emails exchanged behind the scenes. Support may also be passively exchanged when members read others' exchanges, but do not participate in exchange the support themselves. Wellman and Gulia (1999) have argued that the public exchange of support may increase members' perceptions of being a supportive group when in fact, few people are actually involved in the supportive exchange. Thus, there is a perception that the group is very supportive, even if only a few of the members actually help each other. Yet, because everyone can read the message, all group members benefit from the support exchange even if they were not active in creating it.

Using social exchange theory and theories about the norms of reciprocity, previous research has demonstrated that both participating in the exchange of support and observing the exchange of support by others are positively related to SOVC (Blanchard, 2008; Blanchard & Markus, 2004; De Koster & Houtman, 2008). The relationship between actively participating and SOVC may be higher than passively observing support exchanges, but both relationships are independently related to SOVC. Social exchange of support has also been linked to the development of online trust (Kollock, 1994; Ren, et al., 2007)

Group Identity

The development of a group identity is also attracting attention in trust and SOVC research (Postmes, Spears, Lee, & Novak, 2005; Ren, et al., 2007; Spears, Lea, & Postmes, 2007; Tanis & Postmes, 2005). Much of this line of empirical and theoretical research considers group identity as the antecedent to other group outcomes; it finds that as members develop a stronger identity with each other in the group, they will experience stronger positive group outcomes, such as commitment, SOVC, and group trust.

Some of this research, particularly by Postmes and his colleagues, has previously argued that online group members must remain completely anonymous, otherwise individuation of group members will occur and the salience of group identity will break down. While this may have been true in laboratory experiments conducted in chatrooms, this mode of reasoning is no longer appropriate. Today's technologies have a wide variety of identifying technology options. Indeed, interacting FtF groups can still have a group identity, even though no one is anonymous. Other researchers (Ren, et al., 2007) and even Postmes himself (Postmes, et al., 2005) has started to examine group identity with the use of technology identity cues. We will discuss this in more detail as well as expand upon the long history of group identity research in FtF groups below.

In summary, current research on online groups both theoretically and empirically suggests that the exchange of support and the development of a group identity among members all lead to SOVC and trust. We propose that SOVC at least partially mediates the relationship between these variables and trust because of the important role SOVC plays in preceding trust.

The preceding section has focused on the online group research literature important to our model of trust. While this provides essential information in developing our model of trust, we feel we would be remiss to neglect the substantial amount of research on groups in FtF environments. While not all of this research is directly applicable to online groups due to the differences of interacting online compared to FtF, we feel it can provide relevant insights into developing our model.

In particular, we want to focus on the development of group identity. While previous researchers (notably Postmes et al., 2005) have focused on group identity in their online group research, they have focused mostly on what happens *after* a group has developed a group identity, not on what facilitates (or hinders) the development of group identity online. We feel that by drawing on the research on the development of group identity, conducted mostly in FtF environments, we can better understand the role of technology in developing trust in online groups.

Development of Group Identity

To begin our discussion of group identity, we first want to present the differences between a super-ordinate identity (i.e., a social identity) and a sub-ordinate identity (i.e., a group identity). Although there are similarities between these two forms of identity (Hogg, Abrams, Otten, & Hinkle, 2004), there are also differences which are important to our model.

Super-Ordinate Identity

Super-ordinate identities involve societal level groups. This can include identity with diffuse individual characteristics (e.g., gender, ethnicity, college alumnus), identity with a particular professional or occupational group (e.g., human resource professional, doctor, plumber), identity with hobbies and interests (e.g., marathoner, Harley Davidson rider, gardener), or even with health or family issues (e.g., cancer survivor, new mother, diabetic). The distinguishing feature of super-ordinate groups is that the members do not generally interact with each other and cannot interact with other as a whole. Nonetheless, these groups very important to an individual's social identity (Hogg, et al., 2004; Meyer, Becker, & Van Dick, 2006), i.e., her or his super-ordinate identity. These identities form the frame around FtF groups; we do not include super-ordinate identities in our model.

Sub-Ordinate Identity

Sub-ordinate identity is related to specific groups where the members interact with one another. These groups may be focused around the same super-ordinate groups listed above (i.e., individual characteristics, professional groups, hobbies and health concerns), but the members of these groups can and do interact with each other. A main difference, then, is that sub-ordinate identity is attached to a particular interacting group, even though it is likely to be related to the super-ordinate identity. For example, a doctor may feel like a member of a particular interacting group, but his or her overall identity as a "doctor" has not diminished. On the other hand, a marathoner may identify as a person who competitively runs 26.2 miles, but also be attached to the regular, local training group that helps him or her participate in marathons.

In this chapter, we focus on the sub-ordinate identity, i.e., group identity. We highlight this because we have noted that researchers often use the term "identity" when they are referring both to non-interacting groups (i.e., super-ordinate identity) was well as interacting groups (i.e., sub-ordinate identity). We are interested in interacting groups in order to understand both socially and technologically what contributes to the group identity and, ultimately, group trust.

Now that we have established our focus on the group identity, we can turn to the antecedents of group identity which are most relevant to online groups. We feel that the recent research in FtF groups demonstrating the strong effects of entitativity and uncertainty are highly relevant to group identity in online groups (Hogg, Sherman, Dierselhuis, Maitner, & Moffit, 2007).

Entitativity and Uncertainty

Entitativity is the feeling of "groupy-ness" members have in a group (Hogg, et al., 2007; Lickel, Hamilton, & Sherman, 2001; Lickel, et al., 2000). It is a cognitive assessment of how much a group feels like a group to its members. Entitativity research suggests that feelings of groupy-ness come from clear group boundaries, internal homogeneity, high rates of social interaction, clear group structure, and common goals. Entitativity is important because members must believe that they are interacting in a group in order for the important subsequent group processes, such as cohesion, influence, persuasion, commitment, identity, and trust to occur.

Recently, Hogg et al. (2007) have demonstrated in FtF groups that entitativity is a key component of group identity. Members who perceive a higher level of entitativity in a group also experience a higher level of group identity. However, that relationship is moderated by the member's feelings of uncertainty. In a highly entitative group, when members felt uncertain about themselves and their role within the group, they felt a much higher level of group identity than members who felt very certain about themselves. That is, when members perceive a group to be very groupy and

they experience a high level of uncertainty, they identify more strongly with the group.

We think this research is quite relevant to the online groups in which we are interested. First, the issues of entitativity are essential in online groups. What makes an online group feel like a group? Since it cannot (by definition) be FtF interaction with all of the accompanying nonverbal communication cues and visible boundaries, other methods of creating entitativity must be considered. Clearly, members' exchange of support discussed above, which would provide evidence of social interaction and common goals, is positively related to entitativity. However, we posit that technology also plays an important role in entitativity which we will discuss further in the following section on technologies.

We also note that the feelings of uncertainty may be especially important. Members may feel uncertain due to some function of their super-ordinate identity. For example, online group members searching for help with issues stemming from super-ordinate identities such as diffuse characteristics ("How do I deal with covert sexism?"), professional issues ("How do I solve this work problem that is important to my job?"; "How do I get into graduate school?"), health issues ("What is the best treatment for my cancer?"; How do I get my child to sleep through the night?") or even hobbies ("How do I train for a marathon?"; "Why do my plants keep dying?"), are more likely to feel a social identity with an online group that has strong entitativity.

While uncertainty related to super-ordinate identity is important, we also propose to that uncertainty about how to behave in the online group itself may play a factor in this relationship. For example, new members may enter into an online group with some trepidation about how to interact. Even experienced online group members may be uncertain about how to act in a new group. If a group has a strong entitativity, uncertain members may more easily be able to pick up the established behavioral patterns and thus have a stronger social identity.

GROUP AND PERSONAL IDENTITY TECHNOLOGIES

At this point, we have established a model of trust based on relevant research on online and FtF groups. While this could be sufficient as the starting place for our model, we feel that it neglects the important role that technology characteristics play in online groups. The varying characteristics of technology, we feel, have been neglected for some time. We trace this back to the historical beginnings of computer-mediated communication research in which many researchers proposed what was essentially a deterministic view of how technology affected interpersonal and group behavior (e.g., Kiesler, Seigel, & McGuire, 1984). This research approach was thoroughly criticized as "technological determinism," which substantially neglected the role of context in how the technology was used (Baym, 1995; Culnan & Markus, 1987; Markus, 1994a, 1994b; Walther, 1992). However, more recently, some of these same critics have argued that researchers have neglected the role that particular technologies play in interpersonal interactions and group behavior for fear of being labeled a technological determinist. This neglect has lead to a stream of research ignoring how characteristics of certain technologies can help or hinder online interactions (Culnan, 2008; Markus, 2005).

Our goal then is to address this problem by including particular technological features in our model. However, we do not focus on concrete technology examples, but instead take our conceptualization of technology up to the construct level. We hope this will make our model more generalizable from the examples we have already considered to new (or simply different) technologies with different features and characteristics. Additionally, instead of examining "technology" as a single, unitary construct, we divide it into two types: technology related to group identity and technology related to personal identity. We propose that these two types of technology have different effects at different times on the development of group trust. At this time, of course, we lack the empirical evidence that will allow us to describe the importance of the two types of technology, both relative to one another and relative to the other elements of the model.

Group Technologies

Group technologies are related to the interacting group as it exists online. In this section, we describe the technologies that the user may interpret as being related to how the interacting group functions. These technologies are likely to affect users early on in their decisions about the group and general member interactions.

Group technology characteristics include:

- Indications of communication activity: number of sub-topics, number of threads, number of posts, dates posts started, dates of last reply, interval latency for responses.
- Presence of moderators: names or other signifiers of moderation, either human or technological.
- Introduction to the group: a place where new members can go to learn more about the rules and purposes of the group. This often takes the form of a Frequently Asked Questions (FAQs) page, group rules, or an online tutorial.
- Online indications of group identity: group name, group leaders, group boundaries, group membership barriers, use of group related nicknames, use of group specific acronyms and emoticons, references to group activities that occur online and FtF.

Our conceptualization of group technologies is clearly related to entitativity. These group technology characteristics affect social interaction, clear boundaries, clear group structure, and common goals, all of which have been linked to entitativity in FtF groups (Hogg, et al., 2007; Lickel, et al.,

2001; Lickel, et al., 2000). Not all online groups may use all these technologies, but the more of them that are present, the more likely that group members will perceive higher entitativity.

Personal Identity Technologies

Personal identity technologies differ from the technologies described above, which demonstrate the viability of the group. Personal identity technologies allow a user to focus on particular individuals. However, we do not assume that the technologies will necessarily individuate others. Instead, these technologies allow users to form impressions about the individual *group* members (i.e., Is this group full of similar types of people?). Along those lines, we think these personal individual technologies play a significant role in allowing users to make decisions about the trustworthiness of the group members.

Personal identity technology characteristics include:

- Access to knowledge about member institution: tenure in the group (i.e., date joined), numbers of messages posted, number of messages directed to the person, about the person, or referencing the person
- Access to knowledge about member role: group leader, moderator, administrator, other role in the group
- Member forthcomingness: real picture, real name and other "real life" information present in avatar, signature file, and/or in message content
- Member super-ordinate group similarity: information in avatar or signature file which indicate membership to the larger purpose of the group
- Member sub-group identity cues: information in avatar or signature file which indicate identity or attachment to the specific online group.

When a member uses these technologies to make judgments about the individuals in a group, there are two decision points: 1) does the group have these technologies?; and 2) does the user take advantage of them? The first two personal identity technology characteristics are likely to be automated by the group software, with little user input. The last three are more clearly related to user choices about what to share and how to present oneself to the group. We think all of these technology characteristics are positively related to trust and also that "more is better" for these technologies, as with the group technology characteristics.

Because members cannot physically see each other in these online groups, the process of learning about the personal identity of other members is more important in online groups than in FtF groups. Research on personal identity in FtF groups does not gather as much attention because people form impressions so quickly (Hancock & Dunham, 2001; Walther, 1995). In online groups, on the other hand, the process of forming an impression takes much longer (Walther, 1996, 2002). Our focus in this model remains on learning the personal identity of others *qua* members of the group. The importance of personal identity in online groups is the determination of like-me/like-the-group versus not-like-me/not-like-the-group (see also Ren, et al., 2007).

Personal identity is communicated through the technological options members enact in the online group as well as from the content of comments they make in the group. We propose that personal identity technology allows other members to determine of the speaker/writer is credible, trustworthy, and overall a worthy member of the community. Specifically, personal identity technologies moderate the relationship between exchanging support and SOVC as well as group identity and SOVC. When a member sees others using the technology to be forthcoming about their identity and can identify others' position in the group, they will interpret that person's supportive communication to be more strongly related to a SOVC and for that member to be more trustworthy.

Personal identity technologies also affect the relationship between subgroup identity and SOVC by helping individuals determine if they are like the group or not like the group. Like-the-group personal identity technology cues will lead to a higher SOVC. So these technologies have different but important moderating relationships between support and group identity and SOVC.

Additionally, some personal identity technology should positively affect entitativity. In particular, the technology that shows how similar the members are with each other such as technologies that promote super-ordinate identity and sub-ordinate identity should increase entitativity.

FUTURE RESEARCH DIRECTIONS

We can envision a number of research questions related to this new model. We believe that the role of various characteristics of both types of technology needs to be tested empirically. Some examples of the kinds of research questions we foresee include:

- How does communication activity level increase online entitativity? Which features related to member interaction have the strongest effects?
- When do Frequently Asked Questions and group role pages increase entitativity? Are they more important for new or experienced users?
- How do moderators and other indicators of group structure and roles affect entitativity? Are indicators of technical moderators or roles (as opposed to human ones) sufficient?
- What do members perceive as the group's boundaries? How do entry barriers affect entitativity? Are some stronger than others?

- How do avatar choices affect the development of SOVC and trust?
- How salient are technological features (e.g., post dates, number of replies, number of times post read) to perceptions of entitativity? Is the effect stronger for newer or more experienced members?
- Do constant messages (e.g., in a signature file) increase the effect of group identity on SOVC most, or are consistent but different messages more effective?
- When do personal identity technologies lead a group member to define the others as like-me or not-like-me? How does that effect the relationship between support and SOVC?
- How does super-ordinate uncertainty differ from sub-ordinate uncertainty in moderating the entitativity to group identity relationship?

CONCLUSION

We have created and presented a model that will help to elucidate the relationship that various aspects of technology and the development of group trust for online groups. Our model draws on theories of group trust, sense of virtual community, social exchange, social identity, and entitativity as well as research from online and FtF groups. A primary contribution of this model is in understanding how technology characteristics can influence both directly and through moderation key points of our model.

The history, stability, and popularity of the online groups for which we have developed this model will provide a rich stream of research to better understand technology and trust in online groups. As the technologies develop, especially as they allow for more and more personalization and identity markers, this model will become even more relevant to understanding how members of online groups, like bulletin boards, discussion groups, chat rooms, blogs and comments on blogs, and social networking site groups, develop trust for those groups.

REFERENCES

Baym, N. (1995). The emergence of community in computer mediated communication. In Jones, S. G. (Ed.), *Cybersociety: Computer mediated communication and community* (pp. 138–163). Thousand Oaks, CA: Sage.

Baym, N. (1997). Interpreting soap operas and creating community: Inside an electronic fan culture. In Keisler, S. (Ed.), *Culture of the Internet*. Manhaw, NJ: Lawrence Erlbaum Associates.

Birchmeier, Z., Joinson, A. N., & Dietz Uhler, B. (2005). Storming and forming a normative response to a deception revealed online. *Social Science Computer Review*, *23*(1), 108–121. doi:10.1177/0894439304271542

Blanchard, A. L. (2008). Testing a Model of Sense of Virtual Community. *Computers in Human Behavior*, *24*, 2107–2123. doi:10.1016/j.chb.2007.10.002

Blanchard, A. L., & Markus, M. L. (2004). The experienced sense of a virtual community: Characteristics and processes. *The Data Base for Advances in Information Systems*, *35*(1), 65–79.

Chipuer, H. M., & Pretty, G. H. (1999). A review of the sense of community index: Current uses, factor structure, reliability and further development. *Journal of Community Psychology*, *27*, 643–658. doi:10.1002/(SICI)1520-6629(199911)27:6<643::AID-JCOP2>3.0.CO;2-B

Culnan, M. J. (2008). Online communities: Infrastructure, relational cohesion and sustainability. *Computerization Movements and Technology Diffusion: From Mainframes to Ubiqutous Computing*.

Culnan, M. J., & Markus, M. L. (1987). Information technologies: electronic media and interorganizational communication. In Jablin, F. M., Putnam, L. L., Roberts, K. H., & Porter, L. W. (Eds.), *Handbook of Organizational Communication: An Interdisciplinary Perspective*. Newbury Park, CA: Sage.

Cummings, L. L., & Bromiley, P. (1996). The organizational trust inventory (OTI), Development and validation. In Kramer, R. M., & Tyler, T. R. (Eds.), *Trust in Organizations: Frontiers in Theory and Research* (pp. 302–330). Thousand Oaks, CA: Sage Publications.

De Koster, W., & Houtman, D. (2008). 'Stormfront is like a second home to me': On virtual community formation by right-wing extremists. *Information. Communication and Technology*, *11*(8), 1155–1176.

Finholt, T., & Sproull, L. (1988). Electronic Groups at Work. *Organization Science*, *1*(1), 41–64. doi:10.1287/orsc.1.1.41

Fisher, A. T., Sonn, C. C., & Bishop, B. J. (2002). *Psychological sense of community: Research, applications and implications*. New York: Kluwer Academic/Plenum Publishers.

Foster, P. M. (2004). Psychological sense of community in groups on the Internet. *Behaviour Change*, *21*(2), 141–146. doi:10.1375/bech.21.2.141.55421

Gambetta, D. (1988). *Trust: making and breaking cooperative relations*. New York: B. Blackwell.

Goulder, A. W. (1960). The norm of reciprocity: A preliminary statement. *American Sociological Review*, *25*, 161–178. doi:10.2307/2092623

Hancock, J. T., & Dunham, P. J. (2001). Impression formation in computer-mediated communication revisited: An analysis of the breadth and intensity of impressions. *Communication Research*, *28*(3), 325–347. doi:10.1177/009365001028003004

Hogg, M. A., Abrams, D., Otten, S., & Hinkle, S. (2004). The social identity perspective: intergroup relations, self-conception and small groups. *Small Group Research, 35*(3), 246–276. doi:10.1177/1046496404263424

Hogg, M. A., Sherman, D. K., Dierselhuis, J., Maitner, A. T., & Moffit, G. (2007). Uncertainty, entitativity, and group identification. *Journal of Experimental Psychology, 43*, 135–142. doi:10.1016/j.jesp.2005.12.008

Joinson, A. N., & Dietz-Uhler, B. (2002). Explanations for the perpetration of and reactions to deception in a virtual community. *Social Science Computer Review, 20*(3), 275–289.

Kiesler, S., Seigel, J., & McGuire, T. (1984). Social Psychological aspects of computer-mediated communication. *The American Psychologist, 39*, 1123–1134. doi:10.1037/0003-066X.39.10.1123

Koh, J., & Kim, Y.-G. (2003). Sense of virtual community: A conceptual framework and empirical validation. *International Journal of Electronic Commerce, 8*(2), 75.

Kollock, P. (1994). The Emergence of Exchange Structures: An Experimental Study of Uncertainty, Commitment, and Trust. *American Journal of Sociology, 100*(2), 313–345. doi:10.1086/230539

Lickel, B., Hamilton, D. L., & Sherman, S. J. (2001). Elements of a Lay Theory of Groups: Types of Groups, Relational Styles, and the Perception of Group Entitativity. *Personality and Social Psychology Review, 5*(2), 129–140. doi:10.1207/S15327957PSPR0502_4

Lickel, B., Hamilton, D. L., Wieczorkowska, G., Lewis, A., Sherman, S. J., & Uhles, A. N. (2000). Varieties of groups and the perception of group entitativity. *Journal of Personality and Social Psychology, 78*(2), 223–246. doi:10.1037/0022-3514.78.2.223

Luhmann, N. (1979). *Trust and power: two works* (Davis, H., Raffan, J., & Rooney, K., Trans.). Chichester, NY: Wiley.

Markus, M. L. (1994a). Electronic mail as the medium of managerial choice. *Organization Science, 5*, 502–527. doi:10.1287/orsc.5.4.502

Markus, M. L. (1994b). Finding a happy medium: Explaining the negative effects of electronic communication on social life at work. *ACM Transactions on Information Systems, 12*, 119–149. doi:10.1145/196734.196738

Markus, M. L. (2005). Technology-shaping effects of E-collaboration technologies: Bugs and features. *International Journal of e-Collaboration, 1*(1), 1–23.

McMillan, D. W., & Chavis, D. M. (1986). Sense of community: A definition and theory. *Journal of Community Psychology, 14*, 6–23. doi:10.1002/1520-6629(198601)14:1<6::AID-JCOP2290140103>3.0.CO;2-I

Meyer, J. P., Becker, T. E., & Van Dick, R. (2006). Social identities and commitments at work: Toward and integrative model. *Journal of Organizational Behavior, 27*, 665–683. doi:10.1002/job.383

Obst, P., & White, K. M. (2004). Revisiting the sense of community index: A confirmatory factor analysis. *Journal of Community Psychology, 32*(6), 691–705. doi:10.1002/jcop.20027

Obst, P., Zinkiewicz, L., & Smith, S. G. (2002). Sense of community in science fiction fandom, Part 1: Understanding sense of community in an international community of interest. *Journal of Community Psychology, 30*(1), 87–103. doi:10.1002/jcop.1052

Postmes, T., Spears, R., Lee, A. T., & Novak, R., J. (2005). Individuality and social influence in groups: Inductive and deductive routes to group identity. *Journal of Personality and Social Psychology, 89*(5), 747–763. doi:10.1037/0022-3514.89.5.747

Ren, Y., Kraut, R., & Kiesler, S. (2007). Applying Common Identity and Bond Theory to Design of Online Communities. *Organization Studies, 28*(3), 377–408. doi:10.1177/0170840607076007

Rheingold, H. (1993). *The virtual community: Homesteading on the electronic frontier.* Reading, MA: Addison-Wesley.

Roberts, L. D., Smith, L. M., & Pollock, C. M. (2002). MOOing till the cows come home: The sense of community in virtual environments. In Sonn, C. C. (Ed.), *Psychological sense of community: research, applications, implications.* New York: Kluwer Academic/Plenum.

Rothaermel, F. T., & Sugiyama, S. (2001). Virtual Internet communities and commercial success: Individual and community-level theory grounded in the atypical case of TimeZone.com. *Journal of Management, 27*(3), 297–312. doi:10.1016/S0149-2063(01)00093-9

Schwartz, M. (2008, August 3). The Trolls Among Us. *New York Times.*

Spears, R., Lea, M., & Postmes, T. (2007). CMC and social identity. In Joinson, A. N., McKenna, K. Y. A., Postmes, T., & Reips, U.-D. (Eds.), *The Oxford Handbook of Internet Psychology.* London: Oxford University Press.

Sproull, L., & Keisler, S. (1991). *Connections: New ways of working in the networked organization.* Cambridge, MA: MIT Press.

Sztompka, P. (1999). *Trust: a sociological theory.* Cambridge, UK: Cambridge University Press.

Tanis, M., & Postmes, T. (2005). A social identity approach to trust: Interpersonal percpetion, group membership and trusting behaviour. *European Journal of Social Psychology, 35*, 413–424. doi:10.1002/ejsp.256

Utz, S. (2005). Types of deception and underlying motivation: What people think. *Social Science Computer Review, 23*(1), 49–56. doi:10.1177/0894439304271534

Walther, J. B. (1992). Interpersonal effects in computer-mediated interaction: A relational perspective. *Communication Research, 19*(1), 52–91. doi:10.1177/009365092019001003

Walther, J. B. (1995). Relational aspects of computer-mediated communication: Experimental observations over time. *Organization Science, 6*(2), 186–203. doi:10.1287/orsc.6.2.186

Walther, J. B. (1996). Computer mediated communication: Impersonal, interpersonal and hyperpersonal interaction. *Communication Research, 22*, 33–43.

Walther, J. B. (2002). Time effects in computer-mediated groups: Past, present, and future. In Hinds, P., & Kiesler, S. (Eds.), *Distributed work* (pp. 235–257). Cambridge, MA: MIT Press.

Welch, M. R., Rivera, R. E. N., Conway, B. P., Yonkoski, J., Lupton, P. M., & Giancola, R. (2005). Determinants and consequences of social trust. *Sociological Inquiry, 75*(4), 453–473. doi:10.1111/j.1475-682X.2005.00132.x

Wellman, B., & Guilia, M. (1999). Net Surfers don't ride alone: Virtual communities as communities. In Wellman, B. (Ed.), *Networks in the Global Village: Life in Contemporary Communities.* Boulder, CO: Westview.

Chapter 16
Internet Exchange and Forms of Trust

Denise Anthony
Dartmouth College, USA

James A. Kitts
Columbia University, USA

Christopher Masone
Google, USA

Sean W. Smith
Dartmouth College, USA

ABSTRACT

All economic exchange entails some uncertainty, but uncertainty is exacerbated in periods of social change that disrupt conventional patterns and modes of exchange. The increasing reliance on the Internet as a medium for exchange has greatly increased uncertainty, raising particular problems of trust between parties. This study examines how information that may reduce uncertainty affects individuals' trust in online exchange. Within an experimental marketplace, subjects make purchase decisions with a series of simulated vendors. Subjects receive information about vendors in the form of ratings of transaction security that vary as to the source of reputation information (interpersonal vs. institutional sources) and the content of information (rating of reliability vs. capability for engaging in secure transactions). Subjects are more likely to trust vendors when given reputation information from institutional sources, but they do not differentiate capability from reliability information in evaluating vendors in this context.

INTRODUCTION

A recent radio news story described a now common 21st century event: the closing of a family-owned retailer after 70 years of selling sheet music in New York City (Adler, 2009). Former patrons reminisced

that the shop was a well-known, reliable source not only of musical scores for every imaginable instrument and voice, but also of advice regarding how various editions of the same score were suited to the needs of each buyer. While some noted that online sources now provide access to many of the same scores, they also suggested that customers would no

DOI: 10.4018/978-1-61520-901-9.ch016

longer receive the personalized service that they had previously enjoyed. Leading conductors as well as novices had relied on the shop to reduce their uncertainty surrounding each purchase.

Virtually all economic exchange entails some uncertainty; there is often asymmetry of information between buyer and seller and there is no guarantee that a partner will behave as promised for exchanges that are asynchronous. Periods of social change can exacerbate uncertainty by introducing new exchange partners and situations. For example, in the industrial revolution, major demographic shifts from urban and international migration increased contact among strangers and across cultures, complicating exchange. Industrialization further introduced new forms of organization (e.g., bureaucratic factories) and new types of exchange (e.g., wage labor) (Perrow, 2002). Increased uncertainty regarding potential partners and exchange situations meant that social actors often could no longer rely on *interpersonal* trust, based in established relationships with known others. Instead, new *institutions* were created to reduce uncertainty and facilitate the trust required for exchange (Shapiro, 1987; Zucker, 1986).

Increasing reliance on the Internet as a medium for exchange has greatly increased uncertainty in transactions by inviting contact between unknown trading partners in new and foreign exchange situations. Uncertainty is even greater on the Internet because potential exchange partners may be anonymous or at least have no fixed identity (Friedman & Resnick, 2001). Given such high levels of uncertainty and the unique opportunity to observe exchange in a new environment, it is not surprising that much research across many disciplines has been devoted to the question of trust in online exchange (Baye, 2002; Camp, 2000; Cheshire & Cook, 2004; Falcone *et al*, 2001; Friedman & Resnick, 2001; Kollock, 1999; Lunn & Suman, 2002).

Uncertainty may be mitigated by information received from third parties, whether by peers or institutional actors. This project investigates how different sources and types of information about vendors affect propensity to trust in and purchase from online vendors. In the next section, we describe differences between interpersonal and institutional trust. We then describe some theoretical and empirical studies of trust mechanisms used in online exchange. Next we describe a laboratory experiment that examines how different types of information from interpersonal or institutional sources affect exchange in an online marketplace. Finally, we discuss the implications and limitations of our study, including questions remaining for future research.

BACKGROUND

Social conditions that increase uncertainty are often viewed as problems of trust. When actors depend on each other for valued outcomes, they are vulnerable to others' choices; in these conditions, any uncertainty about others' motives and future actions raises a fundamental dilemma of trust (Coleman, 1990; Hardin, 2002; Heimer, 2001; Luhman, 1979; Molm et al 2000). Trust is generally relevant for situations in which "participants are uncertain and vulnerable – they lack information about what others can and will do, but they also have a stake because they cannot achieve their objectives without the cooperation of others" (Heimer, 2001, p.42). According to Bacharach and Gambetta (2001), uncertainty is the primary problem of trust.

Uncertainty and Forms of Trust

We specifically define trust as an actor's positive expectations of an exchange partner's conduct, such that the actor is willing to take some action that makes her vulnerable to her partner's behavior (Barber, 1983; Coleman, 1990; Garfinkle, 1967; Hardin, 2002; Luhman, 1979; Schutz, 1970). Russell Hardin specifies trust as a three-part relation, such that A trusts B to do X, though we rarely talk about trust in such complete terms (Hardin, 2002, p.5). For example, if Alice trusts Bob to repay her, she loans him $10. Alice is now vulnerable because she risks losing her ten dollars, and possibly more if Bob's failure to repay will jeopardize their relationship. However, Alice may feel more certain about Bob repaying the loan if she has information that Bob is reliable.

Although information is a straightforward remedy to uncertainty, gathering and evaluating information is costly and difficult (Simon, 1955; Kollock & O'Brien, 1992). Further, information asymmetries in exchange result because "minds are private"; that is, intentions are not known (Rasmusen, 1984; Kreps, 1990). Thus, social conditions can influence the availability and accessibility of information about potential exchange partners. Actors embedded in a social network may have information about a partner's history either from direct experience or from others in the network (Granovetter, 1985; Greif, 1989, 1993). In the example of interpersonal trust above, Alice may trust Bob, and thus be willing to lend him money, because he has honored her trust in the past or she may have information from others who vouch for Bob's reliability. Information about a partner's past reliability increases the likelihood of successful exchange (Burt & Knez, 1996; Dawes, 1980; Raub & Weesie, 1990). Somewhat differently, social relationships also can assure reliability not by providing information about a partner's past, but rather through providing incentives or constraints that ensure his good conduct in the future. Axelrod (1984) described how the "shadow of the future" in ongoing interaction can dissuade opportunistic behavior because mistreating a partner will have negative consequences for oneself. According to Hardin (2002, p.19), "shared interests make for the reliability of the trusted."

Uncertainty in exchange can also stem from lack of information about an exchange partner's competence to deliver on promises (Barber, 1983, pp.9-15; Heimer, 2001, p.44) or about the quality of the commodities traded (Akerlof, 1970; Greif, 1993; Kollock, 1994). That is, a trustee may fail to honor trust either because she is unwilling to do so or because she is unable, a distinct problem of *capability* or competence (Coleman, 1990 p. 96). Perceptions also matter: A party may be unwilling to trust another actor who she believes is incapable of honoring trust, even when such concerns are unjustified. When there is uncertainty about either competence or quality in exchange, actors will seek committed relationships (DiMaggio & Louch, 1998; Greif, 1989, 1993; Kollock, 1994). That is, they seek out social ties in order to use the reliability that they expect from their stable relationships to compensate for lack of information regarding capabilities. For example, high reliability through social relationships compensates for deficits in creditworthiness in microcredit borrowing groups (Anthony, 2005; Anthony & Horne, 2003) and in credit card markets (Guseva & Rona-Tas, 2001; see also Cook *et al*, 2004). Research on interpersonal trust typically avoids these complications by focusing on the problem of reliability, using ensured capability as an implicit scope condition (see Hardin, 2002; Gambetta, 1988; Luhman, 1988; Snijders, 1996). As a result, such theories of interpersonal trust only apply where a trustee's *capability* is not in question. Although researchers acknowledge that capability varies in empirical situations of interpersonal trust (e.g. Hardin, 2002: p. 8), they typically focus attention on motivational issues and leave questions of competence aside. The interplay of reliability and capability in interpersonal trust thus remains largely unexplored.

In the absence of social relationships, third party institutions can provide information regarding actors' reliability or capability to facilitate trusted exchange[1] (Heimer, 2001; Shapiro, 1987; Yamagishi, 1995; Zucker, 1986). As noted above, increased uncertainty regarding trading partners and transactions during the late 19th and early 20th centuries led to the creation of new institutions to provide information to unknown exchange partners or in new types of transactions. New

Table 1. Dimensions of reputation information for reducing uncertainty in trust dilemmas

Content of Information	Source of Information	
	INTERPERSONAL	**INSTITUTIONAL**
RELIABILITY	Direct experience Reputation: history of past reliable behavior Assurance mechanisms: norms, threat of peer sanctions	Record of past behavior Assurance mechanisms: contracts, laws, criminal and civil penalties
CAPABILITY	Observation: evidence of ability Reputation: performance history	Licensure and accreditation bodies Certification

third-party institutions for the licensure and accreditation of occupations and organizations, for example, became a source of information about actors' capabilities. Other institutions began to assure reliability, either through information about past behavior (e.g., Better Business Bureau) or by providing incentives to deliver on promises regardless of exchange partner identities (e.g., laws and regulatory bodies). Consistent with economic sociology claims regarding the role of institutions in markets, it is by "establishing particular legal, social and *informational* conditions, [that] institutions make the production, distribution, and exchange of commodities possible (Carruthers *et al*, 2001, p.94, italics added). Yamagishi and Yamagishi (1994) refer to these third party institutions as assurance rather than trust mechanisms to distinguish the sources of information and enforcement in institutional trust from those for interpersonal trust. For institutional trust, information comes from an organization, not peers, and may be regarding the reliability of an exchange partner, the capability, or both.

We can distinguish interpersonal from institutional forms of trust by considering differences along two dimensions of uncertainty-reducing information: (1) the content of the information about the trustee, and (2) the source of that information (see Table 1). The content of evaluative information about the trustee may be either the trustee's *reliability*, that is, the likelihood that the trustee *will* do the trusted action based on assessments of past behavior or future incentives and

constraints, or the trustee's *capability*, that is, the likelihood that the trustee *can* do the trusted action. There are also two general types of sources for evaluative information, *interpersonal sources* (whether direct ties to peers or indirect diffusion of information, such as reputations or gossip) or *institutional* sources (such as licensure and accreditation bodies).

Information from interpersonal sources, including both direct experience and reputation information from peers, may ameliorate uncertainty about the trustee's reliability. Interpersonal sources may also supply evaluative information on the trustee's capabilities, such as through a reputation for competence or resourcefulness. Information from institutional third parties may ameliorate uncertainties about either reliability of the trustee (either by an official record of past dealings, such as a criminal record, or legal constraints on future actions) or may provide a formal assessment of capabilities (such as licensure and accreditation). In this study, we present a set of individuals with a problem of uncertainty in exchange, and examine how these two different kinds of information from these two different sources may affect trust in online exchange.

Trust and Internet Exchange

Recent years have seen the rapid proliferation of online reputation and recommender systems, which rely on individuals sharing information about their experiences with individual sellers

(Cheshire & Cook, 2004; Resnick *et al,* 2000). Such systems provide low-cost reliability information from peers consistent with interpersonal trust (Kollock, 1999), despite the vast size of the network and the limited availability of personally identifying information online. Some argue that reputation systems could be the basis for all trusted Internet-based communication and exchange (e.g., Camp *et al*, 2002). In the large, open transaction system of the Internet, however, interpersonal trust is likely to become less effective over time, as suggested by Güth and Kliemt (2004; see also Yamagishi & Matsuda, 2003) because reputation systems work best in closed networks (Cheshire & Cook, 2004) and online reputations are vulnerable to strategic abuse (David & Pinch, 2005). However, new institutionalized sources of information that can overcome the limitations of interpersonal trust have yet to be established online.[2]

A SOCIAL EXPERIMENT FOR TRUST IN INTERNET EXCHANGE

To investigate how interpersonal and institutional trust mechanisms influence exchange, we developed a laboratory version of an online marketplace, in which consumers encounter simulated vendors. Each of 73 subjects took part in a series of purchase decisions from different vendors. More specifically, subjects visited a simulated website called "*WhatsThePrice.com*" which gave them an opportunity to either accept or decline a purchase from each of 12 vendors. Subjects earned points for making purchases from 'legitimate' vendors, but not for exchanges with vendors that were 'not legitimate' (i.e., where the vendor would not successfully complete the exchange, regardless of reason such as incompetence or fraud). Subjects began each round with a pool of 5 points and decided whether to make a purchase or not. If subjects chose to make a purchase and the vendor was legitimate, they tripled their 5 points to 15; if they chose to make a purchase but the vendor was not legitimate, they lost their 5 points; if they chose not to make a purchase they kept the 5 points.

The experiment simulates the truster's move in a standard trust game when the truster has the opportunity to engage in the exchange (trust the trustee) or not. Subjects were informed that they were helping to evaluate the characteristics and usability of a new website for consumers seeking information about online vendors. Subjects were not deceived in this experiment, and were completely aware that they were not making actual purchases from online vendors on a real web page.

For each vendor, subjects received information about the commodity for sale: the seller's asking price and a range of prices that contained the true fair market value of the item. For example, a subject may receive an invitation to buy an item for $9, along with the information that the item is truly worth anywhere from $6 to $15. The subjects also received a rating of the vendor; the source and the basis of this rating were manipulated in the experiment. Some of the items were cheap (with asking price from $8 to $25) and others were expensive (with asking price from $85 to $110). Each subject was exposed to 6 cheap items and 6 expensive items (within-subject exposure) and the fair market value range was held constant across vendors as a fixed proportion of the asking price.

Subjects were shown a rating of each vendor on a 1-5 scale (though all subjects saw ratings only in the range of 3-5). The scale was described as similar to a grading scale of A through F, in which 5=A or the highest rating possible, and 1=F or the lowest rating possible. The information content that was the basis for the rating (reliability versus capability) and the source of the rating (peers or institutions) varied across subjects for a 2 X 2 between-subjects design. Table 2 shows the four types of providers of the vendor ratings by the two dimensions of reputation information for trusted exchange. Subjects were informed of the different providers of vendor ratings, but each received ratings from only one provider (between subject exposure).

Table 2. Vendor rating providers by information dimensions for WhatsThePrice.com experimental online marketplace

Content of Information	Source of Information	
	INTERPERSONAL Rating	**INSTITUTIONAL Rating**
RELIABILITY *Vendor has history of conducting secure online transactions*	Customers' feedback about their experiences of the security of transactions with online vendors ~ www.BuyReliable.org ~ Reliable information from *consumers* like you!	Center for Online Purchase Reporting (COPR), an independent evaluation of vendors' record of secure transactions ~ www.COPR.org ~ Your independent *source* for reliable information!
CAPABILITY *Vender has technical capacity to conduct secure online transactions*	Customer assessments and discussion of the security of online vendors ~ www.BuySecure.org ~ Use the power of *consumer* feedback for online security!	Center for Secure Online Transactions (CSOT), a technical evaluation of vendors online security system ~ www.CSOT.org~ Your source for independent security information!

Consumer feedback and rating systems (column one in Table 2) provide information similar to word-of-mouth information in offline settings, that is, similar to social ties for interpersonal trust. Feedback systems provide information on a vendor's reliability based on the experiences of customers. Consumer rating systems offer customers the ability to evaluate vendors along various dimensions; here we define the rating as based on evaluations of security. Similarly, the two types of institutional sources (column two in Table 2) are independent third-party organizations that evaluate vendors on either their history of secure transactions (reliability) or their technical capability for conducting secure transactions.

In response to a recruitment advertisement, undergraduate students visited a website at which they completed an Informed Consent form and a brief survey regarding their experience in Internet commerce, risk preferences, generalized trust, and demographic characteristics. Upon completing the survey, subjects received a numeric identifier (ID). Subjects brought the ID to an experiment session in a public computer lab, where they received instructions and each subject completed the experiment at a private computer terminal. Subjects did not communicate with one another during the experiment and could not see other subjects' choices or outcomes.

At the end of the session, subjects completed a brief post-survey and were debriefed. The numeric ID was used to anonymously link the survey responses to the experiment results. Participation in the study required approximately 30-45 minutes of subjects' time, including both surveys and the experiment session. For this time, subjects were paid at least $5 and up to $20, depending on their outcomes in the experiment. The actual legitimacy of vendors was random and uncorrelated with ratings, regardless of the information content or source. Subjects did not learn the results of individual purchase decisions and did not receive even overall feedback on their performance until the end of the game, so no learning about vendor characteristics or other feedback on subject strategies was possible. We found no evidence of order effects.

Experiment Results

A total of 73 subjects participated in the experiment, with 12 rounds per session, for a total of n=876 observations. Two-thirds of the subjects were women (n=50) and 60% were white (n=44). Analyses treat information *content* (reliability, capability), information *source* (interpersonal, institutional), *price* (cheap, expensive), and *rating* (low, medium, high) as categorical independent

Figure 1. Likelihood of making purchase by price of goods and rating of vendor, n=876

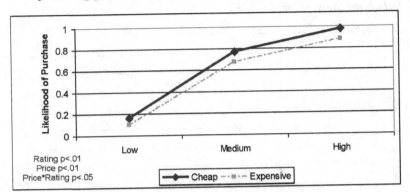

variables. Specifically, we model the odds of accepting purchases using logistic regression, with Huber-White robust standard errors for repeated observations by subject.

Figure 1 presents the predicted probabilities from models including only dummy variables for price and the three vendor rating levels. We see that few subjects were willing to make a purchase from vendors with low ratings, while the majority of subjects purchased at medium ratings, and almost all purchased from vendors with high ratings. The price of the goods also influenced subjects' willingness to purchase from online vendors; they were significantly more likely to purchase cheaper items overall (main effect of price is significant). The interaction of price and rating is statistically significant, although the effect of price is qualitatively similar for all vendor ratings, and vice versa.

The fact that subjects responded strongly and positively to vendor ratings is unsurprising. However, the mild negative effect of item price is intriguing, as subjects were aware that their performance in the experiment (and thus their rewards for participating) was not related to the money they spent in purchases; they were asked to judge only whether or not vendors were 'legitimate.' Apparently, they were less likely to judge a vendor as legitimate if the price was greater. It may be that they scrutinized high-cost goods

more carefully, even though the same amount of information was provided for all vendors, and subjects knew their outcomes were not related to price. Given that the fair value range was computed in proportion to the asking price, and thus the fair value range was greater in absolute terms for the more expensive items, it is possible that subjects may have perceived a higher uncertainty in the exchanges for expensive items. This uncertainty may have led them to judge the vendor as less legitimate, but further work is needed to investigate this conjecture.

Figure 2 shows the main experimental results for the effect of information content (reliability versus capability) on likelihood of making a purchase. While price and rating are still significant, there is no significant difference in likelihood of purchase between those who received reliability information versus those who received capability information. the two-way and three-way interactions between content, rating and price are also not significant (data not shown).

Figure 3 shows the results for the effect of information source (institutional vs. interpersonal ratings) on likelihood of purchase. The effects for price and rating are similar to those shown in Figure 1. Subjects were generally more likely to purchase when vendors were rated by an institutional rather than interpersonal source (consumers), but the main effect of source is not

Figure 2. Likelihood of making an online purchase by price of goods, vendor rating and content of information provided about the vendor, n=876

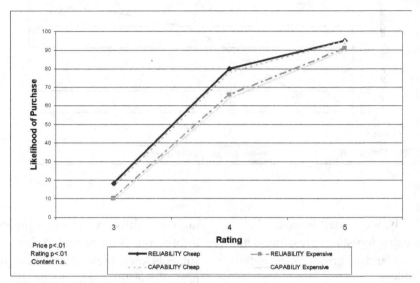

Figure 3. Likelihood of making an online purchase by price of goods, vendor rating and source of information about vender, n-876

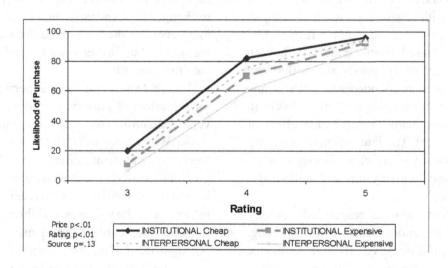

statistically significant. The two-way interaction between source and price is not significant but the interaction between source and rating is significant (p<.05). It appears that subjects felt most uncertain about, and therefore showed more variation in purchasing for vendors with a rating of 4. In contrast, the subjective strength of a 5 rating or the weakness of a 3 rating appear so salient that subjects do not discriminate very much by either information source or content in those conditions. If we look at the effect of source on willingness to purchase from vendors with a rating of 4 only, we find that source is significant (p<.05), with subjects more willing to trust institutional than interpersonal sources (data not shown). For these vendors, content remains not significant, and the interaction between source and content also is not significant.

In the full model for likelihood of purchase with rating, price, content and source, price ($p<.01$), rating ($p<.10$) and source ($p<.05$) are significant, but content again is not nor is the interaction between source and content (data not shown).

These findings indicate that consumers appear to be somewhat more willing to make an online purchase when they have information about vendors from institutional third parties rather than feedback from other consumers especially when they have greater uncertainty about the vendor (e.g., vendors with a rating of 4). This finding is notable given the prevalence of peer reputation and recommender systems on the Internet. Subjects were very responsive to ratings of vendors regardless of the basis of the rating; the content of information consumers receive regarding vendors' security (reliability versus capability) had no effect on purchase decisions here. Perhaps subjects attended so strongly to the value of the rating that they paid little attention to the content.

FUTURE RESEARCH DIRECTIONS

We have presented suggestive findings that subjects appear more likely to trust when reputation information comes from an institutional source, but that they do not differentiate capability information from reliability information in choosing to trust a vendor. It may be the case that this experimental setting does not adequately capture the online marketplace or that our focus on transaction security may not apply to other trust problems that arise in online exchange. Whether these findings generalize to other domains of uncertainty in online exchange remains a question for future research.

The very limited information regarding vendors provided in this experiment is not consistent with real-world websites. However, by designing and controlling an experimental online marketplace, we were able to investigate how specific forms and sources of information relevant to interpersonal and institutional trust influence consumers' willingness to make purchases from online vendors. Here we examined the simple question of whether subjects trusted in the vendor's legitimacy, controlling for price differences and holding constant the fair market value range as a proportion of the asking price. Future work may manipulate the fair market value range to represent uncertainty in product quality, such that some vendors offer items with much greater or lesser ambiguity in value. It also will allow subjects to bid what they would be willing to pay in the fair value range, giving a continuous measure of subjects' trust in the vendor.

This chapter has focused on the implications of uncertainty in Internet exchange but the advent of online exchange also increased vulnerability in transactions (the size of the potential loss). for example, to the extent that Internet infrastructure is not secure, such that aspects of the exchange are open to more than the two exchanging parties, entering a credit card number or bank account information may put one's account or identity at risk. Actors may be particularly concerned about losses to privacy because such damages are more difficult to quantify and therefore compensate. While important, the direct implications of increased vulnerability in Internet exchange are left to future work.

Future research may also consider differences in individual personality, including general attitudes toward trust (Simpson & McGrimmon 2008) as well as variations across cultures (Cook *et al*, 2005; Kuwabara *et al*, 2007) in attitudes and behavior toward risk and uncertainty. These may affect how individuals respond to different types and sources of reputation information. Such questions may be addressed through straightforward extensions of the experiment presented here.

CONCLUSION

Trust plays an important role in economic exchange. As new technologies emerge for conducting exchanges online, established mechanisms of trust are disrupted or distorted because of increased uncertainty, which can lead to a breakdown of exchange. Despite the high levels of uncertainty among exchange partners on the Internet, prevalent online trust mechanisms appear to be based on a model of interpersonal rather than institutional trust. This is somewhat surprising given the crucial role served by institutional third parties in evaluating the reliability and capability of trading partners before the advent of online exchange. Further, the evidence shown here from an experimental online marketplace indicates that although consumers are responsive to reputation information from either interpersonal or institutional sources, they are more likely to trust in exchange with anonymous vendors when given reputation information from institutional third parties. This provides some preliminary evidence that creation and dissemination of institutional sources of information may facilitate online trust and commerce, but more importantly provides a number of specific directions for future research, which may elaborate and refine this goal.

REFERENCES

Adler, M. (2009). History of NYC Sheet Music Store to Close. *NPR*. Retrieved from http://www.npr.org/templates/story/story.php?storyId=103728928

Akerlof, G. (1970). The market for lemons. *The Quarterly Journal of Economics, 84*, 488–500. doi:10.2307/1879431

Anthony, D. L. (2005). Cooperation in Micro-Credit Borrowing Groups: Identity, Sanctions and Reciprocity in the Production of Collective Goods. *American Sociological Review, 70*(1), 496–515. doi:10.1177/000312240507000307

Anthony, D. L., & Horne, C. (2003). Gender and Cooperation: Explaining loan repayment in micro-credit borrowing groups. *Social Psychology Quarterly, 66*(3), 293–302. doi:10.2307/1519827

Axelrod, R. (1984). *The Evolution of Cooperation*. New York: Basic Books.

Ba, S., Whinston, A. B., & Zhang, H. (2003). Building trust in online auction markets through an economic incentive mechanism. *Decision Support Systems, 35*(3), 273–286. doi:10.1016/S0167-9236(02)00074-X

Bacharach, M., & Gambetta, D. (2001). Trust in Signs. In Cook, K. S. (Ed.), *Trust in Society* (pp. 148–184). New York: Russell Sage Foundation.

Barber, B. (1983). *Logic and Limits of Trust*. New Brunswick, NJ: Rutgers University Press.

Baye, M. (2002). Special Issue on The economics of the Internet and e-commerce. *Advances in Applied Microeconomics, 11*.

Burt, R. S., & Knez, M. (1996). Trust and Third-Party Gossip. In Kramer, R. M., & Tyler, T. R. (Eds.), *Trust in Organizations: Frontiers of Theory and Research* (pp. 68–89). Thousand Oaks, CA: Sage.

Camp, L. J. (2000). *Trust and Risk in Internet Commerce*. Cambridge, MA: The MIT Press.

Camp, L. J., Nissenbaum, H., & McGrath, C. (2002). Trust: A collision of paradigms. *Lecture Notes in Computer Science, 2339*, 91–105. doi:10.1007/3-540-46088-8_10

Carruthers, B., Babb, S., & Halliday, T. (2001). Institutionalizing Markets, or the Market for Institutions? In Campbell, J. L., & Pedersen, O. K. (Eds.), *The Rise of Neoliberalism and Institutionalism Analysis* (pp. 94–126). Princeton, NJ: Princeton University Press.

Cheshire, C., & Cook, K. S. (2004). The Emergence of trust networks under uncertainty – Implications for Internet interactions. *Analyse & Kritik*, 26, 220–240.

Coleman, J. (1990). *Foundations of Social Theory*. Cambridge, MA: Belknap Press.

Cook, K. S., Rice, E. R., & Gerbasi, A. (2004). The Emergence of Trust Networks under Uncertainty: The Case of Transitional Economies – Insights from Social Psychological Research. In Ackerman, S. R., Rothstein, B., & Kornai, J. (Eds.), *Problems of Post Socialist Transition: Creating Social Trust*. New York: Palgrave.

Cook, K. S., Yamagishi, T., Cheshire, C., Cooper, R., Matsuda, M., & Rie, M. (2005). Trust Building via Risk Taking: A Cross-Societal Experiment. *Social Psychology Quarterly*, 68, 121–142. doi:10.1177/019027250506800202

Datta, P., & Chatterjee, S. (2008). The economics and psychology of consumer trust in intermediaries in electronic markets: the EM-Trust framework. *European Journal of Information Systems*, 17, 12–28. doi:10.1057/palgrave.ejis.3000729

David, S., & Pinch, T. (2005). Six Degrees of Reputation: The Use and Abuse of Online Review and Recommendation Systems. *Social Science Research Network Working Paper Series*.

Dawes, R. (1980). Social Dilemmas. *Annual Review of Psychology*, 31, 169–193. doi:10.1146/annurev.ps.31.020180.001125

DiMaggio, P., & Louch, H. (1998). Socially embedded consumer transactions: For what kinds of purchases do people most often use networks? *American Sociological Review*, 63, 619–637. doi:10.2307/2657331

Falcone, R., Singh, M., & Tan, Y. H. (2001). *Trust in Cyber-societies*. Berlin: Springer. doi:10.1007/3-540-45547-7

Friedman, E., & Resnick, P. (2001). The Social Costs of Cheap Pseudonyms. *Journal of Economics & Management Strategy*, 10(2), 173. doi:10.1162/105864001300122476

Froomkin, A. M. (1996). The essential role of trusted third parties in electronic commerce. In Kalakota, R., & Whinston, A. B. (Eds.), *Readings in Electronic Commerce*. Reading, MA: Addison-Wesley.

Gambetta, D. (1988). Can We Trust Trust? In Gambetta, D. (Ed.), *Trust Making and Breaking Cooperative Relations*. New York: Basil Blackwell.

Garfinkle, H. (1967). *Studies in Ethnomethodology*. Englewood Cliffs, NJ: Prentice Hall.

Granovetter, M. (1985). Economic Action and Social Structure: The Problem of Embeddedness. *American Journal of Sociology*, 91, 481–510. doi:10.1086/228311

Greif, A. (1989). Reputation and Coalitions in medieval trade: Evidence on the Maghribi traders coalition. *The Journal of Economic History*, 49, 857–882. doi:10.1017/S0022050700009475

Greif, A. (1993). Contract enforceability and economic institutions in early trade: The Maghribi traders coalition. *The American Economic Review*, 83, 525–548.

Guseva, A., & Rona-Tas, A. (2001). Uncertainty, Risk and Trust: Russian and American Credit Card Markets Compared. *American Sociological Review*, 66(5), 623–646. doi:10.2307/3088951

Güth, W., & Kliemt, H. (2004). The Evolution of Trust(worthiness) in the Net. *Analyse & Kritik*, 26, 203–219.

Hardin, R. (2002). *Trust and Trustworthiness*. New York: Russell Sage.

Heimer, C. A. (2001). Solving the problem of trust. In Cook, K. S. (Ed.), *Trust in Society* (pp. 40–88). New York: Russell Sage Foundation.

Kollock, P. (1994). The Emergence of Exchange Structures: An Experimental Study of Uncertainty, Commitment and Trust. *American Journal of Sociology, 100*, 313–345. doi:10.1086/230539

Kollock, P. (1999). The Production of trust in online markets. *Advances in Group Processes, 16*, 99–123.

Kollock, P., & O'Brien, J. (1992). The Social Construction of Exchange. *Advances in Group Processes, 9*, 89–112.

Kreps, D. (1990). *Game Theory and Economic Modeling*. New York: Oxford University Press. doi:10.1093/0198283814.001.0001

Kuwabara, K., Willer, R., Macy, M. W., Mashima, R., Shigeru, T., & Yamagishi, T. (2007). Culture, Identity, and Structure in Social Exchange: A Web-based Experiment in the United States and Japan. *Social Psychology Quarterly, 70*, 461–479. doi:10.1177/019027250707000412

Luhmann, N. (1979). *Trust and Power*. Chichester, UK: Wiley.

Luhmann, N. (1988). Familiarity, Confidence, Trust: Problems and Alternatives. In Gambetta, D. (Ed.), *Trust Making and Breaking Cooperative Relations* (pp. 94–107). New York: Basil Blackwell.

Lunn, R., & Suman, M. (2002). Experience and Trust in Online Shopping. In Wellman, B., & Haythornthwaite, C. (Eds.), *The Internet in Everyday Life*. Oxford, UK: Blackwell. doi:10.1002/9780470774298.ch19

Molm, L. D., Takahashi, N., & Peterson, G. (2000). Risk and Trust in Social Exchange: An Experimental Test of a Classical Proposition. *American Journal of Sociology, 105*, 1396–1427. doi:10.1086/210434

Perrow, C. (2002). *Organizing America*. Princeton, NJ: Princeton University Press.

Rasmusen, E. (1994). *Games and Information* (2nd ed.). Cambridge, MA: Blackwell.

Raub, W., & Weesie, J. (1990). Reputation and Efficiency in Social Interactions: An Example of Network Effects. *American Journal of Sociology, 96*, 626–654. doi:10.1086/229574

Resnick, P., Zeckhauser, R., Friedman, E., & Kuwabara, K. (2000). Reputation systems: Facilitating trust in Internet interactions. *Communications of the ACM, 43*, 45–48. doi:10.1145/355112.355122

Schutz, A. (1970). *On Phenomenology and Social Relations: Selected Writings*. Chicago, IL: University of Chicago Press.

Shapiro, S. P. (1987). The Social Control of Impersonal Trust. *American Journal of Sociology, 93*, 623–658. doi:10.1086/228791

Simon, H. (1955). A Behavioral Model of Rational Choice. *The Quarterly Journal of Economics, 63*, 129–138.

Simpson, B., & McGrimmon, T. (2008). Trust and Embedded Markets: A Multi-method Investigation of Consumer Transactions. *Social Networks, 30*, 1–15. doi:10.1016/j.socnet.2007.04.004

Snijders, C. (1996). *Trust and Commitments*. Gronigen, Netherlands: Interuniversity Center for Social Science Theory and Methodology.

Yamagishi, T. (1995). Social Dilemmas. In Cook, K. S., Fine, G. A., & House, J. (Eds.), *Sociological Perspectives on Social Psychology*. Boston: Allyn & Bacon.

Yamagishi, T., & Matsuda, M. (2003). The Role of Reputation in Open and Closed Societies: An Experimental Study of Online Trading. *Center for the Study of Cultural and Ecological Foundations of Mind, Working Paper Series 8*. Retrieved May 1, 2009, from http://lynx.let.hokudai.ac.jp/COE21/english/workingpaper/index.html

Yamagishi, T., & Yamagishi, M. (1994). Trust and Commitment in the United States and Japan. *Motivation and Emotion, 18*, 129–166. doi:10.1007/BF02249397

Ye, Z., Smith, S. W., & Anthony, D. (2005). Trusted Paths for Browsers. [TISSEC]. *ACM Journal Transactions on Information and System Security, 8*(2), 153–186. doi:10.1145/1065545.1065546

Zucker, L. G. (1986). Production of Trust: Institutional Sources of Economic Structure, 1840-1920. In Staw, B. M., & Cummings, L. L. (Eds.), *Research in Organizational Behavior* (*Vol. 8*, pp. 53–111). Greenwich, CT: JAI Press Inc.

ENDNOTES

[1] Third party institutions also facilitate trust by limiting truster's vulnerability in exchange (see Heimer, 2001).

[2] Of course some institutional third parties do exist to promote online exchange, such as certification authorities (CAs) like Veri-Sign, which authenticate the identity of trading parties in an online transaction (Ba *et al*, 2002; Froomkin, 1996). CAs play an important role in electronic commerce by authenticating actors (websites) and attesting to certain facts about them, making it somewhat more difficult for an online actor to change his identity. However, consumers do not necessarily understand the role or limits of CAs (Datta & Chatterjee, 2008), nor are such entities resistant to corruption or abuse (Ye *et al*, 2005).

Chapter 17
Millennials, Social Networking, and Trust

Kurt Komaromi
Ithaca College, USA

Fahri Unsal
Ithaca College, USA

G. Scott Erickson
Ithaca College, USA

ABSTRACT

Trust in exchanges is an important concept in business and has become of topic of some interest in e-commerce. Substantial work has been done on how institutional mechanisms, technology, word-of-mouth, and numerous other variables affect trust in a website and potential customers' willingness to conduct business there. This study continues that line of research by considering how the millennial generation perceives the trustworthiness of three types of online sites: a retailer, an auction site, and a social networking site. Little work has been done on whether social network sites have more or less trust than other types of websites and what aspects of trust are affected. Given the broad trend toward utilizing these social network sites for commercial purposes, it makes sense to assess how targeted users view and interact with them. This study presents preliminary data on all of these issues, suggesting that there do appear to be differences between social network sites and more traditional online vendors.

INTRODUCTION

The advent of the Internet has thrust the concept of trust into a number of new and exciting contexts. Specifically, the ability to communicate and interact on an on-demand basis though without face-to-face contact has created a variety of new situations and issues with which we have never before had to deal.

Virtual commercial relationships have been a topic of special interest, as a number of things taken for granted in the physical world are more problematic when buyer and seller do not meet face-to-face. A substantial literature has developed on trust and Internet transactions, a literature we will reference. But relatively little scholarship has considered the impact of social networking sites on

DOI: 10.4018/978-1-61520-901-9.ch017

trust, particularly within the millennial generation most comfortable with a Web 2.0 world and targeted by such sites.

This paper examines the differences in trust levels between different types of websites, specifically those offering traditional e-commerce transactions with an established retailer, those based on more of a peer-to-peer relationship, and those based on a social network. The comparison of the three allows a mix of factors such as institution, website characteristics, word-of-mouth, and others. In particular, we can review whether reviews and recommendations from social network site peers matter more or less than those found at an established retail site or those at an open exchange.

BACKGROUND

As trust issues have developed as a key and much-studied topic in e-commerce, our literature review will concentrate chiefly on the established scholarship in that area. Initially, however, we can define some of the major issues regarding trust, particularly in business relationships, from a more general perspective.

The conceptual basis of trust came out of sociology (e.g. Gambetta 1988). Garfinkel (1963) established a number of critical ideas: trust is apparent in individual action; it is interactive in terms of relationships, expectations and behavior of others; and it is based on symbiosis and exchange. Further, trust is dependent on situation and circumstance (Baier 1986), and individuals develop routines based on the conditions of a particular trust relationship (Giddens 1991).

This general framework has then been applied to the more business-oriented applications including organization to organization, organization to individual (employees), and organization to individual (customers). Under such conditions, a more rational view of trust developed, particularly from the aspect of calculative self-interest (Coleman 1990). The reduction in transaction costs

and deeper relationships accomplished through trusting an opposite party can be weighed and evaluated by both individuals and organizations, leading to more cooperation and more efficiency when trust is present (Axelrod 1990).

Specifically in the field of marketing and exchange, trust also has a long history. Obviously again, a situational application that defines the nature of trust involved, marketing typically looks at a commercial exchange and the trust found in the trading partners. Trust can be defined in this context as expectations concerning the behavior of the opposite party (Mayer, et. al. 1995). And it is conceptualized as having three parts (Bakker, et. al. 2006; Collins & Smith 2006; Marshall, et. al. 2005):

- Capability, a belief that an exchange partner is able to perform as promised,
- Benevolence, a belief that an exchange partner wants to perform as promised, and
- Integrity, a belief that an exchange partner will live up to the agreement.

The overall level of trust is further influenced by factors such as strength of the relationship (Collins & Smith 2006; Foos, et. al. 2006), shared fields of experience (Lin 2006), power (Collins & Smith 2006; Nielsen 2005), and virtuality (Choi & Lee 2003).

Strength of relationship and the closely related concept of social capital (Vainio 2005; Tsai 2000) also have an impact on trust. Strength in a relationship builds up over time as partners successfully complete transactions, also referred to as repeated interactions (Lewis and Weigert 1985). Partners with such a satisfactory history will, of course, have more belief in the capability, benevolence, and integrity of their counterparties. Further, from a social capital perspective, partners with a high structural component (central to many relationships) and high relational component (perceived trustworthiness by others in the network) will be viewed more favorably based on the strength of relationship with numerous past partners and potential for numerous future relationships (Anderson & Naurus 1990).

Shared fields of experience (often used in the communication literature) relates to similar backgrounds, be they cultural ties, interests, and other such connectors, referred to in the trust literature as shared norms and/or shared experiences. When the party on the other side of the exchange is someone or something to which one can relate, trust comes more easily.

Power possessed or power released in an exchange also affect trust. If one side of a relationship has power, the other side is unlikely to act opportunistically as retribution may occur. When power is transferred, trust may decline on one side and increase on the other as the perceived potential for payback changes.

Virtual relationships raise difficulties regarding trust as in-person interaction has been seen as critical to the process (O'Hara-Devereaux & Johansen 1994). Common measures used to assess trustworthiness such as eye contact and body language are impossible in an online environment. As a consequence, establishing trust in other ways is critical.

So although there continues to be some discussion among scholars about precisely what trust might be in different situations, we have a fairly clear definition for exchange relationships in business. An individual or organization's willingness to be vulnerable based on a belief in the other party's capability benevolence, and integrity. Further research in this area has suggested that trust can be influenced by strength of relationship and social capital, shared fields of experience, power, and virtuality. As we shall discuss, not all necessarily apply to the situation described in this paper, but they provide a basis for study and analysis.

But a number of these issues, most obviously virtuality, have indeed echoed in scholarly work on trust in e-commerce. As we all know, e-commerce has a special interest in returning customers as opposed to constantly recruiting new custom-

ers at high expense (though new customers are important, too). Since trust is associated with return customers, it is a particularly important and challenging factor in online business (Reichheld & Schefter 2000, Gefen 2000). Moreover, because there is more uncertainty with virtual online vendors, the perceived risk in executing an exchange is higher and trust more difficult to establish (Jarvenpaa & Tractinsky 1999).

One broad stream in the literature is that loyalty and trust in e-commerce is based on the site's information technology (IT) and trust in the vendor (Gefen, Karahanna & Straub 2003). The IT component can be measured by an existing technology acceptance model (TAM) (Davis 1989; Davis, Bagozzi & Warshaw 1989). TAM considers the usefulness of the site and the perceived ease of use. Incorporating these measures into a trust study both focuses the trust variables and indicates when the IT may influence the trust variables themselves.

Trust in the vendor, on the other hand, flows from several things, including the individual's personality and disposition to trust, cognition (perceived similarity), familiarity, calculative reassurance, and situational variables (Kim & Ahn 2006; Chen & Dhillon 2003; Gefen, Karahanna & Straub 2003). Most of these should be familiar from the above discussion. In short:

- **Disposition:** some individuals are more trusting, in general, than others.
- **Cognition:** if an individual can relate to the site, other users, or the community that makes up the site, he/she are more willing to extend trust.
- **Familiarity:** if a site is familiar to an individual, especially through past use, he/she is more willing to extend trust.
- **Calculative reassurance:** if an individual can convince themselves that an established firm or brand is unlikely to behave opportunistically, he/she is more willing to extend trust.

- **Situational:** the nature of the product, the IT of the website, and other such factors may also impact the willingness to extend trust.

Implicit in this general description are a number of related issues that can be assessed to get a better handle on what kinds of e-commerce approaches inspire more or less trust. Initially, there is the effect of outside validators. Seals and certifications, affiliations, and other institution-based reassurances via third parties can obviously help (McKnight, Cummins & Chavarty 1998). The "normality" of the site, whether it works as a similar site is expected to work, requesting similar information, processing the exchange in an appropriate manner is also an issue (McKnight, Cummins & Chavarty 1998). So the prospective buyer reviews a website, looking at the IT structure, the third party assurances, the normality of the experience, and a number of other features to assess the trustworthiness of the vendor.

Closely related to this is the power of word-of-mouth in enhancing trust (Awad & Ragowsky 2008). E-vendors have rapidly adopted a capability to provide feedback from exchange partners concerning the products purchased, satisfaction with the overall experiences, and other such feedback. Customer ratings and customer reviews both help to build trust in the e-vendor itself and in specific products or brands offered for sale on the site.

Finally and again closely related, there is the potential for site-based communities or social networking sites to further enhance trust. We've already noted how the literature has included cognition, familiarity, and now word-of-mouth as important variables in building trust. When one starts putting those together at a social networking site, with members similar to the potential buyer, with whom the buyer deals on a regular basis, and which might include reviews and recommendations from members, there are some quite interesting questions regarding trust. We explore these in the following study.

CONCEPTUAL FOUNDATION AND METHODOLOGY

The basic thrust of this research is to determine the impact of social network sites on trust toward e-vendors. As established in the literature above, we can conceptualize the framework as follows:

- Trust, based on capability, benevolence, integrity
- General factors influencing trust:
  - Strength of relationship
  - Shared experience
  - Power
  - Virtuality
- E-commerce factors (extending virtuality)
  - Personal orientation
  - Nature of the vendor (IT, outside certifications, reputation)
  - Word-of-mouth

Through the design of the study, we were able to use the existing TAM framework and associated survey to address this conceptualization of trust as well as potential factors of perceived ease of use of the site and perceived usefulness of the site. Further extensions on the framework were able to better verify trust through specific behaviors (turning over personal information) while also bringing intended use and word-of-mouth factors into the mix. Other factors in the framework were either not included (power seemed immaterial to these circumstances) or muted by the study design (all vendors/sites are well-established, reputable and certified; all respondents should have similar personal orientations and shared experience). One key difference in all this is the crux of the study, whether institutional credibility of the site engenders more trust than the shared experience of a social networking site. Further, do other factors such as word-of-mouth vary in this context?

For the study, we chose a single product, the Blackberry Storm from Research in Motion (RIM), with which we thought the sample would

Figure 1.

	Institutional Credibility		Social Network	
Amazon	Yes		No	
eBay	No		No	
Facebook	No		Yes	

be familiar and have some interest. We identified the product offered for sale or promoted by RIM with a direct link to a purchase page at Amazon, eBay, and Facebook. As noted above, we chose these sites for a number of reasons suggested in the literature:

- All are well-known and well-established, mitigating any impact from disposition, familiarity, calculative reassurance, and situation.
- All have numerous outside validators.
- All offer the product for sale or, in the case of Facebook, a product page with a direct link back to a purchase site at RIM.
- All have product or vendor reviews and recommendations.
- Amazon has the highest level of institutional credibility as the company stands behind both the website and direct transactions.
- Facebook, as a social network, has the highest level of cognition as users interact with and relate to the community. Facebook is not the actual vendor, however, and does not offer any institutional support for products.
- eBay does not have as strong a social network nor does it have a strong institutional commitment, as sellers are independent, often unfamiliar vendors. The site does provide feedback on vendors but lacks the direct oversight of an Amazon (which does include independent vendors, too, but to a lesser degree). The community, to some

extent, polices the vendors, but the community is less connected than is the case with Facebook.

And in terms of the critical distinction between the sites, we have the established business site of Amazon on one hand, with certain perceptions and expectations of behavior because it is commercial vs. the social networking site of Facebook, with high shared experience but limited (though growing) commercial applications. These distinctions, with eBay as something of a control, can be summarized as follows:

Our sample included college students from a small, private school in the Northeastern US. This is a convenience sample but also one that obviously includes the millennial generation we were targeting with this research (because they are the group targeted by a social network site such as Facebook). While results should be extended to other demographic groups only with great care, they are relevant in terms of how technology users of this age and socioeconomic group view online vendors or related sites. As noted, the sample was homogeneous in a number of ways, but that was also by design so as to focus on the technology and trust variables, not differences in the sample. The one demographic variable we did track was gender, which has been shown to have an impact on trust in a previous study (Awad & Ragowsky 2008).

A sample of approximately 285 (over 300 students were targeted, but there was some unknown overlap and students were instructed to participate

Table 1. Trust perception, ANOVA results

Statement	Amazon	eBay	Facebook	F calculated (F critical = 3.05)	p-Value (95%*, 99%**)
T1: Honest	2.06	2.32	2.75	12.84	0.000006**
T2: Cares about consumers	2.18	2.65	2.72	8.11	0.0004**
T3: Not opportunistic	2.83	3.03	3.06	1.33	0.26
T4: Good service	2.13	2.26	2.76	11.13	0.00003**
T5: Trustworthy	2.10	2.56	3.03	22.06	3.0 E-9**
T6: Knows its market	2.04	2.32	2.31	2.23	0.11

only once) was constructed. Respondents were given extra credit in classes for participating. Respondents were alerted by email and guided to two links, one to a webpage featuring the Blackberry device on one of the three websites and one to the survey. Respondents were also sent a reminder email a few days after the initial request. Respondents were directed to review the website, including reviews and recommendations, and then complete the survey. The survey was constructed from a number of the sources already cited, particularly the TAM model as employed by Gefen, Karahanna & Straub (2003) and some word-of-mouth additions from Awad & Ragoswky (2008). The verbatim survey is included in the appendix.

DATA ANALYSIS AND DISCUSSION

Data are reported in the accompanying tables. The responses totaled 68 for Amazon, 67 for Facebook, and 34 for eBay, with a little minor variation (a respondent or two) on some questions. The lower response rate for eBay was due to logistical problems, not a different propensity for response among the sample. As eBay is included for context, the problem was not deemed critical. The response rate was approximately 59%.

As noted, the questionnaire and exact wording is included in an appendix. The following tables report the responses, according to a five-point Likert scale (coded 1, SA, to 5, SD). Although categorical data, we did analyze the results using means and standard deviations, as is commonly done. ANOVA results, testing differences among the multiple means, are included in the following tables.

As noted in the above sections, the questions were validated in previous studies. They specifically measure a number of aspects of overall trust in a website (reported in Table 1), technological acceptance in terms of perceived ease of use and perceived usefulness (Tables 2 & 3), and intended use (Table 4). The last grouping includes several outcomes relating to trust, including willingness to use the site for search, willingness to surrender personal information, willingness to trust site

Table 2. Ease of use perception, ANOVA results

Statement	Amazon	eBay	Facebook	F calculated (F critical = 3.05)	p-Value (95%*, 99%**)
PEU1: Easy to use	1.71	1.85	1.92	1.80	0.17
PEU2: Easy to become skillful	1.79	1.88	1.92	0.61	.054
PEU3: Interaction clear	1.82	1.88	1.89	0.22	0.80

Table 3. Usefulness perception, ANOVA results

Statement	Amazon	eBay	Facebook	F calculated (F critical = 3.05)	p-Value (95%*, 99%**)
PU1: Useful for searching and buying	1.84	2.09	3.00	35.93	1.0 E-13**
PU2: Improves searching and buying performance	2.27	2.56	3.24	20.14	1.5 E-8**
PU3: Provide useful information	1.83	2.15	2.79	21.11	6.7 E-9**

recommendations and willingness to trust customer reviews. Shorthand descriptions of each question/variable are included in the tables. The full language of each, once again, is included in the appendix.

The survey is constructed in a fashion to allow factor analysis and other correlation techniques, so we have also included partial correlation matrices. These reflect only the relationship of the individual questions/variables to the trust variables. The internal correlations of each section are not reported here, but they were satisfactorily strong.

As the data clearly show, Amazon is more trusted on every single variable, to a highly significant degree on the vast majority of them. Facebook is less trusted on almost every single variable, and eBay consistently takes the middle position, sometimes closer to Amazon. The overall conclusion has to be that Amazon is perceived a significantly more trustworthy.

Not surprisingly, Table 2 suggests that respondents see little difference between the ease of use of the technology at each site. Again, by intention, we included sites that were slick and contained the latest technology.

The results are more varied in terms of usefulness, depicted in Table 3, a group of measures also used to separate technology from trust in terms of willingness to use. Generally, Amazon and eBay are perceived as much more useful, at least in this context of searching for and purchasing a personal electronics product. Facebook is not seen as providing useful search and buying

information, does not improve that process, and doesn't have particularly useful information. In some ways, this is not surprising, as Facebook is a social networking site, not a vendor. On the other hand, given the substantial interest in using social networks for commercial purposes, this is an extremely interesting result. We can explore this further with some of the following questions and results, but the natural conclusion is that these respondents, the millennial generation that uses social networking sites extensively, doesn't see them as a place to look for thinking about buying products or actually executing the purchase.

Table 4 breaks out some of the concepts in more detail. The search and research question obviously mirrors the usefulness perception questions but add some additional and subtle distinctions including research; differences among search, research, and purchase; and, most importantly, can be used to evaluate the technology access perceptions and the overall trust perceptions with the activities for which the respondents are willing to use the websites. The reported results are fairly emphatic, with uniformly higher acceptance of Amazon, then eBay, and then Facebook far behind along all variables. In particular, Amazon is decidedly favored when anything regarding purchase is included in the question. Again, the institutional reassurances seem to be the most powerful in instilling enough trust to conduct activities related to commerce. And, interestingly, the cognition reassurances, the impact of a social network or community with which this

Table 4. Intended use, ANOVA results

Statement (*negatively worded)	Amazon	eBay	Facebook	F calculated (F critical = 3.05)	p-Value (95%*, 99%**)
Search and Research					
Increases my productivity in searching	2.25	2.35	2.93	14.06	2.3 E-6**
Enables me to search and buy faster	2.10	2.32	3.09	21.01	7.3 E-9**
Improves my performance in searching and researching information	2.18	2.56	2.88	12.08	1.3 E-5**
Enhances my effectiveness for search, researching, and buying	2.12	2.47	2.96	18.19	7.2 E-8**
Security with Personal Information					
Willing to use credit card	1.81	2.21	3.50	48.44	2.6 E-17**
Willing to provide personal information	2.96	3.00	3.39	3.09	0.048*
Product Recommendations					
Recommendations not the information I need*	3.31	3.09	3.21	0.82	0.44
Provides useful recommendations	2.22	2.62	2.58	4.66	0.011*
Provides relevant recommendations	2.26	2.44	2.54	2.00	0.14
Provides helpful recommendations	2.35	2.45	2.43	0.25	0.78
Customer Reviews					
Customer reviews not the information I need*	3.66	3.29	3.13	5.60	0.004**
Provides useful customer reviews	1.87	2.38	2.43	7.99	0.0005**
Provides relevant customer reviews	2.00	2.18	2.45	4.82	0.009**
Provides helpful customer reviews	1.96	2.27	2.38	4.54	0.012*

group feels comfortable does not add much to commercial trust. Indeed, given the other results, it may subtract from it.

The second group of responses in Table 4 have to do with surrendering credit card and/ or personal information. Again, this is a further aspect of trust—how far will the respondents go with surrendering information given the level of trust in the site. These results are also very interesting as respondents readily turn over credit card information to both Amazon and eBay but not to a Facebook page sponsored by a producer. At the same time, however, they are much less willing to provide other personal information. One could speculate that perhaps this generation effectively differentiates sites and similarly differentiates what types of information the sites need or don't need to conduct business. They provide what they feel is needed and are more skeptical of other requests. This perspective would go naturally

Table 5. Partial correlation matrix: Amazon

Statement	T1	T2	T3	T4	T5	T6
PEU1	.117	-.015	.088	-.067	.085	.388**
PEU2	.041	.009	.147	.076	.146	.281*
PEU3	.135	.119	.021	.156	.149	.402**
PU1	.216	.215	.140	.009	.187	.043
PU2	.243*	.250*	.310*	.152	.354**	.174
PU3	.289*	.401**	.071	.224	.316**	.221
I1	.200	.316**	.046	.207	.239	.109
I2	.248*	.298*	-.025	.194	.246*	.154
I3	.352**	.320**	.306*	.189	.414**	.020
I4	.383**	.347**	.199	.160	.353**	.209
I5	.234	.222	.029	.197	.489**	.161
I6	.321**	.382**	.209	.251*	.393**	.177
I7	.080	.014	.337**	-.014	-.030	-.143
I8	.221	.174	-.028	.046	.235	.046
I9	.309*	.288*	.081	.138	.452**	.296*
I10	.310*	.278**	-.083	.265*	.349**	.202
I11	-.001	-.050	.188	-.114	-.079	-.090
I12	.233	.238	.112	.236	.302*	.146
I13	.280*	.127	.292*	.063	.283*	.218
I14	.217	.144	-.013	.192	.300*	.196

with some of the earlier results and discussion, that social networking sites don't add much to commercial-related trust as users don't view them as participating in that part of their lives.

The third group of responses in Table 4 relate to product recommendations ("if you like/bought this…, then you might like this…"). This result is quite compelling as we finally see the social networking site have an impact equal to or above the other sites. And this makes sense. We're now talking about recommendations (word-of-mouth in the literature) from either a peer community or one designated a peer community by the vendor (based on common purchasing characteristics). Purchase doesn't even necessarily come into it, as it's more a matter of checking into music, video, media, or other things that might be purchased but that the subject would probably research first

anyway. So although trusting recommendations doesn't have high agreement relative to some other aspects of this survey, the relative level of the Facebook ratings is distinct and compelling.

Finally, the fourth group in Table 4 is somewhat similar, looking to product/vendor reviews by other users/customers. On one hand, we are back to purchase and commerce concerns (I bought it, now what do I think of it?), and the institutional trust in Amazon reappears, with high levels of trust in reviews posted there. On the other hand, the reviews are posted by a community with some similarity to the respondents, a particularly close community in the case of Facebook. Consequently, both the institutional and the community factors appear to be at work with this aspect of word-of-mouth.

Tables 5, 6, and 7 indicate the correlations between the questions, providing insights into

Table 6. Partial correlation matrix: eBay

	T1	T2	T3	T4	T5	T6
PEU1	-.029	.085	.087	.026	.132	-.225
PEU2	.102	.186	.169	.258	.172	-.049
PEU3	.146	.266	.072	.277	.264	.017
PU1	.183	.224	.239	.273	.552**	-.212
PU2	.343*	.427*	.285	.233	.573**	.149
PU3	-.031	.174	.146	.091	.356*	-.162
I1	.442**	.210	.586**	.165	.335	.006
I2	.300	.378*	.362*	.205	.358*	.183
I3	-.007	.078	.124	-.002	.315	-.140
I4	.142	.213	.383*	.149	.446**	-.230
I5	.506**	.516**	.201	.558**	.574**	.053
I6	.127	.290	.193	.273	.561**	-.197
I7	.047	-.163	-.004	-.136	-.136	.201
I8	.286	.479**	.157	.318	.507**	-.073
I9	.144	.345*	.210	.099	.340*	-.034
I10	.135	.280	.373*	.322	.389*	.025
I11	-.065	-.356*	-.016	-.149	-.132	-.057
I12	-.008	.195	.217	-.018	.214	-.108
I13	.305	.360*	.342*	.390*	.366*	.155
I14	.382*	.360*	.345*	.335	.414*	-.143

the specific items that relate to higher trust levels in the websites.

Perceived Ease of Use (PEU) appears to have little to do with Trust for any of the websites, especially eBay. The exceptions are the very strong correlations between all the PEU variables and the "knows its market" variable for both Amazon and Facebook—essentially a measure of competence. So an easy to use website may have something to do with establishing credibility but little else that has to do with trust, regardless of the type of website.

Perceived Usefulness (PU) appears to be more of a factor. In particular the patterns of the correlations are very similar for Amazon and Facebook once again, with strong relationships between the PU variables and the trust variables of honesty, care, and trustworthiness (related to benevolence and integrity). eBay also has a very strong correlation along the trustworthiness dimension. A useful website, and this may relate to past experience that has formed the perception, is perceived as more trustworthy.

Search and Research (SR, I1-I4)), the next four questions/variables, shows much the same thing, as would be expected. Again, what we see in Amazon and Facebook are very similar patterns, again correlating with the honesty, care, and trustworthiness variables. eBay is again somewhat less correlated and has a different pattern than the other two sites, showing particular strength with SR correlating to the "not opportunistic" trust variable as well as in the trustworthiness column. How a respondent means to use the website correlates to trust is almost identical for Amazon and Facebook, less so for eBay.

Table 7. Partial correlation matrix: Facebook

	T1	T2	T3	T4	T5	T6
PEU1	.117	-.015	.088	-.067	.085	.388**
PEU2	.041	.009	.147	.076	.146	.281*
PEU3	.135	.119	.021	.156	.149	.402**
PU1	.216	.215	.140	.009	.187	.043
PU2	.243*	.250*	.310*	.152	.354**	.174
PU3	.289*	.401**	.071	.224	.316**	.221
I1	.200	.316**	.046	.207	.239	.109
I2	.248*	.298*	-.025	.194	.246*	.154
I3	.352**	.320**	.306*	.189	.414**	.020
I4	.383**	.347**	.199	.160	.353**	.209
I5	.234	.222	.029	.197	.489**	.161
I6	.321**	.382**	.209	.251*	.393**	.177
I7	.080	.014	.337**	-.014	-.030	-.143
I8	.221	.174	-.028	.046	.235	.046
I9	.309*	.288*	.081	.138	.452**	.296*
I10	.310*	.378**	-.083	.265*	.349**	.202
I11	-.001	-.050	.188	-.114	-.079	-.090
I12	.233	.238	.112	.236	.302*	.146
I13	.280*	.127	.292*	.063	.283*	.218
I14	.217	.144	-.013	.192	.300*	.196

Personal Information (PI, I5-I6) has some very interesting results. For Amazon and Facebook, the willingness to share personal information correlates very strongly with a number of trust variables, the willingness to share a credit card number with trustworthiness. For eBay, it's just the opposite, with the credit card variable correlating closely with several trust variables, personal information with trustworthiness. This may have something to do with the tendency of Amazon and Facebook to collect information explicitly and implicitly, and then use it to tailor the site to individuals. Regardless, the personal information to be surrendered is different and important to establishing trust at these sites.

Product Recommendations (PR, I7-I10) continues the theme of similar patterns with Amazon and Facebook, with a number of variables linked to trust, most of them the same between the two sites. eBay also shows several correlations, though not necessarily the same variables. Belief in product recommendations seems to have clear links to trust in the site.

Finally, Customer Reviews (CR, I11-I14) shows much the same thing, with some correlations between these variables and trust (particularly trustworthiness) for the Amazon and Facebook sites. What is different are the much more numerous significant correlations in the eBay results, with variables across the board in both the trust group and the CR group showing relationships. With the nature of eBay, that's really not surprising as customer reviews establish the credibility of the individual vendors, not eBay itself (at least not to the extent of a more controlling Amazon). But it is good to see it verified in the data.

Given these results, what overall conclusions can we draw? The major one is that even though the respondents had significantly greater trust in Amazon than Facebook, the same factors (and the same variables in the factors) drive trust. So if Facebook doesn't have the same level of trust, it's because it's perceived as less useful, less effective in search and research, less secure, less believable in product recommendations, and less believable in customer reviews. The same things drive confidence in the site as with Amazon, so if it is to succeed in becoming more commercial, it needs similar perceived performance in all these areas that drive trust. Even though social network rather than institutionally credible, it requires similar tools to gain success.

eBay, on the other hand, seems something of a different animal. Having neither a social network nor institutional credibility to the same extent as the comparison sites, it appears to be able to drive trust in different ways. Usage priorities and how they relate to trust are different, personal information surrender's link to trust is different, and both product recommendations and customer reviews are perceived differently in how they correspond to trust. The task for eBay management is different in establishing trust in its users, and they should have different priorities in moving forward.

FUTURE RESEARCH DIRECTIONS

A number of potential future research directions have already been alluded to in the discussion. But several others are immediately obvious. Probably most important is the additional analysis that can be conducted on the existing data. The format of the questions is designed for formal factor analysis, with creation of the aggregate factors already alluded to in the results and the discussion. With that level of data analysis we can propose some more specific hypotheses and conduct some formal tests. Before doing so, we'd like to gather some additional data, particularly looking to better balance the responses between websites. But a more full factor analysis can only add heft to some of the preliminary conclusions drawn in this chapter.

The format of the questions also allows for some more specific parsing of the data and, again, formal hypothesis testing. In the intended use section, for example, there are individual questions that differ only according to a single aspect of web behavior—searching and researching, for example, vs. searching, researching, and purchasing. Again, a more formal and structured analysis can be done of these slight variations in the responses, including hypothesis testing. As can be determined from the Appendix, there is also available information on experience with the websites in question and gender, two additional variables that may have an influence on all the aspects of trust already discussed.

In terms of further research, these initial results and initial analysis have suggested some directions for further research. Initially, social networks have their place in establishing trust, but it is conditional. As commerce and purchasing push into a community, the community does not really add its reassurances to those types of activities. To recommendations, yes. To purchase, no. This apparent implicit or explicit division of the millenials' internet life into sectors (community vs. commerce) would be an extremely interesting direction to explore. How is it done, is it conscious, and can anything be done about it in marketing terms (to better utilize social networking sites for marketing purposes).

This research stream also has obvious limitations, such as including only millenials. While that was the purpose of the study, the sample could certainly be expanded to include other demographic groups. Further, it did include only Northeast US college students, a limited pool and was focused solely on a single consumer electronics product. Given the apparent usefulness of the results shown here or in future articles, the methodology could be improved and applied to any number of other scenarios.

CONCLUSION

This article presents preliminary results from a study of trust perceptions of millennial generation respondents related to a phone/personal digital assistant product offered by or through three different online presences. Amazon is an established e-retailer with certain institutional reassurances that help to instill trust. Facebook is an established social networking site with community reassurances that help to instill trust. eBay is an established auction site with not so many institutional or community reassurances, landing somewhere in the middle on both dimensions.

The study compared perceptions of respondents of all three sites on the basis of overall trust, technology acceptance (perceived usefulness, perceived ease of use), and certain aspects of use (search, research and purchase, personal information, and word-or-mouth such as reviews and recommendations). There were clear similarities as well as clear distinctions in several areas. Initially, the institutional reassurances seem to be more powerful in establishing trust in almost all circumstances. This was, of course, a study about commercial applications of the web, so a well-established and trusted online retailer would, not surprisingly have advantages in this area. The community reassurances were noticeably weaker in a number of areas, particularly those involving purchase or other buying-related activities. Where the community variable had a greater impact was in areas such as recommendations, related to purchase but not necessarily the same thing. But the data also suggested that Amazon and Facebook were very much alike in terms of what variables/factors drive trust. While Facebook may lag on perceptions regarding most of those variables, the way to greater trust for commercial applications is clear—it's the same as what is found at an explicitly commercial site such as Amazon.

The results beg for deeper and more formal analysis, which will be done. But it appears that very different things are going on with institutional and community reassurances and their effect on trust. Trust, as we know, is multidimensional, and it is unsurprising that different circumstances affect trust in different ways. Further analysis should provide deeper insights into this issue.

REFERENCES

Anderson, J. C., & Naurus, J. A. (1990). A model of distributor firm and manufacturing firm working partnerships. *Journal of Marketing, 54*, 42–58. doi:10.2307/1252172

Awad, N. F., & Ragowsky, A. (2008). Establishing trust in electronic commerce through online word of mouth: An examination across genders. *Journal of Management Information Systems, 24*(4), 101–121. doi:10.2753/MIS0742-1222240404

Axelrod, R. (1990). *The evolution of cooperation*. Harmondsworth, UK: Penguin.

Baier, A. (1986). Trust and antitrust. *Ethics, 96*, 231–260. doi:10.1086/292745

Bakker, M., Leenders, R., Gabbay, S., Kratzer, J., & Engelen, J. (2006). Is trust really social capital? Knowledge sharing in product development projects. *The Learning Organization, 13*, 594–605. doi:10.1108/09696470610705479

Chen, S. C., & Dhillon, G. S. (2003). Interpreting dimensions of consumer trust in e-commerce. *Information Technology and Management, 4*(2/3), 303–318. doi:10.1023/A:1022962631249

Choi, B., & Lee, H. (2003). An empirical investigation of knowledge management styles and their effect on corporate performance. *Information & Management, 40*, 403–417. doi:10.1016/S0378-7206(02)00060-5

Coleman, J. (1990). *Foundations of social theory.* Cambridge, MA: Harvard University Press.

Collins, C. J., & Smith, K. G. (2006). Knowledge exchange and combination: the role of human resource practices in the performance of high-technology firms. *Academy of Management Journal, 49,* 544–560.

Davis, F. D. (1989). Perceived usefulness, perceived ease of use and user acceptance of information technology. *Management Information Systems Quarterly, 13*(3), 319–340. doi:10.2307/249008

Davis, F. D., Bagozzi, R. P., & Warshaw, P. R. (1989). User acceptance of computer technology: A comparison of two theoretical models. *Management Science, 35*(8), 982–1003. doi:10.1287/mnsc.35.8.982

Foos, T., Schum, G., & Rothenberg, S. (2006). Tacit knowledge transfer and the knowledge disconnect. *Journal of Knowledge Management, 10,* 6–18. doi:10.1108/13673270610650067

Gambetta, D. G. (Ed.). (1988). *Trust, making and breaking of cooperative relations.* New York: Basil Blackwell.

Garfinkel, H. (1963). A conception of, and experiments with, trust as a condition of stable concerted action. In Harvey, O. J. (Ed.), *Motivation and social interaction* (pp. 187–238). New York: Ronald Press.

Gefen, D. (2000). E-commerce: The role of familiarity and trust. *Omega, 28*(6), 725–737. doi:10.1016/S0305-0483(00)00021-9

Gefen, D., Karahanna, E., & Straub, D. W. (2003). Trust and TAM in online shopping: An integrated model. *Management Information Systems Quarterly, 27*(1), 51–90.

Giddens, A. (1991). *Modernity and self-identity.* Cambridge, UK: Polity.

Jarvenpaa, S. L., & Tractinsky, N. (1999). Consumer trust in an internet store: A cross-cultural validation. *Journal of Computer-Mediated Communication, 5*(2), 1–35.

Kim, M.-S., & Ahn, J.-H. (2006). Comparison of trust sources of an online market-maker in the e-marketplace: Buyer's and seller's perspectives. *Journal of Computer Information Systems, 47*(1), 84–94.

Lewis, J. D., & Weigert, A. (1985). Trust as a social reality. *Social Forces, 63*(4), 967–985. doi:10.2307/2578601

Lin, H.-F. (2006). Impact of organizational support on organizational intention to facilitate knowledge sharing. *Knowledge Management Research & Practice, 4,* 26–35. doi:10.1057/palgrave.kmrp.8500083

Marshall, R. S., Nguyen, T. V., & Bryant, S. E. (2005). A dynamic model of trust development and knowledge sharing in strategic alliances. *Journal of General Management, 31,* 41–57.

Mayer, R. C., Davis, J. H., & Shoorman, F. D. (1995). An integrative model of organizational trust. *Academy of Management Review, 20*(3), 709–734. doi:10.2307/258792

McKnight, D. H., Cummings, L. L., & Chervany, N. L. (1998). Initial trust formation in new organizational relationships. *Academy of Management Review, 23*(3), 472–490. doi:10.2307/259290

Nielsen, B. B. (2005). The role of knowledge embeddedness in the creation of synergies in strategic alliances. *Journal of Business Research, 58,* 1194–1204. doi:10.1016/j.jbusres.2004.05.001

O'Hara-Devereaux, M., & Johansen, R. (1994). *Globalwork: Bridging distance, culture and time.* San Francisco: Jossey Bass.

Reichheld, F. F., & Schefter, P. (2000). E-loyalty: Your secret weapon on the web. *Harvard Business Review, 78*(4), 105–113.

Tsai, W. (2000). Social capital, strategic relatedness and the formation of intraorganizational linkages. *Strategic Management Journal, 21*, 925–939. doi:10.1002/1097-0266(200009)21:9<925::AID-SMJ129>3.0.CO;2-I

Vainio, A. M. (2005). Exchange and combination of knowledge-based resources in network relationships. *European Journal of Marketing, 39*, 1078–1095. doi:10.1108/03090560510610734

APPENDIX

Questionnaire Text

Trust

Based on my perception of the website, I know it is honest.
Based on my perception of the website, I know it cares about consumers.
Based on my perception of the website, I know it is not opportunistic.
Based on my perception of the website, I know it provides good service.
Based on my perception of the website, I know it is trustworthy.
Based on my perception of the website, I know it knows its market.

Perceived Ease of Use

The website is easy to use.
It is easy to become skillful at using the website.
My interaction with the website is clear and understandable.

Perceived Usefulness

The website is useful for searching and buying electronic products
The website improves my performance in searching and buying electronic products.
The website provides useful information for buying electronic products

Intended Use

The website increases my productivity in searching.
The website enables me to search and buy faster.
The website improves my performance in searching and researching information about electronic products.
The website enhances my effectiveness for search, researching, and buying electronic products.
I would use my credit card to purchase from the online vendor.
I am very likely to provide the online vendor with the personal information it needs to better serve my needs.
As this website, the product recommendations are usually not the information I need
The website provides useful recommendations about electronic products.
At this website, the product recommendations are relevant for me.
At this website, the product recommendations are helpful
At this website, the product reviews are usually not the information I need.
The website is useful for finding customer review information about electronic products.
At this website, the product reviews are relevant for me.
At this website, the product reviews are helpful.

Other

How often do you visit the site?
At least once a day, weekly, monthly, 3-4 times a year, never
Have you ever purchased a product based on the recommendations made on this site?
What is your gender?

Chapter 18
Trust in Online Customer–Firm Interaction:
A Literature Review and Directions for Research

Sandro Castaldo
SDA Bocconi School of Management, Italy

Monica Grosso
SDA Bocconi School of Management, Italy

Charles Hofacker
Florida State University, USA

Katia Premazzi
SDA Bocconi School of Management, Italy

ABSTRACT

Trust is a key element in developing customer-firm relationships in the virtual marketplace. The peculiarities of the online setting, however, threaten firms' capability to exploit opportunities derived from such environments. This can lead to customers mostly using the online setting as an information source rather than as a place to conduct transactions. Trust is a key antecedent of online transactions. In this chapter, the authors focus on trust's role in the virtual marketplace by reviewing a series of relevant studies and proposing directions for future research.

INTRODUCTION

The development of Internet technology has led many authors to emphasize the relevance of trust in the online context – a context in which there is spatial separation between the retailer and the consumer, and a temporal separation between pay-

ment and delivery (Gupta, Yadav and Varadarajan 2009). This separation threatens firms' effective interaction with customers, as requires the latters to trust the vendor. Trust is therefore a critical element in enabling online relationships and information exchange.

This chapter thus focuses on the concept of trust and its role in the online setting. It also has a twofold

DOI: 10.4018/978-1-61520-901-9.ch018

objective: firstly, we underline the relevance of trust in the online setting by analysing the threats and opportunities in the virtual marketplace and presenting a brief review of the literature on trust in the online context. Secondly, we pose what we believe are key research questions on this topic, developing hypotheses for testing. The chapter concludes with a report on the results of a preliminary study that tested some of the hypotheses and a description of potential research directions that could develop the study more realistically.

THREATS AND OPPORTUNITIES IN THE VIRTUAL MARKETPLACE: THE CRITICAL ROLE OF TRUST

At the turn of the century, the development of technologies and the consequent increase in the use of electronic channels led to an excessively positive forecast of the virtual marketplace's short-term potential. In turn, this led to the now well-known 'Internet bubble' phenomenon and its subsequent crash. Following that collapse, many studies investigated its causes. Their results converged, revealing that online transaction problems are mainly due to the high level of risk and uncertainty characterizing this marketplace and the lack of trust that might otherwise have overcome this. Customers seem to increasingly rely on the Internet as an information tool, but do not actually purchase anything (MacGraw, 1999; Everard and Galletta, 2005).

For online retailing to succeed, firms must receive extremely sensitive customer information, including names, street addresses, and credit card numbers. Furthermore, data on customers and their habits are frequently required to provide them with quality service. Indeed, customers almost always need to assist with the service production process. This assistance often originates from information that customers provide. If a client, for example, orders an item of clothing, such as a dress, she has to provide details of her dress

size, taste, and so on. Customization – whether the classic version or mass-customization – requires even more detailed information.

Marketing theory increasingly emphasizes the strategic management of customer relationships (e.g., Payne and Frow, 2005), which requires a strong flow of information, specifically from the customer to the firm. The information and communication technologies (ICT) evolution has provided firms with the opportunity to acquire a huge quantity and variety of data from Web visitors and shoppers (Cespedes and Smith, 1993; DeCew, 1997). However, the ease with which data can be acquired and disseminated across the Web, and the peculiarities of the electronic setting, have led to growing concerns about consumer privacy (e.g., Culnan, 1993; Milne and Gordon, 1993; Milne, 2000; Phelps, Novak and Ferrell, 1999).

Furthermore, online transactions often do not involve a simultaneous exchange of goods and money, as a spatial and temporal separation between the partners is common (Gupta, Yadav, Varadarajan, 2009). Consequently, the delay between payment and delivery creates uncertainty about Internet shopping as well as increasing its risk (Hee-Woong et al., 2004). These are exacerbated by the anonymity of the transaction (Grabner-Krauter and Kalusca, 2003) and the information asymmetry between the involved parties (Hee-Woong et al., 2004), which can easily lead to a perceived lack of control and fear of opportunism (Grabner-Krauter and Kalusca, 2003). Furthermore, when information is directly requested from consumers who are unsure about how information will be used, this is regarded as a subtle form of privacy invasion (Milne, 2000). This kind of threat is becoming progressively more prevalent with the development of transactions that require the provision of information. Consequently, one of the key questions that concerns managers, academics, and policy makers is online consumers' response to the constant requests for information (Equifax-Harris, 1996; Milne, 2004).

A growing debate has emerged on how consumers protect themselves against privacy invasion, and how they have modified their online behaviour in response to these threats. Customers have developed "protecting behaviours" (e.g., Milne and Boza, 1999; Sheehan and Hoy, 2000; Raman and Pashupati, 2005) that seem to be aimed at reducing information sharing with online firms. This unwillingness to share information is one reason why the amount of retailing executed online is still minuscule, even in Web-friendly countries such as the US (Everard and Galletta, 2005). This lack of online purchases creates a further dilemma for companies, since they could realize cost saving if customers were to use self-service technologies such as the Web. Cost savings through the use of alternative electronic channels such as the Web are, however, overshadowed by electronic channels' extreme flexibility. This flexibility allows a firm to optimize its marketing information mix, to automatically suggest complementary products, and to implement relationship-friendly tools such as product comparison aides (Viswanathan, 2005). In addition, multi-channel shoppers have a higher purchase volume and are more profitable (Venkatesan, Kumar and Ravishankar, 2007). Electronic channels can, moreover, serve an important communication function in terms of attracting new customers and be used to retain current clients, while extending and leveraging pre-existing relationships (Sawhney and Zabin, 2002). Newsletters, customized specials, price discrimination, couponing, frequent buyer programmes, online communities, friends and family deals, collaborative filtering, all are dependent on an extensive information flow from the customer to the firm.

Marketers will lose all the above-mentioned opportunities that the technology evolution has brought about unless they find a way to manage the threats of consumer privacy protection behaviours. A lack of trust has been identified as one of the greatest barriers inhibiting Internet transactions (Hoffman et al., 1999; MacGraw,

1999; Luo, 2002). Researchers have shown that trust encourages the purchase intention of both potential customers (Gefen et al., 2003; Jarvenpaa et al., 2000) and repeat customers (Garbarino and Johnson, 1999), while increasing the loyalty of repeat customers (Gefen, 2002). Therefore, scholars regard trust as one of the most important prerequisites for electronic commerce's success (Hoffman et al., 1999).

It is not surprising then that many studies on online interaction focus on trust as a key variable. In the following section, we review such studies.

TRUST IN THE VIRTUAL MARKETPLACE: LITERATURE REVIEW

A review of the main contributions to the literature on trust in the virtual setting identifies four main topics (Castaldo, 2007): the conceptualization of trust, the multi-level dimensionality of trust, trust antecedents and consequences and, finally, the evolutionary process of trust. Each of these four topics is analyzed in more detail in this section.

Conceptualization

Efforts to conceptualize online trust have tended to rely on previous research on the off-line environment. In an important attempt to conceptualize trust, McKnight et al. (2002a) identified the following four aspects of the trust concept as found in e-commerce: disposition to trust (general willingness to trust others), institution-based trust (perceptions of the Internet environment), trusting beliefs (perceptions of Web vendor attributes), and trusting intentions (intentions to engage in trust-related behaviours with a Web vendor). Another relevant contribution is by Bhattacherjee (2002), who specifically addresses the concept of individual trust in online firms (the 'trusting beliefs' of McKnight et al.) by developing a seven-item scale for the construct.

Nah and Davis (2002) adapted McAllister's (1995) concepts of cognition-based and affect-based trust to online settings. These authors all argue that, in the e-commerce context, cognition-based trust refers to the trustee's reliability and dependability, which Mayer et al. (1995) call 'integrity'. Affect-based trust refers to care and concern for the other party, or, according to Mayer et al., 'benevolence'. Integrity and benevolence are two frequent themes in the online trust literature.

Several empirical studies have also developed measuring instruments for online customer trust. Newholm et al. (2004), for example, classify the tools identified in the literature into five categories: interface features, offer fulfilment, reputation policies, website transactions, and multiple contact points.

Finally, various authors have analysed the relationship between trust and distrust in e-commerce and argue that they are not merely two opposite ends of a single bipolar construct, but two distinct constructs with differing effects on behaviour (Kramer, 1999; Lewicki et al., 1998). McKnight and Chervany (2001), for instance, argue that distrust is based on different emotions than trust: the former comes from feelings such as fear and worry, while trust is based on feelings of calm and security. In a subsequent study, McKnight et al. (2004a) provide evidence of trust and distrust's distinct natures.

Multi-Level Dimensions

A unique aspect of the online setting is that it does not simply involve trust between the customer and a vendor, but also between the customer and the transaction medium – the Internet environment (Lee and Turban, 2001; McKnight et al., 2002b; Shankar et al., 2002). Unlike the vendor–customer relationship in traditional business settings, the primary interface that connects buyers, sellers and third parties is an electronic market structure supported by ICT, i.e. the website (Gefen et al.,

2003). Many studies have therefore highlighted the concept of 'technology trust', which Ratnasingam (2005: 22) defines as 'the subjective probability by which organizations believe that the underlying technology infrastructure is capable of facilitating transactions according to their confident expectations'. Given a set of different trust objects, a multi-level analysis of e-trust has emerged in the literature. This analysis is based on studies demonstrating that online shoppers may simultaneously trust and distrust (Harris and Goode, 2004):

- The *e-vendor* (e.g., Fukuyama, 1995; Urban et al., 2000) in a form of interpersonal trust;
- The *payment system* (e.g., Hoffman et al., 1999a), which concerns technology trust; and
- The very nature of the *Internet and online shopping* (e.g., Hoffman et al., 1999b; Schoder and Yin, 2000), which entails institutional trust.

Given the reality of the online setting, and contrary to the traditional environment, interpersonal trust seems to play a secondary role to technology and institutional trust in Internet transactions. By means of a simulation experiment, Gefen and Straub (2004) investigate which of the established dimensions of trust in interpersonal relationships, as well as in traditional commerce, feature in consumer e-trust. Their study shows that e-trust is composed of four distinct beliefs: the vendor's integrity, benevolence, ability, and predictability and that among these beliefs, only integrity and predictability are significant antecedents of purchase intentions in e-commerce. Furthermore the authors' results indicate that a disposition to trust and familiarity affect these beliefs and that e-trust, especially the belief in benevolence, is increased by the perception of social presence on the website.

Antecedents and Consequences

Many off-line trust antecedents and consequences can also be found in the virtual setting (Shankar et al., 2002). Indeed, certain empirical results (e.g., Javarpaa et al., 2000; Yoon, 2002) regarding e-trust have included antecedents such as a firm's reputation and size as well as a user's past experience and communication – and consequences – such as commitment, long-term interaction, satisfaction, uncertainty reduction, and loyalty. Many of these variables have also been identified in the off-line literature.

Although trust in the online setting is similar to the off-line one, there is an important distinction between the two environments from which unique e-trust antecedents and consequences are derived: while the object of trust is usually an individual or an organization in the traditional environment, in the virtual setting, the absence of a physical relationship implies that the object of trust is basically the technology (mainly the Internet) and the firm's website (Shankar et al., 2002).

Studies on the antecedents and consequences of e-trust can be classified into two main groups: 'general' and 'clustering' studies (Castaldo, 2007). The former group of studies is aimed at identifying trust antecedents and consequences that can be generalized to all virtual settings. The latter group of studies has investigated how e-trust antecedents and consequences change according to certain contexts such as across different types of sites or customers.

The 'general' study by Jarvenpaa et al. (2000) is among the most quoted on this topic in the online trust literature. These authors conducted causal research by assuming that two independent variables – the perceived size of an Internet store and its perceived reputation – are positively related to the consumers' initial trust in that store. They posited that trust in the store would have a direct positive effect on the attitude towards it and an indirect positive effect on the attitude through the perceived risk associated with buying from

that store as the mediating variable. Additionally, they assumed that both the latter constructs would have a direct effect on the consumers' willingness to buy from the Internet store. Their model provided a good fit for the data, while perceived reputation had a much stronger effect on trust than perceived size.

Gefen and Straub's (2003) model treats social presence on the web site as a predicting variable with trust in an e-service provider as endogenous. These authors further assumed that trust in the e-service provider would be positively related to consumers' purchase intention. In addition, they hypothesized that the perceived usefulness of a web site would affect the purchase intention, which would in turn be affected by the web site's perceived ease of use and social presence on it.

Lee and Turban (2001) presented an even more comprehensive model that introduced the multi-level dimensions of trust in a study of its antecedents and consequences. Their framework hypothesized four antecedent dimensions of trust: trustworthiness of the Internet merchant, trustworthiness of the Internet shopping medium, contextual factors, and other factors not fitting the other three dimensions but possibly influencing trust. The dependent variable in these authors' model is consumers' trust in Internet shopping. Consumers' propensity to trust (dispositional trust) is included as a moderating variable that impacts all relationships between trust and its antecedents. The variable trustworthiness of the Internet shopping medium and contextual factors are predictors of system trust.

Some of the studies of the 'cluster' group classified e-trust antecedents and consequences on the basis of customers' typology, while others tried to verify whether sites with different characteristics would require different antecedents of trust. Hee-Woong et al. (2004) investigated trust antecedents by distinguishing two different consumer typologies: potential and repeat customers. Owing to the unavailability of a complete purchase experience, the institutional mode of trust building (Zucker, 1986) can be an important way for potential customers to build trust. For repeat customers, personal experience offers further evidence of trust in addition to the institutional basis. Potential customers tend to be more exploratory with an Internet store, carrying out tasks like product searches, comparison shopping, and evaluating service policies. At this stage, potential customers only experience the quality of an Internet store's website, not its fulfilment of service quality. In addition, potential customers may interpret the website information (e.g., service policy) and attempt to determine the vendor's intentions (vendor's concern for customers) with the exchange, implicitly invoking intentionality in trust building. Thus, in Internet shopping, legal and technological safeguards are not only important for potential customers, but also for repeat customers. As system users, these customers have a more comprehensive experience with a vendor's website, as well as having full transaction experience with the store. They are therefore able to evaluate both the website quality and the fulfilment of service quality.

Bart et al. (2005) investigated trust antecedents' strengths across different web site categories according to the following site factors: financial risk, information risk, involvement with or price of the product or service on the web site, and the information on the website. The results of the study show that these different site characteristics require different e-trust antecedents.

To develop a synthetic framework (illustrated in Table 1), we categorize e-trust antecedents into three main classes according to whether they refer to the firm, user or website characteristics. Firm characteristics include trust antecedents (such as size, trustworthiness, and reputation) that are common to the off-line environment.

Although users' characteristics are essentially similar to what one might observe in an off-line setting, in e-trust studies they are linked to the virtual medium and the technology involved.

Authors therefore refer to IT-related individual characteristics (such as a predisposition to technology and past experience with online transaction) as e-trust antecedents.

The antecedents of e-trust that are truly unique to the online environment are those that can be classified as website characteristics. They appear to be the most important elements that lead to trust in the virtual setting, since the site is the medium for the exchange between the firm and its customers. The site is more than a shop; it is the tool (especially for firms that have no off-line presence) through which the organization communicates its value and trustworthiness. Hence, navigation, user-friendliness, lack of errors, presentation, links to other relevant sites and the selection of items are very important elements in developing trust. Conversely, the high level of uncertainty derived from the lack of direct contact with the firm and other customers is an important issue that inhibits online transactions. Consequently, online firms try to overcome this lack of direct contact by including e-advisors on their websites and by encouraging the development of online communities of customers. Finally, policies ensuring privacy and security (certified by trustworthy parties), refund systems and the longevity of the site are crucial elements in reducing customers' perception of risk.

The most relevant consequences of e-trust that emerge from the literature are the adoption of new technologies and the conclusion of online transactions, especially at the beginning of the relationship (Gefen et al., 2003; Jarvenpaa et al., 2000).

Trust Evolution

Most studies on online trust have focused on trust building in the initial relationship period by analysing the concept of 'initial trust' (Koufaris and Hampton-Sosa, 2004). In the e-commerce context, online retailers face the challenge of having to

Table 1. E-trust antecedents: main contributions

Typology	Antecedents	Authors
FIRM CHARACTERISTICS	Perceived size Perceived reputation Communication	Jarvenpaa, Tractinsky and Vitale, 2000 Pavlou, 2003 Jarvenpaa, Tractinsky and Vitale, 2000 Yoon, 2002 Pavlou, 2003 Hee-Woong, Xu, Koh, 2004 Koufaris and Hampton-Sosa, 2004 McKnight, Kacmar and Choudhury, 2004b Newholm, et al., 2004 Jarvenpaa, Tractinsky and Vitale, 2000
USER CHARACTERISTICS	Past experience/familiarity with Internet shopping/web site Predisposition to technology	Gefen Karahanna and Straub, 2003 Yoon, 2002 Gefen Karahanna and Straub, 2003 Koufaris and Hampton-Sosa, 2004
WEB SITE CHARACTERISTICS	Navigation and user friendliness Error-freeness Selection of items Site Design Virtual advisor/ information Community Privacy and security Refund policies Site longevity	Koufaris and Hampton-Sosa, 2004 Newholm, et al., 2004 Bart, Shankar, Sultan and Urban, 2005 Newholm, et al., 2004 Bart, Shankar, Sultan and Urban, 2005 Smith, Bailey and Brynjolfsson, 2000 Shneiderman, 2000 Urban, Sultan. Qualls, 2000 Hee-Woong, Xu and Koh, 2004 Bart, Shankar, Sultan and Urban, 2005 Smith, Bailey and Brynjolfsson, 2000 Luo, 2002 Newholm, et al., 2004 Dayal, Landesberg and Zeisser, 1999 Hoffma, Novak and Peralta, 1999a Palmer, Bailey and Faraj, 2000 Smith, Bailey and Brynjolfsson, 2000 Luo, 2002 Gefen Karahanna and Straub, 2003 Koufaris and Hampton-Sosa, 2004 Newholm, et al., 2004 Bart, Shankar, Sultan and Urban, 2005 McKnight, Choudhury and Kacmar 2002a,b Suh and Han, 2003 Jarvenpaa, Tractinsky and Vitale, 2000 Smith, Bailey and Brynjolfsson, 2000

Source: Castaldo (2007)

build consumer trust prior to online transactions, because shoppers perceive more risk online than they do in traditional channels (Van den Poel and Leunis, 1999) and are therefore less likely to enter into an initial exchange. The initial period is critical, because the consumer decides very quickly whether to purchase on a specific website or not. If online retailers therefore fail to persuade consumers to overcome the initial trust barrier, all other efforts will be in vain (McKnight et al., 2004a).

Consequently, many studies have investigated how online retailers can build this initial customer trust, while the concept of ongoing or long-term trust in e-commerce has not yet been comprehensively investigated (Nah and Davis, 2002).

Of the studies focusing on initial trust building, those of McKnight et al. are the most significant (2002a/b, 2004a). These authors argue that a disposition to trust is a particularly important antecedent in the relationship's initial stage.

Finally, Kim et al. (2005) maintain that the online trust-building process has two main characteristics:

- It is a *cumulative* process, as the level of trust in previous stages affects the trust level in later phases;
- It is an *interactive* process.

THE ROLE OF TRUST IN INCREASING INFORMATION SHARING WITH E-VENDORS: HYPOTHESIS DEVELOPMENT

Research indicates that familiarity with the entities (such as websites) collecting information will influence consumers' willingness to share information with them (Sheehan, 2005). Consequently, individuals tend to be more willing to share private information with companies with which they are familiar, as familiarity has taught them how their information is used (or misused). Trust can therefore be a critical element with respect to online relationships and information exchange while, conversely, a lack of trust has been identified as one of the greatest barriers to Internet transactions (Hoffman, Novak and Peralta, 1999).

Consequently, if the consumer trusts the entity collecting personal information, privacy concerns are likely to decrease (Milne and Boza, 1999) and information disclosure is likely to be maximized (Grabner-Krauter, 2002). Therefore, we hypothesize:

H$_1$: The higher the trust, the greater the information disclosure.

An interesting research focus would be the analysis of trust's interaction with a tool that previous studies have shown increases information sharing: the offer of compensation. Even though compensation can function as an announcement that information is being collected from consumers (Sheehan and Hoy, 2000), past research has found that it eliminates some consumer privacy concerns up front, particularly in situations such as market research (Milne and Gordon, 1993).

Compensation thus indicates an exchange of benefits derived from the act of providing information (Sheehan and Hoy, 2000). Westin-Harris (1997) notes that people often consider the nature of the benefit offered in exchange for information when deciding whether an activity violates their personal privacy. Furthermore, other studies have found that consumers are also aware that not all relationships are mutually beneficial and, consequently, often don't want to enter into long-term relationships or don't value relationships with organizations (Szmigin and Bourne, 1998; Phelps, Novak and Ferrell, 2000). Receiving some form of incentive also supports Milne and Gordon's (1993) position that certain people are willing to give up a degree of privacy to obtain desired products and services. As Sheehan and Hoy (2000) point out, consumers may not mind receiving unsolicited marketing communications about products and services in which they are interested, even if some of their personal information is used to identify them as potential clients.

Finally, the strategy of compensating consumers in exchange for divulging personal attitudes or behaviours is well documented in the survey methodology literature as a means of increasing response rates (e.g., Barker, 1989; Chebat and Cohen, 1993).

Hence, on-line consumers' willingness to concede a certain loss of privacy could also be increased by providing them with some sort of compensation that can either be monetary or non-monetary. Empirical evidence shows that consumers receiving tangible benefits, such as discounts, access to websites, future savings, and rewards, may be less concerned with privacy because they feel an equal exchange has been established (Goodwin, 1991). Therefore, as in the case of trust, compensation can be a way of increasing information disclosure:

Table 2. Number of participants in each cell

		Compensation condition		
		No compensation	Compensation (monetary, certain)	Total
Trust condition	Low Trust	22	20	42
	High Trust	21	21	42
	Total	*43*	*41*	84

H_2: *Information disclosure increases if compensation is offered.*

As mentioned, the interaction between these two variables, which have previously always been investigated separately, would be an interesting research area.

Although previous studies have also focused on a variety of other issues, they have been unable to provide evidence of interaction between the relevant variables. In particular, there have been separate studies on: the definition and measurement of privacy concern (e.g., Sheehan, 2005; Smith, Milberg and Burke, 1996), the antecedents and consequences of privacy concern (e.g., Phelps, Nowak and Ferrell 2000; Phelps, D'Souza and Nowak, 2001), the impact of trust (e.g., Miyazaki and Krishnamurthy, 2002; Grabner-Krauter, 2002), and compensation for information (Sheehan and Hoy, 2000).

We hypothesise trust as a moderating variable that affects the relationship between compensation and information disclosure. We specifically suggest that, in addition to high trust, individuals will be more inclined to provide information online if they are offered compensation or incentives:

H_3: *Under condition of high trust, subjects are more willing to provide information when offered compensation than when offered no compensation.*

In the following section, we illustrate the results of a preliminary study aimed at testing the identified hypotheses.

SOME PRELIMINARY RESULTS

A preliminary study was designed to test the three hypotheses proposed in the previous section.

Design and Procedure

The study was undertaken by means of a 2 (trust: high vs. low) x 2 (compensation: no compensation vs. compensation) between-subjects experiment. The participants were 84 students from a large Northern Italian university, who were randomly assigned to the four cells (Table 2).

The experiment was conducted in an on-campus controlled laboratory with groups of 20 to 22 participants and lasted approximately 20 minutes.

The experimental materials consisted of a set of vignettes (Appendix 1). Once the participants entered the laboratory, they were provided with a scenario on a handout telling them to assume that they had to purchase a product online, but the website they regularly used for online shopping was temporarily closed for maintenance activities[1] and they therefore had to use a website they had never used before. Different versions of the vignettes instructed the participants they should act as if they had different levels of trust in the website. In order to choose and buy the product, and to conclude the purchase, this web site required registration, which meant that certain personal data had to be entered. The registration form was depicted in the handout. The compensation manipulation occurred at this stage, as one version of the form (compensation) informed the subjects that after their registration they would receive a discount

Table 3. Trust measure

Trust Items
Based on what you have read, how strongly do you agree or disagree with the following? · I feel I can trust this web site · This web site makes truthful claims · This web site is honest · I do not believe what this web site tells me · I can rely on this web site · This web site is safe · I will feel secure when I buy from this web site because I know it will never let me down · This web site can not be counted on to do its job

coupon for purchases on this website, while the second version (no compensation) simply asked them to register.

The participants were then asked to answer a one-page questionnaire containing two key questions: a trust manipulation check, and a measure of their willingness to provide online information.

Measures

Dependent Variable. The dependent variable "information disclosure" was measured as the average score on a multi-item question investigating willingness to provide information. Specifically, the participants rated their willingness to provide six different types of personal data, using a 7-point scale (1 = no willingness, 7 = high willingness). The average rating across the items was calculated for each subject and considered the measure of the subject's willingness to disclose information. The higher the average, the greater the information disclosure.

Two other dependent variables, which took the "quality" of the information the subject was willing to provide into consideration, were created for a post hoc analysis. The dependent variable "disclosure of non problematic information" was calculated as the average score expressed by each subject across the following items: data related to lifestyle (number of cars owned, ownership or rental of a house, etc.), demographic data (age, ethnic group, height, etc.), and data that referred to media usage habits (television programmes

watched, magazines read, etc.). The dependent variable "willingness to provide problematic information" was calculated as the average score expressed by each subject across the following items: identification data (name, address, etc.), medical data, financial data (credit card number, type, expiry date, etc.).

Trust To perform the manipulation check, trust was measured using a 7-point (1 = strongly disagree, 7 = strongly agree) multi-item scale that was adapted from existing scales found in the literature (Table 3). The scale was translated into Italian and back into English by a second translator to ensure validity. The items were factor analyzed to create a single measure of trust with high scores indicating a higher level of trust in the web site (Cronbach alpha = 0.949).

Manipulation Check and Assumptions

Tests were conducted to ensure that statistical assumptions associated with analysis of variance (ANOVA) were met. Levene's test of equality of error variance was not rejected, suggesting that the dependent variable's error variance is equal across the four conditions. Consequently, a one-way ANOVA was used to assess the trust manipulation. The participants in the group under condition of high trust reported a higher level of trust than those in the group under condition of low trust (M_{HIGH} = 4.1654, M_{LOW} = 2.4107; $F_{(1, 82)}$= 69.038, p=0.000).

Results

A factorial analysis of variance (ANOVA) was performed to test the hypotheses. The analysis confirmed only H_1, meaning that just the main effect of trust on information disclosure was confirmed (M_{HIGH} = 4.524, M_{LOW} = 3.360; $F(1, 82)$= 29.198, p=0.000).

Compensation had no effect (H_2), nor was the interaction effect significant, thus H_3 was not confirmed.

We then performed a post hoc analysis, classifying the information as either "problematic" or "non problematic" data to control whether the type of information could have an effect on these results. Past research demonstrated that the type of personal information requested influences customers' willingness to provide such information (Nowak and Phelps, 1997; Long et. al, 1999; Phelps, Novak and Ferrell 2000; Phelps, D'Souza and Nowak 2001). Hence, while customers may be willing to provide general information about their attitudes, they are more concerned about information requests pertaining to values, identification or financial variables. Our results show that once again only the main effect of trust was significant ($M_{HIGH-PROB}$ = 3.611, $M_{LOW-PROB}$ = 2.218, $F(1, 82)$= 41.114, p=0.000; $M_{HIGH-NO PROB}$ = 5,4365, $M_{LOW-NO PROB}$ = 4.4921, $F(1,82)$= 10.199, p=0.002) in respect of both kinds of information, confirming prior research.

Discussion

The study proposed above supports the critical role of trust in information disclosure. Compensation appears to be far less important, as neither the main nor the interaction effects were significant in our study. Trust appears to be the only variable that can influence consumers' willingness to provide e-vendors with information, regardless of the type of information exchanged. This supports the literature on trust's role in information sharing (e.g., Grabner-Krauter, 2002; Milne and Boza, 1999), while simultaneously questioning findings of studies that have just examined compensation (e.g., Goodwin, 1991). By reviewing the literature on trust in an online setting and proposing a preliminary study on information sharing with online firms, this chapter highlights the relevance of such sharing in the virtual marketplace.

However, as we recognize that this study is a very simplified, preliminary investigation into the phenomenon, we also hope to see more work by other researchers interested in the topic. This project also has a number of limitations that should be addressed in further research to deepen our knowledge and possibly arrive at more conclusive remarks. In the following section, we propose directions that researchers could follow to reach this aim.

FUTURE RESEARCH DIRECTIONS

Below we indicate some issues that, basing on our experiment, should be taken into account by researchers aiming to investigation of the role of trust in information disclosure.

First, more fine-grained measure of information disclosure would be needed. In the study described above, we operationalized information disclosure and willingness to provide information; however, attitudinal willingness to provide information could differ from actual information-giving behaviour. The following point provides indications of how such a limitation could be overcome and actual behaviour could be measured.

Another concern relates to a more realistic experimental setting. The use of a controlled experimental setting could allow respondents' actual behaviour - instead of their attitudes and perceived intentions or past behaviour - to be measured. The use of surveys has been a common element in many studies on responses to privacy invasion[2]. The problem of a research design using surveys is threefold. Firstly, surveys just measure past or intentional behaviour, not actual behaviour. Secondly, this methodology tends to heighten privacy concerns, because respondents are sensitized to the topic since they are forced to focus on it. Indeed, some research suggests that many consumers ignore the implications of privacy invasion either due to denial (Raman and Pashupati, 2005) or to the way in which choices are presented (Johnson, Bellman and Lohse, 2002). According to this view, consumers may not be aware of the implications of sharing their information with an online website, as well as being unable to predict their own behaviour. The use of a behavioural approach would allow both the sensitizing effects and the lack of awareness that plague surveys to be avoided. Such a behavioural approach could be undertaken using a designed website in which the participants could be asked to register as they would normally do. A system registering the information provided would allow the researchers to measure the participants' actual information disclosure.

Third, participants of an experiment should be selected bearing in mind the differing socio-economic and behavioural characteristics of various groups. Even though students are recognized as an acceptable target in experimental marketing research, their actual online behaviour could differ from that of other target markets. The replication of the experiment using different segments of customers could allow the type of online e-shopper to be controlled, potentially providing marketers with more general insights.

Next, the measure of trust is critical for the research project. As mentioned in our text, trust is a process; hence, trust's impact on information disclosure and consumers' perception of compensation could differ depending on the stage of the relationship with the site. In our view, researchers should focus on the stages previous to initial trust, thus controlling for past experience with a website. This could be done by using a completely unknown website (specifically built for the experiment) as an experimental tool. Eventually, a longitudinal study could be undertaken by conducting sequen-

tial experiments with the same respondents to take the relationship evolution into account.

Furthermore, the use of a more realistic experimental setting could allow researchers to utilize the trust manipulation more effectively by leveraging its antecedents. The website could be built so that it would provide the participants with different perceptions of the firm and website characteristics (see Table 1).

Additionally, a research project where the object being trusted is manipulated would be very interesting. As mentioned in the literature review, trust is a multi-level construct in the virtual marketplace, as in this setting, the object being trusted could be: the e-vendor (e.g., Fukuyama, 1995; Urban et al., 2000), the payment system (e.g., Hoffman et al., 1999a) or the very nature of Internet and online shopping (e.g., Hoffman et al., 1999b; Schoder and Yin, 2000). Trust could therefore be manipulated and measured on these three levels to investigate the presence of differences in its impact on information disclosure.

Since firms use different types of compensation (money vs. gift; certain vs. uncertain, i.e. lottery, etc.) to stimulate information disclosure, the type of compensation offered could impact information provision behaviour and interact with trust. Thus, further studies could attempt more complex manipulation of type of compensation than we did.

Finally, the controls used in the study can be more complex. Researchers could include variables that impact relationships as possible covariates. Firstly, the participants' characteristics regarding their attitude towards online shopping and predilection for technology (see Table 1) could be recorded, as the literature has proven them a relevant trust antecedents and they could, consequently, have an impact on both the manipulation and the study results. Other relevant variables could be privacy concerns,[3] attitude towards the product category sold on the website, etc.

In general, future experiments could be designed to overcome the limits of this first exploratory effort. By thoroughly investigating the relationship between digital trust, privacy concerns and compensation, new and fascinating paths could be uncovered for a better understanding of online search and shopping behaviour.

REFERENCES

Barker, L. B. (1989). Survey Research. In Emmert, P., & Barker, L. B. (Eds.), *Measurement of Communication Behavior* (pp. 25–39). New York: Longman.

Bart, Y., Shankar, V., Sultan, F., & Urban, G. L. (2005). Are the Drivers and Role of Online Trust the Same for All Web Sites and Consumers? A Large-Scale Exploratory Empirical Study. *Journal of Marketing*, 69(4), 133–152. doi:10.1509/jmkg.2005.69.4.133

Bhattacherjee, A. (2002). Individual Trust in Online Firms: Scale Development and Initial Test. *Journal of Management Information Systems*, 19(1), 211–241.

Castaldo, S. (2007). *Trust in Marketing Relationships*. Cheltenham, UK: Edward Elgar.

Cespedes, F. V., & Smith, H. J. (1993). Database Marketing: new rules for policy and practice. *Sloan Management Review*, 34(Summer), 8–12.

Chebat, J. C., & Cohen, A. (1993). Response speed in mail surveys: beware of shortcuts. *Marketing Research*, 5(Spring), 20–26.

Culnan, M. J. (1993). How did they get my name? An exploratory investigation of consumer attitudes toward secondary information use. *Management Information Systems Quarterly*, 17(3), 341–363. doi:10.2307/249775

Dayal, S., Landesberg, H., & Zeisser, M. (1999). How to build trust online. *Marketing Management Fall*, 8(3), 64-69.

DeCew, J. (1997). *In Pursuit of Privacy. Law, Ethics, and the Rise of Technology*. Ithaca, NY: Cornell University Press.

Equifax-Harris. (1996). *Consumer Privacy Survey*. Atlanta, GA: Louis Harris and Associates, Inc.

Everard, A., & Galletta, D. F. (2005). How presentation flaws affect perceived site quality, trust, and intention to purchase from an online store. *Journal of Management Information Systems*, 6(3), 55–95.

Fukuiama, F. (1995). *Trust: The social virtues and the creation of prosperity*. New York: Free Press.

Garbarino, E., & Johnson, M. S. (1999). The Different Roles of Satisfaction, Trust, and Commitment in Customer Relationships. *Journal of Marketing*, 63(2), 70–87. doi:10.2307/1251946

Gefen, D. (2000). E-Commerce: the role of familiarity and trust. *The International Journal of Management Science*, 28(6), 725–737.

Gefen, D. (2002). Consumer Loyalty in e-commerce. *Journal of the Association for Information Systems*, 3, 27–51.

Gefen, D., Karahanna, E., & Straub, D. W. (2003). Trust and TAM in Online Shopping: An Integrated model. *MIS Quartely*, 27(1), 51–90.

Gefen, D., & Straub, D. W. (2004). Consumer Trust in B2C e-Commerce and the importance of social presence: experiments in e-Products and e-Services. *Omega: The International Journal of Management Science*, 32(6), 407–424. doi:10.1016/j.omega.2004.01.006

Goodwin, C. (1991). Privacy: recognition of a consumer right. *Journal of Public Policy & Marketing*, 10(1), 149–166.

Grabner-Krauter, S. (2002). The Role of Consumers' Trust in Online-Shopping. *Journal of Business Ethics*, 39, 43–50. doi:10.1023/A:1016323815802

Grabner-Krauter, S., & Kalusca, E. A. (2003). Empirical research in on-line trust: a review and critical assessment. *International Journal of Human-Computer Studies*, *58*(6), 783–812. doi:10.1016/S1071-5819(03)00043-0

Gupta, P., Yadav, M. S., & Varadarajan, R. (2009). How task-facilitative interactive tools fosters buyer's trust in online retailers: a process view of trust development. *Journal of Retailing*, *85*(2), 159–176. doi:10.1016/j.jretai.2009.02.001

Harris, L. C., & Goode, M. M. H. (2004). The four levels of loyalty and the pivotal role of trust: a study of online service dynamics. *Journal of Retailing*, *80*(2), 139–158. doi:10.1016/j.jretai.2004.04.002

Hee-Woong, K., Xu, Y., & Koh, J. (2004). A Comparison of Online Trust Building Factors Between Potential Customers and Repeat Customers. *Journal of the Association for Information Systems*, *5*(10), 392–420.

Hoffman, D., Novak, T. P., & Peralta, M. A. (1999). Building consumer trust online environment: the case for information privacy. *Communications of the ACM*, *42*(4), 80–85. doi:10.1145/299157.299175

Jarvenpaa, S. L., Tractinsky, J., & Vitale, M. (2000). Consumer trust in an internet store. *Information Technology and Management*, *1*(1/2), 45–71. doi:10.1023/A:1019104520776

Johnson, E. J., Bellman, S., & Lohse, G. L. (2002). Defaults, framing and privacy: why opting in-opting out. *Marketing Letters*, *13*(1), 5–15. doi:10.1023/A:1015044207315

Kim, H. W., Xu, Y., & Koh, J. (2004). A comparison of online trust building factors between potential customers and repeat customers. *Journal of the Association for Information Systems*, *5*(10), 392–420.

Koufaris, M., & Hampton-Sosa, W. (2004). The development of initial trust in an online company by new customers. *Information & Management*, *41*, 377–397. doi:10.1016/j.im.2003.08.004

Lee, M. K. O., & Turban, E. (2001). A trust model for consumer internet shopping. *International Journal of Electronic Commerce*, *6*(1), 75–91.

Lewicki, R. J., & Bunker, B. B. (1996). Developing and Maintaining Trust in Work Relationships. In Kramer, R. M., & Tyler, T. R. (Eds.), *Trust in Organizations: Frontiers of Theory and Research* (pp. 114–139). Thousand Oaks, CA: Sage.

Lewicki, R. J., McAllister, D. J., & Bies, R. J. (1998). Trust and Distrust: New Relationships and Realities. *Academy of Management Review*, *23*(3), 438–458. doi:10.2307/259288

Luo, X. (2002). Trust production and privacy concerns on the Internet. A framework based on relationship marketing and social exchange theory. *Industrial Marketing Management*, *31*, 111–118. doi:10.1016/S0019-8501(01)00182-1

MacGraw, H. (1999). Managing the privacy revolution. *Direct Marketing*, *62*, 36–38.

Mayer, R. C., Davis, J. H., & Schoorman, F. D. (1995). An Integrative Model of Organizational Trust. *Academy of Management Review*, *20*(3), 709–734. doi:10.2307/258792

McAllister, D. J. (1995). Affect- and Cognition-Based Trust as Foundations for Interpersonal Cooperation in Organizations. *Academy of Management Journal*, *38*(1), 24–59. doi:10.2307/256727

McKnight, D. H., & Chervany, N. L. (2001). What Trust Means in e-commerce Consumer Relationships: An Interdisciplinary Conceptual Typology. *International Journal of Electronic Commerce*, *6*(2), 35–59.

McKnight, D. H., Choudhury, V., & Kacmar, C. (2002a). Developing and Validating Trust Measures for e-commerce: An Integrative Typology. *Information Systems Research*, *13*(3), 334–359. doi:10.1287/isre.13.3.334.81

McKnight, D. H., Choudhury, V., & Kacmar, C. (2002b). The impact of initial consumer trust on intentions to transact with a Web site: a trust building model. *The Journal of Strategic Information Systems, 13*(4), 297–323. doi:10.1016/S0963-8687(02)00020-3

McKnight, D. H., Kacmar, C., & Choudhury, V. (2004a). Dispositional Trust and Distrust, Distinctions in Predicting High- and Low-Risk Internet Expert Advice Site Perceptions. *e-Service Journal, 3*(2), 35-58.

Milne, G. R. (2000). Privacy and ethical issues in database/interactive marketing and public policy: a research framework and overview of the special issue. *Journal of Public Policy & Marketing, 19*(1), 1–6. doi:10.1509/jppm.19.1.1.16934

Milne, G. R., & Boza, M. E. (1999). Trust and concern in consumers' perceptions of marketing information management practices. *Journal of Interactive Marketing, 13*(1), 5–24. doi:10.1002/(SICI)1520-6653(199924)13:1<5::AID-DIR2>3.0.CO;2-9

Milne, G. R., & Gordon, M. E. (1993). Direct mail privacy-efficiency trade-offs within an implied social contract framework. *Journal of Public Policy & Marketing, 12*(2), 206–215.

Miyazaki, A. D., & Krishnamurthy, S. (2002). Internet seals of approval: effects on online privacy policies and consumer perceptions. *The Journal of Consumer Affairs, 36*(1), 28–49.

Moellering, G. (2006). *Trust: Reason, Routine, Reflexivity*. Amsterdam: Elsevier Science Publishing Company.

Nah, F. F. H., & Davis, S. (2002). HCI research issues in e-commerce. *Journal of Electronic Commerce Research, 3*(3), 98–113.

Newholm, T., McGoldrick, P., Keeling, K., Macaulay, L., & Doherty, J. (2004). Multi-Story Trust and Online Retailer Strategies. *International Review of Retail, Distribution and Consumer Research, 14*(4), 437–456. doi:10.1080/0959396042000260889

Palmer, J., Bailey, J. P., & Faraj, S. (2000). The role of intermediaries in the development of trust in the WWW: the use of prominence of trusted third parties and privacy statements. *Journal of Computer-Mediated Communication, 5*(3).

Pavlou, P. A. (2003). Consumer acceptance of electronic commerce – integrating trust and risk with the technology acceptance model. *International Journal of Electronic Commerce, 7*(3), 69–103.

Phelps, J., Nowak, G. J., & Ferrell, E. (2000). Privacy concerns and consumer willingness to provide personal information. *Journal of Public Policy & Marketing, 19*(1), 27–41. doi:10.1509/jppm.19.1.27.16941

Phelps, J. E., D'Souza, G., & Nowak, G. J. (2001). Antecedents and consequences of consumer privacy concerns: an empirical investigation. *Journal of Interactive Marketing, 15*(4), 2–17. doi:10.1002/dir.1019

Raman, P., & Pashupati, K. (2005). Online Privacy: Consumer Concerns and Technological Competence. In Krishnamurthy, S. (Ed.), *Contemporary Research in E-Marketing* (pp. 200–225). Hershey, PA: Idea Group Publishing.

Ratnasingam, P. (2005). Trust in inter-organizational exchanges: a case study in business to business electronic commerce. *Decision Support Systems, 39*(3), 525–544. doi:10.1016/j.dss.2003.12.005

Rust, R. T., & Kannan, R. K. (2003). E-service: a new paradigm for business in the electronic environment. *Communications of the ACM, 46*(6), 36–42. doi:10.1145/777313.777336

Sawhney, M., & Zabin, J. (2002). Managing and measuring relational equity in the network economy. *Journal of the Academy of Marketing Science*, *30*(4), 313–332. doi:10.1177/009207002236908

Schoder, D., & Yin, P. L. (2000). Building firm trust online. *Communications of the ACM*, *43*(12), 73–79. doi:10.1145/355112.355127

Shankar, V., Urban, G. L., & Sultan, F. (2002). Online Trust: a stakeholder perspective, concepts implications and future directions. *The Journal of Strategic Information Systems*, *11*(4), 325–344. doi:10.1016/S0963-8687(02)00022-7

Sheehan, K. B. (2005). Public Opinions of Online Privacy: Definitions, Assessment and Implications for Industry and Public Policy. In Krishnamurthy, S. (Ed.), *Contemporary Research in E-Marketing* (pp. 186–199). Hershey, PA: Idea Group Publishing.

Sheehan, K. B., & Hoy, M. G. (2000). Dimensions of privacy concern among online consumers. *Journal of Public Policy & Marketing*, *19*(1), 62–73. doi:10.1509/jppm.19.1.62.16949

Shneiderman, B. (2000). Designing Trust into Online experiences. *Communications of the ACM*, *43*(12), 57–59. doi:10.1145/355112.355124

Smith, H. J., Milberg, S. J., & Burke, S. J. (1996). Information privacy: measuring individuals' concerns about organizational practices. *Management Information Systems Quarterly*, *16*(June), 167–196. doi:10.2307/249477

Smith, M., Bailey, J., & Brynjolfsson, E. (2000). Understanding digital markets: review and assessment. In Bryonjolfsson, E., & Kahim, B. (Eds.), *Understanding the digital economy*. Cambridge, MA: MIT Press.

Suh, B., & Han, I. (2002). The Impact of Consumer trust and Perception of Security Control on the Acceptance of Electronic Commerce. *International Journal of Electronic Commerce*, *7*(3), 135–161.

Szmigin, I., & Bourne, H. (1998). Consumer equity in relationship marketing. *Journal of Consumer Marketing*, *15*(6), 544–557. doi:10.1108/07363769810240545

Urban, G. L., Sultan, F., & Qualls, W. J. (2000). Placing Trust at the Center of Your Internet Strategy. *Sloan Management Review*, *42*(1), 39–48.

Van den Poel, D., & Leunis, J. (1999). Consumer acceptance of the internet as a channel of distribution. *Journal of Business Research*, *45*, 249–256. doi:10.1016/S0148-2963(97)00236-1

Venkatesan, R., Kumar, V., & Ravishankar, N. (2007). Multichannel shopping: causes and consequences. *Journal of Marketing*, *71*(2), 114–132. doi:10.1509/jmkg.71.2.114

Viswanathan, M., Rosa, J. A., & Harris, J. E. (2005). Decision making and coping of functionally illiterate consumers and some implications for marketing management. *Journal of Marketing*, *69*(January), 15–31. doi:10.1509/jmkg.69.1.15.55507

Westin-Harris. (1997). *Privacy and American Business Study*. A survey.

Yoon, S. J. (2002). The antecedents and consequences of trust in online purchase decisions. *Journal of Interactive Marketing*, *16*(2), 47–63. doi:10.1002/dir.10008

Zucker, L. G. (1986). Production of Trust: Institutional Sources of Economic Structure, 1840-1920. *Research in Organizational Behavior*, *8*, 53–111.

ENDNOTES

[1]   This allowed the researchers to control their level of familiarity with the website, which could impact information disclosure.

[2]   Some exceptions include a series of experiments by Miyazaki and Krishnamurthy (2002) indicating that the presence of seals

of approval (e.g., TRUSTe, BBBOnline) could make consumers more positive about a website's privacy policy.

[3] Previous research suggests that the level of individuals' privacy concerns influences their willingness to share information (Phelps et al. 2000; Sheehan and Hoy 2000).

APPENDIX

The Vignettes Used In the Study

Figure 1.

| | no INCENTIVE yes |
| high TRUST low | |

high

You have to buy a product online. The website you usually use is temporarily closed for maintenance works. You therefore decide to visit another website that you never used but that you trust.
To access some information you need to buy the product you need you have to sign in the website by providing some personal data:

> **SIGN IN!**
>
> To sign in, please provide the following data:
>
> NAME: _____
> ADDRESS: _____
> CITY: _____
> ZIPCODE: _____
> COUNTRY: _____
> EMAIL: _____
> PHONE: _____
> SSN CODE: _____
> CREDIT CARD TYPE: _____
> CC NUMBER: _____
> CC EXPIRATION: _____

You have to buy a product online. The website you usually use is temporarily closed for maintenance works. You therefore decide to visit another website that you never used but that you trust.
To access some information you need to buy the product you need you have to sign in the website by providing some personal data:

> **SIGN IN!**
>
> To sign in, please provide the following data – at the end of the process you will receive a discount coupon to be used in our website:
>
> NAME: _____
> ADDRESS: _____
> CITY: _____
> ZIPCODE: _____
> COUNTRY: _____
> EMAIL: _____
> PHONE: _____
> SSN CODE: _____
> CREDIT CARD TYPE: _____
> CC NUMBER: _____
> CC EXPIRATION: _____

You have to buy a product online. The website you usually use is temporarily closed for maintenance works. You therefore decide to visit another website that you never used but that you do not trust.
To access some information you need to buy the product you need you have to sign in the website by providing some personal data:

> **SIGN IN!**
>
> To sign in, please provide the following data:
>
> NAME: _____
> ADDRESS: _____
> CITY: _____
> ZIPCODE: _____
> COUNTRY: _____
> EMAIL: _____
> PHONE: _____
> SSN CODE: _____
> CREDIT CARD TYPE: _____
> CC NUMBER: _____
> CC EXPIRATION: _____

You have to buy a product online. The website you usually use is temporarily closed for maintenance works. You therefore decide to visit another website that you never used but that you do not trust.
To access some information you need to buy the product you need you have to sign in the website by providing some personal data:

> **SIGN IN!**
>
> To sign in, please provide the following data – at the end of the process you will receive a discount coupon to be used in our website:
>
> NAME: _____
> ADDRESS: _____
> CITY: _____
> ZIPCODE: _____
> COUNTRY: _____
> EMAIL: _____
> PHONE: _____
> SSN CODE: _____
> CREDIT CARD TYPE: _____
> CC NUMBER: _____
> CC EXPIRATION: _____

low

no   **INCENTIVE**   **yes**

T R U S T

Legend:
    in blue: trust manipulation;
    in red: compensation manipulation.

Compilation of References

Abraham, R. (2006). *Mobile phones and economic development: Evidence from the fishing industry in India.* In The international conference on information and communications technologies and development, (ICTD 2006) conference proceedings. Berkeley, CA: IEEE.

Abrahamson, E. (1991). Managerial fads and fashions: The diffusion and rejection of innovations. *Academy of Management Review, 16*, 586–612. doi:10.2307/258919

Adler, M. (2009). History of NYC Sheet Music Store to Close. *NPR*. Retrieved from http://www.npr.org/templates/story/story.php?storyId=103728928

Advisory Conciliation and Arbitration Service (ACAS). (2006, September). *Internet and e-mail policies.* Retrieved June 22, 2007, from http://www.acas.org.uk/index.aspx?articleid=808

Advisory Conciliation and Arbitration Service. A. (2004). *Internet and e-mail policies.* Retrieved November 30, 2006, from http://www.acas.org.uk/index.aspx?articleid=808

Ahn, T.-K., Ostrom, E., Schmidt, E., & Walker, J. (2003). Trust in two-person games: Game structures and linkages. In Ostrom, E., & Walker, J. (Eds.), *Trust and reciprocity.* New York: Russell Sage Foundation.

Ajzen, I. (1991). The theory of planned behavior. *Organizational Behavior and Human Decision Processes, 50*(2), 179–211. doi:10.1016/0749-5978(91)90020-T

Ajzen, I., & Fishbein, M. (1980). *Understanding attitudes and predicting social behavior.* Englewood Cliffs, NJ: Prentice-Hall.

Akerlof, G. A. (1970). The market for Lemons: Quality uncertainty and the market mechanism. *The Quarterly Journal of Economics, 84*(3), 488–500. doi:10.2307/1879431

Akinci, S., Aksoy, S., & Atilgan, E. (2004). Adoption of Internet banking among sophisticated consumer segments in an advanced developing country. *International Journal of Bank Marketing, 22*(3), 212–232. doi:10.1108/02652320410530322

Alchian, A., & Demsetz, H. (1973). The property rights paradigm. *The Journal of Economic History, 33*, 16–27.

American Management Association. A. (2005). *2005 Electronic Monitoring and Surveillance Survey--Many companies monitoring, recording, videotaping and firing employees.* Retrieved November 30, 2006, from http://www.amanet.org/press/amanews/ems05.htm

Aminuzzaman, S. (2002). Cellular phones in rural Bangladesh: A study of the village pay phone of Grameen bank. In Goldstein, A., & O'Connor, D. (Eds.), *Electronic commerce for development.* Paris: OECD Development Centre Studies.

Anderson, B. (1991). *Imagined communities: Reflections on the origin and spread of nationalism.* London: Verso.

Anderson, J. C., & Naurus, J. A. (1990). A model of distributor firm and manufacturing firm working partnerships. *Journal of Marketing, 54*, 42–58. doi:10.2307/1252172

Anderson, J. L. (2006). A structured approach for bringing mobile telecommunications to the world's poor. *Electronic Journal of Information Systems in Developing Countries, 27*(2), 1–9.

Anderson, P., & Tushman, M. L. (1990). Technological discontinuities and dominant designs: A cyclical model of technological change. *Administrative Science Quarterly, 35*, 604–633. doi:10.2307/2393511

Anglaise, P. (2005a, September 21). Hotel. *Petite Anglaise*. Retrieved June 19, 2007, from http://www.petiteanglaise. com/archives/2005/09/

Anglaise, P. (2005b, May 13). Titillation. *Petite Anglaise*. Retrieved June 18, 2007, from http://www.petiteanglaise. com/archives/2005/05/

Anglaise, P. (2006a, July 20). Suspendered. *Petite Anglaise*. Retrieved June 18, 2007, from http://www.petiteanglaise. com/archives/2006/07/20/suspendered/#comments

Anglaise, P. (2006b, July 18). Things fall apart. *Petite Anglaise*. Retrieved June 18, 2007, from http://www. petiteanglaise.com/archives/2006/07/

Anglaise, P. (2007a). *About Petite Anglaise*. Retrieved June 18, 2007, from http://www.petiteanglaise.com/ about-this-site/

Anglaise, P. (2007b, March 22). Twist. *Petite Anglaise*. Retrieved June 20, 2007, from http://www.petiteanglaise. com/archives/2007/03

Anthony, D. L. (2005). Cooperation in Micro-Credit Borrowing Groups: Identity, Sanctions and Reciprocity in the Production of Collective Goods. *American Sociological Review, 70*(1), 496–515. doi:10.1177/000312240507000307

Anthony, D. L., & Horne, C. (2003). Gender and Cooperation: Explaining loan repayment in micro-credit borrowing groups. *Social Psychology Quarterly, 66*(3), 293–302. doi:10.2307/1519827

Aoki, A. Hayashi, K., Kishida, K., Nakakoji, K., Mishawaka, Y., Reeves, B., Tkashima, A., & Yamamoto, Y. (2001). A case study of the evolution of Jun. An object oriented open source 3D multimedia library. In *Proceedings of the 23rd International Conference on Software Engineering*, Toronto, Ontario, Canada (pp. 524 - 533).

Ariss S., Nykodym, N., & Cole-Laramore, A. A. (2002). Trust and Technology in the Virtual Organization. *SAM Advanced Management Journal*, 22-25.

Aronson, E. (1972). *The social animal*. New York: Viking.

Arrow, K. (1974). *The limits of organization*. New York: Norton.

Arrow, K. J. (2000). Observations on social capital. In Dasgupta, P., & Serageldin, I. (Eds.), *Social capital: A multifaceted perspective* (pp. 3–5). Washington, D.C.: The World Bank.

Awad, N. F., & Ragowsky, A. (2008). Establishing trust in electronic commerce through online word of mouth: An examination across genders. *Journal of Management Information Systems, 24*(4), 101–121. doi:10.2753/ MIS0742-1222240404

Awamleh, R., & Fernandes, C. (2006). Diffusion of Internet Banking amongst educated consumers in a high income non-OECD country. *Journal of Internet Banking and Commerce, 11*(3).

Axelrod, R. (1984). *The Evolution of Cooperation*. New York: Basic Books.

Axelrod, R. (1990). *The evolution of cooperation*. Harmondsworth, UK: Penguin.

Ba, S., Whinston, A. B., & Zhang, H. (2003). Building trust in online auction markets through an economic incentive mechanism. *Decision Support Systems, 35*(3), 273–286. doi:10.1016/S0167-9236(02)00074-X

Bacharach, M. O. L., & Gambetta, D. (2001). Trust in signs. In Cook, K. (Ed.), *Trust and social structure* (pp. 148–184). New York: Russell Sage Foundation.

Bacharach, M., & Gambetta, D. (2001). Trust in Signs. In Cook, K. S. (Ed.), *Trust in Society* (pp. 148–184). New York: Russell Sage Foundation.

Bacharach, M., & Gambetta, D. (2001). Trust in signs. In Cook, K. S. (Ed.), *Trust in Society* (pp. 148–184). New York: Russell Sage Foundation.

Baier, A. (1986). Trust and antitrust. *Ethics, 69*(2), 231–260. doi:10.1086/292745

Baier, A. (1986). Trust and Antitrust. *Ethics, 96*, 231–260. doi:10.1086/292745

Bailenson, J., & Blascovich, J. (2004). Avatars. In Bainbridge, W. S. (Ed.), *Encyclopedia of human-computer interaction* (pp. 64–68). Great Barrington, MA: Berkshire Publishing Group.

Bailey, J., & Bakos, J. Y. (1997). An exploratory study of the emerging role of electronic intermediaries. *International Journal of Electronic Commerce, 1,* 7–20.

Bakker, M., Leenders, R., Gabbay, S., Kratzer, J., & Engelen, J. (2006). Is trust really social capital? Knowledge sharing in product development projects. *The Learning Organization, 13,* 594–605. doi:10.1108/09696470610705479

Barbalet, J. (2009). A characterization of trust, and its consequences. *Theory and Society, 38*(4), 367–382. doi:10.1007/s11186-009-9087-3

Barber, B. (1983). *Logic and Limits of Trust.* New Brunswick, NJ: Rutgers University Press.

Barker, L. B. (1989). Survey Research. In Emmert, P., & Barker, L. B. (Eds.), *Measurement of Communication Behavior* (pp. 25–39). New York: Longman.

Barsoux, J.-L. (1993). *Funny business: Humour, management and business culture.* London: Cassell.

Bart, Y., Shankar, V., Sultan, F., & Urban, G. L. (2005). Are the Drivers and Role of Online Trust the Same for All Web Sites and Consumers? A Large-Scale Exploratory Empirical Study. *Journal of Marketing, 69*(4), 133–152. doi:10.1509/jmkg.2005.69.4.133

Bartle, R. (2003). *Designing virtual worlds.* Indianapolis, IN: New Riders Publishing.

Baruch, Y. (2004). Transforming careers: from linear to multidirectional career paths: Organizational and individual perspectives. *Career Development International, 9*(1), 58–73. doi:10.1108/13620430410518147

Batson, C. D., Polycarpou, M. P., Harmon-Jones, E., Imhoff, H. J., Mitchener, E. C., & Bednar, L. L. (1997). Empathy and attitudes: Can feeling for a member of a stigmatized group improve feelings toward the group. *Journal of Personality and Social Psychology, 72,* 105–118. doi:10.1037/0022-3514.72.1.105

Batt, R., Christopherson, S., Rightor, N., & van Jaarsveld, D. (2001). *Net working: Labor market challenges for the new media workforce.* Washington, DC: Economic Policy Institute.

Battaglia, T. A., Finley, E., & Liebschutz, J. M. (2003). Survivors of intimate partner violence speak out: Trust in the patient-provider relationship. *Journal of General Internal Medicine, 18,* 617–623. doi:10.1046/j.1525-1497.2003.21013.x

Bauman, Z. (1997). *Postmodernity and its discontents.* Cambridge, MA: Polity Press.

Baye, M. (2002). Special Issue on The economics of the Internet and e-commerce. *Advances in Applied Microeconomics, 11.*

Baym, N. (1995). The emergence of community in computer mediated communication. In Jones, S. G. (Ed.), *Cybersociety: Computer mediated communication and community* (pp. 138–163). Thousand Oaks, CA: Sage.

Baym, N. (1997). Interpreting soap operas and creating community: Inside an electronic fan culture. In Keisler, S. (Ed.), *Culture of the Internet.* Manhaw, NJ: Lawrence Erlbaum Associates.

Baym, N. K. (2000). *Tune in log on: soaps, fandom and online community.* Thousand Oaks, CA: Sage.

Beatty, R. W., & Ulrich, D. O. (1993). *Re-energising the Mature Organisation. Managing Change: Cases and Concepts.* New York: McGraw-Hill.

Beaulieu, A. (2004). Mediating ethnography: Objectivity and the making of ethnographies of the Internet. *Social Epistemology, 18*(2-3), 139–163. doi:10.1080/0269172042000249264

Becerra, M., & Gupta, A. (2003). Perceived trustworthiness within the organization: The moderating impact of communication frequency on trustor and trustee effects. *Organization Science, 14*(1), 32–45. doi:10.1287/orsc.14.1.32.12815

Beck, U. (1992). *Risk society: Towards a new modernity.* Newbury Park, CA: SAGE Publications.

Beckert, J. (2005). Trust and the performative construction of markets. *MPIfG Discussion Paper* 05/8. Koeln, Germany: Max Planck Institut fuer Gesellschaftsforschung. Retrieved May 1, 2009, from http://www.mpifg.de/pu/mpifg_dp/dp05-8.pdf

Beem, C. (1999). *The necessity of politics. Reclaiming American public life.* Chicago: University of Chicago Press.

Begole, J., Struble, C. A., Shaffer, C. A., & Smith, R. B. (1997). Transparent Sharing of Java Applets: A Replicated Approach. In G. Robinson, & C. Schmandt (Ed.), *Proceedings of the 10th annual ACM symposium on User interface software and technology*, Banff, Alberta, Canada, October 14 - 17, 1997 (pp. 55-64). New York: ACM Press

Belanger, F., Hiller, J. S., & Smith, W. J. (2002). Trustworthiness in electronic commerce: the role of privacy, security, and site attributes. *The Journal of Strategic Information Systems*, *11*(3/4), 245–270. doi:10.1016/S0963-8687(02)00018-5

Bell, G. (2005). The age of the thumb: A cultural reading of mobile technologies from Asia. In Thumb culture: The meaning of mobile phones for society, eds. P. Glotz, S. Bertschi and C. Locke, Boslego, J. (2005). Engineering social trust what can communities and institutions do? International Health, 27 (1) – Spring.

Beninger, J. R. (1987). Personalization of mass media and the growth of pseudo-community. *Communication Research*, *14*, 352–371. doi:10.1177/009365087014003005

Benkler, Y. (2006). *The wealth of Networks. How Social Production transforms Markets and Freedom.* New Haven, CT: Yale University Press.

Ben-Ner, A., & Putterman, L. (2002). *Trust in the new economy.* Minneapolis, MN: University of Minnesota, Industrial Relations Centre.

Ben-Ze'ev, A. (2004). *Love online: Emotions on the Internet.* Cambridge, UK: Cambridge University Press. doi:10.1017/CBO9780511489785

Berger, J., & Fişek, M. H. (2006). Diffuse status characteristics and the spread of status value: A formal theory. *American Journal of Sociology*, *111*, 1038–1079. doi:10.1086/498633

Berger, J., & Webster, M. (2006). Expectations, status, and behavior. In Burke, P. (Ed.), *Contemporary social psychological theories* (pp. 268–300). Stanford, CA: Stanford University Press.

Berger, J., Fisek, M. H., Norman, R. Z., & Wagner, D. G. (1985). The formation of reward expectations in status situations. In Berger, J., & Zelditch, M. Jr., (Eds.), *Status, reward, and influence: How expectations organize behavior* (pp. 215–261). San Francisco: Jossey-Bass.

Berger, J., Fisek, M. H., Norman, R. Z., & Zelditch, M. Jr. (1977). *Status characteristics and social interaction.* New York: Elsevier.

Berger, P. L., & Luckmann, T. (1966). *The Social Construction of Reality.* Garden City, NY: Doubleday.

Berggren, N., & Jordahl, H. (2006). Free to trust: Economic freedom and social capital. *Kyklos*, *59*, 141–169. doi:10.1111/j.1467-6435.2006.00324.x

Berhnheim, B. D., & Whinston, M. D. (1998). Incomplete contracts and strategic ambiguity. *The American Economic Review*, *88*, 902–932.

Best, A. L. (2006). Introduction. In Best, A. L. (Ed.), *Representing Youth: Methodological Issues in Critical Youth Studies* (pp. 1–38). New York: NYU Press.

Bhattacherjee, A. (2002). Individual Trust in Online Firms: Scale Development and Initial Test. *Journal of Management Information Systems*, *19*(1), 211–241.

Bierhoff, H.-W., & Vornefeld, B. (2004). The social psychology of trust with applications in the Internet. *Analyse & Kritik*, *26*, 48–62.

Bijker, W. E. (1995). Sociohistorical Technology Studies. In Jasanoff, S., Markle, G. E., Peterson, J. C., & Pinch, T. (Eds.), *Handbook of Science and Technology Studies* (pp. 229–256). Thousand Oaks, CA: Sage.

Bimber, B. (2000). Measuring the gender gap on the internet. *Social Science Quarterly, 81,* 868–876.

Birchall, D. W., & Giambona, G. (2007). SME manager development in virtual learning communities and the role of trust: A conceptual study. *Human Resource Development International, 10*(2), 187–202. doi:10.1080/13678860701347164

Birchall, D. W., & Tovstiga, G. (2005). *Capabilities for Strategic Advantage – Leading through Technological Innovation.* London: Palgrave.

Birchall, D. W., Giambona, G., & Gill, J. (2008). Who is on the other side of the screen? Learning in a virtual environment. In Kautonen, T., & Karjaluoto, H. (Eds.), *Trust and New Technologies.* Cheltenham, UK: Edward Elgar Publishing.

Birchall, D., & Lyons, L. (1995). *Creating Tomorrow's Organisation.* London: Pitman.

Birchmeier, Z., Joinson, A. N., & Dietz Uhler, B. (2005). Storming and forming a normative response to a deception revealed online. *Social Science Computer Review, 23*(1), 108–121. doi:10.1177/0894439304271542

Bjørnskov, C. (2003). The happy few. Cross-country evidence on social capital and life satisfaction. *Kyklos, 56,* 3–16. doi:10.1111/1467-6435.00207

Bjørnskov, C. (2007). Determinants of generalized trust: A cross-country comparison. *Public Choice, 130,* 1–21. doi:10.1007/s11127-006-9069-1

Blachman, J. (2005, August 31). Job posting. *New York Times,* p. 19.

Blais, D. (2001). 'Walla chat': An Ethnographic View of an Israeli Internet Chat Site [in Hebrew]. *Kesher, 30,* 77–92.

Blanchard, A. L. (2008). Testing a Model of Sense of Virtual Community. *Computers in Human Behavior, 24,* 2107–2123. doi:10.1016/j.chb.2007.10.002

Blanchard, A. L., & Markus, M. L. (2004). The experienced sense of a virtual community: Characteristics and processes. *The Data Base for Advances in Information Systems, 35*(1), 65–79.

Blau, P. (1964). *Exchange and power in social life.* New York: Wiley.

Blau, P. (1973). *The Dynamics of Bureaucracy.* Chicago: University of Chicago Press.

Blumer, H. (1969). *Symbolic interaction: Perspective and method.* Englewood Cliffs, NJ: Prentice Hall.

Bogdan, R. C., & Biklen, S. K. (1982). *Qualitative Research for Education: An Introduction to Theory and Methods* (2nd ed.). Boston: Allyn and Bacon.

Bohnet, I., Frey, B. S., & Huck, S. (2001). More order with less law: On contract enforcement, trust, and crowding. *The American Political Science Review, 95,* 131–144. doi:10.1017/S0003055401000211

Bolton, G. E., & Ockenfels, A. (2006). *The Limits of Trust in Economic Transactions. Investigations of Perfect Reputation Systems.* Retrieved from http://ockenfels. uni-koeln.de/uploads/tx_ockmedia/Bolton_Ockenfels_Limits_of_Trust.pdf

Bolton, G. E., Katok, E., & Ockenfels, A. (2004). Trust among internet traders. A behavioral economics approach. *Analyse & Kritik, 26,* 185–202.

Bolton, G., Loebecke, C., & Ockenfels, A. (2008). Does competition promote trust and trustworthiness in online trading? An experimental study. *Journal of Management Information Systems, 25*(2), 145–169. doi:10.2753/MIS0742-1222250207

Boon, S., & Holmes, J. (1991). The dynamics of interpersonal trust: Resolving uncertainty in the face of risk. In Hinde, R. A. (Ed.), *Cooperation and prosocial behavior* (pp. 167–182). New York: Cambridge University Press.

Boutin, P. (2008, October 20). Twitter, Flickr, Facebook make blogs look so 2004. *Wired Magazine,* 16.

Bowman, E. H., & Singh, H. (1993). Corporate restructuring: Reconfiguring the firm. *Strategic Management Journal, 14*(2), 5–14. doi:10.1002/smj.4250140903

Boyd, D. (2007, June 24). Viewing American class divisions through Facebook and MySpace. *Apophenia Blog Essay.* Retrieved June 20, 2009, from http://www.danah.org/papers/essays/ClassDivisions.html

Boyd, D. M., & Ellison, N. B. (2007). Social network sites: Definition, history, and scholarship. *Journal of Computer-Mediated Communication, 13*(1). Retrieved from http://jcmc.indiana.edu/vol13/issue1/boyd.ellison.html.

Boyns, D., Forghani, S., & Sosnovskaya, E. (2009). MMORPG worlds: On the construction of social reality in World of Warcraft. In Heider, D. (Ed.), *Living virtually: Researching new worlds* (pp. 67–92). New York: Peter Lang.

Bracken, C. C., & Lombard, M. (2004). Social presence and children: Praise, intrinsic motivation, and learning with computers. *The Journal of Communication, 54,* 22–37. doi:10.1111/j.1460-2466.2004.tb02611.x

Brann, P., & Foddy, M. (1988). Trust and the consumption of a deteriorating resource. *The Journal of Conflict Resolution, 31*(4), 615–630. doi:10.1177/0022002787031004004

Brave, S. B., Nass, C., & Hutchinson, K. (2005). Computers that care: Investigating the effects of orientation of emotion exhibited by an embodied computer agent. *International Journal of Human-Computer Studies, 62,* 161–178. doi:10.1016/j.ijhcs.2004.11.002

Brave, S., & Nass, C. (2008). Emotion in Human-Computer Interaction. In Sears, A., & Jacko, J. A. (Eds.), *The Human-Computer Interaction Handbook: Fundamentals, Evolving Technology and Emerging Applications* (2nd ed., pp. 77–92). New York: Taylor & Francis.

Bremner, C. (2007, March 30). Secretary sacked for blog on office life wins £30,000. *The Times.*

Brewer, M. B. (1981). Ethnocentrism and its role in interpersonal trust. In Brewer, M. B., & Collins, B. E. (Eds.), *Scientific inquiry and the social sciences* (pp. 345–359). New York: Jossey-Bass.

Brickham, P., Becker, L. J., & Castle, S. (1979). Making trust easier and harder. *Journal of Personality and Social Psychology, 62*(6), 989–1002.

Brinkmann, U., & Seifert, M. (2001). Face to Interface: Zum Problem der Vertrauenskonstitution im Internet am Beispiel von elektronischen Auktionen. *Zeitschrift für Soziologie, 30*(1), 23–47.

Brinton, M. (1992). *Women and the economic miracle: Gender and work in postwar Japan.* Berkeley, CA: University of California Press.

Brinton, M., & Nee, V. (Eds.). (1998). *The new institutionalism in sociology.* Stanford, CA: Stanford University Press.

Bunting, M. (2004). *Willing slaves: How the overwork culture is ruling our lives.* London: HarperCollins.

Burke, P. J., & Stets, J. E. (2009). *Identity Theory.* Oxford, UK: Oxford University.

Burleson, B. R., & Goldsmith, D. J. (1998). How the comforting process works: Alleviating emotional distress through conversationally induced reappraisals. In Andersen, P. A., & Guerrero, L. K. (Eds.), *Handbook of communication and emotion: Research, theory, applications, and contexts* (pp. 245–279). San Diego, CA: Academic Press.

Burt, R. (1987). Social contagion and innovation: Cohesion versus structural equivalence. *American Journal of Sociology, 92,* 1287–1335. doi:10.1086/228667

Burt, R. S. (2005). *Brokerage and Closure.* Oxford, UK: Oxford University.

Burt, R. S., & Knez, M. (1996). Trust and Third-Party Gossip. In Kramer, R. M., & Tyler, T. R. (Eds.), *Trust in Organizations: Frontiers of Theory and Research* (pp. 68–89). Thousand Oaks, CA: Sage.

Butler, P. (2005, February 4). Reality bytes: What's up, Doc? NHS blogger in mystery moonlight flit. *The Guardian.*

Byrne, D., Griffitt, W., & Stefanik, D. (1967). Attraction and similarity of personality characteristics. *Journal of Personality and Social Psychology, 5,* 82–90. doi:10.1037/h0021198

Byrne, M. D. (2008). Cognitive Architecture. In Sears, A., & Jacko, J. A. (Eds.), *The Human-Computer Interaction Handbook: Fundamentals, Evolving Technology and Emerging Applications* (2nd ed., pp. 93–113). New York: Taylor & Francis.

Callon, M., & Latour, B. (1992). Don't Throw the Baby out with the Bath School! A Reply to Colins and Yearley. In Pickering, A. (Ed.), *Science as Practice and Culture* (pp. 343–368). Chicago, IL: University of Chicago.

Calvert, S. L., Rideout, V. J., Woolard, J. L., Barr, R. F., & Strouse, G. A. (2005). Age, ethnicity, and socio-economic patterns in early computer use: A national survey. *The American Behavioral Scientist, 48*, 590–607. doi:10.1177/0002764204271508

Camp, L. J. (2000). *Trust and Risk in Internet Commerce*. Cambridge, MA: The MIT Press.

Camp, L. J., Nissenbaum, H., & McGrath, C. (2002). Trust: A collision of paradigms. *Lecture Notes in Computer Science, 2339*, 91–105. doi:10.1007/3-540-46088-8_10

Campos, C., & Schultz, M. (2009). *Status-based trust and its effects on workplace mobility.* Presented at the annual meeting of the American Sociological Association, San Francisco, CA.

Carley, K. M. (2002). Smart Agents and Organizations of the Future. In Lievrouw, L., & Livingstone, S. (Eds.), *The Handbook of New Media* (pp. 206–220). Thousand Oaks, CA: Sage.

Carruthers, B., Babb, S., & Halliday, T. (2001). Institutionalizing Markets, or the Market for Institutions? In Campbell, J. L., & Pedersen, O. K. (Eds.), *The Rise of Neoliberalism and Institutionalism Analysis* (pp. 94–126). Princeton, NJ: Princeton University Press.

Cassell, J., & Bickmore, T. (2000). External manifestations of trustworthiness in the interface. *Communications of the ACM, 43*(12), 50–56. doi:10.1145/355112.355123

Cassell, J., Sullivan, J., Prevost, S., & Churchill, E. (2000). *Embodied conversational agents*. Cambridge, MA: MIT Press.

Castaldo, S. (2007). *Trust in Marketing Relationships*. Cheltenham, UK: Edward Elgar.

Castells, M. (2001). *The Internet galaxy: Reflections on the Internet, business and society*. Oxford, UK: Oxford University Press.

Castells, M. (2004). *Informationalism, Networks and the Network Society: A Theoretical Blueprint*. Retrieved March 27, 2009, from http://ascweb.usc.edu/pubs/faculty/Informationalism.pdf

Castells, M., Qiu, J. l., Fern'andez-Ard'evol, M., & Sey, A. (2007). *Mobile communication and society: A global perspective (information revolution and global politics)*. Cambridge, MA: MIT Press.

Castronova, E. (2005). *Synthetic worlds: The business and culture of online games*. Chicago: University of Chicago Press.

Castronova, E. (2007). *Exodus to the virtual world: How online fun is changing reality*. New York: Palgrave Macmillian.

Cespedes, F. V., & Smith, H. J. (1993). Database Marketing: new rules for policy and practice. *Sloan Management Review, 34*(Summer), 8–12.

Chaikin, A. L., & Derlega, V. J. (1974). *Self-disclosure*. Morristown, NJ: General Learning Press.

Chang, M. K., Cheung, W., & Lai, V. S. (2005). Literature derived reference models for the adoption of online shopping. *Information & Management, 42*, 543–559. doi:10.1016/S0378-7206(04)00051-5

Charmaz, K. (2006). *Constructing grounded theory: A practical guide through qualitative analysis*. Thousand Oaks, CA: Sage Publications.

Chau, P. Y. K., & Lai, V. S. K. (2003). An Empirical Investigation of the Determinants of User Acceptance of Internet Banking. *Journal of Organizational Computing and Electronic Commerce, 13*(2), 123–145. doi:10.1207/S15327744JOCE1302_3

Chaudhuri, A., & Holbrook, M. B. (2001). The chain of effects from brand trust and brand affect to brand performance: The role of brand loyalty. *Journal of Marketing, 65*, 81–93. doi:10.1509/jmkg.65.2.81.18255

Chebat, J. C., & Cohen, A. (1993). Response speed in mail surveys: beware of shortcuts. *Marketing Research, 5*(Spring), 20–26.

Chen, S. C., & Dhillon, G. S. (2003). Interpreting dimensions of consumer trust in e-commerce. *Information Technology and Management*, *4*(2/3), 303–318. doi:10.1023/A:1022962631249

Cheshire, C., & Antin, J. (2008). The Social Psychological Effects of Feedback on the Production of Internet Information Pools. *Journal of Computer-Mediated Communication*, *13*(3). doi:10.1111/j.1083-6101.2008.00416.x

Cheshire, C., & Antin, J. (in press). Order, Coordination and Uncertainty. In Cook, K. S., Snijders, C., Buskins, V., & Cheshire, C. (Eds.), *eTrust and Reputation*. New York: Russell Sage Foundation.

Cheshire, C., & Cook, K. S. (2004). The Emergence of trust networks under uncertainty – Implications for Internet interactions. *Analyse & Kritik*, *26*, 220–240.

Cheshire, C., & Cook, K. S. (2004). The Emergence of Trust Networks: Implications for Online Interaction. *Analyse & Kritik*, 28.

Cheshire, C., & Cook, K. S. (2004). Uncertainty and the emergence of trust networks: Implications for research on the internet. *Analyse & Kritik*, *28*, 220–240.

Cheshire, C., Gerbasi, A., Cook, K. S., & Harkness, S. (2009, August). *Trust and Structural Shifts in Modes of Exchange*. Paper presented at the meeting of the American Sociological Association, San Francisco, CA.

Chetty, S., & Blankenburg, H. D. (2000). Internationalisation of small to medium-sized manufacturing firms: a network approach. *International Business Review*, *9*(1), 77–93. doi:10.1016/S0969-5931(99)00030-X

Cheung, C. M. K., & Lee, M. K. O. (2006). Understanding consumer trust in internet-shopping: a multidisciplinary approach. *Journal of the American Society for Information Science and Technology*, *57*(4), 479–492. doi:10.1002/asi.20312

Cheung, S. (1974). A theory of price control. *The Journal of Law & Economics*, *12*, 53–71. doi:10.1086/466784

Chipuer, H. M., & Pretty, G. H. (1999). A review of the sense of community index: Current uses, factor structure, reliability and further development. *Journal of Community Psychology*, *27*, 643–658. doi:10.1002/(SICI)1520-6629(199911)27:6<643::AID-JCOP2>3.0.CO;2-B

Choi, B., & Lee, H. (2003). An empirical investigation of knowledge management styles and their effect on corporate performance. *Information & Management*, *40*, 403–417. doi:10.1016/S0378-7206(02)00060-5

Christopherson, S. (2004). The divergent worlds of new media: How policy shapes work in the creative economy. *Review of Policy Research*, *21*(4), 543–558. doi:10.1111/j.1541-1338.2004.00093.x

Cialdini, R. (1996). The Triple tumor structure of organizational behavior. In Messick, D. M., & Tenbrunsel, A. E. (Eds.), *Codes of conduct* (pp. 44–58). New York: Russell Sage Foundation.

Cialdini, R. B. (1993). *Influence: Science and practice*. New York: HarperCollins.

Ciborra, C. U. (1993). *Teams, markets and systems*. Cambridge, UK: Cambridge University Press.

CIDA. (2002). CIDA's strategy on knowledge for development through information and communications technologies, available at: www.acdi-cida.gc.ca/ict, (accessed 5 January 2009).

Clay-Warner, J., & Robinson, D. T. (2008). *Social Structure and Emotion*. Amsterdam: Elsevier.

Cleary, M., & Stokes, S. C. (2006). *Democracy and the culture of skepticism: Political trust in Argentina and Mexico*. New York: Russell Sage Foundation.

Coase, R. (1937). The nature of the firm. *Economica*, *4*, 386–405. doi:10.1111/j.1468-0335.1937.tb00002.x

Coase, R. (1960). The problem of social cost. *The Journal of Law & Economics*, *3*, 1–44. doi:10.1086/466560

Cobbetts. (2005, February). Danger! Bloggers at work. *Employment Matters*.

Coleman, J. (1990). *Foundations of social theory*. Cambridge, MA: Harvard University Press.

Coleman, J. S. (1988). Social capital in the creation of human capital. *American Journal of Sociology, 94*, S95–S120. doi:10.1086/228943

Coleman, J. S., Katz, E., & Menzel, H. (1957). The diffusion of an innovation among physicians. *Sociometry, 20*, 253–270. doi:10.2307/2785979

Collins, C. J., & Smith, K. G. (2006). Knowledge exchange and combination: the role of human resource practices in the performance of high-technology firms. *Academy of Management Journal, 49*, 544–560.

Collins, H. M. (1995). Science Studies and Machine Intelligence. In Jasanoff, S., Markle, G. E., Peterson, J. C., & Pinch, T. (Eds.), *Handbook of Science and Technology Studies*. Thousand Oaks, CA: Sage.

Consalvo, M. (2007). *Cheating: Gaining Advantage in Videogames*. Cambridge, MA: MIT Press.

Cook, K. (2005). Networks, norms, and trust: The Social psychology of social capital. *Social Psychology Quarterly, 68*(1), 4–14. doi:10.1177/019027250506800102

Cook, K. S., & Emerson, R. M. (1978). Power, Equity and Commitment in Exchange Networks. *American Sociological Review, 43*, 721–731. doi:10.2307/2094546

Cook, K. S., & Levi, M. (1990). *The limits of rationality*. Chicago: University of Chicago Press.

Cook, K. S., Cheshire, C., & Gerbasi, A. (2006). Power, Dependence, and Social Exchange. In Burke, P. J. (Ed.), *Contemporary Social Psychological Theories*. Stanford, CA: Stanford University Press.

Cook, K. S., Cheshire, C., Gerbasi, A., & Aven, B. (in press). Assessing Trustworthiness in Online Goods and Services. In Cook, K. S., Snijders, C., Buskins, V., & Cheshire, C. (Eds.), *eTrust and Reputation*. New York: Russell Sage Foundation.

Cook, K. S., Emerson, R. M., Gillmore, M. R., & Yamagishi, T. (1983). The Distribution of Power in Exchange Networks: Theory and Experimental Results. *American Journal of Sociology, 89*(2), 275–305. doi:10.1086/227866

Cook, K. S., Hardin, R., & Levi, M. (2005). *Cooperation without trust?* New York: Russell Sage Foundation.

Cook, K. S., Rice, E. R., & Gerbasi, A. (2004). The Emergence of Trust Networks under Uncertainty: The Case of Transitional Economies – Insights from Social Psychological Research. In Ackerman, S. R., Rothstein, B., & Kornai, J. (Eds.), *Problems of Post Socialist Transition: Creating Social Trust*. New York: Palgrave.

Cook, K. S., Yamagishi, T., Cheshire, C., Cooper, R., Matsuda, M., & Rie, M. (2005). Trust Building via Risk Taking: A Cross-Societal Experiment. *Social Psychology Quarterly, 68*, 121–142. doi:10.1177/019027250506800202

Copeland, D. G., & McKenney, J. L. (1988). Airline Reservation Systems: Lessons from History. *Management Information Systems Quarterly, 12*(3), 353–370. doi:10.2307/249202

Cordella, A. (2006). Transaction costs and information systems: Does IT add up? *Journal of Information Technology, 21*, 195–202. doi:10.1057/palgrave.jit.2000066

Corritore, C. L., Kracher, B., & Wiedenbeck, S. (2003). On-line trust: concepts, evolving themes, a model. *International Journal of Human-Computer Studies, 58*, 737–758. doi:10.1016/S1071-5819(03)00041-7

Crisp, C. B., & Jarvenpaa, S. L. (2000). *Trust over Time in Global Virtual Teams*. Austin, TX: University of Texas Publishing.

Culnan, M. J. (1993). How did they get my name? An exploratory investigation of consumer attitudes toward secondary information use. *Management Information Systems Quarterly, 17*(3), 341–363. doi:10.2307/249775

Culnan, M. J. (2008). Online communities: Infrastructure, relational cohesion and sustainability. *Computerization Movements and Technology Diffusion: From Mainframes to Ubiqutous Computing*.

Culnan, M. J., & Markus, M. L. (1987). Information technologies: electronic media and interorganizational communication. In Jablin, F. M., Putnam, L. L., Roberts, K. H., & Porter, L. W. (Eds.), *Handbook of Organizational Communication: An Interdisciplinary Perspective*. Newbury Park, CA: Sage.

Cummings, L. L., & Bromiley, P. (1996). The organizational trust inventory (OTI), Development and validation. In Kramer, R. M., & Tyler, T. R. (Eds.), *Trust in Organizations: Frontiers in Theory and Research* (pp. 302–330). Thousand Oaks, CA: Sage Publications.

Cunningham, L. F., Gerlach, J., & Harper, M. D. (2005). Perceived risk and e-banking services: An analysis from the perspective of the consumer. *Journal of Financial Services Marketing, 10*(2), 165–178. doi:10.1057/palgrave.fsm.4770183

D'Aveni, R. A. (1994). *Hypercompetition: Managing the Dynamics of Strategic Manoeuvring*. New York: The Free Press.

Dabholkar, P. A., & Bagozzi, R. (2002). An attitudinal model of technology-based-self-service: Moderating effects of consumer traits and situational factors. *Journal of the Academy of Marketing Science, 30*(3), 184–201.

Daft, R. L., & Lengel, R. H. (1986). Organizational Information Requirements, Media Richness and Structural Design. *Management Science, 32*(5), 554–571. doi:10.1287/mnsc.32.5.554

Damarin, A. K. (2004). *Fit, flexibility, and connection: Organizing employment in emerging web labor markets. New York City 1993-2003.* Unpublished doctoral dissertation, Columbia University, New York.

Damarin, A. K. (2006). Rethinking occupational structure - The case of web site production work. *Work and Occupations, 33*(4), 429–463. doi:10.1177/0730888406293917

Danet, B. (1996). Text as mask: Gender, play and performance on the Internet. In Jones, S. G. (Ed.), *Cybersociety 2.0: Revisiting computer-mediated communication and community* (pp. 122–138). Thousand Oaks, CA: Sage.

Danet, B. (2001). *Cyberpl@y*. London: Berg.

Dani, S. S., Burns, N. D., Backhouse, C. J., & Kochhar, A. K. (2006). The implications of organizational culture and trust in the working of virtual teams. *Journal of Engineering Manufacture, 220*(B), 951-960.

Das, T. K., & Teng, B. (1998, July). Between trust and control: developing confidence in partner cooperation in alliances. *Academy of Management Review, 23*, 491–512. doi:10.2307/259291

Das, T. K., & Teng, B.-S. (1998). Resource and Risk Management in the Strategic Alliance Making Process. *Journal of Management, 24*(1), 21–42. doi:10.1016/S0149-2063(99)80052-X

Dasgupta, P. (1988). Trust as a commodity. In Gambetta, D. (Ed.), *Trust: Making and breaking cooperative relations* (pp. 49–72). New York: Basil Blackwell.

Dasgupta, P. (in press). Trust and Cooperation among Economic Agents. In Philosophical Transactions of the Royal Society B

Datta, P., & Chatterjee, S. (2008). The economics and psychology of consumer trust in intermediaries in electronic markets: the EM-Trust framework. *European Journal of Information Systems, 17*, 12–28. doi:10.1057/palgrave.ejis.3000729

David, S., & Pinch, T. (2005). Six Degrees of Reputation: The Use and Abuse of Online Review and Recommendation Systems. *Social Science Research Network Working Paper Series*.

Davies, S. (1979). *The diffusion of process innovations*. New York: Cambridge University Press.

Davis, F. D. (1989). Perceived usefulness, perceived ease of use and user acceptance of information technology. *Management Information Systems Quarterly, 13*(3), 319–340. doi:10.2307/249008

Davis, F. D., Bagozzi, R. P., & Warshaw, P. R. (1989). User acceptance of computer technology: A comparison of two theoretical models. *Management Science, 35*(8), 982–1003. doi:10.1287/mnsc.35.8.982

Davis, M. H. (1996). *Empathy: A social psychological approach*. Boulder, CO: Westview Press.

Dawes, R. (1980). Social Dilemmas. *Annual Review of Psychology, 31*, 169–193. doi:10.1146/annurev.ps.31.020180.001125

Dawes, R. M. (1994). *House of cards: Psychology and psychotherapy built on myth*. New York: Free Press.

Dayal, S., Landesberg, H., & Zeisser, M. (1999). How to build trust online. *Marketing Management Fall, 8*(3), 64-69.

De Koster, W., & Houtman, D. (2008). 'Stormfront is like a second home to me': On virtual community formation by right-wing extremists. *Information. Communication and Technology, 11*(8), 1155–1176.

Deal, T. E., & Kennedy, A. A. (1982). *Corporate cultures: The rites and rituals of corporate life*. Reading, MA: Addison-Wesley.

DeCew, J. (1997). *In Pursuit of Privacy. Law, Ethics, and the Rise of Technology*. Ithaca, NY: Cornell University Press.

Deci, E. L. (1971). Effects of externally mediated rewards on intrinsic motivation. *Journal of Personality and Social Psychology, 18*, 105–115. doi:10.1037/h0030644

Deci, E. L., Koestner, R., & Ryan, R. M. (1999). A meta-analytic review of experiments examining the effects of extrinsic rewards on intrinsic motivation. *Psychological Bulletin, 125*, 627–668. doi:10.1037/0033-2909.125.6.627

Defilippi, R. J. (2002). Organizational models for collaboration in the new economy. *Human Resource Planning, 25*(2), 24–35.

Delhey, J., & Newton, K. (2005). Predicting cross-national levels of social trust: Global pattern or Nordic exceptionalism? *European Sociological Review, 21*, 311–327. doi:10.1093/esr/jci022

Demsetz, H. (1967). Towards a theory of property rights. *The American Economic Review, 57*, 347–359.

Dennis, A. R., & Kinney, S. T. (1998). Testing media richness theory in the new media: The effects of cues, feedback, and task equivocality. *Information Systems Research, 9*(3). doi:10.1287/isre.9.3.256

Diaz, A. (2008). Through the Google Goggles: Socio-political bias in Search Engine Design. In Zimmer, M., & Spink, A. (Eds.), *Web Search. Multidisciplinary Perspectives* (pp. 11–34). Heidelberg, Germany: Springer.

Dibbell, J. (1998). *My tiny life: Crime and passion in a virtual world*. New York: Holt.

Digman, J. M. (1990). Personality structure: Emergence of the five-factor model. *Annual Review of Psychology, 41*, 417–440.

DiMaggio, P. J., & Powell, W. W. (1983). The iron cage revisited: Institutional isomorphism and collective rationality in organizational fields. *American Sociological Review, 48*(2), 147–160. doi:10.2307/2095101

DiMaggio, P., & Louch, H. (1998). Socially embedded consumer transactions: For what kinds of purchases do people most often use networks? *American Sociological Review, 63*, 619–637. doi:10.2307/2657331

DiMaggio, P., & Powell, W. W. (1983). The iron cage revisited: Institutional isomorphism and collective rationality in organizational fields. *American Sociological Review, 63*, 147–160. doi:10.2307/2095101

DiMaggio, P., Hargittai, E., Neuman, W. R., & Robinson, J. P. (2001). Social Implications of the Internet. *Annual Review of Sociology, 27*, 307–336. doi:10.1146/annurev.soc.27.1.307

Doctorow, C. (2005, July 24). Would you give a fiver a month for a UK tech/civil liberties org? *BoingBoing*. Retrieved 30 November 2006, from http://boingboing.net/2005_07_01_archive.html.

Donath, J. (1998). Identity and Deception in the Virtual Community. In Smith, M., & Kollock, P. (Eds.), *Communities in Cyberspace*. London: Routledge.

Donath, J. (in press). *Signals, Truth and Design*. Cambridge, MA: MIT Press.

Drucker, P. (1973). *Management*. New York: Harper & Row.

Drucker, P. (1994). *Knowledge work and knowledge society: The social transformations of this century*. Paper presented at the 1994 Edwin L. Godkin Lecture. Retrieved 1 August 2006, from http://www.ksg.harvard.edu/ifactory/ksgpress/www/ksg_news/transcripts/drucklec.htm

Duarte, D., & Tennant-Snyder, N. (1999). *Mastering Virtual Teams: Strategies, Tools and Techniques that Succeed*. San Francisco: Jossey-Bass Publishers.

Ducheneaut, N., & Moore, R. J. (2004). The social side of gaming: A study of interaction patterns in a massively multiplayer online game. In *Proceedings of the ACM conference on computer-supported cooperative work,* Chicago, IL (pp. 360-369).

Ducheneaut, N., Moore, R. J., & Nickell, E. (2004). Designing for sociability in massively multiplayer games: an examination of the third places of SWG. In J. H. Smith & M. Sicart (Eds.), *Proceedings of the other players conference.* Copenhagen, Denmark: IT University of Copenhagen.

Ducheneaut, N., Yee, N., Nickell, E., & Moore, R. J. (2006). Alone together? Exploring the social dynamics of massively multiplayer games. *Conference proceedings on human factors in computing systems CHI2006* (pp. 407-416). Montreal, PQ, Canada.

Ducheneaut, N., Yee, N., Nickell, E., & Moore, R. J. (2007). The life and death of online gaming communities: A look at guilds in World of Warcraft. In *Proceedings of CHI 2007* (pp. 839-848). New York: ACM.

Durkheim, E. (1893). *The division of labor in society.* London: MacMillan. (Original work published 1984)

Durkheim, E. (1949). *The Division of Labor in Society.* Glencoe, IL: Free Press.

Durkheim, E. (1982). *The rules of sociological method.* New York: The Free Press. (Original work published 1895)

Durkheim, E. (1984). *Division of labor in society.* New York: The Free Press. (Original work published 1893)

Dutton, W. H., & Shepard, A. (2006). Trust in the Internet as an experience technology. *Information Communication and Society, 9*(4), 433–451. doi:10.1080/13691180600858606

Dutton, W. H., & Shepherd, A. (2006). Trust in the Internet as an experience technology. *Information Communication and Society, 9*(4), 433–451. doi:10.1080/13691180600858606

Dyer, J. H., & Nobeoka, K. (2000). Creating and managing a high-performance knowledge-sharing network: The Toyota case. *Strategic Management Journal, 21*(3), 345–367. doi:10.1002/(SICI)1097-0266(200003)21:3<345::AID-SMJ96>3.0.CO;2-N

Eggertsson, T. (1990). *Economic behavior and institutions.* Cambridge, UK: Cambridge University Press. doi:10.1017/CBO9780511609404

Eimeren, B., & Frees, B. (2008). *Internetzuwachs: Größter Zuwachs bei den Silversurfern. Ergebnisse der ARD/ZDF-Onlinerstudie 2008.* Retrieved from http://www.daserste.de/service/studie08_1.pdf

Einwiller, S., & Will, M. (2001). *The Role of Reputation to Engender Trust in Electronic Markets.* Paper presented at the Proceedings of the 5th International Conference on Corporate Reputation, Identity, and Competitiveness, Paris.

Eisenstadt, S. N. (1974). Friendship and the structure of trust and solidarity in society. In Leyton, E. (Ed.), *The compact: Selected dimensions of friendship* (pp. 138–145). Toronto, Canada: University of Toronto Press.

Ekman, P., & Friesen, W. V. (1969). Nonverbal leakage and clues to deception. *Psychiatry, 32,* 88–95.

Ekman, P., & Friesen, W. V. (1974). Detecting deceeption from the body or face. *Journal of Personality and Social Psychology, 29,* 288–298. doi:10.1037/h0036006

Electronic Frontier Foundation. (2005a, May 31). *How to blog safely (about work or anything else).* Retrieved January 5, 2006, from http://www.eff.org

Electronic Frontier Foundation. E. (2005b). *Bloggers' FAQ: Labor Law.* Retrieved November 30, 2006, from http://www.eff.org/bloggers/lg/faq-labor.php

Ellickson, R. (1991). *Order without law.* Cambridge, MA: Harvard University Press.

Ellison, N., Heino, R., & Gibbs, J. (2006). Managing Impressions Online: Self-Presentation Processes in the Online Dating Environment. *Journal of Computer-Mediated Communication, 11*(2). doi:10.1111/j.1083-6101.2006.00020.x

Emerson, R. M. (1962). Power-Dependence Relations. *American Sociological Review, 27*(1), 31–41. doi:10.2307/2089716

Enzle, M. E., & Anderson, S. C. (1993). Surveillant intentions and intrinsic motivations. *Journal of Personality and Social Psychology*, *64*, 265–279. doi:10.1037/0022-3514.64.2.257

Equifax-Harris. (1996). *Consumer Privacy Survey*. Atlanta, GA: Louis Harris and Associates, Inc.

Erikson, E. H. (1968). *Identity: Youth and Crisis*. New York: Norton.

Erikson, E., & Parent, J. M. (2007). Central authority and order. *Sociological Theory*, *25*, 245–267. doi:10.1111/j.1467-9558.2007.00307.x

Eriksson, K., Kerem, K., & Nilsson, D. (2008). The adoption of commercial innovations in the former Central and Eastern European markets. The case of internet banking in Estonia. *International Journal of Bank Marketing*, *26*(3), 154–169. doi:10.1108/02652320810864634

Ertel, M., & Pröll, U. (2004). Arbeitssituation und Gesundheit von „neuen Selbständigen im Dienstleistungssektor. [Working situation and health of new self-employed in the service sector]. *Arbeit*, *1*, 1–12.

Everard, A., & Galletta, D. F. (2005). How presentation flaws affect perceived site quality, trust, and intention to purchase from an online store. *Journal of Management Information Systems*, *6*(3), 55–95.

Fairweather, N. B. (1999). Surveillance in employment: The case of teleworking. *Journal of Business Ethics*, *22*(1), 39–49. doi:10.1023/A:1006104017646

Falcone, R., Singh, M., & Tan, Y. H. (2001). *Trust in Cybersocieties*. Berlin: Springer. doi:10.1007/3-540-45547-7

Fehr, E., & Falk, A. (2002). Psychological foundations of incentives. *European Economic Review*, *46*, 687–724. doi:10.1016/S0014-2921(01)00208-2

Feldman, M. S., & March, J. G. (1981). Information in organization as signal and symbol. *Administrative Science Quarterly*, *26*, 171–186. doi:10.2307/2392467

Fenwick, T. (2006). Contradictions in portfolio careers: Work design and client relations. *Career Development International*, *11*(1), 65–79. doi:10.1108/13620430610642381

Ferdig, R. E., & Mishra, P. (2004). Emotional Responses to Computers: Experiences in Unfairness, Anger, and Spite. *Journal of Educational Multimedia and Hypermedia*, *13*(2), 143–161.

Fetterman, D. M. (1998). *Ethnography: Step by Step*. London: Sage Publication.

Field, J. (2003). *Social Capital*. London: Routledge.

Fine, G. A. (1984). Negotiated orders and organizational cultures. *Annual Review of Sociology*, *10*, 239–262. doi:10.1146/annurev.so.10.080184.001323

Finholt, T. A. (2003). Collaboratories as a new form of scientific organization. *Economics of Innovation and New Technology*, *12*(1), 5–25. doi:10.1080/10438590303119

Finholt, T., & Sproull, L. (1988). Electronic Groups at Work. *Organization Science*, *1*(1), 41–64. doi:10.1287/orsc.1.1.41

Fiore, A. T., & Donath, J. S. (2004). Online Personals: An Overview. *Extended abstracts of ACM Computer-Human Interaction 2004*.

Fiore, A. T., Shaw Taylor, L., Mendelsohn, G. A., & Hearst, M. (2008). Assessing Attractiveness in Online Dating Profiles. In *Proceedings of ACM Computer-Human Interaction 2008*, Florence, Italy.

Fisher, A. T., Sonn, C. C., & Bishop, B. J. (2002). *Psychological sense of community: Research, applications and implications*. New York: Kluwer Academic/Plenum Publishers.

Flavian, C., Guinalıu, M., & Torres, E. (2006). How bricks-and-mortar attributes affect online banking adoption. *International Journal of Bank Marketing*, *24*(6), 406–423. doi:10.1108/02652320610701735

Fogg, B. J. (2003). *Persuasive Technology: Using Computers to Change What We Think and Do*. San Francisco: Morgan Kaufmann.

Fogg, B. J., & Nass, C. (1997). Do users reciprocate to computers? In *Proceedings of the CHI Conference '97* (pp. 331-332).

Fogg, B. J., Cuellar, G., & Danielson, D. (2008). Motivation, Influencing, and Persuading Users: An Introduction to Captology. In Sears, A., & Jacko, J. A. (Eds.), *The Human-Computer Interaction Handbook: Fundamentals, Evolving Technology and Emerging Applications* (2nd ed., pp. 133–146). New York: Taylor & Francis.

Foos, T., Schum, G., & Rothenberg, S. (2006). Tacit knowledge transfer and the knowledge disconnect. *Journal of Knowledge Management, 10*, 6–18. doi:10.1108/13673270610650067

Foreman-Peck, J. (1995). *A history of the world economy.* Hempstead, UK: Harvester Wheatsheaf.

Fornell, C., & Larcker, D. F. (1981). Evaluating structural equation models with unobservable variables and measurement error. *JMR, Journal of Marketing Research, 18*, 39–50. doi:10.2307/3151312

Foschi, M. (2000). Double standards for competence: Theory and research. *Annual Review of Sociology, 26*, 21–42. doi:10.1146/annurev.soc.26.1.21

Foster, P. M. (2004). Psychological sense of community in groups on the Internet. *Behaviour Change, 21*(2), 141–146. doi:10.1375/bech.21.2.141.55421

Fox, D. R. (1985). Psychology, ideology, utopia, and the commons. *The American Psychologist, 40*, 48–58. doi:10.1037/0003-066X.40.1.48

Freeman, D. (1999). *The Fateful Hoaxing of Margaret Mead: A Historical Analysis of Her Samoan Research.* Boulder, CO: Westview Press.

Friedman, B., Kahn, P., & Howe, D. (2000). Trust online. *Communications of the ACM, 43*, 34–40. doi:10.1145/355112.355120

Friedman, E., & Resnick, P. (2001). The Social Costs of Cheap Pseudonyms. *Journal of Economics & Management Strategy, 10*(2), 173. doi:10.1162/105864001300122476

Froomkin, A. M. (1996). The essential role of trusted third parties in electronic commerce. In Kalakota, R., & Whinston, A. B. (Eds.), *Readings in Electronic Commerce.* Reading, MA: Addison-Wesley.

Frost, V. (2006, July 24). Virtually famous. *The Guardian.*

Fukuiama, F. (1995). *Trust: The social virtues and the creation of prosperity.* New York: Free Press.

Gallivan, M. J. (2001). Striking a balance between trust and control in a virtual organization: a content analysis of open source software case studies. *Information Systems Journal, 11*(4), 277–304. doi:10.1046/j.1365-2575.2001.00108.x

Gambetta, D. (1988). Can We Trust Trust? In Gambetta, D. (Ed.), *Trust Making and Breaking Cooperative Relations.* New York: Basil Blackwell.

Gambetta, D. (1988). Introduction. In Gambetta, D. (Ed.), *Trust: Making and breaking co-operative relations.* Oxford, UK: Basil Blackwell.

Gambetta, D. (1988). Mafia: the Price of Distrust. In Gambetta, D. (Ed.), *Trust: Making and breaking cooperative relations* (pp. 158–175). New York: Basil Blackwell.

Gambetta, D. (1988). *Trust: making and breaking cooperative relations.* New York: B. Blackwell.

Gambetta, D. (1998). *Can We Trust Trust?* Oxford, UK: University of Oxford.

Gambetta, D. G. (1988). Can we trust trust? In Gambetta, D. G. (Ed.), *Trust* (pp. 213–237). New York: Basil Blackwell.

Gambetta, D. G. (Ed.). (1988). *Trust, making and breaking of cooperative relations.* New York: Basil Blackwell.

Gan, C., Clemes, M., Limsombunchai, V., & Weng, A. (2006). A logit analysis of electronic banking in New Zealand. *International Journal of Bank Marketing, 24*(6), 360–383. doi:10.1108/02652320610701717

Garbacz, C., & Thompson, H. G. (2007). Demand for telecommunication services in developing countries. *Telecommunications Policy, 31*(5), 276–289. doi:10.1016/j.telpol.2007.03.007

Garbarino, E., & Johnson, M. S. (1999). The Different Roles of Satisfaction, Trust, and Commitment in Customer Relationships. *Journal of Marketing, 63*(2), 70–87. doi:10.2307/1251946

Gardner, H. (2006). *Five minds for the future*. Boston, MA: Harvard Business School Press.

Gardner, M. W., & Dorling, S. R. (1998). Artificial neural networks (the multilayer perceptron) – A review of applications in the atmospheric sciences. *Atmospheric Environment, 32*(14-15), 2627–2636. doi:10.1016/S1352-2310(97)00447-0

Garfinkel, H. (1963). A conception of, and experiments with, trust as a condition of stable concerted action. In Harvey, O. J. (Ed.), *Motivation and social interaction* (pp. 187–238). New York: Ronald Press.

Garfinkel, H. (1967). *Studies in Ethnomethodology*. Englewood Cliffs, NJ: Prentice Hall.

Geertz, C. (1973). *The interpretation of cultures*. New York: Basic Books.

Geertz, C. (1977). *The Interpretation of Cultures: Selected Essays*. New York: Basic Books.

Geertz, C. (2000). *Local knowledge: Further essays in interpretive anthropology*. New York: Basic Books.

Gefen, D. (2000). E-Commerce: the role of familiarity and trust. *The International Journal of Management Science, 28*(6), 725–737.

Gefen, D. (2000). E-commerce: the role of familiarity and trust. *Omega-The International Journal of Management Science, 28*, 725–737. doi:10.1016/S0305-0483(00)00021-9

Gefen, D. (2002). Consumer Loyalty in e-commerce. *Journal of the Association for Information Systems, 3*, 27–51.

Gefen, D., & Straub, D. W. (2004). Consumer Trust in B2C e-Commerce and the importance of social presence: experiments in e-Products and e-Services. *Omega: The International Journal of Management Science, 32*(6), 407–424. doi:10.1016/j.omega.2004.01.006

Gefen, D., Karahanna, E., & Straub, D. W. (2003). Trust and TAM in online shopping: An integrated model. *Management Information Systems Quarterly, 27*(1), 51–90.

Gemünden, H. G. (1985). Perceived risk and information search. A systematic meta-analysis of the empirical evidence. *International Journal of Research in Marketing, 2*, 79–100. doi:10.1016/0167-8116(85)90026-6

Gerbasi, A., & Cook, K. S. (2008). The Effect of Perceived Trustworthiness on Affect in Negotiated and Reciprocal Exchange. In Clay-Warner, J., & Robinson, D. T. (Eds.), *Social Structure and Emotions* (pp. 142–166). Amsterdam: Elsevier. doi:10.1016/B978-0-12-374095-3.00009-4

Geroski, P. (2000). Models of technology diffusion. *Research Policy, 29*, 603–625. doi:10.1016/S0048-7333(99)00092-X

Gerrard, P., & Cunningham, B. J. (2003). The diffusion of Internet banking among Singapore consumers. *International Journal of Bank Marketing, 21*(1), 16–28. doi:10.1108/02652320310457776

Ghoshal, S., & Moran, P. (1996). Bad for practice: A critique of the transaction costs theory. *Academy of Management Review, 21*, 13–47. doi:10.2307/258627

Giambona, G., Silburn, N. J. L., & Birchall, D. W. (2009). Trust, virtual teams and grid technology. In Bessis, N. (Ed.), *Grid Technology for Maximising Collaborative Decision Management and Support: Advancing Effective Virtual Organisations*. Hershey, PA: IGI Publishing.

Gibbons, R. (2001). Trust in social structures: Hobbes and Coase meet repeated games. In Cook, K. S. (Ed.), *Trust in Society* (pp. 332–353). New York: Russell Sage Foundation.

Gibbs, J. L., Ellison, N. B., & Heino, R. D. (2006). Self-presentation in online personals: The role of anticipated future interaction, self-disclosure, and perceived success in Internet dating. *Communication Research, 33*(2), 1–26. doi:10.1177/0093650205285368

Gibson, C. B., & Manuel, J. A. (2003). Building Trust: Effective Multicultural Communication Processes in Virtual Teams. In Cohen, S. G., & Gibson, C. B. (Eds.), *Virtual Teams That Work Creating Conditions for Virtual Team Effectiveness*. San Francisco: Jossey-Bass.

Giddens, A. (1990). *The Consequences of Modernity*. Stanford, CA: Stanford University Press.

Giddens, A. (1991). *Modernity and self-identity: Self and society in the late modern age*. Stanford, CA: Stanford University Press.

Giffin, K. (1967). The contribution of studies of source credibility to a theory of interpersonal trust in the communication process. *Psychological Bulletin, 68*(2), 104–120. doi:10.1037/h0024833

Gilovich, T., Savitsky, K., & Medvec, V. H. (1998). The Illusion of Transparency: Biased Assessments of Others' Ability to Read One's Emotional States. *Journal of Personality and Social Psychology, 75*(2), 332–346. doi:10.1037/0022-3514.75.2.332

Glaeser, E. L., Laibson, D. L., Scheinkman, J. A., & Soutter, C. L. (2000, August). Measuring Trust. *The Quarterly Journal of Economics*, 811–847. doi:10.1162/003355300554926

Glaser, B. G., & Straus, A. L. (1968). *The discovery of grounded theory: Strategies for qualitative research*. London: Weidenfeld and Nicholson.

Godar, S. H., & Ferris, S. P. (2004). *Virtual and Collaborative Teams: Process, Technologies And Practice*. Hershey, PA: IGI Publishing.

Goffman, E. (1956). *The Presentation of Self in Everyday Life*. New York: Doubleday.

Goffman, E. (1959). *The presentation of self in everyday life*. Garden City, NY: Basic Books.

Goffman, E. (1967). *Interaction ritual: Essays on face-to-face behavior*. New York: Anchor Books.

Golan, O. (2010). Symbols and Language of Youth on the Internet: Rhetoric, idioms and icons [in Hebrew]. *Israeli Sociology, 11*(2), 389–416.

Golding, B. (2009, June 10). Dot-com has 'Date' in Court. *New York Post*. Retrieved August 26, 2009, from http://www.nypost.com/seven/06102009/news/regionalnews/dot_com_has_date_in_court_173449.htm

Goldsmith, S., & Siemasko, C. (2009, March 23). This isn't AIG...it's AIU! Insurance giant takes down sign on Water St. offices. *New York Daily News*. Retrieved on May 28, 2009, from http://www.nydailynews.com/money/2009/03/23/2009-03-23_this_isnt_aig__its_aiu_insurance_giant_t.html

Gong, L., & Nass, C. (2007). When a talking-face computer agent is half-human and half-humanoid: Human identity and consistency preference. *Human Communication Research, 33*, 163–193. doi:10.1111/j.1468-2958.2007.00295.x

Goodwin, C. (1991). Privacy: recognition of a consumer right. *Journal of Public Policy & Marketing, 10*(1), 149–166.

Gorman, G. E. (2007). Who am I, and where's my money? Issues in online security. *Online Information Review, 31*(5), 561–565. doi:10.1108/14684520710832298

Gottschall, K., & Henninger, A. (2005). Freelancer in den Kultur- und Medienberufen: Freiberuflich, aber nicht frei schwebend. [Freelancer in the culture and media professions: freelance but not free pending] In Mayer-Ahuja, N., & Wolf, H. (Eds.), *Entfesselte Arbeit- Neue Bindungen* (pp. 156–184). Berlin, Germany: Ed. Sigma.

Goulder, A. W. (1960). The norm of reciprocity: A preliminary statement. *American Sociological Review, 25*, 161–178. doi:10.2307/2092623

Gounaris, S., & Koritos, C. (2008). Investigating the Drivers of Internet Banking Adoption Decision: A Comparison of Three Alternative Frameworks. *International Journal of Bank Marketing, 26*(5), 282–304. doi:10.1108/02652320810894370

Govier, T. (1997). *Social Trust and Human Communities*. Montreal, Canada: McGill-Queen's Press.

Grabner-Kräuter, S. (2002). The Role of Consumers Trust in Online Shopping. *Journal of Business Ethics, 39*, 43–50. doi:10.1023/A:1016323815802

Grabner-Kräuter, S., & Faullant, R. (2008). Consumer Acceptance of Internet Banking: the Influence of Internet Trust. *International Journal of Bank Marketing, 26*(7), 483–504. doi:10.1108/02652320810913855

Grabner-Krauter, S., & Kalusca, E. A. (2003). Empirical research in on-line trust: a review and critical assessment.

International Journal of Human-Computer Studies, 58(6), 783–812. doi:10.1016/S1071-5819(03)00043-0

Granovetter, M. (1985). Economic action and social structure: A theory of embeddedness. *American Journal of Sociology, 91*(3), 481–510. doi:10.1086/228311

Granovetter, M. (1985). Economic action and social structure: The problem of embeddedness. *American Journal of Sociology, 91*, 481–510. doi:10.1086/228311

Green, D., Sternberg, B., & Lepper, M. R. (1976). Overjustification in a token economy. *Journal of Personality and Social Psychology, 34*, 1219–1234. doi:10.1037/0022-3514.34.6.1219

Green, M. (2007). Trust and social interaction on the Internet. In Joinson, A., McKenna, K., Postmes, T., & Reips, U.-D. (Eds.), *The Oxford Handbook of internet psychology* (pp. 43–52). New York: Oxford University Press.

Green, M. C. (2007). Trust and social interaction on the Internet. In Joinson, A., McKenna, K., Postmes, T., & Reips, U.-D. (Eds.), *The Oxford Handbook of Internet Psychology*. Oxford, UK: Oxford University Press.

Greif, A. (1989). Reputation and Coalitions in medieval trade: Evidence on the Maghribi traders coalition. *The Journal of Economic History, 49*, 857–882. doi:10.1017/S0022050700009475

Greif, A. (1993). Contract enforceability and economic institutions in early trade: The Maghribi traders coalition. *The American Economic Review, 83*, 525–548.

Greif, A. (1994). Cultural beliefs and the organization of society: Historical and theoretical reflection on collectivist and individualist societies. *The Journal of Political Economy, 102*, 912–950. doi:10.1086/261959

Greif, A. (2006). *Institutions and the path to the modern economy: Lesson from medieval trade*. Cambridge, UK: Cambridge University Press.

Groom, V., & Nass, C. (2007). Can Robots be Teammates? *Interaction Studies: Social Behaviour and Communication in Biological and Artificial Systems, 8*(3), 483–500.

Gross, P. (1983). *Die Verheißungen der Dienstleistungsgesellschaft* [The promises of the service society]. Opladen, Germany: Westdeutscher Verlag.

Grudin, J., & Poltrock, S. E. (1997). Computer-Supported Cooperative Work and Groupware. In M. Zelkowitz (Ed.), Advances in Computers, 45, 269–320.

Guenther, T., & Schmidt, J. (2008). Wissenstypen im Web 2.0 – eine wissenssoziologische Deutung von Prodnutzung im Internet. In Willems (Ed.). Weltweite Welten. Figurationen aus wissenssoziologischer Perspektive (pp. 167-187). Wiesbaden, Germany: VS-Verlag.

Guerra, G. A., Zizzo, D. J., Dutton, W. H., & Peltu, M. (2003). *Economics of trust in the information economy: Issues of identity, privacy and security*. OII Research Report No. 1.

Gulati, R., & Sytch, M. (2008). The dynamics of trust. [Book review]. *Academy of Management Review, 33*(1), 276–278.

Gupta, P., Yadav, M. S., & Varadarajan, R. (2009). How task-facilitative interactive tools fosters buyer's trust in online retailers: a process view of trust development. *Journal of Retailing, 85*(2), 159–176. doi:10.1016/j.jretai.2009.02.001

Guseva, A., & Rona-Tas, A. (2001). Uncertainty, Risk and Trust: Russian and American Credit Card Markets Compared. *American Sociological Review, 66*(5), 623–646. doi:10.2307/3088951

Güth, W., & Kliemt, H. (2004). The Evolution of Trust(worthiness) in the Net. *Analyse & Kritik, 26*, 203–219.

Gwartney, J., Lawson, R., & Samida, D. (2000). *Economic freedom of the world 2000: Annual report*. Retrieved from http://www.freetheworld.com.

Habermas, J. (1989). *The Structural Transformation of the Public Sphere: An Inquiry into a Category of Bourgeois Society*. Cambridge, MA: Polity Press. (Original work published 1962)

Haddon, L. (1999, June). *European perceptions and use of the Internet*. Paper presented at the conference Usages and Services in Telecommunications, Arcachon.

Haddon, L. (2003). Domestication and mobile telephony. In Katz, J. (Ed.), *Machines that become us: The social context of personal communication technology* (pp. 43–56). New Brunswick, NJ: Transaction.

Haddon, L. (2006). The contribution of domestication research to in-home computing and media consumption. *The Information Society*, *22*(4), 195–203. doi:10.1080/01972240600791325

Hair, J. F., Anderson, R. E., Tatham, R. L., & Black, W. (1998). *Multivariate data analysis*. Upper Saddle River, NJ: Prentice-Hall.

Hakken, D. (1999). *Cyborgs@Cyberspace? An ethnographer looks to the future*. New York: Routledge.

Halal, W. E. (1998). *The New Management: Bringing Democracy and Markets Inside Organisations*. San Francisco: Berrett-Koehler Publishers.

Hall, J. (2005, April 9). Big Business battles to keep up with the bloggers. *Daily Telegraph*.

Hamilton, H. (2002, February 27). Tell it to their face for Christ's sake. *Dooce*. Retrieved June 14, 2007, from http://www.dooce.com/archives/daily/02_27_2002.html

Hamilton, H. (2002a, February 6). Intimidation. *Dooce*. Retrieved November 30, 2006, from http://www.dooce.com/archives/daily/02_06_2002.html

Hamilton, H. (2002b, February 17). The proper way to hate a job. *Dooce*. Retrieved November 30, 2006, from http://www.dooce.com/archives/daily/01_17_2002.html

Hancock, J. T., & Dunham, P. J. (2001). Impression formation in computer-mediated communication revisited: An analysis of the breadth and intensity of impressions. *Communication Research*, *28*(3), 325–347. doi:10.1177/009365001028003004

Hancock, J. T., Toma, C., & Ellison, N. (2007). The truth about lying in online dating profiles. *Extended abstracts of ACM Computer-Human Interaction 2007*.

Handy, C. (1995). *The Age of Unreason*. New York: Arrow Business Books.

Hannan, M. T., & Freeman, J. H. (1984). Structural inertia and organizational change. *American Sociological Review*, *49*, 149–164. doi:10.2307/2095567

Hardin, G. (1968). Tragedy of the commons. *Science*, *162*, 1243–1248. doi:10.1126/science.162.3859.1243

Hardin, R. (1993). The Street-Level Epistemology of Trust. *Politics & Society*, *21*, 505–529. doi:10.1177/0032329293021004006

Hardin, R. (2002). *Trust and Trustworthiness*. New York: Russell Sage Foundation.

Hardin, R. (2006). *Trust*. Cambridge, UK: Polity.

Harigopal, K. (2006). *Management of Organizational Change: Leveraging Transformation*. Thousand Oaks, CA: Sage.

Harris, L. C., & Goode, M. M. H. (2004). The four levels of loyalty and the pivotal role of trust: a study of online service dynamics. *Journal of Retailing*, *80*(2), 139–158. doi:10.1016/j.jretai.2004.04.002

Hayashi, N. (1995). Emergence of Cooperation in One-shot Prisoner's Dilemmas and the Role of Trust. *Japanese Journal of Phycology*, *66*(3), 184–190.

Hearn, F. (1997). *Moral order and social disorder: The American search for civil society*. New York: Aldine de Gruyter.

Hecht, J. (2001). Digital Youth. *Mashabei Enosh*, *167*, 38–50.

Hechter, M. (1987). *Principles of group solidarity*. Berkeley, CA: California University Press.

Hechter, M., & Opp, K.-D. (Eds.). (2001). *Social norms*. New York: Russell Sage Foundation.

Hee-Woong, K., Xu, Y., & Koh, J. (2004). A Comparison of Online Trust Building Factors Between Potential Customers and Repeat Customers. *Journal of the Association for Information Systems*, *5*(10), 392–420.

Heilman, M. E. (1979). High school students' occupational interest as a function of projected sex ratios in male-dominated occupations. *The Journal of Applied Psychology*, *64*, 275–279. doi:10.1037/0021-9010.64.3.275

Heim, M. (1992). The Erotic Ontology of Cyberspace. In Benedikt, M. (Ed.), *Cyberspace: First steps* (pp. 59–80). Cambridge, MA: MIT Press.

Heimer, C. A. (2001). Solving the problem of trust. In Cook, K. S. (Ed.), *Trust in Society* (pp. 40–88). New York: Russell Sage Foundation.

Heise, D. R. (1970). The Semantic Differential and Attitude Research. In Summers, G. F. (Ed.), *Attitude Measurement*. Chicago: Rand McNally.

Heise, D. R. (1979). *Understanding Events: Affect and the Construction of Social Action*. New York: Cambridge University Press.

Heise, D. R. (2004). Enculturating Agents with Expressive Role Behavior. In Payr, S., & Trappl, R. (Eds.), *Agent Culture: Human-Agent Interaction in a Multicultural World* (pp. 127–142). Mahwah, NJ: Lawrence Erlbaum Associates.

Heise, D. R. (2007). *Expressive Order: Confirming Sentiments in Social Actions*. New York: Springer.

Heise, D. R. (2009). *Interact*. Retrieved from http://www.indiana.edu/~socpsy/ACT/interact.htm

Heise, D. R. (2010). *Surveying Cultures: Discovering Shared Conceptions and Sentiments*. Hoboken, NJ: Wiley.

Heise, D. R., & Thomas, L. (1989). Predicting Impressions Created by Combinations of Emotion and Social Identity. *Social Psychology Quarterly, 52*(2), 141–148. doi:10.2307/2786913

Henderson, S., & Gilding, M. (2004). 'I've Never Clicked this Much with Anyone in My Life': Trust and Hyperpersonal Communication in Online Friendships. *New Media & Society, 6*, 487–506. doi:10.1177/146144804044331

Hendrick, C. (1972). Effects of salience of stimulus inconsistency on impression formation. *Journal of Personality and Social Psychology, 22*, 219–222. doi:10.1037/h0032599

Henttonen, K., & Blomqvist, K. (2005). Managing distance in a global virtual team: the evolution of trust through technology-mediated relational communication. *Strategic Change, 14*, 107–119. doi:10.1002/jsc.714

Hernandez, J. M. C., & Mazzon, J. A. (2007). Adoption of internet banking: proposition and implementation of an integrated methodology approach. *International Journal of Bank Marketing, 25*(2), 72–88. doi:10.1108/02652320710728410

Herreros, F. (2004). *The problems of forming social capital. Why trust?* London: Palgrave. doi:10.1057/9781403978806

Herreros, F., & Criado, H. (2008). The state and the development of social trust. *International Political Science Review, 29*, 53–71. doi:10.1177/0192512107083447

Herring, S. C. (2001). Computer-mediated discourse. In Schiffrin, D., Tannen, D., & Hamilton, H. (Eds.), *The Handbook of Discourse Analysis* (pp. 612–634). Oxford, UK: Blackwell.

Hess, A. (2008). Reconsidering the Rhizome. A textual analysis of Web Search engines as Gatekeepers of the Internet. In Zimmer, M., & Spink, A. (Eds.), *Web Search. Multidisciplinary Perspectives* (pp. 35–50). Heidelberg, Germany: Springer.

Hine, C. (2001). *Virtual ethnography*. London: Sage.

Hochschild, A. R. (1997). *The Time bind: When work becomes home and home becomes work*. New York: Metropolitan Books.

Hodgson, G. M. (1988). *Economics and institutions: A manifesto for a modern institutional economics*. Cambridge, UK: Polity Press.

Hoffman, D., Novak, T. P., & Peralta, M. A. (1999). Building consumer trust online environment: the case for information privacy. *Communications of the ACM, 42*(4), 80–85. doi:10.1145/299157.299175

Hogg, M. A., Abrams, D., Otten, S., & Hinkle, S. (2004). The social identity perspective: intergroup relations, self-conception and small groups. *Small Group Research, 35*(3), 246–276. doi:10.1177/1046496404263424

Hogg, M. A., Sherman, D. K., Dierselhuis, J., Maitner, A. T., & Moffit, G. (2007). Uncertainty, entitativity, and group identification. *Journal of Experimental Psychology, 43*, 135–142. doi:10.1016/j.jesp.2005.12.008

Holloway, S. L., & Valentine, G. (2003). *Cyberkids: Children in the Information Age*. London: Routledge.

Holm, H. J., & Danielson, A. (2005). Tropic trust versus Nordic trust: Experimental evidence from Tanzania and Sweden. *The Economic Journal*, *115*, 505–532. doi:10.1111/j.1468-0297.2005.00998.x

Hooghe, M., Reeskens, T., Stolle, D., & Trappers, A. (2009). Ethnic diversity and generalized trust in Europe. A cross-national multilevel study. *Comparative Political Studies*, *42*, 198–223. doi:10.1177/0010414008325286

Hopcroft, R. (1994). The social origins of agrarian change in late medieval England. *American Journal of Sociology*, *99*, 1559–1595. doi:10.1086/230454

Hopkins, C. (2009, January 29). Statistics on fired bloggers. *Morpheme Tales*. Retrieved March 18, 2008, from http://morphemetales.wordpress.com/2009/01/29/statistics-on-fired-bloggers/

Horne, C. (2000). Community and the state: The relationship between normative and legal controls. *European Sociological Review*, *16*, 225–243. doi:10.1093/esr/16.3.225

Hu, L., & Bentler, P. M. (1999). Cutoff criteria for fit indexes in covariance structure analysis: Conventional criteria versus new alternatives. *Structural Equation Modeling*, *6*, 1–55. doi:10.1080/10705519909540118

Huberman, B. A., Loch, C. H., & Önçüler, A. (1994). Status as a valued resource. *Social Psychology Quarterly*, *67*, 103–114. doi:10.1177/019027250406700109

Hudson, H. E. (2006). From rural village to global village: Telecommunications for development. In *The information age*. Mahwah, NJ: Lawrence Erlbaum Associates.

Hughes, N., & Lonie, S. (2007). M-PESA:Mobile Money for the "unbanked": Turning cellphones into 24-hour tellers in Kenya. *Innovations*, Winter and Spring.

Hunt, P. M. (2008). From Festies to Tourrats: Examining the Relationship between Jamband Subculture Involvement and Role Meanings. *Social Psychology Quarterly*, *71*(4), 356–378. doi:10.1177/019027250807100405

Husted, B. W. (1998). the ethical limits of trust in business relations. *Business Ethics Quarterly*, *8*, 233–248. doi:10.2307/3857327

Igbaria, M., & Iivari, J. (1995). The effects of self-efficacy on computer usage. *Omega*, *23*(6), 587–605. doi:10.1016/0305-0483(95)00035-6

Igbaria, M., Guimaraes, T., & Davis, G. B. (1995). Testing the determinants of microcomputer usage via a structural equation model. *Journal of Management Information Systems*, *11*, 87–114.

Ilako, F., & Kimura, M. (2004). *Provision of ARVs in a resource-poor setting*: *Kibera slum*. Paper presented at the International Conference on AIDS, Nairobi.

Ingram, P., & Clay, K. (2000). The choice-within-constraints new institutionalism and implications for sociology. *Annual Review of Sociology*, *26*, 525–546. doi:10.1146/annurev.soc.26.1.525

International Telecom Union. (2008). *The global information society: A statistical view*. New York: United Nations Publication.

iRobot Corporation. (2008). *About iRobot, 2008*. Retrieved from http://www.irobot.com/sp.cfm?pageid=74

Isbister, K., & Layton, T. (1995). Agents: What (or who) are they? In Nielsen, J. (Ed.), *Advances in human-computer interaction* (*Vol. 5*). Norwood, NJ: Ablex Publishing Corporation.

Isbister, K., & Nass, C. (2000). Consistency of Personality in Interactive Characters: Verbal Cues, Non-Verbal Cues, and User Characteristics. *International Journal of Human-Computer Studies*, *53*, 251–267. doi:10.1006/ijhc.2000.0368

Ishaya, T., & Macaulay, L. (1999). The role of trust in virtual teams. In P. Sieber, & J. Griese (Eds.), *Organizational Virtualness & Electronic Commerce, Proceedings of the 2nd International VoNet* - Workshop, September 23-24, Bern (pp. 135-152).

Ishihara, S. (2003). *The informal economy of Kibera slums*. Unpublished doctoral dissertation, SOAS, London.

Ivatury, G., & Pickens, M. (2006). *Mobile phone banking and low-income customers: Evidence from South Africa.* Consultative Group to Assist the Poor/The World Bank.

Jacobson, D. (1999). Impression Formation in Cyberspace: Online Expectations and Offline Experiences in Text-based Virtual Communities. *Journal of Computer-Mediated Communication, 5*(1).

Jahansoozi, J. (2006). Organization-stakeholder relationships: exploring trust and transparency. *Journal of Management Development, 25*(10), 942–955. doi:10.1108/02621710610708577

Jain, A., McClendon, R. W., Hoogenboom, G., & Ramyaa, R. (2003). *Prediction of frost for fruit protection using artificial neural networks.* American Society of Agricultural Engineers.

Jarrett, R. L., Sullivan, P. J., & Watkins, N. D. (2005). Developing social capital through participation in organized youth programs: Qualitative insights from three programs. *Journal of Community Psychology, 33*, 41–55. doi:10.1002/jcop.20038

Jarvenpaa, S. L., & Leidner, D. E. (1999). Communications and trust in global virtual teams. *Organization Science, 10*(6), 791–815. doi:10.1287/orsc.10.6.791

Jarvenpaa, S. L., & Shaw, T. R. (1998). Global virtual teams: Integrating models of trust. In P. Sieber & J. Griese (Eds.), *Organizational Virtualness Proceedings of the 1st Vo Net - Workshop*, April, Bern, (pp. 35-51).

Jarvenpaa, S. L., & Tractinsky, N. (1999). Consumer trust in an internet store: A cross-cultural validation. *Journal of Computer-Mediated Communication, 5*(2), 1–35.

Jarvenpaa, S. L., Shaw, T. R., & Staples, S. (2004). Toward Contextualized Theories of Trust: The Role of Trust in Global Virtual Teams. *Information Systems Research, 15*(3), 250–267. doi:10.1287/isre.1040.0028

Management, 1, 45–71. doi:10.1023/A:1019104520776

Jarvenpaa, S. L., Tractinsky, N., & Vitale, M. (2000). Consumer Trust in an Internet store. *Information Technology and Management, 1*, 45–71. doi:10.1023/A:1019104520776

Jasanoff, S., Markle, G. E., Peterson, J. C., & Pinch, T. (1995). *Handbook of Science and Technology Studies.* Thousand Oaks, CA: Sage.

Johnson, B. (2007, March 30). Briton sacked for writing Paris blog wins tribunal case. *The Guardian.*

Johnson, E. J., Bellman, S., & Lohse, G. L. (2002). Defaults, framing and privacy: why opting in-opting out. *Marketing Letters, 13*(1), 5–15. doi:10.1023/A:1015044207315

Johnson, S. (1997). *Interface Culture: How New Technology Transforms the Way we Create and Communicate.* New York: Basic Books.

Johnson, S. M., Makinen, J. A., & Millikin, J. W. (2001). Attachment injuries in couple relationships: A new perspective on impasses in couples therapy. *Journal of Marital and Family Therapy, 27*, 145–155. doi:10.1111/j.1752-0606.2001.tb01152.x

Johnson, W. L., Rickel, J. W., & Lester, J. C. (2000). Animated pedagogical agents: Face-to-face interaction in interactive learning environments. *International Journal of Artificial Intelligence in Education, 11*, 47–78.

Johnsson-Smaragdi, U. (2001). Media use styles among the young. In Livingston, S., & Bovill, M. (Eds.), *Children and their changing media environment: A European comparative study* (pp. 113–140). London: Lawrence Erlbaum Associates Publishers.

Joinson, A. N. (2001). Self-disclosure in computer-mediated communication: The role of self-awareness and visual anonymity. *European Journal of Social Psychology, 31*, 177–192. doi:10.1002/ejsp.36

Joinson, A. N., & Dietz-Uhler, B. (2002). Explanations for the perpetration of and reactions to deception in a virtual community. *Social Science Computer Review, 20*(3), 275–289.

Jones, G. R., & George, J. M. (1998). The Experience and Evolution of Trust: Implications for Cooperation and Teamwork. *Academy of Management Review, 23*(3), 473–490. doi:10.2307/259293

Jones, S. M., & Burleson, B. R. (1997). The impact of situational variables on helpers' perception of comforting messages: An attributional analysis. *Communication Research*, *24*, 530–555. doi:10.1177/009365097024005004

Jones, W. H., Couch, L., & Scott, S. (1997). Trust and betrayal: The psychology of getting along and getting ahead. In Hogan, R., Johnson, J., & Briggs, S. (Eds.), *Handbook of Personality Psychology* (pp. 465–483). San Diego: Academic Press. doi:10.1016/B978-012134645-4/50020-2

Kahane, R. (1975). Informal Youth Organizations: A General Model. *Sociological Inquiry*, *45*(4), 17–28. doi:10.1111/j.1475-682X.1975.tb00345.x

Kahane, R. (1997). *The Origins of Postmodern Youth*. Berlin: De Gruyter.

Kalakota, R., & Robinson, M. (1999). e-Business: Roadmap for success. Reading, MA: Addison Wesley.

Kalleberg, A. L. (2003). Flexible firms and labour market segmentation. *Work and Occupations*, *30*(2), 154–175. doi:10.1177/0730888403251683

Kaluscha, E. A. (2004). *The importance of Initial Consumer Trust in B2C Electronic Commerce*. University of Klagenfurt, Klagenfurt.

Kamssu, A. J. (2005). Global connectivity through wireless network technology: A possible solution for poor countries. *International Journal of Mobile Communications*, *3*(3), 249–262. doi:10.1504/IJMC.2005.006583

Karat, J., Karat, C.-M., & Brodie, C. (2008). Human-Computer Interaction Viewed from the Intersection of Privacy, Security, and Trust. In Sears, A., & Jacko, J. A. (Eds.), *The Human-Computer Interaction Handbook: Fundamentals, Evolving Technology and Emerging Applications*. New York: Taylor & Francis.

Karjaluoto, H., Mattila, M., & Pento, T. (2002). Factors underlying attitude formation towards online banking in Finland. *International Journal of Bank Marketing*, *20*(6). doi:10.1108/02652320210446724

Karney, B. R., McNulty, J. K., & Bradbury, T. N. (2002). Cognition and the Development of Close Relationships. In *The Blackwell Handbook of Social Psychology: Interpersonal Processes*. Hoboken, NJ: Wiley-Blackwell.

Kasper-Fuehrer, E. C., & Ashkanasy, N. M. (2001). Communicating trustworthiness and building trust in virtual organizations. *Journal of Management*, *27*, 235–254. doi:10.1016/S0149-2063(01)00090-3

Katz, M. L., & Shapiro, C. (1986). Technology adoption in the presence of network externalities. *The Journal of Political Economy*, *94*, 822–841. doi:10.1086/261409

Katz, M. L., & Shapiro, C. (1992). Product introduction with network externalities. *The Journal of Industrial Economics*, *40*, 55–83. doi:10.2307/2950627

Kayworth, T. R., & Leidner, D. (2000). The global virtual manager: A prescription for success. *European Management Journal*, *18*(2), 183–194. doi:10.1016/S0263-2373(99)00090-0

Kemper, T. D. (1991). Predicting Emotions from Social Relations. *Social Psychology Quarterly*, *54*, 330–342. doi:10.2307/2786845

Kendall, L. (2002). *Hanging out in the virtual pub: Masculinities and relationships online*. Berkeley, CA: University of California Press.

Kenny, C. (2002). Information and communication technologies for direct poverty alleviation: Costs and benefits. *Development Policy Review*, *20*, 141–157. doi:10.1111/1467-7679.00162

Kiesler, S., Seigel, J., & McGuire, T. (1984). Social Psychological aspects of computer-mediated communication. *The American Psychologist*, *39*, 1123–1134. doi:10.1037/0003-066X.39.10.1123

Kim, H. W., Xu, Y., & Koh, J. (2004). A comparison of online trust building factors between potential customers and repeat customers. *Journal of the Association for Information Systems*, *5*(10), 392–420.

Kim, K., & Prabhakar, B. (2000). *Initial trust, perceived risk and the adoption of internet banking*.

Kim, M.-S., & Ahn, J.-H. (2006). Comparison of trust sources of an online market-maker in the e-marketplace: Buyer's and seller's perspectives. *Journal of Computer Information Systems*, *47*(1), 84–94.

Kim, P. H., Ferrin, D. L., Cooper, C. D., & Dirks, K. T. (2004). Removing the shadow of suspicion: The effects of apology versus denial for repairing competence- versus integrity-based trust violations. *The Journal of Applied Psychology, 89*, 104–118. doi:10.1037/0021-9010.89.1.104

King, A. B. (2001). Affective Dimensions of Internet Culture. *Social Science Computer Review, 19*(4), 414–430. doi:10.1177/089443930101900402

Kiyonari, T., Yamagishi, T., Cook, K. S., & Cheshire, C. (2006). Does Trust Beget Trustworthiness? Trust and Trustworthiness in Two Games and Two Cultures: A Research Note. *Social Psychology Quarterly, 69*(3), 270–283. doi:10.1177/019027250606900304

Klopp, J., & Kamungi, P. (2008). Violence and elections: Will Kenya collapse? *World Policy Journal, 24*(4), 11–18. doi:10.1162/wopj.2008.24.4.11

Knack, S. (2002). Social capital and the quality of government: Evidence from the state. *American Journal of Political Science, 46*, 772–785. doi:10.2307/3088433

Knack, S., & Keefer, P. (1997). Does social capital have an economic payoff? A cross-country investigation. *The Quarterly Journal of Economics, 112*, 1251–1288. doi:10.1162/003355300555475

Knight, F. H. (1971). *Risk, Uncertainty, and Profit.* Chicago: University of Chicago Press, Phoenix Books. (Original work published 1921)

Knight, J. (1992). *Institutions and social conflict.* Cambridge, UK: Cambridge University Press. doi:10.1017/CBO9780511528170

Koh, J., & Kim, Y.-G. (2003). Sense of virtual community: A conceptual framework and empirical validation. *International Journal of Electronic Commerce, 8*(2), 75.

Kollock, P. (1994). The Emergence of Exchange Structures: An Experimental Study of Uncertainty, Commitment, and Trust. *American Journal of Sociology, 100*(2), 313–345. doi:10.1086/230539

Kollock, P. (1999). The economies of online cooperation. In Smith, M. A., & Kollock, P. (Eds.), *Communities in Cyberspace* (pp. 220–239). New York: Routledge.

Kollock, P. (1999). The production of trust in online markets. *Advances in Group Processes, 16*, 99–123.

Kollock, P., & O'Brien, J. (1992). The Social Construction of Exchange. *Advances in Group Processes, 9*, 89–112.

Kollock, P., & Smith, M. A. (1999). Communities in Cyberspace. In Smith, M. A., & Kollock, P. (Eds.), *Communities in Cyberspace* (pp. 3–28). London: Routledge.

Koufaris, M., & Hampton-Sosa, W. (2004). The development of initial trust in an online company by new customers. *Information & Management, 41*, 377–397. doi:10.1016/j.im.2003.08.004

Kozinets, R. V. (2006). Netnography 2.0. In R. W. Belk (Ed.), Handbook of qualitative research methods in marketing (129-142). Northampton, MA: Edward Elgar Publishing.

Kramer, R. (1999). Trust and distrust in organizations: Emerging perspectives, enduring questions. *Annual Review of Psychology, 50*, 569–598. doi:10.1146/annurev.psych.50.1.569

Kreps, D. (1990). *Game Theory and Economic Modeling.* New York: Oxford University Press. doi:10.1093/0198283814.001.0001

Kreps, D. M. (1990). Corporate Culture and Economic Theory. In Alt, J. E., & Shepsle, K. A. (Eds.), *Perspectives on Positive Political Economy* (pp. 90–143). New York: Cambridge University Press.

Krishna, A. (2000). Creating and harnessing social capital. In Dasgupta, P., & Serageldin, I. (Eds.), *Social capital: A multifaceted perspective* (pp. 71–93). Washington, DC: The World Bank.

Kuhlmeier, D., & Gary, K. (2005). Antecedents to internet-based purchasing: a multinational study. *International Marketing Review, 22*(4), 460–473. doi:10.1108/02651330510608460

Kuisma, T., Laukkanen, T., & Hiltunen, M. (2007). Mapping the reasons for resistance to Internet banking: A means-end approach. *International Journal of Information Management, 27*, 75–85. doi:10.1016/j.ijinfomgt.2006.08.006

Kunda, G. (1992). *Engineering culture: Control and commitment in a high-tech corporation.* Philadelphia: Temple University Press.

Kurian, G. T. (2001). *The book of world rankings.* New York: Facts on File.

Kurzban, R. (2003). Biological foundations of reciprocity. In E. Ostrom & J. Walker, Trust and reciprocity (pp. 105-127). New York: Russell Sage Foundation.

Kuwabara, K., Willer, R., Macy, M. W., Mashima, R., Shigeru, T., & Yamagishi, T. (2007). Culture, Identity, and Structure in Social Exchange: A Web-based Experiment in the United States and Japan. *Social Psychology Quarterly, 70,* 461–479. doi:10.1177/019027250707000412

Laforet, S., & Li, X. (2005). Consumers' attitudes towards online and mobile banking in China. *International Journal of Bank Marketing, 23*(5), 362–380. doi:10.1108/02652320510629250

LaFrance, M. (1996). Why we trust computers too much. *Technology Studies, 3*(1), 163–178.

Lai, V. S., & Li, H. (2005). Technology acceptance model for Internet banking: an invariance analysis. *Information & Management, 42,* 373–386. doi:10.1016/j.im.2004.01.007

Lally, E. (2002). *At home with computers.* Oxford, UK: Berg.

Lassar, W. M., Manolis, C., & Lassar, S. S. (2005). The relationship between consumer innovativeness, personal characteristics, and online banking adoption. *International Journal of Bank Marketing, 23*(2), 176–199. doi:10.1108/02652320510584403

Latour, B. (1996). *Armis, or the Love of Technology* (Porter, C., Trans.). Cambridge, MA: Harvard University.

Latour, B. (2005). *Reassembling the Social: An Introduction to Actor-Network Theory.* Oxford, UK: Oxford University.

Laurel, B. (1993). *Computers as theater.* Reading, MA: Addison-Wesley Publishing Company.

Lawler, E. J. (2001). An Affect Theory of Social Exchange. *American Journal of Sociology, 107*(2), 321–352. doi:10.1086/324071

Lawler, E. J., & Yoon, J. (1993). Power and the Emergence of Commitment Behavior in Negotiated Exchange. *American Sociological Review, 58*(4), 465–481. doi:10.2307/2096071

Lawler, E. J., & Yoon, J. (1996). Commitment in Exchange Relations. *American Sociological Review, 61*(1), 89–108. doi:10.2307/2096408

Lawler, E. J., Thye, S. R., & Yoon, J. (2000). Emotion and Group Cohesion in Productive Exchange. *American Journal of Sociology, 106,* 616–657. doi:10.1086/318965

Lawler, E. J., Thye, S. R., & Yoon, J. (2008). Social Exchange and Micro Social Order. *American Sociological Review, 73,* 519–542. doi:10.1177/000312240807300401

Lee, G. K., & Cole, R. E. (2000). *The Linux Kernel Development as a Model of Open Source Knowledge Creation. Unpublished working paper.* Berkeley, CA: Haas School of Business, University of California.

Lee, J. D., & See, K. A. (2004). Trust in automation: Designing for appropriate reliance. *Human Factors, 46,* 50–80.

Lee, J. R., Nass, C., Brave, S., Morishima, Y., Nakajima, H., & Yamada, R. (2007). The case for caring co-learners: The effects of a computer-mediated co-learner agent on trust and learning. *The Journal of Communication, 57,* 183–204. doi:10.1111/j.1460-2466.2007.00339.x

Lee, M. K. O., & Turban, E. (2001). A trust model for consumer internet shopping. *International Journal of Electronic Commerce, 6*(1), 75–91.

Lei, D., Slocum, J. W., & Pitts, R. A. (1999). Designing organizations for competitive advantage: the power of unlearning and learning. *Organizational Dynamics,* (Winter): 24–38. doi:10.1016/S0090-2616(99)90019-0

Lenhart, A., & Fox, S. (2006). *Bloggers: A portrait of the internet's new storytellers.* Pew Internet and American Life Project.

Lenhart, A., Rainie, L., & Lewis, O. (2001). Teenage Life Online. *Pew Internet & American Life Project Reports.* Retrieved April 11, 2009, from http://www.pewinternet. org/pdfs/PIP_Teens_Report.pdf

Lessig, L. (2004). *Free Culture. The nature and future of creativity.* New York: Penguin.

Levi, M. (1988). *Of rule and revenue.* Berkeley, CA: California University Press.

Levi, M. (1998). A state of trust. In Braithwaite, V., & Levi, M. (Eds.), *Trust and governance* (pp. 77–101). New York: Russell Sage Foundation.

Levi, M., & Stoker, L. (2000). Political trust and trustworthiness. *Annual Review of Political Science, 3,* 475–507. doi:10.1146/annurev.polisci.3.1.475

Levy, S. (2006). *The perfect thing: How the iPod shuffles commerce, culture, and coolness.* New York: Simon & Schuster.

Lewandowsky, S., Mundy, M., & Tan, G. P. A. (2000). The dynamics of trust: Comparing humans to automation. *Journal of Experimental Psychology. Applied, 6,* 104–123. doi:10.1037/1076-898X.6.2.104

Lewicki, R. J., & Bunker, B. B. (1996). Developing and Maintaining Trust in Work Relationships. In Kramer, R. M., & Tyler, T. R. (Eds.), *Trust in Organizations: Frontiers of Theory and Research* (pp. 114–139). Thousand Oaks, CA: Sage.

Lewicki, R. J., McAllister, D. J., & Bies, R. J. (1998). Trust and Distrust: New Relationships and Realities. *Academy of Management Review, 23*(3), 438–458. doi:10.2307/259288

Lewis, J. D., & Weigert, A. (1985). Trust as a social reality. *Social Forces, 63*(4), 967–985. doi:10.2307/2578601

Lewis, V. (2004). Doing Research with Children and Young People: An Introduction. In Fraser, S., Lewis, V., Ding, S., Kellett, M., & Robinson, C. (Eds.), *Doing Research with Children and Young People* (pp. 1–11). London: Sage.

Lickel, B., Hamilton, D. L., & Sherman, S. J. (2001). Elements of a Lay Theory of Groups: Types of Groups, Relational Styles, and the Perception of Group Entitativity. *Personality and Social Psychology Review, 5*(2), 129–140. doi:10.1207/S15327957PSPR0502_4

Lickel, B., Hamilton, D. L., Wieczorkowska, G., Lewis, A., Sherman, S. J., & Uhles, A. N. (2000). Varieties of groups and the perception of group entitativity. *Journal of Personality and Social Psychology, 78*(2), 223–246. doi:10.1037/0022-3514.78.2.223

Lie, M., & Sørensen, K. (1996). Making technologies our own? Domesticating technology into everyday life. In Lie, M., & Sørensen, K. (Eds.), *Making technologies our own? Domesticating technology into everyday life* (pp. 1–30). Oslo: Scandinavian University.

Liker, J. K., Haddad, C. J., & Karlin, J. (1999). Perspectives on Technology and Work Organizations. *Annual Review of Sociology, 25,* 575–596. doi:10.1146/annurev. soc.25.1.575

Lin, H.-F. (2006). Impact of organizational support on organizational intention to facilitate knowledge sharing. *Knowledge Management Research & Practice, 4,* 26–35. doi:10.1057/palgrave.kmrp.8500083

Lipnack, J., & Stamps, J. (2000). *Virtual Teams.* New York: John Wiley.

Littler, D., & Melanthiou, D. (2006). Consumer perceptions of risk and uncertainty and the implications for behaviour towards innovative retail services: The case of Internet Banking. *Journal of Retailing and Consumer Services, 13,* 431–443. doi:10.1016/j.jretconser.2006.02.006

Livingstone, S. (2002). *Young people and new media: Childhood and the changing media environment.* London: Sage.

Loch, C. H., & Huberman, B. A. (1999). A punctuated-equilibrium model of technology diffusion. *Management Science, 45,* 160–177. doi:10.1287/mnsc.45.2.160

Lock, S. E., Ferguson, S. L., & Wise, C. (1998). Communication of sexual risk behavior among late adolescents. *Western Journal of Nursing Research, 20,* 273–294. doi:10.1177/019394599802000302

Long, C. P., & Sitkin, S. B. (2006). Trust in balance: How managers integrate trust-building and task control. In Bachmann, R., & Zaheer, A. (Eds.), *Handbook of Trust Research* (pp. 87–106). Cheltenham, UK: Elgar.

Lorenz, E. H. (1988). Neither friends nor strangers: Informal networks of subcontracting in French industry. In Gambetta, D. (Ed.), *Trust: Making and Breaking Cooperative Relations* (pp. 194–210). New York: Blackwell.

Luarn, P., & Lin, H.-H. (2005). Toward an understanding of the behavioral intention to use mobile banking. *Computers in Human Behavior, 21*, 873–891. doi:10.1016/j.chb.2004.03.003

Luhmann, N. (1979). *Trust and Power.* New York: Wiley.

Luhmann, N. (1979). *Trust and power: two works* (Davis, H., Raffan, J., & Rooney, K., Trans.). Chichester, NY: Wiley.

Luhmann, N. (1979). *Trust and power: Two works by Niklas Luhmann.* Chichester, UK: Wiley. (Original work published 1967)

Luhmann, N. (1988). Familiarity, Confidence, Trust: Problems and Alternatives. In Gambetta, D. (Ed.), *Trust Making and Breaking Cooperative Relations* (pp. 94–107). New York: Basil Blackwell.

Luhmann, N. (1989). Vertrauen. Ein Mechanismus der Reduktion sozialer Komplexität (3rd ed.). Stuttgart.

Luhmann, N. (1995). *Social Systems.* Stanford, CA: Stanford University Press.

Luk, K. C., Ball, J. E., & Sharma, A. (2000). A study of optimal model lag and spatial inputs for artificial neural network for rainfall forecasting. *Journal of Hydrology (Amsterdam), 227*, 56–65. doi:10.1016/S0022-1694(99)00165-1

Lunn, R. J., & Suman, M. W. (2002). Experience and trust in online shopping. In B. Wellman & C. Haythornthwaite (Eds.), The Internet in everyday life (549-577). Malden, MA: Blackwell Publishing.

Lunn, R., & Suman, M. (2002). Experience and Trust in Online Shopping. In Wellman, B., & Haythornthwaite, C. (Eds.), *The Internet in Everyday Life*. Oxford, UK: Blackwell. doi:10.1002/9780470774298.ch19

Luo, X. (2002). Trust production and privacy concerns on the Internet. A framework based on relationship marketing and social exchange theory. *Industrial Marketing Management, 31*, 111–118. doi:10.1016/S0019-8501(01)00182-1

Lynch, G. (2008). Courting the Kalenjin: The failure of dynasticism and the strength of the ODM wave in Kenya's Rift Valley province. *African Affairs, 107*(429), 541–568. doi:10.1093/afraf/adn060

Macaulay, S. (1963). Non-contractual relations in business: A preliminary study. *American Sociological Review, 28*, 55–67. doi:10.2307/2090458

MacGraw, H. (1999). Managing the privacy revolution. *Direct Marketing, 62*, 36–38.

MacKinnon, N. J. (1994). *Symbolic Interactionism as Affect Control.* New York: State University of New York.

Macy, M. W., & Skvoretz, J. (1998). The evolution of trust and cooperation between strangers: A computational model. *American Sociological Review, 63*(5), 638–660. doi:10.2307/2657332

Madden, M., & Lenhart, A. (2006). Online Dating. *Pew Internet and American Life Project.* Retrieved August 26, 2009, from http://www.pewinternet.org/~/media/Files/Reports/2006/PIP_Online_Dating.pdf.pdf

Maes, P. (1994). Agents that reduce work and information overload. *Communications of the ACM, 37*(7), 31–40. doi:10.1145/176789.176792

Maines, D. R., & Charlton, J. (1985). Negotiated order approach to the analysis of social organization. *Studies in Social Interaction,* (Supplement 1), 271–308.

Malhotra, D., & Murnighan, J. K. (2002). The effects of contracts on interpersonal trust. *Administrative Science Quarterly, 47*, 534–559. doi:10.2307/3094850

Malone, T. W., Laubacher, R., & Scott Morton, M. S. (2003). *Inventing the organizations of the 21st Century.* Cambridge, MA: MIT Press.

Malone, T. W., Yates, J., & Benjamin, R. I. (1987). Electronic markets and electronic hierarchies: Effects of information technology on market structure and corporate strategies. *Communications of the ACM, 30*, 484–497. doi:10.1145/214762.214766

Mandelli, A. (2002). Bounded sociability: Relationship costs and intangible resources in complex digital networks. *IT & Society, 1*(1), 251–274.

Mandrik, C. A., & Bao, Y. (2005). Exploring the Concept and Measurement of General Risk Aversion. *Advances in Consumer Research. Association for Consumer Research (U. S.), 32*, 531–539.

Mansbridge, J. (1999). Altruistic trust. In Warren, M. E. (Ed.), *Democracy and trust* (pp. 290–309). Cambridge, UK: Cambridge University Press. doi:10.1017/CBO9780511659959.010

Marker, P., McNamara, K., & Wallace, L. (2002). *The significance of information and communication technologies for reducing poverty*. London: DFID.

Markham, A. (1998). *Life online: Researching real experience in virtual space*. Lanham, MD: AltaMira Press.

Markham, A. (2004). Internet communication as a tool for qualitative research. In Silverman, D. (Ed.), *Qualitative research: Theory, method, and research* (pp. 95–124). Thousand Oaks, CA: Sage.

Markham, A. (2004). The methods, politics, and ethics of representation in online ethnography. In Denzin, N. K., & Lincoln, Y. S. (Eds.), *Handbook of qualitative research* (3rd ed., pp. 793–820). Thousand Oaks, CA: Sage.

Markus, M. L. (1994a). Electronic mail as the medium of managerial choice. *Organization Science, 5*, 502–527. doi:10.1287/orsc.5.4.502

Markus, M. L. (1994b). Finding a happy medium: Explaining the negative effects of electronic communication on social life at work. *ACM Transactions on Information Systems, 12*, 119–149. doi:10.1145/196734.196738

Markus, M. L. (2005). Technology-shaping effects of E-collaboration technologies: Bugs and features. *International Journal of e-Collaboration, 1*(1), 1–23.

Markus, M. L., Manville, B., & Agres, C. E. (2000). What makes a virtual organization work? *Sloan Management Review, 42*, 26.

Marsh, S., & Dibben, M. R. (2003). The Role of Trust in Information Science and Technology. *Annual Review of Information Science & Technology, 37*, 465–498. doi:10.1002/aris.1440370111

Marshall, C., & Rossman, G. (1995). *Designing Qualitative Research*. Thousand Oaks, CA: Sage Publications.

Marshall, M., Jaggers, K., & Gurr, T. R. (2005). Polity IV dataset. Computer file version p4v2004. College Part, MD: Center for International Development and Conflict.

Marshall, R. S., Nguyen, T. V., & Bryant, S. E. (2005). A dynamic model of trust development and knowledge sharing in strategic alliances. *Journal of General Management, 31*, 41–57.

Massaro, D. M. (1998). *Perceiving talking faces: From speech perception to a behavioral principle*. Cambridge, MA: MIT Press.

Matzat, U. (2009). The Acceptance and Effectiveness of Social Control on the Internet: A Comparison between Online Auctions and Knowledge Sharing Groups. In Cook, K., Snijders, C., & Buskens, V. (Eds.), *Trust and Reputation*. New York: Russell Sage Foundation.

Mayer, R. C., & Davis, J. H. (1999). The effect of the performance appraisal system on trust for management: A field quasi-experiement. *The Journal of Applied Psychology, 84*(1), 123–136. doi:10.1037/0021-9010.84.1.123

Mayer, R. C., Davis, J. H., & Schoorman, D. F. (1995). An integrative Model of organizational trust. *Academy of Management Review, 20*(3), 709–734. doi:10.2307/258792

McAlister, D. J. (1995). Affect- and cognition based trust as foundations for interpersonal cooperation in organizations. *Academy of Management Review, 38*(1), 24–59. doi:10.2307/256727

McCall, G. J. (2006). Symbolic Interaction. In Burke, P. J. (Ed.), *Contemporary Social Psychological Theories*. Stanford, CA: Stanford University Press.

McCrae, R. R., & Costa, P. T. (1992). Discriminant validity of NEO-PIR facet scales. *Educational and Psychological Measurement, 52*, 229–237. doi:10.1177/001316449205200128

McElroy, J. C., Hendrickson, A. R., Townsend, A. M., & DeMarie, S. M. (2007). Dispositional Factors in internet use: Personality versus cognitive style. *Management Information Systems Quarterly, 31*(4), 809–820.

McEvily, B., Perrone, V., & Zaheer, A. (2003). Trust as an organising principle. *Organization Science, 14*(1), 91–103. doi:10.1287/orsc.14.1.91.12814

McKenna, K. Y. A., Green, A. S., & Gleason, M. E. J. (2002). Relationship Formation on the Internet: What's the Big Attraction? *The Journal of Social Issues, 58*(1), 9–31. doi:10.1111/1540-4560.00246

McKnight, D. H., & Chervany, N. L. (1996). The Meanings of trust. *MISRC Working Paper.* Retrieved October 2002, from http://www.misrc.umc.edu/wpaper/Working-Papers/9604.pdf

McKnight, D. H., & Chervany, N. L. (2001). What Trust Means in e-commerce Consumer Relationships: An Interdisciplinary Conceptual Typology. *International Journal of Electronic Commerce, 6*(2), 35–59.

McKnight, D. H., & Chervany, N. L. (2002). What trust means in e-commerce customer relationships: An interdisciplinary conceptual typology. *International Journal of Electronic Commerce, 6*(2), 35–59.

McKnight, D. H., Choudhury, V., & Kacmar, C. (2002). Developing and Validating Trust Measures for e-Commerce: An Integrative Typology. *Information Systems Research, 13*(3), 334–359. doi:10.1287/isre.13.3.334.81

McKnight, D. H., Choudhury, V., & Kacmar, C. (2002). The impact of initial consumer trust on intentions to transact with a web site: A trust building model. *The Journal of Strategic Information Systems, 11*(3/4), 297–323. doi:10.1016/S0963-8687(02)00020-3

McKnight, D. H., Choudhury, V., & Kacmar, C. (2002b). The impact of initial consumer trust on intentions to transact with a Web site: a trust building model. *The Journal of Strategic Information Systems, 13*(4), 297–323. doi:10.1016/S0963-8687(02)00020-3

McKnight, D. H., Cummings, L. L., & Chervany, N. L. (1998). Initial trust formation in new organizational relationships. *Academy of Management Review, 23*(3), 472–490. doi:10.2307/259290

McKnight, D. H., Kacmar, C., & Choudhury, V. (2004a). Dispositional Trust and Distrust, Distinctions in Predicting High- and Low-Risk Internet Expert Advice Site Perceptions. *e-Service Journal, 3*(2), 35-58.

McKnight, H. D., & Chervany, N. L. (2002). What trust means in e-commerce customer relationships: An interdisciplinary conceptual typology. *International Journal of Electronic Commerce, 6*(2), 35–59.

McMillan, D. W., & Chavis, D. M. (1986). Sense of community: A definition and theory. *Journal of Community Psychology, 14*, 6–23. doi:10.1002/1520-6629(198601)14:1<6::AID-JCOP2290140103>3.0.CO;2-I

Meuter, M. L., Bitner, M. J., Ostrom, A. L., & Brown, S. W. (2005). Choosing Among Alternative Service Delivery Modes: An Investigation of Customer Trial of Self-Service Technologies. *Journal of Marketing, 69*, 61–83. doi:10.1509/jmkg.69.2.61.60759

Meyer, J. P., Becker, T. E., & Van Dick, R. (2006). Social identities and commitments at work: Toward and integrative model. *Journal of Organizational Behavior, 27*, 665–683. doi:10.1002/job.383

Meyer, J. W., & Rowan, B. (1977). Institutionalized organizations: Formal structure as myth and ceremony. *American Journal of Sociology, 83*, 340–363. doi:10.1086/226550

Meyer, T. (2006). *Online banking. What we learn from differences in Europe.* Frankfurt am Main: Deutsche Bank Research.

Meyerson, D., Weick, K., & Kramer, R. (1996). Swift trust and temporary group. In Kramer, R., & Tyler, T. (Eds.), *Trust in Organizations: Frontiers of Theory and Research.* Thousand Oaks, CA: Sage.

Miles, R. E., Snow, C. C., Mathews, J. A., Miles, G., & Coleman, H. J. (1997). Organizing in the knowledge age: Anticipating the cellular form. *The Academy of Management Executive, 11*(1), 7–20.

Miller, A. S., & Mitamura, T. (2003). Are surveys on trust trustworthy? *Social Psychology Quarterly, 66*, 62–70. doi:10.2307/3090141

Miller, D., & Slater, D. (2000). *The Internet: An ethnographic approach.* Oxford, UK: Berg.

Milne, G. R. (2000). Privacy and ethical issues in database/interactive marketing and public policy: a research framework and overview of the special issue. *Journal of Public Policy & Marketing, 19*(1), 1–6. doi:10.1509/jppm.19.1.1.16934

Milne, G. R., & Boza, M. E. (1999). Trust and concern in consumers' perceptions of marketing information management practices. *Journal of Interactive Marketing, 13*(1), 5–24. doi:10.1002/(SICI)1520-6653(199924)13:1<5::AID-DIR2>3.0.CO;2-9

Milne, G. R., & Gordon, M. E. (1993). Direct mail privacy-efficiency trade-offs within an implied social contract framework. *Journal of Public Policy & Marketing, 12*(2), 206–215.

Mishler, W., & Rose, R. (2001). What are the origins of political trust? Testing institutional and cultural theories in post-communist societies. *Comparative Political Studies, 34*(1), 30–62. doi:10.1177/0010414001034001002

Mishra, A. (1996). The Centrality of Trust. In Kramer, R., & Tyler, T. (Eds.), *Trust in Organizations: Frontiers of Theory and Research.* Thousand Oaks, CA: Sage.

Mishra, P. (2006). Affective Feedback from Computers and its Effect on Perceived Ability and Affect: A Test of the Computers as Social Actors Hypothesis. *Journal of Educational Multimedia and Hypermedia, 15*(1), 107–131.

Misztal, B. A. (1996). *Trust in modern societies.* Cambridge, UK: Polity Press.

Mitchell, V.-W. (1998). Consumer perceived risk: conceptualisations and models. *European Journal of Marketing, 33*(1/2), 163–195. doi:10.1108/03090569910249229

Miyazaki, A. D., & Krishnamurthy, S. (2002). Internet seals of approval: effects on online privacy policies and consumer perceptions. *The Journal of Consumer Affairs, 36*(1), 28–49.

Moellering, G. (2006). *Trust: Reason, Routine, Reflexivity.* Amsterdam: Elsevier Science Publishing Company.

Möllering, G. (2001). The nature of trust: From Georg Simmel to a theory of expectation, interpretation and suspension. *Sociology, 35*(2), 403–420.

Möllering, G. (2005). The trust/control duality: An integrative perspective on positive expectations of others. *International Sociology, 20*(3), 283–305. doi:10.1177/0268580905055478

Möllering, G. (2006). *Trust: Reason, Routine, Reflexivity.* Amsterdam: Elsevier.

Möllering, G. (2009). Leaps and lapses of faith: Exploring the relationship between trust and deception. In Harrington, B. (Ed.), *Deception: From Ancient Empires to Internet Dating* (pp. 137–153). Stanford, CA: Stanford University Press.

Molm, L. D. (1997). *Coercive Power in Social Exchange.* Cambridge, UK: Cambridge University.

Molm, L. D. (2003). Theoretical Comparison of Forms of Exchange. *Sociological Theory, 21*(1), 1–17. doi:10.1111/1467-9558.00171

Molm, L. D. (2008). The Structure of Reciprocity and Integrative Bonds: The Role of Emotions. In Clay-Warner, J., & Robinson, D. T. (Eds.), *Social Structure and Emotions.* Amsterdam: Elsevier. doi:10.1016/B978-0-12-374095-3.00010-0

Molm, L. D., Quist, T. M., & Wiseley, P. A. (1993). Reciprocal Justice and Strategies of Exchange. *Social Forces, 72*(1), 19–44. doi:10.2307/2580158

Molm, L., Takahashi, N., & Peterson, G. (2000). Risk and trust in social exchange: An experimental test of a classical proposition. *American Journal of Sociology, 105*(5), 1396–1427. doi:10.1086/210434

Moon, Y. (2000). Intimate exchanges: Using computers to elicit self-disclosure from consumers. *The Journal of Consumer Research, 26*, 323–339. doi:10.1086/209566

Moon, Y., & Nass, C. (1996). How "Real" Are Computer Personalities? *Communication Research, 23*(6), 651–674. doi:10.1177/009365096023006002

Moon, Y., & Nass, C. (1996). How "real" are computer personalities?: Psychological responses to personality types in human-computer interaction. *Communication Research, 23*, 651–674. doi:10.1177/009365096023006002

Moon, Y., & Nass, C. (1998). Are computers scapegoats?: Attributions of responsibility in human-computer interaction. *International Journal of Human-Computer Interaction, 49*, 79–94.

Mooradian, T., Renzl, B., & Matzler, K. (2006). Who Trusts? Personality, Trust and Knowledge Sharing. *Management Learning, 37*(4), 523–540. doi:10.1177/1350507606073424

Muir, B. M. (1987). Trust between humans and machines, and the design of decision aids. *International Journal of Man-Machine Studies, 27*, 527–539. doi:10.1016/S0020-7373(87)80013-5

Mukherjee, A., & Nath, P. (2003). A model of trust in online relationship banking. *International Journal of Bank Marketing, 21*(1), 5–15. doi:10.1108/02652320310457767

Mulder, L. B., Dijk, E. V., De Cremer, D., & Wilke, H. A. M. (2006). Undermining trust and cooperation: The paradox of sanctioning systems in social dilemmas. *Journal of Experimental Social Psychology, 42*, 147–162. doi:10.1016/j.jesp.2005.03.002

Muller, E. N., & Seligson, M. A. (1994). Civic culture and democracy: The question of causal relations. *The American Political Science Review, 88*, 635–652. doi:10.2307/2944800

My, I. B. M. *Baby*. (1965, November 19). Time Magazine. Retrieved August 26, 2009, from http://www.time.com/time/magazine/article/0,9171,834652,00.html

MySecureCyberspace. (n.d.). *Online Dating*. Carnegie Mellon University. Retrieved August 26, 2009, from http://www.mysecurecyberspace.com/encyclopedia/index/online-dating.html

Nah, F. F. H., & Davis, S. (2002). HCI research issues in e-commerce. *Journal of Electronic Commerce Research, 3*(3), 98–113.

Nannestad, P. (2008). What have we learned about generalized trust, if anything? *Annual Review of Political Science, 11*, 413–436. doi:10.1146/annurev.polisci.11.060606.135412

Narayan, D., Chambers, R., Shah, M. K., & Petesch, P. (2000). *Voices of the Poor: Crying out for Change*. New York: Oxford University Press. doi:10.1596/0-1952-1602-4

Nass, C. I., Steuer, J., & Tauber, E. R. (1994). Computers are social actors. In *Proceedings of ACM Computer-Human Interaction 1994*, Boston, MA.

Nass, C., & Brave, S. B. (2005). *Wired for speech: How voice activates and advances the human-computer relationship*. Cambridge, MA: MIT Press.

Nass, C., & Lee, K. M. (2001). Does computer-synthesized speech manifest personality?: Experimental tests of recognition, similarity-attraction, and consistency-attraction. *Journal of Experimental Psychology. Applied, 7*, 171–181. doi:10.1037/1076-898X.7.3.171

Nass, C., & Moon, Y. (2000). Machines and Mindlessness: Social Responses to Computers. *The Journal of Social Issues, 56*(1), 81–103. doi:10.1111/0022-4537.00153

Nass, C., & Reeves, B. (1996). Technology and Roles: A Tale of Two TVs. *The Journal of Communication, 46*(2), 121–128. doi:10.1111/j.1460-2466.1996.tb01477.x

Nass, C., & Steuer, J. (1993). Voices, Boxes, and Sources of Message: Computers and Social Actors. *Human Communication Research, 19*(4), 504–527. doi:10.1111/j.1468-2958.1993.tb00311.x

Nass, C., Fogg, B. J., & Moon, Y. (1996). Can Computers be Teammates? *International Journal of Human-Computer Studies, 45*, 669–678. doi:10.1006/ijhc.1996.0073

Nass, C., Moon, Y., & Green, N. (1997). Are computers gender-neutral? Gender stereotypic responses to computers. *Journal of Applied Social Psychology, 27*, 864–876. doi:10.1111/j.1559-1816.1997.tb00275.x

Nass, C., Moon, Y., Fogg, B. J., Reeves, B., & Dryer, D. C. (1995). Can Computer Personalities be Human Personalities? *International Journal of Human-Computer Studies, 43*, 223–239. doi:10.1006/ijhc.1995.1042

Nass, C., Steuer, J., & Tauber, E. R. (1994). *Computers are Social Actors*. Paper presented at the SIGCHI Conference on Human Factors in Computing Systems: Celebrating Interdependence.

Nass, C., Takayama, L., & Brave, S. B. (2006). Socializing consistency: From technical homogeneity to human epitome. In Zhang, P., & Galletta, D. (Eds.), *Human-computer interaction in management information systems: Foundations*. Armonk, NY: M. E. Sharpe.

Ndubisi, N. O., & Sinti, Q. (2006). Consumer attitudes, system's characteristics and internet banking adoption in Malaysia. *Management Research News, 29*(1/2), 16–27. doi:10.1108/01409170610645411

Nee, V. (2005). The new institutionalism in economics and sociology. In Smelser, N. J., & Swedberg, R. (Eds.), *The handbook of economic sociology* (pp. 49–74). Princeton, NJ: Princeton University Press.

Nee, V., & Ingram, P. (1998). Embeddedness and beyond: Institutions, exchange, and social structure. In Nee, V., & Brinton, M. (Eds.), *New institutionalism in sociology* (pp. 19–45). Stanford, CA: Stanford University Press.

Nee, V., & Sanders, J. (2001). Trust in ethnic ties: Social capital and immigrants. In K. S. Cook (Ed.), Trust in society: Vol. 2. The Russell Sage Foundation Series on Trust (1st ed., pp. 374-392). New York: Russell Sage Foundation.

Newholm, T., McGoldrick, P., Keeling, K., Macaulay, L., & Doherty, J. (2004). Multi-Story Trust and Online Retailer Strategies. *International Review of Retail, Distribution and Consumer Research, 14*(4), 437–456. doi:10.1080/0959396042000260889

Neyland, D. (2007). Achieving Transparency: The Visible, Invisible and Divisible in Academic Accountability Networks. *Organization, 14*(4), 499–516. doi:10.1177/1350508407078050

Nielsen, B. B. (2005). The role of knowledge embeddedness in the creation of synergies in strategic alliances. *Journal of Business Research, 58*, 1194–1204. doi:10.1016/j.jbusres.2004.05.001

Nissenbaum, H. (2004). Will Security Enhance Trust Online, or Supplant It? In Kramer, R., & Cook, K. (Eds.), *Trust and Distrust Within Organizations: Emerging Perspectives, Enduring Questions* (pp. 155–188). New York: Russell Sage Publications.

Nooteboom, B. (1996). Trust, opportunism and governance: A process and control model. *Organization Studies, 17*(6), 985–1010. doi:10.1177/017084069601700605

North, D. (1981). *Structure and change in economic history*. New York: Norton.

North, D. (1990). *Institutions, institutional change, and economic performance*. New York: Cambridge University Press.

Norton, M., Frost, J., & Ariely, D. (2007). Less is more: The lure of ambiguity, or why familiarity breeds contempt. *Journal of Personality and Social Psychology, 92*(1), 97–105. doi:10.1037/0022-3514.92.1.97

Nugroho, A. S., Kuroyanagi, S., & Iwata, A. (2002). A solution for imbalanced training sets problem by CombNET-II and its application on fog forecasting. *IEICE Transactions on Information and Systems. E (Norwalk, Conn.), 85-D*(7), 1165–1174.

O'Hara-Devereaux, M., & Johansen, R. (1994). *Globalwork: Bridging distance, culture and time*. San Francisco: Jossey Bass.

O'Leary, M., Orlikowski, W., & Yates, J. (2001). Distributed work over the centuries: trust and control in the Hudson's Bay Company (1670-1826). In Hinds, P., & Kiesler, S. (Eds.), *Distributed Work*. Cambridge, MA: MIT Press.

Obst, P., & White, K. M. (2004). Revisiting the sense of community index: A confirmatory factor analysis. *Journal of Community Psychology, 32*(6), 691–705. doi:10.1002/jcop.20027

Obst, P., Zinkiewicz, L., & Smith, S. G. (2002). Sense of community in science fiction fandom, Part 1: Understanding sense of community in an international community of interest. *Journal of Community Psychology, 30*(1), 87–103. doi:10.1002/jcop.1052

Obstfeld, M., & Taylor, A. M. (2003). *Global capital markets: Growth and integration.* Cambridge, UK: Cambridge University Press.

Olive, J. P. (1997). The talking computer: Text to speech synthesis. In Stork, D. (Ed.), *Hal's legacy: 2001's computer as dream and reality* (pp. 101–130). Cambridge, MA: MIT Press.

Olson, G. M., & Olson, J. S. (2001). Distance Matters. *Human-Computer Interaction, 15*(2), 139–178. doi:10.1207/S15327051HCI1523_4

Olson, G. M., Finholt, T. A., & Teasley, S. D. (2000). Behavioral aspects of collaboratories. In Koslow, S. H., & Huerta, M. F. (Eds.), *Electronic Collaboration in Science.* Mahwah, NJ: Lawrence Erlbaum Associates.

Olson, J. S., & Olson, G. M. (2000). i2i trust in e-commerce. *Communications of the ACM, 43*, 41–44. doi:10.1145/355112.355121

Olson, M. Jr. (1965). *The logic of collective action.* Cambridge, MA: Harvard University Press.

Orbell, J. M., & Dawes, R. M. (1993). Social Welfare, Cooperators' Advantage and the Option of Not Playing the Game. *American Sociological Review, 58*, 787–800. doi:10.2307/2095951

Osgood, C. E., May, W. E., & Miron, M. S. (1975). *Cross-Cultural Universals of Affective Meaning.* Urbana: University of Illinois.

Osgood, C. E., Suci, G. J., & Tannenbaum, P. H. (1957). The Measurement of Meaning. [University of Illinois.]. *Urbana (Caracas, Venezuela), IL.*

Osterloh, M., & Frey, B. S. (2000). Motivation, knowledge transfer and organisational forms. *Organization Science, 11*(5), 538–550. doi:10.1287/orsc.11.5.538.15204

Oyserman, D., Croon, H. M., & Kemmelmeier, M. (2002). Rethinking individualism and collectivism: Evaluation of theoretical assumptions and meta-analyses. *Psychological Bulletin, 128*, 3–72. doi:10.1037/0033-2909.128.1.3

Palmer, A., & Bejou, D. (1994). Buyer-Seller Relationships: A Conceptual Model and Empirical Investigation. *Journal of Markeliiig Management, 10*, 495–512.

Palmer, J. W., Bailey, J. P., & Faraj, S. (2000). The Role of Intermediaries in the Development of Trust on the WWW: The Use and Prominence of Trusted Third Parties and Privacy Statements. *Journal of Computer-Mediated Communication, 5*(3).

Pantzar, M. (1997). Domestication of everyday life technology: Dynamic views on the social histories of artifacts. *Design Issues, 13*(3), 52–65. doi:10.2307/1511941

Papert, S. (1980). *Mindstorms: Children, computers and powerful ideas.* New York: Basic books.

Parasuraman, R., & Riley, V. (1997). Humans and automation: Use, misuse, disuse, abuse. *Human Factors, 39*, 230–253. doi:10.1518/001872097778543886

Parasuraman, S., Singh, I. L., Molloy, R., & Parasuraman, R. (1992). Automation-related complacency: A source of vulnerability in contemporary organizations. *IFIP Transactions A – Computer Science and Technology, 13*, 426–432.

Parke, F. I., & Waters, K. (1996). *Computer facial animation.* Wellesley, MA: A. K. Peters.

Parks, M. R., & Floyd, K. (1996). Making Friends in Cyberspace. *The Journal of Communication, 46*(1). doi:10.1111/j.1460-2466.1996.tb01462.x

Parsons, T. (1951). *The social system.* New York: The Free Press.

Parsons, T. (1971). *The system of modern societies.* New York: Prentice Hall.

Pauleen, D. J., & Yoong, P. (2001). Relationship building and the use of ICT in boundary-crossing virtual teams: A facilitator's perspective. *Journal of Information Technology, 6*(4), 205–221. doi:10.1080/02683960110100391

Paunonen, S., Haddock, G., Forsterling, F., & Keinonen, M. (2003). Broad versus Narrow Personality Measures and the Prediction of Behaviour Across Cultures. *European Journal of Personality, 17*, 413–433. doi:10.1002/per.496

Pavlou, P. A. (2002). *What drives electronic commerce? A theory of planned behavior perspective.* Academy of Management Proceedings.

Pavlou, P. A. (2003). Consumer acceptance of electronic commerce – integrating trust and risk with the technology acceptance model. *International Journal of Electronic Commerce, 7*(3), 69–103.

Pavlou, P. A. (2003). Consumer Acceptance of Electronic Commerce: Integrating Trust and Risk with the Technology Acceptance Model. *International Journal of Electronic Commerce, 7*(3), 101–134.

Pavlou, P. A., & Fygenson, M. (2006). Understanding and predicting electronic commerce adoption: an extension of the theory pf planned behavior. *Management Information Systems Quarterly, 30*(1), 115–143.

Paxton, P. (2002). Social capital and democracy: An interdependent relationship. *American Journal of Sociology, 67*, 254–277. doi:10.2307/3088895

Paxton, P. (2007). Association memberships and generalized trust: A multilevel model across 31 countries. *Social Forces, 86*, 47–76. doi:10.1353/sof.2007.0107

Pelto, P. J. (1970). *Anthropological research: The structure of inquiry.* Cambridge, UK: Cambridge University Press.

Pennington, R., Wilcox, D. H., & Grover, V. (2003/2004). The Role of System Trust in Business-to-Consumer Transactions. *Journal of Management Information Systems, 20*(3), 197–226.

Perrow, C. (2002). *Organizing America.* Princeton, NJ: Princeton University Press.

Peters, T., & Waterman, R. H. (1982). *In search of excellence.* New York: Harper and Row.

Petersen, A., Anderson, A., Wilkinson, C., & Allan, S. (2007). Nanotechnologies, risk and society. *Health Risk & Society, 9*, 117–124. doi:10.1080/13698570701306765

PEW Internet & American Life Project. (2007a). *Online identity management and search in the age of transparency.* Retrieved from http://www.pewinternet.org/pdfs/PIP_Digital_Footprints.pdf

PEW Internet & American Life Project. (2008a). *Online Shopping. Internet users like the convenience but worry about the security of their financial information.* Retrieved from http://www.pewinternet.org/pdfs/PIP_Online%20Shopping.pdf

Phelps, J. E., D'Souza, G., & Nowak, G. J. (2001). Antecedents and consequences of consumer privacy concerns: an empirical investigation. *Journal of Interactive Marketing, 15*(4), 2–17. doi:10.1002/dir.1019

Phelps, J., Nowak, G. J., & Ferrell, E. (2000). Privacy concerns and consumer willingness to provide personal information. *Journal of Public Policy & Marketing, 19*(1), 27–41. doi:10.1509/jppm.19.1.27.16941

Picard, R. W. (1997). *Affective Computing.* Cambridge, MA: MIT Press.

Piccoli, G., & Ives, B. (2003). Trust and the unintended effects of behavior control in virtual team. *Management Information Systems Quarterly, 27*(3), 365–395.

Pikkarainen, T., Pikkarainen, K., Karjaluoto, H., & Pahnila, S. (2004). Consumer acceptance of online banking: an extension of the technology acceptance model. *Internet Research, 14*(3), 224–235. doi:10.1108/10662240410542652

Podolny, J. M. (1993). A status-based model of market competition. *American Journal of Sociology, 98*, 829–872. doi:10.1086/230091

Podolny, J. M., & Stuart, T. E. (1995). A Role-Based Ecology of Technological Change. *American Journal of Sociology, 100*(5), 1224–1260. doi:10.1086/230637

Podolny, J. M., Toby, E. S., & Hannan, M. T. (1996). Networks, Knowledge, and Niches: Competition in the Worldwide Semiconductor Industry, 1984-1991. *American Journal of Sociology, 102*(3), 659–689. doi:10.1086/230994

Polatoglu, V. N., & Ekin, S. (2001). An empirical investigation of the Turkish consumers' acceptance of Internet banking services. *International Journal of Bank Marketing, 19*(4), 156–165. doi:10.1108/02652320110392527

Porteous, D. (2006). *The enabling environment for mobile banking in Africa.* Boston: DFID.

Porteous, D. (2007). *Just how transformational is m-banking?* Finmark Trust.

Postmes, T., Spears, R., Lee, A. T., & Novak, R., J. (2005). Individuality and social influence in groups: Inductive and deductive routes to group identity. *Journal of Personality and Social Psychology, 89*(5), 747–763. doi:10.1037/0022-3514.89.5.747

Powell, W., & DiMaggio, P. J. (Eds.). (1991). *The new institutionalism in organizational analysis.* Chicago: The University of Chicago Press.

Power, M. (2007). *Organized Uncertainty. Designing a World of Risk Management.* Oxford, UK: Oxford University Press.

Pugh, M. D., & Wahrman, R. (1983). Neutralizing sexism in mixed-sex groups: Do women have to be better than men? *American Journal of Sociology, 88*, 746–762. doi:10.1086/227731

Putnam, R. (1993). *Making democracy work: Civic traditions in modern Italy.* Princeton, NJ: Princeton University Press.

Putnam, R. (2000). *Bowling alone: The collapse and revival of American community.* New York: Simon and Schuster.

Putnam, R. (2007). E pluribus unum: Diversity and community in the twenty-first century. The 2006 Johan Skytte Prize Lecture. *Scandinavian Political Studies, 30*, 137–174. doi:10.1111/j.1467-9477.2007.00176.x

Putnam, R. D. (1995). Bowling alone: America's declining social capital. *Journal of Democracy, 6*(1), 65–78. doi:10.1353/jod.1995.0002

Putnam, R. D. (2000). *Bowling along: The collapse and revival of American community.* New York: Simon & Schuster.

Raessens, J. (2005). Computer games as participatory media culture. In Raessens, J., & Goldstein, J. (Eds.), *Handbook of compute game studies* (pp. 373–388). Cambridge, MA: MIT Press.

Raiser, M., Haerpfer, C., Nowotny, T., & Wallace, C. (2001). *Social capital in transition: a first look at the evidence.* Working Paper No. 61, European Bank.

Raman, P., & Pashupati, K. (2005). Online Privacy: Consumer Concerns and Technological Competence. In Krishnamurthy, S. (Ed.), *Contemporary Research in E-Marketing* (pp. 200–225). Hershey, PA: Idea Group Publishing.

Randall, C. (2006, July 17). Wrote blog and got the sack. V bad. Will sue. *Colin Randall's Paris Blog.* Retrieved June 18, 2007, from http://www.telegraph.co.uk/news/main.jhtml?xml=/news/2006/07/18/wblog18.xml

Rao, M., & Mendoza, L. (Eds.). (2005). *Asia unplugged: The wireless and mobile media boom in the Asia-Pacific.* Thousand Oaks, CA: Sage.

Rasmusen, E. (1994). *Games and Information* (2nd ed.). Cambridge, MA: Blackwell.

Ratnasingam, P. (2005). E-Commerce relationships: The impact of trust on relationship continuity. *International Journal of Commerce & Management, 15*(1), 1–16.

Ratnasingam, P. (2005). Trust in inter-organizational exchanges: a case study in business to business electronic commerce. *Decision Support Systems, 39*(3), 525–544. doi:10.1016/j.dss.2003.12.005

Ratnasingham, P. (1999). Risks in low trust among trading partners in eletronic commerce. *Computers & Security, 18*, 587–592. doi:10.1016/S0167-4048(99)82005-7

Raub, W., & Weesie, J. (1990). Reputation and Efficiency in Social Interactions: An Example of Network Effects. *American Journal of Sociology, 96*, 626–654. doi:10.1086/229574

Ravi, V., Carr, M., & Sagar, N. V. (2006). Profiling Of Internet Banking Users In India Using Intelligent Tequniques. *Journal of Service Research, 6*(2), 61–73.

Raymond, E. S. (2001). *The cathedral and the bazaar: Musings on Linux and Open Source by an accidental revolutionary.* Cambridge, MA: O'Reilly.

Reeves, B., & Nass, C. (1996). *The media equation: How people treat computers, television, and new media like real people and places.* New York: Cambridge University Press.

Reichheld, F. F., & Schefter, P. (2000). E-loyalty: Your secret weapon on the web. *Harvard Business Review, 78*(4), 105–113.

Reinganum, J. F. (1981). On the diffusion of new technology: A game theoretic approach. *The Review of Economic Studies, 48*, 395–405. doi:10.2307/2297153

Ren, Y., Kraut, R., & Kiesler, S. (2007). Applying Common Identity and Bond Theory to Design of Online Communities. *Organization Studies, 28*(3), 377–408. doi:10.1177/0170840607076007

Resnick, P., Zeckhauser, R., Friedman, E., & Kuwabara, K. (2000). Reputation systems: Facilitating trust in Internet interactions. *Communications of the ACM, 43*, 45–48. doi:10.1145/355112.355122

Resnick, P., Zeckhauser, R., Swanson, J., & Lockwood, K. (2006). The value of a reputation on eBay: A controlled experiment. *Experimental Economics, 9*, 79–101. doi:10.1007/s10683-006-4309-2

Rheingold, H. (1995). *The virtual community: Homesteading on the electronic frontier.* Reading, MA: Addison-Wesley.

Richards, J. (2007). *Unmediated workplace images from the Internet: An investigation of workblogging.* Paper presented at the 25th International Labour Process Conference.

Rickett, J. (2006, September 30). Joel Rickett on the latest news from the publishing industry. *The Guardian.*

Rideout, V., Roberts, D. F., & Foehr, U. G. (2005). Generation M: Media in the lives of 8-18 Year-Olds. *Kaiser Family Foundation.* Retrieved April 11, 2009, from http://www.kff.org/entmedia/upload/Generation-M-Media-in-the-Lives-of-8-18-Year-olds.pdf

Ridgeway, C. L. (1982). Status in groups: The importance of motivation. *American Sociological Review, 47*, 76–88. doi:10.2307/2095043

Ridgeway, C. L. (1991). The social construction of status value: Gender and other nominal characteristics. *Social Forces, 70*, 367–386. doi:10.2307/2580244

Ridgeway, C. L., & Correll, S. J. (2004). Motherhood as a status characteristic. *The Journal of Social Issues, 60*, 683–700. doi:10.1111/j.0022-4537.2004.00380.x

Ridgeway, C. L., & Correll, S. J. (2006). Consensus and the creation of status beliefs. *Social Forces, 85*, 431–453. doi:10.1353/sof.2006.0139

Ridgeway, C. L., & Erickson, K. G. (2000). Creating and spreading status beliefs. *American Journal of Sociology, 106*, 579–615. doi:10.1086/318966

Ridgeway, C. L., Boyle, E. H., Kuipers, K. J., & Robinson, D. T. (1998). How do status beliefs develop? The role of resources and interactional experience. *American Sociological Review, 63*, 331–378. doi:10.2307/2657553

Riegelsberger, J., Sasse, A. M., & McCarthy, J. D. (2005). The mechanics of trust: a framework for research and design. *International Journal of Human-Computer Studies, 62*, 381–422. doi:10.1016/j.ijhcs.2005.01.001

Riegelsberger, J., Sasse, M. A., & McCarthy, J. D. (2003). The researcher's dilemma: Evaluating trust in computer-mediated communication. *International Journal of Human-Computer Studies, 58*, 759–781. doi:10.1016/S1071-5819(03)00042-9

Riegelsberger, M., Sasse, A., & McCarthy, J. D. (2007). Trust in mediated interactions. In Joinson, A., McKenna, K., Postmes, T., & Reips, U.-D. (Eds.), *The Oxford Handbook of Internet Psychology.* Oxford, UK: Oxford University Press.

Robbins, S. P. (1998). *Organizational Behavior: Concepts, Controversies, Applications*. Upper Saddle River, NJ: Prentice Hall.

Roberts, L. D., Smith, L. M., & Pollock, C. M. (2002). MOOing till the cows come home: The sense of community in virtual environments. In Sonn, C. C. (Ed.), *Psychological sense of community: research, applications, implications*. New York: Kluwer Academic/Plenum.

Robertson, M., & Hammersley, G. (2000). Knowledge management practices within a knowledge-intensive firm: the significance of the people management dimension. *Journal of European Industrial Training, 24*(2), 241–253. doi:10.1108/03090590010321205

Robinson, D. T. (1996). Identity and Friendship: Affective Dynamics and Network Formation. *Advances in Group Processes, 13*, 91–111.

Robinson, D. T. (2007). Control Theories in Sociology. *Annual Review of Sociology, 33*, 157–174. doi:10.1146/annurev.soc.32.061604.123110

Robinson, D. T., & Smith-Lovin, L. (1999). Emotion Display as a Strategy for Identity Negotiation. *Motivation and Emotion, 23*(2), 73–104. doi:10.1023/A:1021325011770

Robinson, D. T., & Smith-Lovin, L. (2006). Affect Control Theory. In Burke, P. J. (Ed.), *Social Psychology*. Stanford, CA: Stanford University Press.

Robinson, D. T., Smith-Lovin, L., & Tsoudis, O. (1994). Heinous Crime or Unfortunate Accident? The Effects of Remorse on Responses to Mock Criminal Confessions. *Social Forces, 73*(1), 175–190. doi:10.2307/2579922

Rockmann, K. W., & Northcraft, G. B. (2008). To be or not to be trusted: The influence of media richness on defection and deception. *Organizational Behavior and Human Decision Processes, 107*(2), 106–122. doi:10.1016/j.obhdp.2008.02.002

Rogers, E. (1995). *Diffusion of Innovations*. New York: Free Press.

Rogers, E. M. (1995). *Diffusion of Innovations*. New York: Simon & Schuster.

Ross, A. (2002). *No collar: The humane workplace and its hidden costs*. New York: Basic Books.

Rotchanakitumnuai, S., & Speece, M. (2003). Barriers To Internet Banking Adoption: a qualitative study among corporate customers in Thailand. *International Journal of Bank Marketing, 21*(6), 312–323. doi:10.1108/02652320310498465

Rothaermel, F. T., & Sugiyama, S. (2001). Virtual Internet communities and commercial success: Individual and community-level theory grounded in the atypical case of TimeZone.com. *Journal of Management, 27*(3), 297–312. doi:10.1016/S0149-2063(01)00093-9

Rothstein, B. (2000). Trust, social dilemmas and collective memories. *Journal of Theoretical Politics, 12*, 477–501. doi:10.1177/0951692800012004007

Rothstein, B., & Stolle, D. (2008). How political institutions create and destroy social capital: An institutional theory of generalized trust. *Comparative Politics, 40*.

Rotter, J. B. (1967). A new scale for the measurement of interpersonal trust. *Journal of Personality, 35*, 651–665. doi:10.1111/j.1467-6494.1967.tb01454.x

Rotter, J. B. (1971). Generalized expectancies for interpersonal trust. *The American Psychologist, 26*, 443–452. doi:10.1037/h0031464

Rotter, J. B. (1980). Interpersonal trust, trustworthiness, and gullibility. *The American Psychologist, 35*, 1–7. doi:10.1037/0003-066X.35.1.1

Rousseau, D. M., Sitkin, S. B., Burt, R. S., & Camerer, C. (1998). Not so different after all: A Cross-discipline view of trust. *Academy of Management Review, 23*, 393–404.

Rust, R. T., & Kannan, R. K. (2003). E-service: a new paradigm for business in the electronic environment. *Communications of the ACM, 46*(6), 36–42. doi:10.1145/777313.777336

Sanderson, C. (2007, April 2). Blogger beware! *Comment is Free*. Retrieved June 18, 2007, from http://commentisfree.guardian.co.uk/catherine_sanderson/2007/04/blogger_beware.html

Sarel, D., & Marmorstein, H. (2003). Marketing online banking services: The voice of the customer. *Journal of Financial Services Marketing, 8*(2), 106–118. doi:10.1057/palgrave.fsm.4770111

Sauder, M., & Lancaster, R. (2006). Do rankings matter? The effects of *U.S. News and World Report* rankings on the admissions process of law schools. *Law & Society Review, 40*, 105–134. doi:10.1111/j.1540-5893.2006.00261.x

Sawhney, M., & Zabin, J. (2002). Managing and measuring relational equity in the network economy. *Journal of the Academy of Marketing Science, 30*(4), 313–332. doi:10.1177/009207002236908

Sayar, C., & Wolfe, S. (2007). Internet banking market performance: Turkey versus the UK. *International Journal of Bank Marketing, 25*(3), 122–141. doi:10.1108/02652320710739841

Schelling, T. C. (1960). *The strategy of conflict.* Cambridge, MA: Cambridge University Press.

Schneider, F. B. (Ed.). (1999). *Trust in Cyberspace. Commission on Information Systems' Trustworthiness.* Washington, DC: National Research Council.

Schoder, D., & Yin, P. L. (2000). Building firm trust online. *Communications of the ACM, 43*(12), 73–79. doi:10.1145/355112.355127

Schoneboom, A. (2007). Diary of a working boy: Creative resistance among anonymous workbloggers. *Ethnography, 8*(4), 403–423. doi:10.1177/1466138107083559

Schoorman, F. D., Mayer, R. C., & Davis, J. H. (2007). Editor's Forum: An Integrative model of organizational trust: Past, Present, and Future. *Academy of Management Review, 32*(2), 344–354.

Schul, Y., Burnstein, E., & Martinez, J. (1983). The informational basis of social judgments: Under what conditions are inconsistent trait descriptions processed as easily as consistent ones? *European Journal of Social Psychology, 13*, 143–151. doi:10.1002/ejsp.2420130205

Schutz, A. (1970). *On Phenomenology and Social Relations: Selected Writings.* Chicago, IL: University of Chicago Press.

Schwartz, M. (2008, August 3). The Trolls Among Us. *New York Times.*

Selnes, F. (1998). Antecedents and consequences of trust and satisfaction in buyer-seller relationships. *European Journal of Marketing, 32*(3), 305–322. doi:10.1108/03090569810204580

Semmes, C. E. (1991). Developing trust: Patient-practitioner encounters in natural health care. *Journal of Contemporary Ethnography, 19*, 450–470. doi:10.1177/089124191019004004

Shank, D. B. (2008). *Affect Toward Computers Who Coerce in Social Exchange.* Athens, GA: University of Georgia.

Shank, D. B. (2009). *Perceived Justice of Computers.* Paper presented at the Southern Sociological Society Annual Meeting, New Orleans, LA.

Shank, D. B. (2010). *Georgia 2008 Affect Control Theory Technology Dictionary.* Unpublished manuscript.

Shank, D. B., Hoogenboom, G., & McClendon, R. W. (2008). Dew Point Temperature Prediction Using Artificial Neural Networks. *Journal of Applied Meteorology and Climatology, 47*(6), 1757–1769. doi:10.1175/2007JAMC1693.1

Shank, D. B., McClendon, R. W., Paz, J., & Hoogenboom, G. (2008). Ensemble Artificial Neural Networks for Prediction of Dew Point Temperature. *Applied Artificial Intelligence, 22*(6), 523–542. doi:10.1080/08839510802226785

Shankar, V., Smith, A. K., & Rangaswamy, A. (2003). Customer satisfaction and loyalty in online and offline environments. *International Journal of Research in Marketing, 20*(2), 153–175.

Shankar, V., Urban, G. L., & Sultan, F. (2002). Online Trust: a stakeholder perspective, concepts implications and future directions. *The Journal of Strategic Information Systems, 11*(4), 325–344. doi:10.1016/S0963-8687(02)00022-7

Shapiro, D. L., Sheppard, B. H., & Cheraskin, L. (1992). Business on a handshake. *Negotiation Journal, 8*(4), 365–377. doi:10.1111/j.1571-9979.1992.tb00679.x

Shapiro, S. P. (1987). The Social Control of Impersonal Trust. *American Journal of Sociology*, *93*, 623–658. doi:10.1086/228791

Sheehan, K. B. (2005). Public Opinions of Online Privacy: Definitions, Assessment and Implications for Industry and Public Policy. In Krishnamurthy, S. (Ed.), *Contemporary Research in E-Marketing* (pp. 186–199). Hershey, PA: Idea Group Publishing.

Sheehan, K. B., & Hoy, M. G. (2000). Dimensions of privacy concern among online consumers. *Journal of Public Policy & Marketing*, *19*(1), 62–73. doi:10.1509/jppm.19.1.62.16949

Shinozawa, K., Reeves, B., Wise, K., Maldonado, H., & Naya, F. (2002). Robots as New Media: A Cross-Cultural Examination of Social and Cognitive Responses to Robotic and On-Screen Agents. Submitted to the Information Systems Division of the International Communication Association.

Shneiderman, B. (2000). Designing Trust into Online experiences. *Communications of the ACM*, *43*(12), 57–59. doi:10.1145/355112.355124

Shortliffe, E. H. (1993). Doctors, Patients, and Computers: Will Information Technology Dehumanize Health-Care Delivery? *Proceedings of the American Philosophical Society*, *137*(3), 390–398.

Siegrist, M., Gutscher, H., & Earle, T. C. (2005). Perception of risk: the influence of general trust, and general confidence. *Journal of Risk Research*, *8*(2), 145–156. doi:10.1080/1366987032000105315

Sifry, D. (2004, October 17). Oct 2004 State of the Blogosphere: Corporate bloggers. *Sifry's Alerts*. Retrieved November 30, 2006, from http://www.sifry.com/alerts/archives/000390.html

Sifry, D. (2005, September 14). Welcome to the Blogosphere, Google! *Sifry's Alerts*. Retrieved November 30, 2006, from http://www.sifry.com/alerts/archives/000340.html

Silverstone, R. (1995). *Television and everyday life*. London: Routledge.

Silverstone, R. (1999). *Why Study the Media?* London: Sage.

Silverstone, R., & Haddon, L. (1996). Design and the domestication of information and communication technologies: Technical change and everyday life. In Silverstone, R., & Mansell, R. (Eds.), *Communication by design: The politics of information and communication technologies* (pp. 44–74). Oxford, UK: Oxford University Press.

Silverstone, R., Hirsch, E., & Morley, D. (1992). Information and communication technologies and the moral economy of the household. In Silverstone, R., & Hirsch, E. (Eds.), *Consuming technologies: Media and information in domestic spaces* (pp. 15–31). London: Routledge. doi:10.4324/9780203401491_chapter_1

Simmel, G. (1978). *The Philosophy of Money*. London: Routledge. (Original work published 1900)

Simon, H. (1955). A Behavioral Model of Rational Choice. *The Quarterly Journal of Economics*, *63*, 129–138.

Simpson, B., & McGrimmon, T. (2008). Trust and Embedded Markets: A Multi-method Investigation of Consumer Transactions. *Social Networks*, *30*, 1–15. doi:10.1016/j.socnet.2007.04.004

Sitkin, S. B., & Roth, N. L. (1993). Explaining the limited effectiveness of legalistic 'remedies' for trust/distrust. *Organization Science*, *4*, 367–392. doi:10.1287/orsc.4.3.367

Slater, D., & Kwani, J. (2005). *Embeddedness and escape: Internet and mobile use as poverty reduction strategies in Ghana*. Report No. 4, Information Society Research Group, London.

Smallbone, D., & Rogut, A. (2005). The challenge facing SMEs in the EU's new member states. *The International Entrepreneurship and Management Journal*, *1*(2), 219–240. doi:10.1007/s11365-005-1130-x

Smith, B. A., McClendon, R. W., & Hoogenboom, G. (2006). Improving air temperature prediction with artificial neural networks. *International Journal of Computational Intelligence*, *3*(3), 179–186.

Smith, H. J., Milberg, S. J., & Burke, S. J. (1996). Information privacy: measuring individuals' concerns about organizational practices. *Management Information Systems Quarterly, 16*(June), 167–196. doi:10.2307/249477

Smith, M. (2007). *Confianza a la Chilena: A comparative study of how e-services influence public sector institutional trustworthiness and trust.* Unpublished doctoral dissertation, London School of Economics, London.

Smith, M., Bailey, J., & Brynjolfsson, E. (2000). Understanding digital markets: review and assessment. In Bryonjolfsson, E., & Kahim, B. (Eds.), *Understanding the digital economy.* Cambridge, MA: MIT Press.

Smith-Lovin, L. (1987). Impression from Events. *The Journal of Mathematical Sociology, 13*, 35–70.

Smith-Lovin, L., & Douglass, W. (1992). An Affect-Control Analysis of Two Religious Groups. In Franks, D. D., & Gecas, V. (Eds.), *Social Perspectives on Emotion.* Greenwich, CT: Jai Press.

Snell, J. (2005, May 16). Blogging@IBM. *Chmod 777 Web.* Retrieved November 30, 2006, from http://www-128. ibm.com/developerworks/blogs/dw_blog_comments. jspa?blog=351&entry=81328

Snijders, C. (1996). *Trust and Commitments.* Gronigen, Netherlands: Interuniversity Center for Social Science Theory and Methodology.

Sorrentino, R. M., Hanna, S. E., Holmes, J. G., & Sharp, A. (1995). Uncertainty orientation and trust in close relationships: individual differences in cognitive styles. *Journal of Personality and Social Psychology, 68*(2), 314–327. doi:10.1037/0022-3514.68.2.314

Souter, D., Scott, N., Garforth, C., Jain, R., Mascarenhas, O., & McKemey, K. (2005). *The economic impact of telecommunications on rural livelihoods and poverty reduction: A study of rural communities in India (Gujarat).* Mozambique and Tanzania: Report, Commonwealth Telecommunications Organisation Report for U.K. Department for International Development.

Sparrow, R. (2002). The March of the Robot Dogs. *Ethics and Information Technology, 4*, 305–318. doi:10.1023/A:1021386708994

Spears, R., Lea, M., & Postmes, T. (2007). CMC and social identity. In Joinson, A. N., McKenna, K. Y. A., Postmes, T., & Reips, U.-D. (Eds.), *The Oxford Handbook of Internet Psychology.* London: Oxford University Press.

Spence, M. A. (1974). *Market signaling: Informational transfer in hiring and related screening processes.* Cambridge, MA: Harvard University Press.

Sproull, L., & Keisler, S. (1991). *Connections: New ways of working in the networked organization.* Cambridge, MA: MIT Press.

Steidley, C., Sadovski, A., Tissot, P., & Bachnak, R. (2005). *Using an artificial neural network to improve predictions of water level where tide charts fail.* Paper presented at the Innovations in Applied Artificial Intelligence, Bari, Italy.

Stewart, K. J. (2003). Trust transfer on the World Wide Web. *Organization Science, 14*(1), 5–17. doi:10.1287/orsc.14.1.5.12810

Stewart, T. A. (1993). Welcome to the Revolution. *Fortune, 128*(15), 66–80.

Stiff, J. B. (1994). *Persuasive Communication.* New York: Guilford Press.

Stinchcombe, A. L. (1965). Social structure and organizations. In March, J. G. (Ed.), *Handbook of Organizations* (pp. 219–223). Chicago: Rand-McNally.

Stoll, C. (1995). *Silicon Snake Oil.* New York: Doubleday.

Strauss, A. (1978). *Negotiations: Varieties, processes, contexts, and social order.* San Francisco: Jossey-Bass.

Strauss, A. (1987). *Qualitative analysis for social scientists.* Cambridge, UK: Cambridge University Press. doi:10.1017/CBO9780511557842

Strauss, A. L., & Corbin, J. (1998). *Basics of qualitative research: Techniques and procedures for developing grounded theory* (2nd ed.). Thousand Oaks, CA: Sage.

Strauss, A., & Corbin, J. (1990). *Basics of qualitative research: Grounded theory procedures and techniques.* London: Sage Publications.

Stuart, T. E. (2000). Interoganizational alliances and the performance of firms: A study of growth and innovation rates in a high-technology industry. *Strategic Management Journal*, *21*, 791–811. doi:10.1002/1097-0266(200008)21:8<791::AID-SMJ121>3.0.CO;2-K

Stuart, T. E., & Podolny, J. M. (1996). Local Search and the Evolution of Technological Capabilities. *Strategic Management Journal*, *17*, 21–38.

Stuart, T. E., Hoang, H., & Hybels, R. C. (1999). Interorganizational endorsements and the performance of entrepreneurial ventures. *Administrative Science Quarterly*, *44*, 315–349. doi:10.2307/2666998

Suh, B., & Han, I. (2002). The Impact of Consumer trust and Perception of Security Control on the Acceptance of Electronic Commerce. *International Journal of Electronic Commerce*, *7*(3), 135–161.

Suh, B., & Han, I. (2003). The Impact of Customer Trust and Perception of Security Control on the Acceptance of Electronic Commerce. *International Journal of Electronic Commerce*, *7*(3), 135–161.

Sukkar, A. A., & Hasan, H. (2005). Toward a Model for the Acceptance of Internet Banking in Developing Countries. *Information Technology for Development*, *11*(4), 381–398. doi:10.1002/itdj.20026

Szmigin, I., & Bourne, H. (1998). Consumer equity in relationship marketing. *Journal of Consumer Marketing*, *15*(6), 544–557. doi:10.1108/07363769810240545

Sztompka, P. (1999). *Trust: A sociological theory*. Cambridge, UK: Cambridge University Press.

Sztompka, P. (2008). Trust Review of Democracy and the Culture of Skepticism: Political Trust in Argentina and Mexico by M. Cleary & S. C. Stokes. *International Sociology*, *23*(2), 215–234. doi:10.1177/0268580907086377

Tadelis, S. (1999). What's in a name? Reputation as a tradable asset. *The American Economic Review*, *89*, 548–563.

Takayama, L., & Kandogan, E. (2006). *Trust as an underlying factor of system administrator interface choice.* Paper presented at the Conference on Human Factors in Computing Systems, Montréal, Canada.

Tanis, M., & Postmes, T. (2005). A social identity approach to trust: Interpersonal percpetion, group membership and trusting behaviour. *European Journal of Social Psychology*, *35*, 413–424. doi:10.1002/ejsp.256

Taylor, M. (1987). *The possibility of cooperation*. Cambridge, UK: Cambridge University Press.

Taylor, P. A. (1999). *Hackers: Crime in the Digital Sublime*. London: Routledge. doi:10.4324/9780203201503

Taylor, T. L. (2006). *Play between worlds: Exploring online game culture*. Cambridge, MA: MIT Press.

Teo, T. S. H., & Liu, J. (2007). Consumer trust in e-commerce in the United States, Singapore and China. *Omega-The International Journal of Management Science*, *35*, 22–38. doi:10.1016/j.omega.2005.02.001

Teven, J. J., & Hanson, T. L. (2004). The impact of teacher immediacy and perceived caring on teacher competence and trustworthiness. *Communication Quarterly*, *52*, 39–53.

Thatcher, J. B., Loughry, M. L., Lim, J., & McKnight, D. H. (2007). Internet anxiety: An empirical study of the effects of personality, beliefs, and social support. *Information & Management*, *44*, 353–363. doi:10.1016/j.im.2006.11.007

Thiedecke, U. (2007). *Trust, but test! Das Vertrauen in virtuellen Gemeinschaften*. Konstanz, Germany: UVK.

Thomas, D., & Bostrom, R. (2008). Building trust and cooperation through technology adaptation in virual teams: Empirical field evidence. *Information Systems Management*, *25*(1), 45–56. doi:10.1080/10580530701777149

Thompson, J. D. (1967). *Organizations in action: Social science bases of administrative theory*. New York: McGraw Hill.

Thompson, P., & Ackroyd, S. (1995). All quiet on the workplace front? A critique of recent trends in British industrial sociology. *Sociology*, *29*(4), 615–633. doi:10.1177/0038038595029004004

Thurlow, C., & McKay, S. (2003). Communication Technologies in Adolescence. *Journal of*

Language and Social Psychology, 22(1), 94–103. doi:10.1177/0261927X02250060

Thye, S. R. (2000). A status value theory of power in exchange relations. *American Sociological Review, 65,* 407–432. doi:10.2307/2657464

Tönnies, F. (1963). *Gemeinschaft und gesellshaft.* Darmstadt, Germany: Wissenschaftliche Buchgessellschaft. (Original work published 1887)

Torkzadeh, G., Chang, J. C.-J., & Demirhan, D. (2006). A contingency model of computer and Internet self-efficacy. *Information & Management, 43,* 541–550. doi:10.1016/j.im.2006.02.001

Troyer, L. (2004). *Affect Control Theory as a Foundation for the Design of Socially Intelligent Systems.* Paper presented at the American Association for Artificial Intelligence Symposium on Architectures for Modeling Emotion: Cross Disciplinary Foundations, Menlo Park, CA.

Troyer, L. (2008). A Strategy for Incorporating Social Intelligence in the Design of Virtual Environments. In Clay-Warner, J., & Robinson, D. T. (Eds.), *Social Structure and Emotion* (pp. 95–106). Amsterdam: Elsevier. doi:10.1016/B978-0-12-374095-3.00006-9

Troyer, L., & Younts, C. W. (1997). Whose expectations matter? The relative power of first- and second-order expectations in determining social influence. *American Journal of Sociology, 103,* 692–732. doi:10.1086/231253

Tsai, W. (2000). Social capital, strategic relatedness and the formation of intraorganizational linkages. *Strategic Management Journal, 21,* 925–939. doi:10.1002/1097-0266(200009)21:9<925::AID-SMJ129>3.0.CO;2-I

Turkle, S. (1995). *Life on the screen: Identity in the age of the Internet.* New York: Simon and Schuster.

Tyler, T. R., & Kramer, R. M. (1996). Whither trust? In Kramer, R. M., & Tyler, T. R. (Eds.), *Trust in Organizations* (pp. 1–15). Thousand Oaks, CA: Sage.

Ullmann-Margalit, E. (1978). *The emergence of norms.* Oxford, UK: Oxford University Press.

Ullmann-Margalit, E. (2004). Trust, distrust, and in between. In Hardin, R. (Ed.), *Distrust* (pp. 60–82). New York: Russell Sage Foundation.

Urban, G. L., Sultan, F., & Qualls, W. J. (2000). Placing Trust at the Center of Your Internet Strategy. *Sloan Management Review, 42*(1), 39–48.

Uslaner, E. M. (2000). Producing and consuming trust. *Political Science Quarterly, 115,* 569–590. doi:10.2307/2657610

Uslaner, E. M. (2002). *The moral foundations of trust.* Cambridge, UK: Cambridge University Press. doi:10.1017/CBO9780511614934

Utz, S. (2005). Types of deception and underlying motivation: What people think. *Social Science Computer Review, 23*(1), 49–56. doi:10.1177/0894439304271534

Vainio, A. M. (2005). Exchange and combination of knowledge-based resources in network relationships. *European Journal of Marketing, 39,* 1078–1095. doi:10.1108/03090560510610734

Van den Poel, D., & Leunis, J. (1999). Consumer acceptance of the internet as a channel of distribution. *Journal of Business Research, 45,* 249–256. doi:10.1016/S0148-2963(97)00236-1

Vaughan, P. (2007). Early lessons from the deployment of M-Pesa. In *The transformational potential of m-transactions* (pp. 6–10). Newbury, UK: Vodafone Group PLC.

Venkatesan, R., Kumar, V., & Ravishankar, N. (2007). Multichannel shopping: causes and consequences. *Journal of Marketing, 71*(2), 114–132. doi:10.1509/jmkg.71.2.114

Venkatesh, V., Morris, M. G., Davis, G. B., & Davis, F. D. (2003). User Acceptance of Information Technology: Toward a Unified View. *Management Information Systems Quarterly, 27*(3), 425–478.

Vishwanath, A. (2004). Manifestations of interpersonal trust in online interaction: A cross-cultural study comparing the differential utilization of seller ratings by eBay participants in Canada, France, and Germany. *New Media & Society*, 6(2), 219–234. doi:10.1177/1461444804041441

Viswanathan, M., Rosa, J. A., & Harris, J. E. (2005). Decision making and coping of functionally illiterate consumers and some implications for marketing management. *Journal of Marketing*, 69(January), 15–31. doi:10.1509/jmkg.69.1.15.55507

Voswinkel, S. (2000), Das mcdonaldistische Produktionsmodell - Schnittstellenmanagement interaktiver Dienstleistungsarbeit. [The mcdonald production modell- Interface management in interactive service work] In H. Minssen (Ed.), Begrenzte Entgrenzungen. Wandlungen von Organisation und Arbeit (pp. 177-203). Berlin, Germany: Ed. sigma.

Vygotsky, L. (1978). *Mind in society: The development of higher psychological processes*. Cambridge, MA: Harvard University Press.

Walczuch, R., & Lundgren, H. (2004). Psychological antecedents of institution-based consumer trust in e-retailing. *Information & Management*, 42, 159–177.

Wallace, P. (1999). *The Psychology of the Internet*. Cambridge, UK: Cambridge University Press.

Wallace, P. (2001). *The psychology of the Internet*. Cambridge, UK: Cambridge University Press.

Wallace, P. (2001). *The psychology of the Internet*. Cambridge, UK: Cambridge University Press.

Walther, J. B. (1992). Interpersonal effects in computer-mediated interaction: A relational perspective. *Communication Research*, 19(1), 52–91. doi:10.1177/009365092019001003

Walther, J. B. (1995). Relational aspects of computer-mediated communication: Experimental observations over time. *Organization Science*, 6(2), 186–203. doi:10.1287/orsc.6.2.186

Walther, J. B. (1996). Computer mediated communication: Impersonal, interpersonal and hyperpersonal interaction. *Communication Research*, 22, 33–43.

Walther, J. B. (2002). Time effects in computer-mediated groups: Past, present, and future. In Hinds, P., & Kiesler,

S. (Eds.), *Distributed work* (pp. 235–257). Cambridge, MA: MIT Press.

Walther, J. B., Slovacek, C., & Tidwell, L. C. (2001). Is a picture worth a thousand words? Photographic images in long term and short term virtual teams. *Communication Research*, 28(1), 105–134. doi:10.1177/009365001028001004

Wan, W. W. N., Luk, C.-L., & Chow, C. W. C. (2005). Customers' adoption of banking channels in Hong Kong. *International Journal of Bank Marketing*, 23(3), 255–272. doi:10.1108/02652320510591711

Wang, Y. D., & Emurian, H. H. (2005). An overview of online trust: concepts, elements, and implications. *Computers in Human Behavior*, 21, 105–125. doi:10.1016/j.chb.2003.11.008

Wang, Y.-S., Wang, Y.-M., Lin, H.-H., & Tang, T.-I. (2003). Determinants of user acceptance of Internet banking: an empirical study. *International Journal of Service Industry Management*, 14(5), 501–519. doi:10.1108/09564230310500192

Ward, K. (2005). Internet consumption in Ireland—Towards a connected life. In Silverstone, R. (Ed.), *Media, technology and everyday life in Europe* (pp. 107–123). Aldershot, UK: Ashgate.

Weber, M. (1947). *The theory of economic and social organization*. New York: Oxford Press.

Weber, M. (1979). *Economy and society*. Berkeley, CA: University of California Press.

Webster, M., & Hysom, S. J. (1998). Creating status characteristics. *American Sociological Review*, 63, 351–379. doi:10.2307/2657554

Wedge, D., Ingram, D., McLean, D., Mingham, C., & Bandar, Z. (2005). *A global-local artificial neural network with application to wave overtopping prediction*. Paper presented at the Artificial Neural Networks: Formal Models and Their Applications - ICANN 2005, Warsaw, Poland.

Weick, K. E. (1995). *Sensemaking in organization*. Thousand Oaks, CA: Sage.

Welch, M. R., Rivera, R. E. N., Conway, B. P., Yonkoski, J., Lupton, P. M., & Giancola, R. (2005). Determinants and consequences of social trust. *Sociological Inquiry*, *75*(4), 453–473. doi:10.1111/j.1475-682X.2005.00132.x

Welker, M., Werner, A., & Scholz, J. (2005). Online-Research. Markt- und Sozialforschung mit dem Internet. Heidelberg, Germany: dpunkt.verlag.

Wellman, B. (2001). Computer Networks as Social Network. *Science*, *293*, 2031–2034. doi:10.1126/science.1065547

Wellman, B., & Guilia, M. (1999). Net Surfers don't ride alone: Virtual communities as communities. In Wellman, B. (Ed.), *Networks in the Global Village: Life in Contemporary Communities*. Boulder, CO: Westview.

Westin-Harris. (1997). *Privacy and American Business Study*. A survey.

Wheeless, L. R., & Grotz, J. (1977). The measurement of trust and its relationship to self-disclosure. *Human Communication Research*, *3*, 250–257. doi:10.1111/j.1468-2958.1977.tb00523.x

Whitty, M. (2007). Love letters: The development of romantic relationships throughout the ages. In Joinson, A., McKenna, K., Postmes, T., & Reips, U.-D. (Eds.), *The Oxford Handbook of Internet Psychology*. Oxford, UK: Oxford University Press.

Wilhelm, A. G. (2000). *Democracy in the digital age: Challenges to political life in cyberspace*. New York: Routledge.

Willer, R. (2009). Groups reward individual sacrifice: The status solution to the collective action problem. *American Sociological Review*, *74*, 23–43. doi:10.1177/000312240907400102

Williamson, O. E. (1975). *Markets and hierarchies: Analysis and antitrust implications*. New York, NY: Free Press.

Williamson, O. E. (1981). The economics of organization: The transaction cost approach. *American Journal of Sociology*, *87*, 548–577. doi:10.1086/227496

Williamson, O. E. (1985). *The economic institutions of capitalism*. New York: The Free Press.

Williamson, O. E. (1993). Calculativeness, trust, and economic organization. *The Journal of Law & Economics*, *36*(2), 453–486. doi:10.1086/467284

Wilson, J. M., Straus, S. G., & McEvily, B. (2006). All in Due Time: The Development of Trust in Computer Mediated and Face-to-Face Teams. *Organizational Behavior and Human Decision Processes*, *99*, 16–33. doi:10.1016/j.obhdp.2005.08.001

Wilson, K. R., Wallin, J. S., & Reiser, C. (2003). Social stratification and the digital divide. *Social Science Computer Review*, *21*, 133–143. doi:10.1177/0894439303021002001

Winter, D. G., John, O. P., Stewart, A. J., Klohnen, E. C., & Duncan, L. E. (1998). Traits and motives: Toward an integration of two traditions in personality research. *Psychological Review*, *105*, 230–250. doi:10.1037/0033-295X.105.2.230

Wolfe, A. (1989). *Whose keeper? Social science and moral obligation*. Berkeley, CA: University of California Press.

Wu, I.-L., & Chen, J.-L. (2005). An extension of trust and TAM model with TPB in the initial adoption of online tax: an empirical study. *International Journal of Human-Computer Studies*, *62*, 784–808. doi:10.1016/j.ijhcs.2005.03.003

Yamagishi, T. (1988). The Provision of a Sanctioning System in the United States and Japan. *Social Psychology Quarterly*, *51*(3), 265–271. doi:10.2307/2786924

Yamagishi, T. (1995). Social Dilemmas. In Cook, K. S., Fine, G. A., & House, J. (Eds.), *Sociological Perspectives on Social Psychology*. Boston: Allyn & Bacon.

Yamagishi, T. (1998). *The Structure of Trust*. Tokyo, Japan: University of Tokyo Press.

Yamagishi, T. (2001). Trust as a form of social intelligence. In Cook, K. S. (Ed.), *Trust in Society* (pp. 121–147). New York: Russell Sage Foundation.

Yamagishi, T., & Cook, K. S. (1993). Exchange and Social Dilemmas. *Social Psychology Quarterly*, *56*(4), 235–248. doi:10.2307/2786661

Yamagishi, T., & Matsuda, M. (2003). The Role of Reputation in Open and Closed Societies: An Experimental Study of Online Trading. *Center for the Study of Cultural and Ecological Foundations of Mind, Working Paper Series 8.* Retrieved May 1, 2009, from http://lynx.let.hokudai.ac.jp/COE21/english/workingpaper/index.html

Yamagishi, T., & Yamagishi, M. (1994). Trust and Commitment in the United States and Japan. *Motivation and Emotion, 18,* 129–166. doi:10.1007/BF02249397

Yamagishi, T., & Yamagishi, M. (1994). Trust and commitment in the United States and Japan. *Motivation and Emotion, 18,* 129–166. doi:10.1007/BF02249397

Yamagishi, T., & Yamagishi, M. (1994). Trust and Commitment in the United States and Japan. *Motivation and Emotion, 18,* 129–166. doi:10.1007/BF02249397

Yamagishi, T., Foddy, M., Makimura, Y., Matsuda, M., Kiyonari, T., & Platow, M. (2005). Comparisons of Australians and Japanese on group-based cooperation. *Asian Journal of Social Psychology, 8*(2), 173–190. doi:10.1111/j.1467-839x.2005.00165.x

Yamagishi, T., Kikuchi, M., & Kosugi, M. (1999). Trust, gullibility and social intelligence. *Asian Journal of Social Psychology, 2*(1), 145–161. doi:10.1111/1467-839X.00030

Yamagishi, T., Matsuda, M., Yoshikai, N., Takahashi, H., & Usui, Y. (in press). Trust and Reputation. In Cook, K. S., Snijders, C., Buskins, V., & Cheshire, C. (Eds.), *eTrust and Reputation.* New York: Russell Sage Foundation.

Ye, Z., Smith, S. W., & Anthony, D. (2005). Trusted Paths for Browsers. [TISSEC]. *ACM Journal Transactions on Information and System Security, 8*(2), 153–186. doi:10.1145/1065545.1065546

Yoon, S. J. (2002). The antecedents and consequences of trust in online purchase decisions. *Journal of Interactive Marketing, 16*(2), 47–63. doi:10.1002/dir.10008

Yousafzai, S. Y., Pallister, J. G., & Foxall, G. R. (2003). A proposed model of e-trust for electronic banking. *Technovation, 23,* 847–860. doi:10.1016/S0166-4972(03)00130-5

Zak, P., & Knack, S. (2001). Trust and growth. *The Economic Journal, 111,* 207–243. doi:10.1111/1468-0297.00609

Zakaria, N., Amelinckx, A., & Wilemon, D. (2004). Working together apart? Building a knowledge-sharing culture for global virtual teams. *Creativity and Innovation Management, 13*(1), 15–29. doi:10.1111/j.1467-8691.2004.00290.x

Zimmer, E. A., & Hunter, C. D. (2003). The Internet and risk: Perception and reality. In Strate, L., Jacobson, R., & Gibson, S. B. (Eds.), *Communication and Cyberspace: Social Interaction in an Electronic Environment* (pp. 183–202). Cresskill, NY: Hampton Press.

Zimmer, M. (2008). The Gaze of the Perfect Search Engine: Google as an Infrastructure of Dataveillance. In Zimmer, M., & Spink, A. (Eds.), *Web Search. Multidisciplinary Perspectives* (pp. 77–99). Heidelberg: Springer.

Zimmer, T. (1972). The impact of Watergate on the public's trust in people and confidence in the mass media. *Social Science Quarterly, 59,* 743–751.

Zucker, L. (1986). Similarity based trust. *Research in Organizational Behavior, 8,* 53–111.

Zucker, L. G. (1986). Production of trust: Institutional sources of economic structure, 1840–1920. In Staw, B. M., & Cummings, L. L. (Eds.), *Research in Organizational Behavior* (*Vol. 8,* pp. 53–111). Greenwich, CT: JAI Press.

About the Contributors

Dominika Latusek is an assistant professor of management and organization theory at Kozminski University in Warsaw, Poland. She conducts research on cooperation between organizations with an emphasis on trust and culture. She was a Fulbright Visiting Scholar at Stanford University, where she conducted field studies of Silicon Valley companies.

Alexandra Gerbasi is an assistant professor of sociology at California State University, Northridge. She received her Ph.D. from Stanford University. Her primary research interest is how network structures influence the exchange process and the emergent sentiments of the interactions, particularly trust, commitment and emotions.

* * *

Denise Anthony is Associate Professor and Chair of the Department of Sociology at Dartmouth College. She is also Research Director of the Institute for Security, Technology, and Society (ISTS at www.ists.dartmouth.edu/), which explores the widespread use of information technology in society, and its implications for behavior, privacy, and security.

David W. Birchall is an Emeritus Professor at Henley Business School, University of Reading. David's research interests are in the area of management learning and innovation practices in organizations. He has particular expertise in the development of systems to support remote workers and learners. David has consulted and lectured throughout the world on aspects of innovation, technology and organization capabilities, organizational learning and knowledge management.

Anita Blanchard is associate professor of Psychology and Organization Science at the University of North Carolina Charlotte. She has her PhD from Claremont Graduate University in Organizational Psychology. Her research interests include how successful virtual communities function, particularly within organizations. She examines the application of behavior setting theories to virtual communities, the effects of virtual community participation on face-to-face communities' trust and social capital, the development and experience of a sense of community within virtual communities, and how virtual groups come to be experiences as "groups."

David Boyns is an Associate Professor of Sociology at California State University, Northridge. His research interests include sociological theory, cultural sociology, media studies, and the sociology of emotions. His current research investigates forms of technologically mediated social interaction in virtual environments, and draws upon Massive Multiplayer Role Playing Games as case studies.

Celeste Campos-Castillo is currently an ASA Minority Fellowship Program Fellow with funds from the National Institute of Mental Health as well as a doctoral candidate in the department of sociology at the University of Iowa. Her primary research interests include the emergence of trust and commitment, computer-mediated interaction, mental health, and specialist organizations and their environments. She is currently working on her dissertation, which will examine the relationship between trust and health in physician-patient relationships.

Sandro Castaldo is Chairman of the Marketing Department of the SDA Bocconi School of Management and Full Professor of the Management Department of the Bocconi University where he teaches marketing and channel management. He has a Ph.D. in Business Administration and Management from Bocconi University. His current research interests are trust, retailing and channel relationships. His work has appeared in Journal of Business Ethics, Industrial Marketing Management, Journal of Service Management and other outlets. He recently co-edited the book 'Coopetition Winning Strategies for the 21st Century' (edited by S. Castaldo, G. Dagnino, F. Le Roy, S. Yami) Edward Elgar, Cheltenham, UK, forthcoming and published the book 'Trust in Market Relationship', Edward Elgar, Cheltenham, UK, 2007.

Coye Cheshire is assistant professor in the School of Information at the University of California, Berkeley. As a sociological social psychologist, he studies cooperation, trust, collective action and interpersonal relationships in computer-mediated systems. He lives in Concord, CA with his wife, two charming beagles and a very large cat.

G. Scott Erickson is associate professor and chair of the Marketing/Law Department in the School of Business at Ithaca College, Ithaca, NY. He holds a PhD from Lehigh University and masters degrees from Thunderbird and SMU. He has published widely on intellectual property, intellectual capital, competitive intelligence, and a number of related topics. His book with Helen Rothberg, From Knowledge to Intelligence, was published by Elsevier in 2005. His consulting work began 25 years ago with Alexander Proudfoot and continues today.

Rita Faullant is assistant professor at the Department of Innovation Management and Entrepreneurship at the University of Klagenfurt, Austria. Her research centers on consumer co-creation and customer integration in new product development, adoption and diffusion processes of new products and technologies, and on organizational innovativeness.

Andrew T. Fiore is a Ph.D. candidate in the School of Information at the University of California, Berkeley, where he studies computer-mediated communication and relationship formation from the perspective of psychological social psychology. In 2006, he was named a Microsoft Research Fellow, and he holds master's degrees from UC Berkeley in Statistics and from the MIT Media Lab in Media Arts and Sciences. He prefers ordinary least squares to hierarchical linear modeling and North Carolina-style barbecue to just about everything.

Genoveffa (Jeni) Giambona is a Research Manager/Research Fellow at the Research Institute for the Built Environment, University of Reading. Jeni's research interests are in the area of leadership development, management learning (e-learning especially), virtual teams and trust. She also researches meta-evaluation and the study of how learning mechanisms work in different contexts and cultures. She has led projects on the meta-evaluation of e-learning programs aimed at leadership development. Jeni also has an interest in the application of realist synthesis, narrative analysis and discourse analysis.

Oren Golan is a Fulbright postdoctoral scholar at NYU's Center for Media, Culture and History. For several years he has lectured at the Department of Sociology and Social Anthropology at the Hebrew University and at the unit for Informal Education at Beit Berl College. His PhD is entitled: "Computing Friendship: the Social Construction of Relationships within CMC among Israeli Adolescents" (available on his website http://cyber-youth.blogspot.com/). His research interests include: Internet studies, the sociology of youth, popular culture, informal education, social trust, friendship, entrepreneurship, and of late – online religion.

Sonja Grabner-Kräuter is Associate Professor of Marketing and International Management at the Klagenfurt University, Austria. Her research focus is on business ethics, consumer trust, and electronic commerce. She has published in Journal of Advertising, Journal of Business Ethics, International Journal of Human-Computer Studies, Innovative Marketing, Journal of Product and Brand Management, and International Journal of Bank Marketing.

Maria Grigoryeva is a graduate student in the department of sociology at the University of Washington. Her broad interests are in social influence and social networks, and her research addresses the intersection of institutional analysis and criminology. Her master's thesis examines the effects of differential parenting practices on early childhood development and adolescent delinquency. Her other research investigates the utility of neighborhood social ties and informal control mechanisms in reducing crime and the influence of new social relationships on individual attitudes and behaviors after the transition to college.

Monica Grosso is a Ph.D. Candidate in Business Adminstration and Management at the Bocconi University and SDA Bocconi School of Management. She collaborates as a researcher with the Retailing Observatory of the SDA Bocconi School of Management. Her research interests are retailing and channel management and in particular private label and collaborative relationships within distribution channels.

Tina Guenther is a researcher, academic lecturer in sociology, blogger and author of "sozlog". She received her PhD from the University of Bamberg, Germany with a dissertation on structural change at "Germany Inc." entitled "Struktur- und Kulturwandel international tätiger deutscher Unternehmen" (DUV, 2007). Tina is interested in both economic sociology and sociological research of online social life, particularly in trust online.

Charles F. Hofacker has a Ph. D. in Mathematical Psychology from the University of California, Los Angeles, and is Professor of Marketing at Florida State University. His current research interests are at the intersection of marketing and information technology. His work in that and other areas has appeared in the Journal of Marketing Research, Journal of the Academy of Marketing Science, Psychometrika,

Management Science and other outlets. Along with Ed Malthouse, he is co-editor of the Journal of Interactive Marketing. Dr. Hofacker currently serves as Webmaster for the American Marketing Association's Academic Resource Center (ARC) and is also the moderator of ELMAR, an electronic newsletter and community platform for academic marketing with over 6,300 subscribers.

James A. Kitts is an Assistant Professor in the Graduate School of Business at Columbia University. He is broadly interested in the dynamics of cooperation and competition among organizations and among their members, with specific focus on collective action and exchange in social networks. His work has been published recently in the American Sociological Review, Social Forces, and Demography.

Kurt Komaromi is an Instructor of Marketing and Integrated Marketing Communications at Ithaca College. His research focuses on the impact of new media on marketing strategy. Prior to teaching, Kurt had an extensive career in corporate marketing and sales management with companies such as American Hospital Supply, Merck KGaA, and Abbott Laboratories. He maintains a consultancy providing marketing services and sales training to clients across North America. Kurt holds a master's degree in Communications from Ithaca College along with an undergraduate degree from the University of Notre Dame.

Jong-Eun Roselyn Lee received her Ph.D. in Communication at Stanford University, and is now assistant professor in the Department of Communication at Hope College in Michigan. She conducts research on social responses to technology in the context of human-computer interaction; social identity dynamics in computer-mediated communication; and psychological effects of social media.

Christopher Masone received his PhD in Computer Science from Dartmouth College in 2008, focusing on bridging the gap between usability and security. His dissertation, "Attribute-Based, Usefully Secure Email," used real-world examples of person-to-person trust building to inform the design of an email system that enables trustworthy communication among users who do not know each other a priori. He currently designs and builds software at Google, Inc.

Gianluca Miscione's research activity is focused on the interplay between information technologies and organizational processes. It is situated between science and technology studies, and development studies. Particular attention is paid to understanding what happens at the intersection of the global and the local. Since completing his Master's dissertation on the social boundaries of the Internet, he has been exploring what happens on the borders of the so-called "knowledge society", with the aim of bridging the gap between mainstream research and development.

Guido Möllering is a Senior Research Associate at the Max Planck Institute for the Study of Societies in Cologne, Germany. He received his PhD from the University of Cambridge, UK. Trust has been among his main research interests for more than twelve years. His book "Trust: Reason, Routine, Reflexivity" was published by Elsevier in 2006.

Olga Morawczynski is a PhD candidate in the discipline of Science and Technology Studies at the University of Edinburgh. Her research examines the adoption, usage and impact of m-banking applications in general and M-PESA in particular. Olga's research is funded by Microsoft Research in conjunction with the University of Edinburgh.

Clifford Nass is the Thomas M. Storke Professor at Stanford University, with appointments in Communication; Computer Science; Education; Science, Technology, and Society; Sociology; and Symbolic Systems. He is the Director of the CHIMe Lab and the co-Director of the Kozmetsky Global Collaboratory. His research focuses on the social aspects of human-interactive media interaction, with particular attention to cars, mobile, robots, adaptation and personalization, and multitasking. He is the author of two books (The Media Equation and Wired for Speech) as well as over 125 articles on human-technology interaction and statistical methodology. He has been involved in the design of over 200 interfaces for numerous consumer, automotive, and financial services companies.

Katia Premazzi has a Ph. D. in Business Administration & Management from Bocconi University, Milano, and is currently an Assistant Professor at the Management Department of the same university. She teaches marketing, channel management and retailing courses at the undergraduate and graduate level, in both Italian and English. She is also a Professor in the Marketing Department of SDA Bocconi School of Management, where she teaches in the distance learning modules of the EMMS (Executive Master in Marketing and Sales), and in the executive education programs. She also collaborates, as a researcher, with the Retailing Observatory. Her current research interests are retail innovation, shopping behaviour, and Corporate Social Responsibility in retailing.

Lisa Rashotte received her Ph.D. in Sociology from the University of Arizona in 1998. She joined the UNC Charlotte faculty as Assistant Professor of Sociology in 1998, and was promoted to Associate Professor in 2004. She became Chair of the Sociology Department in 2008. She is a member of American Sociological Association's sections on Social Psychology, Theory, Mathematical Sociology, and the Sociology of Emotions. Her research focuses on small group interaction, nonverbal behaviors, emotions, gender, and expectations. Recently, she has conducted projects on altering the status meaning of gender and, with Murray Webster, on the effect of behaviors on inequality structures in small groups. Her current laboratory project, also with Murray Webster, addresses how characteristics come to have status value.

Blaine Robbins is a PhD candidate in the department of sociology at the University of Washington. His research interests center on the quantitative analysis of social exchange theory and network formation; the connection between social capital and violent crime; and the dynamic relationship between trust and control. He is currently working on his dissertation, which focuses on the effects of (de)centrally administered (non)monetary sanctions on trust, cooperation, and morality.

Abigail Schoneboom is a sociologist based at The City University of New York (CUNY), where her research focuses on "creative resistance," looking at workers who reclaim time from the labor process in order to pursue their own intellectual and artistic projects. She recently obtained her Ph.D. from CUNY Graduate Center, writing a dissertation entitled Hiding Out: Creative Resistance Among Anonymous Workbloggers. She also has a Master of Engineering degree from Oxford University and over ten years of professional experience working in industry and academia with a focus on organizational development and information technology.

Daniel B. Shank is a doctoral student in Sociology at the University of Georgia where he has received an M.S. in Artificial Intelligence and an M.A. in Sociology. His primary foci are social psychology, emotions, and identities especially as they relate to human-technology interaction. Mr. Shank's M.A. thesis laboratory research led to a paper Perceived Justice of Coercive Computers which received best graduate paper awards from both the Southern Sociological Society and the Social Psychology section of the American Sociological Association. He is also the manager of the Laboratory for the Study of Social Interaction, overseeing social psychological experiments in emotion, affect, identities, and justice.

Sean Smith has been working in information security---attacks and defenses, for industry and government---since before there was a Web. As a post-doc and staff member at Los Alamos National Laboratory, he performed security reviews, designs, analyses, and briefings for a wide variety of public-sector clients; at IBM T.J. Watson Research Center, he designed the security architecture for (and helped code and test) the IBM 4758 secure coprocessor, and then led the formal modeling and verification work that earned it the world's first FIPS 140-1 Level 4 security validation. In July 2000, Sean left IBM for Dartmouth, since he was convinced that the academic education and research environment is a better venue for changing the world. His current work, as PI of the Dartmouth PKI/Trust Lab, investigates how to build trustworthy systems in the real world. At Dartmouth, his courses---on Operating Systems, Security, and Theory---have all been named "favorite classes" by graduating seniors. His book Trusted Computing Platforms: Design and Applications (Springer, 2005) provides a deeper presentation of this research journey; his book The Craft of System Security (Addison-Wesley, 2007) resulted from the educational journey.

Matthias Thiemann holds a Diplom in Social Sciences from Humboldt-Universitaet zu Berlin, and an MA in Economics from the New School for Social Research, New York. Since 2007, he is a PhD-student in Sociology at Columbia University. He is interested in the way workers adapt to unregulated labor markets, which entails the necessity of trust-building strategies. Other research looks at the state-finance relationship, pointing to the symbiosis of both in the case of the US in the last decades.

Fahri Unsal is a professor of Marketing/International Business in the School of Business at Ithaca College. He has also taught for Maryland University in Germany and Bilkent University in Turkey during sabbatical years. He has received his PhD from Cornell University and his M.S. degree from the American University of Beirut. He has widely published on electronic commerce, online trust, file sharing, European Union enlargement, and online education topics.

Andrew Wong is a senior scientist at the Telenor Group Business Development and Research Center Asia Pacific. His work focuses on communication theory and behavior practice of the low-income segment of emerging nations.

Index